THE LETTERS OF
THOMAS BABINGTON
MACAULAY

EDITED BY

THOMAS PINNEY

PROFESSOR OF ENGLISH
POMONA COLLEGE, THE CLAREMONT COLLEGES
CLAREMONT, CALIFORNIA

VOLUME V

JANUARY 1849 – DECEMBER 1855

DULCE·PERICULUM

CAMBRIDGE UNIVERSITY PRESS
CAMBRIDGE
LONDON · NEW YORK · NEW ROCHELLE
MELBOURNE · SYDNEY

Published by the Press Syndicate of the University of Cambridge
The Pitt Building, Trumpington Street, Cambridge CB2 IRP
32 East 57th Street, New York, NY 10022, USA
296 Beaconsfield Parade, Middle Park, Melbourne 3206, Australia

First published 1981

Printed in Great Britain
by Western Printing Services Ltd, Bristol

Library of Congress Cataloguing in Publication Data
Macaulay, Thomas Babington Macaulay, Baron, 1800–1859.
The Letters of Thomas Babington Macaulay.
On spine: The letters of Macaulay.
Includes indexes.
Contents: v. 1. 1807 – February 1831 – v. 2. March 1831 – December 1833 –
v. 3. January 1834 – August 1841 – v. 4. September 1841 – December 1848 –
v. 5. January 1849 – December 1855 – v. 6. January 1856 – December 1859.
I. Pinney, Thomas, ed. II. Title. III. Title: The letters of Macaulay.

DA3.M3A4   828'.8'09 [B]   73–75860
ISBN 0 521 22749 6

The title-page device is
the Macaulay coat of arms, taken from Macaulay's seal
on a letter of 17 December 1833;
it was later the basis of Macaulay's arms as Baron Macaulay.
Acknowledgement is made to the Master and Fellows of
Trinity College, Cambridge.

THE LETTERS OF
THOMAS BABINGTON MACAULAY

VOLUME V

Volumes in the series

Macaulay in his study at the Albany, F.3. Portrait in oil by Edward Matthew Ward, painted in May 1853 (National Portrait Gallery). The view through the window is of the roof of Anglesey House, where a weathercock showed Macaulay the changes of weather. The clock, writing desk, and statuette of Voltaire (a gift of Lady Holland) may now be seen at Wallington Hall, Northumberland. Macaulay, as usual, failed to be pleased by the portrait: 'He has made me uglier than a daguerreotype' (Journal, XI, 76: 25 May 1853).

CONTENTS

PREFACE

The years between the publication of the first two and the second two volumes of Macaulay's *History* exhibit a mingled pattern of light and shade. While the public man was showered with national and international honors, the private person found his once robust health beginning to give way until, midway in the period covered in this volume, it broke, never to be fully restored. Macaulay bore the irony of his situation with determined good spirits, but he could hardly help seeing his triumphs under the shadow of mortality.

The honors were certainly abundant. As he wrote to Ellis in February of 1853:

> You little know the dignity of your correspondent. I now sign myself
>
> T B Macaulay FRS, MRIA, M P late fellow of Trin Coll Cambridge late Lord Rector of the University of Glasgow, Knight of the Order of Merit of Prussia, Member of the Royal Academies of Munich and Turin, Member of the Historical Society of Utrecht, and, – die of envy – Member of the French Institute in the Department of Moral Science!!!

Later in the year he was to receive an honorary D.C.L. from Oxford. He was already a Trustee of the British Museum, the (honorary) Professor of Ancient Literature of the Royal Academy, a Bencher of Lincoln's Inn, and a Senator of the University of London. The profits from his books grew with every year. In England, the first installment of the *History of England* had reached an eleventh edition – a total of 35,000 copies in the expensive library format – before the second installment appeared to set off a wave of even greater sales. The *Essays*, first published in book form in 1843, had by the next decade become one of the staple commodities of English letters, available in a bewildering variety of editions, formats, and prices. The *Lays of Ancient Rome* issued in a steady stream from the presses of Messrs Spottiswoode, 2,000 copies being automatically reordered by the publisher each time the preceding 2,000 had been exhausted, as they were at brief intervals; by 1855 some 23,000 copies had been sold.

In the United States the Bible was the only rival of Macaulay's *History* for popularity among the book buyers. Within a few weeks of publication, 100,000 copies had been sold there. The absence of international copyright meant that this literary gold mine was open for exploitation by any one who could manage it, and the heated competition between the many pirates who ventured perhaps had something to do with Macaulay's unparalleled American popularity. 'No work, of any kind, has ever so completely taken our whole country by storm,' Macaulay's authorized American publishers, the Harpers, wrote to him early in 1849.

On the Continent, too, Macaulay at the beginning of the 1850s was both celebrated among the public and profitable to the publishers. The English-language edition of the *History* published by Baron Von Tauchnitz of Leipzig in his well-known paper-back series, the 'Collection of British Authors,' did so well that Tauchnitz eagerly sought to add anything he could get of Macaulay's: within a few years the 'British Authors' included not only the *History* but the *Lays*, the *Speeches*, and three series of *Essays* – a total of nineteen volumes. Tauchnitz also wanted Macaulay to do a book for him on modern British writers, but this Macaulay wisely declined to attempt. The Germans were evidently the most avid of Macaulay's European audiences, for, as he was able to boast in 1856, there were then no less than six translations of the *History* into German in progress – two at Leipzig, two at Braunschweig, and one each at Stuttgart and Vienna. There were at least three translations of the *History* into French, two into Italian, and single renderings into Dutch, Russian, Polish, Danish, Swedish, Hungarian, Spanish, Bohemian, and – if Trevelyan is to be trusted – Persian!

With such popularity, Macaulay began to grow rich. He already had, thanks to his Indian years and the inheritance from his Uncle Colin, what it pleased him to call a 'competence;' that competence now began to verge upon opulence. From the incomplete figures available in Macaulay's Journal and in his letters I calculate that he received at least £18,000 from Longman between 1849 and 1854; on the publication of the second part of the *History* at the end of 1855 the figures, of course, went even higher. The famous check for £20,000 written by Longman to Macaulay in March of 1856 represented a large part, but still only a part, of what Macaulay was to earn from that source in the next few years. As early as 1852 Macaulay could estimate that he was 'worth 40,000£ realised – besides some hundreds at my banker's – my furniture, books etc., and copyrights worth, at a moderate calculation some thousands' (Journal, VI, 14: 22 December 1852). Seven years later, in the year of his death, Macaulay's annual income exceeded £5,000, and he put his fortune at not less than £80,000. As he wrote with pardonable complacency: 'Twenty five years ago I was worth exactly and literally nothing. I had paid my debts, and had not a penny. My whole fortune – except about 8000£ from my uncle Colin – is of my own acquisition' (Journal, XI, 599–600: 3 December 1859).

Literary fame and substantial fortune, excellent things in themselves, were made even sweeter to Macaulay by an unlooked-for event in 1852. The Whigs of Edinburgh, dazzled by the splendor of their former parliamentary representative, resolved to atone for their rejection of Macaulay in 1847. He would not have to campaign; he would not be compelled to make any promises; he would not have to spend a penny on the entire affair; all they sought was the chance to redeem themselves by persuading Macaulay to allow them to return him once again to Parliament. At first, even this abject surrender was not enough. Macaulay affirmed that he would not stand. The Edinburgh people, however, persisted; Macaulay must allow them to complete their penance. The negotiations between the offended statesman and the contrite electors make a delicate comedy in which Macaulay, the aloof object of desire, willing to be won but unwilling to give a sign, is finally wrought upon to say 'yes' when the terms are irresistible. 'On full consideration,' he wrote, 'I did not think that I could, consistently with my duty, refuse.' It was, he added, 'a very signal, I may say, an unprecedented, reparation' (19 June 1852). The reparation was made perfect when, at the election, he was returned at the head of the poll.

Macaulay had always struck observers as a man of vigorous, even rude, physical health. To the fastidious Emerson, for example, he seemed to have 'the strength of ten men; immense memory, fun, fire, learning, politics, manners, and pride'.* His prodigies of efficiency in handling the voluminous paper work of political office were the admiration and despair of his colleagues. He was an indefatigable walker. And he was, to quote Emerson again, 'the king of diners-out.' The program of a week at the end of May 1850 will do to illustrate this claim.

On Sunday, the 26th, Macaulay dined at Sir William Molesworth's with Thackeray, Lord and Lady Ashburton, the Portuguese minister, Lord Monteagle, and Lord and Lady Lovelace. The next day he took a long walk to Greenwich and dined at his favorite tavern, the Trafalgar. On Tuesday he breakfasted at Lord Mahon's – such breakfasts began at 10 and lasted for several hours – with Eugène Scribe, Lord Carlisle, Lord and Lady Ashley, M. Van de Weyer, and Monteagle. That evening he dined at The Club, where he presided in the chair over a group including Sir Henry Holland, the Bishop of Oxford, Henry Hallam, William Whewell, Sir David Dundas, and Dean Milman – 'we sate till past eleven,' Macaulay noted, and the Bishop told a good joke. 'Scribes and Pharisees,' he said, on hearing that Macaulay had breakfasted that morning with Scribe and the

* *Letters of Ralph Waldo Emerson,* ed. R. L. Rusk, IV, 42: 23 March 1848.

Evangelical Lord Ashley. On the next night, Wednesday, he dined at his friend Ellis's with Tom Taylor, Frederick Pollock, and other lawyers of Ellis's set. On Thursday, the 30th, Macaulay dined at the Duke of Somerset's – a 'stupid party' consisting of 'Murray the Hippopotamus man, Rawlinson, a bore – two Sardinians, Hamilton, Panizzi, Lady Palmerston, Tufnell.' Later in the evening they were joined by Lord Aylesbury, Lord Shrewsbury, and 'a pretty Miss Talbot.' On Friday, for the only time in the week, Macaulay dined alone at home. On Saturday he gave a breakfast party of his own to the Bishop of Oxford, Lord Carlisle, Hallam, Milman, Thackeray, and Van de Weyer – a group of men every one of whom he had either dined with or breakfasted with at least once already in the week. That night he dined with Sir Robert Peel – 'How odd!' he exclaimed to his Journal; Peel's other guests were Lord and Lady Villiers, Lord and Lady Ashburton, Lord and Lady Granville, and Lord and Lady Canning. After dinner Macaulay looked in at Palmerston's – 'immense crowd' – and ended the week 'glad to get home to bed.'

It would not be difficult to match this crowded account with many others like it. Yet Hannah Trevelyan, in her MS Memoir of her brother, can affirm that

It was with an effort he even dined out, and few who met him in society and enjoyed his brilliant conversation could guess how much rather he would have remained at home, and how much difficulty I had to force him to accept invitations and prevent his growing sauvage. . . . I am quite sure not one in ten invitations were accepted by him (35).

Signs of warning began to appear as early as the winter of 1849–50, when the Journal is filled with complaints about respiratory afflictions, troubled sleep, and a general feeling of oppression. At the end of June 1852 he felt himself 'unstrung, – a weight at my heart, and an indescribable sense of anxiety. These are the penalties of advancing life.' A few days later he speaks of a 'vile asthmatic attack,' and then of a 'bilious attack,' as his doctors had called it. We should no doubt speak of a 'heart attack,' but under any name it meant that Macaulay's old vigor and the physical confidence that went with it were gone for ever. This week in his life proved to be a serious crisis, turning him from the careless health of the past to the anxious care that shadowed all the rest of his years. The permanent symptoms of his ill-health were oppression of the chest, shortness of breath, attacks of coughing, and a general nervousness and weakness. To all appearances he was a changed man – 'I became twenty years older in a week' he wrote in 1853 – but he was determined that his physical weakness should make no change in the life of his mind and of his affections, even though he was now compelled in every other way to accept the self-indulgences of a valetudinarian.

Damaged as he was in health, Macaulay's public career after his return to Parliament was very limited. He was unable for months even to address his Edinburgh constituents, and did so at last on an occasion of intense emotion for all concerned and of great strain for Macaulay (see 2 November 1852). In the House of Commons he made only three speeches, all of them in 1853; after that his voice was heard no more in Parliament, though he did important work on committees in connection with the new India Bill of 1853, the reform of the universities, and the opening of the Indian civil service to competition. Long before his official retirement from the House early in 1856 Macaulay had recognized his inability to meet the demands of his position and sought to be relieved of the burden.

Beginning in 1853 he found an agreeable substitute for the Edinburgh reviewing he had done for so many years by writing for another Edinburgh enterprise, the *Encyclopaedia Britannica*. The proprietor, Adam Black, Macaulay's old Edinburgh political manager, was bringing out the eighth edition of the work, and for this Macaulay volunteered to contribute biographical sketches without a fee, reserving only the right to reprint them in a separate volume should he choose to do so. Between 1853 and 1858 Macaulay did five of these biographies – Atterbury, Bunyan, Goldsmith, Johnson, and Pitt; they were written, if not exactly without book, at least largely from the impressions that Macaulay had long since formed about his beloved seventeenth and eighteenth century subjects. Free from the polemical element of the *Edinburgh Review* articles, these sketches show Macaulay at his best in a short space; they were for many years and through many editions one of the ornaments of the *Britannica*.

After all else has been said about the years following the publication of the first part of the *History*, their chief story remains the composition of the next part of that work. This second part presents the decade following the revolution of 1688, and describes the consolidation of the new reign in England, Scotland, and Ireland as well as the unfolding of William's policy on the Continent. Macaulay set to work upon it at once, while the noise of acclamation for the first part was still loud in his ears. As he had done before, he made tours of inspection to the scenes of his narrative – the Boyne and Killiecrankie among the most notable of them – and did original research in archives and libraries. Mostly, however, his work was in London, at the State Paper Office, at the British Museum, at the libraries of the Houses of Parliament, at the bookstores of London, and, pre-eminently, amidst his own collection of books and documents. The frontispiece to this volume, a portrait made in 1853 that shows Macaulay seated in his study while politely but impatiently attending to the viewer, presents him, I think, as he essentially was now: no longer a public man but wholly the scholar and historian, surrounded by his books and familiar domestic ornaments, and impatient of the interruption that separates him from the writing desk prominent on the right of the picture.

Interruptions there were, of course. One occurred in the summer of 1853, when a pirated edition of Macaulay's speeches appeared in both England and the United States. Macaulay was very angry, and determined to protect his reputation as an orator by issuing an edition of his own. This was based partly on corrected texts published at the time, and partly, as he ingenuously put it, upon his sense of the 'words which I might have used.' To this labor of reconstruction he devoted most of his summer retreat at Tunbridge Wells, and he was occupied with the details of correction and proof-reading at intervals until the publication of the volume early in December.

By the beginning of 1855, his field trips and his visits to archives completed, his materials surrounding him, and a number of chapters already written, Macaulay settled in to push the manuscript through to publication. Early in March he ceased to keep his Journal, and the flow of his correspondence diminished at the same time. The intensity of his absorption in his *History* is amusingly expressed in a letter to the clerk of the City of London in June 1855 asking to see records in the clerk's keeping: the letter is dated 1689, and Macaulay has forgotten to sign it – two rare inadvertences in his letters. By the end of November 1855 Macaulay had completed his labor and stepped back to await, with mixed anxiety and confidence, the judgment of the public. 'I am more nervous than I was about the first part,' he wrote in resuming his Journal at this time:

For then I had no highly raised expectations to satisfy. And now people expect so much that the Seventh Book of Thucydides would hardly content them. On the other hand the general sterility – the miserably enervated state of literature – is all in my favor. We shall see.

He was not disappointed.

BIOGRAPHICAL CHRONOLOGY

1849 February 1
Begins second part of *History*
— March 21
Speech on inauguration as Lord
Rector of University of Glasgow
— March 22
To Edinburgh: last visit to Jeffrey
— April 5–9
Easter tour to Chester, Bangor,
Lichfield
— July 1
Prince Albert offers TBM the chair
of history at Cambridge
— August 16–September 3
Tour of Ireland to visit scenes for
History: Dublin, the Boyne,
Limerick, Killarney, Cork,
Londonderry
— September 6–17
French tour with Ellis: works in
French archives
1850 Winter
First serious complaints about
health
— January 18
Elected Bencher of Lincoln's Inn
— February
Elected Professor of Ancient
Literature, Royal Academy
— March 28–April 1
Easter tour to Norwich and Ely
— April
Elected member of Senate,
University of London
-- June 21–July 6
Scottish tour to inspect scenes for

History: Perth, Killiecrankie,
Inverness, Glencoe, Inverary
— September 2–28
At Ventnor, Isle of Wight
1851 January
Sets up carriage
— April 17–21
Easter tour: Southampton,
Portsmouth, Winchester
— May 1
At opening of Great Exhibition
— August 2
Elected to Royal Bavarian Acad-
emy
— August 7–September 29
At Malvern
1852 January 19
Offered cabinet post following
Palmerston's dismissal
— March
Elected member of Academy of
Turin
— April 8–12
Easter tour: Peterborough, Boston,
Lincoln
— June [14]
Invited to stand for Edinburgh
— June 30
Crisis in his health begins
— July 13
Elected at Edinburgh
— July 22
Further heart attack
— August 3–September 27
Recuperating at Clifton
— August

Resumes work on *History* 'after a
long intermission'
– November 2
Speech to Edinburgh electors
– November 6
Takes seat in Parliament
– November 16
Appointed to Committee on Indian
Territories
– November 30
Elected to Royal Irish Academy
– November
Made Knight of Prussian Order of
Merit
1853 January
Begins vol. 4 of *History*
– February
Elected to French Institute
– March 21
Finishes life of Atterbury for
Encyclopaedia Britannica
– March 22–30
To Paris with the Trevelyan
family
– June 1
Speech on Exclusion of Judges Bill
– June 7
Receives honorary D.C.L. at
Oxford
– June 24
Speech on India
– July 12–August 19
At Tunbridge Wells
– July 19
Speech on Annuity Tax: last
speech in Parliament
– August 26–September 19
European tour with Ellis: Cologne,
Heidelberg, Geneva, Lyons, Paris
– December 2
Finishes life of Bunyan for
Encyclopaedia Britannica

– December 7
Publishes *Speeches*
1854 March
Appointed chairman of Committee
on Indian Civil Service
– April 13–17
Easter tour: York, Castle Howard,
Durham
– May 17
Elected President of the Edinburgh
Philosophical Institution
– June
Further crisis in health
– July 5–September 30
At Thames Ditton
– September 7–18
French tour with Ellis: Bourges,
Orléans, Tours, Paris; examines
French War Office records
– September 30–October 6
Reading MSS at All Souls, Oxford
– December 27
Report on Indian Civil Service
published
1855 January–November
Concentrated work on finishing
History, volumes 3 and 4: ceases to
keep Journal, reduces correspond-
ence, rarely ventures out during
winter
– June 28–September 29
At Richmond
– August 27
Finishes life of Goldsmith for
Encyclopaedia Britannica
– November 21
Finishes proofs of *History*, vols. 3
and 4
– December 17
History, vols. 3 and 4 published;
first edition of 25,000 copies

THE LETTERS

TRIUMPHANT YEARS
1 JANUARY 1849 – 23 DECEMBER 1851

1849 February 1
Begins second part of *History*

– March 21
Speech on inauguration as Lord Rector of University of Glasgow

– March 22
To Edinburgh: last visit to Jeffrey

– April 5–9
Easter tour to Chester, Bangor, Lichfield

– July 1
Prince Albert offers TBM the chair of history at Cambridge

– August 16–September 3
Tour of Ireland to visit scenes for *History*: Dublin, the Boyne, Limerick, Killarney, Cork, Londonderry

– September 6–17
French tour with Ellis: works in French archives

1850 Winter
First serious complaints about health

– January 18
Elected Bencher of Lincoln's Inn

– February
Elected Professor of Ancient Literature, Royal Academy

– March 28–April 1
Easter tour to Norwich and Ely

– April
Elected member of Senate, University of London

– June 21–July 6
Scottish tour to inspect scenes for *History*: Perth, Killiecrankie, Inverness, Glencoe, Inverary

– September 2–28
At Ventnor, Isle of Wight

1851 January
  Sets up carriage

— April 17–21
  Easter tour: Southampton, Portsmouth, Winchester

— May 1
  At opening of Great Exhibition

— August 2
  Elected to Royal Bavarian Academy

— August 7–September 29
  At Malvern

TO LADY TREVELYAN, 1 JANUARY 1849

MS: Trinity College.

Albany Jan 1. 1849

Dearest Hannah,

A sad beginning this new year has had. Poor Auckland died at seven this morning. Miss Emily Eden is not expected to live till night. The whole look of the Admiralty is as sad as if every clerk had lost a relation. Poor Ward[1] I found crying bitterly.

Auckland was taken with an apoplectic fit on Saturday afternoon while shooting at the Grange with Lord Ashburton. His sister Fanny went down immediately. He had one short interval of recollection yesterday afternoon, and knew her.

A steamer started this morning from Liverpool for the Bishop. He will now be a peer, – the first Bishop of Sodor and Man who has been so.

My success is beyond all precedent. The second edition will be out of print as soon as it appears. What they call the subscription was opened to day. Eleven hundred were subscribed for in Paternoster Row alone by twelve o'clock, – by two o'clock near 1500. Eight hundred are bespoken for the country. A new edition of four thousand is to be put in hand immediately.[2]

Ever yours,
T B Macaulay

TO DR HENRY HOLLAND, 2 JANUARY 1849

MS: Gennadius Library, American School of Classical Studies, Athens. *Partly published: Griffon* (Spring, 1966), p. 8.

Albany Jan 2. 1849

Dear Dr. Holland,

Thanks for all your kindness. Your advice comes barely in time for the third edition. The second, I learn from Longman, will disappear almost as soon as it appears. I shall make some alteration in the passage which you mention. But I own that, to my thinking, Cartwright's evidence, which I had overlooked, seems to confirm the Quaker tradition. What could be more natural than that James, on his return from mass, should be told

---

[1] (Sir) Henry George Ward (1797–1860: *DNB*), Secretary to the Admiralty, 1846–9, and afterwards Governor of Ceylon. TBM had called at the Admiralty about the question discussed in his letter to Finlaison, 25 December 184[8]: 'Ward promises me full information' (Journal, 1, 456: 1 January).

[2] TBM corrected the sheets for this on the 2nd and 3rd; on the 5th Longman told him that the print order had been raised to 5,000 copies. By the end of January a further 2,000 copies, still called the third edition, had to be printed, and all 7,000 copies were sold by the end of March (Journal, 1, 457–553).

that Penn was holding forth in the tennis court, and should look in for a moment?[1]

I am to be honored by a visit from a deputation of Quakers who mean to give me a lecture, or, as they call it, an opportunity, touching the character of William Penn.[2] I have all my proofs in order for them, and hope to reduce them to the state of a silent meeting.

Ever yours,

T B Macaulay

TO LORD JOHN RUSSELL, 3 JANUARY 1849

MS: Public Record Office. *Partly published:* Russell, *Later Correspondence*, 1, 191.

Albany London / January 3. 1849

My dear Lord John,

Thanks for your kind note. Your approbation is most gratifying to me. I am not surprised that you think me too much of a Trimmer. It is natural that a Russell should be partial to the Exclusionists. And indeed if the question were merely this – Ought the Exclusion Bill to have passed? – I should without hesitation answer in the affirmative. But the question is whether, when it was clear that the exclusion bill would not pass, it was wise to reject all compromise, and, instead of framing laws which might have secured the liberties and religion of the nation, to proceed to excesses which produced a violent reaction in the public mind. This was Burnet's view; and I can hardly wish to be a more zealous Whig

---

[1] TBM had written that, on the King's progress through Chester, Penn 'was most graciously received by James, who even condescended to go to the Quaker meeting, and to listen with decency to his friend's melodious eloquence' (*History*, II, 295–6: ch. 8). TBM expanded the passage in the fourth edition, adding a reference to the evidence of Bishop Thomas Cartwright's *Diary*, 30 August 1687, and changing the statement about Penn and James thus: '[Penn] was permitted to harangue in the tennis court, while Cartwright preached in the Cathedral, and while the King heard mass at an altar. . . . It is said, indeed, that His Majesty deigned to look into the tennis court and to listen with decency to his friend's melodious eloquence.' Cartwright's evidence says only that on this occasion James 'went to his devotions in the Shire Hall, and Mr. Penn held forth in the Tennis Court' (*Diary*, 1843, p. 74).

[2] The delegation called on 5 February to ask TBM for the evidence justifying his hostile (and mistaken) treatment of Penn in the *History*. The anticipation of the encounter created a mildly amused stir in TBM's circle; Lord Shelburne, Charles Austin, and Milman were there to witness the event (Trevelyan, II, 251–2), and *Punch*, 17 February, devoted a page of comic verse and drawing to it. The members of the delegation were Samuel Gurney (see 7 February), Josiah Forster, George Stacey, John Hodgkin, and Joseph Bevan Braithwaite. One of them recalled long afterwards that TBM 'was extremely rude, treating the Friends with contempt' (Allen C. Thomas, 'William Penn, Macaulay, and "Punch,"' *Bulletin of the Friends' Historical Society*, VII [1916], 94).

than Burnet. Just look at his first volume, page 459, and at a very short, but very sensible note of Swift's, which contains the whole case.[1]

I have grieved most sincerely for the loss of poor Lord Auckland. / Ever, my dear Lord John,

Yours most truly

T B Macaulay

TO BISHOP SAMUEL WILBERFORCE, 3 JANUARY 1849

MS: Bodleian Library.

Albany London / Jany. 3. 1849

My dear Bishop of Oxford,

I thank you most sincerely for your kind invitation, though I cannot at present avail myself of it. Hereafter I propose to rummage some of the Oxford libraries; and I should be delighted to have your company and help.[2] Before that time however we shall, I hope, meet in London.

You will find in my book not a little about old Obadiah and the songs which the gownsmen chaunted under the windows of his lodgings.[3] He was a wretched fellow.

I should be truly glad to be set right, if I have fallen into any error as to the views of our reformers on the subject of episcopacy. But I can scarcely think that I am wrong. The following facts I take to be undeniable, (1) that Cranmer pronounced bishops to be mere lieutenants of the King *ad spiritualia* just as the Chancellor and Treasurer were lieutenants of the King *ad temporalia;*[4] (2) that, in Cranmer's judgment, the imposition of hands was an unnecessary form, and that the King's mandate sufficed to make a priest; (3) that, according to Cranmer, there was, in the primitive times, no distinction between priests and bishops; (4) that Cranmer considered the episcopal office as determined by a demise of the Crown; (5) that Henry the Eighth granted commissions authorising bishops to ordain etc. in his name and during his pleasure; (6) that Bishop Parkhurst[5] pronounced the polity of the Church of

---

[1] Swift's note is this: 'It [the plan to limit James's authority rather than exclude him] was the wisest, because it would be less opposed; and the king would consent to it; otherwise an exclusion would have done better' (Burnet, *History of His Own Time*, Oxford, 1823, II, 208). TBM wrote that the Exclusionists, on the defeat of the bill, 'found some consolation in shedding the blood of Roman Catholics' (*History*, I, 259: ch. 2).

[2] Wilberforce had been Bishop of Oxford since 1845.

[3] Obadiah Walker (1616–99: *DNB*), Roman Catholic Master of University College, Oxford. TBM reports that the undergraduates sang a ballad of which the burden was 'Old Obadiah / Sings Ave Maria' (*History*, II, 281: ch. 7).

[4] On this and the other points respecting church government, see TBM's controversial letters to Bishop Phillpotts, 8 and 22 January.

[5] John Parkhurst (1512?–75: *DNB*), Bishop of Norwich.

Zurich preferable to the polity of the Church of England; (7) that Bishop Ponet[1] recommended the abolition of the title of Bishop and the substitution of the word *superintendent*; (8) that neither in the Articles nor in the Homilies is episcopacy asserted to be of divine or apostolical institution; (9) that till the Restoration persons who had been ordained after the Presbyterian fashion held livings in the Church of England without reordination; and (10) that at Dort an English Bishop sate in a spiritual Council with divines not episcopally ordained, and voted with them on the gravest questions of theology. I do not apprehend that any one of these propositions will be disputed: and, if this be so, it is surely impossible to deny that in the seventeenth century a great change did take place in the opinion of the rulers of the Anglican Church touching the episcopal office. Whether the change were or were not for the better is a point on which I do not say one word. I have treated the question as a historian and not as a theologian. But I assure you that, if you can show me that I am wrong, I will candidly acknowledge my mistake.

Ever yours truly

T B Macaulay

TO LORD MAHON, 4 JANUARY 1849

MS: Stanhope Papers, Chevening. *Published:* Lord Stanhope, *Miscellanies*, 2nd Series, 1872, pp. 142–3.

Albany London / Jan. 4, 1849

My Dear Mahon,

P.M.A.C.F. has set as many people to work as the authorship of Junius.[2] I am delighted to think that I have been the humble instrument of calling forth so much industry and ingenuity. Among the conjectures which have been communicated to me one comes from a noble person whom I had never in my life seen or heard of, Lord Sidney Osborne.[3]

---

[1] John Ponet (1514?–56: *DNB*), Bishop of Rochester and of Winchester. The recommendations of both Parkhurst and Ponet are noticed in the *History*, I, 50: ch. 1.

[2] In his account of the death of Charles II, TBM says that the Duke of York, at the suggestion of the Duchess of Portsmouth, a former mistress of Charles, brought in a Catholic priest, Father Huddleston, to receive the dying king's confession. Among the authorities cited is a 'curious broadside' in which it is said that the Duke of York acted on the suggestion of 'P.M.A.C.F.' TBM adds that 'I must own myself quite unable to decipher the last five letters' (*History*, I, 440n). Mahon wrote to suggest that the initials referred to a Portuguese chaplain in the service of Queen Catherine and that they stood for 'Pereyra (Manoel) A Capuchin Friar' (see his letter of 3 January in *Miscellanies*, 2nd Series, p. 141). In a note added to the *History* in 1850 TBM says that despite 'several very ingenious conjectures touching these mysterious letters...I am convinced that the true solution has not yet been suggested.' A note of 1856 states that the most plausible identification is 'Père Mansuete, A Cordelier Friar.' For this conjecture, see 24 January 1849.

[3] Osborne (1808–89: *DNB*) was Rector of Durweston, Dorset.

I can without flattery assure you that yours is the best guess that, as far as I know, has yet been made. Nevertheless I am not satisfied. It appears from the Chaillot M.S. that the Queen applied to the Duchess[1] about the King's spiritual state, and that the Duchess applied to the Duke. Why should the Duchess, who undoubtedly was, during part of that day, in the same room with her husband, employ a messenger? If she employed a messenger, why should she select one of the Queen's servants rather than one of her own? Observe too that none of the Queen's priests knew any language in which it was possible to communicate with Charles. That was the reason which made it necessary to call in Huddlestone. Now, if Manuel Pereira, or, as you are forced to call him, Pereira Manuel, could not make himself understood by Charles, he would hardly, I think, have been selected to carry a message to James, who does not appear to have been a better linguist than his brother.

I will give you my own explanation in order that you may take your revenge upon it. It seems clear to me that the writer of the broadside meant the letters P.M.A.C.F. to be understood by somebody; or he would not have used them. It seems to me equally clear that he did not mean them to be understood by everybody or he would have used clearer signs, such as *her M. the Q.* or *her R.H. the D.* How then do men act when they insert, in a paper likely to be seen by all sorts of persons, some things meant to be understood only by a few? They use a cipher. Is it not highly probable that there was in that age a Roman Catholic cipher? It was the age of ciphers. The Scotch Whigs had one. The agents of the Prince of Orange had one. Coleman[2] used one in his letters to his fellow Papists. I think it therefore very likely that there may have been a cipher known to every Jesuit and Franciscan in the kingdom, and that in this cipher every person of great note in the State may have been designated by some letter or combination of letters. If once this supposition be admitted, all difficulty is at an end. We may find ten solutions in a minute. For the notation may have been purely arbitrary. P.M. may have meant the Queen and A.C.F. the Duchess, or vice versa.

I think with you that the agency of the mistress would not have been mentioned in a paper written by a Roman Catholic for the edification of his brethren.

Ever yours truly
T B Macaulay

[1] The Duchess of York, not the Duchess of Portsmouth (see note 2, p. 8).
[2] Edward Coleman (d. 1678: *DNB*), one of the victims of Titus Oates.

TO JOHN LEYCESTER ADOLPHUS, 5 JANUARY 1849

MS: Princeton University.

Albany Jan 5 / 1849

Dear Adolphus,

Many thanks. Your remarks are too late, I grieve to say, for the third edition which is now fast printing off. The publishers seem determined, after the third edition, to stereotype; and, before this is done, I will carefully consider your suggestions.

One word however as to my parts of speech, about which I am as sensitive as Mrs. Malaprop. Balderdash[1] is a good word and come of a good family. It is in Johnson, with an Anglo Saxon derivation. Observe too that I have not honored it with a place in the text, but have kept it in the notes, – the Court of the Gentiles, – with French, Spanish, Italian and Dutch, – a very proper place for second rate English.

Ever yours truly
T B Macaulay

Pray exhort Mrs. Adolphus to persist in criticizing. She was right so far as this, that I had not made my meaning sufficiently clear. I have added a word or two in the second edition. And, where she was wrong, she had Jeffrey to keep her in countenance, the most celebrated critic of our age and country.

TO JOHN EVELYN DENISON, 5 JANUARY 1849

MS: University of Nottingham.

Albany London / January 5. 1849

Dear Denison,

Many thanks for your kind letter. I was perfectly aware that much of the uninclosed land was cultivated: but I see that I expressed myself ambiguously. The mistake shall be rectified.[2] I can however hardly be wrong in supposing that the uninclosed land was generally very ill cultivated. Indeed it was for the most part common; and common land never is well cultivated.

---

[1] In a note to chapter 3 TBM refers to Ned Ward's *London Spy* and then apologizes: 'I am almost ashamed to quote such nauseous balderdash' (*History*, 1, 351).

[2] As evidence for his statement that little more than half the area of England was under cultivation in 1688, TBM cites the maps of Ogilby's *Itinerarum Angliæ*, showing that the 'proportion of uninclosed country' was 'very great' (*History*, 1, 311n). This is changed in the third edition thus: 'The proportion of uninclosed country, which, if cultivated, must have been wretchedly cultivated, seems to have been very great.' Although TBM's letter of this date to Adolphus says that it is then too late to make corrections in the third edition, evidently some things could still be altered.

Pray convey to Lady Charlotte my kind regards; and assure her that her approbation has given me great pleasure. / Ever, dear Denison,

Yours very truly

T B Macaulay

TO BISHOP HENRY PHILLPOTTS, 8 JANUARY 1849

Text: Correspondence between the Bishop of Exeter and…T. B. Macaulay, 2nd edn, 1861, pp. 12–16.

Albany, London, January 8, 1849.

My Lord,

I beg you to accept my thanks for your highly-interesting letter.[1] I have seldom been more gratified than by your approbation; and I can with truth assure you that I am not solicitous to defend my book against any criticisms to which it may be justly open. I have undertaken a task which makes it necessary for me to treat of many subjects with which it is impossible that one man should be more than superficially acquainted – law, divinity, military affairs, maritime affairs, trade, finance, manufactures, letters, arts, sciences. It would therefore be the height of folly and arrogance in me to receive ungraciously suggestions offered in a friendly spirit, by persons who have studied profoundly branches of knowledge to which I have been able to give only a passing attention. I should not, I assure you, feel at all mortified or humbled at being compelled to own that I had been set right by an able and learned prelate on a question of ecclesiastical history.

I really think, however, that it is in my power to vindicate myself from the charge of having misrepresented the sentiments of the English Reformers concerning Church Government.

Your Lordship admits that I have given a correct account of the opinions which Cranmer held in 1540 touching the royal supremacy and the episcopal function.[2] But you say that he soon afterwards changed his mind, and expressed opinions very different; and you think that I ought in candour to have mentioned this. Perhaps it would have been as well if I had inserted the words "at one time," or "on one occasion." But it matters very little. I had said, a few lines before, that on this class of subjects, the founders of the Anglican Church were constantly changing their minds, that they contradicted each other, that they contradicted

---

[1] Phillpotts wrote to TBM a long letter, dated 6 January, criticizing TBM's account of Cranmer's views of church government and of the history of the church under Henry VIII, calling it 'uncandid and scarcely reconcileable with your pervading tone of justice and sincerity' (*Correspondence*, 2nd edn, p. 6).

[2] *History*, I, 57.

themselves, and that the word "supremacy" had very different significa-
tions in the same mouth at different conjunctures. The truth is that you
altogether misapprehend the use which I meant to make of Cranmer's
answers of 1540. The fault is probably my own. I ought to have made my
meaning clearer. Yet I think that, if you will do me the honour to read
again pages 55, 56, and 57 of my first volume, you will see that I never
meant to make the Church responsible for Cranmer's vagaries. I cited his
dicta, not to prove what was the genuine Anglican doctrine, but to prove
in how unsettled a state the minds even of very eminent Doctors were,
in that troubled age, on questions of the utmost gravity. I say expressly
that this notion of the supremacy gave scandal not only to Papists, but
also to Protestants; and I quote the article by which our Church contradicts point blank Cranmer's main proposition. I persuade myself that
your Lordship will, on reexamination, acquit me of everything worse
than some want of lucidity.

I have looked again at the Commission which Bonner received from
Henry, and at that which Cranmer took out after Henry's death; and must
own that my opinion as to the sense of these documents remains unchanged. Your Lordship directs my attention to the words "præter et
ultra ea quæ tibi ex sacris literis divinitus commissa esse dignoscuntur."[1]
No doubt these words recognise an episcopal power derived from God.
But do they recognise an episcopal power derived immediately from God?
I think not. I am strongly of opinion that those who drew up these
commissions held that the episcopal power was derived from God through
the King, and was to be exercised in subordination to the King; as your
Lordship probably holds that the priestly power is derived from God
through the Bishop, and is to be exercised in subordination to the Bishop.
My reason for thinking this is that the words quoted by your Lordship are
immediately followed by these very significant words, "vice, nomine, et
auctoritate nostris exequendum." I really believe that the sense of these
instruments may fairly be summed up thus: – 'Whereas all spiritual as well
as temporal jurisdiction is derived from the Sovereign, and may be
resumed by him, we empower you to ordain, to institute, to grant letters
of administration, to take cognisance of ecclesiastical offences, and to
perform all functions which appear from Holy Writ to belong by Divine
appointment to Bishops, as our lieutenant, in our name, by our authority,
and during our pleasure.'

Your Lordship says that I ought to have consulted the public Acts of
our Kings and of the Church, instead of culling here and there instances
of ill-judged actions and expressions of private men. This charge is made

[1] In Bonner's commission: Burnet, *History of the Reformation,* Appendix of Records, Part 1,
book 3, no. 14.

in language so kind and flattering, that I cannot complain of it. Yet I cannot plead guilty. For it seems to me that I have mentioned three facts of the highest importance which indicate, in a manner not to be mistaken, the opinion, not of individuals, but of the Church and State, on the subject of Episcopacy.

First, I have remarked that the Church has not, in her doctrinal confessions and discourses, asserted any form of ecclesiastical government to be essential to the welfare of a Christian Society.[1] This is surely a most important fact. It is strange that, if the Church really held episcopacy to be essential, not a word should be said on that subject in the 19th Article. Still stranger would seem the language of the 36th Article. The subject of that Article is the consecration of Bishops. Not a word is said about the divine origin of the office, or about the necessity of the imposition of hands. It is only affirmed that the Anglican form of consecration contains nothing that *of itself* is superstitious or ungodly. It is not easy to take lower ground than this. I am convinced that half the ministers of the established Church of Scotland would have the candour to admit as much. The second part of the Homily on Whitsunday is equally remarkable. Three notes of a true Church are given, but not a word about episcopacy. I had mentioned these things in my first chapter, but omitted them from fear of prolixity. I do not wish to lay more stress on them than is reasonable. But let me ask your Lordship whether you think that Laud, or Sheldon, or Ken, would have drawn up such Articles and such Homilies?

Secondly, I have mentioned the very important circumstance that, till the Restoration, episcopal ordination was not required by law as a qualification for holding a cure of souls in the Church of England.[2] I have no doubt that your Lordship remembers a remarkable passage on this subject in Clarendon's Life, ii. 152, fol.[3] How can I believe that a Church in which, during three generations, numerous ministers not episcopally ordained were admitted to the charge of parishes can have held episcopal ordination essential to the administration of the sacraments?

Thirdly, I have mentioned the fact that James I., as head of the Church, sent a Bishop and several priests to the Synod of Dort.[4] These divines joined in solemn acts of public worship with ministers not episcopally ordained, and sate in council with those ministers on the gravest questions of theology. One of the Anglican Presbyters who was sent on this embassy afterwards became a bishop; and his writings are highly esteemed to this day. He always considered himself as highly honoured by having been selected for such a mission, and spoke of himself as unworthy to form a

[1] *History*, I, 53.   [2] *History*, I, 53; 76–7.
[3] TBM quotes this at length in his letter to Phillpotts of 22 January.
[4] *History*, I, 76.

part of so illustrious a congress.[1] Imagine Sancroft or South rising to address the Moderator in the General Assembly of the Church of Scotland.

I therefore cannot admit that I have neglected to consult the public Acts of our kings and of the Church. I have, I think, proved from those Acts that there did take place in the seventeenth century a very great change in the opinion of the clerical body, and of the heads of that body, touching ecclesiastical policy. Your Lordship, I understand, admits that there was some change. The difference between us is a difference of degree, and differences of degree are not easily expressed with precision in words. I do not, I must own, feel satisfied that the language which I have used requires any modification. But if reading and reflection should lead me to a different opinion, false shame shall not prevent me from making a public retractation.[2]

I beg your Lordship to excuse the faults of this letter. It has been written in a sick-room, with considerable difficulty and pain:[3] but I could not delay my acknowledgements for your great kindness and courtesy. / I have the honour to be, / My Lord, with great respect,

Your Lordship's most faithful servant,

T. B. Macaulay.

TO FRANCES MACAULAY, 9 JANUARY [1849]

MS: Trinity College.

Albany Jan 9

Dearest Fanny,

Pray do not plague yourself about Thornton's letter. The delay was of no consequence.

After Hannah left me yesterday I got much worse, had a painful night, and am now suffering a good deal, and can scarcely limp across the room. There is however nothing at all serious; and my spirits are extremely good. Bright[4] prescribes strict abstinence and the poor man's plaister among other remedies.[5]

---

[1] The reference is to Robert Hall, Bishop of Norwich. TBM quotes Hall's humble acknowledgement of his unworthiness to assist at the Synod and adds: 'to high churchmen this humility will seem not a little out of place' (*History*, 1, 76n).

[2] TBM changed none of the passages in dispute between him and Phillpotts.

[3] TBM began to complain of ill health on 1 January and on 7 January called in Dr Bright to treat an attack of rheumatism; he did not leave his room again until 14 January (Journal, 1, 458; 466).

[4] John Bright (1783–1870: *DNB*), physician, attended TBM until his death. The *DNB* says that Bright 'never practised extensively, having an ample private fortune' and quotes the *Lancet*'s description of him as one of 'that old school of physicians whose veneration for Greek and Latin certainly exceeded their estimation of modern pathological research.'

[5] 'I obeyed him and ate nothing during twenty four hours except a porringer of broth and

I have sent to tell the Dowager Lady Grey that I shall not be able to dine with her to morrow. Love to all.

Ever yours
T B M

TO THOMAS FLOWER ELLIS, 10 JANUARY 1849

MS: Trinity College. *Extract published:* Trevelyan, II, 252.

Albany Jany. 10 / 1849

Dear Ellis,

I have been during several days close prisoner to my room with a sharp attack of rheumatism. However after several nights of pain and restlessness I have at last had a night of ease and repose; and, except a slight difficulty in walking, am pretty well again. I shall however keep house a little longer, seeing that the climbing of my stairs requires a sound pair of legs. Will you dine here to morrow – Thursday – at seven?

I have had a pastoral epistle in three sheets from St Henry of Exon, and have sent him three sheets in answer. We are the most courteous and affectionate of adversaries. You cannot think how different an opinion I entertain of him since he has taken to subscribing himself, "with very high esteem

My admiring reader."

I will have him to breakfast some morning in the spring; and I bespeak you to meet him.

Sale capital. The whole second edition gone, and 1250 of the third already ordered.

Ever yours
T B Macaulay

TO MRS SYDNEY SMITH, 10 JANUARY 1849

MS: New College, Oxford.

Albany Jan 10. 1849

Dear Mrs. Sydney Smith,

I shall be truly obliged to you for a sight of the letters which you mention.[1]

---

a slice of toast....thought often how I should bear to be a regular valetudinarian, and determined that I could endure it' (Journal, 1, 460: 9 January).

[1] The letters of Sydney Smith were being edited by Mrs Austin, and to accompany them Mrs Smith was anxious to obtain a memoir from one of Sydney's friends. None of them, apparently, dared make the attempt. A *Memoir* by Sydney's daughter Saba, Lady Holland, was published in 1855: see 17 November 1854.

If, after full consideration, I should see reason to think that a few pages written by me could be useful to your design, assuredly I will do what you ask. But I own that I do not like the thought of giving what looks like a certificate or a testimonial to one who was my older and better. If I had it in my power, as Jeffrey doubtless has, to tell interesting anecdotes which are not generally known, the case would be different. But I am afraid that I might incur the reproach of arrogance by coming forward to pronounce an eulogy on talents acknowledged by the whole world, and on works which have taken a permanent place in the literature of my country. I will however think the matter over, and consult some judicious friends. / Believe me, / My dear Madam,

Yours most truly

T B Macaulay

TO THOMAS FLOWER ELLIS, 11 JANUARY 1849

MS: Trinity College. *Extract published:* Trevelyan, II, 252–3.

Albany Jan 11. 1849

Dear Ellis,

I am getting better and better: but the weather does not tempt me to venture out even by day; and I should not like to expose myself so early as Saturday to the air of a January night. I shall therefore expect you then at seven o'clock, unless I hear to the contrary.

As to my Lord of Exeter, I must and will have you to meet him, if I am forced to get you a long ladle for the occasion. How is it possible to hold out against a man whose censure is conveyed in the following sort of phrase? – "Pardon me if I say that a different course would have been more generous, more candid, more philosophical, all which I may sum up in the words, more like yourself."[1] This is the extreme point of his severity. And to think how long I have denied to this man all share of Christian charity. Surely surely, he is filled with that grace of which it is written, πάντα πιστεύει, πάντα ἐλπίζει, πάντα ὑπομένει.[2]

As the channel islands are in the diocese of Exeter I will turn the conversation to that subject, and set my Lord and you to compare your estimates of the Jersey beauties. I have no doubt that you will agree like brothers.

Ever yours

T B Macaulay

[1] 'Forgive me if I say, that I think it would have been better and wiser, and therefore more like yourself. . .' (Phillpotts to TBM, 8 January, *Correspondence*, 2nd edn, p. 9).
[2] I Corinthians 13:7.

TO MRS SARAH AUSTIN, 12 JANUARY 1849

MS: Trinity College.

Albany London / January 12. 1849

Dear Mrs. Austin,

Your anecdotes are delightful and most welcome. I shall treasure them up for future use. But were they less interesting than they are I should value them as marks of your kindness. I hope that they are not the last contributions that I shall receive from you. / Believe me, / Dear Mrs. Austin,

Most truly yours
T B Macaulay

TO SIR EDWARD BULWER-LYTTON, 21 JANUARY 1849

MS: Hertfordshire County Council.

Albany London / January 21. 1849

Dear Sir Edward Lytton,

I ought not to be surprised, and yet I cannot help being surprised, by your versatility and fertility. I have passed some very pleasant hours over King Arthur.[1] I do not know how many years have elapsed since any poem has appeared which has charmed me so much. Numerous passages have already fixed themselves in my memory. At the same time I do not quite like the way in which you renounce and disinherit all your fine progeny for the sake of this youngest offspring.[2] You remind me of the unfatherly indifference with which Jacob, in the Book of Genesis, treats the goodly sons whom Leah had borne to him, and reserves all his tenderness for the two children of his beloved Rachael. You will give your friends leave, I hope, to praise your poetry without throwing any disparaging reflections on your prose.

I like your versification much. Indeed, I have long been of opinion that the *sesta rima* was the stanza best fitted for English romantic poetry. Frere, Byron, and others who imported and tried to naturalise the *ottava rima* had not sufficiently considered the difference between our language and the languages of the south. As soon as an Italian or Spanish poet has a

[1] Bulwer's poem, *King Arthur*, 2 vols.; the second volume had just appeared, with Bulwer's name; the first volume was published anonymously in March 1848. TBM wrote in his Journal that he praised the work 'not insincerely – for it is marked by his characteristic ability. Yet I think it will hardly be popular' (1, 471: 23 January).

[2] At the end of his preface to the poem, Bulwer-Lytton calls it 'the child of my most cherished hopes' to which he confides 'the task to uphold, and the chance to continue, its father's name.'

thought rhymes come pouring in upon him by scores. His difficulty is merely the difficulty of selection. He must be a poor artist if he cannot write poems in *terza rima*, poems in *ottava rima*, nay even sonnets, which shall flow as easily as Prior's tales. But an English versifier is in a very different situation. There are not, I firmly believe, ten stanzas in Don Juan in which sense or grace has not been sacrificed to rhyme.

Ever yours most truly

T B Macaulay

TO BISHOP HENRY PHILLPOTTS, 22 JANUARY 1849

Text: Correspondence between the Bishop of Exeter and. . .T. B. Macaulay, pp. 43–51. Extract published: Trevelyan, II, 253n.

Albany, London, Jan. 22, 1849.

My Lord,

I should be most ungrateful if I did not thankfully acknowledge my obligations to your Lordship for the highly interesting and very friendly letters with which you have honoured me.[1] Before another edition of my book appears I shall have time to weigh your observations carefully, and to examine the works to which you have called my attention. You have convinced me of the propriety of making some alterations. But I hope that you will not accuse me of pertinacity if I add that, as far as I can at present judge, those alterations will be slight, and that, on the great points in issue, my opinion is unchanged.

I cannot, for example, see that I was wrong in saying that Henry considered himself, and was represented by his favourite Courtiers, as a kind of Pope, the channel of Sacramental graces, and the expositor of Catholic verity. That he was so represented by Cranmer in the very remarkable answers which Burnet published from the Stillingfleet MS., your Lordship does not deny. But you conceive that this was a notion peculiar to Cranmer, and that even Cranmer held it only for a short time. Yet surely the paper to which I have referred in the Note to page 56 of my first volume is to the same effect. That paper was evidently meant as a kind of brief for the courtly party in the Convocation. I will give two sentences. "This text, Matt. xvi., *Quodcunque ligaveritis,* etc., gave authority to all the Apostles jointly to make laws and keep councils, until such time as a convenient number of the lay people were converted to the

---

[1] TBM received Phillpotts's second letter, dated 16 January, on the 18th and noted that 'he is civil, clever and learned, but, I think, utterly in the wrong'; Phillpotts sent a third letter on the 18th and a fourth on the 20th. TBM began his reply to these on the 22nd but did not finish it until the next day (Journal, I, 469–71).

faith; and then the said text ceased." "This text of Actuum xx., *Attendite vobis et universo gregi, in quo Spiritus Sanctus vos posuit Episcopos,* was not meant of such Bishops only as be now of the Clergy, but was as well meant and spoken of every ruler and governor of the Christian people."[1] Strype believed this paper to be in the handwriting of Gardiner;[2] and this is a very significant circumstance; for as the contents were clearly not such as Gardiner would have written of his own accord, he must have written them like a timeserver, as he was, because he knew that they would please Henry.

But I lay still more stress on the two Commissions – that given to Bonner in 1539, and that taken out by Cranmer in 1546. They are instruments of high dignity and importance – they run in very similar language; and they must be held to express the deliberate sense of those who ruled the Church and State during a period of more than seven years. Your Lordship will, I think, admit that, in both Commissions, the Bishop is empowered to ordain, not merely *auctoritate regis,* a phrase which might perhaps be so construed as to save the spiritual independence of the Episcopate, but *vice regis,* a phrase which seems to be susceptible of no such construction. The best comment on this word *vice* will be found in Cranmer's Declaration, contained in the Stillingfleet MS. – "A Bishop may make a Priest by the Scripture; and so may Princes and Governors also, and that by the authority of God committed to them."[3] I really do not think that I exaggerate when I say that in these Commissions the King does claim to be the channel of Sacramental Graces.

Then as to the claim of the King to be the expositor of doctrine, I cannot think that the passages which your Lordship cites prove my view to be erroneous. It appears from those passages that the King, before he propounded dogmas and commanded his people to accept them as orthodox, consulted Bishops and other learned men. It appears also that he acknowledged a certain spiritual authority in General Councils. But does it follow hence that he did not claim to be the Pope of England, the expositor of Catholic verity? Does not the Pope, before he condemns a heresy, consult theologians? Were not the books of the Jansenists and Quietists sifted by many grave Doctors before the Supreme Pontiff, having weighed the reports and authorities, pronounced his anathema? And do not all Roman Catholics hold that General Councils congregated *in Spiritu Sancto* have a very high and venerable authority? Nay, many Roman Catholics, we know, have maintained that a General Council

[1] John Strype, *Ecclesiastical Memorials,* Oxford, 1822, vol. 1, part 1, ch. 17, pp. 209–10.
[2] *Ibid.,* p. 208: 'it seems to be the hand of Stephen Gardiner.' Phillpotts says that TBM's readiness to accept such evidence '*astonishes* me' (*Correspondence,* 2nd edn, p. 53).
[3] Cranmer's answer to question 11 in the document printed in Burnet, *History of the Reformation,* Appendix of Records, part 1, book 3, no. 21.

might be called without the consent, nay, in defiance of the prohibition, of the Supreme Pontiff. The two Councils of Pisa were actually so called, and one of them at least has always been held by a large party to have been a good and regular Council. The Anglican Church, in declaring that a Council cannot be held *in Spiritu Sancto* without the Royal Consent, has really ascribed a higher spiritual power to the King than the most illustrious Gallican Divines have ever ascribed to the Pope.

I have carefully considered what your Lordship has written concerning that great change which, as I hold, took place in the sentiments of our Ecclesiastical rulers during the seventeenth century. It seems to me that the whole question is decided by this single fact, that, till the Act of Uniformity was passed after the Restoration, Episcopal Ordination was not necessary, either in law or in practice, to the exercise of any priestly function in the Church of England. "The Act of Uniformity," says Clarendon, "admitted no person to have any Cure of Souls or any Ecclesiastical dignity in the Church of England, but such who had been or should be ordained Priest or Deacon by some Bishop. This," he goes on, "was *new*. For there had been *many*, and at present there were some, who possessed Benefices with Cure of Souls and other Ecclesiastical promotions, who had never received orders but in France or Holland; and these men must now receive new Ordination, which had always been held unlawful in the Church, or by this Act of Parliament must be deprived of their livelihood, which they enjoyed in the most flourishing and peaceable time of the Church. And therefore it was said that this had not been the opinion of the Church of England, and that it would be a great reproach on all other Protestant Churches who had no Bishop, as if they had no Ministers, and consequently were no Churches; for that it was well known the Church of England did not allow reordination, as the ancient Church never admitted it: inasmuch as, if any priest of the Church of Rome renounces the Communion thereof, his ordination is not questioned. And, therefore, the not admitting the Ministers of other Protestants to have the same privilege here, can proceed on no other ground than that they looked not upon them as Ministers, having no ordination, which is a judgment the Church of England had not ever owned."[1]

Thus far Clarendon. But the Statute-book contains evidence still more decisive. I refer to the Act of Parliament, 13 Eliz. c. 12. "In order," says the Act, "that the Churches of the Queen's Majesty may be supplied with Pastors of sound religion, it is enacted that every person pretending to be a Priest or Minister of God's Holy Word and Sacraments, by reason of

[1] *Life of Clarendon*, Oxford, 1759, II, 152. In a note on this passage, Phillpotts observes that Clarendon was merely reporting one side of the argument in Parliament (*Correspondence*, 2nd edn, p. 57).

any other form of institution, consecration, or ordination, than the form set forth by Parliament," shall be episcopally ordained, if not ordained already? No; but shall subscribe the Articles, or shall be incapable of holding any benefice. And with this law the practice was in perfect harmony.[1] Elizabeth made Whittingham Dean of Durham. He had been ordained at Geneva. The Archbishop of York questioned the appointment. The case was tried, and finally decided in Whittingham's favour. Dr. Delaune, who had been ordained at Leyden by the Presbytery, was presented in the reign of James I. to a living in the diocese of Norwich, and was instituted by Bishop Overall. In Strype's Life of Grindal is the license which the Archbishop gave to John Morrison, who had been ordained by the Presbytery of Lothian. The preamble recites that Morrison had been admitted to the Ministry according to the laudable rite of the Reformed Church of Scotland, and that he was orthodox in the faith. He is, therefore, empowered by the Primate to celebrate divine offices, and *to minister the Sacraments* throughout the whole province of Canterbury.[2]

The Convocation, unless I greatly mistake, ratified the judgment of the Parliament on this subject. For surely the 55th Canon of 1603 must be understood as a distinct recognition of Presbyterian orders. That Canon directs all preachers, before their sermons, to exhort the people to pray for Christ's Holy Catholic Church, and especially for the Churches of England, Scotland, and Ireland. Now, in 1603, Episcopal Ordination was unknown in the Scotch Church. The only Bishops in Scotland were those Tulchan bishops[3] who had never been consecrated, and who were just such bishops as his late Royal Highness the Bishop of Osnaburg.[4] Here then we have a Presbyterian Church mentioned, between two Episcopal Churches, as being, not less than those Episcopal Churches, a branch of Christ's Holy Catholic Church. Is it possible to believe that either the Upper or the Lower House of Convocation, when this Canon was voted, held that the Church of Scotland was not within the definition of a true Church given in the Articles?

I have trespassed so long on your Lordship's patience that I will not venture to discuss the important question, whether the framers of our

---

[1] Phillpotts replied that the law 'applies to those who had been ordained in the preceding reign of Mary, or earlier, by the *Roman Ordinal*' (*ibid.*, p. 51).

[2] John Strype, *The History of the Life and Acts of. . .Edmund Grindal*, Oxford, 1821, book II, ch. 13, and Appendix of Original Papers, book II, no. 17. To the cases of William Whittingham (1524?–79: *DNB*) and William Delaune (d. 1610: *DNB*) Phillpotts replied that ' *Whittingham's* Case was *not* of a *Cure of Souls. Dr. DeLaune's* Case was of the *Institution*, which is not denied of a person not Episcopally Ordained.' As for Morrison, Grindal's license to him 'is the case of an unauthorized act of an individual' (*ibid.*, pp. 51–2).

[3] A term of contempt for the nominal Bishops of Scotland created by the restoration of ecclesiastical titles in 1572.

[4] Frederick, Duke of York.

Articles and Homilies took the Calvinistic or the Arminian view of the great problems of metaphysical theology. In truth I could not, without writing a pamphlet, give one half of the reasons which have led me to the conclusion at which I have arrived. I will, however, just mention one circumstance which seems to me important, and which I do not remember to have seen noticed. The Act of Toleration was specially intended for the relief of the Calvinistic Dissenters. The relief given by that Act was confined to persons who should subscribe all the Articles of the Church of England, with the exception of the 34th, the 35th, the 36th, and some words of the 20th and 27th. The Legislature absolutely required the disciples of Owen[1] and Bunyan, the old members of the Assembly of Divines, men who avowedly held the doctrines of the Confession of Faith, to sign the Articles of the Church of England on Free Will, Justification, Election, and Predestination: and these men made not the least objection. Now surely, if the sense of the Articles were plainly Arminian, it would have been as absurd to offer toleration to the Puritans on condition of their subscribing the Articles as it would have been to offer toleration to the Socinians on condition of their subscribing the Athanasian Creed, or to Papists on condition of their taking the declaration against Transubstantiation. The fact that a law intended for the relief of sects notoriously Calvinistic was framed in this way, I consider as a distinct declaration of the Legislature that the Doctrinal Articles may honestly, and without any straining, be understood in a Calvinistic sense.

You are probably aware that the strictly Calvinistic Dissenters long continued to attach great importance to the rule about subscription, and were alarmed and indignant when it was relaxed. They actually petitioned Parliament against any relaxation in 1773. A very remarkable speech of Burke on the subject will be found in his works.[2] The writings of William Huntington, S.S., who was something more than a Calvinist, contain several curious passages on this subject. He evidently wished the subscription to be retained for the purpose of discouraging Arminianism among the Non-Conformists.

But I must stop. I again assure your Lordship that I will carefully reconsider the opinion which I have formed on these important matters, and will weigh with attention the many valuable observations contained in your letters.[3]

---

[1] John Owen (1616–83: *DNB*), the leading Congregationalist preacher and theologian of his day.
[2] Speech on a Bill for the Relief of Protestant Dissenters, 17 March 1773.
[3] TBM received Phillpotts's answer to this letter on the 26th and wrote in his Journal that there was 'nothing in it – he is beaten hollow and is beginning to lose his temper. I need not answer him, and I will not' (1, 478). Phillpotts had concluded his remarks on TBM's use of Strype's evidence thus: 'Do not think me very saucy, when I say, that a person *willing* to

I beg again to repeat the expression of my respectful gratitude for your great kindness. When your parliamentary duties call you to London I will do myself the honour of repeating my thanks in person. In the mean time / I have the honour to be, / My Lord,

Your Lordship's most faithful servant,

T. B. Macaulay.

TO MRS HENRY HART MILMAN, 23 JANUARY 1849

MS: McGill University.

Albany Jany. 23. 1849

Dear Mrs. Milman,

I am very sorry that I am engaged on the 30th.[1] It is shocking to think that for that awful anniversary – indeed centenary – when all good churchmen should be fasting, I have had four invitations to dinner, and two from clergymen, one indeed from a Bishop. To think that, on such an occasion, there should be feasting at once in the Deanery of St Paul's and in the Cloisters of Westminster! I heartily wish however that I could take part of your calf's head.

Ever yours truly

T B Macaulay

TO UNIDENTIFIED RECIPIENT, 23 JANUARY 1849

MS: Trinity College.

Albany London / January 23. 1849

Sir,

It has been a great pleasure to me to be of any service to a family in which my valued friend Hallam is interested. I wish all success and honor to your son in the career on which he is entering. / I have the honor to be, / Sir,

Your faithful Servant

T B Macaulay

come to such a conclusion on such evidence would make an invaluable foreman of a jury to convict another *Algernon Sidney*. Seriously, I never met with so monstrous an attempt to support a foregone conclusion' (*Correspondence*, 2nd edn, p. 54).

[1] The anniversary of the execution of Charles I. TBM dined at home on that day, with Ellis (Journal, 1, 484).

TO JOSEPH EDLESTON,[1] 24 JANUARY 1849

MS: Trinity College. *Envelope:* The Reverend Joseph Edleston / etc. etc. etc. / Trinity College / Cambridge. *Subscription:* TBM.

Albany London / January 24. 1849

Sir,

I am truly obliged to you for your kind letter. Your suggestion, coupled with one from Lord Mahon, has, I really think, led me to the discovery of the meaning of the letters which I thought undecipherable. Father Mansuete, a Franciscan, was James's confessor. P.M.A.C.F. may well be Père Mansuete, a Catholic Friar.[2] I do not find in the list of the Portuguese ecclesiastics about the Queen a single name which will suit. Barillon mentions too that the Portuguese priests could not speak French or English enough to communicate with Charles.[3] It is therefore not very likely that they would have been able to communicate with James: and his own confessor was the person who would most naturally have discharged that duty.

I do not think that I bore hard upon Jeffreys.[4] Consider that Stanhope[5] was, though young, the man whom the University evidently put forward, through the whole matter, as the public advocate. He had been in charge of the Academical records, and was well acquainted with them. He had been sent up to London to engage the good offices of the Duke of Albemarle. He had been twice in conference with Sunderland. Perhaps his high birth had something to do with this: for he was one of the few divines who, in that age, could boast of noble descent. But he was also a man of eminent learning, and was afterwards thrice prolocutor of the Convocation. His colleagues in the syndicate evidently put him forward as the person best qualified to speak for them. Jeffreys, like an unjust and cruel judge as he was, silenced the man who had the knowledge and self-possession which the occasion required, and crossexamined with severity the man who knew nothing and who was frightened out of his wits. Observe too that Jeffreys was almost as rude to Dr. Cook[6] as to Stanhope.

---

[1] Edleston (1816?–95) was Fellow and Bursar of Trinity, 1840–63, and Vicar of Gainsford, Durham, 1862–95.

[2] See 4 January.

[3] *History,* I, 436.

[4] The reference in what follows is to TBM's account of Jeffreys' treatment of a delegation from Cambridge summoned before the Court of High Commission to explain why the University refused to admit a Benedictine monk recommended by James for a degree (*History,* II, 280–4).

[5] George Stanhope (1660–1728: *DNB*), then a Fellow of Kings, was among the deputies that Jeffreys refused to hear; TBM's information is from Thomas Howell, ed., *A Complete Collection of State Trials,* 34 vols., 1809–28, XI, 1313–39.

[6] Dr William Cook (1633?–1707), Fellow of Jesus; the quotation from Jeffreys is in Howell, *State Trials,* XI, 1329.

"How came you who never were Vice Chancellor to know the Vice Chancellor's oath better than one who has taken it?"

One error about Newton is corrected in the third edition.[1] Your other hints shall be carefully considered.

It is always gratifying to me to be brought into any sort of communication with my beloved College. Of all the titles which I have a right to add to my name that of late Fellow of Trinity is the one of which I am proudest. / I have the honor to be, / Sir,

Your faithful Servant,

T B Macaulay

TO LORD MAHON, 2 FEBRUARY 1849

MS: Stanhope Papers, Chevening. *Partly published:* Stanhope, *Miscellanies,* 2nd Series, p. 144.

Albany Feby. 2. 1849

Dear Lord Mahon,

I am more gratified than I can express by the Duke's approbation;[2] and I most sincerely thank you for communicating it to me. You shall have Mr. Arbuthnot's letter back in a day or two. I could not deny myself the pleasure of sending it to my sister.

I really think that out of your guess and out of a piece of information which I received the other day from Cambridge, I have made a correct explanation of P.M.A.C.F. I will tell it you when we meet.[3] I do not claim more than a third part of the merit of the discovery, indeed hardly so much.

Ever yours truly

T B Macaulay

[1] TBM's statement that Newton's *Principia* was printed at the expense of the Royal Society (*History*, II, 282) is corrected to 'with the sanction of the Royal Society' in the third edition. Edleston was editing the *Correspondence of Sir Isaac Newton and Professor Cotes*, published in 1850.

[2] Mahon had sent TBM a letter from Charles Arbuthnot, confidential friend of the Duke of Wellington, reporting the Duke's compliment to TBM's *History:* 'He says that this History makes one as well and even better acquainted with the times of which it is written than we are with those in which we live. I can assure you that I never knew the Duke so unbounded as he is in praise of Mr. Macaulay's Work' (Arbuthnot to Mahon, 1 February: MS, Chevening). 'Though I am almost callous to praise now,' TBM wrote in his Journal, 'this praise made me happy for two minutes. A fine old fellow!' (Trevelyan, II, 249).

[3] Seeing Mahon on 10 February at a meeting of the British Museum Trustees, TBM wrote down the name 'Père Mansuete a Franciscan of Loraine' and handed it to Mahon. This note, with Mahon's explanation of it, is now among the papers at Chevening.

TO LORD MAHON, 3 FEBRUARY 1849

MS: Trinity College.

Albany Feb 3. 1849

Dear Lord Mahon,

I now return you Mr. Arbuthnot's letter with many thanks.

Ever yours truly

T B Macaulay

TO SIR JAMES STEPHEN, 7 FEBRUARY 1849

MS: Cambridge University Library.

Albany London Feb 7. 1849

Dear Stephen,

I am suffering, not only with fortitude, but with great complacency, those inflictions which prove me to be an honest historian. The Bishop of Exeter thinks me unfair to the Church of England: Sam Gurney[1] thinks me unfair to the Quakers: Dr. Vaughan[2] thinks me unfair to the Puritans; and Lord Shrewsbury thinks me unfair to the Roman Catholics. I believe my position to be perfectly defensible on all the four sides: but if any side be more assuredly impregnable than the others, it is that which Lord Shrewsbury has attacked.

Will any person seriously deny that, since the time of Leo the Tenth and of Charles the Fifth, Italy and Spain have been going down politically and intellectually, and that England, Scotland, and Northern Germany have been rising?[3] Spain to be sure produced a few eminent writers during the century which followed the Reformation. Then she became barren. Italy was not quite so barren. Yet what is the value of the Italian literature since 1600? And observe that the best Italian writers since 1600 were men emancipated from the yoke of the Church. Fra Paolo, my favourite historian, was, as Bossuet says, a Protestant in a friar's gown.[4] What Alfieri, Parini,[5] and other eminent Italians of the eighteenth century

---

[1] Samuel Gurney (1786–1856: *DNB*), one of the Gurneys of Norfolk, a banker, philanthropist, and leader of the Quaker community. He was one of the delegation of Quakers who called on TBM to protest against his treatment of Penn: see 2 January.

[2] Charles James Vaughan (1816–97: *DNB*), Headmaster of Harrow since 1844. Vaughan was one of Arnold's best pupils at Rugby, had a distinguished career at Trinity, and restored the fortunes of Harrow.

[3] TBM had asserted in the *History*, I, 48, that in the last three centuries the chief object of the Church of Rome had been 'to stunt the growth of the human mind' and that 'whatever advance has been made in knowledge, in freedom, in wealth, and in the arts of life, has been made in spite of her, and has everywhere been in inverse proportion to her power.'

[4] *Histoire des Variations des Églises Protestantes*, book 7, section 109 (*Oeuvres*, Versailles, XIX [1816], 495): 'un Protestant habillé en moine.'

[5] Giuseppe Parini (1729–99), Italian poet.

were it is unnecessary to say. I will venture to affirm that the single city of Edinburgh has done more for the human mind during the last hundred years than Italy, Spain and Portugal together during the last two hundred.

Lord Shrewsbury says that the whole literary glory of France is posterior to the Reformation. The truth is that the exception proves the rule which I have laid down. For, though France is called Roman Catholic, her literary glory is almost entirely derived from the two struggles which her great intellects maintained against the Church of Rome. Deduct all the writings of the Jansenist party and all the writings of the philosophers, and a pretty *caput mortuum* you will have left. It is amusing to see Rome claim the glory of the Port Royalists whom she persecuted. As to the Jesuits, what single great original work did any Jesuit ever produce? Bourdaloue's[1] sermons and Fray Gerundio[2] are the two best Jesuit books that I know of; and you will hardly place either very high. The Jesuits wrote good Latin. Of Greek they seem to have known but little. In no modern language has any member of the order produced any work which ranks above the third rate.

As to Germany little can be inferred from comparing together principalities and towns in which Catholics and Protestants are much intermixed. Look at the great line of separation; and say on which side of that line the intellectual glory of Germany is to be found. On which side of that line are Klopstock, Herder, Wieland, Goethe, Schiller, Lessing? Who would take the trouble to learn German, if it were not for what the Protestant part of Germany has produced?

Lord Shrewsbury asks how it is possible that a system which was favourable to civilisation up to the fifteenth century can then have become unfavourable to civilisation. I see no difficulty. In my opinion the part of the Roman Catholic system which has had the greatest effect on the well being of mankind is not the invocation of Saints, or the doctrine of purgatory, or the praying for the dead; but the authority given to the priesthood over the laity. Whether that authority be good or bad for the temporal interests of mankind must depend on this, whether the priesthood be or be not wiser than the laity. For it is on the whole desirable that intelligence should govern. Now up to the fifteenth century I believe that the priests were decidedly the most intelligent part of the community. Therefore the superstition – as I hold it to be – which induced the rest of the society to submit to their guidance, was a salutary superstition. In the sixteenth century the clergy had no intellectual superiority. From that

---

[1] Louis Bourdaloue (1632–1704), French Jesuit.
[2] José De Isla, *Fray Gerundio*, Madrid, 1758. On re-reading it in 1856 TBM remarked that 'as a picture of the state of learning among the educated classes in Spain a century ago the work has great value' and that the author 'seems...to have been a sincerely religious man, as well as a man of wit and taste' (Journal, IX, 34; 37).

time, therefore, I hold that the superstition which induced the rest of the society to submit to them was unmixedly noxious. This view may be erroneous: but surely it is not inconsistent. – But I must stop. Keep this letter to yourself. But you can use it as a brief for me, if Lord S. should harangue you again.

Ever yours
T B Macaulay

TO UNIDENTIFIED RECIPIENT, 7 FEBRUARY 1849

MS: Trinity College.

Albany London / February 7. 1849

Sir,

I am extremely obliged to you for the interesting little work which you have sent me. I wish that every old town in the kingdom had inhabitants as studious of local antiquities and history as yourself and the gentleman whose assistance you acknowledge. / I have the honor to be, / Sir,

Your faithful Servant
T B Macaulay

TO LORD MAHON, 19 FEBRUARY 1849

MS: Stanhope Papers, Chevening.

Albany Feby. 19. 1849

Dear Lord Mahon,

I am not quite well this afternoon; and, that I may not be worse, I must undergo medical discipline to day and to morrow. I must therefore deny myself the pleasure of breakfasting with you in the morning and of meeting you at the club. I reckon on seeing you here on Wednesday.

Ever yours truly,
T B Macaulay

TO WILLIAM STRADLING,[1] 20 FEBRUARY 1849

MS: Yale University. *Envelope:* W Stradling Esq / Chilton Priory / Bridgewater. *Subscription:* T B M.

Albany London / February 20. 1849

Dear Sir,

I am much obliged to you for your letter and for the interesting drawings which accompanied it. I have little hope of being able to revisit

---

[1] See 13 January 1843.

Bridgewater at present. When I am free to leave London, it will be necessary for me to travel through Scotland and Ireland. I must see Glencoe and Killiecrankie, Londonderry, the Boyne, and Athlone. But should any accident call me into your neighbourhood, I shall certainly not omit to look again at your curious collections, and to thank you in person for your kind invitation. / I have the honor to be, / Dear Sir,

Your faithful Servant,

T B Macaulay

TO JOHN PARTRIDGE,[1] 21 FEBRUARY 1849

MS: National Portrait Gallery.

Albany Feb 21 / 1849

Dear Sir,

I will call in Brook Street at one on Thursday if that will suit you. I hope that a single sitting will suffice. For at present I find it difficult to spare time.

Very truly yours,

T B Macaulay

TO CHARLES MACAULAY, 3 MARCH 1849

MS: University of London. *Mostly published:* Rae, *Temple Bar,* LXXXVI, 199–200.

Albany London March 3. / 1849

Dear Charles,

Whether this letter will reach you in the Mauritius, I do not know. I write at a venture. I learned yesterday that Lord Grey has resolved, without any solicitation on the part of anybody connected with you, to offer you the Secretaryship of the Colony.

I do not wish to influence your decision. But I think it right to tell you that, in my opinion, your chances of obtaining public employment in England are not great, and that the situation now offered to you puts you in the way of whatever promotion the Colonial Office has to give. I should hope that, in a very few years, you would obtain a good government. If, on consideration, you make up your mind to pass the years of your most vigorous manhood in serving your country abroad, the advantages are

---

[1] Partridge (1790–1872: *DNB*), a portrait painter, was at work on a group portrait of the Fine Arts Commissioners; the painting is now in the National Portrait Gallery, but has been ruined by the effects of bitumen. An oil sketch of the whole and a number of finished oil studies of individual sitters still survive, including one of TBM. Partridge's studies have been discussed in detail by Richard Ormond, 'John Partridge and the Fine Arts Commissioners,' *Burlington Magazine,* CIX (July 1967), 397–402. TBM notes in his Journal for 22 February that he 'sate two hours to Partridge' (I, 515).

obvious. You will get over the years of your boy's education.[1] You will be able, I presume, to live on your appointments, and your private income will be saved. I should hope that, in time, part even of your official income may be laid by. By the time that you are fifty you will have a comfortable independence honorably earned; and we may then hope to be able to put your son into some place in which he will not be a burden to you.

This is one side of the question. Whether you think these advantages worth years of expatriation is a point of which you alone are the proper judge. Trevelyan, as usual, is decidedly of opinion that you ought to accept the offer of the colonial office.[2] My own wishes, I confess, are rather on the same side. But I am sensible that no man knows what will make another man happy. I would infinitely rather read and write by my quiet fireside in the Albany than be first Lord of the Treasury or Governor General of India; and I shall not think that we have the smallest right to blame you if, on full consideration, you prefer a quiet and modest rural life in England to the more lucrative path which is open before you. I only beg you again to consider that you are now called to chuse between public employment and privacy. I should deceive you if I suffered you to hope that any place here is likely to be attainable. Reduction is going on in every department; and I have no longer any pretence for asking favours of the ministers.

Mary's feeling is among the matters which you will have to consider. I do not pretend to guess at what her wishes may be. Hannah will write to her without delay, and will apprise her of what is in contemplation. We are all well and prospering. The sale of my book has been enormous, – twelve thousand copies in three months. None of Sir Walter's novels went faster. The demand still keeps up at 400 a week, and we are going to stereotype. I expect to make some thousands pleasantly enough by this success. I should have sent you a copy long ago if I had felt any assurance that it would reach you. I shall now await for the publication of the stereo-type edition, which will be Auctior et emendatior.[3] The Americans have doubtless taken care to supply our colonies. / Ever, my dear Charles,

Yours most affectionately

T B Macaulay

P.S. We were all most pleased by your literary exertions.

[1] Thomas George Macaulay (1842–64).

[2] Trevelyan wrote to Charles on the same day as TBM, saying that all the family agreed that Charles should accept the appointment, that 'Macaulay and I should write to you, to advise you to do so, and that I should tell Lord Grey that we were going to do so....Now, My dear Charles, I hope you will think that we have done the best for you' (Trevelyan Letter Books: University of Newcastle).

[3] TBM had been preparing corrections for this edition since late January (Journal, 1, 476); 3,000 copies were published in April.

TO THOMAS FLOWER ELLIS, 6 MARCH 1849

MS: Trinity College. *Mostly published:* Trevelyan, II, 253.

Albany London / March 6. 1849

Dear Ellis,

I am truly glad to hear that I have cured a Serjeant at law of many prejudices. When I receive the learned gentleman's epistle, I will return a most gracious answer.

I am to harangue at Glasgow on the 21st or 22nd.[1] You will then, I suppose, be at Liverpool.

Pray tell Adolphus how much I am obliged to him for his criticisms. I have generally followed his advice. I see that I now and then fell into Gough's error.[2] I got into a passion with the Stuarts as he did with the Sikhs, and consequently did less damage than I should have done if I had kept my temper.

I hear that Croker has written a furious article against me,[3] and that Lockhart wishes to suppress it, declaring that the current of public opinion runs strongly on my side, and that a violent attack by a personal enemy will do no harm to me and much harm to the Quarterly Review. How they settle the matter I care not, as the Duke says, one twopenny damn.[4]

Ever yours,
T B Macaulay

TO ARTHUR KNIGHT,[5] 6 MARCH 1849

MS: Trinity College. *Address:* For / Arthur Knight Esq.

Albany London / March 6. 1849

My dear Sir,

I am truly grateful to your relation for the interesting portrait which he has sent me, and to you for taking charge of it. I shall value it much.

---

[1] TBM gave his inaugural address at Glasgow on 21 March.

[2] Sir Hugh Gough (1779–1869: *DNB*), first Viscount Gough, commander in India during the first and second Sikh wars, had just fought the battle of Chillianwallah with heavy losses; the news of the battle aroused much noise against him at home. TBM wrote in his Journal that 'this fool Gough has done all that he could do to lose a battle, and was saved from defeat solely by the pluck of his men' (I, 521: 3 March).

[3] 'Mr. Macaulay's *History of England*,' *Quarterly Review*, LXXXIV (March 1849), 549–630. The article is of extraordinary length, and, like TBM's review of Croker's Boswell, is full of minute criticisms.

[4] 'It was the Duke of Wellington who invented this oath, so disproportioned to the greatness of its author' (Trevelyan, II, 253n).

[5] 'I have not succeeded in identifying him or his brother: the latter may possibly be John Prescott Knight (1803–81: *DNB*), portrait painter and Secretary to the Royal Academy, 1848–73.

I have the pleasure of knowing your brother, and I occasionally meet him. I need not say that there are very few persons whose approbation I prize so highly as his.

I hear bad accounts of Combe Florey from several quarters.[1] To be sure no parish can expect a succession of Sydneys. Indeed there was but one in England; and I never shall, I am afraid, see another. / Believe me, / My dear Sir,

Your faithful Servant,

T B Macaulay

TO THOMAS FLOWER ELLIS, 8 MARCH 1849

MS: Trinity College. *Partly published:* Trevelyan, II, 253–4.

Albany March 8 / 1849

Dear Ellis,

Mr. Broderip's offer[2] is most kind and liberal. I accept it with much gratitude. A collection made by Heber[3] cannot but be highly valuable and curious. I should be able, probably in a few days, certainly in a few weeks, to make all the notes and extracts which I should require.[4]

Do you think that it would be intrusive in me to write to Mr. Broderip or to call on him?

At last I have attained true glory. As I walked through Fleet Street the day before yesterday, I saw a copy of Hume at a bookseller's window with the following label. "Only £2 " 2 " 0 – Hume's History of England in eight volumes, highly valuable as an introduction to Macaulay." I laughed so convulsively that the other people who were staring at the books took me for a poor demented gentleman. Alas for poor David! As for me, only one height of renown yet remains to be attained. I am not yet in Madame Tussaud's Wax work.[5] I live however in hope of seeing some day an advertisement of a new groupe of figures, Mr. Macaulay, in one of his own

---

[1] Sydney Smith had been succeeded as Rector of Combe Florey by Thomas Prowse Lethbridge (1810–51); he was in delicate health and kept a curate there, who was too poor to live in the Rectory (Empson to Napier, 10 April [1845]: MS, British Museum).

[2] W. J. Broderip (1789–1859: *DNB*), a London magistrate and a well-known amateur naturalist, had offered to lend TBM a collection of ballads and broadsides. TBM acknowledges his use of it in the *History*, calling it 'an excellent collection formed by Mr. Richard Heber, and now the property of Mr. Broderip, by whom it was kindly lent to me' (III, 54).

[3] Richard Heber (1773–1833: *DNB*), one of the greatest of English book-collectors; his library was dispersed by sale in the 1830s.

[4] TBM kept the books until January 1853, when Broderip at last asked for their return (Journal, VI, 26).

[5] He has been there since 1861.

coats, conversing with Mr. Silk Buckingham in oriental costume, and Mr. Robert Montgomery in full canonicals.

I return Broderip's letter.

Ever yours

T B Macaulay

TO EDWARD EVERETT, 8 MARCH 1849

MS: Massachusetts Historical Society. *Extract published:* Frothingham, *Everett*, p. 302.

Albany London / March 8. 1849

My dear Everett,

I assure you that I have not for a long time been more delighted than when, on entering my library this morning, I saw a letter from you on the table. I have long been resolving to write to you, and blaming myself for delay. Yet I felt that sort of difficulty which, I believe, is the chief impediment to the correspondence of friends who really value each other. It is easy to write to a person to whom you write daily. It is easy also to write an occasional letter when something important is to be communicated. But to write an occasional letter, containing nothing very particular, is to me, and, I imagine, to many other people, a very arduous task. I am truly obliged to you for forcing me to do what I ought to have done before.

I need not tell you how gratifying your approbation is to me. And yet, much as I delight in your praise, I wish that you had spared one page at least to tell me about yourself. We hear that you are out of trammels,[1] and that you are perfectly your own master; and we hope that we shall profit by your liberty: I assure you that there is not a breakfast party or dinner party assembled by any of your old friends, at which the probability of your paying England a visit is not discussed. I am quite sure that every American whom you have furnished with letters of recommendation will tell you that a line from you is the best passport into the best society of London. Even your patriotism ought to impel you to come over often, and to stay with us long. For I am quite sure that you can do more than any man living to promote good feeling between New England and Old England: and we are both, I am confident, equally convinced that the concord of the two great branches of the English race is of the highest importance to the happiness of both.

You will write, however, shortly, and tell me what you are doing, and whether there is any chance of our seeing you here soon. You will find me still in the Albany, but in much larger, brighter, and better rooms than those in which I had the great pleasure of seeing you formerly. I have done

[1] Everett resigned as President of Harvard in January.

with politics. I have competence, liberty, leisure, tolerable health, very dear and affectionate relations. The serious business of the rest of my life will be my history; and that business will be a pleasure. I am one of the few people to whom Horace's "Qui fit Mæcenas"[1] is inapplicable. For, really, if I had to chuse my own lot in life, I should carefully pick out from the whole vast heap the precise ticket which has fallen to my share. I write all this egotism in the hope of drawing forth some egotism from you in return.

Thanks for your hint about the Archives of Simancas.[2] I hope to be at Paris shortly,[3] and I will profit by your suggestions.

Pray remember me kindly to Mrs. Everett and to Miss Everett, and believe me ever yours most truly

T B Macaulay

TO MRS WILLIAM HARDY COZENS-HARDY,[4] 10 MARCH 1849

MS: Trinity College. *Envelope:* Mrs. Cozens Hardy / Letheringsett Hall / Holt / Norfolk. *Subscription:* TBM.

Albany London / March 10. 1849

Madam;

I do not see that the text which you quote has any reference whatever to the transmission of political power. The elevation of Solomon to the throne by the choice of David, acting under the advice of Nathan, seems to prove the contrary. Besides, the doctrine which you cite from the History of Palestine is of itself sufficient to refute Filmer's whole theory.[5] "The patriarchs," says the historian, "exercised the power of giving priority to any son, but the Mosaic law overruled this practice in favour of the first born."[6] Filmer's theory was that the law of primogeniture was patriarchal and Ante Mosaical. Had it not been patriarchal and Ante Mosaical there would have been no pretence for representing it as binding on Christians. / I have the honor to be, / Madam,

Your most obedient Servant,
T B Macaulay

[1] *Satires,* I, i, I.

[2] The Spanish national archives, near Valladolid. TBM had transcripts from the Spanish archives in the Mackintosh papers and also from Guizot, who loaned him copies of Ronquillo's despatches: see the note acknowledging TBM's pleasure in 'this mark of the friendship of so great a man' (*History,* I, 465–6).

[3] TBM went to Paris in September.

[4] Sarah Theobald (d. 1891), of Norwich, married William Hardy Cozens-Hardy in 1830.

[5] TBM summarizes Sir Robert Filmer's theories of divine right in *History,* I, 71; they held, among other things, that 'the rule of succession in order of primogeniture was a divine institution, anterior to the Christian, and even to the Mosaic dispensation....'

[6] A passage like this is in John Kitto, *The History of Palestine,* 1843, pp. 65–6.

TO W. J. BRODERIP, 12 MARCH 1849

Text: Copy, Huntington Library.

Albany March 12 / 1849

My dear Sir,

I am truly grateful to you for intrusting me with a collection so valuable as this, at the first glance, appears to be.[1] I have only turned over six or eight leaves, and I have found already much curious information.

I have alluded to the charge which Jeffreys delivered at Bristol in page 337 of my first volume.[2] Being myself a Bristol man on the mother's side, I am sorry to be forced to own that his scurrility was, on that occasion, not altogether without excuse.

Lord Campbell had seen a Dutch copy of the engraving of the Chancellor's capture.[3] The English copy, I have no doubt, is the original.

With repeated thanks, believe me, / My dear Sir

Your faithful Servant,

T B Macaulay

TO UNIDENTIFIED RECIPIENT, 12 MARCH 1849

MS: Mr Joseph Hamburger.

Albany London / March 12. 1849

Sir,

I have just found on my table the volume which you did me the honor to send me.[4] I hope very soon to find leisure to become acquainted with the contents. The lines on which I opened struck me much. / I have the honor to be, / Sir,

Your faithful Servant,

T B Macaulay

TO JOHN HILL BURTON, 14 MARCH 1849

MS: National Library of Scotland.

Albany London / March 14. 1849

My dear Sir,

I should like much to look at the Edinburgh Records with you, and to

[1] See *to* Ellis, 8 March.
[2] Jeffreys reprimanded the magistrates of Bristol for their connivance in the trade of kidnapping to supply the American labor market.
[3] TBM makes no reference to an engraving of the scene of Jeffreys' capture in his account (*History*, II, 562–3); C. H. Firth includes what is probably the print in question in his edition of the *History*, III (1914), 1211.
[4] TBM's Journal for this date gives no clue to the identity of the recipient.

talk over the question of the Duke's visit.[1] Mr. Robertson's[2] very accurate and sensible letter seems to me to leave the matter where it was. The Duchess's letter, even if we suppose it to have been written in January 1684, does not at all prove that the Duke ran down to Scotland in July 1684: and the silence of all historians, of the Gazette, and of Lord Fountainhall, seems to me to be all but decisive. Mr. Laing tells me that the entry in the Council Book is apparently in a different hand from that in which the other entries of that time were made, and may therefore probably be of later date.[3] At least so I understood his letter which I cannot at this moment find. But you of course know all that is to be known on that subject.

I shall be most anxious to see your book. / Ever, my dear Sir,

Yours most truly

T B Macaulay

TO EPES SARGENT,[4] 15 MARCH 1849

MS: Boston Public Library. *Envelope:* Epes Sargent Esq / Boston / Massachusetts / United States. *Subscription:* TBM.

Albany London / March 15. 1849

Sir,

I have received several friendly communications from America on the subject to which your letter relates.[5] My answer to all those communications has been the same. The question is one to be decided, not by me, but by the American public. I should have thought myself injured if the Messrs. Harpers had taken on themselves to alter the substance or the

[1] See 22, 26, and 30 September and 6 October 1848.
[2] Probably Joseph Robertson (1810–66: *DNB*), a schoolfellow and lifelong friend of Burton, newspaper editor in Glasgow and Edinburgh, and, from 1853, Curator of the Records in the Edinburgh Register House.
[3] See *to* Laing, 13 December 1848.
[4] Sargent (1813–80) was an American journalist and miscellaneous writer.
[5] Sargent has noted on this letter that it 'was in reply to one from me on the question of the alteration of the spelling in his History by the American publishers,' Harper and Brothers. The subject was one that stirred a commotion in the American press. Sampson Low, Harpers' London agent, wrote to TBM on 8 March begging that TBM would send a letter to New York affirming that the altered spelling made no difference in the work (MS, Trinity); I do not know whether TBM sent a reply. He writes in his Journal that 'I cannot but think that the outcry on this subject has been raised merely by some booksellers who wish to invade the quasi copyright of the Harpers, and are ashamed to do so without some excuse' (I, 528: 9 March 1849). So anxious were the Harpers on the matter that they persuaded Chauncey Goodrich, Professor of Theology at Yale, son-in-law of Noah Webster, and editor of the 1847 Webster's *Dictionary* on which Harpers based the spelling of the *History*, to draw up a statement of facts as 'one who has no interested motives in the case'; Goodrich's statement, which was sent to TBM, suggests that the clamor had been gotten up by rival publishers (20 February 1849: MS, Trinity).

style of my book. But I do not conceive that I have a right to complain because they have adopted a mode of spelling which, in some respects, differs from mine. I write *traveller, dulness, defence,* because all Englishmen write so, and because, if I wrote otherwise, I should be accused of affectation or eccentricity. But if your countrymen prefer *traveler, dullness, defense,* I cannot blame a publisher for consulting their taste. Whether the Websterian spelling be or be not generally approved in the United States is a question which I am quite incompetent to decide. / I have the honor to be, / Sir,

Your most obedient Servant,
T B Macaulay

TO LEIGH HUNT, 15 MARCH 1849

MS: British Museum.

Albany March 15 / 1849

Dear Sir,

I did not observe you yesterday night in the crowd at Lord John's.[1] I am sorry that the expectation of meeting me should have caused you any disturbance. I am still more sorry to learn that the Queen's goodness has failed of producing the effect which I had anticipated.[2] / Believe me

Yours very truly
T B Macaulay

TO WILLIAM WHEWELL, 18 MARCH 1849

MS: Trinity College.

Albany March 18. 1849

Dear Whewell,

Your letter has given me more pleasure than I can well express. I was very desirous from the first to send a copy of my book to our library; and I refrained from doing so only because I was afraid of appearing presumptuous. I should now like to wait a few weeks. The third edition,

---

[1] TBM went to 'Lady John's great party in Downing Street' with Hannah: 'Staid close to Hannah and pointed out people to her. She was much amused and interested, and I was glad to see her so' (Journal, I, 535–6).

[2] I have found no further letters from TBM to Hunt, and perhaps for a time there was a break between the two men. In July TBM re-read Hunt's *Byron* and found it so offensive that, he wrote, 'had I remembered the odious nature of the work, I should, I think, have avoided all intercourse with the writer.' And, again, 'I ought never to have assisted him, or used my interest to get him a pension' (Journal, II, 64–5: 16 and 17 July). But next year he shook hands with Hunt on meeting him again (Journal, II, 231: 14 February 1850), and he was still lending money to Hunt in 1857 (Journal, XI, 142: 10 July).

though it consisted of seven thousand copies, is almost exhausted. The fourth will, I believe, be ready by the middle of April, and will be free from some blemishes which disfigure the first three editions. I will direct Longman to get a copy bound for the library of Trinity.[1]

Next week I leave town for Glasgow, where I must pass two days, much against my will, in exhibiting myself and haranguing. I hope to find you in town when I return. Pray remember me very kindly to Mrs. Whewell.

By the bye, what sort of person is Mr. Blackburn,[2] a fellow of our college, who is a candidate for the mathematical chair at Glasgow? Would he really do us honour? If your report be favourable, I may possibly be able to serve him.

Ever yours truly,

T B Macaulay

TO THOMAS LONGMAN, [19 MARCH 1849][3]

Text: Trevelyan, II, 230n.

[London]

I am very unwilling to seem captious about such a work as an Index. By all means let Mr. ————[4] go on. But offer him, with all delicacy and courtesy, from me this suggestion. I would advise him to have very few heads, except proper names. A few there must be, such as Convocation, Nonjurors, Bank of England, National Debt. These are heads to which readers who wish for information on those subjects will naturally turn. But I think that Mr. ———— will on consideration perceive that such heads as Priestcraft, Priesthood, Party Spirit, Insurrection, War, Bible, Crown, Controversies, Dissent, are quite useless.[5] Nobody will ever look at them; and, if every passage in which party-spirit, dissent, the art of war, and the power of the Crown are mentioned is to be noticed in the Index, the size of the volumes will be doubled. The best rule is to keep close to proper names, and never to deviate from that rule without some special occasion.

---

[1] The copy TBM sent is inscribed: 'This Book is presented to Trinity College Cambridge in token of the respect, gratitude and affection of Thomas Babington Macaulay. London May 11. 1849.'

[2] Hugh Blackburn (1823–1909), B.A., Trinity, 1845, and Fellow, 1846, was Professor of Mathematics at Glasgow, 1849–79.

[3] Dated from TBM's Journal of this date: 'a stupid index – I sent it back declining to have anything to do with correcting it' (I, 539–40). An index to each volume was added to the fourth edition of the *History*, printed in April.

[4] Perhaps the Mr Woolcombe to whom a copy of the index was sent on 28 May 1849, according to Longman's records.

[5] Only 'Crown' survives from this list in the published index.

TO UNIDENTIFIED RECIPIENT,[1] 25 MARCH 1849

MS: Buffalo Public Library. *Extract published: Catalogue of the Gluck Collection. . . ,*Buffalo, N.Y., 1899, p. 74.

Albany London March 25. 1849

My dear Sir,

I have received a very kind and welcome letter from you which it would be ungrateful in me not promptly to acknowledge. What you tell me of the reception which my book has found in the United States gratifies me much, but at the same time surprises me. For it seems to me that very few books have in as high a degree the merit or demerit of being intensely English; and I should have thought that this peculiarity, which has conduced not a little to the success of my volumes here, would have made them seem dull to a people who have never seen anything resembling our Court, our Bishops, our country gentlemen, our country clergymen, to a people who are strangers to the feelings of loyalty to a family, respect for an aristocracy, zeal for the privileges of an established Church. I should have thought that our disputes about the patriarchal theory of government, the divine right of kings, regency, abdication, and so forth, would have been as uninteresting to you as the controversy between the followers of Omar and the followers of Ali.[2] I am glad to find that I was mistaken.

I should greatly enjoy a trip to the United States if I could be sure that I should be as free and as obscure there as I am when I go to Paris or Brussels, that I should be at liberty to chuse my own associates, and that I should never be forced to make a show of myself at dinners and public meetings. But my dislike of exhibition, which was always strong, and which never yielded except to clear public duty, has, since I quitted politics, become almost morbid. And what I hear of the form in which your countrymen shew their kindness and esteem for men whose names are at all known deters me from visiting you. I need not tell you that I mean no national reflection. Perhaps the peculiarity to which I allude is honorable to the American character; but it must cause annoyance to sensitive and fastidious men. Brougham or O'Connell would have liked nothing better. But Cowper would have died or gone mad; Byron would have insulted his admirers, and have been shot or tarred and feathered; and, though I have stronger nerves than Cowper's, and, I hope, a better temper than Byron's, I should suffer much pain and give much offence.

---

[1] This letter is listed in the catalogue of W. E. Benjamin, March 1886, offering the collection of James R. Osgood and others for sale. Osgood (1836–92), the American publisher, was too young in 1849 to have been the recipient, but it is conceivable that the letter may have been written to another American publisher and editor, James T. Fields (1817–81), with whom Osgood was associated at a later period. Fields had made the first of his many visits to England in July–September 1847.

[2] I.e., between the two great Muslim sects.

I assure you that I and many others remember your visit to us with pleasure, and hope to see you here again. We have gone through rough times; but a quiet season seems to be before us. – But I must stop.

Ever yours truly
T B Macaulay

TO MRS SARAH AUSTIN, 26 MARCH 1849

MS: Mr F. R. Cowell.

Albany London / March 26. 1849

Dear Mrs. Austin,

I am most grateful for your kindness. The Paston Letters[1] I know well. I am also fortunate enough to have a copy of the memoir of Mr. John Meadows,[2] lent me by a lady, who, like you, claims kindred with him. The more anecdotes and recollections you can send me the more thankful I shall be. But I would rather hear them from you than read them.

This week I hope to be freed from the labour of correcting proofs, and to be able to begin the second portion of my work.[3] I am not in high spirits about it. I am afraid that, even if better executed than the first two volumes, it will be less attractive; and I know that the world always punishes its favourites for its own folly in overpraising them. However I cannot well flinch; and I must do my best.

Ever yours most truly
T B Macaulay

TO SELINA MACAULAY, 27 MARCH 1849

MS: Trinity College.

Albany London / March 27. 1849

Dearest Selina,

I inclose you a cheque. I had a very quick journey to and from Glasgow. The retrospect is pleasant enough. But such exhibitions, while they last, are very distasteful to me. I brought back a superb box which now adorns the drawing room at Clapham.[4]

---

[1] First published between 1787 and 1823. The first two volumes were included in the sale of TBM's library (item 309).

[2] Edgar Taylor, *The Suffolk Bartholomeans: a Memoir of...John Meadows...Ejected under the Act of Uniformity from the Rectory of Ousden in Suffolk,* 1840. Mrs Austin, a Taylor of Norfolk, was descended from Meadows.

[3] TBM had already begun, at least tentatively, the next part of the *History* (Journal, 1, 486: 1 February 1849).

[4] The 'superb box' was a silver gilt box containing the freedom of the City of Glasgow. TBM left London for Glasgow on the 20th; the next day he addressed the University. The speech (it is included in the authorized *Speeches*), published as 'Inaugural Address Delivered

The last copy of my third edition – an edition of seven thousand – went out of Longman's shop on Saturday. The whole sale since the first of December has been thirteen thousand copies. It is very many years since any book of the same price or anything near the same price has had such a sale.

Love to Edward and to Mrs. Edward. The children will hardly understand a message from me, I am afraid.

Ever yours
T B Macaulay

TO LADY THERESA LEWIS, 28 MARCH 1849

MS: New York Public Library.

Albany March 28 1849

Dear Lady Theresa,

I shall have very great pleasure in dining with you on Wednesday next.[1] I am glad that you liked my Glasgow speech. It produced an effect as great as the lyre of Orpheus. For it prevented the boys from pelting the Professors with peas, an effect never before, within living memory, achieved by any orator.

Ever yours truly
T B Macaulay

TO UNIDENTIFIED RECIPIENT,[2] 31 MARCH 1849

MS: Cambridge University Library.

Albany March 31. 1849

My dear Sir,

I am grateful for your suggestions, though I am not convinced that I

by the Right Honourable Thomas Babington Macaulay, on His Installation as Lord Rector of the University of Glasgow,' Glasgow, 1849, was reprinted in London with the following dedication: 'To the Students of the University of Glasgow, this address, published at their request, is inscribed, by their friend, Thomas Babington Macaulay.' TBM attended a dinner at which he gave a toast to the historian Archibald Alison (see 18 November 1850). On the next day he delivered a short speech at the Glasgow Town Hall on receiving the freedom of the city; this was reported in the newspapers at the time, but is not included in the *Speeches*. On the same day TBM left Glasgow for Edinburgh, where he had his last meeting with Jeffrey at Craigcrook. The next day, 23 March, he returned to London (Journal, I, 541–52: 20–23 March 1849).

[1] The party included Clarendon, Luttrell, Greville, and Labouchere (Journal, I, 562: 4 April).
[2] It seems likely, despite the discrepancy in dates, that this letter was written to the person mentioned in TBM's Journal for 12 March: 'an absurd letter from a man at Cambridge telling me. . .that, as a father of a family, he wished me to leave out all mention of the story about Kirke [*History*, I, 635–6]. I answered that. . .I wrote history not solely or chiefly for

ought to adopt them. If I were conscious of having anywhere disgraced myself by trying to gratify prurient imaginations with licentious descriptions, I should, I hope, with shame and sorrow, hasten to repair so great an offence. I have always thought the indelicacy of Gibbon's great work a more serious blemish than even his uncandid hostility to the Christian religion. But I cannot admit that a book like mine is to be regarded as written for female boarding schools. I open a school for men: I teach the causes of national prosperity and decay: and the particular time about which I write is a time when profligacy, having been compelled during some years to wear the mask of hypocrisy, had just thrown that mask away, and stood forth with a brazen impudence of which there is scarcely any other example in any modern society. How is it possible to treat a subject like mine without inserting a few paragraphs, – perhaps there may be, in my two thick volumes, two pages, – which it would be better that a young lady should not read aloud? How many of the most instructive chapters in the Bible, Chapters of the highest value as illustrating the frailty of human nature, the tendency of crime to draw on crime, and the frightful effect of private vices on public affairs, are such as no parent would desire his daughter to read aloud? I am not aware that there is a single line in my work which can sully the imagination of anybody who is in the habit of listening to the morning and evening lessons at Church.

As to the other point to which you advert, I have done my best to tell truth, and have consequently been abused by High Churchmen, Low Churchmen, Papists, Quakers, Presbyterians and Voluntaries. I see no reason to retract a syllable. I have never denied that our Reformers, with one exception, were, in the main, honest men. The exception is Cranmer whom I believe, and can prove, to have had as little claim to the praise of honesty as old Talleyrand himself. / Believe me, / My dear Sir,

Yours very truly

T B Macaulay

TO JOHN EVELYN DENISON, [2 APRIL 1849][1]

MS: University of Nottingham.

Albany / Monday

Dear Denison,

I am extremely vexed about this mistake. I wrote to you, as soon as I

young ladies but for men, and could not omit everything that might be unfit for a girl to read aloud' (1, 533). Perhaps this letter is a second letter to the same person on the same subject.

[1] The date must be that of the breakfast party that TBM gave on 2 April to Mahon, Bancroft, Whewell, Austin, Rogers, and Henry Hallam (Journal, 1, 559) just before leaving on an Easter tour, 5 April.

received your letter, begging you to breakfast here this morning; and I was a little surprised at having no answer: but I supposed that you might have left town for the Easter holidays. My servants have committed some blunder; but I cannot detect the offender.

I am truly obliged to you for your kind invitation. But our course lies very far from Lincolnshire. We are bound for Chester and the Menai Straits.[1]

Kindest remembrances and thanks to Lady Charlotte.

Ever yours truly,

T B Macaulay

TO GEORGE BANCROFT, 9 APRIL 1849

Text: Copy, Massachusetts Historical Society.

Albany April 9 1849

My dear Sir,

Many thanks for your present,[2] which I found today on my table, when I arrived in town after a short excursion into the country. I am, I own, particularly gratified by the popularity of my book in the United States, because that popularity was altogether unexpected by me. I thought my book too English to please anywhere but in England: and I am still puzzled to understand how, even if it were a much better work than my vanity can persuade me that it is, it should interest any great number of your countrymen. You have no Court, no aristocracy, no established Church. You have not the sentiment of loyalty to a family. The doctrines of divine right and non resistance must seem to you a mere gibberish. I should have thought that to most Americans a history like mine would have been as unattractive as a history of the disputes between the followers of Omar and the followers of Ali, or between the Greens and the Blues at Constantinople. And I am glad to find that I was wrong.

Ever yours truly

T B Macaulay

---

[1] TBM, Trevelyan, Hannah, Fanny, Margaret, and George left on 5 April for Chester, went to Bangor on the 6th, to Lichfield on the 7th, and returned to London on the 9th (Journal, I, 562–9).

[2] TBM identifies this as 'a cheap American edition of my book...sent me by Bancroft' (Journal, I, 570: 9 April). The edition is very likely that published at Boston by Phillips, Sampson and Co., 1849. A MS note in a copy at Yale says that 'This edition of the first volume of Macaulay's History was issued at Boston in consequence of the feeling excited by the issue on the part of the Messrs. Harper of the work with the orthography sanctioned by Webster's Dictionary. Ed. 1847. N. Porter.' Porter, then Professor of Philosophy and later President of Yale, succeeded his colleague Chauncey Goodrich as editor of Webster's *Dictionary:* for the spelling controversy, see 15 March 1849.

TO ALFRED WESTWOOD,[1] 11 APRIL 1849

MS: Trinity College. *Envelope:* Alfred Westwood Esq / Leytonstone / Essex. *Subscription:* TBM.

Albany London / April 11. 1849

Sir,

I am much obliged to you for the interest which you are so kind as to take in the reputation of my work. But you may be quite easy. No man, as Bentley said, was ever written down but by himself.[2]

There is scarcely one criticism in Croker's silly article which does not admit of complete refutation. It is quite true that I was led by Coxe into the mistake of calling Sir Winston Churchill a baronet instead of a knight.[3] But that mistake was corrected three months ago; and seven thousand copies have been sold which are free from it. I have discovered many errors in my book which have escaped the Reviewer. They will be rectified in the fourth edition which is about to appear. I doubt not that I shall hereafter discover others; for no work so extensive was ever free from inaccuracies. But I am convinced that the general view which I have taken of the History of our Revolution will, the more it is examined, appear the more correct.

I have no intention of engaging in a controversy with an antagonist whom I despise. If I should see reason to think that this attack has produced any effect on the public mind, I may consider whether it would be worth while to employ two hours in exposing his blunders. But my belief is that, in a few weeks, his paper will be as much forgotten as everything else that he ever wrote. / I have the honor to be, / Sir,

Your obedient Servant,

T B Macaulay

TO LADY TREVELYAN, [12 APRIL 1849]

MS: Trinity College.

Albany Thursday

Dearest Hannah,

Longman has just been here to tell me that my fourth edition, of three

---

[1] I have not identified him.

[2] See 24 May 1844.

[3] TBM calls Marlborough's father a 'poor Cavalier baronet' (*History*, 1, 459); the error was corrected in the third edition. Croker notes the mistake in his review of the *History*, *Quarterly Review*, LXXXIV, 608. Though TBM blames William Coxe's *Memoirs of Marlborough*, 3 vols., 1818–19, for the error, Coxe says correctly that Marlborough's father was rewarded for his loyalty by a knighthood.

thousand copies, which will not appear till next week, is already bespoken, and that a fifth edition, also of three thousand, must be immediately put in hand.[1] This makes sixteen thousand copies sold since the first week in December. I am really almost frightened by this rush of prosperity.

Ever yours

T B M

I have a letter from an honest man in Essex[2] who has been enraged and dismayed by Croker's article and calls on me to give the fellow a sound castigation. I shall leave the matter to other people who, I have no doubt, will do all that is necessary.

TO LORD MONTEAGLE, 17 APRIL 1849

MS: Trinity College.

Albany London / April 17. 1849

Dear Lord Monteagle,

I hope that the University will have a good Professor:[3] but I am afraid that I can contribute nothing to that desirable event. I have heard no candidate mentioned: but I will make inquiry to day in the Temple. I need not tell you that for £200 a year or thrice that sum it is impossible to obtain the services of a lawyer in high practice. A promising young man, or an eminent man who has retired and wishes for honorable, useful, and easy employment, would be the thing. The latter is what I should recommend. Charles Austin would be the very man, if he would accept the situation.[4] He seems in want of employment; I should think that he would like to be connected in so honorable a manner with the University; and I have no doubt that his lectures would produce a great effect among the lads. But I am writing at random. Kindest remembrances to all at The Lodge.

Ever yours

T B Macaulay

---

[1] TBM made a few corrections in this edition, which appeared in May.
[2] See the preceding letter.
[3] Thomas Starkie (1782–1849: *DNB*), Downing Professor of Law at Cambridge, had died on 15 April.
[4] Austin had retired from practice in the year before. He did not accept the appointment, if it was offered to him.

TO THOMAS FLOWER ELLIS, 17 APRIL 1849

MS: Trinity College.

Albany April 17 / 1849

Dear Ellis,

I wished to have some talk with you – Frank will have told you why. I have a slight cold, however; and I do not like to expose myself to the cold air of this evening. Could you dine with me to morrow – Wednesday?[1] If not what I have to say must keep till Thursday. I take it for granted that you would not take this Professorship. Of course if you had any thought of it, the thing could without the smallest difficulty be managed.

Ever yours

T B Macaulay

Send an answer by post directly.

TO FRANCES MACAULAY, 18 APRIL 1849

MS: Trinity College.

Albany April 18 / 1849

Dearest Fanny,

I am sorry to find that it will be impossible for me to have John and his boy to lunch on Tuesday. I have a letter from Empson which tells me that he shall pass through London on Tuesday, and wants to have a talk with me about the Review on that day. As the matter is of some consequence, I must keep clear of all engagements.[2] Explain this to John.

I hope that Mary and Parker will be able to join our party on Thursday the 26th.[3]

Ever yours

T B Macaulay

---

[1] TBM had gone to call on Ellis but found him out on 17 April; the two men then dined together the next day, when TBM found Ellis 'not unwilling to hold the Professorship, if it could be made compatible with his practice' (Journal, I, 579). In the event, the appointment went to Andrew Amos, TBM's successor on the Council of India.

[2] Empson called on TBM on Tuesday, 24 April, when TBM gave him notes for use in the *ER*'s reply to Croker's review of the *History* – 'sufficient to smash twenty Crokers' (Journal, I, 587). The article was by James Moncrieff, 'Macaulay's *History of England*,' *ER*, XC (July 1849), 249–92. TBM describes it as having 'much sugar, but a squeeze of acid which perhaps was desirable' (Journal, II, 54–5: 5 July).

[3] TBM entertained Fanny, the Trevelyans, and the Parkers that day at the Trafalgar Tavern, Greenwich, where they had 'a most luxurious repast' (Journal, I, 590).

TO [JOHN HILL BURTON], 20 APRIL 1849

MS: National Library of Scotland.

Albany London / April 20. 1849

My dear Sir,

Many thanks. I will consider whether the expression about the English Judges may not with advantage be slightly modified. Perhaps the mere omission of *The* would do all that is required.[1]

The article in the Quarterly is a mere succession of untruths, blunders and mares' nests. If the effect of the whole had been striking, it might have been necessary for me to go minutely through the charges, and to expose their futility. But the failure has been so complete that I shall content myself with pointing out a dozen or two of the grossest mistakes to Empson, that he may, if he thinks it worth while, notice them in the Edinburgh Review. I believe however that, long before the next Number of the Edinburgh Review appears, the whole matter will be forgotten.

Very truly yours,

T B Macaulay

Pray tell the gentleman who defended me so ably how much I was gratified by such an exhibition of skill and vigour in my cause.

TO FRANCES MACAULAY, 21 APRIL 1849

MS: Trinity College.

Albany April 21 / 1849

Dearest Fanny,

I will not trouble you to take me to Battersea Rise. I shall probably walk out to Clapham and sleep there.[2]

I intend to order dinner at six *precisely* on Thursday. I shall see you however before that time.

I am quite concerned to hear about Alice. But all the world has colds – I am sure I have – and sickness makes a greater difference in her than in any child that I ever saw.

I send you a letter which you may, if you please, add to your collection. I am glad to find that my poor Amanuensis at New York[3] has at last got a situation in which he seems likely to prosper.

Ever yours

T B Macaulay

[1] No doubt the reference is to some passage in the first two volumes of the *History*, but I have not found it.

[2] TBM dined at Battersea Rise on Tuesday, 24 April, and spent the night at Clapham (Journal, 1, 588).

[3] William Parker Snow (1817–95: *DNB*), a sailor, explorer, lecturer, and writer, had, after a

TO WILLIAM WHEWELL, 26 APRIL 1849

MS: Trinity College.

Albany London / April 26. 1849

My dear Whewell,

Rutherfurd and I are strongly tempted to visit Cambridge on Saturday the 5th of May, turning our backs on the Royal Academy, its dinner, and its annual acre of daubed canvass. But, as Cambridge is nothing without the Master of Trinity, we wish to know whether you will be there. Of course we count on a Sunday dinner in the dear old hall.[1]

Would it be possible to procure for Ellis the place of University Counsel which poor Starkie held?[2] I do not think that there is any fellow of Trinity at the bar whose claims stand higher than Ellis's. The profit is, I suppose, nothing. But he loves the place, and would like to have some official connection with it; and I should like to see him have anything on which he sets a value.

Ever yours truly
T B Macaulay

TO WILLIAM WHEWELL, 28 APRIL 1849

MS: Trinity College.

Albany April 28 / 1849

Dear Whewell,

We accept your hospitality with the greatest delight. We shall certainly be in time for dinner. Indeed if the day should be fine, I shall bring Rutherfurd down in time for a long walk.

What you say about the place of University Council seems decisive.

Ever yours,
T B Macaulay

variety of experiences all over the world, worked briefly in the early part of 1848 as TBM's amanuensis, transcribing the first two volumes of the *History*. TBM tried to help settle Snow, paying his passage to America in 1849 (Journal, I, 446: 21 December 1848); he continued to help Snow with money after Snow's return to England, calling him 'almost the only person to whom I ever gave liberal assistance without having cause to regret it' (Journal, III, 51: 14 October 1850). But Snow proved unable to settle to anything, and finally TBM grew disgusted with his 'romantic' plans (Journal, VIII, 140: 19 October 1854). He continued, however, to send gifts of money as late as March 1858 (Journal, XI, 281). Snow's last years were obsessed with the fate of Sir John Franklin and the history of arctic exploration.

[1] Rutherfurd and TBM made the trip, leaving on the 5th and returning on the 7th; they stayed with Whewell at the Lodge (Journal, II, 2–5).

[2] Ellis did not get the position; no new university counsel was appointed until 1857.

TO LORD MAHON, 28 APRIL 1849

MS: Huntington Library.

Albany April 28. 1849

Dear Lord Mahon,

I shall have great pleasure in breakfasting with you next Saturday.[1]

Yours ever,

T B Macaulay

TO THOMAS FLOWER ELLIS, [2? MAY 1849][2]

MS: Trinity College. *Partly published:* Trevelyan, II, 389.

[London]

Dear Ellis,

I will do what I can to please Hammond.[3] When I see Longman next I will tell him to let you have a copy of the fifth edition. I shall expect you here at seven on Monday.

Yours ever

T B Macaulay

I have a most intoxicating letter from Everett. He says that no book has ever had such a sale in the United States, except (note the exception) the Bible and one or two school books of universal use.[4] This, he says, he has been assured by booksellers of the best authority.

TO ELIOT WARBURTON,[5] 2 MAY 1849

MS: Alexander Turnbull Library, Wellington.

Albany London / May 2. 1849

My dear Sir,

I have just received your present; and I assure you that I shall value it both for its intrinsic merit, and as a mark of your kindness. I have of course

---

[1] The company were Hallam, Milman, Frederic Peel, the Duke of Argyll, and Samuel Wilberforce (Journal, II, 2).

[2] Dated from the reference to Everett's letter, which TBM received on 2 May (Journal, I, 594).

[3] Possibly the 'young Hammond' of 10 May.

[4] In his Journal, 3 May, TBM adds the detail that '100 000 copies have already gone off' (I, 596).

[5] Warburton (1810–52: *DNB*), traveller and writer, was a graduate of Trinity and a particular friend of Milnes; he published his Eastern travels as *The Crescent and the Cross*, 2 vols., 1844. The work referred to in this letter is his *Memoirs of Prince Rupert and the Cavaliers*, 3 vols., published on 28 April. TBM's copy is in the library at Wallington. Meeting Warburton on 21 May, TBM 'chatted with him in a friendly way. He is a very deserving man apparently. His book would be good if it were only half as long as it is' (Journal, II, 13).

only dipped into it as yet. But I have read enough to be convinced that it will be an important and interesting addition to our historical literature.

Little specks there will inevitably be in every such work. If any should strike me, I will point them out to you, that they may be removed in a future edition; and I should be truly grateful to you if you would do me the same service.

I may mention that in page 152 of vol. 1 you speak of South as a Bishop. He never was so. He died a Prebendary of Westminster. Charles talked of making him a Bishop: but the thing ended in talk.

Ever yours sincerely

T B Macaulay

TO JOHN MACAULAY, 4 MAY 1849

MS: Trinity College.

Albany London / May 4. 1849

Dear John,

I inclose you a line which I have just received.[1] I have notified your acceptance without waiting for your answer. For it is not impossible that there may be a change of ministry next week, though I hope better things. However you are now well provided for. The news will give great joy at Clapham.

You will judge whether you ought to come up to town instantly. I go to Cambridge to morrow and shall not return till Monday. In any case you ought to write a short note of warm thanks to Lord John whose kindness has been great indeed. Congratulations to your wife. Love to the children.

Ever yours,

T B Macaulay

TO LORD JOHN RUSSELL, 4 MAY 1849

MS: Public Record Office.

Albany May 4 / 1849

Dear Lord John,

I really cannot express to you the gratitude with which I have just read your note. It will spread happiness through a large circle of deserving

---

[1] 'A letter from Lord John to say that he has given my brother John the living of Aldingham worth 1100£ a year – in a fine country – fine population – was there ever such prosperity?' (Journal, II, 1). Aldingham is in north Lancashire, on Morecambe Bay. John spent the rest of his days there.

people. There can be no doubt that my brother will accept the living with delight.

Most truly yours,
T B Macaulay

TO SELINA MACAULAY, 4 MAY 1849

MS: Trinity College.

Albany London / May 4. 1849

Dearest Selina,

Lord John has just given our brother John a living – a country living in the diocese of Chester – worth more than a thousand a year. This is indeed great prosperity; and you will, I know, sincerely rejoice in it.

Ever yours
T B Macaulay

TO FRANCES MACAULAY, 5 MAY 1849

MS: Trinity College.

Albany May 5 / 1849

Dearest Fanny,

I am just starting for Cambridge. I am not surprised at your joy. For it is a great thing indeed. Eleven hundred a year and a house to a country clergyman is as much as two thousand a year in London. I apprehend too that the duties must be very light. For the population is little more than nine hundred.

As to gratitude, my sisters owe me none. I have done no more for them than my duty required. John certainly has some reason to feel obliged to me. And I shall with all delicacy give him to understand that the only return that I expect from him will be the utmost attention on all occasions to you and Selina.

I suppose that John will come up to town with as little delay as possible.

Ever yours
T B Macaulay

TO [LADY TREVELYAN?], [7 MAY 1849]

MS: Fragment, Trinity College.

[London]

[. . . .] I have this moment arrived after a pleasant excursion. I am sorry that I cannot dine at Clapham on the 15th.[1] I have promised Hallam, Milman and Mahon

[.   .   .   .   ][2]

of John's letter to Lord J Russell. I think it proper, simple, and expressive.

Ever yours,
T B Macaulay

TO EDWARD EVERETT, 7 MAY 1849

MS: Massachusetts Historical Society. *Extracts published:* Frothingham, *Everett,* p. 303; Trevelyan, II, 389–90n.

Albany London / May 7. 1849

My dear Everett,

I have very seldom been so much gratified as by your most kind letter.[3] We Anglo-Saxons are not much given to expressing all that we feel. We leave that to the Celts, who generally overdo the matter as much at least as we underdo it. But when either the New Englander or the Old Englander really does pour his heart out, the effusion is not to be despised. –

It would be mere affectation in me not to own that I am greatly pleased by the success of my history in America.[4] But I am almost as much puzzled as pleased. For the book is quite insular in spirit. There is nothing cosmopolitan about it. I can well understand that it might have an interest for a few highly educated men in your country. But I do not at all understand how it should be acceptable to the body of a people who have no king, no Lords, no knights, no established Church, no Tories, nay, I might say, no Whigs in the English sense of the word. The dispensing power, the Ecclesiastical Supremacy, the doctrines of divine right and passive obedience, must all, I should have thought, seemed strange unmeaning things to the vast majority of the inhabitants of Boston and Philadelphia. Indeed so very English is my book that some Scotch critics, who have praised me far beyond my deserts, have yet complained that I have said so much of the crotchets of the Anglican high churchmen, crotchets which scarcely any Scotchman seems able to comprehend.

I have had as yet no assailant worth mentioning. Croker did his worst, but produced no effect except that of bringing on himself a storm of obloquy

---

[1] On that day TBM dined at The Club and then went to a party at Lansdowne House (Journal, II, 10).

[2] All that survives of this letter is the lower two-thirds of the last leaf; probably about four lines are missing in the gap between the bottom of the recto and the remaining lines on the verso.

[3] TBM calls it 'a most affectionate letter' (Journal, I, 594: 2 May 1849).

[4] See *to* Ellis, [2? May].

from all quarters. I hear that Lingard is to plead the cause of his Church against me in the Dublin Review.[1] He is an infinitely more respectable and more formidable antagonist than Croker. But he will have to struggle both against truth and against an immense force of prejudices.

You are in the right about Gottingen. Croker would have hugged you for such a criticism. He was unable to find one such blot in four months of research. I discovered my error some weeks ago, and, in the third edition, altered Gottingen to Leipsic.[2]

But enough about my book, – too much indeed, if I were not writing to an indulgent friend. I do not quite like your account of yourself.[3] Yet if your maladies just suffice to drive you over to us for recreation, change of air, and medical advice, I am afraid that my condolence will be somewhat hypocritical. I should be glad to hear that you had been appointed minister,[4] but, on the whole, more glad if you would come as plain Edward Everett, and let your countrymen see how little the high office which you once held had to do with your place in the esteem of Englishmen. Come however in any way; and I shall be well pleased. In the meantime be assured that your letters of recommendation will be duly honoured by your friends. I shall be most happy to see Mr. Henry Colman;[5] and indeed I wonder that I have never met him; for I find that he is well known to Hallam and to others with whom I daily associate.

I send you a trifling pamphlet[6] which may amuse you for two minutes. It is but a poor return for your speech of the 7th of February[7] which I found on my table the other day, and which, though it bears no inscription, I flatter myself came from the author. My friends in the Education

---

[1] John Lingard (1771–1851: *DNB*), Catholic historian; his *History of England from the First Invasion by the Romans to the Accession of William and Mary* appeared in 8 vols., 1819–30. Lingard wrote that it was 'out of the question' for him to review TBM's work; Lingard's private opinion of the *History* was that it 'abounds in claptrap of every description' (Donald F. Shea, *The English Ranke: John Lingard*, New York, 1969, pp. 34; 65). The *History* was reviewed by Dr Charles William Russell, *Dublin Review*, XXVI (June 1849), 390–441. TBM said of this that it was 'not unhandsome, nor, for Roman Catholics, unfair' (Journal, II, 37: 30 June 1849).

[2] I have not found this passage in the *History*.

[3] Everett had been exhausted by his labors as President of Harvard and had gone off to a spa soon after his resignation.

[4] 'There was talk that Everett might be reappointed to his former post' (Frothingham, *Everett*, p. 303).

[5] Colman (1785–1849) retired from the Unitarian ministry and devoted himself to the study of agriculture; he was in England and on the Continent, 1843–8, investigating agricultural conditions. In 1849, in bad health, he returned to England and died there on 17 August. Colman's *Fourth Report on the Agriculture of Massachusetts*, 1841, is item 18 in the sale catalogue of TBM's library.

[6] Probably TBM's inaugural address at Glasgow, 21 March.

[7] A speech before the Massachusetts House of Representatives, in support of state aid to the colleges in the state: Everett, *Orations and Speeches on Various Occasions*, 11th edn, II (1887), 605–29.

Committee[1] will be obliged to you for strengthening their hands. It is painful to think that, in England, the only class which obstinately opposes every attempt of the government to instruct the people is the old Puritan body, the body to which your Pilgrim fathers belonged. / Ever, dear Everett,

Yours affectionately
T B Macaulay

TO FRANCES MACAULAY, 8 MAY 1849

MS: Trinity College.

Albany May 8. 1849

Dearest Fanny,

If eleven on Thursday will suit you, I will be in Chester Terrace at that hour.[2]

John seems to feel his good fortune very properly. The truth is that, with the exception of great dignities to which he has no pretension, the Crown has few better things to give. I consider his living for example as a better thing than Lord Monteagle's place of Comptroller of the Exchequer. I believe eleven hundred a year with a house in the lake country to be a better thing than two thousand a year with the necessity of taking a house in London and of residing there during the greater part of the year.

I had a very pleasant trip to Cambridge, and brought back Rutherfurd and Craig converted to the organ and the surplice.[3]

Ever yours
T B M

TO THOMAS FLOWER ELLIS, 10 MAY 1849

MS: Trinity College.

Albany May 10. / 1849

Dear Ellis,

I shall be happy to dine with you on Friday the 25th. But I am engaged

---

[1] Of the Privy Council.

[2] Fanny was staying with James and Mary Parker at 21 Chester Terrace, Regent's Park. On Thursday, 10 May, TBM took Fanny and the Parkers on a tour of the British Museum (Journal, II, 8).

[3] Craig had joined Rutherfurd and TBM on their Cambridge visit. In his Journal for 7 May TBM wrote that 'The Chapel worship of yesterday [at Trinity], which indeed was finely and decorously performed and extremely well attended, affected the Lord Advocate much. When we sate down after the psalms he whispered to me: "This is magnificent. This is something like public worship"' (II, 5).

on both Saturday and Tuesday next. If Wednesday the 16th would suit you, I could dine with you on that day.[1]

I am glad to hear of young Hammond's success.[2]

Have you seen the last Man in the Moon?[3] It is worth looking at.

Ever yours,

T B M

I hear all that is most delightful about my brother's living – excellent parsonage in perfect repair, nice garden, good neighbours, quiet well disposed peasantry, the waves breaking against the wall of the churchyard, delightful scenery all round, healthy air, and a probable increase of income. I understand that Earls have been at Lord John for the appointment, which is considered as the best of the kind in a circle of many miles. I am the more obliged to him.

Ever yours,

T B M

TO MARGARET TREVELYAN, 24 MAY 1849

MS: John Rylands Library. *Extracts published: Bulletin of the John Rylands Library*, xxv (1941), 132–3.

Albany London / May 24. 1849

My dearest Margaret,

A thousand thanks for your letter. I am glad to hear that, what with the hawthorns in the hedges and what with the trinkets in the bazaars, you are leading a pleasant life.[4] I shall miss you much on Saturday and Sunday at Clapham, and shall long for one of our rambles and for a game at chess. Eddis has all but finished my portrait.[5] Mamma thinks it very like. I hope

---

[1] The page of TBM's Journal for 25 May is missing; so is that for Saturday, 12 May. On Tuesday, 15 May, TBM dined at The Club. He dined with Ellis on 16 May (Journal, II, 10).

[2] James Lempriere Hammond (1829–80: *Boase*), a sizar of Trinity, had just won two prizes for Latin verse, a place in the first-class list of freshmen, and a Trinity scholarship. He was Fellow of Trinity, 1853, Tutor, 1854–64, and Bursar, 1863–70.

[3] The May number begins with 'Macaulay's England Dramatised,' pp. 249–62, an illustrated farce in three acts, inspired by the fact that 'all the world is raving about Mr. Macaulay's History. . .gents at the Casino discuss the character of William of Orange, and crossing-sweepers may soon be expected to differ on the true motives of Strafford' (249); the piece ends with a 'terrific combat between Mr. Macaulay and Mr. Wilson Croker.'

[4] Margaret was at Liverpool with the Croppers.

[5] Between 26 April and 30 May TBM gave six sittings to Eden Upton Eddis for a portrait commissioned by Longman. It was engraved by William Greatbach and used as the frontis-piece to the 1850 edition of TBM's *Essays,* but was received in that form as a 'failure' (Journal, II, 241: 24 February 1850). To redeem himself, Eddis made a drawing in chalk of TBM in March 1850; this was reproduced in an engraving by J. Brown as a plate in *Bentley's Miscellany,* XXXI (January 1852), opp. p. 1. TBM sat to Eddis a third time in May 1852 (Journal, V, 40–2), for a portrait probably worked up from the 1850 drawing. This is the

it is like: for I appear as a very meek, gentle, smiling person. My other effigies by no means do justice to my moral qualities. In Richmond's drawing[1] I look extremely sensual, in Parke's bust[2] extremely impudent, and, in Marochetti's medallion,[3] which I gave you, extremely sulky. In the daguerreotype by which I am known to the Yankees[4] I look sensual, impudent, and sulky at once. Eddis has seized the truly seraphic expression of my countenance. What Longman means to do with the picture I cannot guess. But if I get it, it will, I suppose, find its way to Westbourne Terrace.[5]

Àpropos of Westbourne Terrace, I have not seen the house yet. Indeed I am not certain that it is yet absolutely taken.

Àpropos of *yet*. Yet is sometimes an adverb and sometimes a conjunction. In my sentence above it is an adverb. In the following sentence it is a conjunction. "Baba was a naughty girl; yet her uncle was fond of her."

portrait reproduced as the frontispiece to vol. 12 of the Albany Edition, 1898, and is now in the possession of Lady Elizabeth Longman. Eddis (1812–1901: *DNB*) was a fashionable portrait painter. He did the portrait of Trevelyan that was presented to the family by the Commissariat officers in 1850: see 30 November 1850.

1 TBM sat for a crayon drawing by George Richmond in 1844; it is now in the collection of Sir William Dugdale, Bart., and is reproduced as the frontispiece to vol. 3 of this edition. Richmond (1809–96: *DNB*), one of the most successful and agreeable of Victorian portrait painters, was patronized by Sir Robert Inglis and became almost painter-in-ordinary to the Evangelicals and their children. His first success was a portrait of Wilberforce, and there are few Evangelical families that he did not illuminate thereafter. Richmond did a second portrait of TBM: see 30 November 1850.

2 See *to* Mrs Charles Trevelyan, 5 November 1846.

3 A bronze medallion portrait, 1848, now in the National Portrait Gallery (various plaster copies are extant). Baron Carlo Marochetti (1805–67: *DNB*), sculptor, educated in France, came to England in 1848 and quickly established a reputation for portrait sculpture.

4 A daguerreotype, commissioned by Harpers and taken by Richard Beard, was engraved for the frontispiece to volume one of the American edition of the *History*. TBM received copies of it on 4 December 1848 (Journal, I, 430) and observed that it was 'very like, I doubt not, but with the usual faults of daguerreotype likenesses'; later he called it a 'hideous caricature' (30 May 1849). Edward Marston, a partner in the Harpers' English agency, recalled that 'I once saw [TBM] much annoyed by a steel engraving of himself which had been made from a Daguerreotype for an American edition of "The History of England"; he did not like it at all, and it had to be cancelled....it was difficult to understand why he objected, for it seemed to us to be an excellent likeness, though perhaps it had somewhat too stern a look' (*After Work: Fragments from the Workshop of an Old Publisher*, 1904, p. 36). If Marston is correct in saying that the engraving was cancelled, it is clear that another was made from the same picture. Richard Beard (1801?–85: *Boase*) had operated a studio for daguerreotype portraits at the Royal Polytechnic Institution since 1841.

5 The Trevelyans had been looking for a London house since early in the year and had found one at 20 Westbourne Terrace. The region was newly-developed and was thus described in 1843: 'This terrace being half a mile in length, and 40 feet wider than Portland Place, will, when completed, be the most splendid in the Metropolis' (Janet Dunbar, *The Early Victorian Woman*, 1963, p. 40). On 1 June TBM gave Trevelyan, who, despite his work at the Treasury, must have remained innocent of the city's wickedness, 'some hints about London life, and cautioned him not to walk late in the Parks, or to talk to strangers, particularly soldiers, as his simple good nature sometimes inclines him to do' (Journal, II, 19–20).

I think I have now answered all your questions. Give my love to everybody great and small. I do not know exactly at what house you are. But I suppose that a letter addressed to Mr. Edward Cropper's will reach you.

Ever yours, my darling,

T B Macaulay

TO UNIDENTIFIED RECIPIENT, 26 MAY 1849

MS: Trinity College.

Albany May 26. 1849

Sir,

I am very sensible of the honour which you do me. But I am at present sitting to several artists;[1] and I find their demands on my time so exorbitant that I cannot consent to make any new engagement of the same kind. With many thanks for your courtesy I have the honour to be, / Sir,

Your most obedient Servant

T B Macaulay

TO UNIDENTIFIED RECIPIENT, 30 MAY 1849

MS: Trinity College.

Albany May 30 / 1849

Sir,

One of the pictures for which I am sitting contains numerous figures, and will, when it is finished, be the property of his Royal Highness Prince Albert.[2] The other is for Messrs. Longman;[3] and they mean to have it engraved. You will perceive that I cannot exercise any right of ownership in either case.

The daguerreotype[4] is common property. You may do what you will with it. But you must excuse me from being a party to the multiplication of so hideous a caricature of myself. / I have the honour to be, / Sir,

Your obedient servant,

T B Macaulay

[1] 'Several artists' is presumably a polite exaggeration. TBM was sitting to Eddis and had been sitting earlier to Partridge; I know of no other portraits from this period.
[2] Albert encouraged Partridge's work on 'The Fine Arts Commissioners,' but the picture was never sold. See Richard Ormond, 'John Partridge and the Fine Arts Commissioners,' *Burlington Magazine,* CIX (July 1967), 398.
[3] The Eddis portrait: see 24 May.
[4] By Beard: see 24 May.

TO THE DUCHESS OF ARGYLL,[1] 2 JUNE 1849

MS: New York Public Library.

Albany June 2. 1849

Dear Duchess of Argyll,

I shall have very great pleasure in breakfasting with you next Monday.[2]

Ever yours most truly,

T B Macaulay

TO JOHN LEYCESTER ADOLPHUS, 3 JUNE 1849

MS: Mrs Michael Millgate.

Albany June 3. 1849

Dear Adolphus,

You understand that you are engaged to me for Friday the 22nd – the Trafalgar, Greenwich – 6 1/2 precisely.[3]

Ever yours

T B Macaulay

TO MRS GEORGE BANCROFT,[4] 6 JUNE 1849

MS: Massachusetts Historical Society.

Albany June 6. 1849

Dear Mrs. Bancroft,

Will you and Mr. Bancroft give me the pleasure of your company to breakfast on Monday next at ten?[5]

Very truly yours,

T B Macaulay

TO FRANCES MACAULAY, 12 JUNE 1849

MS: Trinity College.

Albany June 12. 1849

Dearest Fanny,

I will settle the demand of the Railway Company.[6] You can then con-

[1] Lady Elizabeth Leveson-Gower (1824–78), eldest daughter of the second Duke of Sutherland, married George Douglas, eighth Duke of Argyll, in 1844.

[2] The company included Hallam and Mahon (Journal, II, 21: 4 June).

[3] TBM gave what he thought 'a very good dinner' that evening to a party of old friends from the Northern Circuit: Ellis, Adolphus, Dundas, and Parker (Journal, II, 35).

[4] Mrs Elizabeth Davis Bliss, a widow, married Bancroft in 1838; she died in 1886.

[5] The party were Mr and Mrs Bancroft, Lord Glenelg, Hallam, and Milman (Journal, II, 27: 11 June).

[6] 'Wrote to Fanny to say that I should pay the 45£ for her railway call' (Journal, II, 28: 12 June).

sider at leisure, after consulting Edward, whether it would be desirable for you to change your investment. My own inclination is to think that the worst is over. But I judge without any minute knowledge of circumstances. I have every reason to believe that my affairs are in so prosperous a state as to make it my duty, as it is my pleasure, to render you this little service.

I am glad to find that Hannah's complaint is nothing worse than a cold. If she is tolerably well, I shall dine with you on Friday.[1]

Ever yours,
T B Macaulay

TO SELINA MACAULAY, 16 JUNE 1849

MS: Trinity College.

Albany London / June 16. 1849
Dearest Selina,

I will settle about the call. I can do so without inconvenience, and am truly glad that it is in my power to render you this small service.

I have written scarcely a page of William's reign. I am however daily employed in collecting materials, reading Dutch histories and French Gazettes, and making extracts from despatches and private letters which have never been published. I do not expect to publish the two next volumes till Christmas 1853. I should be glad to be sure that I should then have completed the task; I do not say to my satisfaction, but in a manner not inferior to that in which the two first volumes are executed. [. . .][2]

TO THOMAS LONGMAN, 16 JUNE 1849

MS: Longman Group Ltd.

Albany London / June 16 1849
My dear Sir,

I give you joy very sincerely on the birth of your boy and on Mrs. Longman's safety.[3]

As to the plan which you propose, I do not much like it.[4] But I can

---

[1] TBM spent Friday, 15 June, at Clapham (*Journal,* II, 30).

[2] The closing and signature have been cut away.

[3] Longman's first son, Thomas Norton Longman (1849–1930), was born on 15 June. He was a member of the firm, 1869–1919.

[4] A new edition of TBM's essays was being prepared. It appeared in January 1850, in one volume, with the engraving of Eddis's portrait, an index, and three essays added to the 1843 text: 'Madame D'Arblay,' 'Addison,' and 'The Earl of Chatham.' The first printing of 1,000 copies was followed by 2,000 in February 1850, 2,000 in December 1850, and 3,000 in October 1852.

suggest nothing better. A big book is proverbially a big evil; and the proverb holds good especially when the big book is twice as large as its fellow volumes. However I shall not contend.

I hear great complaints of false references and inaccuracies in the Index to the History.[1] But I have neither time nor heart to look into the matter. I have made out a list of mistakes in the text which must be altered before you reprint.[2]

Ever yours truly
T B Macaulay

to John Holmes,[3] 22 June 1849

MS: British Museum. *Envelope:* J Holmes Esq / etc. etc. etc. / British Museum. *Subscription:* T B Macaulay.

Albany June 22. / 1849

My dear Sir,

Will you be so kind as to send the Catalogues by the bearer?[4]

You are right about Madame de Montespan.[5] The error shall be corrected. The more blemishes you point out, the more I shall be obliged to you.

Very truly yours,
T B Macaulay

to Selina Macaulay, 25 June 1849

MS: Trinity College.

Albany London / June 25. 1849

Dearest Selina,

I inclose a cheque for the quarter. You are aware that hitherto poor Edward has very kindly contributed a hundred pounds towards the two hundred and fifty pounds a year which I have allowed to you and Fanny.

---

1 See [19 March].
2 The sixth edition, of 3,000 copies, appeared in December. TBM made corrections for it between July and late October (Journal, II, 60; 121).
3 Holmes (1800–54: *DNB*), bibliographer and cataloguer, was employed in the Department of Manuscripts, British Museum, from 1830. TBM went to the Museum on 21 June, where he received 'some hints for corrections from Holmes, kindly given and perhaps correct, but of little importance' (Journal, II, 34). On hearing of Holmes's death TBM wrote that 'he was a very good courteous intelligent friendly person – I sincerely regret him' (Journal, VIII, 39–40: 4 April 1854).
4 On the 26th TBM lists among his reading the 'Catalogue of the M.S.S. in the British Museum' (Journal, II, 38).
5 'The Duchess of Montespan' (*History*, II, 266: ch. 7, end) is corrected to 'Marchioness' in the sixth edition.

As the sale of my book has made a very comfortable addition to my income, I think it right to pay the whole two hundred and fifty myself. I communicated my determination last week to Edward. But, poor fellow, this last calamity has prevented him from answering me.[1] I do not know that I ever heard of a human being in real life whom fate seemed to pursue, as a heathen would say, with such inveterate and implacable cruelty. You would translate this language into a more Christian and salutary form of expression. But really the trial seems to be beyond even the patience of the most saintly mind.

I will take care that your call shall be paid up punctually to the day.

Ever yours affectionately

T B Macaulay

TO LORD JOHN RUSSELL, 30 JUNE 1849

MS: Public Record Office. *Mostly published:* Russell, *Later Correspondence,* 1, 196.

Albany June 30. 1849

Dear Lord John,

You will, I am sure, allow me, as a Cambridge man anxious for the welfare and honor of Cambridge, to say one word about the vacant Professorship of modern History.[2] If Stephen be a candidate, I have done. My regard for him is such that I cannot but wish him success in any competition in which he may engage; and I have no doubt that, if his lectures should be less profoundly learned than those of men whose whole lives have been passed in study, the defect would be more than supplied by the practical statesmanship which nothing but long experience of great affairs can give. But, if Stephen be out of the question, I would venture to suggest that the claims of Kemble are entitled to your careful consideration.[3] You have been too busy, I imagine, to read his book on our Anglo Saxon polity.[4] I really believe that I speak the sense of all who

---

[1] TBM wrote to Cropper on 19 June; on the 23rd he learned from Hannah that 'poor Edward's baby is dying – and he brokenhearted. No wonder. Was ever such a curse on a house? It reminds me of the Greek stories. Alas Alas.' News of the child's death came on the next day (Journal, 11, 33–7). Cropper afterwards had three living children by this, his third marriage.

[2] William Smyth died on 24 June. On the day that this letter was written, TBM received a note from Prince Albert asking to see him the next day: when TBM appeared at the Palace 'the Prince, to my extreme astonishment, offered me the Professorship' (Trevelyan, 11, 261).

[3] TBM had some trouble in steering a course between Kemble and Stephen. At the end of the day on which this letter was written he went to Clapham, where he learned that 'Stephen has completely withdrawn. That sets me partly at ease. Awkward stories about Kemble's drinking. However I am in for it' (Journal, 11, 48–9).

[4] *The Saxons in England,* 2 vols., published in early December 1848. TBM received a copy on 15 December (Journal, 1, 441).

are entitled to judge when I say that it is a most valuable addition to our stock of historical knowledge, and, though not likely to be popular with the multitude, will always be held in high esteem by scholars and thinkers.

Do not take the trouble to answer these lines. I well know how busy you are, and should be unwilling to steal a minute from your scanty time of recreation.

Ever yours most truly
T B Macaulay

Everything that we hear of Adlingham [*sic*] increases our gratitude to you. It seems to be the very pearl of Crown livings.

TO THOMAS FLOWER ELLIS, 9 JULY 1849

MS: Trinity College.

Albany July 9 / 1849

Dear Ellis,

Remember that you dine here to morrow – Tuesday.

I have corrected the translation of the passage in Tzetzes.[1] Empson writes that he took it for granted that the translation was yours, and had therefore not even read it. "I told him," he says, "not to trust anything to the Scotch Hellenists."

Ever yours
T B Macaulay

TO LADY THERESA LEWIS, 19 JULY 1849

MS: New York Public Library.

Albany July 19. 1849

Dear Lady Theresa,

The story about which you inquire is a mere romance.[2] Harrison[3] was not at that time within three hundred miles of Lord Capel. The siege of Colchester was throughout directed by the Lord General Fairfax, who, of all men, was the least likely to perpetrate or threaten any monstrous

---

[1] A passage from the twelfth-century Byzantine writer John Tzetzes; this was cited, with a translation, in the *ER* review of TBM's *History* in order to refute Croker's charge that TBM had misunderstood a passage from Procopius (see *History*, I, 5; *Quarterly Review*, LXXXIV, 556; and *ER*, XC, 288–9). TBM had corrected the translation himself before the *ER* was published (Journal, II, 55: 7 July).

[2] Lady Theresa wrote 'asking me about an idle story which Lord Essex had told her concerning his ancestor the 1st Lord Capel' (Journal, II, 68: 19 July). The first Lord Capel (1610?–49: *DNB*) surrendered to Lord Fairfax on the taking of Colchester in 1648.

[3] Thomas Harrison (1606–60: *DNB*), the Regicide.

act of atrocity. Harrison, who was then only a Colonel, was fighting under Cromwell against the Scotch near Appleby. Look at Whitelock's Memorials,[1] page 322.

It is a curious circumstance that the defenders of Colchester were accused of almost exactly the same crime which your story imputes to the besiegers. If you will look at the Royalist account of the siege by Carter,[2] printed in 1650, you will see that the Roundheads charged the garrison with putting prisoners in the way of the fire from the trenches. This charge Carter solemnly, and no doubt quite truly, denies. I cannot help suspecting that the story which Lord Essex[3] mentions is nothing but this very story turned round. For, odd as it may seem, stories are very often turned round in this way. I dare say you know the origin of the plot of the Merchant of Venice. In the original tale the unhappy debtor was a Jew, and the barbarous creditor a Christian.[4] But, as the Christians were the stronger party, they inverted the relation between the believer and the unbeliever. Just so, I imagine, when the Cavaliers became the stronger party, they inverted this rumour about the siege of Colchester, and, in their ballads and broadsides, represented the parliamentary commanders as exposing the children of loyal parents to the fire from the town. As such wickedness could not well be imputed to Fairfax, whose humanity was known, and who had made his peace with the royal family, Harrison, who was regarded as worse than the devil, was brought from Westmoreland to Essex, and promoted from the rank of Colonel to the supreme command. Much of what is called history originates in this way. / Believe me / Dear Lady Theresa,

Yours very truly
T B Macaulay

TO SELINA MACAULAY, 25 JULY 1849

MS: Trinity College. *Envelope:* Miss Macaulay / Mrs. Power's / Sion Hill / Clifton / Bristol. *Subscription:* T B M.

Albany London / July 25. 1849

Dearest Selina,

Your letter has brought to my mind the circumstances to which it relates. I had quite forgotten them; nor do I remember the name of your

---

[1] Bulstrode Whitelocke, *Memorials of the English Affairs*, 1682. TBM's copy is item 1007 in the sale catalogue of his library.

[2] Matthew Carter, *A Most True and Exact Relation of that as Honourable as Unfortunate Expedition of Kent, Essex, and Colchester*, 1650.

[3] Arthur Capel (1803–92), sixth Earl of Essex.

[4] A version of the pound-of-flesh plot, with the Jew as debtor, is outlined by Bishop Percy in a note to the *Reliques:* see the New Variorum edition of *The Merchant of Venice*, 1888, p. 295.

friend. I did not order five copies of her book, which indeed did not, from what she told me, seem likely ever to be published. I merely, as she appeared to be in distress, sent her a cheque for five pounds. No copy of the book has been sent me; nor do I expect one. If I should receive one, you are perfectly welcome to it. I only beg that you will keep what I tell you to yourself, lest it should wound the feelings of this lady, who seems, not unnaturally, unwilling to have it known that she has accepted pecuniary assistance.

I was much pleased with the account of the ceremony at Bovey Tracey.

Ever yours,

T B Macaulay

TO THOMAS FLOWER ELLIS, 6 AUGUST 1849

MS: Trinity College.

Albany August 6 / 1849

Dear Ellis,

I have an answer from Baring. He says "Ellis is a very good man, both quâ lawyer and quâ liberal. But I can say nothing till I know whether Lord John will want an M.P."[1]

I do not see that I can do more. But if anything occurs to you let me know.

Ever yours

T B Macaulay

TO SIR HENRY ELLIS,[2] 14 AUGUST 1849

MS: British Museum.

Albany August 14 / 1849

My dear Sir,

I am not quite sure that I shall be so fortunate as to see you before I start for Ireland.[3] I therefore write these few lines to request that every

---

[1] On 3 August TBM 'found a note from Ellis about the place of counsel to the Admiralty – wrote immediately to Baring – strongly' (Journal, II, 80). On 6 August: 'Heard from Baring. I am afraid that this business cannot be managed for Ellis' (II, 84). Sir Francis Baring was First Lord of the Admiralty, 1849–52.

[2] Ellis (1777–1869: *DNB*), in the service of the British Museum since 1800, had been Principal Librarian since 1827; following a parliamentary inquiry in 1835–6 he had been virtually though not nominally superseded in the direction of the Museum, but he retained his position until 1856. On 15 August TBM went to the Museum to speak to Ellis about Stephen (Journal, II, 93).

[3] TBM left for Ireland on 16 August, visited Dublin, the Boyne, Limerick, Killarney, Cork, and Londonderry, and returned to London on 4 September (Journal, III, 1a–49a).

facility and convenience consistent with our rules may be afforded to Sir James Stephen whenever he may wish to make use of the Library. His public character you well know. He is now Professor of Modern History in the University of Cambridge;[1] and it is therefore matter of national interest that no advantage should be withheld from him. I am very sorry that it will not be in my power to introduce him. But I have had so much experience of your kindness, and am so well acquainted with your zeal for the interests of literature that I leave him without any misgivings to your care. / Believe me, / My dear Sir,

Yours very truly,

T B Macaulay

TO THOMAS FLOWER ELLIS, 19 AUGUST 1849

MS: Trinity College. *Extract published:* Trevelyan, II, 266n.

Dublin August 19 / 1849

Dear Ellis,

I now see my way pretty clearly; and I think that I shall certainly be in England again about the 6th of September. There can therefore be no difficulty at all as to our passing ten days at Paris.[2] Just send me a line directed hither to let me know what your plans are.

Dublin is a fine city. If you put Churches out of the question, – for the Churches here are but mean, – the public buildings are in better taste than those of London, and would be thought fine even at Paris. Of the peculiarities of the national character and manners I have seen next to nothing. Nobody that I ever saw is here except the Lord Lieutenant and the Archbishop. The whole aristocracy has fled into the country. I am in a capital hotel, equal to the best at Brighton or Cheltenham. On Tuesday I go to the Boyne. What my next move will be is not quite settled.

I wish that you had been at Church with me to day. The sermon beat even that which we heard at St Mary Redcliff. The preacher compared the state of the damned in hell to that of Smith O'Brien on his way to the Antipodes.[3] "How gladly would that unhappy man welcome any who would save him from the consequences of his misdeeds! And will not you, my brethren, welcome the glad tidings? etc. etc. etc."

---

[1] Stephen received the appointment on 26 July.

[2] TBM and Ellis left London for Paris on 5 September and returned on 17 September (Journal, III, 94a–97a).

[3] William Smith O'Brien (1803–64: *DNB*), Irish M.P. and nationalist leader, led a hapless insurrection in July 1848 – TBM calls it ' that contemptible abortion of a rebellion' (Journal, III, 14a: 20 August). His sentence of death was commuted to transportation for life, and he had been sent out to Tasmania in July 1849. O'Brien received an unconditional pardon in 1856.

As to political agitation it is dead and buried. Never did I see a society apparently so well satisfied with its rulers. The Queen made a conquest of all hearts.[1]

Ever yours
T B Macaulay

TO LORD CLARENDON, 22 AUGUST 1849

MS: Trinity College.

Morrison's Hotel / August 22. 1849

Dear Lord Clarendon,

Many thanks for your kindness. I went over the field of battle at the fords of the Boyne yesterday with three excellent Ciceroni,[2] and learned much that is curious. But I have no doubt that the sources of information indicated by Dr. Taylor[3] are of great value. I am just about to start for Killarney. When I return I will not fail to call on him.

With repeated thanks believe me, / Dear Lord Clarendon,

Yours most truly
T B Macaulay

TO LADY TREVELYAN, 26 AUGUST 1849

MS: University of London.

Cork August 26. 1849

Dearest Hannah,

Here I am comfortably rested in a very good hotel after wandering through a hundred and thirty miles of wild country, jolting on poneys up rugged mountain passes, and riding on Irish cars between places where there was neither poste chaise nor stage coach to be had.[4] You know

---

[1] Victoria arrived in Dublin on 2 August and left on the 10th, just a week before TBM's arrival.

[2] TBM spent 21 August touring the field of the Boyne with a Mr Mahony, Captain Thomas Larcom (see 2 September), and William Robert Wills Wilde (1815–76: *DNB*), surgeon and antiquary, the father of Oscar (Journal, III, 16a). In his account of the battle TBM acknowledges Wilde's 'pleasing volume entitled "Beauties of the Boyne and Blackwater" ' (*History*, III, 621–2n). The acknowledgement is perhaps a return for Wilde's having dedicated the second edition of the book (1850) to TBM 'in Testimony of the Respect and Admiration of the Author.'

[3] William Cooke Taylor (1800–49: *DNB*), Irish journalist and editor, on the staff of the *Athenaeum* (for which he reviewed TBM's *History*), returned to Ireland on Clarendon's invitation to be statistical writer to the government. TBM called on him on 29 August for information about Irish history (Journal, III, 40a).

[4] TBM left Dublin for Limerick on 22 August; on the next two days he toured the lakes of Killarney; on the 25th he went on to Cork. All of this travel beyond Limerick was by carriage and by horseback (Journal, III, 21a–31a).

pretty well how little I like to be put out of my way, and how little horse-
manship is in my way. You will therefore form a high notion of Killarney
when I tell you that I think all my trouble overpaid. Even William's
poetical feelings were aroused, and he declared that he had never seen
anything so beautiful in his life. As a set off against the pleasure of seeing
this most lovely of all spots I have had the pain of seeing a people, the
most miserable that I ever fell in with in any part of the world. I passed
scores, I may say hundreds of dwellings lying in ruin. My guide told me
that the people had left their houses and gone to America. And yet there
was nothing to be said against the landlords of that region. Lord Kenmare,[1] the late Lord Headley,[2] and the present Lady Headley are celebrated all over Ireland and beyond it for benevolence and judicious liberality. Then the clothes of the people: – you never saw a beggar in such
things. And the endless mendicant whine which follows you mile after
mile, – the dozens of children who run after you in every village and up
every hill crying "Give me halfpenny – mother dead in workhouse – "
Their strange appearance sometimes made me laugh, and I yet could
hardly help crying. But what use is there in making oneself miserable?
These things must not be thought on after this way.

So, it will make us mad.[3]

I shall stay here to day and to morrow. On Tuesday I go back to Dublin.
Wednesday I must pass in some researches at Dublin. On Thursday I
run down to Londonderry. Friday I spend there. On Saturday I return to
Dublin. On Monday I propose to come back to England, and on Wednesday or Thursday following (the 5th or 6th of September), I shall start
with Ellis for Paris. Possibly I may just catch you before you set out for
Enmore.

I have an invitation from the Archbishop to his villa. I am happy to say
that I shall be able to excuse myself. I have also a very polite letter from
Colonel Jones,[4] offering me help at Athlone, where I shall not be. Possibly,
if I should find it necessary, I may three years hence, make another short
trip to Ireland for some finishing touches, and may then find a railway
open to Athlone and Aughrim.

I have a letter from our brother Charles who seems delighted with
your girls, especially with Baba. He talks of sending his boy immediately
to school.

---

[1] The first Baron Kenmare (1788–1853), of Kenmare House, Killarney, Lord Lieutenant of
County Kerry, 1831–53.
[2] The second Baron Headley (1784–1840), of Aghadoe House, Killarney.
[3] *Macbeth*, II, ii, 33–4.
[4] Colonel Sir Harry David Jones (1791–1866: *DNB*), an officer of the Royal Engineers and a
Peninsular veteran, was Chairman of the Irish Board of Works, 1845–50, and thus immediately concerned with the work of famine relief under Trevelyan.

I suppose that Trevelyan's holiday is about to commence. It is high time. Everybody here talks with astonishment of the business which he gets through; and yet they can know only a part of what he has to do.[1] Kindest love to him and to all. Tell Baba to send me a line. When shall you be in Westbourne Terrace. It makes me a little sad to think that I shall never again walk out to you at Clapham. But this is what the Scotch, I believe, call sinning my mercies.

Ever yours
T B Macaulay

TO THOMAS FLOWER ELLIS, 26 AUGUST 1849

MS: Trinity College. *Partly published:* Trevelyan, II, 266, notes 1,2.

Cork August 26. 1849

Dear Ellis,

I am delighted to learn that you can go with me to Paris. I shall try to be in London on Tuesday the 4th of September. We shall then be able to start on Thursday at latest, and shall have ten days clear. I hope that we shall be able to make trips to Rouen and Chartres and to see two of the finest churches in the world, – I might say three; for the Cathedral of Rouen, though far inferior to St. Ouen, is a noble building. Beauvais, which is more astonishing than any of them, we shall, I am afraid, hardly be able to visit, for want of a railway. But this we will consider.

I have written about a courier, and hope to find a respectable one. If you would do what is necessary about passports it might save time. I am told that they are much more strict on that head now than under the monarchy. And small blame to them – but so much for the blessed effects of revolutions. I do not know that it will be worth while to get a foreign office passport. But, if it would, my name may be of use; for they are always most attentive to me there. See that I am "Conseiller de Sa M.B. dans son Conseil privé." I have found the advantage of such foolery. You may be "Procureur de Sa M. B. dans son Duché de Lancaster;" – or "Juge de la Ville de Leeds," or both.[2]

Well, here I am, after such adventures as would have amazed you. I often thought how you would have stated to have seen me – me who had not crossed a horse since I rode, in June 1834, through the mango park at Arcot in the Carnatic, – jolting on a Kerry poney up the wildest and finest of all mountain passes. But really Killarney is worth some trouble.

---

[1] See 3 February 1847.

[2] Ellis had been both Attorney-General to the Duchy of Lancaster and Recorder of Leeds since 1839.

I never in my life saw anything more beautiful, I might say so beautiful. The best part of Windermere is in the same style, but inferior; and all our lakes and the Scotch lakes have the disadvantage of a sterile soil and a cold climate. Imagine a finer Windermere in that soft part of Devonshire where the myrtle grows wild. The exuberance and freshness of vegetation at Killarney is marvellous. The wood is everywhere. The grass is greener than anything that I ever saw. There is a positive sensual pleasure in look- ing at it. No sheep is suffered to remain more than a few months on any of the islands of the lakes. I asked why not. I was told that they would die of fat; and indeed those that I saw looked like Aldermen who had passed the chair. The ash berries are redder, the heath richer, the very fern more delicately articulated than elsewhere. Unfortunately the price paid for all this beauty is that the sky is charged with all the vapours of the Atlantic, and that it is thought a miracle to have two fine days together. I had however one fine day and one tolerable day, no rain except while I was in a gloomy pass which perhaps was made more striking by the rain.

But when one turns from the scenery to the people! – I was agreeably disappointed by what I saw of Meath and Louth when I went to the Boyne, and not much shocked by anything that I fell in with in going by railway from Dublin to Limerick. But from Limerick to Killarney, and from Killarney to Cork, I hardly knew whether to laugh or cry. Hundreds of dwellings in ruins, abandoned by the late inmates who have fled to America – the labouring people dressed literally – not rhetorically, – worse than the scarecrows of England – the children of whole villages turning out to beg of every coach and car that goes by. But I will have done. I cannot mend this state of things; and there is no use in breaking my heart about it. I am comforted by thinking that between the poorest English peasant and the Irish peasant there is ample room for ten or twelve well marked degrees of poverty. Send me a line to Dublin.

> Ever yours
> T B Macaulay

TO THOMAS FLOWER ELLIS, 2 SEPTEMBER 1849

MS: Trinity College.

Dublin September 2 1849

Dear Ellis

This morning at five I arrived here from Londonderry[1] and found your letter on my table. I agree to all that you say. Boulogne is the place. We

---

[1] TBM returned to Dublin from Cork on 28 August; on the 30th he went to Strabane, then to Londonderry on the 31st, and returned to Dublin on the 1st (Journal, III, 37a–48a).

had better go from Folkestone.[1] If we reach France early in the day we can at once proceed to Paris. If we are late, we can sleep at Boulogne and make a second pilgrimage to the spot where Walmesley[2] sleeps in the odour of sanctity.

I expect to be at the Albany soon after four on Tuesday morning.[3] Tuesday will amply suffice for my arrangements; and therefore on Wednesday I shall be at your orders as early as you please. Since you must be back by the 17th you had better gain a day at the beginning. I hope to find that a courier has been engaged. But if it should be impossible to secure the services of a good man at so short a notice and for so short a time, I will procure one at Paris, after consulting with our hotel keeper.

By the bye you know our contract. I promised to treat you. I do not mean that I will pay for your tubs and towels. But I insist upon it that I order all the dinners and settle the bills. I will give you a round of restaurateurs – Very, – the Frères Provençaux, – the Café de Paris, – Vefour etc. And when we have tried them we will stick to the best. If you have any scruples about going through this course of experimental gastronomy at the expense of a Plutus like me, – a fellow rolling in wealth, and about to receive six thousand pounds more in a few weeks, – I will promise to let you take me to Rome in your carriage and at your own proper charge the first autumn after you are a Judge of the Common Pleas.

I assure you that Marian's letter reached me through the agency of my friend Captain Larcom,[4] – a capital fellow. What the letter contained is safe in the breast of a man of honor. You are the last person who shall know one syllable. Fathers have flinty hearts. I have been ungallant enough not to write an answer, for the very homely reason that I did not know whither to direct it.

I shall bore you to death with my Irish adventures when we meet. But one story I must give you. It is a real and undoubted fact. The Lee overflowed a great quantity of land round Cork, and did much mischief. Accordingly a meeting of the citizens was called by advertisement, "for the purpose of taking steps to prevent the late inundations."

I shall call on you on Tuesday morning. I would ask you to dine at the

---

[1] This is what they did: to Folkestone on the 5th, to Boulogne on the 6th, and to Paris on the 7th, where they stayed at the Hotel Bristol (Journal, II, 94).

[2] John Walmesley (1799?–1832), a barrister of the Inner Temple, died at Boulogne. I do not know what connection he had with Ellis and TBM; he does not appear to have been on the Northern Circuit.

[3] He was (Journal, III, 49a).

[4] Captain Thomas Larcom (1801–79: *DNB*), of the Royal Engineers, had an important part in directing famine relief in Ireland. He was made permanent Under-Secretary for Ireland in 1853 and was knighted in 1860. Larcom had called on TBM in Dublin on 18 August (Journal, III, 10a) and had accompanied him on his tour to the Boyne.

Albany that day. But my man is very poorly.[1] It will be all that I can do to bring him safe home to be nursed by his wife; and since I left Londonderry I have been forced to be his servant.

Ever yours

T B Macaulay

TO CHRISTIAN BERNHARD TAUCHNITZ,[2] 8 SEPTEMBER 1849

Text: [Christian Karl Bernhard von Tauchnitz], *Fünfzig Jahre der Verlagshandlung Bernhard Tauchnitz, 1837 bis 1887*, Leipzig, 1887, p. 106.

Paris, Septbr. 8, 1849

The translation which you were so good as to send seems to me excellent.[3] I am no judge of the delicacies of a German style. But my meaning has, as far as I have seen, been completely seized and clearly exhibited. The notes also, though not absolutely free from small mistakes, show a knowledge of English laws and literature such as few Englishmen attain. ... The specimen which you have sent of your edition of my history is extremely handsome.

TO LADY NAPIER,[4] [*c.* 10 SEPTEMBER 1849][5]

MS: Haverford College.

[Paris]

Dear Lady Napier,

    Ellis and I are going on an excursion to St Germains to day; and I much

---

1 William came down with a heavy cold on 31 August (Journal, III, 42a).

2 Tauchnitz (1816–95), created Freiherr von Tauchnitz in 1860, was a Leipzig publisher specializing in the reprint of English works for circulation on the Continent, the small, paper-covered volumes of the 'Collection of British Authors' begun in 1841. Tauchnitz was the first among foreign reprint publishers to operate under the new international copyright agreements. He sought fair contracts with his authors and scrupulously observed their terms: TBM calls him 'a pearl of a bookseller' (Journal, IV, 13: 9 March 1851). Tauchnitz had called on TBM on 21 July. They then 'made an agreement very favourable to me,' as TBM wrote in his Journal (II, 71), though this was evidently not finally confirmed until later: see 24 March 1850. Tauchnitz published the *History*, 10 vols., 1849–61; *Essays*, 5 vols., 1850; *Lays of Ancient Rome*, 1851; *Speeches*, 2 vols., 1853; *Biographical Essays*, 1857; and the essays on Pitt and Atterbury, 1860.

3 The first volume of the German translation by Prof. Friedrich Bülau, Leipzig, 1849–51. TBM found it at the Albany on his return from Ireland: 'the translator has given the meaning faithfully and is evidently a man well read in our history, laws, manners, and literature' (Journal, III, 50a: 4 September).

4 Frances Dorothea, second wife of General Sir George Thomas Napier (1784–1855: *DNB*), Peninsular veteran, formerly Governor of the Cape of Good Hope, and brother of Sir Charles James and Sir William Napier. TBM dined with Napier on 12 September: 'a capital fellow – good natured as brave – the only Napier that I like....His wife a fine woman' (Journal, II, 96).

5 TBM's Journal at this point is very summary and does not mention any excursion to St Germain; the 10th or the 11th seems the likeliest date.

fear that we shall not be at the Hotel till too late to trespass on you. If we should be earlier than we expect it will give us the greatest pleasure to join your party.

Ever yours truly
T B Macaulay

TO FRANCES MACAULAY, 11 SEPTEMBER 1849

MS: Trinity College.

Paris Septr. 11 / 1849

Dearest Fanny,

We are amusing ourselves here pleasantly enough. We have been to Rouen, and are going to Chartres.[1] Thackeray[2] is in the Hotel Bristol with us, and is to be of our party to Chartres. Yesterday I gave him a dinner at the Frères Provençaux.[3] Our old friend Dumont,[4] who, by the bye, asked very kindly after you, was there, and played his part well. Paris is quite unchanged in aspect. There is no token of the Revolution except here and there a withered miserable poplar, called a tree of liberty, and the words Liberté, Egalité, Fraternité, on the public buildings. No private person shows, as far as I have seen, the least love or respect for the present form of government. The word republic is hardly uttered without a sneer.

The best thing that I have observed is the extraordinary advance which our neighbours have made in taste for Gothic architecture. There are several buildings in progress which are equal, indeed superior, to the best of Barry and Hardwicke.[5] I must stop. For I am engaged to go with

---

[1] They went to Rouen on the 8th and to Chartres on the 12th (Journal, II, 95).

[2] The first meeting between Thackeray and TBM is reported in TBM's Journal for 8 March 1849: 'Thackeray – glad to know him. He told me that he knew how I had spoken of his book and thanked me quite touchingly' (I, 528). They met frequently after this, and though there was no close friendship between them, each evidently liked and genuinely respected the other. When they first met, Thackeray was still excited by the success of *Vanity Fair* and inclined to talk too much about it. On this, TBM shrewdly remarked: 'I suspect that success, coming late, has turned his head. "L'on voit bien, messieurs, que vous n'etes pas accoutumés a vaincre"' (Journal, II, 25–6: 8 June 1849). On the day after this letter, TBM and Thackeray dined with Sir George Napier, when, Thackeray reported, 'I am afraid I disgusted Macaulay...we were told that an American lady was coming in the evening, whose great desire in life was to meet the Author of Wanaty Fair and Author of the Lays of A. Rome, so I proposed to Macaulay to enact me, and let me take his character – but he said solemnly that he did not approve of practical jokes, & so this sport did not come to pass' (to Mrs Brookfield, 13 September: Ray, *Letters of Thackeray*, II, 593).

[3] 'Thackeray and Dumont dined with us at the Frères Provençaux. I took more wine than agreed with me, though not enough to disorder my head' (Journal, II, 95).

[4] See [26 September 1830].

[5] Philip Hardwick (1792–1870: *DNB*), eclectic architect, designed the Great Western and Victoria hotels and the new hall and library of Lincoln's Inn.

Dumont to the Archives. I shall be in London, I hope, on Monday next.
Kind regards to George and Sarah Anne.[1]

Ever yours
T B Macaulay

TO FRANCES MACAULAY, 18 SEPTEMBER 1849

MS: Trinity College.

Albany London / September 18 / 1849

Dearest Fanny,

I arrived safe and well yesterday evening after a not unpleasant tour.[2]
I inclose your certificates. But I wish you to understand that I mean to pay
whatever further demands may be made on you in respect of these shares.
I can very well afford to do so; and it is a pleasure to me to lay out my
money so well.

I write in haste: for I have a large arrear of correspondence in consequence of my late rambles. Remember me most kindly to George and
Sarah Anne.

Ever yours,
T B Macaulay

TO FRANCES MACAULAY, 21 SEPTEMBER 1849

MS: Trinity College.

Albany London / September 21. 1849

Dearest Fanny,

You must allow me to insist on what I mentioned in my last letter.
When do you expect the next call? The price of your stock is now, I
think, lower than it can long continue to be. This is no time therefore for
selling. If there should not be a rise before Xmas, I shall probably buy
instead of parting with what I now have.

Poor Empson is very ill in bed at Craig Crook. His wife writes his
letters from his dictation. He has had a congestion on the brain, – a
complaint which has a very disagreeable sound. Longman – but do not
talk of this – seems to think that it will be necessary to look out for another
editor. I am truly distressed about it.

---

[1] Babington.
[2] TBM worked at the National Archives on the 13th, 14th, and 15th, left for Boulogne on the
16th, and arrived in London on the 17th (Journal, II, 96–7).

I am regularly at work.[1] I write a foolscap sheet and a half of narrative daily. If this holds I shall, by Christmas, have prepared a tolerable specimen of my history of the reign of William. Kindest messages to George and Sarah Anne.

Ever yours
T B Macaulay

TO LADY TREVELYAN, 21 SEPTEMBER 1849

MS: Trinity College.

Albany London / September 21. 1849

Dearest Hannah,

I am glad to have so good an account of you all. I look forward to the 1st of October with great delight.[2] To me at least your migration will be an unmixed benefit.

I am most uneasy about Empson. He has had a congestion on the brain, and, though better, is still in bed, unable to write. I had a letter yesterday dictated by him but written by his wife. He has obtained a month's holiday from the Court of Directors. This is bad in itself, and worse when we consider all that it indicates. Longman seems to think it impossible that a person so affected can go through the harrassing business of editing the Review. It is painful to think of the state of that once happy house at Craig Crook; Mrs. Jeffrey dropsical – Empson in bed with this alarming malady, Jeffrey, himself an invalid requiring a nurse, and nearer eighty than seventy, forced to work at the new Number of the Edinburgh Review instead of his son in law.

Love to Trevelyan and the dear girls. I long for a walk with Baba across the Parks. Kind regards to Mrs. Trevelyan.

Ever yours
T B Macaulay

---

1 'Began to write in earnest – Irish expedition of James. I am resolved that there shall be no day without a page or so' (Journal, II, 97: 18 September). Lady Trevelyan told Marianne Thornton a little later than this that 'Tom has come back such a hot Orangeman, that he says if he had stayed in Ireland he should have joined an Orange Lodge. He wont hear a word against Lord Roden [Grand Master of the Orange Society] and says he cannot trust himself to write the siege of Derry as yet he feels so excited' (to Louisa Inglis, [October?] 1849: MS, Cambridge University Library). This sounds more violent than anything in TBM's letters or Journal.

2 When the Trevelyans moved from Clapham to Westbourne Terrace.

TO MARGARET TREVELYAN, 26 SEPTEMBER 1849

MS: Trinity College.

Albany London / September 26. 1849

My dearest girl,

I am most thankful for your letter. You cannot think how often I have missed you and longed for you during the last week, which I have passed in solitude as complete as that of Robinson Crusoe before he fell in with Friday. Yet I was glad that you were enjoying yourself in the fresh air among the trees and not in streets that have been black with coffins and mourning coaches all day long. Now however the danger is all but over; and it will, I trust, be quite over before you return.[1]

I saw hardly any change in Paris. Here or there was a miserable stunted poplar stuck in the pavement, and called a tree of liberty. On some of the public buildings are the words "Liberté. Egalité. Fraternité." In other things I saw no change. The shops, the galleries, the gardens of the Thuilleries, look just as they did. Véry's crawfish soup and partridges are just as good as ever. But every human being that I saw, high and low, was cursing the revolution, and breathing vengeance on the Red Party. I went to St Germains in company with a very intelligent and polished man, evidently a considerable proprietor. He had been in the fight last June year. "I am not young," he said, "I am the father of a family. I am a man of peace. Is it not cruel that I should have had to turn out, to take my fusil-de-chasse, and to fight in the streets to save my house and my children from those mad dogs. There we were, Sir, thousands of us, grey headed men, husbands and parents who had never drawn a trigger before except against a partridge." He described the fight at the point where he was. The first volley that he and his friends fired killed seven of the insurgents. "I had never seen a man die by violence before. I could not sleep for weeks without dreaming of their horrible faces." But there was no tenderness for them in his heart. "We have been too lenient with them. There should have been no prisoners made. They want to rob, to burn, to murder. They are as bad as ever. They will soon be up again. And then we will have no mercy. It shall be the last time. They shall be treated like dogs – like mad dogs." And he repeated this over and over. You may be shocked: but I quite sympathized with him. Had I been in Cavaignac's[2] place at that time I would have made such an example of the rabble of the Faubourg St Antoine that the ears of all the world should have tingled. But how I run on to my darling about politics for which she does not

---

[1] There had been an epidemic of cholera in England this summer; the number of deaths in London for the week ending 15 September exceeded the weekly average by 2,000.

[2] Louis Eugène Cavaignac (1802–57), the general in command against the revolt of June 1848.

care one straw. Love to Mamma and Papa and the Lady of the Castle; and tell her Ladyship how much I long to have a game of play with her. Pray remember me kindly to Grandmamma. M. Dumont wished me to present his homages to your uncle Otto.[1] Pray convey them properly.

Ever yours dearest

T B Macaulay

TO [FRANCES MACAULAY?], [3? OCTOBER 1849][2]

MS: Fragment, Trinity College.

[London]

I called in Westbourne Terrace, and found everything in confusion, as usual on such occasions. It reminded me of our moving thirty one years ago this very month from Clapham to Cadogan Place. I hope that this removal will be a happier one than that proved.

TO DR JAMES DIXON,[3] 10 OCTOBER 1849

MS: Cambridge University Library.

Albany Octr. 10 / 1849

Sir,

I am much obliged to you for your suggestions. I will attend to them.

You are wrong about the shout in Palace Yard. I did not invent the circumstance, but strictly followed the narrative of an ear witness, – Johnstone, the confidential agent of William the Third.[4] Remember that, across the water, the distance from Westminster Hall to the Temple is not very great, and that water is an excellent conductor of sound. I was myself on one of the roofs of the Temple when William the Fourth opened London Bridge, and I heard, or fancied that I heard, the shouting at London Bridge.[5]

Bayonets were used by James the Second's Dragoons, but the French name had not come in. The ordinary word was *dagger*.[6]

---

[1] Edward Otto Trevelyan (1810–80), Charles Trevelyan's younger brother, was curate of Stogumber, Somerset, from 1841.

[2] On this date TBM called, apparently for the first time, at Westbourne Terrace, where he 'found Hannah in the midst of her troubles, – handsome house handsomely furnished' (Journal, II, 106).

[3] Dixon (1813–96: *Boase*) was a surgeon specializing in ophthalmology; he also had antiquarian interests and contributed materials to the *Oxford English Dictionary* and *Notes and Queries*.

[4] The roar of the crowd outside Westminster Hall on the acquittal of the seven bishops 'was heard at Temple Bar' (*History*, II, 386).

[5] See 3 August 1831.

[6] See *History*, I, 296.

Of course I did not suppose the legs of a badger to be uneven.[1] I was merely speaking in the language of the contemporary lampoons. Perhaps it might be as well to alter the sentence.

Authorities differ about the spelling of Bryse's name.[2] I followed his own signature to his deposition at Edinburgh. / I have the honor to be, / Sir,

Your most obedient Servant
T B Macaulay

TO THOMAS LONGMAN, 11 OCTOBER 1849

MS: Longman Group Ltd.

Albany October 11 / 1849

My dear Sir,

I am at a loss to conceive what the Professor can mean. Of course the matter will easily be cleared up.

I return the M.S.S. and his former letter as well as this last.

Surely it ought not to be difficult to make him understand that you and I must see such a publication as he contemplates in two different points of view, – that the value of papers as materials for history and their value in the bookselling market are two very different things. It is no affront to the genius of Sir Isaac Newton to say that you would rather be the publisher of Pickwick than of the Principia.

Ever yours truly
T B Macaulay

TO SIR EDWARD BULWER-LYTTON, 12 OCTOBER 1849

MS: Hertfordshire County Council.

Albany October 12 / 1849

Dear Sir Edward,

Thanks for the Caxtons.[3] I am truly glad to have made their acquaintance. You have written more powerful books, but none, I think, that leaves a more pleasing or a more salutory impression on the mind.

---

[1] 'His legs uneven as those of a badger' is an item in TBM's description of Titus Oates (*History*, I, 483). He did not change the passage.

[2] John Bryce was a Covenanter executed in 1685 (*History*, I, 499); the spelling 'Bryce' is the same in all editions.

[3] Published on 8 October. TBM received the book on the 9th and found it 'more amusing' than Bulwer-Lytton's standard (Journal, II, 111).

I generally read your works too fast to make minute observations. I noted however three or four slips of the pen which you may as well correct in your second edition. You make Dr. Heman and the learned Mr. Caxton place the accent on the first syllable of Peisistratos. The Greeks never put the accent further back than the antepenultimate syllable. I should not have thought this worth mentioning, – for there is no more unprofitable study than that of the Greek accents, – were it not that in this case the smallest inexactness is a dramatic impropriety. You or I may make such mistakes unreproved. But it is otherwise with the master of the Philhellenic Institute and with the author of the History of Human Error. I may notice another inaccuracy which, unimportant as it is, does not suit the character of Mr. Austin Caxton. He says that Sphinx and Enigma are feminine words. Ἄινιγμα, you will remember, is neuter.

You describe a roundhead mob, which, in the time of the civil war, attacked a royalist's house, as a Malignant mob, – Malignant with a capital. Now the word Malignant was never so used. It was exclusively applied to the Cavaliers. I am confident that it is impossible to point out a single exception. When I have added that you have, in one place, written Lord Wellesley for Lord Wellington, or perhaps for Sir Arthur Wellesley, I have exhausted my budget of criticisms. They are the merest trifles: but, judging by myself, I think that you may be glad to have your attention called to them.[1] With repeated thanks for the great pleasure which you have given me, believe me, dear Sir Edward,

> Very truly yours,
> T B Macaulay

TO JOHN MACAULAY, 23 OCTOBER 1849

MS: Mr D. R. Bentham.

Albany Octr. 23 / 1849

Dear John,

Many thanks for your letter. I have read it with much interest and pleasure. What you say of the Northern peasantry confirms the opinion which I have always held about them. I remember many years ago saying to poor Lord Kerry that, if Bowood were only in Lancashire, it would be the most enviable place in the world, but that the pauperism and broken spirit of the Wiltshire labourers would make it painful to me to live among them even in a palace.

---

[1] Bulwer-Lytton wrote to his publisher that TBM 'with his usual critical acumen' had pointed out 'one or two rather important oversights of mine' (Margaret Oliphant, *Annals of a Publishing House: William Blackwood and His Sons*, 1897, II, 420).

I am glad that you are

[.   .   .   .]¹

making [yourself]² respected and loved by your parishioners.

I shall show your letter to Hannah to morrow. I am sure

[.   .   .   .]¹

I have just come back from a visit to Lord Lansdowne.³ To morrow I shall be at work again. I am getting on pleasantly and satisfactorily. The sale still keeps up beyond all expectations. The sixth edition goes to press to morrow, which will bring the whole number of copies up to 22,000 for England.

TO WILLIAM EMPSON, 27 OCTOBER 1849

MS: Trinity College.

Albany London / Oct 27. 1849

Dear Empson,

So far so good. But pray take care of yourself. Your amanuensis,⁴ I hope, takes care both of herself and of you. My kindest regards to her.

I like your last Number better and better. Rogers's is a very able paper.⁵ But there are plenty of blots in it. I have however no inclination to list them.

I have been asked to ask you to insert a paper on the Marriage question.⁶

---

1 The top half of the last leaf has been cut away, removing about six lines from the recto and perhaps as many from the verso. The concluding words of the letter are written at the top of the first leaf and are not followed by a signature.

2 Most of the word has been removed with the missing part of this letter.

3 TBM went down to Bowood on the 20th and returned on this day (Journal, II, 117–21). It was on this occasion that TBM's first recorded meeting with Matthew Arnold, then Lord Lansdowne's private secretary, took place.

4 Mrs Empson: see *to* Frances Macaulay, 21 September.

5 Henry Rogers, 'Reason and Faith; Their Claims and Conflicts,' *ER*, XC (October 1849), 293–356. Rogers (1806?–77: *DNB*), a frequent contributor to the *ER* on theological, philosophical, and literary topics, was Professor of English, Mathematics, and Mental Philosophy at the Congregational Spring Hill College, Birmingham. TBM, in common with most of those who knew him, was very fond of Rogers – 'excellent fellow' is a characteristic response (Journal, II, 357: 19 July 1850).

6 The request almost certainly came from Henry Thornton; TBM received a letter from him on this day, which, he says, 'plagued me' (Journal, II, 127). Thornton's wife Harriet had died in 1840 and he now intended to marry her sister, Emily Dealtry. Such a marriage was rendered illegal by the Marriage Act of 1835, making marriage with the 'deceased wife's sister' carry civil as well as canonical disabilities. TBM regarded Thornton as a man afflicted with a mania: 'and for what an object – ugly, sickly, bad hearted, indelicate, stupid, ill-educated' (Journal, III, 169: 15 February 1851). In 1852 Thornton married despite the law, and much of his time thereafter was occupied in an obsessive and unsuccessful struggle to get it changed: see chapter six of Forster's *Marianne Thornton*. A marriage bill was introduced in 1850, one of a long series of such bills, which, year after year, were introduced and rejected, until 1907. The *ER* published a paper on the question in 1853 by Henry Rogers, who had himself married his deceased wife's sister.

I have answered that I could not with any propriety press you to do anything on that subject except in strict conformity with your own judgment.
I think the argument is decidedly in favour of the proposed change in the
law. But I am not zealous about the matter. I should be sorry if the
Edinburgh Review took what I think the wrong side. But I do not
conceive that you are under any obligation to say anything.

Ever yours,
T B Macaulay

TO BENJAMIN HAWES, 1 NOVEMBER 1849

MS: Duke University.

Albany November 1 / 1849

My dear Hawes,

I am truly grateful for your kindness, and so, I assure you, is Ellis.[1]
The young man has written most warmly to his father about the kindness
of the official gentlemen at Adelaide. I heartily wish all prosperity to your
boy in the career on which he is entering.[2]

Ever yours truly,
T B Macaulay

TO FRANCES MACAULAY, 10 NOVEMBER 1849

MS: Trinity College.

Albany London / November 10. 1849

Dearest Fanny,

I inclose the letter. Everett will, I am certain, show Henry[3] every kindness and civility possible. I wish, between ourselves, that I were as sure of

---

[1] Hawes had written to Ellis the day before with good news about Arthur Ellis (Journal, II,
129). Arthur Danvers Ellis, Ellis's third son and fifth child, went out to South Australia
early in 1849 with a small sum of capital; both TBM and Trevelyan had done what they
could for him through their connections with Hawes and the Colonial Office. The first
reports were encouraging, but in 1850 and for two years thereafter there are many anxious
entries in TBM's Journal about Arthur's debts, which TBM helped to pay. Arthur was first
employed as a clerk to the Stipendiary Magistrate at Port Adelaide but resigned after a few
months. In October 1853 he applied unsuccessfully for the position of inspector of police;
he disappears from the archives of South Australia after that (information from the
Archivist). Arthur left three children, who inherited their grandfather's property through
their Aunts Marian and Louisa Ellis.

[2] Hawes's son, Benjamin Park Hawes (1828–59), had just entered the Indian Army.

[3] Henry Babington, who had resigned from the East India Company's service in this year. He
called on TBM next year, so evidently he survived his American tour (Journal, II, 350: 9
July 1850).

Henry's good temper and good breeding. He is so bitter, sulky and cynical that I am afraid of his getting into scrapes among the Yankees who are to the last degree sensitive about the deportment of English travellers, and prone to suspect that some affront is intended even when there is no ground for suspicion. I should not in the least wonder if he were to have a bullet or a bowie knife put into him before he reaches Boston.

Kind remembrances to Price[1] and Lydia.

> Ever yours
> T B Macaulay

TO FRANCES MACAULAY, 13 NOVEMBER 1849

MS: Trinity College.

Private

Albany Nov 13. 1849

Dearest Fanny,

I have not a line of Praed's writing. As to recollections, I will tell you, though I must beg you not to tell Moultrie or anybody else, that what I recollect I would much rather forget myself than publish to others.[2] I hate public ruptures with friends. If they use me basely, – and Praed alone of all my friends ever used me basely, – my rule is

> "Le bruit est pour le fat: la plainte est pour le sot:
> L'honnête homme trompé s'éloigne et ne dit mot."[3]

You had better merely tell Moultrie that I am afraid that I have no materials which can be of any use to him.

It is a very foolish thing, I think, to publish any biography or any remains of Praed. He was a wonderful boy at seventeen; and a wonderful boy he continued to be till he died at near forty. The best thing for his fame is that his early poetry should be read in the Etonian, where it appears as the work of a lad and is compared with the works of other lads. He never afterwards wrote better. I am not sure that he ever afterwards wrote so well. The proposed collection will, I am confident, do him no

---

[1] Bonamy Price (1807–88: *DNB*) had married TBM's cousin Lydia Rose in 1834. Price was a mathematics and classics master at Rugby from 1830 to 1850. Fanny Macaulay was often the guest of the Prices at Rugby, and that is how she was able to read TBM's *Lays* to Dr Arnold (see 14 July 1842). Price was later Drummond Professor of Economics at Oxford, 1868–88.

[2] John Moultrie was planning an edition of Praed's works and was seeking recollections for a memoir; the plan was not carried out. In Derwent Coleridge's 'Memoir' prefixed to Praed's *Poems*, 1864, TBM is only briefly mentioned and no reference is made to their estrangement.

[3] M. Delanoue, *La Coquette Corrigée* (1756), I, iii; see Trevelyan, I, 122n.

honour; and I have just so much kindness for him remaining as to wish that the plan were abandoned.

I hear nothing about the Rugby mastership.[1] Malden was a candidate last time; and then he told me that he should not object, if elected, to go into the Church. I have heard nothing from him on this occasion. Remember me to Mr. and Mrs. Price.

> Ever yours,
> T B Macaulay

TO UNIDENTIFIED RECIPIENT, 17 NOVEMBER 1849

MS: University of California, Los Angeles.

Albany London / November 17. 1849

My dear Sir,

I am much obliged to you for your letter, and highly gratified by your approbation. I was well acquainted with Lord Huntingdon's deposition.[2] It was published by authority together with the other evidence taken by the Council held on the 22nd of October 1688. I do not, however, think that, when you consider the position in which Lord Huntingdon then stood, you will blame me for not excepting him from the general censure which I have passed on the witnesses. He was a most unpopular man. He was a favourite at court in times when to be a favourite at court was to be an enemy of the nation. He was loaded with places. He had a regiment. He was Chief Justice in Eyre north of Trent. He had recently been induced to accept offices taken from eminent noblemen on account of their fidelity to the constitution. The Earl of Rutland, Lord Lieutenant of Leicestershire, and the Earl of Scarsdale, Lord Lieutenant of Derbyshire, had refused to be the agents of the government for the purpose of packing a House of Commons.[3] They had both been turned out: Lord Huntingdon had been put in their room; and he had exerted himself to coerce the freeholders of two counties by most irregular means and for a most pernicious end. I cannot therefore think that I do him injustice when I say that his name did not, at that time, command public respect and confidence.

---

[1] Arnold's successor, Archibald Campbell Tait (1811–92: *DNB*), had just been made Dean of Carlisle; Tait was succeeded as headmaster by Edward Goulburn (1818–97: *DNB*), appointed on 18 November.

[2] The seventh Earl of Huntingdon (1650–1701: *DNB*), though not named in TBM's account, was among the witnesses to the genuineness of the birth of the Prince of Wales in 1688: TBM says of them that they included 'not a single name which commanded public confidence and respect' (*History*, II, 473). Huntingdon's deposition is in Howell, *State Trials*, XII, 142–3.

[3] See *History*, II, 326.

That his deposition was true I do not in the least doubt. But that is not the point in issue.

With many thanks for your kindness, believe me, / My dear Sir,

Your faithful Servant

T B Macaulay

TO LORD MAHON, 20 NOVEMBER 1849

MS: Stanhope Papers, Chevening.

Albany Nov 20. 1849

Dear Lord Mahon,

Your theory is at least plausible. Niebuhr takes a very different view. Look at his Lectures in Schmitz's work – Vol iii pages 170. and 232.[1] But I do not think that Niebuhr represents the passage in Jerome correctly.

Ever yours truly

T B Macaulay

TO FRANCES MACAULAY, 7 DECEMBER 1849

MS: Huntington Library. *Extract published:* Trevelyan, II, 230.

Albany London / Dec 7. 1849

Dearest Fanny,

I read a portion of my history to Hannah and Trevelyan with great effect. Hannah cried, and Trevelyan kept awake.[2] But I have not written three chapters, – only parts of two. I think what I have done as good as any part of the former volumes; and so Ellis thinks.

The reason that the clergy were, as compared with other classes, poorer then than now I had, I thought, explained, or at least suggested.[3] The tithe and the rent follow quite different laws. The tithe increases in proportion to the increase of the produce; the rent, in quite a different proportion. While the rent of a parish in Leicestershire has been increasing from five hundred pounds to two thousand, the tithe has probably increased from a hundred pounds to seven hundred.

---

[1] *Lectures on the History of Rome,* trans. Leonhard Schmitz, 3 vols., 1844–8; Niebuhr believes that the *Annals* of Tacitus were originally in twenty books, not sixteen, and, on St Jerome's authority, that the *History* contained thirty books. Mahon has endorsed the letter: 'In consequence of the conversation turning to that subject when I breakfasted in Macaulay's rooms (Nov. 19) I sent him my little tract "On the Lost Books of Tacitus".' Mahon's tract, first published in 1836, is reprinted in his *Miscellanies,* 2nd Series, 1872, pp. 90–3.

[2] The reading was from ch. 12, the 'Irish narrative' (Trevelyan, II, 269).

[3] See the discussion in *History,* I, 324–5.

It is true that, as Mrs. Rose says, a certain number of country gentle-men in the Seventeenth Century, passed some years at the Temple. But these were the minority, the select cases. In one of the best plays of that age – pity that it is not a lady's play – there is a scene in which two brothers dispute as to the two methods of education. "I sent my boy," says the fine gentleman, "to Westminster, then the University, then the Temple, then to travel." Sir William the country gentleman answers in a fury "My son knows a sample of grain as well as e'er a fellow in the north – can handle a sheep or a bullock – understands all sorts of manures. As for travelling he has travelled about my estate and knows every corner of it." "Yes," says the Londoner, "and lives as nastily as his swine and keeps worse company than they."[1]

I am truly sorry to have no better account of Lydia.[2] My love to her.

Ever yours

T B Macaulay

TO CAPTAIN THOMAS LARCOM, 10 DECEMBER 1849

MS: Trinity College.

Albany London / Dec 10. 1849

Dear Captain Larcom,

I return by this day's post the very curious little volume which Dr. Anster[3] was so kind as to intrust to me. Pray thank him for me. I have registered the parcel, and hope that it will arrive safe.

Ever yours truly

T B Macaulay

TO FRANCES MACAULAY, 19 DECEMBER 1849

MS: Trinity College. *Extracts published:* Trevelyan, II, 237; 269.

Albany London / Decr. 19. 1849

Dearest Fanny,

I am just starting for Althorp, where I shall stay till the end of the week.[4] Lord Spencer has invited me to rummage his family papers; a great proof of liberality when it is considered that he is the lineal descendant of Sunderland and Marlborough. In general it is ludicrous to see how sore people are at seeing the truth told about their ancestors. I am curious too

---

[1] Thomas Shadwell, *The Squire of Alsatia*, act II.
[2] Fanny's hostess, Lydia Rose Price.
[3] John Anster (1793–1867: *DNB*), Registrar to the High Court of Admiralty in Ireland and later Regius Professor of Civil Law in the University of Dublin.
[4] TBM returned on 22 December (Journal, II, 183).

about that noble library, the finest private library, I believe, in England. I shall therefore be able to get through three days well enough.[1] When I come back I will see about Bernard Barton.[2]

Denman, I hear, has at last sent in his resignation.[3] There is little doubt that Campbell will be on the bench at the opening of Hilary Term in January. I hope that the Chancellor[4] will soon take himself off too, and that Rolfe will succeed. In that case we may be able to do something for Edward.[5]

I have heard that something has been written against Stephen.[6] If he were not so morbidly sensitive it would matter little. I have never been able to discover that a man is at all the worse for being written against. One foolish line written by himself does him more harm than the ablest books written by other people.

Love to Lydia.

Ever yours

T B Macaulay

TO LORD SPENCER, 24 DECEMBER 1849

MS: The Earl Spencer.

Albany London / December 24. 1849

My dear Lord,

I send to day by railway a copy of Barry O'Meara's book in which you

---

[1] The party included Lady Davy, the Dowager Lady Lyttelton, and two of her sons, the fourth Lord Lyttelton and Spencer Lyttelton, with their wives (Journal, II, 176).

[2] The Quaker poet (1784–1849: *DNB*); I do not know what Fanny may have asked.

[3] Denman had already suffered two strokes and was under pressure from all sides to resign, but he did not wish to see Campbell succeed him as Lord Chief Justice and delayed his resignation until 28 February 1850. Campbell then did succeed him.

[4] Lord Cottenham resigned on 19 June 1850. For some reason there was hostility towards Cottenham on the part of TBM's family: the 'Sketch of the Life of Sir James Parker' asserts that Cottenham 'soon showed himself to be a tyrannical bad man, full of unjust prejudices, ignorant of law and obstinate in his ignorance. . . . Before he left the Court he was detested by the whole Bar' (typescript, Mrs Lancelot Errington). TBM wrote that Cottenham's 'grossly unjust and unhandsome conduct to Trevelyan has destroyed all my regard for him' (Journal, II, 20–1: 2 June 1849). Cottenham was succeeded by Thomas Wilde, Lord Truro.

[5] Edward Joseph Rose (1818–82), second son of Lydia Babington Rose, was Curate of Dalby-on-the-Wolds, Leicestershire, 1845–55; TBM finally did get preferment for him: see 24 June 1855.

[6] In the epilogue to his collected *Essays in Ecclesiastical Biography*, 2 vols., 1849, Stephen had expressed doubts as to eternal damnation. The formidable Dr Corrie, Master of Jesus, said of Stephen: 'You know, my friend, in healthier times he would have been burnt' (M. Holroyd, ed., *Memorials of George Elwes Corrie*, Cambridge, 1890, p. 277). Leslie Stephen says of this episode in his father's life that 'certain learned dons discovered on his appointment to the professorship of history that he was "Cerinthian." I do not pretend to guess at their meaning' (*Life of Sir James Fitzjames Stephen*, 1895, p. 56). TBM says that Stephen was called a 'Semi Sabellian' (29 April 1850).

will find an engraving of your Cameo.[1] Pray honour the volumes with a place in your notable collection.

I have found, I believe, the words which Lady Spencer[2] recollects to have seen written in your gallery. They are, as I supposed, in Horace Walpole's Anecdotes of Painting, under the head of Lely. The words are – "the gallery at Althorp, one of those enchanted scenes which a thousand circumstances of history and art endear to a pensive spectator."[3]

With many thanks for your kindness and for Lady Spencer's, believe me ever, / My dear Lord,

Yours very truly
T B Macaulay

TO UNIDENTIFIED RECIPIENT, 24 DECEMBER 1849

MS: Yale University.

Albany Dec 24. 1849

Sir,

Lord Clarendon has transmitted to me a letter which you wrote to him respecting the family of Dr. Cooke Taylor.[4] My own knowledge of Dr. Cooke Taylor was very slight. I was in his company only once, and then only for about ten minutes. But all that I have heard of him has led me to form a high opinion of his abilities and of his character. I have great pleasure in sending you what I can afford to contribute for the benefit of his widow and children. I wish that it were more. But you must excuse me from taking the chair at the meeting which you propose to call. Reasons which, I am persuaded, you would yourself admit to be of great weight have forced me to lay down a rule from which I could not now depart without giving just cause of offence to many respectable persons. / I have the honor to be, / Sir,

Your most obedient servant
T B Macaulay

[1] Lord Spencer had just purchased some relics of Napoleon that had belonged to Barry O'Meara, including a cameo of Napoleon that had been engraved for one of the illustrations to O'Meara's *Napoleon in Exile* (see 5 October 1822). Not finding this illustration in the copy of the book that he examined at Althorp, TBM sent one containing it. His gift is now in the library at Althorp (I owe this information to the present Earl Spencer).

[2] Georgiana Elizabeth Poyntz (1799–1851) married Lord Spencer in 1830.

[3] *Anecdotes of Painting in England,* 2nd edn, III (1765), 18n.

[4] Taylor (see 22 August) died on 12 September, leaving his widow, a son, and three daughters. TBM sent £10 to the fund for their relief (Journal, II, 183: 23 December).

TO FRANCES MACAULAY, 26 DECEMBER 1849

MS: Trinity College.

Albany London / Dec 26. 1849

Dearest Fanny,

Send me the letter. I shall pay this call;[1] and then I would strongly advise you to sell. When I dissuaded you a few weeks ago,[2] it was because I had a notion – whence derived I know not – that you were liable to no more calls. I now find that a hundred pounds will not clear you of your engagements.

Perhaps you had better wait till after the next dividend is declared, and then sell.

I wished much for you yesterday.[3] Kindest messages and Xtmas wishes to all at the Temple.

Ever yours
T B Macaulay

TO MRS SYDNEY SMITH, 29 DECEMBER 1849

MS: Mr D. C. L. Holland.

Albany Dec 29 1849

My dear Mrs. Sydney Smith,

I am most grateful to you for your kind present.[4] I shall read the lectures with the greatest interest. I have often heard of them.

Ever yours most truly
T B Macaulay

TO ELIOT WARBURTON, 16 JANUARY 1850

MS: Alexander Turnbull Library, Wellington.

Albany London / January 16. 1850

My dear Sir,

The subject which I suggested to you was, if I recollect rightly, the

---

[1] 'Fresh call on Selina for railway shares – 40£. I shall pay it, and I shall do the same for Fanny who does not ask it' (Journal, II, 184: 24 December).

[2] See *to* Fanny, 21 September.

[3] TBM spent Christmas with the Trevelyans and his brother Charles's family: 'I had sent as usual the fish, the turkey, and the chine' (Journal, II, 187).

[4] Sydney Smith's *Elementary Sketches of Moral Philosophy*, originally delivered as lectures at the Royal Institution in 1804–6 and privately printed in 1849. They were published in 1850. Smith thought he had destroyed the manuscript, but Mrs Smith had rescued it from the fire (Sydney Smith, *Letters*, I, 101n).

resistance of the Roman Catholic party to our Protestant Princes.[1] It would include the insurrections against Henry the Eighth and Edward the Sixth, the rising of the Northern Earls against Elizabeth, – Norfolk's plottings with Mary, Babington's conspiracy, and the Gunpowder plot. You might give a lively picture of the manners of the Roman Catholic gentry, of the secret missions of Jesuits in disguise, and so on. I feel at the same time that the difficulties of such a work would be very great; and, though I might mention it in conversation, I would by no means advise any friend to undertake it without very serious consideration.

The subject of which you speak is of much greater extent. It would be the entire business of a long life. The history of the English Reformation cannot be studied to any purpose, unless it is studied in connection with the history of the German Reformation, of the Swiss Reformation, of the French Huguenots, of the followers of Knox in Scotland. You would have to speak also of the abortive attempt at reformation in Italy and Spain. The proceedings of the Councils of Constance and Trent alone, – both of which would enter into the plan, – would furnish work for years. If you feel a generous ambition to attempt this enterprise, after mature reflection, I should be sorry to discourage you. Only remember that it will be a thankless as well as a laborious task, and that, if you tell the truth courageously, you will assuredly be a mark for the malevolence of Roman Catholics, high Churchmen, Low Churchmen, Presbyterians, Independents, Baptists, everybody in short except a few candid and impartial men whose voices will hardly be heard. / Believe me, / My dear Sir,

Yours very truly,

T B Macaulay

TO THOMAS LONGMAN, [16? JANUARY 1850][2]

Text: Trevelyan, II, 239.

[London]

I have looked through the tenth volume of Lingard's History in the new edition.[3] I am not aware that a single error has been pointed out by Lingard in my narrative. His estimate of men and of institutions naturally differs from mine. There is no direct reference to me, but much pilfering

---

1 TBM dined with Warburton at Sir John Romilly's on 15 December but does not describe their conversation (Journal, II, 173). Nothing came of the subjects discussed in this letter.

2 On 11 January TBM heard from Longman that 'Lingard has written something against me'; on the 16th he looked through Lingard's tenth volume and recorded his response in his Journal in language closely resembling that of this letter (II, 202; 207).

3 This had just appeared. The tenth volume treats the Revolution of 1688.

from me, and a little carping at me. I shall take no notice either of the pilfering or the carping.[1]

TO THOMAS FLOWER ELLIS, 22 JANUARY 1850

MS: Trinity College.

Albany Jany. 22. 1850

Dear Ellis,

Dine here on Saturday – if not on Monday. I make my first appearance at the Benchers' Table on Friday.[2] I hope that Brougham will be there.[3] My fiercest opponent was a great fool whom I remember with horror as one of the pre-eminent bores of the House of Commons, a Mr. Stuart[4] whom the Standard has repeatedly proposed for the custody of the Great Seal. He considers himself one of the royal House of Stuart, and looks on me as an enemy of his name. There were only two negatives, I understand.

Ever yours truly
T B Macaulay

TO [DUNCAN MACFARLAN?],[5] 26 JANUARY 1850

Text: Sotheby's Catalogue, 24 July 1905, item 333, 3 1/2 pp. 8vo: dated Albany, London, 26 January 1850.

I have been to the Treasury, and have read your memorial.[6] Your case, as

---

[1] In his Journal, II, 207, TBM mentions a 'small piece of impotent envy directed against me' in Lingard's Preface; perhaps he means the passage from the end in which Lingard explains that he has not introduced into his *History* those 'many curious and miscellaneous subjects, which, however foreign to the general purpose of history, are usually welcome to readers of fanciful or limited tastes and pursuits' (the Preface is dated 20 December 1849).

[2] On 14 January TBM learned that he had been proposed for election as a Bencher of Lincoln's Inn; the idea is said to have originated with the Vice-Chancellor, Sir James Knight-Bruce (*Daily News*, cited in *Scotsman*, 26 January). 'I must of course accept with gratitude,' TBM wrote. 'If Brougham were in England he would move heaven and earth to keep me out. What a fury he will be in' (Journal, II, 205). TBM's election was carried on the 18th, and he paid his fees on the 22nd (Journal, II, 210; 212). A window in the Chapel of Lincoln's Inn contains TBM's arms.

[3] He is not mentioned in TBM's account of the banquet on the 25th (Journal, II, 215).

[4] (Sir) John Stuart (1793–1876: *Boase*), son of Dugald Stewart; Bencher of Lincoln's Inn, 1839; M.P. for Newark, 1846–52, and for Bury St Edmund's, 1852. He was Vice-Chancellor, 1852–71, and was knighted in 1853.

[5] Macfarlan (1771–1857: *Boase*) had been Principal of the University of Glasgow since 1823.

[6] TBM's Journal for this date records a visit 'To the Treasury – Glasgow Memorial' (II, 215). The University of Glasgow was in litigation with a Glasgow railway company which had contracted to make an exchange of land and to pay for new buildings for the University but which was now seeking for an act of dissolution from Parliament. The matter was settled in May 1850: see James Coutts, *A History of the University of Glasgow*, pp. 415–19.

it is there put, seems to me quite unanswerable. That the Legislature should pass an Act annulling a contract on which an action is depending before the ordinary tribunals, seems to me a monstrous proposition. The bill, I feel sure, can never pass the Commons. At all events, it will be stopped by the Lords.[1]

TO THOMAS FLOWER ELLIS, 28 JANUARY 1850

MS: Trinity College.

Albany Jany. 28 / 1850

Dear Ellis,

I have written to Mr. Barnett. I return his letter. You are engaged to me on Thursday.

I am much cut up by this news about Jeffrey.[2] I loved him as much as it is easy to love a man who belongs to a preceding generation. However it is a comfort to think that he went off at a ripe age, honoured, prosperous, with faculties bright and affections warm to the very last. I wish you and myself such a death. Poor Denman's state makes J[effrey]'s end seem enviable. The report which I heard at Brookes's yesterday is that the physicians have at last extorted the resignation which ought to have been given earlier.

Ever yours
T B Macaulay

TO JOHN HILL BURTON, 29 JANUARY 1850

MS: National Library of Scotland.

Albany London / Jany. 29. 1850

My dear Sir,

I am sorry that I cannot do what is asked of me. The plan is an Edinburgh plan.[3] The Committee consists of Edinburgh men. Any paper which I

---

1 The rest of the letter is summarized thus in the catalogue: 'He will tell his correspondent the course the College should take after further enquiry. He has sent four vols. on Freemasonry presented to the College Library by Henry Gassett, Esq., Boston, United States.' TBM's Journal entry is more vivid: 'a letter from a fool at Boston who sent me some trash about Freemasonry for Glasgow College' (II, 215: 25 January).

2 Jeffrey died on 26 January.

3 Burton was actively promoting a plan for a national system of education in Scotland without religious teaching and had presumably asked TBM for a public statement in favor of it. The resolutions of the Committee on National Education, which included Burton, Adam Black, and other of TBM's old political associates in Edinburgh, had just been published (*Scotsman,* 26 January).

might write would be considered, and justly considered, as addressed to the citizens of Edinburgh; and my motives for writing it would be misconstrued in a manner which would be peculiarly disagreeable to me.

I am deeply distressed about my dear old friend Jeffrey. I loved him more than I ever loved any man who was so much my Senior. I hope that some public mark of respect and gratitude will be paid to him.

Ever yours truly
T B Macaulay

TO [C. DAWSON?],[1] 30 JANUARY 1850

MS: Historical Society of Pennsylvania. *Published: Notes and Queries*, 10 January 1874, p. 26.

Albany London / January 30. 1850

Sir,

I am much obliged to you for the trouble which you have kindly taken. I think Penn a poor shallow half crazy creature: but I am satisfied that he was not a Papist. That he corresponded with Cardinal Howard[2] is probable enough. But what then? Burnet had a good deal of intercourse with Cardinal Howard; and nobody suspected Burnet of being a Papist. Howard was an honest, sensible, moderate man who was connected by blood and friendship with many of the most respectable Protestants in England. It would have been well if Penn had never kept worse company or followed worse advice than Howard's.

As to the other story, to what does it amount? A nameless priest, talking to a nameless gaoler, calls Penn Father Penn. A gossiping Prebendary runs open mouthed with this silly story to Sherlock. Sherlock questions Penn; and Penn resents the suspicion, and ceases to call on Sherlock.[3] I see no sign of guilt in the conduct of the accused person. Any man of spirit would have acted in the same way. / I have the honour to be, / Sir,

Your most obedient Servant
T B Macaulay

---

[1] The recipient is identified as 'C. Dameron' in *Notes and Queries*; as 'C. Dawson' in the *Catalogue* of the F. J. Dreer collection, Philadelphia, 1890; and as 'C. Davison' in the catalogue of the Historical Society of Pennsylvania. I have arbitrarily chosen Dawson. The *Notes and Queries* text adds the address 'Hartlepool,' but this is not in the MS.

[2] Philip Thomas, Cardinal Howard (1629–94: *DNB*), Chaplain to Queen Catherine; as 'chief counsellor of the Holy See in matters relating to his country' he disapproved of James's policy and 'recommended patience, moderation, and respect for the prejudices of the English people' (*History*, 1, 468).

[3] This story is told of Penn and Tillotson (not Sherlock) in William Hepworth Dixon, *William Penn*, 1851, pp. 310–12.

TO RICHARD MONCKTON MILNES, 11 FEBRUARY 1850

MS: Trinity College.

Albany February 11 / 1850

Dear Milnes,

Many thanks for the tracts. Will you breakfast here at ten on Wednesday?[1]

Ever yours,

T B Macaulay

TO THOMAS FLOWER ELLIS, 13 FEBRUARY 1850

MS: Trinity College.

Albany Feby. 13 / 1850

Dear Ellis,

I return your friend's letter. What can I say? The proceedings of the Privy Council have been in print more than a hundred and sixty years, and are given at length in Howell's State Trials. I have made all the use of them that appeared to me to be desirable: and I have mentioned that the Queen Dowager was present, as you will see if you look at my book.[2] Nothing is more difficult than to answer people who find mare's nests of this sort, and expect to be thanked and applauded for such discoveries. Write something civil – no great matter what.

Ever yours,

T B Macaulay

TO WILLIAM EMPSON, 16 FEBRUARY 1850

Text: D. Cleghorn Thomson, 'Two Macaulay Letters,' *Review of English Literature,* I (1960), 38–9.

Albany, / London. / February 16, 1850.

Dear Empson,

I return Lord Cockburn's[3] letter. He seems to me to be quite on the

---

1 'Thackeray, Tom Taylor, Milnes to breakfast. Stupid party' (Journal, II, 229–30: 13 February).

2 The reference is to TBM's account of the council at which James presented proofs of the birth of the Prince of Wales: see 17 November 1849.

3 Henry Cockburn (1779–1854: *DNB*), Lord Cockburn, a friend and contemporary of Jeffrey and, like him, an Edinburgh Whig through the lean days of Tory domination. Both Jeffrey and Cockburn were made Judges of the Court of Session in 1834. Cockburn occasionally contributed to the *ER*, and his *Memorials of His Time*, 1856, and *Journal...* *1831–1854*, 2 vols., 1874, are attractive records of his lifetime.

right track. If the object were to procure a dissertation like that which Stewart wrote on Robertson,[1] many people would do it well, nobody better than yourself. But the object is to have a portrait of Jeffrey such as he was long before you and I knew him, and of that remarkable society of which he was the centre. None but an Edinburgh man, and an old Edinburgh man can do this; and I should doubt whether there be a single competent man except Lord Cockburn.[2]

The book which I should propose, not certainly as a faultless model but as something like a model, is Hardy's Life of Charlemont.[3] Lord Charlemont was in Dublin, something like what Jeffrey was in Edinburgh – the centre of literary society and especially of good Whig society. Round each of these centres was collected a large number of eminent persons whose names were well known in London, but of whose characters, manners and style of conversation we were very imperfectly informed. Hardy has grouped around Lord Charlemont the figures of Hood,[4] Grattan, Hutchinson,[5] Tottenham[6] and twenty others. I think that Cockburn might group round Jeffrey the Erskines,[7] Playfairs,[8] Cranstouns,[9] Leslies and others.

There ought above all to be a lively picture of that set of men who started the Edinburgh Review – their habits, their amusements, their studies. To a certain extent even their levities might properly be exhibited.

As to letters, there can be no doubt that plenty will be forthcoming. The difficulty will be to select. I should advise that no letter should be printed which did not contain some indication of our dear friend's genius or his excellent heart.

---

[1] Dugald Stewart, *Account of the Life and Writings of William Robertson*, 1801.

[2] Cockburn's *Life of Lord Jeffrey, with a Selection from His Correspondence*, 2 vols., appeared in 1852.

[3] Francis Hardy, *Memoirs of the Political and Private Life of James Caulfield, Earl of Charlemont*, 1810. TBM had read it on 4 and 5 January (Journal, II, 197–8).

[4] Thus in text, but TBM probably wrote Flood – i.e., Henry Flood (1732–91: *DNB*), Irish reform politician.

[5] John Hely-Hutchinson (1724–94: *DNB*), advocate of home rule, Catholic emancipation, and parliamentary reform.

[6] Col. Charles Tottenham (1685–1758: *DNB*), Irish politician (he is only briefly mentioned in Hardy's *Charlemont*).

[7] Henry Erskine (1746–1817: *DNB*), Dean of the Faculty of Advocates, twice Lord Advocate; a leading Edinburgh Whig.

[8] John Playfair (1748–1819: *DNB*), Professor of Mathematics and of Natural Philosophy at the University of Edinburgh, 1785–1819.

[9] George Cranstoun (d. 1850: *DNB*), Lord Corehouse, Dean of the Faculty of Advocates and Judge of the Court of Session.

TO [HENRY COCKBURN?], [*c.* 16 FEBRUARY 1850]

Text: D. Cleghorn Thomson, 'Two Macaulay Letters,' *Review of English Literature*, I, 38.

[London]

I have found no letters which I should choose to give to the public. Perhaps people might be interested by knowing that dear Jeffrey, a judge of seventy-four, condescended to revise the proofs of my history with all the diligence and minute care of a corrector of proofs working for bread – that he looked after the very commas and colons.[1] I send you a specimen of his care and kindness – a single sheet. I have dozens. But the letters which accompanied these sheets do more honour to our kind old friend's heart than to his critical sagacity; and nothing shall induce me to make myself ridiculous by publishing them.

TO THOMAS FLOWER ELLIS, 25 FEBRUARY 1850

MS: Trinity College.

Albany February 25 / 1850

Dear Ellis,

You will be amused to learn that I have just received a letter from Brougham. As I have declared everywhere during some days that I stayed away from the meeting about Jeffrey's monument because I would not enter Brougham's house,[2] I fully expected a declaration of war, and was perfectly ready to send back a defiance. To my extreme amusement and embarrassment I found that the epistle begins Dear T.M. Then come hints about the inquiry in 1690 into the death of Lord Essex, and offers of papers that are at Cashiobury.[3] What on earth can I do? It is plain that he wishes to do me all the harm that he can and yet that he shrinks from an open quarrel. I think that I shall send an ironical answer, – an answer, that is to say, which may be read in two senses. I shall tell him that I well know how deep and sincere an interest he takes in my success, and that I feel all

[1] This fact appears in Cockburn's *Life of Jeffrey*, I, 402. Jeffrey himself wrote to TBM that he thought some passages of the *History* 'a little too rhetorical' but that in correcting the proofs he had dealt only in 'commas and semicolons' (9 November [1848]: MS, Lord Knutsford).

[2] On 16 February TBM writes that he came away from a breakfast party at Senior's with Hallam, but that when Hallam went to Brougham's about Jeffrey's monument 'I would not go. I never will enter B's house' (Journal, II, 233).

[3] Evidently refused; TBM refers to Essex's suicide, 1683, in *History*, I, 268, but not thereafter. Cassiobury was Lord Essex's estate in Hertfordshire.

the gratitude which his kindness deserves.[1] I cannot help laughing at the fellow's pranks, much as I dislike him.

Remember that you dine here on Wednesday.

Ever yours,

T B Macaulay

TO CHURCHILL BABINGTON,[2] 26 FEBRUARY 1850

MS: Trinity College.

Albany London / February 26. 1850

Dear Sir,

I am much obliged to you for the very beautiful volume[3] which has just been left here. It does great honor to our University press. Your part seems, as far as I can judge, to have been very well performed. I have looked through the fragments in the hope of finding some specimens of the peculiarities attributed by the ancient critics to the style of Hyperides. But I can find nothing but the qualities common to all the Attic orators of his age, perspicuity, purity, and manly simplicity. / I have the honour to be, / Dear Sir,

Your faithful Servant,

T B Macaulay

TO FRANCES MACAULAY, 2 MARCH 1850

MS: Huntington Library.

Albany London / March 2. 1850

Dearest Fanny,

Thanks for your letter. I am always delighted to hear from you and of you. Hannah and I have been planning a visit of a day to Brighton:[4] but we must wait till the spring is further advanced.

---

[1] On 27 February TBM writes that Ellis 'advised me against sending an ironical letter which I had written to Brougham. I yielded with some reluctance' (Journal, II, 245–6). On the next day he notes: 'Sent Brougham an answer extremely dry, yet not absolutely uncivil' (*ibid.*, 246).

[2] Babington (1821–89: *DNB*), a cousin of the Rothley Temple family, was Fellow of St John's, Cambridge, and afterwards Professor of Archaeology in the University. In 1849 he published *Mr. Macaulay's Character of the Clergy in the Seventeenth Century Considered*, noted thus in TBM's Journal: 'Silly book by Churchill Babington....He sent it with a sillier letter' (II, 26: 9 June 1849).

[3] *The Oration of Hyperides against Demosthenes, Respecting the Treasure of Harpalus...*, printed at Cambridge, 1850, the first of a two-volume edition based on newly-discovered fragments. The book is item 614 in the catalogue of TBM's library sale.

[4] Fanny and Selina were now permanently residing at Temple House, Brighton.

I thought that I mentioned to you the change in my book cases.[1] I have added two new rows of shelves; and am now pretty well able to accommodate my whole library. I have counted the books. There are more than seven thousand volumes, a tolerable collection, when you consider that only three or four hundred of them were our father's.

I am glad you like Campbell's Chancellors. It is a most amusing book. The life of Lord Mansfield is the best in his new work.[2] You know probably that Denman has at last taken himself off, and that Lord C[ampbell] succeeds. It was high time.

It is generally believed that the Gorham case[3] will be decided to day: but there have been so many postponements that I feel no confidence in reports. There is no doubt that the decision will be against the Bishop. Some people talk of a secession. My own belief is that it will be a very unimportant one, that no man eminent in learning or station will be among the seceders.[4] Indeed if the Bishop himself, against whom the decision is, does not think himself bound to retire, why should others go?

I work quietly every morning, and get on, – not very fast, – but still I get on, and am tolerably satisfied. The difficulties are immense, chiefly because nobody has cleared the way for me. On the other hand I have the advantage of telling a story much of which will be quite new even to diligent students of history. I wrote a sheet yesterday about a landing of the French in Devonshire. I think it as interesting as any passage in my two first volumes: and it is my belief that the materials from which it is taken have never been examined by any person living except myself.[5]

I have just been elected by the Royal Academy Professor of Ancient Literature,[6] and approved by the Queen – fully approved Her Majesty

---

[1] TBM had new cases constructed in mid-February (Journal, ɪɪ, 232: 15 February).

[2] Campbell's *Lives of the Chief Justices of England*, a sort of supplement to his *Lives of the Lord Chancellors*, was published in two volumes in December 1849. Campbell says that Jeffrey 'gratified' him by repeating 'a favourable account of the book which he had received from Macaulay' (Hardcastle, *Life of Lord Campbell*, ɪɪ, 258).

[3] The Bishop of Exeter, Phillpotts, had refused to institute George Gorham (see 21 June 1819) to a living presented to Gorham in 1847, objecting to Gorham's Calvinistic views on baptismal regeneration. When the Court of Arches found for the Bishop, Gorham appealed to the Judicial Committee of the Privy Council, which, on 8 March, reversed the Court's judgment. Phillpotts applied to the Court of Queen's Bench, the Court of Common Pleas, and the Court of Exchequer without success before yielding. The case was an important contest between High Church and Low Church principles.

[4] The seceders included Henry, later Cardinal, Manning, and Henry Wilberforce.

[5] These are listed in the note on p. 655 of the *History*, ɪɪɪ.

[6] TBM was appointed to the office on 21 February. The office, in common with the other honorary professorships of the Academy, is not filled by election but by the nomination of the Queen on the recommendation of the President. TBM was put forward by Sir Martin Archer Shee in succession to the Bishop of Llandaff, Edward Copleston, who died on 14 October 1849.

was graciously pleased to declare. The Duke of Cambridge[1] tells me that she speaks very handsomely of me. As to this Professorship it is purely honorary. The duties and the emoluments are identical and consist in dining with the Academy once a year at the opening of the Exhibition. Even speechmaking after dinner is not required. Dr. Johnson was my predecessor. The last professor was the Bishop of Llandaff. Hallam is my colleague as professor of Ancient History. He succeeds Goldsmith.

We all expect you here in little more than three weeks for our Easter tour.[2] When the spring is further advanced I hope to see you and dear Selina at Brighton. My love to her.

Ever yours,
T B Macaulay

TO SIR CHARLES TREVELYAN, 2 MARCH 1850

MS: Trinity College.

Albany March 2 / 1850

Dear Trevelyan,

Your paper[3] is excellent. I see no reason to alter it.

Perhaps you might strengthen the last illustration. There was a time when the E[ast] I[ndia] Company underpaid its servants. What was the consequence? All the monstrous misgovernment which is still a reproach to our national character belonged to the time when the salaries of the civil service were barely enough to afford an European in India the necessaries of life. I think that the salary of a member of council was only 300 Rs a month when every fleet brought back Nabobs able to buy boroughs and to build palaces. Lord Clive always laid it down that the first step to a reform was to give good salaries. Indeed Sir Thomas Roe, one of the ablest of the old commercial servants, had said the same long before Lord Clive – "Give good wages to their content; and then you know what you part from."[4] You might add that, in the highest ranks of the public service, the love of distinction will always secure a supply of able men whose private fortune makes salary a matter of little importance.

---

[1] Adolphus Frederick (1774–1850: *DNB*), seventh and most popular of the sons of George III. TBM knew him as one of the trustees of the British Museum.

[2] To Norwich and Ely, 28 March–1 April (Journal, II, 273–6).

[3] I have not identified the paper, but it was probably written in anticipation of the work of a select committee on official salaries, which began hearing evidence on 26 April and before which Trevelyan appeared on 7 May.

[4] See the essay on Lord Clive, *ER*, LXX, 346, where TBM quotes this remark. Roe (1581–1644: *DNB*) was ambassador to the Mogul, 1615–18.

But you will never have a Lord Lansdowne or a Lord Stanley Deputy Secretary at War or Permanent Secretary to the Admiralty.

Ever yours,

T B Macaulay

TO [LONDON AND NORTHWESTERN RAILWAY AGENT], 3 MARCH 1850

MS: University of Indiana.

Albany March 3. 1850

Sir,

I now reside, not at E.1. but at F.3. Albany Piccadilly. I shall be obliged to you to direct all future communications accordingly. / I have the honor to be, / Sir,

Your obedient Servant

T B Macaulay

The Dividend warrant[1] for the last half year has arrived safe, after a delay of a few hours.

TO RICHARD MONCKTON MILNES, 4 MARCH 1850

MS: Trinity College.

Albany March 4 / 1850

Dear Milnes,

I am very sorry that I am engaged early on Saturday morning.[2]

Yours very truly

T B Macaulay

TO THOMAS FLOWER ELLIS, 9 MARCH 1850

MS: Trinity College. *Extracts published:* Trevelyan, II, 254.

Albany London / March 9. 1850

Dear Ellis,

I could not go to the ceremony at Lincoln's Inn,[3] as I had a breakfast party at home. Every thing, I am assured, went off well. Brougham's

[1] 'My London and North Western Dividend came in' (Journal, II, 247: 3 March).
[2] When he attended a trustees' meeting at the British Museum.
[3] Campbell took formal leave of the Society of Lincoln's Inn on 5 March before being admitted a member of Serjeants' Inn, consequent on his elevation to Chief Justice; until 1873 this was a process required of all judges on their appointment. Brougham delivered an address of congratulation on the occasion (*The Times*, 6 March).

speech is said by persons who do not like him to have been in excellent taste. But there was one droll incident of which the fame may not have reached York. Brougham was provided with a purse of gold which was to be presented to Campbell. It is an old usage at our Inn that when a Bencher is called to the coif we give him some guineas as a retaining fee to be of counsel for the Society. Brougham justly remarked that this form would be grossly improper in the present case. Campbell is the first peer of the realm that was ever made a Serjeant at Law; and a peer of the realm cannot be of counsel for anybody. To offer a retainer to a noble Lord would have been an insult. Brougham therefore very coolly put the purse into his own pocket, and there it still remains awaiting the decision of some competent authority on this curious question.[1]

Campbell, I am told, is in high spirits. Yet in all situations there are compensating circumstances. Would you take a judgeship of the Common Pleas, – your *Summum Bonum,* – on consideration that Frank should expose himself as young Campbell[2] did on Thursday. It was, every body tells me, the most lamentable exhibition of idiotic egotism that ever was seen.

I called on Denman the day before yesterday at his own request. Poor fellow – he is much changed, not, as far as I could see, intellectually, but physically. His daughter says that he is as clear minded as ever, but nervous and irritable. He was very kind to me.

I hope that Roebuck will do well.[3] If he fails it will not be from the strength of his competitors. What a nerveless, milk and water set the young fellows of the present day are. Grey declares that there is not in the whole House of Commons any stuff, under five and thirty, of which a junior Lord of the Treasury can be made. It is the same in literature, and, I imagine, at the bar. It is odd that the last twenty five years which have witnessed the greatest progress ever made in physical science, the greatest victories ever achieved by man over matter, should have produced hardly a volume that will be remembered in 1900, and should have seen the breed of great advocates and parliamentary orators become extinct among us.

One good composition of its kind was produced yesterday – the judgment in Gorham's case. I hope you like it. I think it excellent, – worthy of

[1] 'Brougham tried to play me a dog's trick by running away with my fee of ten guineas as a retainer to plead, when become a serjeant, for the Society of Lincoln's Inn. I made him disgorge the money at the House of Lords by threatening to sentence him to the gallows as a thief, and so commencing my judicial career with a notorious culprit' (Hardcastle, *Life of Lord Campbell,* II, 274).

[2] William Frederick Campbell (1824–93), second Baron Stratheden and Campbell, M.P. for the borough of Cambridge, 1847–52; for Harwich, 1859–60. I do not know what TBM refers to.

[3] I am not sure which of several issues to which this might plausibly refer is meant.

D'Aguesseau[1] or Mansfield. I meant to have heard it delivered: but when I came to Whitehall, I found the stairs, the passages and the very street so full of parsons, Puseyite and Simeonite, that there was no access even for Privy Councillors; and, not caring to elbow so many successors of the Apostles, I walked away.

I will give you a classical criticism of mine which I told to Mahon and Cornwall Lewis at the levee, and which they thought happy. How do you construe the famous words "Qualem pateris libamus et auro."[2] The vulgar notion that "pateris et auris" is put for "pateris aureis," I hold in the highest contempt. Find anything like that in any good writer, if you can. Virgil was not such an idiot. I hold the two words to have each of them an emphatic substantive meaning. All libations were not poured from the patera. Libations to some Gods were poured from the scyphus, to others from the cantharus. All libations were not poured from gold. There were libations from silver and from earthenware. But the patera was the bowl used for the highest solemnities; and gold of course was, on such occasions, the metal employed. Virgil therefore, when he means to extol a particular wine, says "This is the wine which we pour from the patera, and from gold, at sacrifices etc. etc." Just as, if I saw a man sipping Barclay's Entire from a wine glass I should say "That is stuff to be drunk from quart pots and from pewter." I suppose a grammarian would tell me that this was a ἓν διὰ δυοῖν[3] and that I merely meant pewter quart pots. Tell me how you like my explanation. Shall I send it to the Philological?[4]

You will find Lord Carlisle a delightful person to do business with.[5]

When do you come back. My sister went to see Marian, and found that she had been gone, I think, about an hour.

Ever yours,

T B Macaulay

TO FRANCIS KYFFIN LENTHALL,[6] 13 MARCH 1850

MS: Trinity College. *Envelope:* F. K. Lenthall Esq / 36 Mount Street / Grosvenor Square. *Subscription:* T B M.

Albany March 13 / 1850

Sir,

    I have no doubt that you put the right construction on your ancestor's

---

[1] Henri François d'Aguesseau (1668–1751), Chancellor of France.

[2] Virgil, *Georgics*, II, 192.   [3] Hendiadys.

[4] The *Proceedings* of the Philological Society.

[5] He had just been made Chancellor of the Duchy of Lancaster, of which Ellis was attorney-general.

[6] Lenthall (1824–92), a barrister, was a member of the Oxford Circuit, and later Recorder of Woodstock.

expressions,[1] and that I have used language which may be misinterpreted. The truth is that I was not thinking about him, but about the parliament of which he was a member: and the words in which he was reprimanded prove how strong the Roundhead spirit was in that parliament. I will try in the next edition to remove what you justly consider as an inaccuracy. / I have the honour to be, / Sir,

Your most obedient Servant

T B Macaulay

TO UNIDENTIFIED RECIPIENT, 20 MARCH 1850

MS: Morgan Library.

Albany March 20 / 1850

Sir,

I beg you to accept my thanks for your very pleasing volumes. I hope that the public will like them as much as I do, and that your literary career will be honourable and prosperous. / I have the honor to be, / Sir,

Your obedient Servant

T B Macaulay

TO CHRISTIAN BERNHARD TAUCHNITZ, 24 MARCH 1850

Text: Bernhard Tauchnitz, 1837–1887, p. 106.

Albany, London, March 24, 1850.

I am quite satisfied with the form in which the agreement is drawn. . . .[2]

---

[1] The reference is to a paragraph describing the House of Commons in 1660, which reprimanded a speaker for declaring that 'all who had drawn the sword against Charles the First are as much traitors as those who cut off his head' (*History*, I, 167). The speaker, unnamed in TBM's text, was Sir John Lenthall (1625–81: *DNB*). The original text of the paragraph begins by asserting that the Commons 'by no means represented the general sense of the people, and showed a strong disposition to check the intolerant loyalty of the Cavaliers.' This was altered in the seventh edition thus: 'by no means represented the general sense of the people, and, while execrating Cromwell and Bradshaw, reverenced the memory of Essex and Pym.'

[2] For the *History* in the Tauchnitz edition: on 22 April TBM went to the City and 'executed the contract with Tauchnitz before a notary' (Journal, II, 299).

TO SIR ALEXANDER DUFF GORDON,[1] 2 APRIL 1850

MS: University of Texas.

Albany April 2. 1850

My dear Sir,

I am truly sorry that I am engaged to dinner on Wednesday the 10th.[2]

Very truly yours,

T B Macaulay

TO MRS CATHERINE GORE,[3] 3 APRIL 1850

MS: Berg Collection, New York Public Library.

Albany London / April 3. 1850

Madam,

I have just arrived in London after a short excursion, and have found on my table a volume which you have done me the honour to present to me.[4] I shall always prize this gift highly for its own sake, and for that of the giver, to whom I have owed many pleasant hours. I read the *Hamiltons* long ago with much interest; and the glance which I have just given to the first pages convinces me that a second perusal will confirm the impression which the first made.

I earnestly hope that you will reprint more of your novels in the same form.[5] I cannot refrain from putting in a word for *Pinmoney* and the *Manners of the Day* which, I own, are still my favourites.[6]

With repeated thanks for your kindness, believe me, / Madam,

Your most faithful Servant,

T B Macaulay

[1] Duff Gordon (1811–72: *Boase*), third Baronet, was a clerk in the Treasury and later a Commissioner of Inland Revenue. He married Lucie, only child of John and Sarah Austin, in 1840. The Duff Gordons, noted as a remarkably handsome couple, became a familiar part of the same social world that TBM knew. He was not fond of them; he calls Sir Alexander 'an illconditioned ass' (Journal, II, 228: 10 February 1850), and Lady Duff Gordon an 'indelicate woman – repeatedly saying things that made me ashamed for her' (Journal, VIII, 94: 7 August 1854).

[2] TBM dined at home that day (Journal, II, 285).

[3] Mrs Gore (1799–1861: *DNB*) began publishing fiction in 1824 and produced a steady stream of novels until her death. Thackeray satirized them in ' "Lords and Liveries", by the authoress of "Dukes and Déjeuners," "Hearts and Diamonds," and "Marchionesses and Milliners." ' Mrs Gore also wrote successfully for the London theater.

[4] 'I found the Hamiltons a present from Mrs. Gore. I read a good deal of it with interest. I remember that I read it some eleven years ago' (Journal, II, 277: 1 April). *The Hamiltons, or the New Æra,* was first published in 1834.

[5] *The Hamiltons* (with a new subtitle, 'Official Life') was re-issued in the format of Bentley's Standard Novels: 'It can hardly be doubted that this ingenious "large paper" issue was Mrs Gore's idea – was perhaps prepared mainly for her personal use' (Michael Sadleir, *XIX Century Fiction*, 1951, II, 107).

[6] See *to* Hannah, 3 and 7 September 1831.

TO FRANCES MACAULAY, 6 APRIL 1850

MS: Trinity College.

Albany London / April 6. 1850

Dearest Fanny,

Many thanks for the Journal. It is delightful. I am not much amiss.[1] The cough and cold are gone. But Bright thinks that I have suppressed gout about me which is always shewing itself in some form or other, sometimes in eruption on the hands, sometimes in asthmatic symptoms, sometimes in determination of blood to the head. He is treating me accordingly, and will, I dare say, set me up. I have nothing in the meantime to complain of except a little languor and heaviness.

I shall certainly visit you at Brighton before long. We will then consider about St Leonards. Have you ever been to Chichester?

I am truly glad that Selina is so well. She has, I hope, some fine months before her.

Remember to send me that fool Montgomery's letters.[2] I want to show them to Ellis. He will not believe without seeing. Love to Selina.

Ever yours
T B Macaulay

TO SELINA MACAULAY, 8 APRIL 1850

MS: Trinity College.

Albany London / April 8. 1850

Dearest Selina,

Thanks for your kind letter. I am pretty well. The cough and cold have ceased to trouble me; and Bright seems to be treating very properly the symptoms which remain. I cannot hope to have as much enjoyment of life during the years which are before me as I have hitherto had. But I have no reason to complain.

Miss Shore[3] must be a very silly person. Which Miss Shore is she?

[1] TBM's first serious complaints about his health date from this winter of 1849–50, when his Journal is full of details about coughs, asthma, broken sleep, occasional giddiness, and general oppression. On his Easter tour he had a heavy cold and, at least once, a 'fit of coughing which evidently distressed and alarmed Hannah, Fanny and Baba, but to which I am more accustomed than they guess' (Journal, II, 274: 28 March). On 4 April he called in Bright, feeling 'my whole frame unstrung' (II, 279).

[2] TBM received letters from Montgomery in late March 'begging, in fact, that I will let him out of the pillory' (Trevelyan, II, 276). The occasion must have been the publication of the one-volume edition of the *Essays* in January, which retains the review of Montgomery. TBM calls one of the letters 'exquisitely ridiculous. . . . What a fool and what a coxcomb he must be' (Journal, II, 278: 2 April).

[3] John Shore, the first Baron Teignmouth, had six daughters, only one of whom, Charlotte, was still alive and unmarried at the date of this letter. Some other family may be meant.

I have just seen Lord Monteagle. He met Stephen yesterday at Trinity Lodge, and gives a better account of our friend than I had expected. The persecution seems to be going off in mere growling and snarling.[1] It never had any importance but what it derived from Stephen's sensibility.

So poor Galloway[2] is gone. He was presiding at the India House a few days ago. And old Rogers, I am afraid, is going. Love to Fanny.

Ever yours
T B Macaulay

TO WILLIAM JOHN ALEXANDER,[3] 11 APRIL 1850

MS: Scottish Record Office.

Albany April 11. 1850

My dear Sir,

I return the Chandos M.S.[4] It is highly curious and interesting. To be sure it would not be safe to draw general conclusions from the proceedings of a man so rich and so eccentric as Timon. His wealth, for those times, must have been stupendous. It appears that near 200,000£ were sunk in building, furniture, books, pictures and plate at Cannons alone; and Cannons was but one of His Grace's houses.[5] His passion for splendour, expense and etiquette seems also to have amounted to a monomania.

It is a great pity that this M.S. was never seen by Warton,[6] by Roscoe,[7] or by any other editor of Pope's Poems. It is by far the best commentary that I ever saw on the Fourth Epistle. / Believe me, / My dear Sir,

Yours very truly,
T B Macaulay

1 See 19 December 1849.
2 Sir Archibald Galloway died on the 6th.
3 Alexander (1797–1873: *Boase*) was a barrister on the Oxford Circuit and a Bencher of the Middle Temple; he succeeded as third Baronet in 1859.
4 TBM notes in his Journal for this day (II, 286) that Alexander had sent him a MS volume about the household of the first Duke of Chandos (1673–1744: *DNB*), traditionally held to be the original of Timon in Pope's 'Epistle to Burlington.'
5 The Duke of Chandos spent lavishly on houses at Cannons (near Edgware), at Cavendish Square, and at St James's Square.
6 Joseph Warton (1722–1800: *DNB*), edited Pope, 1797.
7 William Roscoe (1753–1831: *DNB*); his edition of Pope, 1824.

TO THOMAS FLOWER ELLIS, 11 APRIL 1850

MS: Trinity College.

Albany April 11. 1850

Dear Ellis,

Will you breakfast here on Wednesday next at ten?[1]

Ever yours
T B Macaulay

I have read the Parasitus. It is in parts delicious, but not, as a whole, in the first rank of Lucian's pieces. The answer to the objection – "How miserable the parasite must be who gets no invitations,"[2] is exquisite, and perhaps the happiest banter on the Socratic sophistry that ever was.

TO LORD MAHON, 15 APRIL 1850

MS: Stanhope Papers, Chevening.

Albany April 15 / 1850

Dear Lord Mahon,

I have so bad a rheumatism that [I] cannot have the pleasure of seeing you here on Wednesday to breakfast.

Ever yours,
T B Macaulay

TO THOMAS FLOWER ELLIS, 15 APRIL 1850

MS: Trinity College.

Albany April 15 / 1850

Dear Ellis,

My dining out is altogether out of the question; and I am afraid that I must put off my breakfast party. I have been suffering two days under a severe attack of rheumatism which has almost crippled me. I sit in my dressinggown because I cannot put on my coat; and I live on milk because I cannot cut bread and butter.

Lady Trevelyan has a bad cold; and I have not let her know how poorly I am lest she should make herself worse by coming here. I am therefore quite alone. I know how busy you are; but, if you should happen to have a spare hour, it would be a kindness to pass it here. The pain which kept me awake two nights has now, I think, begun to abate.

I have amused myself, as becomes a professor of Ancient Literature

---

[1] The party was cancelled: see *to* Mahon, 15 April.
[2] *The Parasite,* 54.

(invidia rumpantur ut ilia Codro)[1] with Greek and Latin. I found out one odd thing. I am confident that a line of Ovid of which I never at all doubted the genuine Ovidianism is from some lost Greek source. It is in the second book where he recapitulates the mountains which Phaeton set on fire.

> "Caucasus ardet,
> Ossaque cum Pindo, majorque ambobus Olympus."[2]

Now in Lucian's Charon, alias οἱ ἐπισκοποῦντὲς, Mercury proposes to get on some high mountain for the purpose of commanding a view of the world. He says ἆρ' οὖν ὁ Καύκασος ἐπιτήδειος, ἢ ὁ Παρνασσὸς ὑψηλοτερος, ἢ ἀμφοῖν ὁ Ὄλυμπος ἐκεινοσί;[3] Observe that throughout this piece of Lucian scraps of the poets are constantly mixed up with the prose. I have no doubt that these words are taken from some lost poem in which there was an enumeration of mountains, – perhaps some Chorus in some lost play about Phaeton. How do you like this criticism? – Or does it "sentir furieusement le rheumatisme?"

Ever yours
T B Macaulay

TO LADY TREVELYAN, 16 APRIL 1850

MS: Trinity College.

Albany April 16. 1850

Dearest Hannah,

Tell me how you are. Pray do not think of going to the Mansion House[4] unless you are quite well. I am really anxious about this. The best proof of my anxiety is that I did not ask you to come here on Sunday or yesterday, when it would have been a great comfort to me to see you. I have had a severe attack of rheumatism, two sleepless nights, and near forty eight hours of sharp pain and utter helplessness. I could neither feed myself nor dress myself. That is over. I am at ease and getting well fast, so that there is not the least reason for your coming at the risk of increasing your cold. Pray nurse yourself. I had not the same reason for abstaining from summoning Ellis who has been very kind. He sate by my bed an hour and a half yesterday, and is to pass this evening here.

---

[1] Virgil, *Eclogues*, VII, 26. On 12 April TBM read three speeches of Cicero and then took up *The Acharnians,* noting that 'I was in a very classical mood' (Journal, II, 288); on the 14th he read Cicero's 'De Divinatio' and Lucian's 'Charon' (II, 291).

[2] *Metamorphoses*, II, 224–5.

[3] 'Charon,' 3: 'Well then, will Caucasus do, or Parnassus, or Olympus yonder, which is higher than either?' (Loeb translation).

[4] The Lord Mayor's banquet for the Ministers was given on 17 April. Sir Charles and Lady Trevelyan are named among the guests (*The Times*, 18 April).

Did you ever read anything like the Sellon correspondence?[1] The lady's letters are written by the Bishop of Exeter. I am as certain of it as if I had seen him write them. Lord Campbell's are only too good natured and courteous and magnanimous – too Grandisonian in short.

I have put off my breakfast party: but I hope to dine with you on Saturday.

Ever yours

T B Macaulay

TO FRANCES MACAULAY, 20 APRIL 1850

MS: Trinity College.

Albany London / April 20. 1850

Dearest Fanny,

I am pretty well again, and am looking forward to some months of good health. This last attack has, I hope, carried off much that has been plaguing me during several weeks. I well know how kind and attentive a nurse you would have been if I had needed your help. But in truth my pain and helplessness lasted little more than forty eight hours.

I never saw anything so absurd as Miss Sellon's last letter.[2] There is nobody more scrupulous than myself about the publishing of confidential communications. But who ever heard that a communication from the head of a benevolent institution, signed officially with the title added to the name, and informing one of the subscribers that he can no longer be suffered to contribute, was of a confidential nature? I sent ten pounds the other day to the Literary Fund.[3] Suppose that it had been sent back with a letter informing me that, on account of my Whiggish opinions, I could not be permitted to subscribe, and that this letter had been signed "Octavian Blewitt[4] Secretary and Treasurer." Should not I have been at perfect liberty to send such a piece of impertinent folly, if I had thought fit, to any newspaper?

---

[1] Priscilla Lydia Sellon (1821–76: *DNB*) founded, under the patronage of Bishop Phillpotts, the Society of Sisters of Mercy of the Holy Trinity, devoted to work among the poor and instantly the object of Evangelical suspicion. On 19 March she wrote to Lord Campbell to say that she was dropping his name from the Committee of the Order for his part in the Gorham case (see *to* Frances Macaulay, 2 March). Campbell wrote asking her to reconsider, but Miss Sellon remained firm and Campbell submitted to his dismissal. The letters appeared in *The Times,* 15 April. Miss Sellon's style hardly resembles Phillpotts's, but he may have furnished the doctrinal argument.

[2] She wrote to protest against the publication of her earlier letters to Campbell (*The Times,* 18 April).

[3] The Royal Literary Fund, of which TBM was elected a vice-president in 1855.

[4] Blewitt (1810–84: *DNB*) had been secretary of the Royal Literary Fund since 1839.

Poor old Wordsworth, the poet, is dying.[1] He is turned of eighty, so that there is no cause for wonder.

I saw Empson yesterday, after an interval of near a year. He is less altered than I should have expected from the severe physical and mental sufferings which he has gone through during the last few months. His mother in law is given over.[2]

Love to dear Selina. I hope that it is as fine a day at Brighton as it is here. I am going to enjoy the sun and the fresh air after my long confinement.

Ever yours,
T B Macaulay

TO THE PRESIDENT AND COUNCIL OF THE ROYAL ACADEMY, 20 APRIL 1850

MS: Westminster City Library.

Mr. Macaulay will do himself the honor of waiting on the President and Council of the Royal Academy to the Anniversary dinner on Saturday the 4th of May.[3]
Albany April 20. 1850

TO LORD MAHON, 22 APRIL 1850

MS: Stanhope Papers, Chevening.

Albany April 22 / 1850

Dear Lord Mahon,

I am much better to day, so much that Bright has just told me that he shall discontinue his visits. I hope therefore that I shall have the pleasure of breakfasting with you on the 30th.[4]

Ever yours truly
T B Macaulay

I have not read the article on Leopardi.[5] Gladstone's, I suppose.

---

[1] He died on 23 April.
[2] Mrs Francis Jeffrey died on 18 May.
[3] TBM duly attended, though he refused a request to speak at the dinner (Journal, II, 309: 4 May).
[4] The party were Milnes, Lord and Lady Ashley, and Hallam (Journal, II, 305).
[5] W. E. Gladstone, 'Giacomo Leopardi,' *Quarterly Review*, LXXXVI (March 1850), 295–336.

TO SIR JAMES AND LADY PARKE, 22 APRIL 1850

MS: Mr F. R. Cowell.

Mr. Macaulay is extremely sorry that he has an engagement which will prevent him from having the honor of waiting on Baron[1] and Lady Parke to dinner on Tuesday the 30th.[2]
Albany April 22. 1850

TO FRANCES MACAULAY, 29 APRIL 1850

MS: Trinity College.

Albany London / April 29. 1850

Dearest Fanny,

I return Stephen's letter. I have written to congratulate him on his success.[3] He is so chicken hearted that it is necessary for his friends to keep his spirits up by cordials. Only think of his having seriously intended to run away from Cambridge because two or three dunces raised the cry of "Semi Sabellian."[4]

I am pretty well at present, though the weather is still cold; and I hope that vigorous exercise and regular habits will keep me right through the summer months. As to courses of waters, those are things not to be tried without advice. I mentioned Bath to Bright; but he was quite against the [. . . .][5]

TO SIR RODERICK MURCHISON, 6 MAY 1850

MS: British Museum.

Albany May 6. 1850

Dear Sir Roderick,

I am very unlucky. I have an engagement which will make it impossible for me to have the pleasure of dining with you on the 15th. Do you ever breakfast out? And will you breakfast here at ten on Thursday next?[6]

Ever yours truly
T B Macaulay

[1] Parke was a Baron of the Court of Exchequer.
[2] TBM dined alone at Blackwall that night (Journal, II, 305).
[3] Stephen began his lectures as Regius Professor of Modern History on 16 April. In the 'Dedicatory Letter' to the published lectures, Stephen says that he consulted TBM on the choice of a subject: he recommended the French wars of religion but added that two or three years of preparation would be needed (*Lectures on the History of France*, 2 vols., 1851).
[4] See 19 December 1849.
[5] The lower half of the second leaf has been torn away. Probably only the last word of the last sentence, the closing, and the signature are missing.
[6] He did, together with Lord Carlisle, Lord Ashburton, Lord Glenelg, Hallam, John Shaw

TO BISHOP SAMUEL WILBERFORCE, 6 MAY 1850

MS: Bodleian Library.

Albany May 6. 1850

My dear Bishop of Oxford,

I am truly sorry that I can name no day but Thursday this week. Will you have the kindness to name your own day for the week after?[1]

Ever yours truly

T B Macaulay

TO BISHOP CHARLES JAMES BLOMFIELD, 10 MAY 1850

MS: Trinity College.

Mr. Macaulay will do himself the honor of waiting on the Bishop of London to dinner on Saturday the 25th.[2]

Albany May 10. 1850

TO LORD MAHON, 23 MAY 1850

MS: Stanhope Papers, Chevening.

Albany May 23 / 1850

Dear Lord Mahon,

I am extremely vexed to find that I must disappoint you to morrow morning. For that, as Tony Lumpkin says, I should not so much care; but I don't like disappointing myself.[3] Forgetting your invitation I promised to sit at eleven to morrow to Mr. Watson Gordon[4] for the University of

Lefevre, and Whewell. On the 15th TBM dined with the Trevelyans and then attended a party at Devonshire House (Journal, II, 312; 316–17).

[1] Wilberforce came to breakfast on the 16th, with Lord Monteagle, Lord Mahon, Hallam, Ellis, and Dundas. 'I was surprised,' TBM wrote of this occasion, 'at the Bishop's telling us that his father when young used to drink tea every evening at a brothel – not, said his Lordship, from any licentious purpose. His health alone would then have prevented that. But it was the mode among the young men. I should have kept the secret from my son, if I had been Wilberforce, and from the public if I had been Wilberforce Junior' (Journal, II, 318).

[2] The date of this engagement must have been changed: TBM dined at the Albany with Ellis on 25 May; on 13 June he dined with Blomfield at the Bishop's palace at Fulham (Journal, II, 325; 341).

[3] Goldsmith, *She Stoops to Conquer,* act I.

[4] Sir John Watson-Gordon (1788–1864: *DNB*), the leading Scottish portrait painter, had been commissioned by the Principal and professors of the University of Glasgow to do TBM's portrait. The picture now hangs in the Hunterian Museum of the University; a small copy is in the National Portrait Gallery of Scotland. The fee was paid by James Keith, an Edinburgh print-seller and publisher, in exchange for the right to publish an engraving of the portrait. Keith duly published such an engraving, by James Faed, in 1851. TBM gave Watson-Gordon five sittings between 13 and 27 May (Journal, II, 314–26).

Glasgow; and, as there have been already some disagreeable mischances and misunderstandings about this picture, I prefer throwing myself on your indulgence to breaking my appointment with him.

Ever yours truly
T B Macaulay

TO SIR EDWARD RYAN, 31 MAY 1850

MS: New York University.

Albany May 31. 1850

Dear Ryan,
I am disengaged on Wednesday the 12th, and shall be delighted to dine with you on that day.[1]

Yours ever,
T B Macaulay

We shall meet, I hope, on Grand Day.[2]

TO BISHOP SAMUEL WILBERFORCE, 31 MAY 1850

MS: Bodleian Library.

Albany May 31. 1850

My dear Bishop of Oxford,
I am sorry to say that on the 21st of June I start for Scotland, and that I shall be some weeks there.[3]
Remember that you breakfast here to morrow.[4]

Yours very truly
T B Macaulay

TO HENRY TAYLOR, 6 JUNE 1850

MS: Bodleian Library. *Published:* Edward Dowden, *Correspondence of Henry Taylor,* pp. 188–9.

Albany June 6. 1850

Dear Taylor,
I read the Virgin Widow[5] without being aware that the book which I

---

[1] TBM dined at Sir Edward Ryan's in company with the Trevelyans, Ellis and his daughter Marian, Mr and Mrs Charles Cameron, and Edward Strutt (*Journal,* II, 339).
[2] One of the quarterly gaudy days of the Inns of Court. Ryan, like TBM, was a member of Lincoln's Inn.
[3] TBM went with Hannah and Margaret to Edinburgh, Perth, Inverness, and Glasgow; they were back in London on 6 July. One of TBM's objects was to see the pass of Glencoe, which he visited on 29 June.
[4] With Lord Carlisle, Hallam, Milman, Thackeray, and Sylvain Van de Weyer (*Journal,* II, 331).
[5] *The Virgin Widow, or, a Sicilian Summer,* published on 11 May.

was reading was a present from you. It contained no indication of your kindness; and I supposed that it had been sent me by the Longmans. I have since learned that they were only your agents. Many thanks for the pleasure which you have given me. Your drama is, what you meant it to be, cheerful, graceful, and gentle. Nevertheless Philip Von Artevelde is still, in my opinion, the best poem that the last thirty years have produced; and I wish that you would deprive it of that preeminence, – a feat which nobody but yourself seems likely to accomplish.

I am a little sceptical as to the doctrines of your preface,[1] and a little uneasy as to the effect which they may produce on yourself. Surely, surely, the great works of Sophocles are pure tragedy: and yet they were not written only for the young; and of all human compositions they are the most free from that vile trick of harrowing and breaking on the wheel which you so justly condemn. I might add many other instances; but this is the strongest.

I would not, on such a subject, be guided by Southey's judgment. There is nothing dramatic in his poetry, – much good description, – much good declamation, – but, as far as I can recollect, nothing dramatic.

Ever yours truly

T B Macaulay

TO LORD MAHON, 8 JUNE 1850

Text: Copy (in Lord Mahon's hand),[2] Stanhope Papers, Chevening.

Albany / June 8. 1850

Dear Lord Mahon

I cannot think how I can have been so careless. I was just going out when I received your letter and forgot it when I came in.

I do not think that the words "Court of St James's" can be properly used for the English Court before the reign of Anne.[3] She was the first Sovereign who made St James's her ordinary town residence. William both before and after the burning of Whitehall lived almost entirely at Kensington.

---

[1] In the Preface, an apology for romantic comedy, Taylor says that he finds unrelieved tragedy too oppressive and mentions that Southey once observed that 'pure tragedy was what few but the young could bear.'

[2] Mahon has added a note: 'the original to be offered to Princess Alice at Windsor Castle, Dec. 1860.'

[3] A memorandum by Mahon accompanying this letter explains that Henry Manners-Sutton wished to use 'The Court of St. James's' as part of the title of his edition of Lord Lexington's correspondence, that Mahon considered the phrase anachronistic in this connection, and that the question was referred to TBM. The work appeared as *The Lexington Papers; or Some Account of the Courts of London and Vienna at the Conclusion of the Seventeenth Century*, 1851 (item 512 in the sale catalogue of TBM's library).

His lungs could not bear the air of Westminster. I have a letter in which he mentions the fire to Pensionary Heinsius. "But" he says "it does not matter much to me. For I cannot live in London."[1]

Ever yours truly

T B Macaulay

TO GEORG WILLEM VREEDE,[2] 11 JUNE 1850

MS: General State Archives, The Hague.

Albany London June 11. 1850

Sir,

I beg you to accept my thanks for your kind letter and for the highly interesting work which accompanied it. At a future period, I may, if life be spared to me, wish to examine the repositories in which you have found so much that is valuable. I shall then without scruple remind you of your generous offer and avail myself of your services. I expect however to be occupied during some years with the history of the reign of William the Third; and, till that part of my task is completed, I shall not make minute researches into the transactions of a later time.

With repeated thanks for your goodness, believe me, / Sir,

Your faithful Servant,

T B Macaulay

TO COLONEL WILLIAM MURE, 11 JUNE 1850

MS: National Library of Scotland.

Albany June 11. 1850

Dear Colonel Mure,

I shall be most happy to accompany you,[3] if you will call here at five minutes before seven. We are very punctual.

Yours truly

T B Macaulay

---

[1] TBM quotes this in the note to his account of the burning of Whitehall (*History*, v, 70n). TBM had William's letters to Heinsius from transcripts in the Mackintosh MSS.

[2] Vreede (1809–80), Professor at Utrecht since 1841, published numerous works on Dutch history. His edition of the *Correspondance Diplomatique et Militaire du Duc de Marlborough, de Grand-Pensionnaire Heinsius et du...Jaques Hop...1706–1707*, Amsterdam, 1850, is item 399 in the sale catalogue of TBM's library.

[3] Mure had been elected to The Club on 28 May and was about to attend his first meeting: 'The party not very large – Milman, Dundas, Senior, Staunton. – We did very well' (Journal, II, 337).

TO RICHARD MONCKTON MILNES, 15 JUNE 1850

MS: Trinity College.

Albany June 15. 1850

Dear Milnes,

I shall have much pleasure in breakfasting with you next Thursday.

Very truly yours,

T B Macaulay

TO THE DUKE OF MANCHESTER,[1] 19 JUNE 1850

MS: Huntingdonshire County Record Office.

Albany June 19. 1850

My Lord Duke,

Fifteen volumes of the Manchester M.S.S. were left here yesterday.[2] I am just setting out for Scotland: but in three weeks I shall return, and shall immediately examine the papers. I have seen enough at the first glance to satisfy me that they are of great value. I need not I hope say that the utmost care shall be taken of them, and that I am extremely sensible of the kindness which led you, unsolicited, to intrust me with memorials which you cannot but prize highly. / I have the honor to be, / My Lord Duke

Your Grace's most obedient servant,

T B Macaulay

TO W. F. B. LAURIE,[3] [JUNE 1850]

Text: W. F. B. Laurie, *Some Sketches of Distinguished Anglo Indians,* new edn, 1887, p. 157.

It seems to me that the fate of such a volume as you describe[4] must depend entirely on the execution. There is not, I apprehend, much curiosity on the subject of the French in India. But eloquence and vivacity will make any subject attractive. My own pursuits do not leave me time to give to manuscripts that attentive perusal, without which advice is a mere mockery.

[1] George Montagu (1799–1855), 6th Duke.
[2] Papers relating to the affairs of Charles Montagu (1660?–1722: *DNB*), first Duke of Manchester. They are described in appendix, Part II, to the 8th *Report* of the Historical Manuscripts Commission, 1881, pp. 12ff.
[3] Laurie (1819?–91: *Boase*) was an officer in the Indian army who published several miscellaneous works on Indian and European politics and history.
[4] Laurie explains that in June 1850 he submitted the manuscript of a book on 'The French in India' to TBM to determine whether 'the public would care about such a work at such a time?' (*Sketches*, p. 156). It was not published.

TO ELIOT WARBURTON, 11 JULY 1850

MS: Alexander Turnbull Library, Wellington.

Albany July 11. / 1850

My dear Sir,

I had no authority but the college tradition for saying that Rupert had quarters at Magdalene.[1] But there are some circumstances which make the tradition probable. There is a full length portrait of him there; and, to the best of my belief, all the other portraits there are of inmates of the college. Then I do not think it likely that he was ordinarily lodged at Xt. Church, though he may have occasionally had an apartment there when the King was absent. For the accommodation of Xt. Church seems to have been barely sufficient for Charles himself. Even the Queen was lodged at Merton, and a private communication was made between her residence and her husband's. Indeed, when it is considered that Christchurch, Merton, and Magdalene, have always been peculiarly appropriated to Royal guests, and that, during the civil war, the King was at Christchurch and the Queen at Merton, it seems almost to follow that the Prince would have been at Magdalene. Nevertheless Rupert may occasionally, during the three or four years of the war, have had an apartment at Christ Church; and thus the credit of your M.S. may be completely saved. I mentioned the matter incidentally, and did not think it necessary to verify what I said by any minute inquiry.

I return the paper which you were so kind as to send me. It is very curious and interesting. Believe me, with many thanks,

Yours very faithfully,

T B Macaulay

The name which is illegible is Maumont. Roos is evidently a mistake for Rosen.[2]

TO EDWARD BAINES, JR, 24 JULY 1850

MS: Duke University.

Albany London / July 24. 1850

My dear Sir,

I am much obliged by your kind letter: but I cannot accept the very

---

[1] 'There Rupert had fixed his quarters; and, before some of his most daring enterprises, his trumpets had been heard sounding to horse through those quiet cloisters' (*History*, II, 288).

[2] Count Rosen was commander and Maumont lieutenant-general of the French contingent among James's forces in Ireland (*History*, III, 165).

flattering invitation with which I have been honored.[1] It must be some very strong and special reason that induces me ever again to make a speech in public. I am every day becoming more averse from such exhibitions and more unfit for them. With my excuses, I have sent Mr. Wilson[2] a subscription which, small as it is, is much more valuable than my oratory would be. / Believe me, / My dear Sir,

Yours very truly

T B Macaulay

TO THE DUKE OF MANCHESTER, 26 JULY 1850

MS: Huntingdonshire County Record Office.

Albany London / July 26. 1850

My Lord Duke,

I have finished the examination of the volumes which you were so kind as to intrust to me;[3] and I have made such extracts as were necessary for my purpose. The collection is of high interest and value. The letters of Prior, of Addison, and of Vanbrugh are eminently curious.

Will your Grace be so good as to let me know to what place I shall send the books. Every care shall be taken of them; and a man from Longman's shall look to the packing. With repeated thanks, I have the honor to be, / My Lord Duke,

Your Grace's faithful Servant,

T B Macaulay

TO SELINA MACAULAY, 29 JULY 1850

MS: Trinity College.

Albany London / July 29. 1850

Dearest Selina,

You must not take a joke too seriously. Of course I never imagined that Mrs. Money meant to ask me to go to Glasgow; nor can I suppose that Fanny or Hannah can have so understood me. If I was a little diverted by her recommending a converted Jew for Hebrew Professor, my excuse must be that he is not the first, nor the second, nor the third, nor the

---

[1] Perhaps to the public presentation of a portrait of Edward Baines, Sr, to the Leeds Mechanics' and Literary Institution, 2 September (Leeds *Mercury,* 7 September). The portrait was purchased by public subscriptions limited to five shillings each.

[2] Thomas Wilson, President of the Institution, was in the chair at the presentation ceremonies.

[3] See 19 June.

fourth person whom she has begged me to serve.¹ I have had in my time a good deal to suffer from the unreasonable importunity of place hunters; and, though I am out of office and out of parliament, few days pass in which I do not receive a letter or a visit from some person who fancies that I can provide for him. I had one such letter and one such visit this very day. For the trouble which such solicitors give me my only compensation is my laugh; and you must not grudge it me.

I wish that you gave a better account of yourself. Of course I cannot possibly take anything ill of you; – least of all when you write from feelings of justice and good nature [. . . .]²

TO ROBERT CARRUTHERS,³ [EARLY AUGUST? 1850]⁴

Text: Inverness *Courier,* 30 May 1878.

There is one point on which I would gladly obtain some information. I mean the battle which Keppoch fought with the Mackintoshes in 1689. I think that after the battle Keppoch exacted a ransom from Inverness, and that Dundee was mediator between the Macdonalds and the town.⁵ Are you aware whether any memorials of these events are preserved among your local records? I should be glad to be referred to any book which may contain a description of the state of Inverness before the Union.

TO LORD MAHON, 2 AUGUST 1850

MS: Stanhope Papers, Chevening.

Albany London / August 2. 1850

Dear Lord Mahon,

I am sorry that I cannot go down to you. But, empty as London is, I am at present engaged daily.

---

¹ See *to* Fanny, 14 October 1846.
² A strip from the bottom of the leaf has been torn away. Probably only the closing and signature are missing.
³ Carruthers (1799–1878: *DNB*), editor and proprietor of the Inverness *Courier,* edited a number of literary and historical works. When TBM was in Inverness in June of this year Carruthers had written to him to offer his services (Journal, III, 59a: 26 June). A note to ch. 13 of the *History* acknowledges TBM's obligations to Carruthers, 'who kindly furnished me with much curious information about Inverness' (III, 324).
⁴ The question asked in this letter relates to an episode in Dundee's campaign of 1689. This is narrated in ch. 13 of the *History,* which TBM completed in September (see 7 and 21 September); August therefore seems a likely date for this letter, which probably precedes that to Carruthers of 15 August.
⁵ See the account in *History,* III, 326–9, of the threat to Inverness by Colin Macdonald of Keppoch and the intervention of Dundee.

As to the Museum, I should like Milman much.[1] We thought of him before; and his present situation is of itself a sort of claim. The dean of the Cathedral of the Capital seems to be peculiarly fitted to be one of the superintendants of the great Museum and Library of the Capital.

I have the correspondence between Marlborough and Heinsius.[2] I do not think that there is much in it. But I may hereafter find reason to change my opinion.

Have you seen Wordsworth's Prelude?[3] – It is the Excursion, weaker and more tedious. Before I read the Prelude I was surprised that a man who had finished so long and elaborate a work should keep it near half a century in his desk, and leave it to be published by his executors. But, after I had read it, my astonishment was at an end. The plain truth is that he wrote it when he was a Jacobin and was ashamed to print it after he became an exciseman. He goes all the lengths of Thelwall[4] or Tom Paine; and the poem ends with loud vauntings of his own incorruptible integrity, – vauntings which he might well shrink from publishing when he had become an electioneering agent of the Lowthers.

Kindest regards to Lady Mahon, and to my Valentine[5] of whose favour I am not a little proud.

Ever yours truly

T B Macaulay

TO CHARLES MACAULAY, 4 AUGUST 1850

MS: University of London. *Published:* Rae, *Temple Bar,* LXXXVI, 200–1.

Albany August 4 / 1850

Dear Charles,

There can be no impropriety in your writing to so old a family friend as Inglis. Whether he is likely to have much influence with Lord Ashley I cannot tell.[6] Their views generally agree; and I daresay that they are friends. But I never heard that there was any special intimacy, and I do not remember to have once met Ashley at Inglis's. I wish you all success.

---

[1] To replace the Duke of Cambridge, who died on 8 July. Milman was not appointed a trustee until 1853: see 18 August 1853.

[2] See *to* G. W. Vreede, 11 June.

[3] Published on 27 July.

[4] John Thelwall (1764–1834: *DNB*), one of the Society of the Friends of the People and a member of the Corresponding Society; imprisoned for sedition, 1794.

[5] Lady Mary Stanhope (1844–76); TBM's valentine verses to her, 1851, are included in the *Miscellaneous Writings*; evidently he had written some for her earlier.

[6] Charles was seeking appointment as secretary to the Board of Health, established in 1848; Ashley was one of the Commissioners. Charles received the appointment on 15 August.

I told Trevelyan that a word from Brodie might, in my opinion, be of use.

Ever yours
T B Macaulay

I was vexed at finding that your child[1] had been christened without my hearing of the matter. I should certainly have been there.

TO BISHOP SAMUEL WILBERFORCE, 10 AUGUST 1850

MS: Bodleian Library.

Albany London / August 10. 1850

My dear Bishop of Oxford,

I return your correspondent's letter. I know nothing about him, and was not even aware of his existence.[2] His father was my father's clerk, was an useful servant of the Antislavery Society and was a very respectable man, – is a very respectable man, I should say; for he is still alive though far advanced in years. Some time ago I and others subscribed to buy a small annuity for the old gentleman. It was indeed small; and he contracted some debts about which he wrote to me three weeks ago; and I sent him a few pounds to extricate him. I did not know that he had a son. Your correspondent may be a very deserving man; but as he has no special claim on us except on his father's account, and as his father is still in need of assistance, I can spare nothing for this New Zealand project. I do not think that I can say more.

Very truly yours,
T B Macaulay

TO CHARLES MACAULAY, [15 AUGUST 1850][3]

MS: University of London. *Published:* Rae, *Temple Bar,* LXXXVI, 201.

Albany Thursday

Dear Charles,

I have been much vexed at missing you. If you had left word when you expected to call I would have been at home, if possible. I say *if possible*:

---

[1] Charles Trevelyan Macaulay (1850–1908), born 30 May, was Charles's third child.

[2] The reference is to a son of Robert Stokes (for whom see 10 June 1831), about whom I have found nothing. The obituary of Robert Stokes in the *Gentleman's Magazine,* 1860, I, 84, says that he was survived by 'one only daughter.'

[3] Dated from the reference to Charles's appointment: on 15 August TBM returned from a meeting at the British Museum to find that Charles had been appointed to the secretaryship of the Board of Health 'without my interference, though I would have interfered, if it had been necessary' (Journal, III, 7).

for I am forced to be much at the Museum. Trevelyan has kept me informed of the progress of your affair. If there had been any hitch I should have gone to Lord Seymour.[1] But I was extremely averse to interfere unnecessarily, and this partly on your account. For I thought it very important to your comfort and to your weight that your appointment should have nothing of the character of a job, but should be evidently the result of a proper consideration of what the public interest required. Trevelyan has been most kind, and judiciously so. We are all greatly obliged to him.

I give your wife joy of your success. I shall be glad to hear of your plans when they are settled.

Ever yours,
T B Macaulay

TO ROBERT CARRUTHERS, 15 AUGUST 1850

Text: Inverness *Courier*, 30 May 1878.

Albany, August 15th, 1850.

My dear Sir,

If you should persist in sending me valuable information, you really must not enjoin me to refrain from sending you thanks in return. Your last letter clears up two or three points about which I was doubtful. Mackay's Memoirs[2] are in print. I know them well; and very curious they are. The life of Sir Ewen Cameron of Lochiel,[3] and the strange book of Richard Franck, Philanthropus,[4] I had never seen until I received your letter. I found them both in the Museum, and was much interested by them. I have written to Edinburgh to ask whether it appears from the Privy Council records that James issued letters of fire and sword against Keppoch. Browne asserts this in his History of the Clans,[5] but Browne's assertion is no warrant. The thing, to be sure, is intrinsically probable. I have been amused by observing that Keppoch is in several works

[1] I do not know what Lord Seymour could have done to help, since he was neither in office nor a member of the Board at this time.

[2] Hugh Mackay, *Memoirs of the War Carried on in Scotland and Ireland, 1689–91*, Edinburgh, 1833, published by the Bannatyne Club. This and the other works mentioned in the letter were all used by TBM in writing chapter 13 of the *History*, the story of 1689 in Scotland.

[3] Anonymous, contained in Thomas Pennant's *A Tour in Scotland, 1769*, 3rd edn, 1774.

[4] Franck's *Northern Memoirs*, 1694, was edited by Sir Walter Scott in 1821.

[5] James Browne, *A History of the Highlands and of the Highland Clans*, 4 vols., Glasgow, 1835–8, II, 131 (the book is item 124 in the sale catalogue of TBM's library). '[Keppoch] was proclaimed a rebel: letters of fire and sword were issued against him under the seal of James' (*History*, III, 325).

styled Colonel Macdonald – evidently a mistake occasioned by his odd
name 'Coll.'[1]

Believe me to be, my dear sir, yours very truly,

T. B. Macaulay

TO THOMAS FLOWER ELLIS, 23 AUGUST 1850

MS: Trinity College.

Albany August 23. 1850

Dear Ellis,

I am extremely concerned. I have no doubt however that Maturin's[2]
advice is good; and indeed he seems to be as valuable a friend as a young
fellow in poor Arthur's situation could have.[3]

This will not reach you, I am afraid, before you start for Bromley.[4]
I did not receive your letter till past five.

I shall go to the Isle of Wight on Monday;[5] but I shall see Trevelyan
first; and, if anything passes which you would wish to know, I will send
you a line.

Ever yours,

T B Macaulay

TO FRANCES MACAULAY, 3 SEPTEMBER 1850

MS: Trinity College.

Madeira Hall / Ventnor / Septr. 3. 1850

Dearest Fanny,

Many thanks. I am now quite at ease.[6]

I am glad that I went back to town. It was just after dinner that I
arrived in Westbourne Terrace. They saw me alight and came into the

---

[1] '...such was the skill with which he could track a herd of cattle to the most secret hiding-
place that he was known by the nickname of Coll of the Cows' (*History*, III, 325).

[2] William Henry Maturin (d. 1889), an officer in the Commissariat Department, served in a
number of administrative positions in South Australia between 1843 and 1859; he was
Acting Colonial Treasurer and Acting Registrar General in 1849, when Arthur Ellis arrived.

[3] TBM's Journal for this day reports: 'Bad news of Arthur. Ellis sent me a most distressing
letter from Maturin to Trevelyan – poor young fellow. What fools boys are. Here was his
fortune made if he had had common sense and common firmness. Alas' (III, 12).

[4] Ellis owned a house called Old Cottage, at Widmore, near Bromley, Kent, where he and his
family spent a large part of their time, beginning in 1850.

[5] TBM went to Ventnor on the 26th, took a house, and returned to London the next day; on
2 September he went again to Ventnor and remained there until the 28th (Journal, III,
14–40).

[6] After he had sent his servants off to the house at Ventnor on 31 August, TBM learned that
his niece Alice was ill at Brighton. He at once went down to get a report, stayed the night,
and returned late the next day to say that all was well (Journal, III, 18–21).

hall, evidently in great anxiety which my report effectually relieved. As my chambers were locked up and the key gone with William, I went to Stevens's Hotel in Bond Street, dined slept and breakfasted there, and yesterday came hither. I mean to rise early, to live [. . . . . .]¹ fifteen miles, – much of it climbing.

Kindest love to Selina and to my little Alice. By all means let her use her Sovereign as she thinks best. I love her [. . . .]¹

to THOMAS FLOWER ELLIS, 3 SEPTEMBER 1850

MS: Trinity College. *Published:* Trevelyan, II, 280.

Madeira Hall / Ventnor / Septr. 3. 1850

Dear Ellis,

Here I am, lodged most delightfully. I look out on one side to the crags and myrtles of the Undercliff against which my house is built. On the other side I have a view of the sea which is at this moment as blue as the sky, and as calm as the Serpentine. My little garden is charming. I wish that I may not, like Will Honeycomb, forget the sin and seacoal of London for innocence and haycocks.² To be sure, as Higman³ well knows, innocence and haycocks do not always go together.

When will you come? Take your own time: but I am rather anxious that you should not lose this delicious weather, and defer your trip till the equinoctial storms are setting in. The earlier therefore the better. I can promise you plenty of water and of towels, good wine, good tea, and good cheese from town, good eggs, butter and milk from the farm at my door, a beautiful prospect from your bedroom window, and, if the weather keeps us within doors, Plautus's comedies, Plutarch's lives, twenty or thirty comedies of Calderon, Fra Paolo's history, and a little library of novels, to say nothing of my own compositions which, like Ligurinus, I will read to you stanti, sedenti, cacanti, etc. etc.⁴

I am just returned from a walk of near seven hours and of full fifteen miles, part of it as steep as the monument. Indeed I was so knocked up with climbing Black Gang Chine that I lay on the turf at the top for a quarter of an hour wheezing like a grampus.

Ever yours,

T B Macaulay

¹ The closing and signature, on the verso of the second leaf, have been torn away, taking with them the top third of the text on the recto – about four lines.
² *Spectator*, No. 530 (Addison).
³ John Philips Higman (1793–1855: *Boase*), tutor of Trinity, 1822–34, and Rector of Fakenham, Norfolk, 1834–55. Ellis, as an undergraduate, had been on a reading party at Lyme under Higman; TBM's remark may refer to some story of that time.
⁴ Cf. Martial, III, xliv, 10–11.

TO FRANCES MACAULAY, 7 SEPTEMBER 1850

MS: Huntington Library. *Extract published:* Trevelyan, II, 284n.

Ventnor Isle of Wight / Septr. 7. 1850

Dearest Fanny,

The accompanying letter will insure Gurney[1] a civil reception from Longman. I should think and so I have told my friends in Paternoster Row that the affair would probably be an advantageous one for them. No books go off better than those which bear the names of popular divines.

I am here in utter solitude. Robinson Crusoe was not more alone, even before he fell in with Friday. Except to say "Bread if you please," and "Fetch a bottle of soda water," to William at dinner, I have not, I think, opened my lips to any human being since I arrived here. Yet I have not had a moment's ennui. I rise before seven. The greater part of the day I pass in the open air. I put a volume of a small edition of Plutarch's lives in my pocket, and wander over rocks and through copse wood hour after hour, sitting down and reading when I feel tired. In the house my book is Fra Paolo. He is my favourite modern historian. His subject did not admit of vivid painting. But what he did he did better than anybody. I wish that he had not kept his friar's gown: for he was undoubtedly at heart as much a Protestant as Latimer.[2]

All that you tell me about Selina and my little Alice is very satisfactory. My kindest love to both.

I ought to have mentioned that I write a page or two of my history daily. I am tolerably satisfied with my account of Dundee's campaign. It will be quite new, I think, even to people who have attended to the subject. Macleod to whom I read part of it told me that I had thrown quite a new light on the whole story; and he, as a highland laird, had rather studied the matter.

Ever yours,
T B Macaulay

TO THOMAS FLOWER ELLIS, 8 SEPTEMBER 1850

MS: Trinity College. *Mostly published:* Trevelyan, II, 281.

Ventnor / September 8. 1850

Dear Ellis,

Thanks. I shall be at Ryde to meet you next Saturday. Go straight to

[1] John Hampden Gurney (1802–62: *DNB*) was at Trinity with TBM. He was curate of Lutterworth, Leicestershire, 1827–44, and Rector of St Mary's, Marylebone, 1847–62. Longmans published his *Historical Sketches*, 1852.

[2] Hugh Latimer (1485?–1555: *DNB*), one of the Oxford martyrs.

the Pier Hotel, and ask for me. I only hope that the weather may continue to be just what it is. The evenings are a little chilly out of doors. But the days are glorious. I rise before seven, breakfast at nine, write a page, ramble five or six hours over rocks and through copsewood with Plutarch in my hand, come home, write another page, take Fra Paolo and sit in the garden reading till the sun sinks behind the Undercliff. Then it begins to be cold. So I carry my Fra Paolo into the house and read on till dinner. While I am at dinner the Times comes in, and is a good accompaniment to a delicious dessert of peaches which are abundant here. I have also a novel of Theodore Hook by my side to relish my wine.[1] I then take a short stroll by starlight, and go to bed at ten. I am perfectly solitary, almost as much so as Robinson Crusoe before he caught Friday. I have not opened my lips, that I remember, these six days except to say "Bread if you please," or "Bring a bottle of soda water." Yet I have not had a moment of ennui. Nevertheless I am heartily glad that you can give me nine days. I wish it were eighteen. Of course if you make any change in your plan you will let me know in time. I shall probably walk across the island to Ryde on Saturday next, and breakfast at Shanklin by the way.

Ever yours,

T B Macaulay

to Margaret Trevelyan, 9 September 1850

MS: Trinity College.

Ventnor Isle of Wight / September 9. 1850

Dearest Baba,

I begin to long for a letter from you. Tell me how you are, what you are doing, whom you see, what books you read. Give me the history of a day. I will set you the example. I am quite rural, a perfect Damon or Menalcas. I rise soon after six, and enjoy the fresh sea breeze of the morning. I breakfast before nine. Then I write a page or so. Then I take a book – generally a Greek book – in my pocket, and set out on a ramble. I stray hour after hour over crags and through thickets of laurels and myrtles. When I am tired, I sit down on the grass and read. My walks are prodigious. Yesterday I walked sixteen measured miles without stopping. When I come home, which is generally about four in the afternoon, I sit in my garden, an extremely pretty garden, and read Fra Paolo's History of the Council of Trent. When the sun sinks behind the Undercliff it becomes too cold to sit in the open air. So I go in, and read in my drawing room

---

[1] TBM read Hook's *Gurney Married, Cousin William,* and *Gervase Skinner* while at Ventnor (Journal, III, 22; 25; 32).

till seven. Then I dine, and amuse myself with a novel and with the Times which makes its appearance together with the peaches for my dessert. After dinner I stroll in my garden for an hour by starlight; and by ten I am in bed. I have no acquaintance here; nor have I, since I left you eight days ago at Westbourne Terrace, spoken a word except to give orders to servants. Yet I never found time pass quicker. On Saturday Ellis comes down to stay a week or ten days with me. I think I shall call him Saturday, as Robinson Crusoe, in his desert island, called his only companion Friday.

I hear the best accounts of our dear little Alice. I have heard nothing of or from Mamma yet.[1] Perhaps you can give me news.

Kindest remembrances to Grandmamma. Write, and tell me whether you are happy and well, and above all whether I can be of any use to you.

Ever yours, dearest,

T B Macaulay

TO FRANCES MACAULAY, 21 SEPTEMBER 1850

MS: Trinity College.

Ventnor / September 21 / 1850

Dearest Fanny,

Thanks for your letters. I have heard from Hannah. I am afraid that the fine weather is over. Last night we, and I suppose you, had a fierce equinoctial gale, which is still blowing. The clouds are dark. The trees are beginning to look autumnal; and my delicious rambles through woods and over rocks will soon be over. They have done me good, however, and I shall be tempted to repeat the experiment some other year.

Ellis has been here a week. We have walked, talked and read Greek and Spanish together indefatigably. He goes to town on [Monday. I think . . . .][2] change again. I have finished my battle of Killiecrankie. He likes it much.[3] Some day I hope to have your opinion. Kindest love to Selina. [. . .][2]

---

[1] Trevelyan and Hannah were on a vacation tour to Munich. Margaret was with her grandmother at Enmore.

[2] The closing and signature on the verso of the second leaf have been torn away, taking four or five lines on the recto; parts of the words on the line above the tear are still visible.

[3] In his Journal TBM adds that Ellis liked it 'less however than I like it, I think, which is not often the case' (III, 34: 18 September).

TO UNIDENTIFIED RECIPIENTS, 24 SEPTEMBER 1850

MS: John Rylands Library.

Ventnor Isle of Wight / September 24. 1850

Gentlemen,

I beg you to accept my thanks for your courtesy. I do not know that the letters which you have been so kind as to send me contain anything absolutely new: but both confirm the notions which I had formed from other materials.

It is, as you say, strange that Sir Walter Scott and Mr. Laing should have committed so gross a blunder as to the date of the battle of Killiecrankie.[1] They were, I suspect, misled by a worthless Jacobite Life of Dundee printed in 1714.[2] That Sir Walter was thus misled appears from a very curious circumstance which nobody has yet noticed. The author of the Life of Dundee has misplaced as well as misdated the battle. He puts it on the banks of the Tummel, whereas it was on the banks of the Garry. Sir Walter, familiar as he was with the geography of Scotland, and studious, in all his works, of topographical accuracy even to minuteness, has committed the same error. You may remember the line in the Vision of Don Roderick. "Tummel's rude pass can of its terrors tell."[3]

Now when I find two such mistakes in a Life of Dundee published in Queen Anne's reign, and exactly the same mistakes in a writer of our own time, I cannot much doubt that the modern author was misled by his predecessor.

With repeated thanks I have the honour to be, / Gentlemen,

Your faithful Servant,

T B Macaulay

TO SELINA MACAULAY, 4 OCTOBER 1850

MS: Trinity College. *Envelope:* Miss Macaulay / Temple House / Brighton. *Subscription:* T B M.

Albany October 4 / 1850

Dearest Selina,

You are quite right about the form.[4] It is only meant for a pattern, and will do as well for Fanny's purpose as for yours.

[1] Laing is no doubt David Laing, the antiquary. I do not know to what text by Laing or Scott TBM refers; Scott correctly dates the battle of Killiecrankie in his *Tales of a Grandfather*, 2nd Series, ch. 8.

[2] *Memoirs of the Lord Viscount Dundee...By an Officer of the Army*, 1711. TBM notices this work in *History*, III, 331n, attributing it to 'a stupid and ignorant Grub Street garreteer' and pointing out the errors regarding Killiecrankie.

[3] 'Conclusion,' stanza 17.

[4] For her will. TBM had talked over the subject with her on 1 September and sent her 'instructions for a will' on 1 October (Journal, III, 20; 43).

You will of course both remember to let me know when your railway calls are to be paid. Our property in that investment is looking up.

Dear little Alice. She has given me the histories of her chairmen, the inquisitive chairman who peeped into a lady's card case – the bearded chairman, the coquettish chairman, and the chairman who was found at the ale house. She seems very well; but her nerves are excitable. She was in evident agitation yesterday night, and at last confessed to her Mamma and me that she was afraid of Ghosts. –

Kindest love to Fanny [. . . .][1]

TO LADY TREVELYAN, 9 OCTOBER 1850

MS: Trinity College.

Albany / October 9. 1850

Dearest Hannah,

I will call for Baba on Saturday and dine with you afterwards. I am afraid that I shall not be able to see you in Westbourne Terrace earlier.

I have my account from Longman. – 3002 £ are to be paid me on the 4th December, every farthing of which I shall invest without dipping into the sum. I cannot expect anything of this sort next year. The market is now thoroughly supplied; and I shall be quite content if I can clear four or five hundred pounds in 1851.[2]

Bad news of poor Empson. He had a paralytic seizure two or three days ago, and was for a time unable to articulate. Then he recovered, and wrote to me a letter in which nothing indicates that he was not perfectly himself. I have written in reply advising him to give up the Review. I am convinced that it is a question of life and death.

I have just seen Cameron.[3] He starts for Ceylon on the 20th to look after his estate there; but he leaves the fair Julia[4] behind him, and is doubtless glad to do so.

Ever yours

I will write my name on another piece of paper.[5]

---

[1] The closing and signature have been cut away.

[2] His account with Longman in October 1851 was £1,450, not including the annual £500 he received for the five years 1849–53 (Journal, IV, 272).

[3] Cameron had returned to England from India in 1848. He owned an estate in Ceylon to which he returned at the end of his life and where he died.

[4] Cameron married in 1838 Julia Margaret Pattle, second of the seven celebrated Pattle sisters of Calcutta. She was a managing woman, and a lion-hunter, and TBM therefore disliked her: he calls her 'pert, ugly, absurd' (Journal, II, 339: 12 June 1850). Mrs Cameron took up photography in the 1860s and made some excellent portraits of eminent Victorians.

[5] TBM has attempted his signature twice at the bottom of the page and bungled it both times.

TO UNIDENTIFIED RECIPIENT, 15 OCTOBER 1850

MS: Harvard University.

Albany London October 15 / 1850

Sir,

I am very sensible of your kindness: but the book which you are so good as to offer me is already in my library. / I have the honor to be, / Sir,

Your faithful Servant,

T B Macaulay

TO SELINA MACAULAY, 24 OCTOBER 1850

MS: Trinity College.

Albany London / October 24. 1850

Dearest Selina,

I send back the draft. I would advise you to omit the words which I have put between brackets. They will either be nugatory or embarrassing. If I should survive you they will be nugatory. For I should at once advance the small sum necessary to pay the debts and legacies. If you should survive me, Fanny will be administratrix; and it would be inconvenient to her to be hampered by such directions. Consider too that you may wish to change your investment some time hence; and it will be inconvenient to have to make a new will because you sell your railway stock.

I shall say nothing to any human being about your arrangements respecting Mrs. Crinean and your other friends.[1] You have a perfect right to make such arrangements; and the feeling which leads you to make them does you honour.

Remember to let me know when you have any railway call. Stock is rising in price. I am thriving. Longman is to pay me 3000 £ in five weeks; and I think myself entitled to set up a Brougham, which will be comfortable in the winter evenings when I dine out. Kindest love to Fanny.

Yours ever

T B Macaulay

TO THOMAS LONGMAN, 26 OCTOBER 1850

MS: Trinity College.

Albany October 26. 1850

My dear Sir,

Pray get me the volumes of Cobbett which you mention.

---

[1] In the final version of her will, drawn up in 1858, Selina left £50 to her cousin Mrs Crinean, £20 to a Frances Lawrence, and all the rest to Fanny.

Many thanks for the little volume.[1] It is very pretty. Who was Diana Louisa Macdonald?

I have begged Empson to consult Dr. Bright very particularly as to the Review; and I have little doubt as to what the Doctor's opinion will be.[2]

Ever yours truly

T B Macaulay

TO JOHN HARLAND,[3] 4 NOVEMBER 1850

MS: Manchester Central Library. *Envelope:* J Harland Esq / Guardian Office / Manchester. *Subscription:* T B M.

Albany London / November 4. 1850

Sir,

I am extremely sensible of your kindness, and should be greatly obliged if you would send me those numbers of your paper which contain extracts from your Quaker's Manuscript.[4] I see the Guardian at one of the Clubs. But I should like to have these papers filed for reference. I see at a glance that they will be highly valuable as materials for history.

With repeated thanks believe me, / Sir,

Your faithful Servant,

T B Macaulay

TO UNIDENTIFIED RECIPIENT, 4 NOVEMBER 1850

MS: National Library of Scotland.

Albany London / November 4. 1850

Sir,

I am sorry that it is out of my power to assist you. I have long been under the necessity of refusing to contribute to Albums. In truth if I had

---

[1] Diana Louisa Macdonald, *Villa Verocchio, or, the Youth of Leonardo Da Vinci: a Tale,* published by Longman in October. The title page states that she is the 'late' Diana Louisa Macdonald; I cannot identify her.

[2] In anticipation of Empson's retirement TBM had already sounded out John Shaw Lefevre as a candidate for the editorship, without success (Journal, III, 53: 17 October). Empson continued as editor until his death.

[3] Harland (1806–68: *DNB*), the leading reporter for the Manchester *Guardian* for thirty years, was also a student of Lancashire history and published a number of volumes on that subject.

[4] The autobiography of a seventeenth-century Lancashire Quaker, William Stout, edited by Harland, had been appearing in the *Guardian*. It was afterwards published by the Chetham Society, 1851. TBM refers to the work in *History,* IV, 625. A copy is item 849 in the sale catalogue of his library.

not done so, I should have had no time for any other pursuit: and I have now pleaded my general rule so often and to persons who have such strong claims on me that I cannot now break through it without giving great offence. I wish your undertaking all success and beg you to believe me, / Sir,

Your faithful Servant,
T B Macaulay

TO JOHN HARLAND, 7 NOVEMBER 1850

MS: Manchester Central Library.

Albany London Nov 7. 1850

Sir,
    The papers have arrived safe; and I beg you to accept my thanks for them. There is not a number which does not contain something curious. / I have the honor to be, / Sir,

Your faithful Servant,
T B Macaulay

TO JOHN LEYCESTER ADOLPHUS, 8 NOVEMBER [1850]

MS: Trinity College.

Albany Nov 8

Dear Adolphus,
    I return the book with many thanks. It is, as I supposed, a translation of the Lettres Françoises[1] which I have.
    I am becoming, somewhat of the latest, a No Popery Man,[2] and, if I improve at the rate at which I have lately been improving, I shall soon take to chalking the walls with 'No Wafer Gods,' and such other orthodox inscriptions.

Ever yours,
T B Macaulay

---

[1] There is no evidence from TBM's library lists to identify which of several books having similar titles is meant.

[2] This was the year of the so-called Papal Aggression in England. The Pope, in a brief published on 29 September, had re-established the Catholic hierarchy in England, and the bishops took English place names to designate their sees. The news of the restoration, which reached London about the middle of October, raised a loud clamor that owed as much to popular hostility to the Tractarians as to the Church of Rome. TBM was pleased to see the Tractarians abused, but refused to join what he regarded as a Guy Fawkes outcry.

TO LORD MAHON, 11 NOVEMBER 1850

MS: Stanhope Papers, Chevening.

Albany Nov 11. 1850

Dear Lord Mahon,

I return poor Hallam's letter. It is a heartbreaking business.[1] I wait in painful anxiety for further intelligence. If one could do anything – But what can one do? –

I have read Southey's Life;[2] and a very stupid book it is. The chief materials are his own letters; and he was a bad letter writer. There was nothing light or playful about him. He did indeed sometimes try to gambol, but with miserable effect. That quaint silly conceit which you quote about the Guelphs and Ghibellines[3] is a very fair sample of his pleasantry.

He was in the right as to the idle scheme of rewarding literary merit with stars and ribands. But it surely did not lie in his mouth to blame that scheme. For he was as proud of his laurel as any miss of a new gown, and was constantly perking in every body's face[4] that most absurd of all distinctions. I dare say that he has boasted of it twenty times at least in his verses. Now every argument that can be urged against the instituting of a literary order of Knighthood may be urged against the Laureateship. Moreover the Laureateship is associated with so many contemptible names, Shadwell, Tate, Eusden, Cibber, Whitehead, Pye,[5] that it at once moves laughter. It would be some time at least before a new order of Knighthood could fall so low. I hope and trust that the vacancy of that crown is to be perpetual.[6]

Ever yours truly
T B Macaulay

[1] Hallam's remaining son, Henry Fitzmaurice, died at Siena, 25 October.

[2] Charles Cuthbert Southey, *The Life and Correspondence of Robert Southey*, 6 vols., 1849–50. The final volume appeared on 26 October; TBM read it on 31 October, finding it 'a dull poor biography' (Journal, III, 65).

[3] A letter from Brougham as Lord Chancellor to Southey, January 1831, asked for Southey's advice on the question of government patronage of literature. Brougham mentioned that 'an order of merit has been proposed by some' but that he thought it best, in order to avoid novelty, to adapt 'one of the existing orders of knighthood, as the Guelphic,' to the purpose (*Life of Southey*, VI, 131). To this Southey replied that 'with regard to prizes, methinks they are better left to schools and colleges. . . . For myself, if we had a Guelphic order, I should choose to remain a Ghibelline' (VI, 136).

[4] Cf. Pope, 'Epistle to Arbuthnot,' line 74.

[5] TBM has named them in chronological order: Thomas Shadwell was made laureate in 1688; Nahum Tate, 1692; Laurence Eusden, 1718; Colley Cibber, 1730; William Whitehead 1757; and Henry James Pye, 1790.

[6] Tennyson succeeded Wordsworth as laureate on 19 November.

TO UNIDENTIFIED RECIPIENT, 12 NOVEMBER 1850

MS: Mr W. Hugh Peal.

Albany November 12 / 1850

Madam,

I assure you that I am extremely sensible of your kindness. But I am now employed in writing the history of times anterior by a century to the French Revolution; nor do I at all expect that I shall live long enough to tell the story of the events of 1794. I should therefore not be justified in depriving you for a time of Manuscripts and books which you must prize very highly. To some other historian they will, no doubt, be valuable materials. / I have the honor to be, / Madam,

Your most obedient Servant

T B Macaulay

TO FRANCES MACAULAY, 15 NOVEMBER 1850

MS: Trinity College. *Partly published:* Trevelyan, II, 196n.

Albany London / Nov 15. 1850

Dearest Fanny,

If I told you all that I think about these disputes I should write a volume. The Pope[1] is a fool, and hates the English nation and government. He meant, I am convinced, to insult and annoy the Queen and her ministers. His whole conduct in Ireland has evidently been directed to that end. Nevertheless the reasons popularly urged against this Bull seem to me absurd. We always knew that the Pope claimed spiritual jurisdiction; and I do not see that he now claims temporal jurisdiction. I therefore cannot but despise the vulgar outcry which I hear wherever I turn. Yet I cannot help enjoying the rage and terror of the Puseyites, who are utterly prostrated by this outbreak of popular feeling.

I could wish that Lord John had written more guardedly;[2] and that, I plainly see, is the wish of some of his colleagues: probably by this time it is also his own wish. He has got much applause in England: but, when he was writing, he should have remembered that he had to govern several millions of Roman Catholics in Ireland, that to govern them at all is no easy task, and that anything which looks like an affront to their religion is certain to call forth very dangerous passions. I see plainly that some of the

[1] Pius IX.
[2] Russell's letter to the Bishop of Durham, dated 4 November, was published in *The Times*, 7 November. It denounces 'papal aggression,' but finds a greater threat in 'the danger within the gates from the unworthy sons of the Church of England herself.'

ministers are uneasy; and I have reason to believe that Lord Clarendon[1] is still more so.

In the meantime these things keep London all alive. Yesterday the ballad singers were entertaining a great crowd under my window with bawling.

"Now all the old women are crying for fear:
The Pope is a coming: oh dear! oh dear!"
The wall of Burlington Gardens is covered with "No Popery," – "No Wafer Gods," – "Down with the Pope," and so forth.

I am pretty well, and have not yet felt the change of weather much. I am glad that you give a better account of Selina. Kindest love to her.

Yours ever

T B Macaulay

I am much less disturbed about the Pope than about poor Hallam. He is expected in town to day or to morrow. What a cruel fate his has been. I could find it in my heart to cry for him.

TO LORD PALMERSTON, 18 NOVEMBER 1850

MS: Hampshire Record Office.

Albany November 18. 1850

Dear Lord Palmerston,

You have heard, I suppose, what has happened at Glasgow. I am about to quit the office of Lord Rector; and the lads met to chuse my successor. You and Sheriff Alison,[2] the author of a big, if not a great, history of Europe, were put in nomination. Alison had the majority of votes, 288 to 219. But the students vote, not by the head, but in four sections which are called nations. The nations were two and two. In these circumstances I have the casting voice.[3] Will you let me know exactly what you wish. If you accept the office you must go down in the course of the winter, or early in the spring, and make an oration to the Students. You may not be able to spare the time, or willing to make such an

---

[1] Then Lord Lieutenant of Ireland.

[2] (Sir) Archibald Alison (1792–1867: *DNB*), high Tory Sheriff of Lanarkshire, whose *History of Europe*, 10 vols., 1833–42, became a standard reference. He was personally very popular in Scotland; Cockburn, for example, calls him 'the Sun of the West' (*Journal*, 11, 235). On the occasion of his inaugural at Glasgow TBM was asked to propose a toast to Alison: 'I did so, and from fear of being thought to grudge him his fame, spoke better of his writings than from the very little which I have read of them they seem to me to deserve' (*Journal*, 1, 546: 21 March 1849). I have not been able to find a report of this toast.

[3] Next day TBM learned that he could not determine the election unless he were personally present at the voting. He thereupon wrote to resign his authority to his predecessor: see next letter.

appearance.[1] If such be your feeling, I can easily bring you off, and with a very good grace. But, if you think that you could do any good by visiting Glasgow and by speaking there, I need not tell you how much pleasure I should have in appointing you.

The question is absolutely one for yourself. You can take a little time to consider it. For I have not yet received the official notification; and, after it has reached me, I may without impropriety defer my decision a few days. / Ever, dear Lord Palmerston,

Yours very truly,
T B Macaulay

TO LORD PALMERSTON, 19 NOVEMBER 1850

MS: Hampshire Record Office.

Albany Nov 19. 1850

Dear Lord Palmerston,

Since I wrote to you I have received an official intimation that I cannot give my casting vote without appearing personally in the Comitia of the College. This is quite out of the question; and I have written to the Principal to tell him so. The decision will therefore rest with my predecessor, Colonel Mure, who lives in the neighbourhood of Glasgow, and can easily attend.[2]

Very truly yours,
T B Macaulay

TO DUNCAN MACFARLAN, 19 NOVEMBER 1850

Text: Copy, National Library of Scotland.

Albany November 19 / 1850

Dear Sir,

I would with great satisfaction have resigned my office into the hands of either of the distinguished persons who have divided the votes of the University; but it will be out of my power to appear personally in the Comitia. I must therefore suffer my privilege of giving a casting vote to lapse to my Predecessor. It is a comfort to me to know that he cannot choose amiss.

I have the honor to be, etc. etc. etc.

T. B. Macaulay

---

1 'In his place,' TBM wrote, 'I should certainly decline the office. But he is not a man to decline anything. He would accept the Rectorship of a college in Greenland, and be off by the next whaler' (Journal, III, 78: 18 November).

2 Mure determined the election in favor of Alison.

TO THOMAS FLOWER ELLIS, 22 NOVEMBER 1850

MS: Trinity College. *Partly published:* Jane Millgate, 'History and Politics: Macaulay and Ireland,' *University of Toronto Quarterly,* XLII (1973), 120.

Albany Nov 22. 1850

Dear Ellis,

I will dine with you on Thursday. I wish you would dine here on Tuesday, the 26th. Let me know.

I have seen poor Hallam, and was much affected.[1] I found him pale, thin, and in tears, yet serene. After a few minutes of grief, he turned the conversation to the Pope and the Bishop of London.[2] We agreed perfectly.

I have just had a deputation of my parish here begging me to go and make a Guy Faux harangue to night. I sent them away wiser than they came, which is not saying much.[3] However they will, I believe, abstain from demanding of the Queen a repeal of the Emancipation Act and a general persecution of Papists.

You doubted the other day about Homer's mention of a flood such as that which swept the Barcelona diligence into the Mediterranean.[4] The lines are in the fifth book. Diomede is dismayed by the fury with which the Trojans, suddenly rallied by Hector and Mars, return to the charge:

ὡς δ' ὅτ ἀνὴρ ἀπάλαμνος, ἰὼν πολέος πεδίοιο,
στήῃ ἐπ' ὠκυρόῳ ποταμῷ ἅλαδε προρέοντι,
ἀφρῷ μορμύροντα ἰδών, ἀνά τ' ἔδραμ' ὀπίσσω,
ὡς τότε Τυδείδης ἀνεχάζετο.[5]

Nobody runs back from a known river, or even from a river in a place which he has never seen before, as from a snake on which he has trodden unawares. No doubt Homer meant that the peasant, in the middle of his journey on a road which is ordinarily dry, is crossed by a torrent which comes raving down from the hills to the sea, like this Catalonian stream.

Ever yours,

T B Macaulay

I have seen a delicious account of a meeting held at New York on this.

[1] On the day before: 'he was much upset – we talked about Harry. I could not refrain from weeping with him' (Journal, III, 80).

[2] Blomfield, the Bishop of London, was particularly outspoken against 'papal aggression' and the perversions of Puseyism: see, e.g., *The Times,* 4, 8, 9, and 20 November.

[3] 'I gave them such a harangue as they are little in the habit of hearing, and completely, for the moment, turned the whole current of their feeling. They went away thanking me, owning that they had been rash, and promising to be more discreet' (Journal, III, 81–2).

[4] An account of the accident is in *The Times,* 14 November.

[5] V, 597–600: 'and even as a man in passing over a great plain halteth in dismay at a swift-streaming river that floweth on to the sea, and seeing it seething with foam starteth back-ward, even so now did the son of Tydeus give ground' (Loeb translation).

TO FRANCES MACAULAY, 23 NOVEMBER 1850

MS: Trinity College. *Extract published:* Trevelyan, II, 196n.

Albany London / November 23. 1850

Dearest Fanny,

I return the paper. It is very droll.

I have seen poor Hallam. He was pale, worn and in tears, but composed; and, after a few minutes given to grief, he commanded himself sufficiently to talk, and to talk very well and sensibly about these Guy Faux proceedings. I find scarcely any difference of opinion among judicious men. Palmerston told me the day before yesterday that he thought the whole thing a mare's nest. A deputation of my parish, St James's, came to me yesterday to ask me to move a resolution at a public meeting. I refused, took their resolutions in my hand, and criticized them in such a way as, for the time at least, converted the delegates. For they told me, at parting, that the whole should be recast, that intolerant sentiments should be expunged, and that, instead of calling for laws to punish avowed Roman Catholics, the parish would express its dislike of the concealed Roman Catholics who hold benefices in the established Church.

I have had some plague about that stupid College at Glasgow. There has been a contest for the place which I have just vacated. The majority of the lads was for Alison, the author of a big, but not a great, history of Europe, the minority for Palmerston. But they vote at Glasgow, not by the head, but by what are called nations and though the votes of the students were 288 and 219, the votes of the nations were two and two. I therefore have the casting vote. It would be impossible for me to vote against Palmerston. Yet it would be disagreeable to vote against the sense of so decided a majority. Happily I find that I cannot vote at all without going down to Glasgow; and, as to losing a week and travelling a thousand miles for such nonsense, the thing is not to be thought of. I shall therefore let the casting vote devolve on my predecessor Colonel Mure or on any body else. I am glad that I have done with that silly business. Can anything be conceived more ridiculous than that grown men, of note in the political and literary world, should trouble themselves about the votes of four or five hundred boys of whom the majority are little more than thirteen years old. The number of boys at Eton is much greater, their age equal, their attainments far superior. Yet who would degrade himself by courting the votes of the Etonians as if their good opinion added to the fame of a writer or a statesman? The whole thing is a humbug. What keeps it up is this, – that the English, knowing little about the Scotch Universities, suppose them to bear some resemblance to Oxford and Cambridge, and are also taken in by the pompous title of

Lord Rector. They fancy that he is like a Chancellor of one of our great seats of learning; and they know that both the Duke of Wellington and Prince Albert justly think themselves elevated in dignity by being Chancellors of our Universities. In truth, if there were a Chancellor of Harrow or of Rugby chosen by the boys, that would be the proper parallel. But I am running on very long and idly.

I am writing an account of the theological disputes of 1689,[1] a most memorable year in our ecclesiastical history. I think that you will be interested by the narrative. I have discovered some very curious things which are quite unknown to the public. Among other things I have found, among the forgotten records of the House of Peers, the original copy of a bill which actually passed that house just after the Revolution 'for Uniting their Majestie's Protestant subjects.'[2] This bill dispenses with the signing of the Articles, with the wearing of the surplice, with the sign of the cross in baptism, and with the kneeling at the other sacrament. It is odd to think that it was thrown out at last, not by the high Churchmen, but by the dissenters and their friends.

Kindest love to Selina.

Ever yours

T B Macaulay

TO FRANCES MACAULAY, 30 NOVEMBER 1850

MS: Trinity College.

London November 30 / 1850

Dearest Fanny, –

I am writing at the board of the Trustees of the Museum, where the Secretary is reading a long report. Inglis is in the chair, looking very fat and red, and in the highest state of Protestant zeal. On my left is Lord Mahon, engaged, like me, in writing a letter. This is the way in which board work is always done.[3]

I have no news for you. The Protestant fury is still boiling, and seems to have been reanimated by the brutality of the Irish blackguards at Birkenhead.[4]

[1] The latter part of ch. 11 is devoted to these.

[2] 'Thoms came after breakfast and brought me, to my great delight, the bill for Uniting Protestants – the copy which came up from the Committee with all the erasures and inter-lineations. Most curious. Indeed invaluable for my purpose' (Journal, III, 54: 19 October). See *History*, III, 89–99.

[3] TBM scrawled a note to Mahon at this meeting that Mahon preserved. It reads: 'Is there the slightest use in this reading? Did any good ever come of it? And is it not absurd that half an hour of the time of busy men should be wasted in this mummery?' Mahon's endorsement explains. 'handed to me by Mr. Macaulay during the reading of the Minutes of the former Meeting according to form' (MS, Stanhope Papers, Chevening).

[4] A meeting at Birkenhead to protest Papal aggression, 27 November, was broken up by Irish navvies (*The Times*, 28 November).

Has Hannah told you of the grand ceremony which is to be performed in Westbourne Terrace? A deputation of Officers of the Commissariat, with Sir Randolph Routh[1] at their head, are to present her in form with the portrait of her husband; and she is to make a speech in reply.[2] She is frightened out of her wits at the thought. I advise her to begin, 'Unaccustomed as I am to public speaking.' After the harangue there is to be a fine dinner at which, as well as at the oratorical display, I propose to assist.

Àpropos of portraits, you cannot think how well Baba has copied Richmond's drawing of me.[3] It was her first attempt in that style; and it is really astonishingly good, and has pleased everybody who has seen it.

Do you see what has happened to George Thompson? His supplies from India have been cut off by the abolition of the Sattara Government. He is forced to take to his old trade of lecturing for hire. So he determined to go to America this autumn, and to harangue against the new Fugitive Slave Law. The law is a bad one, and is extremely unpopular at Boston. Thompson therefore thought Boston the best place for his debut. The Yankees however very properly thought it a gross impertinence in a foreigner to read them sermons on a matter which concerned only themselves, and would not hear him. If he persists he will infallibly be well tarred and feathered; and I should enjoy nothing more than to see him in his plumy honours.[4] Your friend Frederic Douglas[5] was with Thompson, and came in for his share of hooting [. . . .][6]

1 Routh (1785–1858: *DNB*), Commissary-General in the army, superintended famine relief in Ireland under Trevelyan's authority.
2 The portrait, by E. U. Eddis, is now at Wallington. The ceremony of presentation took place on 7 January 1851; a printed copy of the address to Lady Trevelyan, of her reply and her husband's, is among the Trevelyan papers at the University of Newcastle. TBM describes Hannah's response as having 'the conversational ease and fluency of a woman among friends who have shown her a kindness which has touched her feelings. It could not be better done' (Journal, III, 129). Trevelyan's reply was corrected by TBM at Trevelyan's request (Journal, III, 132: 10 January 1851).
3 The second Richmond portrait of TBM, a crayon drawing. It was commissioned by Hannah, and TBM sat for it between 30 January–15 February 1850. TBM said of it that 'the face is characteristic. It is the face of a man of considerable mental powers, great boldness, frankness, and a quick relish for pleasure. It is not unlike Mr Fox's face in general expression. I am quite content to have such a physiognomy' (Journal, II, 238: 22 February 1850). The portrait was engraved in 1861 and appears as the frontispiece to Hannah's edition of TBM's *Works*, 1866. Charles Macaulay said of the drawing that, though 'slightly idealised,' it 'preserves the likeness well, and the expression of the face admirably' (to Mary Macaulay Booth, 9 July 1879: MS, University of London).
4 A meeting of abolitionists at Boston, where Thompson attempted to speak, was broken up by a tumultuous crowd: a burlesque account is in *The Times*, 2 December. For Thompson and the Sattara government, see *to* Denison, 6 August 1847.
5 Frederick Douglass (1817?–95), born a slave, became one of the most prominent abolitionists. He was in England in 1845–7, when Fanny no doubt met him. Douglass appeared at the same meeting with Thompson and was equally unable to secure a hearing.
6 The lower two-thirds of the last leaf has been torn away; probably only the closing and signature are missing.

TO LADY THERESA LEWIS, 6 DECEMBER 1850

MS: New York Public Library.

Albany Dec 6 / 1850

Dear Lady Theresa,

I send you the London Gazette which contains the description of Ferguson.[1] It is the first number in the volume – August 6. 1683. I used to think that he was the original of a portrait at Grove.[2] But I am not sure that the Roman nose is to be found in the picture.

Very truly yours,

T B Macaulay

TO SARAH GRANT FRANZ,[3] 9 DECEMBER 1850

Text: Sarah Grant Franz, *Wild Flowers,* 1878, Preface.

Albany, London, December 9, 1850.

Madam,

I am gratified by hearing that my Essays have given you pleasure, but much more grieved by finding that my advice has given you pain. You quite misunderstood me if you thought that I meant to express a low opinion of your compositions. They are beyond the reach of many very clever and accomplished women. Four-fifths of Chalmers's Collection of the British Poets[4] consists of verses far inferior to yours. But, if you ask me whether I think it likely that you will attain a place among those great masters of the art of whom no age or country produces many, of whom England cannot at this moment be said to possess one, of whom in all Christendom there are not six, I should be guilty of flattery if I encouraged you to hope for such success. I myself, when a young man, aspired

---

[1] Robert Ferguson (d. 1714: *DNB*), 'the plotter.' In the *Gazette* he is described thus: 'a tall lean Man, dark brown hair, a great Roman Nose, thin Jawed, Heat in his Face, speaks in the Scotch Tone, a sharp piercing Eye, stoops a little in the shoulders; he hath a shuffling Gate that differs from all Men, wears his Perriwig down almost over his Eyes, about 45 or 46 years old.' In the *History* this becomes: 'his broad Scotch accent, his tall and lean figure, his lantern jaws, the gleam of his sharp eyes which were always overhung by his wig, his cheeks inflamed by an eruption, his shoulders deformed by a stoop, and his gait distinguished from that of other men by a peculiar shuffle, made him remarkable wherever he appeared' (II, 533).

[2] The estate of Lady Theresa's brother, Lord Clarendon.

[3] I have not been able to discover anything about her; the British Museum has no copy of her book, nor is it listed in the National Union Catalogue (though there is a copy at Yale). In the preface, she says that her poems 'would probably never have been printed but for the sympathy displayed by Lord Macaulay when she requested his advice upon them a few years before his death.' In November 1850 TBM notes that he called on Longman 'to ask some questions for Madame Franz' (Journal, IV, 301).

[4] Alexander Chalmers, ed., *The Works of the English Poets,* 21 vols., 1810.

to be one of those great masters. Reflection and observation convinced me that it was impossible. I relinquished all thought of rivalling them, and contentedly took my place at their feet. It is surely no calamity not to be one of so small a class. Nor do I see any reason to think that the few who attain that eminence are happier than those who do not aspire so high. I have myself had a happier life than any man of letters that I ever knew, and the explanation is this – that I loved letters purely for their own sake; that I considered the exercise of the intellect as its own reward; that, if fame did not come, I did not miss it; that, if it came, I reckoned it as a godsend, as clear gain over and above the ample recompense which I had already received in the act of thinking and composing. I ought to apologise for all this egotism, but I shall be quite willing to be thought by you an egotist if my experience can be of any use to you.

I should be very sorry if you were to acquiesce in my judgment without appeal. I am a very fastidious reader of poetry, and ought not to undertake to answer for the public. Let me advise you to take the opinion of some other critic. / I have the honour to be, Madam,

Your faithful servant,
T. B. Macaulay.

TO UNIDENTIFIED RECIPIENT,[1] 9 DECEMBER 1850

MS: Trinity College.

Albany London / December 9. 1850

My dear Cousin,

I take no part whatever in public affairs; and, though I am on terms of personal friendship with many of the ministers, yet, as I can now do nothing for them, I carefully abstain from asking anything of them. I will however send your letter to Trevelyan, and beg his particular attention to it. I shall be truly glad if your application succeeds. If not, you must remember that there is a wide difference between your position and that of the official men here. You are naturally and laudably anxious for the welfare of the particular district where your lot has been cast. They have to take thought for a great empire, and to distribute the very scanty machinery which is at their command in such a manner as may on the whole effect the greatest quantity of good. It is impossible that, however faithfully, ably, and humanely they may discharge this duty, they should not often seem to people whose view is bounded by the limits of a single

---

[1] Perhaps one of TBM's western Highland cousins; the region was in almost as desperate straits as Ireland. But one can only guess. TBM writes as though he had at least some acquaintance with his correspondent.

parish, very unjust and hard hearted. I say this in general, and heartily hope that it may be in their power to do what you ask.

Very truly yours,
T B Macaulay

TO EDWARD EVERETT, 9 DECEMBER 1850

MS: Massachusetts Historical Society.

Albany London / December 9. 1850

Dear Everett,

I found on my table two or three days ago a valuable present from you,[1] valuable intrinsically, and still more valuable as a mark of your kindness. I have already read the greater part of the two volumes with pleasure of many kinds. But my chief pleasure arises from thinking that the author is my friend.

And is this all that we are to see of you? Will you not be tempted across the sea by our crystal palace and our great œcumenical exhibition?[2] We are told that all New York and Boston, all Philadelphia and Baltimore are coming; and will you be left behind. Mivart[3] makes up two thousand beds after Easter. Will not you occupy one of them? In all the great crowd of foreigners which is expected from all corners of Christendom there is none, I will venture to say, who will be cordially welcomed by a greater number of old friends. Foreigner indeed we hardly call you. If New England will spare so good an Englishman for a summer to old England, we will willingly leave Mr. George Thompson in pledge.

But seriously I do hope that we shall soon see you here.[4]

Ever yours most truly
T B Macaulay

[1] *Orations and Speeches on Various Occasions,* 2 vols., Boston, 1850; item 352 in the sale catalogue of TBM's library. In his Journal, TBM says that 'by the quick glance which I have given to them they seem a little more gaudy and interjectional than is to my taste — Ah and Oh' (III, 93: 5 December).

[2] The Great Exhibition of 1851 – properly the Great Exhibition of the Works of Industry of All Nations – had been in preparation, under the patronage of Prince Albert, since 1849. TBM was at first among the skeptics, but soon became an enthusiast. He had already been appointed a member – in company with Gladstone, Milman, Lord Lyttelton, and Dean Liddell – of a committee charged with devising inscriptions for the medals to be awarded: 'most absurd' he thought then (Journal, II, 351: 10 July 1850). The Exhibition opened on 1 May.

[3] James Mivart (1781–1856: *Boase*), proprietor of Mivart's (afterwards Claridge's) Hotel, Brook Street, Grosvenor Square. Two thousand beds is of course a mistake, but typical of the exaggerations that the advent of the Exhibition generated.

[4] Everett has noted on the letter: 'Received 2 Jan. 1851. wrote 11 May 1854!'

TO LORD ASHLEY, 10 DECEMBER 1850

MS: Mr T. S. Blakeney.

Albany December 10, 1850

My dear Lord,

Many thanks for the facsimile which you have been so kind as to send me. Mr. Goodman may possibly be right in his guess: but I think it more probable that his copy of the petition was one of the many copies which doubtless went out in the newsletters of the morning which followed the presentation.

I am truly glad to hear that my brother's services have given you satisfaction.[1] I was sure that his whole heart would be in his work; and I am therefore not surprised at his success.

Ever yours truly,

T B Macaulay

TO CHARLES MACAULAY, 10 DECEMBER 1850

MS: University of London.

Albany Dec 10. 1850

Dear Charles,

I send you a few lines which I have received from Lord Ashley, and which will probably give you, as they have given me, pleasure.[2]

Yours ever,

T B Macaulay

TO JOHN EVELYN DENISON, 16 DECEMBER 1850

MS: University of Nottingham.

Albany Dec 16. 1850

Dear Denison,

I am truly sorry that I have made more engagements for this Christmas than I can easily or conveniently keep.[3] I should really like to pass a day or two at Ossington. But this year the thing is impossible.

---

[1] See next letter.

[2] Ashley's note to TBM, dated 10 December, concludes: 'Allow me to add that your brother's services, as our Secretary at the B[oard] of Health, give us the highest satisfaction' (MS, University of London).

[3] TBM was at Woburn Abbey, 21–4 December, and at Bowood, 27–31 December (Journal, III, 103–20).

What an universal man your Duke[1] is. I remember your Rubens which he retouched. His music is, I suppose, of a piece with his painting. There has been nothing like him since Leonardo de Vinci.

Ever yours truly,

T B Macaulay

By the bye the Duke may well say Nunc Dimittis. For he has lived to hear wiser men than himself bawling No Popery as loudly as he bawled it two and twenty years ago.

TO [JOHN REUBEN THOMPSON?],[2] 23 DECEMBER 1850

MS: Haverford College. *Published: Journal of the Friends' Historical Society,* XLIX (1961), 205.

[Woburn Abbey] Dec 23. 1850

Sir,

I have the honor to acknowledge the receipt of your letter which has followed me to the country. Your Address I hope to find on my table when I return to London.

I have not the smallest doubt that every person who takes the trouble to examine the original evidence will, unless he be blinded by prejudice, admit that I have dealt very leniently with the fame of William Penn. As to the outcry of the Quakers, I was of course prepared for it; and I laugh at it.

I cannot but distrust the correctness of the anecdote which you mention. I have not at this moment books to consult. But I am quite confident that Penn had declared himself a Quaker long before Monmouth was of an age to have mistresses. Indeed Penn made a high religious profession before he left college.[3]

I am most obliged to you for directing my attention to the Westover

---

[1] The Duke of Newcastle; his estate at Clumber Park was not far from Denison's at Ossington. I do not know what TBM's references to his music are about. In his Journal of 4 September 1856 TBM remarks that he remembered once hearing the Duke 'sing and play at the Duchess of Somerset's' (x, 60).

[2] The reference in this letter to the Westover manuscripts, which Thompson later sent to TBM (see *to* Thompson, 17 May 1851), suggests that he is the recipient. Thompson (1823–73), of Richmond, Virginia, was editor of the *Southern Literary Messenger,* 1847–60. An account by Thompson of a visit that he made to TBM in June 1854 appeared in the *Southern Field and Fireside,* February 1860, and is reprinted in S. A. Allibone, 'Sketch of the Life and Writings of Thomas Babington Macaulay,' in *History of England,* Philadelphia, 1875, v, 78–84.

[3] The 'anecdote' is a libel about Penn in William Byrd's *History of the Dividing Line Betwixt Virginia and North Carolina,* asserting that Penn in his youth 'had been a man of Pleasure about the Town,' successful with the ladies, 'particularly with a Mistress of the Duke of Monmouth,' and that the danger of a duel created by this amour drove Penn to take shelter among the Quakers (ed. W. K. Boyd, Raleigh [North Carolina], 1929, p. 9).

M.S.S.[1] I have little doubt that I shall be able to find a copy in the British Museum. / I have the honor to be, / Sir,

Your faithful Servant,

T B Macaulay

TO UNIDENTIFIED RECIPIENT, 24 DECEMBER 1850

MS: Harvard University.

Albany Dec 24. 1850

My dear Sir,

I should be most happy to join your party on the 30th. But unfortunately I shall be at Bowood on that day.

Very truly yours,

T B Macaulay

TO SELINA MACAULAY, 25 DECEMBER 1850

MS: Trinity College.

Albany London / Dec 25. 1850

Dearest Selina,

I inclose a cheque for the quarter. Kindest Christmas wishes to you and dear Fanny.

Of course you remember that I charge myself with your railway calls. I hope that your property will soon rise still higher in value.

I have just returned from a very pleasant visit to Woburn where I was honored by having a farce from the French acted before me by very aristocratical performers, and was presented with a satin play bill as if I had been a prince of the blood. Baba has laid up the playbill among her curiosities.[2] The day after to morrow I go to Bowood. On New Year's day I shall fall vigorously to work. I am in great hopes and spirits about my book. Of late I have pleased myself better; and great difficulties seem to be giving way. But what comforts me most is the state of my health. Last year I thought that my constitution was breaking up. But this winter I

---

[1] *The Westover Manuscripts*, ed. Edmund Ruffin, Petersburgh, Virginia, 1841; item 31 in the sale catalogue of TBM's library.

[2] TBM has preserved a paper copy of the playbill in his Journal. It is headed: 'Woburn Abbey Theatre. / Under the Patronage of / The Lady Frances Hope, / and / The Right Honorable T. B. Macaulay.' The play was *Turning the Tables*, and the cast were Ayshford Sandford, Miss Bulteel, H. Grenfell, Mr Stafford, Lord Valletort, Miss Lister, George Byng, and Mrs Bulteel. TBM recognized the play as an adaptation by John Poole of Scribe's *Le Nouveau Pourceaugnac* (III, 108–11: 23 December).

have been better than for many years past. I wish, my dear Selina, that it were the same with you. Let me hear how you are going on.

Ever yours affectionately
T B Macaulay

TO AUGUSTUS DE MORGAN, 2 JANUARY 185[1][1]

MS: University of London.

Albany Jany. 2. 1850

My dear Sir,

I can say very little in answer to your questions. As to Burnet, there is much indeed to be learned which cannot be found in any biographical dictionary. But whoever wishes to obtain full information must read volume after volume of squibs and controversial pamphlets. I have myself sermons, tracts and lampoons, relating to the honest bishop which would fill a book shelf. Swift's attacks on him are numerous. Arbuthnot's are still more numerous and still more ferocious. There is indeed a journal of Burnet's last days which I would willingly believe not to be Arbuthnot's. For I never read any pasquinade written with such diabolical malignity: and I am inclined to think well of Arbuthnot's heart and principles.[2]

I should say much the same about Holles, Ludlow, Lilburne and Buckingham.[3] From pamphlets, ballads, satires, a great deal may be gleaned about them which would be new and amusing. But I know of no book in which any great quantity of curious information is likely to be found collected. Of course Guizot has all the ordinary books, and indeed many books which are not ordinary.[4] I introduced Rodd the bookseller to him; and Rodd had the largest stock of works on the civil wars which could be found in London.

I suppose that the Oxford edition of Clarendon's History – the Octavo, I mean, with the omitted passages restored, – is the best.[5] As to Mrs. Hutchinson I do not believe that anything is known about her

---

[1] TBM has written 1850 for 1851: his Journal for 1 January 1851 records 'a letter from De Morgan asking historical information for Guizot. Odd that Guizot should not ask directly' (III, 124).

[2] 'Notes and Memorandums of the Six Days Preceding the Death of a Late Right Reverend – – – – – –,' 1715. It is not now attributed to Arbuthnot.

[3] Denzil Holles (1599–1680: *DNB*); Edmund Ludlow (1617?–92: *DNB*); Robert Lilburne (1613–65: *DNB*); George Villiers (1628–87: *DNB*); all figured in the Civil War.

[4] Guizot was at work on his *Histoire de la République d'Angleterre et de Cromwell*, 2 vols., 1854, a part of his *Histoire de la Révolution d'Angleterre*.

[5] *History of the Rebellion*, ed. B. Bandinel, 8 vols., Oxford, 1826.

beyond what is published with her Memoirs of her husband.[1] Her verses are very respectable.

> Ever yours truly
> T B Macaulay

Some interesting facts about Burnet may be found in the pamphlets which Samuel Johnson (Julian Johnson, I mean,) wrote under William the Third.[2] But allowance must be made for Julian Johnson's savage malignity. It is hardly necessary to refer to Birch's Life of Tillotson,[3] which of course Guizot has consulted.

TO LADY THERESA LEWIS, 7 JANUARY 1851

MS: New York Public Library.

> Albany Jany. 7. 1851

Dear Lady Theresa,

I have never paid particular attention to the history of Waller's plot. But you will find a good deal on the subject in Rushworth.[4] Waller's speech at the bar of the House of Commons is there at length. There is also much in the parliamentary journals. The first entry in the books of the Commons is on the 31st of May 1643, which is designated as "Dies Humiliationis." This, you will observe, exactly agrees with Clarendon's narrative.[5] The house, it should seem, after praying and preaching was over, sate on business and appointed a Committee of Public Safety – Pym Chairman. The report, made by Pym, you will find in the journal of June 6. You will easily follow the subsequent notices. At the beginning of July the conspirators were ordered to be tried by a Court Martial with unusual solemnity. Guildhall was filled up for the proceedings.

In the parliamentary history you will find a speech of Pym to the Corporation of London, giving a full account of the plot.[6] The speech was corrected by Pym's own hand. You will find little in Whitlocke's Memorials; and that little is incorrect. He says that Pym died at the end of May 1643, whereas it is certain that Pym lived till the following December.

> Ever yours truly
> T B Macaulay

---

[1] Lucy Hutchinson, *Memoirs of the Life of Colonel Hutchinson*, 1806.
[2] Samuel Johnson (1649–1703: *DNB*), popularly called 'Julian' Johnson after his tract against the doctrine of non-resistance entitled 'Julian the Apostate,' 1682.
[3] Thomas Birch, *Life of Tillotson*, 1752.
[4] John Rushworth, *Historical Collections of Private Passages of State*, 7 vols., 1659–1701.
[5] Clarendon, *History of the Rebellion*, Book VII, 54–73.
[6] *Parliamentary History*, III, 121–9: 8 June 1643.

TO SIR EDWARD BULWER-LYTTON, 11 JANUARY 1851

MS: Hertfordshire County Council.

Albany January 11. 1851

Dear Sir Edward,

I do not believe that Bacon ever used the precise words, "Knowledge is Power."[1] Sentences however are to be found in his works which seem to justify the assertion that he has emphatically pronounced knowledge to be power. One of the passages to which you have referred is much stronger in the Latin than in the English – "Dispiciamus si respiam inveniatur tanta potentia quanta eruditio hominis naturam investit."

As to the value of the aphorism I agree with you; and I believe that Bacon would have agreed with us both. He did not affect mathematical accuracy of language: and it is not by picking a few lines out of the Novum Organum or the De Augmentis, and reasoning on every word as schooldivines would reason on all the particles of a text that the real meaning of his works is to be collected. A few pages from the passage which I have quoted is another passage in which he puts knowledge and power in the strongest antithesis to each other – "Adeo signanter Deus opera potentiæ et sapientiæ discriminavit."[2] He would have laughed, no doubt, at any body who had twitted him with inconsistency, and would have said that knowledge was power in one sense, and not in another.

I should not chuse to use the word "pled." Our translation of the Bible, and, I believe, every good English writer since, may be cited as authority for *pleaded*. Sir Walter used *pled* once or twice in verse.[3] But Sir Walter's style was frequently tainted by archaisms and Scoticisms; and, much as I admire his genius, I should not consider his authority as of much value on such a point. I think very little of mere analogy in a language as irregular as ours, and very little indeed in the present case. For you may observe that our other monosyllable verbs in *ead*, to *lead*, to *read*, are Saxon. To plead is a term of art introduced into our language by lawyers from the Norman French.

I shall always be glad to see and hear from you when you can spare me half an hour.

Ever yours truly
T B Macaulay

---

[1] But see *Meditationes Sacræ*, No. 11, 'De Hæresibus': '*nam et ipsa scientia potestas est.*' In the installment of Bulwer-Lytton's *My Novel* in the April *Blackwood's* (book 4, ch. 19), Riccabocca confidently asserts that 'no such aphorism is to be found in Bacon from the first page of his writings to the last.' Bulwer-Lytton adds a footnote protesting against the injustice of reducing Bacon's meaning to such formulas.

[2] *De Augmentis*, Book 1 (*Works*, ed. Spedding, new edn, I, 464). Bulwer-Lytton uses this example in his note to *My Novel*: see note 1, above.

[3] E.g., *Lord of the Isles*, IV, 14: 'Anxious his suit Lord Ronald pled.'

TO THOMAS FLOWER ELLIS, 13 JANUARY 1851

MS: Trinity College.

Albany Jan 13. 1851

Dear Ellis,

I shall probably not see you till Friday at seven, when we are to meet at the Clarendon.[1] Be punctual. I am going for two days to Windsor. But I shall take care to put no dates to any letters which I may have occasion to write thence.[2]

The Chief Baron[3] leapt at my invitation like a cock at a grossart, as the Scotch say.[4] I begged him to come and keep order among a set of us wild boys who were hardly to be trusted with Johannisberg and Lafitte. Dundas says that His Lordship will certainly be incomparably the most drunk of the party.

Ever yours,

T B Macaulay

TO MRS HENRY HOLLAND, 13 JANUARY 1851

MS: Mr D. C. L. Holland.

Albany Jany. 13. 1851

Dear Mrs. Holland,

I am sorry to say that the Queen has commanded my attendance from Tuesday to Thursday, so that I shall be unable to enjoy the pleasure of breakfasting with you.

Ever yours truly

T B Macaulay

TO UNIDENTIFIED RECIPIENT, 17 JANUARY 1851

MS: Massachusetts Historical Society.

Albany London / January 17. 1851

Sir,

I am much obliged to you for your kind offer: but I already possess all the tracts which you mention. They are not very common, but much more

---

[1] 'I gave a dinner to a small Northern Circuit party – the Chief Baron, Dundas, Parker of the Admiralty, Ellis, and Adolphus. Good company and not unpleasant' (Journal, III, 144: 17 January).

[2] He is remembering his unlucky Windsor Castle letter of 1 October 1839. Part of TBM's Journal account of this later visit is printed in Trevelyan, II, 290–1.

[3] Sir Frederick Pollock.

[4] See Scott, *Redgauntlet*, Letter XIII. A grossart (groset) is a gooseberry.

common probably in this country than with you. / I have the honor to be, / Sir,

Your most obedient Servant,

T B Macaulay

TO LORD MAHON, 18 JANUARY 1851

MS: Stanhope Papers, Chevening.

Albany January 18. 1851

Dear Lord Mahon,

I am quite certain that I was told by one of our club what I told you about poor Sir Robert.[1] Are you quite sure that there was not a second blackballing. Several persons have tried their chance twice.

You will have seen poor Lord Northampton's death[2] announced in the papers. I am extremely desirous that the vacant place at the Museum should be filled by Milman[3]. He is now in rank, as he has long been in literary eminence, the first of the clergy of the capital. Surely the head of the Cathedral of London is the person, who, of all persons, should seem to be the fittest to have a voice in the management of the great Museum of London. He has abundant leisure; and his duties keep him in town during a part of the year at which it is difficult to get a Quorum. I almost wonder that the Dean of St Paul's was not made an official Trustee.

I think that, before Milman was in his present situation, you mentioned his name to the Archbishop. Do you think that you could with propriety do so again? If you do, I will try to secure the Speaker. The Chancellor I do not know sufficiently to take such a liberty.[4]

Kind regards to Lady Mahon, and true love to my Valentine.[5]

Ever yours,

T B Macaulay

---

[1] Mahon had written to TBM to say that on examining the records of The Club he had found that Peel was blackballed in 1818, though TBM had told Mahon that the event 'took place soon after the passing of the Roman Catholic Relief Bill – which might supply a natural excuse for it' (Mahon to TBM, 8 January: copy, Stanhope Papers).

[2] On 17 January. The second Marquess of Northampton (1790–1851: *DNB*) frequently presided at meetings of the British Museum trustees, where his tediousness was a special torment to TBM. On the news of his death TBM wrote that 'if he had not died, I must soon have resigned: for my patience was quite wearied out' (Journal, III, 145–6: 18 January).

[3] See 2 August 1850.

[4] The Archbishop of Canterbury, the Lord Chancellor, and the Speaker of the House of Commons were first among the *ex officio* trustees of the Museum. They were, in 1851, Sumner, Lord Truro, and Charles Shaw Lefevre.

[5] TBM was, during this week, writing the valentine to Lady Mary Stanhope that appears in his *Miscellaneous Writings* (Journal, III, 141–8).

TO LORD MAHON, 21 JANUARY 1851

MS: Stanhope Papers, Chevening.

Albany London / January 21. 1851

Dear Lord Mahon,

I am sorry to say that I shall not be able to leave town even for a day during this week or the next.

We certainly want a man of science. But it seems to me not very easy to find one in all respects fit for the place. Herschel, I believe, does not live in London. Babbage has a vile temper and a strangely twisted understanding. Our friend Murchison is scarcely of the proper calibre. The same may be said of Lyell.[1] Would Faraday[2] suit? I ask in ignorance: for I barely know him by sight.

Ever yours,
T B Macaulay

TO BENJAMIN HAWES, 21 JANUARY 1851

MS: Royal Archives, Windsor Castle.

Albany January 21. / 1851

Dear Hawes,

I am extremely sorry that I am engaged on Friday.[3] I should have liked to see your colonial menagerie – a perfect Noah's ark.

Ever yours,
T B Macaulay

TO LORD CRANWORTH,[4] 23 JANUARY 1851

MS: King's College, Cambridge.

Albany Jany. 23. 1851

Dear Lord Cranworth,

I found both your notes on my table late last night. I am sorry that I am engaged both to day and Saturday.[5]

Ever yours,
T B Macaulay

[1] Sir Charles Lyell (1797–1875: *DNB*), the geologist; TBM and Lyell occasionally met at London dinner parties.
[2] Michael Faraday (1791–1867: *DNB*), chemist and physicist, the protégé and successor of Davy at the Royal Institution. The new trustees added in this year were Sir Philip Grey-Egerton, the paleontologist, and Lord Edward Seymour. Murchison was made a trustee in 1853.
[3] TBM spent the entire day at home, alone (Journal, III, 149).
[4] Rolfe was created Baron Cranworth on 20 December 1850.
[5] TBM entertained Ellis on this evening and dined at Lord Granville's on Saturday (Journal, III, 149–50).

TO JOHN KENT,[1] 28 JANUARY 1851

MS: Trinity College. *Envelope:* J Kent Esq / Nunney Court / Frome. *Subscription:* T B M

Albany London / January 28. 1851

Sir,

You have all the merit of originality, though the explanation which you suggest had occurred to Lord Mahon and to myself. Indeed you are entitled to the whole of the credit which he and I must divide between us. Some months ago he discovered that in some copies the letters were printed thus: P.M.a.C.F.[2] He inferred very naturally that *a* must be the article, and guessed that C.F. must mean Capuchin Friar, or something of that sort. But as to the P.M. he was quite at fault. He found in Chamberlayne's State of England (1684) that one of Queen Catharine's Portuguese priests was named Miguel Pereira. He thought it possible that this might be the person, and that the initials might have been inverted for some not very intelligible object. This last part of his conjecture I could not adopt. But I agreed with him about the C.F. and, after a little thought, I hit on Père Mansuete; and he concurred. That you should have arrived at the same result is a circumstance which will confirm us both in our opinion. / I have the honor to be, / Sir,

Your most obedient Servant,

T B Macaulay

TO JOHN KENT, 31 JANUARY 1851

MS: Trinity College.

Albany London / January 31. 1851

Sir,

I shall be much obliged to you for any suggestions that occur to you, and particularly for any criticisms as to matter of fact. If I live some years longer I shall probably revise with attention the two volumes which I have already published,[3] and shall of course feel it to be a sacred duty to make the narrative as accurate as possible. / I have the honor to be, / Sir,

Your faithful Servant,

T B Macaulay

---

[1] Kent (1807?–88?), had been a schoolmaster and editor in Canada; he returned to England in 1843 and became tutor to Lord Porchester, afterwards 4th Earl of Carnarvon. 'His rectitude, sincerity, and exceptional ability would have made their mark in the world had he possessed any ambition' (Sir Arthur Hardinge, *Life of the Fourth Earl of Carnarvon*, 1 [1925], 33). In a draft of the letter that he sent to TBM on 25 January Kent describes himself as a 'Tory and a High Churchman' (MS, Trinity).

[2] See 4 January 1849.

[3] This he did in the edition of 1857–8: see 27 October 1856.

TO FRANCES MACAULAY, 12 FEBRUARY 1851

MS: Trinity College.

Albany February 12 / 1851

Dearest Fanny,

I send you the lines which you wish to have. Keep them close: for nothing lowers a man so much as the appearing to attach importance to such trifles.

The line about which you inquire is the first of Young's Night Thoughts. Odd that you should not know it. Cowper has driven Young out. Till the Task appeared all grave people who looked prim at other poetry read the Night Thoughts.

Hannah's picture[1] is charming – excellent. Her best look in her best days.

Nobody here troubles himself now much about Popery. Lord John's bill[2] disappointed people who did not in the least know what they expected. But the question – What more do you want to do? – is unanswerable. The excitement is now, I think, going down in good earnest.

Love to Selina.

Ever yours,

T B Macaulay

TO JOHN EVELYN DENISON, 22 FEBRUARY 1851

MS: University of Nottingham.

Albany February 22. 1851

Dear Denison,

Many thanks for the luxuries which you added to my breakfast this morning.[3] Will you breakfast here on Wednesday morning at ten? You will meet a few friends.[4]

Ever yours,

T B Macaulay

[1] At TBM's request Hannah sat to Richmond for her portrait beginning in March 1850, just after Richmond finished TBM's. The picture was delivered on 6 February 1851, and the next day TBM took it to the Trevelyans: 'Hannah's picture – charming – like her best looks in her best days – like her still at moments. I looked and looked and was ready to cry. The hands bad, which is a shame, for her hands are very pretty' (Journal, III, 162). I have not succeeded in learning where this picture now is.

[2] The Ecclesiastical Titles Bill, introduced on 7 February but not passed by both Houses until the end of July. In its first form the bill 'had prevented Roman Catholic prelates from doing any acts, receiving any gifts, or succeeding to any property, under territorial titles.' After Russell's resignation and return, an amended bill introduced in March 'merely made it illegal for them to assume titles of this character' (Walpole, *History of England*, v [1886], 13). The act was not enforced and was repealed in 1871.

[3] Denison sent a gift of bread and butter (Journal, III, 177).

[4] The party were Hallam, Inglis, Milnes, Milman, Lord Carlisle, Dundas, and Denison (Journal, III, 182).

TO JOHN HARLAND, 3 MARCH 1851

MS: Manchester Central Library.

Albany London / March 3. 1851

Sir,

I have the complete Series of the extracts from the Lancashire Quaker's Memoirs.[1] I assure [you] that I am extremely sensible of your great kindness in this matter. Some of the details are highly curious. / I have the honor to be, / Sir,

Your faithful Servant,
T B Macaulay

TO GEORGE CORNEWALL LEWIS, 4 MARCH 1851

MS: New York Public Library. *Envelope:* G Cornewall Lewis Esq M P / etc. etc. etc. / Kent House / Knightsbridge. *Subscription:* T B Macaulay.

Mr. Macaulay will do himself the honor of waiting on Mr. and Lady Theresa Lewis to dinner on Saturday the 8th.[2]
Albany March 4. 1851

TO UNIDENTIFIED RECIPIENT, 12 MARCH 1851

MS: Mrs Michael Millgate.

Albany March 12. 1851

My dear Sir,

I shall have very great pleasure in breakfasting with you next Tuesday.[3]
Yours very truly
T B Macaulay

TO H. G. TOMKINS,[4] 22 MARCH 1851

MS: Trinity College. *Envelope:* H G Tomkins Esq / Launceston. *Subscription:* T B M.

Albany London / March 22. 1851

Sir,

I beg you to accept my thanks for the pamphlet which you have been

---

[1] See *to* Harland, 4 November 1850.

[2] TBM later excused himself on account of a heavy cold (Journal, IV, 12: 8 March).

[3] TBM, still not feeling well, cancelled this engagement too, but without naming the source of the invitation in his Journal (IV, 22: 17 March).

[4] Perhaps the Henry George Tomkins (d. *c.* 1908) who was admitted at Trinity in 1848, held various curacies, and was Vicar of Branscombe, Devonshire, 1868–72. He published several things, especially in Egyptology and biblical archaeology.

so good as to send me. It is very interesting. / I have the honor to be, /
Sir,

Your faithful Servant,

T B Macaulay

TO LORD JOHN RUSSELL, 23 MARCH 1851

MS: Public Record Office. *Mostly published:* Russell, *Later Correspondence*, 1, 207–8.

Albany March 23. 1851

Dear Lord John,

I return the inscription.[1] It is excellent. I have only one criticism, or
hypercriticism, to make. Is it quite in harmony with the rest of so fine a
composition to say that, in Lord Holland, the injured lost a fearless
advocate, and learning an accomplished scholar?[2] An injured man loses an
advocate in a very different sense from the sense in which learning loses a
scholar. Is it in perfect good taste to join together and to balance against
each other the real heartbreaking sufferings of human beings and the
figurative sufferings of an abstraction? I tell you just what strikes me at the
moment. If you, on consideration, do not agree with me, I am probably
wrong. I should not, at all events, have made so slight a remark on any
but a very short composition. In works of ten lines, every syllable should
be malignantly scrutinised.

I will not plague you with my speculations on more important and
exciting subjects. I will only say that it is impossible for any man to wish
another better than I wish you. / Ever, dear Lord John,

Yours most truly,

T B Macaulay

[1] Written by Russell for the monument to Lord Holland in Millbrook Church. Russell also
composed an epitaph for Lady Holland. TBM writes in his Journal that 'I praised more
perhaps than I should have done, because I thought that he must be at present sore, and
because I know by experience that little things sooth or irritate when people have much to
vex them' (IV, 31). Russell's ministry had just survived a crisis, defeat, and resignation, and
was now, after two weeks of uncertainty, back in power but effectively discredited.

[2] Russell originally wrote 'the injured lost in him a fearless advocate, / Society one of its
brightest ornaments, / Learning an accomplished scholar.' In the MS the lines have been
cancelled and these substituted: 'He was an accomplished scholar, / A brilliant ornament of
society' (Public Record Office). The monument itself contains the new lines.

TO LORD JOHN RUSSELL, 24 MARCH 1851

MS: Public Record Office. *Partly published:* Russell, *Later Correspondence,* I, 208.

Albany March 24 / 1851

Dear Lord John,

To day I called on Rogers, and found him examining the inscription.[1] I looked at it again, and I must say that I think that the word *bold,* between *ardent* and *intrepid,* and the word *kind,* between *courteous* and *benevolent,* may be spared.[2]

Rogers showed me Fox's criticisms. I quite dissent from Fox about the word *easy.* I think *courteous* decidedly preferable.[3]

These are trifles: but, as you have consulted me, I do not like to keep back any part of my opinion.

Ever yours truly
T B Macaulay

TO FRANCES MACAULAY, 24 MARCH 1851

MS: Huntington Library.

Albany London March 24 / 1851

Dearest Fanny,

I am pretty well at present, and indeed have had nothing to complain of except a cold which has spared nobody here. I do not expect to be able to leave town before Easter. If I do, I am afraid that I must go, not to Brighton, but to Oxford. I have a good deal of work to do in the Library of All Souls,[4] for which Milman will give me credentials if they are needed.

By the bye Milman tells me that his son,[5] who has just taken orders, thinks it necessary to dress after the present fashion of the young clergy. The lad went accordingly to a great maker of ecclesiastical garments, and ordered one of those long vests which are worn, as you have doubtless observed, by Puseyite parsons. "Oh, Sir," quoth the tailor, "I understand. An M. B. waistcoat. We make thousands of them." "An M. B. waistcoat!"

---

[1] 'Rogers agreed with my criticism; but added a good deal of criticism of his own, in a very severe tone indeed. . . . I never saw the old man more himself, more keen, more fastidious, more sarcastic' (Journal, IV, 32–3).

[2] The original text read: 'He was ardent, bold and intrepid; / In the relations of private life / Courteous, kind and benevolent.' TBM's corrections have been adopted.

[3] 'Courteous' has been substituted for 'Easy' in the line 'Courteous, kind and benevolent.'

[4] TBM does not seem to have gone until 1854: see *to* Ellis, 4 October 1854.

[5] William Henry Milman (1825–1908), B. A., Christ Church, 1847, was then Curate of Hoxton and afterwards Rector of St Augustine and St Faith.

said Milman the younger; "What does an M. B. waistcoat mean?" "Oh, Sir, all the trade know it by that name." "But what does it mean?" "The Mark of the Beast, Sir."[1]

You are right about Drummond, but quite wrong about the Speaker.[2] He acted admirably. The rule of debate is that you must abstain from personalities, but that you may be as severe on opinions, institutions, etc. as you please. You must not say that Mr. John O'Connell is a traitor or a knave. But you may say that conventual institutions are seminaries of vice and madness; and, though the expression may be violent and reprehensibly coarse, it is quite within the limits of parliamentary language. Suppose that, in a debate on the Slave trade, Mr. Wilberforce or Mr. Fox had said that a slave ship was a hell on earth – would it have been competent to a Liverpool merchant who owned slave ships to call the orator to order for indecorum? Surely not. I think Drummond's language such as no man ought to use, but such, at the same time, as is not and ought not to be prohibited by the rules of parliament.

The general aspect of affairs is disagreeable – Lord John extremely unpopular and losing weight in the house, – the schism between the Whigs and the Peelites widening rather than closing,[3] – the Irish absurd and profligate as usual. I comfort myself by thinking that, in this country, the excess of an evil scarcely ever fails to produce a remedy. I am heartily glad that I am out of the arena. I do not know what part I should have taken. My feelings and good wishes are with my old colleagues: but my judgment is with Lord Aberdeen and Sir James Graham.[4] Graham ought not to have quoted me.[5] I have published nothing on the subject. I have said nothing about it except in the security of private conversation, and it is not fair to bring before the parliament and the country what a man

1 Two years later this is told as a familiar joke, the subject being a 'Tractarian customer' (W. J. Conybeare, 'Church Parties,' *ER*, xcviii [October 1853], 315n). But Conybeare (see 20 October 1853), whose wife was the Macaulays' cousin and with whom Fanny sometimes stayed, may well have heard it first from this letter.

2 In his speech on the Ecclesiastical Titles Bill on 20 March Henry Drummond provoked repeated and furious calls to order from the Irish M.P.s by such remarks as that nunneries 'have ever been either prisons or brothels'; when he said 'What! do you think you can bring over here with impunity a cargo of blinking statues, of bleeding pictures of liquefying blood, and of the Virgin Mary's milk?' wild confusion broke out. The Speaker steadily refused to call Drummond to order, since he had made no personal reflections nor shown disrespect to the House (*Hansard*, 3rd Series, cxv, 261–80, especially 275–7).

3 After Russell's resignation on 22 February an effort to form a coalition of Whigs and Peelites failed because the latter would not support the Ecclesiastical Titles Bill.

4 That is, with the Peelites, neither protectionist nor anti-Catholic.

5 Graham is reported not as quoting but as appealing to TBM's example in his speech on the Ecclesiastical Titles Bill: 'I ask – and would that he were here to answer for himself – does the great historian of the Revolution, who is deeply imbued with Protestant feeling, and almost, indeed, with anti-Catholic antipathies – does Macaulay approve of this Bill?' (*Hansard*, 3rd Series, cxv [20 March], 309).

who has nothing to do with politics, says at a breakfast party or at a club.

Ever yours
T B Macaulay

I inclose a few lines for Selina.

TO SELINA MACAULAY, 24 MARCH 1851

MS: Trinity College.

Albany March 24. 1851

Dearest Selina,

I inclose you a cheque for the quarter. I am truly glad to learn from Fanny that you are better than when I saw you last. In a few days we shall have real spring, I hope; and then we shall all be revived. I hope that you mean to have one look at the inside of the Crystal Palace.

I have written the news – such as it is – to Fanny.

Ever yours
T B Macaulay

TO LORD MAHON, 26 MARCH 1851

MS: Stanhope Papers, Chevening.

Albany March 26 / 1851

Dear Lord Mahon,

I shall be delighted to breakfast with you on Tuesday.[1] Can you breakfast with me on Monday?[2]

We had a pleasant meeting yesterday evening at the Thatched House,[3] though we missed you.

Ever yours truly
T B Macaulay

TO FRANCES MACAULAY, 3 APRIL 1851

MS: Trinity College.

Albany April 3. 1851

Dearest Fanny,

I know of no such book as you want. All that I have ever learned

---

[1] The party were Lord and Lady Ashley, Hallam, Spencer Walpole, and Lord Carlisle (Journal, IV, 43).

[2] Hallam, Milman, Panizzi, Lord Carlisle, and Dundas breakfasted with TBM that day (Journal, IV, 41).

[3] Of The Club: Bishop Blomfield, Bishop Wilberforce, Lord Glenelg, the Reverend Charles Parr Burney, Colonel Leake, Colonel Mure, and Whewell were there (Journal, IV, 35).

about the German Universities of the 16th Century I picked up from histories of the Reformation and from tracts on the points controverted between the Lutherans and the Papists.

We are all well and thriving here. There was a great dull dinner at Westbourne Terrace yesterday – Bunsens[1] – Bouveries[2] – Macnaghtens[3] – Hankeys[4] – Nightingales.[5] However it is over; and we are all alive. [. . .][6]

TO FRANCES MACAULAY, 14 APRIL 1851

MS: Trinity College.

Albany London / April 14. 1851

Dearest Fanny,

I have the Literary Gazette.[7] I am glad that you think it satisfactory. As to the George Penne whom Mr. Dixon has discovered,[8] what evidence is there that he was about the Court at all? What evidence that he was employed in the trafficking for pardons in Somersetshire? Mr. Dixon says that he has some evidence, but does not produce it, or drop the least hint as to the place where it is to be found. I must plainly say that I do not believe him. But if such evidence should turn up, I should retract, [. . .][9]

---

[1] Baron Christian von Bunsen (1791–1860), biblical scholar and linguist, was Prussian ambassador to England, 1841–54; his wife was Welsh.

[2] Probably Philip Pleydell-Bouverie (1788–1872: *Boase*), London banker and M.P., 1830–2; 1857–65. His daughter Maria married Trevelyan's youngest brother, William, in 1852.

[3] Perhaps Elliot Macnaghten (1807–88: *Boase*), a younger brother of Sir William, a director of the East India Company, 1842–58, and Chairman, 1855–6.

[4] Thomson Hankey (1805–93: *DNB*), merchant and director of the Bank of England; M.P., 1853–68; 1874–80. He was an old friend of Trevelyan, with whom he had been at Charterhouse.

[5] William Edward Nightingale (1794–1874), Florence's father. Mrs Nightingale was the daughter of Zachary Macaulay's old ally William Smith.

[6] The last leaf of the sheet has been torn away.

[7] The first of a two-part review of Dixon's *Penn* (see next note) in the *Literary Gazette*, 29 March, is a defense of TBM against Dixon's charges on the matter of Penn.

[8] William Hepworth Dixon (1821–79: *DNB*), miscellaneous writer and editor, published on 22 March *William Penn: an Historical Biography, with an Extra Chapter on 'The Macaulay Charges.'* In this, following the lead of W. E. Forster, he argued that the Penn whom TBM attacked in the *History* for his conduct regarding the maids of Taunton was not William Penn the Quaker but a certain George Penne. At one point TBM seemed disposed to accept Dixon's argument: 'I really begin to think,' he wrote in his Journal for 14 April, 'that Penn was not the agent in the case of the Taunton girls' (IV, 55). But the doubt was only momentary: see *to* Ellis, 29 March 1856. Dixon's book is item 719 in the sale catalogue of TBM's library.

[9] The last leaf of the letter has been torn away.

TO RICHARD OWEN,[1] 14 APRIL 1851

MS: British Museum.

Albany April 14. 1851

Dear Sir,

I return, with many thanks, Sir Robert Heron's Memoirs.[2] They have amused me much; but I cannot say that they have much raised the writer in my opinion. I hope that he is a better zoologist than politician.

Ever yours truly

T B Macaulay

TO LADY TREVELYAN, 23 APRIL 1851

MS: Trinity College.

Albany April 23. 1851

Dearest Hannah,

I will dine with you on Saturday.[3] I am pretty well again – languid to be sure, but confinement and ipecacuanha explain that. I got out this fine morning and walked to Birchin Lane and back. I thought Thornton low and taciturn. We were tête a tête; but, though very friendly as he always is, he did not seem quite at ease. Perhaps it was fancy on my part. But I live in hourly dread of hearing that he has done some mad thing. Did you observe a strange advertisement in the Times of to day, put forth by that Society of which he is the chief member?[4]

I am anxious for your answer about Marian Ellis.[5] It would be really painful to me to have to tell them that we could not contrive to do them a little kindness like this.

Ever yours,

T B Macaulay

[1] Owen (1804–92: *DNB*), comparative anatomist and paleontologist, was Curator of the Hunterian Collection, Royal College of Surgeons, 1849–56, and then, partly on TBM's recommendation, was made Superintendent of the Natural History Department of the British Museum (see 27 February 1856). He was knighted on his retirement in 1884. Owen had been elected in 1845 to The Club, where TBM would have known him.

[2] *Notes*, 2nd edn, Grantham, 1851 (the first edition was privately printed). Heron (1765–1854: *DNB*), Whig M.P. for Peterborough, 1819–47, kept a menagerie and published zoological observations in his *Notes*.

[3] TBM, despite a heavy cold, had just completed his annual Easter tour with the Trevelyans, 17–21 April; this year they had gone to Southampton and Netley Abbey, to Portsmouth and the *Victory*, and to Winchester Cathedral (Journal, IV, 57–64). The dinner with the Trevelyans on 26 April was a family party.

[4] An advertisement by the Marriage Law Reform Association, informing 'persons intending to contract marriage with a deceased wife's sister' of the countries where such marriages are lawful. For Thornton's interest in this, see 27 October 1849.

[5] TBM had asked Hannah to chaperone Marian Ellis at the opening of the Great Exhibition on 1 May (Journal, IV, 67: 22 April).

TO THOMAS FLOWER ELLIS, 23 APRIL 1851

MS: Trinity College.

Albany April 23. 1851

Dear Ellis,

Lady Trevelyan will be delighted to be of any use to Marian. But her delight is not without alloy. For a certain Miss Cropper,[1] of enormous tonnage, and in build similar to the well remembered barges of Amsterdam, is to be under her Ladyship's convoy: and Marian must expect to be most particularly squeezed. I think of offering to take Baba in the Brougham,[2] though I hate such shows. In any case, if you can find no better expedient, Marian may rely on Lady Trevelyan.

Remember that you dine here on Friday the 25th.

Ever yours,
T B Macaulay

TO THOMAS FLOWER ELLIS, 24 APRIL 1851

MS: Trinity College.

Albany April 24 / 1851

Dear Ellis,

Hannah has sent me the inclosed note for Marian. It is not directed because they did not know at Westbourne Terrace whether Marian was in town or country. I suppose, after what you told me, that the whole business is otherwise arranged.

Ever yours,
T B Macaulay

TO SELINA MACAULAY, 28 APRIL 1851

MS: Trinity College.

Albany April 28. 1851

Dearest Selina,

I have not much to complain of. I have been pestered with a cold which will, I suppose, be completely removed by the fine weather. Indeed it is nearly well.

---

[1] No doubt one of the six daughters of Edward Cropper's brother John: three were unmarried in 1851. The likeliest is Mary: see 27 September.

[2] TBM had set up his carriage in January of this year: see Trevelyan, II, 291–2. The brougham – 'handsome and neat' TBM calls it – was built to his order by the London firm of Stocken (Journal, III, 143: 16 January).

I heartily wish that this week were over, – not that I entertain any of the absurd apprehensions which haunt some foolish people,[1] – but simply because I shall be bored to death. Shows all day – routs all night. Two great evening parties on Wednesday – two more on Thursday. On Saturday a dinner at the Royal Academy and a Conversazione of the Royal Society: and, from various causes, I am so situated that I cannot shirk any of these meetings without giving offence. To day I must dine, to my great discomfort, with the Benchers of Lincoln's Inn. I consider this as one of the most disagreeable weeks of my life.[2]

Dear little Alice is delightful. We passed half an hour together on Saturday in versifying the histories of the Inquisitive Chairman who looked into the Lady's card case, and of the Property Chairman who was never to be found but at the Ale house.

I should like to run down to Brighton for a day or two: but just at present it is impossible. Love to dear Fanny.

Ever yours
T B Macaulay

TO THOMAS LONGMAN, 30 APRIL 1851

MS: Longman Group Ltd.

Albany April 30 / 1851

My dear Sir,

The printers have sent me a proof of the Article on Chatham to correct.[3] But they have cut it so close that there is absolutely no margin at all. I must have another copy, with good room.

Ever yours truly
T B Macaulay

---

[1] Many nervous prophecies of public disorder to be created by the Great Exhibition had been made: see, for example, Madame de Lieven's fears and TBM's remarks on them, Trevelyan, II, 293.

[2] In the event, TBM managed to avoid the Wednesday and Thursday parties and the conversazione of the Royal Society; he had only the dinners at Lincoln's Inn and at the Royal Academy to endure (Journal, IV, 72–80: 28 April–3 May).

[3] In his Journal for 7 May TBM writes: 'Corrected the two articles on Chatham for the Travellers' Library. The second article out of all comparison the better' (IV, 83–4). The first article is that on Pitt, January 1834; the second, that on Chatham, October 1844: the two were published together this year as number 5 of the 'Traveller's Library,' a series of shilling pamphlets designed for the railway trade. The idea of the series was TBM's (Journal, IV, 2: 28 February); it began in April with his 'Hastings,' and his own essays soon proved to be the most popular items in the series (Journal, VI, 4: 10 December 1852). Since he carefully corrected them and made some revisions (see, e.g., 22 June 1851), the reprints of his essays in this series (it also included his 'Speeches on Parliamentary Reform,' 1854) have some textual authority.

TO LORD MAHON, 7 MAY 1851

MS: Stanhope Papers, Chevening. *Published:* Stanhope, *Miscellanies,* p. 113.

Albany May 7. 1851

Dear Mahon,

It seems to me very strange that, if the story about Charles and his clocks be true, it should not be in Brantome.[1] It is an anecdote after Brantome's own heart. Observe too that he mentions the report that the Emperor "avoit tenu Quelques propos légers de foy."[2]

I strongly suspect that the story originated in a frigid rhetorical conceit of Famianus Strada. You will find it in his first book. "Sæpe fabricandis horologiis, (quorum videlicet rotis multo quam fortunæ facilius tempera-bat).... operam dare."[3] Now I think it almost impossible that Strada could have written thus if the saying ascribed to Charles had already been famous. On the other hand it is easy to see how Strada's expressions, after being inaccurately translated, might be gradually distorted and expanded into something like the popular fable which Robertson has repeated.

This is my present opinion. But I never examined the matter deeply, and may very likely be mistaken.

I return Mr. Stirling's letter. His articles are, as you say, very good.

Ever yours truly

T B Macaulay

TO LORD MAHON, 14 MAY 1851

MS: Stanhope Papers, Chevening.

Albany May 14 / 1851

Dear Mahon,

I will breakfast with you on the 21st;[4] and I hope that I shall keep this engagement better than my engagement with Hallam.[5] I am ashamed of myself.

Ever yours,

T B Macaulay

---

[1] Mahon wrote to TBM enclosing a letter from William Stirling of Keir asking Mahon to enlist TBM's help in tracing an anecdote of Charles V told by Robertson. Charles, Robert-son says (*History of the Reign of Charles V,* 1809, II, 513), finding that no two of his clocks went just alike, observed that perhaps he had erred in trying to compel uniformity in the much more difficult matter of religion. Stirling (1818–78: *DNB*), afterwards Sir William Stirling-Maxwell, Bart., bibliophile, collector, and historian, was then at work on his *The Cloister Life of the Emperor Charles V,* 1852, where the question of this anecdote, with acknowledgement to TBM, is discussed in a note (3rd edn, p. 262).

[2] Pierre Brantôme, 'Charles-Quint, Empereur et Roy d'Espagne,' *Oeuvres Complètes,* Paris, 1822, I, 32.

[3] Famianus Strada, *De Bello Belgico,* Amsterdam, 1645, book I, p. 11.

[4] The other guests were Hallam, Dundas, and Stanley (Journal, IV, 97).

[5] TBM had forgotten an invitation for this day (Journal, IV, 92).

TO LORD LANSDOWNE, 17 MAY 1851

MS: The Marquess of Lansdowne.

Albany May 17. 1851

My dear Lord Lansdowne,

Though I have felt for you most sincerely, I have hitherto abstained from obtruding my feelings on you.[1] Perhaps it would be better that I should still abstain. But I learn from the newspapers of this morning that you have again taken part in the debates of the House of Lords. I therefore hope that the time has come when sympathy may have some little power to sooth even such a grief as yours. Pray do not answer this letter. Only believe that it expresses very imperfectly what is in the heart of one who has never, during twenty years, passed a day without remembering gratefully how much he owes to your kindness. / Ever, my dear Lord Lansdowne,

Your affectionate friend,

T B Macaulay

TO SIR EDWARD BULWER-LYTTON, 17 MAY 1851

MS: Hertfordshire County Council. *Published:* Lytton, *Life of Edward Bulwer, First Lord Lytton,* II, 145–7.

Albany May 17. 1851

Dear Sir Edward,

Thanks for your pamphlet,[2] which I have read, and for your play[3] which I saw yesterday night. If the play amuses and interests me as much in the perusal as it did in the representation I shall rate it much higher than the pamphlet, though the pamphlet is what everything that you write must be.

As to your scheme,[4] I am not aware that, except to four or five people

[1] Lady Lansdowne died, after a long illness, on 3 April.
[2] 'Letters to John Bull,' 1851, setting forth the Protectionist case.
[3] Bulwer-Lytton's comedy, *Not So Bad as We Seem,* was presented at Devonshire House before the Queen with a distinguished amateur company, including Bulwer-Lytton and Dickens, as a benefit for the Guild of Literature and Art (see next note).
[4] The Guild of Literature and Art, a scheme for the relief of needy writers and artists, sought to avoid the indignities of ordinary charity by creating a sort of college community where its members could live and work. The invention was Bulwer-Lytton's; Dickens was the chief supporter. Bulwer-Lytton wrote *Not So Bad as We Seem* expressly for the Guild, and Dickens devoted much of a year's labor to the cause. TBM's pessimism was, however, justified, for the Guild never flourished and was dissolved in 1897. When he first learned of the scheme TBM wrote that 'I utterly abominate it' but that he would not 'talk against the plan except to a very few friends. Let it have fair play. I am confident that it will end in the pensioning of dunces' (Journal, IV, 64–5: 21 April). TBM had long ago used the same argument in his *Knight's Quarterly* essay 'On the Royal Society of Literature,' 1823.

in very small societies, I have expressed any opinion respecting it. But I certainly do believe that its tendency is to give encouragement not to good writers, but to bad, or, at best, middling writers. And I think that you would yourself feel some misgivings if you would try your plan by a simple practical test. Suppose that you succeed beyond your expectations as to pecuniary ways and means. Suppose ten or twelve charming cottages built on the land which you so munificently propose to bestow. Suppose funds to be provided for paying your Warden and ten or twelve fellows. And suppose that you then sit down to make your choice. Whom will you chuse? Form a list of the thirty best writers now living in the United Kingdom. Then strike off from this list first all who require no assistance, and secondly all who do indeed require assistance, but who actually receive from the state pensions as large as you propose to give. I believe that you will find that five or six and twenty, if not more, of your thirty, will fall into one or the other of these classes. I apprehend therefore that you will be driven to fill your Guild with, to use the mildest term, second rate writers; and this I say on the supposition that the selection is made with the greatest judgment and with an impartiality which the history of literary institutions hardly warrants us in expecting.

There is no analogy between the case of authors and the case of actors. A theatrical fund is a very good thing. For to the existence of the theatrical art it is necessary that there should be inferior performers. That Garrick may act Hamlet, he must have a Rosencrantz and Guildenstern. That Mrs. Siddons may perform Lady Macbeth, she must have a waiting woman. Nothing can be more reasonable than that those who derive pleasure from the exertions of genius should encourage that subordinate class of artist without whose help genius would be unable to exert itself. But there is no such connection between the great and the small writer as exists between the great and the small actor. In literature, I am afraid it will always be found that a bounty on mediocrity operates as a fine on excellence.

I could say a great deal more. But I have already plagued you too long. I need not say that I do justice to your motives, and to the motives of those who are joined with you in this undertaking: and you, I am sure, will not suspect me of wanting sympathy for men of merit in distress. If your project turns out well, I shall have real pleasure in taking to myself the shame of an erroneous prediction. Hitherto you have every reason to congratulate yourself. The success of yesterday night was complete. The principal criticism which occurred to me was that the scene in the coffee-room[1] suffers from the crowding of the actors into so small a space. It seems hardly necessary to employ a spy for the purpose of watching

[1] III, i.

conspirators who talk loud treason in so thick a press of people. It is not easy to set this right. Yet perhaps you might a little thin the room of company while the most important and secret things are said. In general the stage effect was admirable: and I was particularly delighted with Lord Wilmot.[1]

Ever yours truly

T B Macaulay

TO JOHN REUBEN THOMPSON, 17 MAY 1851

MS: Columbia University. *Envelope:*[2] J R Thompson Esq / Richmond / Virginia / U.S. *Subscription:* T B M.

Albany London / May 17. 1851

Sir,

I have received the books which you were so good as to send me;[3] and I beg you to accept my thanks for them. I have read a good deal of the Westover M.S.S. and have been much interested by the pictures of Virginian life a hundred and twenty years ago. / I have the honor to be, / Sir,

Your faithful Servant,

T B Macaulay

TO LORD MAHON, 19 MAY 1851

MS: Stanhope Papers, Chevening. *Published:* Stanhope, *Miscellanies*, p. 115.

Albany May 19. 1851

Dear Mahon,

The Duke is certainly right.[4] The army of the commonwealth was clothed in red. Remember Hudibras.

> So Cromwell with deep oaths and vows
> Swore all the Commons out of th' House,
> Vowed that the redcoats would disband,
> Aye marry would they, at command,
> And trolled them on and swore, and swore,
> Till the army turned them out of door.[5]

Ever yours truly

T B Macaulay

[1] The leading role, played by Dickens.

[2] The envelope is not with the MS at Columbia but is included in a photostatic copy of the letter in the New York Public Library.

[3] See 23 December 1850.

[4] Mahon had written to TBM to say that the Duke of Wellington wanted to know when the British army first wore red coats; Mahon thought it was in the reign of Charles II, but the Duke thought that Monk's troops had been redcoats (*Miscellanies*, p. 114).

[5] Part 2, canto II, 181–4.

TO MR AND MRS JOHN SHAW LEFEVRE, 20 MAY 1851

MS: Yale University.

Mr. Macaulay will do himself the honor of waiting on Mr. and Mrs. John Shaw Lefevre to dinner on Wednesday the 28th.[1]

Albany May 20. 1851.

TO JOHN BRUCE,[2] 24 MAY 1851

MS: Trinity College.

Albany May 24. 1851

Sir,

The object which you have in view seems to me a good one;[3] and your memorial is framed in a manner to which no objection can be made. If my name can be of any use to you it is at your service. / I have the honor to be, / Sir,

Your most obedient Servant,

T B Macaulay

TO MRS CATHERINE GORE, 26 MAY 1851

MS: Bodleian Library.

Mr. Macaulay will do himself the honor of waiting on Mrs. Gore to dinner on Saturday the 7th of June.[4]

Albany May 26. 1851

TO WILLIAM EWART GLADSTONE, 7 JUNE 1851

MS: British Museum.

Albany June 7. 1851

My dear Gladstone,

I shall be most happy to breakfast with you next Thursday.[5]

1 'Not a very agreeable party. I knew hardly anybody – and Miss Murray – the maid of honour, – whom I did know – is my aversion' (Journal, IV, 108–9: 28 May).

2 Bruce (1802–69: *DNB*), editor and antiquarian specializing in 16th and 17th century history, was a founder of the Camden Society, an officer of the Society of Antiquaries, and editor of the *Gentleman's Magazine.*

3 Bruce was preparing a memorial to the Master of the Rolls requesting that scholars be permitted to use the public records without payment of fees. The memorial, which includes the signatures of TBM, Mahon, Carlyle, Dickens, and Milman, succeeded in its object. Both the memorial and Romilly's answer are in *Parliamentary Papers*, 1852, XXI, 529–31.

4 TBM's first meeting with Mrs Gore was in February of this year at Sir William Molesworth's (Journal, III, 180). The dinner on 7 June is described thus: 'very luxurious fare and very aristocratic party. Lord Douro, Lord Clanricarde, Lord Cardigan – who seemed to me to be flirting with Mademoiselle. There was Landseer and Molesworth. We had turtle, venison, and heaven knows what' (Journal, IV, 123–4).

5 The party included Lady Clanricarde, Lady Canning, Sir James (Rajah) Brooke, and 'several Puseyites whom I did not know' (Journal, IV, 130–1).

I am not quite sure that I understand the words of Juvenal which you mention. The whole passage of which they form a part is obscure and abrupt. Indeed the satire, though it contains some striking lines, was evidently never finished. Observe the repetition of the word *labor,* and the apparent antithesis between the epithets *æquus* and *pulcher.*

Hunc *labor æquus*
Provehit, et *pulchro* reddit sua dona *labori.*[1]

Does *labor æquus* mean the labour of doing justice, and *labor pulcher* the labour of earning distinction? If so, the verse would be much to our present purpose: but a harsher, stranger form of expression is scarcely to be found. I have no commentary here.

Ever yours truly
T B Macaulay

TO WILLIAM EWART GLADSTONE, 9 JUNE 1851

MS: British Museum. *Published:* John Morley, *The Life of William Ewart Gladstone,* 1903 II, 539.

Albany June 9. 1851

My dear Gladstone,

I am afraid that we must wait till Thursday. I do not much like taking words from a passage certainly obscure and probably corrupt. Could we not do better ourselves? I have made no Latin verses these many years. But I will venture. I send you three attempts.

Pulcher et ille labor, pulchros ornare labores.
Pulchrum etiam, pulchros palma donare labores.
Pulchrum etiam, pulchris meritam decernere palmam.

You will easily make better. If we can produce a tolerable line among us, we may pretend, as Lander did, that it is in Haphorstrus or Masenius.[2]

Yours ever,
T B Macaulay

---

[1] *Satires,* XVI, 56–7; modern texts read 'Hunc *favor* aequus....' The lines were evidently suggested for use on the medals of the Great Exhibition; TBM and Gladstone were both members of the committee responsible for choosing the inscriptions (see *to* Everett, 9 December 1850).

[2] See, e. g., the occasional poems scattered through Landor's *Pericles and Aspasia* (1836) and attributed to such poets as Cleobuline of Lindos, Mimnermus, Hegemon, Aletheia, and others. In the end the committee chose, for the three classes of medals, lines from Manilius, Ovid, and Claudian: see Henry Cole's Introduction to the *Official Descriptive and Illustrated Catalogue* of the Exhibition, 1851, I, 32.

TO JOHN EVELYN DENISON, 17 JUNE 1851

MS: University of Nottingham.

Albany June 17. 1851

Dear Denison,

I shall be most happy to dine with you on Saturday the 28th.[1]

Ever yours truly
T B Macaulay

TO FRANCES MACAULAY, 18 JUNE 1851

MS: Trinity College.

Albany June 18 / 1851

Dearest Fanny,

Selina sent me a packet to day in which was a letter for you. I broke it open supposing it to be for me. The mistake was of no consequence: for the letter was merely a call of the London and N W company for forty five pounds. You are not I suppose curious to see the document. I shall take care that the needful is done in good time.[2]

Love to Mrs. Rose. [. . .][3]

TO SELINA MACAULAY, 18 JUNE 1851

MS: Yale University.

Albany June 18 / 1851

Dearest Selina,

I will take care that all shall be done in good time.

We shall be delighted to see you here; and I think that I can promise you a great treat.[4]

Ever yours,
T B Macaulay

---

1 The party included Drummond, Labouchere, Bishop Wilberforce, Hallam, and Lord and Lady Mahon. 'I thought – perhaps wrongly – that I talked very successfully. Certainly I sometimes fixed their attention and sometimes made them roar with laughter' (Journal, IV, 151).

2 TBM paid the call for both Fanny and Selina – 'they are welcome' (Journal, IV, 142).

3 The last leaf of the letter has been torn away.

4 Selina came to town in July for the Exhibition (Journal, IV, 158).

TO GEORGE ROBERT GLEIG, 22 JUNE 1851

MS: National Library of Scotland.

Albany June 22.[1] 1851

My dear Sir,

Your letter has just been put into my hands.[2] I am very sensible of your good nature, and sorry that I should have wounded your feelings. Had I at all foreseen, when I was writing for the Edinburgh Review, that my papers would be remembered beyond the quarter of a year which is the ordinary life of such compositions, I should have abstained from expressing myself in that acrimonious and scornful manner which has always been but too fashionable in critical journals. I daily regret the asperity with which I inconsiderately treated writers much less deserving of respect than yourself. / Believe me, / My dear Sir,

Your faithful Servant,

T B Macaulay

TO SELINA MACAULAY, 24 JUNE 1851

MS: Trinity College. *Envelope:* Miss Macaulay / Temple House / Brighton. *Subscription:* T B M.

Albany London / June 24. 1851

Dearest Selina,

I send you a cheque for the quarter. We hope to see you here soon. The weather is inviting; and the transept of the Glass Palace, with its trees and fountains, looks glorious in the midsummer sunshine [. . . .][3]

TO FRANCES MACAULAY, 25 JUNE 1851

MS: Huntington Library. *Extracts published:* Trevelyan, II, 226n.

Albany London / June 25. 1851

Dearest Fanny,

It is not from any want of respect or tenderness for my uncle's memory

---

[1] In his Journal TBM says that he answered Gleig on the 23rd (IV, 146); but he may have been bringing up his Journal after a lapse and so have mistaken the date. '22' is quite clear in the MS.

[2] TBM's essay on Warren Hastings, which reviewed Gleig's biography of Hastings, had just been reprinted in the 'Traveller's Library' series. At Longman's request TBM had omitted the first two paragraphs of the essay and a few other passages containing his severer remarks on Gleig (Journal, IV, 18; 25: 13 and 21 March). On the day before this letter was written TBM met Gleig in St James's Street: 'he thanked me for taking him out of the pillory. I had rather that he had left his thanks unuttered. I did not know how to look' (Journal, IV, 143).

[3] A strip about an inch deep has been cut from the bottom of the letter: probably only the closing and signature are missing.

that I have not done what Mary asked.[1] I loved him and honoured him most sincerely. But the truth is that I have not been able to satisfy myself. People who are not accustomed to this sort of literary labour often imagine that a man can do it as he can work a sum in the rule of three, or answer an invitation to dinner. But the truth is that these short compositions in which every word ought to tell strongly, and in which there ought to be at once some point and much feeling, are not to be produced by mere labour. There must be a concurrence of luck with industry. It was some weeks before I could satisfy myself with the inscription for Metcalfe. Lord John has been working many months on epitaphs for Lord and Lady Holland. I have had them submitted to me twice; and I am not sure that they are yet finally settled. Lord Lansdowne talked with me three years ago about an inscription for a monument which he is setting up to his ancestor Sir William Petty. Lord L could not please himself; I could not please myself; and the monument is, I believe, still blank.[2] I mention these to show you how great the difficulty of these little performances is. It is natural that those who have not considered the matter should think that a man who has sometimes written ten or twelve effective pages in a day must certainly be able to write five lines in less than a year. But it is not so; and, if you think over the really good epitaphs which you have read, and consider how small a proportion they bear to the thousands that have been written by clever men, you will own that I am right.

Kindest love to Mrs. Rose. Is Parker at the Temple? If he is remember me to him and all most affectionately.

Ever yours
T B Macaulay

TO WILLIAM EWART GLADSTONE, 25 JUNE 1851

MS: British Museum.

Albany June 25. 1851

Dear Gladstone,

I am sorry that I cannot be with you this afternoon, and still more sorry that I shall not be able to join Mrs. Gladstone's party in the evening.[3] As to the inscription I have really nothing more to suggest. Perhaps three

---

[1] TBM had been asked in November 1850 to write an epitaph for Thomas Babington; for the text see 24 September 1851.
[2] Lansdowne's monument to Petty, dated 1858, is in the Abbey Church, Romsey, Hampshire. The monument bears an inscription of some forty words.
[3] TBM dined alone on this evening (Journal, IV, 148).

or four words of simple Latin prose would be better than that unfortunate line of Juvenal.[1]

> Ever yours truly
> T B Macaulay

TO CHRISTIAN BERNHARD TAUCHNITZ, 5 JULY 1851

Text: Bernhard Tauchnitz, 1837–1887, p. 108.

> Albany, London, July 5, 1851.

I am very sensible of the punctuality and liberality of your dealing. I am glad that our joint speculation has turned out so well.[2]

TO LORD MAHON, 15 JULY 1851

MS: Stanhope Papers, Chevening.

> Albany London / July 15. 1851

My dear Mahon,

I propose to go down by the Express Train which will reach Edenbridge at half after five.[3] I shall write to order a fly to be in readiness. I suppose that I shall be at Chevening by a quarter to seven on Thursday afternoon.

> Ever yours truly
> T B Macaulay

TO FRANCES MACAULAY, 21 JULY 1851

MS: Trinity College.

> Albany London / July 21. 1851

Dearest Fanny,

I do not know with whom Price[4] converses or corresponds. The general, I should say the universal, sentiment of the people that I have seen is that Horseman's[5] case has completely broken down, and that he is

---

[1] See 7 June.

[2] TBM received £64 from Tauchnitz the day before – 'acceptable indeed' (Journal, IV, 160).

[3] TBM went to Chevening – his first visit – on the 17th, made an excursion with Lord and Lady Mahon to Knole on the 18th, and returned to London on the next day (Journal, IV, 170–9).

[4] Bonamy Price, with whom, and his wife Lydia Rose Price, Fanny was staying.

[5] Edward Horsman (1807–76: *DNB*), M.P. for Cockermouth and a regular critic of the ecclesiastical establishment. He attacked Bishop Monk in the House of Commons on 1 July over an estate which, he claimed, Monk had privately sought to lease for his own profit instead of abiding by his predecessors' decision to let the lease fall in for the benefit of the see. Monk replied in *The Times* of 8 July and published a few days later a pamphlet of 'Documents Respecting the Estate of Horfield Manor'; the evidence makes it clear that Horsman's attack was malicious. See also Monk's 'Mr. Horsman's Statement Respecting the

as troublesome, as rancorous, and as paltry a puppy as ever yelped at the heels of a quiet traveller. I have no love for Bishops in general or for Monk in particular. But I always thought that the charge must be grossly exaggerated. For, though a weak, heavy, pompous man, Monk was always not only just but generous in money matters.

I have been at Chevening on a visit to the Mahons. We went to Knowle which I admired more than I can express. To be sure I would sooner live in a cottage or in a garret.

Love to Lydia.

Yours ever

T B Macaulay

TO UNIDENTIFIED RECIPIENT, 28 JULY 18[51]

Text: S. J. Davey, Supplementary Catalogue, n.d. [*c.* 1880?], item 6610, 4pp. 8vo: dated 28 July 1837.[1]

[London]

If you will look into the collection of Records appended to the third Book of Burnet's History of the Reformation . . . . You will find abundant evidence that my account of Cranmer's opinions is correct. . . . To Question 11 – whether any other than a Bishop may make a priest, – Cranmer replies, 'A Bishop may make a priest by the Scripture; and so may Princes and Governors also, and that by the authority of God committed to them; and the people also by their election.'[2]

TO LADY THERESA LEWIS, 2 AUGUST 1851

MS: New York Public Library.

Albany August 2. 1851

Dear Lady Theresa,

I am sorry to say that on the 6th I shall be more than a hundred miles from your very pleasant party at Kent House.[3]

Ever yours truly

T B Macaulay

Horfield Manor Lease Considered,' 1852. Monk was defended in both the Lords and Commons by Bishop Wilberforce, Gladstone, and others, but *The Times*, in leaders of 8 and 17 July refused to allow that he had not acted dishonorably.

1 This date is clearly impossible; TBM's '51' may easily be mistaken for '37'. The same letter is listed in John Waller, Catalogue 129 (1881), item 140, where it is dated 1851.

2 See 22 January 1849.

3 TBM had already taken a house at Malvern. He spent the night of 6 August in the Euston Hotel, his servants having preceded him to Malvern; next day he followed, and remained there until 29 September (Journal, IV, 194; 266).

TO UNIDENTIFIED RECIPIENT, 2 AUGUST 1851

MS: Trinity College.

Albany August 2. 1851

Sir,

I am sorry that I cannot do what you ask. But the work which you propose to me is one, which, even if I had leisure for it, I could not, I am certain, perform in such a way as to satisfy myself.

I am greatly obliged to you for the volume which you have been so good as to send me. The institution of the Society[1] in which you are interested cannot, of course, occupy a large space in the history of the reign of William the third. But it certainly ought to be mentioned. / I have the honour to be, / Sir,

Your most obedient Servant,
T B Macaulay

TO MARGARET TREVELYAN, 10 AUGUST 1851

MS: Trinity College.

Malvern August 10 / 1851

My dearest Baba,

Another letter from my darling. I am much, very much obliged to you. It is a great happiness to me to think that you remember me; and nothing that interests you can be too trivial to interest me.

I live here in utter solitude, and enjoy it much. Yesterday indeed I was accosted by a man whose face I seemed to myself to recollect, but whose name had completely escaped me. He was very familiar, told me that he had been lamed by tumbling from a coach on the Allegany Mountains, gave me the history of his water cure, and asked permission to call. I could not refuse. But where or when I met him, at Calcutta or at Rome, – whether he is a member of parliament or an Edinburgh elector, a barrister on the Northern Circuit or a fellow of Trinity I have not the faintest notion. He will come, I hope, when I am out, and leave his card.[2] He is the only acquaintance, if I can call him so, that I have seen.

I read and walk all day. Walking indeed is matter of choice with me. For there are vehicles without number; and, on the high roads, I am

---

[1] Perhaps the Society for Promoting Christian Knowledge, founded in 1698. It receives no mention in the *History*.

[2] He left a card on the next day (Journal, IV, 201) and proved to be Edward Twistleton (1809–74: *DNB*), a barrister who held places on various official commissions, who had many friends in common with TBM, and who, as a resident of the Albany, was presumably a familiar face to TBM. Twistleton had been in America courting the woman he married in 1852, Ellen Dwight of Boston.

earnestly pressed to mount. Yesterday a hearse passed, returning from a funeral, and the driver, a most solemn looking being, asked me whether I would like a ride "There is plenty of room, Sir." I could not help laughing out. "All in good time," I said; "some day or other I shall want you; but I am not ready for you yet." He did not in the least relax his gravity. "I meant, Sir, that there was room on the box." I declined the privilege however of exhibiting myself to all Malvern on the box of a hearse, and pursued my ramble on foot.

To day I went to the Abbey Church – really a venerable and beautiful Church, and not a bad sermon. I think the Choir was under repair when we were here in 1846; for it did not then please me as it does now. You, I suppose, have forgotten all about that tour, – my rage at Spetchley and the imbecillity of the Worcester waiter excepted.

Love to all.   Ever yours
                                                            T B Macaulay

Just post time.

to THOMAS FLOWER ELLIS, 12 AUGUST 1851

MS: Trinity College.

                                        Malvern August 12 / 1851

Dear Ellis,

I have now been here several days. Fine days they have been, though not very bright. The mornings have been grey and dull; and, though the sun has never failed to shine out, there has always been more or less of haze floating in the air. Such an atmosphere is not without its beauties. It produces some very pleasing effects. But, on the whole, a more brilliant sky would suit better with the scenery of Malvern. It is a charming place, an island of mountain country in the midst of a vast ocean of cornfield, meadow, park, pleasure ground, and orchard. The hills seem wilder and bolder on account of the richness and softness of the plain, and the plain richer and softer on account of the wildness of the hills. The high road is in general a sort of boundary line. You look one way and you might fancy yourself in the Highlands of Scotland. You look the other way, and you see a boundless expanse of English harvest, garden and pasture. But I am getting into the style of the Malvern guide. However I will add that the Abbey Church here is very fine. I have seen worse Cathedrals. I have a very respectable and comfortable house and grounds. The Lodge is the name by which my dwelling is known, and you may, if you chuse, direct to me there. But Malvern, Worcestershire, is sufficient.

I have an acquaintance or two here. But Senior is the only person with whom I am at all intimate. I could do very well alone. For I have plenty of books; and there are few days on which I do not walk six hours at the least. I am reading the Iliad, and find myself forced to modify a little, perhaps I might say not a little, my opinions on the Homeric controversy. I am also reading Lessing's Laocoon with great delight, admiration and edification. I am ashamed to add that in the evenings I amuse myself with *Martin, ou l'Enfant Trouvé.*[1]

I shall however be very glad when you come to play Friday to my Robinson Crusoe. Perhaps you can now tell me what your arrangements are likely to be. If you are certain to be here on Friday the 29th I will get tickets for the Messiah.[2] They are only 15s. each for the best places; and we can most easily do the whole between breakfast and dinner – I might almost say lunch. We must of course see Worcester Cathedral; and we never shall see it to so much advantage. – I should hope that you can come at latest on Tuesday the 26th.

Kindest remembrances to Marian. I am afraid that this will arrive too late to convey birthday felicitations and good wishes to the fair Lucy.[3]

Ever yours
T B Macaulay

TO EDWARD MATTHEW WARD,[4] 12 AUGUST 1851

MS: Berg Collection, New York Public Library. *Published:* James Dafforne, *Life and Works of Edward Matthew Ward R.A.*, 1879, pp. 57–8.

Malvern August 12. 1851

Sir,
I shall be most happy to see you when I return to town, which will be at the beginning of October.

---

[1] By Eugène Sue, 1846–7.
[2] At the Worcester Musical Festival: see 30 August.
[3] TBM writes in his Journal for 19 April 1849 of a Lucy Hayward, 'a handsome girl from Liverpool,' who dined with him at Ellis's (I, 580). This is no doubt Lucy Haywood (see 8 September 1852), daughter of Ellis's Liverpool friend Francis Haywood; TBM also wrote the name as 'Hayward' in his Journal for 23 May 1851 (IV, 103).
[4] Ward (1816–79: *DNB*) was a painter specializing in historical subjects, especially of the 17th and 18th centuries. He had just received a commission to paint eight pictures for the Commons corridor in the new Houses of Parliament, and he found TBM a particularly helpful source in developing these. Their subjects were The Seven Bishops, William and Mary, Monk Declaring for a Free Parliament (see below), the Last Sleep of Argyll, Alice Lisle, Charles II at Dover, the Execution of Montrose, and the Escape of Charles II with Jane Lane. The original sketches for three of these – Argyll, Alice Lisle, and William and Mary – all bear quotations from TBM's *History* (R. J. B. Walker, *A Catalogue of Paintings, Drawings, Sculpture, and Engravings in the Palace of Westminster*, Part IV, 1962). Ward also based his painting of the death of Charles II, now in the Walker Art Gallery, Liverpool, on the description of the scene in the *History*. In May 1853 Ward made an excellent oil sketch of TBM in his study in the Albany, one of a series by Ward of authors in their studies; it is now in the National Portrait Gallery and is reproduced as the frontispiece to this volume.

As to Monk's declaration for a free parliament,[1] you might take the moment, described by Pepys,[2] when the General came out into Westminster Hall, and was received there with rapturous acclamations. I write from memory; for I have not Pepys with me here. But I think the night scene would be the best – the place near the gate of the Temple, where the bonfires were thickest, and where the mob attacked the house of Praise God Barebones and broke the windows. Or you might take the front of Somerset House, where the rejoicings were also very tumultuous. The central group might be round a fire where a rump of beef is roasting – a lawyer's clerk eagerly reading aloud a great black letter broadside headed "The speech of his Excellency the Lord General" – a soldier of the Coldstream regiment, which, I think, was Monk's own, is between two portly citizens, one shaking his hand, the other filling him a large bell mouthed glass out of a flask, – a cavalier in tarnished embroidery cocking up his hat, – an older royalist with a long white beard, nursed ever since the execution of Charles the First, clasping his hands, lifting his eyes, and seeming to be thanking God for the prospect of a reformation, a stern looking Puritan biting his nails in the background, a party of boys and girls making game of him and holding up to him a stuffed effigy of a Saint with lank hair and hideously long face. But I run on, I am afraid, to very little purpose. / I have the honor to be, / Sir,

Your faithful Servant

T B Macaulay

MS: Trinity College.

Malvern August 16 / 1851

Dear Ellis,

I am truly glad to learn that you hope to be here on Tuesday the 26th. I advise you to start from the Euston Square station at a quarter after ten. You will be able to take your place in a carriage which will go the whole journey to Worcester. You will reach Worcester at twenty minutes after three; and I can meet you there. Of course you will let me know what your arrangements are.

Just at this moment a gentle shower is falling, just sufficient to cool the air and lay the dust. In general there has been glorious harvest weather.

---

[1] Ward's painting of 'General Monk Declaring for a Free Parliament' does not follow TBM's suggestions; it is an interior scene based, according to the *Art Journal*, N.S., VII (1868), 7, on the description in Guizot's *Monk: Chute de la République et Rétablissement de la Monarchie en Angleterre*, 1851, p. 126.

[2] *Diary*, 11 February 1660; Pepys saw Monk at the Guildhall, not Westminster Hall.

Yesterday the atmosphere was remarkably clear. I passed a long time on the crest of the hill. I saw not only Worcester which is always an important part of the view, but Gloucester and Hereford, the white villas of Cheltenham, the junction of the Avon and Severn under the fine Church of Tewkesbury, the Wrekin, the Sugar Loaf mountain in Monmouthshire, and the whole range of the Cotswold hills. There is certainly no other place in the Kingdom from which three Cathedrals are visible.

I shall be delighted to see your romance. I hardly know what to say about the task which you have assigned to me,[1] and which is much more arduous than yours. Your two pictures represent what is daily taking place in all parts of the world, with slight differences of costume. But mine represent what can scarcely be supposed to take place in England and in our time. In France it is possible that there may be such scenes. There doubtless were such in England not much more than a hundred years ago. But our modern usages make the thing almost impossible. And the interest is greatly diminished if the action, instead of coming home to our business and bosoms, is laid in a distant age or country. But Genius triumphs over all difficulties; and I have thought of an expedient for reconciling everything. I shall for the present keep my plan to myself –

> Be innocent of the knowledge
> Till thou applaud the deed.[2]

Ever yours,
T B Macaulay

TO MARGARET TREVELYAN, 19 AUGUST 1851

MS: Trinity College. *Partly published:* Trevelyan, II, 210–11.

Malvern August 19 / 1851

Dearest Baba,

I suppose that you are at Enmore again after your Plymouth trip. Pray give me an account of what you saw. My recollections of my only visit to Plymouth are very sad; and so should your mamma's be. I could cry to think of those times, though I managed not to cry then.[3]

My days glide away here strangely fast. Except an occasional walk with Senior, I have no intercourse with anybody. He asked me to dinner. But he dines at two; and I cannot eat at that hour; so that I escaped. I have just

---

[1] TBM began a romance, presumably in response to a request from Ellis, on the day before this letter (Journal, IV, 208); he finished it on 26 August, read it to Ellis on the 28th, and then burned it (Journal, IV, 222; 224), saying that 'none of these idle *facetiæ* shall ever, if I can help it, rise up against me.' He and Ellis had competed in writing romances in the year before (Journal, III, 35–42: 21 September–1 October 1850).
[2] *Macbeth*, III, ii, 45–6.
[3] TBM and Hannah were at Plymouth on their way to India: see 24 February 1834.

now, on returning from a ramble of seven hours into the heart of Herefordshire, found on my table a card from Lord Gainsborough.[1] I must
return his call; and that will be, I hope, all that will pass between us. For
he is the greatest fool and bore in the whole peerage.

No – no society for me, but the society of the hills and woods, of the
flowers and streams, of the rapid Severn and the gentle Wye. Let me hold
communion with nature, and avoid all fellowship with men. Towns, –
who can bear the thought of those labyrinths of brick, overhung by clouds
of smoke, and roaring like Niagara with the wheels of drays, chariots,
flies, cabs, and omnibuses. Give me rural seclusion like this, especially
when I can smell, as I now do, a leg of mutton on the spit for my dinner,[2] –
not your Middlesex mutton, fit only to make tallow candles of, but hill
mutton, fed on the heath round the Worcestershire beacon. Truly
judicious was the poet who sang –

> "Long live the mountain scenery!
> Long live the mountain mutton!
> Hyde Park, with all its Queenery,
> Lace, China, plate, machinery,
> Or Milman's City Deanery
> I prize not at a button."

"Queenery" – a word invented with bold but laudable poetical license:
for, even in his boldness, our poet is always judicious. Àpropos of poets,
I finished the Iliad to day. I had not read it through since the end of 1837,
when I was at Calcutta, and when you often called me away from my
studies to show you pictures and to feed the crows. I never admired the
old fellow so much, or was so strongly moved by him. What a privilege
genius like his enjoys. I could not tear myself away. I read the last five
books at a stretch during my walk to day, and was at last forced to turn
into a by path, lest the parties of walkers should see me blubbering for
imaginary beings, the creations of a ballad-maker who has been dead two
thousand seven hundred years. What is the power and glory of Cæsar and
Alexander to that? – Think what it would be to be assured that the inhabitants of Monomotapa[3] would weep over one's writings, Anno Domini
4551. – That is the parallel case. Loves and kind remembrances to all.

Ever yours,
T B Macaulay

1 Charles Noel, formerly Baron Barham, was created Earl of Gainsborough in 1841; he was
Baptist Noel's brother. His wife, TBM wrote, was worse than her husband: 'for she is blue'
(Journal, IV, 215: 20 August).
2 'Dined on an excellent leg of mountain mutton' (Journal, IV, 213: 19 August).
3 A place name in south-east Africa on old maps. But in his landlady's library TBM had come
across Diderot's *Les Bijoux Indiscrets* with its false imprint *Au Monomotapa* [Paris 1748],
and that is no doubt what put it into his head (see *to* Ellis, 24 August).

TO THOMAS FLOWER ELLIS, 21 AUGUST 1851

MS: Trinity College. *Mostly published:* Trevelyan, II, 295–6.

Malvern August 21 / 1851

Dear Ellis,

I shall expect you on Wednesday next. Remember to get a ticket for Worcester, and a place in a Worcester carriage. I shall meet you at the station, nothing unforeseen preventing. If you do not at once find me there come hither with all speed. I have settled everything about the Messiah. You may go to the Cathedral in your dressing gown and slippers if you like.

There may be some difficulty about conveyances during the festival. But the supply here is immense. On every road round Malvern coaches and flies pass you every ten minutes, to say nothing of irregular vehicles. For example, the other day I was overtaken by a hearse as I was strolling along and reading the night expedition of Diomede and Ulysses. "Would you like a ride, Sir?" said the driver. "Plenty of room." I could not help laughing. "I dare say, I shall want such a carriage some day or other. But I am not ready yet." The fellow with the most consummate professional gravity answered "I meant, Sir, that there was room for you on the box." I was not in the mind, however, to drive through Malvern on the box of a hearse, and excused myself.

Who is Macfarlan?[1] I see no paper here but the Times and the Literary Gazette. If there is any thing remarkable by Panizzi, bring it down with you.

I do not think that I ever, at Cambridge or in India, did a better day's work in Greek than to day. I have read at one stretch fourteen books of the Odyssey, from the sixth to the nineteenth inclusive. I did it while walking to Worcester and back. I have a great deal to say about the old fellow. I admire him more than ever. But I am now quite sure that the Iliad is a piece of mosaic, made very skilfully long after his time out of several of his lays, with bits here and there of the compositions of inferior minstrels. But this we shall have plenty of time to discuss.

Yours ever
T B Macaulay

---

[1] Charles MacFarlane (1799–1858: *DNB*), a miscellaneous writer who produced histories, novels, biographies, and books of travel, many of them for Charles Knight. For the controversy involving him, see 24 August.

TO MRS CATHERINE GORE, 21 AUGUST 1851

Text: Lady Charnwood, *An Autograph Collection and the Making of It,* 1930, pp. 123–4.

Malvern. / August 21. 1851.

Dear Mrs. Gore,

I am here; and here I shall probably remain till the nights grow long and the fires are lighted. I am not indeed undergoing any of the quack remedies for which Malvern is famous. I sit in no wet sheet. I subject the nape of my neck to no water-spout. I dine at seven; and I do not absolutely reject cider cup,[1] or that delicious perry which, within sight of the window where I am writing, was passed upon Tom Jones for Champagne and on Sophia Western for Sack.[2] I walk eighteen or twenty miles a day, rest myself by lying with my book on the crest of a hill from which I can see at once the Wrekin and Lansdowne, the whole Cotswold range on one side and the Black Mountains of Brecknockshire on the other, Cheltenham with its white villas, the Towers of Worcester and Gloucester Cathedrals, and the fine Church of Tewkesbury at the junction of the Severn and the Avon. I know no scenery which suits my taste so thoroughly. The Highlands of Scotland are seldom, as far as my experience goes, seen for more than a very few hours in a week by the light of a brilliant sun; and even when the weather is fine, the sterility and solitude have a depressing effect on my spirits. In grandeur these hills of course will bear no comparison with those of Argyle-shire and Inverness-shire. But here everything is cheerful and bright. You have just as much wildness and boldness as is sufficient to heighten the effect of that boundless expanse of cornfield, meadow, park, apple orchard, which lies below. But I am getting into the style of the Malvern guide; and it is high time to stop.

There is very little chance of my visiting Hampshire[3] for some time to come. But be assured that, if I should be in your neighbourhood, I shall not forget your invitation. It is unnecessary for me, I hope, to say how grateful I am for your good opinion, or how proud of it.

Pray remember me with all kindness to Miss Gore;[4] and believe me ever, / My dear Madam,

Yours most faithfully,

T. B. Macaulay.

---

[1] 'I have got at last a keg of cider which I hope will prove good' (Journal, IV, 214: 19 August).
[2] *Tom Jones,* book 10, ch. 3.
[3] Mrs Gore lived at Linwood, Lyndhurst, Hampshire, in the New Forest.
[4] Cecilia Anne Mary Gore (d. 1879), married Lord Edward Thynne in 1853. TBM had met her earlier this year: see 26 May.

TO THOMAS FLOWER ELLIS, 24 AUGUST 1851

MS: Trinity College. *Extracts published:* Trevelyan, II, 296.

Malvern August 24. 1851

Dear Ellis,

If you have a copy of Æschines's speeches, I wish you would bring it with you. I am reading to day, with the greatest delight, Demosthenes's speech on the Embassy; and I want to see the answer.

I am expecting you on Wednesday, and planning various excursions. We can easily see Hereford between breakfast and dinner one day, and Gloucester on another. Cheltenham and Tewkesbury with its fine Church are still more easily accessible. I only hope that the weather will be fine. To day the change of the moon was attended by violent rain and wind. But the rain is over; the afternoon has been brilliant; and I hope that we have another glorious month before us.

Thank you for the Examiner. I suppose that you were the kind person who sent it. I think the chastisement administered to Mr. Macfarlan most richly deserved.[1] Who is he? Is he the man who wrote history for Charles Knight? If so, he is a poor dirty creature. I remember that he almost transcribed, without acknowledgment, whole pages from my papers on Clive and Hastings, and mentioned my name only to abuse me.[2]

Pray bring your romance. I have begun mine. If you want stimulants, you will find them here in abundance. My hostess, a most respectable maiden lady, has left her library here. I examined it. The very first book on which I lighted was Les Bijoux Indiscrets – the next La Fontaine's Tales: – then came Bernard's Art d'Aimer,[3] Voltaire's novels, Lord Strangford's

---

[1] In July Gladstone had published an open letter to Lord Aberdeen, written with Panizzi's assistance, on the political prisoners in Naples, and had followed this with a second letter a few days later. Gladstone's protests against the cruelty of the Neapolitan government stirred a commotion; among the replies was one by MacFarlane, 'The Neapolitan Government and Mr. Gladstone,' a defense of the Bourbon regime. An article in the *Examiner* for 16 August (no doubt by Panizzi) disposed of MacFarlane's facts; its arguments were repeated in Panizzi's article on the question in the *ER*, XCIV (October 1851), 490–526. TBM, meeting Gladstone in early March 1852, 'spoke, as I thought, highly of his late pamphlets' (Journal, V, 15).

[2] Not quite fair: MacFarlane's *Our Indian Empire*, 1844 (in Knight's 'Library for the Times') makes considerable use of TBM's essays on Clive and Hastings, usually with approval. MacFarlane, who was a friend of Sir Elijah Impey's son, treats TBM roughly for failing to take into account the evidence of Impey's conduct in the matter of Nuncomar's execution (I, 287). In his *Reminiscences*, 1917, p. 180, MacFarlane is even angrier, speaking of 'the reckless aspersions and ignorant, blundering, inconsiderate calumnies of the Right Hon. Thomas Babington Macaulay.'

[3] Pierre-Joseph Bernard, *L'Art d'Aimer*, Paris, 1775: 'Much more indecency than wit or spirit' (Journal, IV, 218: 23 August).

Translations from Camoens,[1] Prior's works, in short a collection fit for Holywell Street.[2]

Carlyle is here undergoing the water cure. I have not seen him. But his water doctor said to Senior the other day, "You wonder at his eccentric opinions, and style. It is all stomach. I shall set him to rights. He will go away quite a different person." If he goes away writing common sense in good English, I shall declare myself a convert to hydropathy. At present I believe that Doctor and patient are quacks alike.[3] You shall however have water in plenty. I have a well polished ἀσάμινθος[4] for you, into which going you may wash, and out of which you may come, looking like a God. If any more of Arthur's bills[5] are come, bring them with you.

Ever yours,

T B Macaulay

TO FRANCES MACAULAY, 26 AUGUST 1851

MS: Trinity College.

Malvern August 26 / 1851

Dearest Fanny,

I am sorry to have missed you in town. But I cannot say that I am sorry to be out of town. For, much as I love London, I find, as I grow older, that it does not do to sleep, three hundred and sixty five nights running, in that great mass of river fog and coal smoke. I have a pleasant hermitage here, rise early, walk twenty miles a day with Homer or Demosthenes in my pocket, come back from my ramble very ready for my dinner, and soon after dinner am very ready for my bed. This has been my life for near three weeks of glorious weather. To day is an exception. A chill ungenial rain is falling; and the whole valley of the Severn is overhung by a dreary damp mist. I could almost find it in my heart to order a fire.

I have little society here. Senior sometimes joins me in a walk. I have no other associate at present. But Lord Lansdowne is expected. Ellis, I hope, will be able to pay me a visit soon. We have long had it in con-

---

[1] *Poems, from the Portuguese of Luis de Camoens*, 1803: 'Poor stuff – the feeble echo of Little's poetry' (Journal, IV, 218).

[2] Where the dealers in indecent literature were concentrated.

[3] The doctor who popularized the Malvern water-cure was James Manby Gully (1808–83: *DNB*). Carlyle wrote to Emerson from Malvern that the town contained various '*litterateurs* (T. B. Macaulay in his hired villa for one): but the mind rather shuns than seeks them' (25 August: Charles Eliot Norton, ed., *Correspondence of Thomas Carlyle and Ralph Waldo Emerson 1834–1872*, 1883, II, 207).

[4] Trevelyan's note explains: 'The Homeric word for a bath. The sentence is, of course, a ludicrously literal translation from the Greek' (II, 296n).

[5] TBM had paid £75 of Arthur's bills on 24 June (Journal, IV, 147).

templation to visit Worcester and Gloucester Cathedrals together; and this is a good opportunity. My history stands still, except that I turn over some subjects in my mind, and I hope not altogether without advantage.

I must tell you of our Uncle James Mills?[1] Just before I left town[2] he came to the Albany, ranted, stormed, pulled out his purse and protested that he had only a sovereign and a few shillings. I refused to shake hands with him, and told him that his infamous conduct had destroyed all ties between us, and that I meant to have no connection with him. But I gave him a cheque for twenty pounds. He took the cheque, put it in his pocket, and began to rant again. 'Money, Sir. Do you think that I came here for money? You shall hear me, Sir. By God you shall hear me. Money is the root of all evil. I hate it. I detest it. I wish never to see it or hear of it.' With these words in his mouth and the cheque in his pocket he walked off.

Well, I was scarcely here when I received a letter from him[3] to say that the twenty pounds were gone, – gone, observe, in a fortnight, – and that I must send him more. I returned no answer. Then came another letter and another. Still I returned no answer. He has been daily at the Albany trying to learn something from the porters there. At last comes a letter from him – to whom do you think? – to Elizabeth,[4] intreating her to write to him by return of post and to explain to him his nephew's extraordinary silence. This would be merely comical. But I foresee that, when I return to London, I shall be forced either to let him draw on me to the extent of two or three hundred a year or to give him in charge to the police; and I am fully determined to take the latter course.[5] It is certainly disagreeable to be obliged to resort to the protection of the law against so near a relation. But everybody that has ever had anything to do with him will acquit me of unnecessary harshness; and, little as I should like to see my name in a Marlborough Street[6] report on such an occasion, I should like still less to be pillaged and insulted during several years by so odious a fellow.

Love to dear Selina. All the news from Enmore is good, except that sweet little Alice complains of the gout in her foot.

Ever yours,
T B Macaulay

---

1 TBM first began this sentence with 'Did I' and then substituted 'I must' without removing the question mark at the end.
2 24 July (Journal, IV, 182–3).
3 15 August (Journal, IV, 206).
4 TBM's housekeeper, wife of his servant William Williams. Elizabeth's age is given as 39 in the Census of 1841 but as 51 in that of 1851.
5 TBM did not go to this length, but he did attempt to break completely with his Uncle James: see 14 October.
6 The police station nearest TBM in London.

TO JOHN HARLAND, 26 AUGUST 1851

MS: Manchester Central Library.

Malvern August 26 / 1851

Sir,

Your letter has followed me hither. When I return to London I shall find there the volume which you have been so good as to send me.[1] I beg you to accept my thanks for this fresh proof of your kindness, and to believe me

Your faithful Servant
T B Macaulay

TO SELINA MACAULAY, 30 AUGUST 1851

MS: Trinity College. *Envelope:* Miss Macaulay / Temple House / Brighton. *Subscription:* T B M.

Malvern August 30 / 1851

Dearest Selina,

I have given orders about the Supplement of the Times; and you will have it regularly.

Our uncle James has at last ceased to write; at least I hear nothing about his letters. He may very likely have addressed one to the page.

Yesterday Ellis and I went to the Worcester Musical Festival. It was a fine sight. The nave of the Cathedral was crowded with all the beauty and gentility of three counties. The Choirs of three Cathedrals, strongly reinforced by singers from London, performed Handel's Messiah. Some parts struck me much, though I am not very sensible to such impressions. The streets of Worcester were almost impassable for the press of carriages, horses, servants in livery. I saw poor Lady Peel and her pretty daughter there, for the first time since Sir Robert's death. Mr. and Mrs. Cradock[2] – he is a canon there, and his wife was a maid of honour and an old acquaintance of mine – showed us every sort of hospitality.

Thanks to dear Fanny for her letter; and love to her.

Ever yours,
T B Macaulay

---

[1] Harland's edition of William Stout's *Autobiography:* see *to* Harland, 4 November 1850.
[2] Edward H. Cradock (1810–86: *Boase*), Canon of Worcester, 1848–54, and Principal of Brasenose College, Oxford, 1853–86. His wife, née Harriet Lister (d. 1884), was the sister of TBM's old friend Thomas Lister and of Lord John Russell's first wife.

TO MARGARET TREVELYAN, 3 SEPTEMBER 1851

MS: Trinity College.

Malvern September 3. 1851

Dearest Baba,

Thanks for two very kind letters. I am glad that you are to have an allowance. It is an epoch in the life of a girl. I shall delight to see you buying on your own account at Howell and James's[1] in our walks. But we shall never have such walks as while the Exhibition was in its glory.

The day before yesterday Ellis and I went to Gloucester to see the Cathedral. At Worcester we got on the railway; and at the station we met Lady Peel, Miss Peel, and Sir Robert's brother Dr. Peel,[2] Dean of Worcester, with whom the ladies had been staying some days. Miss Peel recognised me with a most gracious bow and smile; and her mother was extremely kind. The Dean made excuses for not having asked me to his house, and begged that I would visit him whenever I came to Worcester. There was, I could see, both in the mother and in the daughter a melancholy recollection of our last meeting.[3] They had heard, I dare say, from some of their friends, Mahon, Goulbourn, Lord Hatherton, or Graham, how much I had felt poor Peel's death, and how strongly I had expressed my gratification at thinking that we had been friends before he died. There was something very peculiar in the warmth with which all of them spoke to me. The ladies were going to a house which they have taken in the neighbourhood of Bristol.

We went on to Gloucester, and in the street leading to the Cathedral whom should we meet but Lord Lansdowne walking alone. We shook hands, and he expressed great concern at my having left Malvern to which he was going immediately. I told him that I should return that evening which seemed to comfort him. That is of course a joke. But I wish to heaven that in any way I could comfort or amuse him. We left him and went to the Cathedral, which I admired more than ever. It is quite at the head of the second rank of our Gothic Churches. The choir, the Lady's Chapel, the Tower, the Cloister are beyond all praise. We got back to Malvern in time for a late dinner.

The next day, yesterday, as I was thinking of calling on Lord Lansdowne who is staying at the Foley Arms, I saw him coming up the road through my grounds. I hastened out to welcome him. To my great surprise I found that he knew the house well. A lady of his own family lived here long it seems, and he used to be her guest more than thirty

---

[1] A department store in Waterloo Place.

[2] John Peel (1798–1875: *Boase*), Dean of Worcester, 1845–75.

[3] TBM dined with Peel on 1 June 1850 (Trevelyan, II, 277).

years ago. He particularly remembered drinking tea here with Horner. You have heard of Horner. He was the intimate friend of Jeffrey and Lord Lansdowne, and the rival of Brougham before I can remember. He made a great figure in parliament; and had the highest character for virtue as well as for ability and knowledge. But he died at an early age – that is before he was forty. I once saw him in the street when I was a boy, and remember staring at him intensely. It was, I think, in 1816[1] that he died. Lord L. sate half an hour and was very kind, as he always is, and more cheerful than he has of late been.

But I must stop. We go to Tewkesbury to day to see the fine Church.

Love to Mamma, Papa, George, Alice. Pray remember me to Grand-mamma and Uncle William,[2] and tell me, when next you write, how they are going on.

Ever yours

T B Macaulay

TO GEORG WILLEM VREEDE, 3 SEPTEMBER 1851

MS: General State Archives, The Hague.

Malvern / Worcestershire / September 3. 1851

Sir,

Your letter has just reached me here: but I am sorry that I have missed the pleasure of seeing the gentleman who was the bearer of it.

I am much obliged to you for the valuable hints which you have had the kindness to convey to me. I am already in possession of a copy of the letters of William to Heinsius. It was made for Sir James Mackintosh and fills two folio volumes very closely written.[3]

The letters of L'Hermitage[4] to the States General are in the Dutch Archives at the Hague and a copy of them has lately been placed in the British Museum. I have repeatedly consulted them and have been much interested by them. I will bear in mind what you say about his corres-

---

[1] 1817.

[2] William (1812–1905) was the youngest of the Trevelyan brothers and 'a good fellow as ever I knew' (Journal, IV, 307: 12 November 1851). He was Vicar of Wolverton, Buckinghamshire, 1856–72, and Rector of Calverton, Buckinghamshire, 1872–81.

[3] TBM describes this in the *History*, III, 69n: ch. 11.

[4] TBM identifies him in the *History* as 'a French refugee' living in London 'as agent for the Waldenses.' He adds that 'copies of the despatches of L'Hermitage, and, indeed, of the despatches of all the ministers and agents employed by the States General in England from the time of Elizabeth downward, now are, or will soon be, in the library of the British Museum. For this valuable addition to the great national storehouse of knowledge, the country is chiefly indebted to Lord Palmerston. But it would be unjust not to add that his instructions were most zealously carried into effect by the late Sir Edward Disbrowe, with the cordial cooperation of the enlightened men who have charge of the noble collection of Archives at the Hague' (IV, 417n: ch. 20).

pondence with the Pensionary. I should be extremely glad to see it: but I could scarcely venture to make such a request of M. Van der Hein[1] with whom I have not the honor of being at all acquainted.

With repeated thanks for your kindness I have the honor to be, / Sir,

Your most faithful Servant,

T B Macaulay

TO MARGARET TREVELYAN, 9 SEPTEMBER 1851

MS: Trinity College.

Malvern September 9 / 1851

Dearest Baba,

Thanks for your kind letter. I am almost sorry that you are in town again. I shall hear no more about the Agapemonites[2] or the beautiful Somersetshire rides and walks, or Papa's exploits with his gun, and depredations on his mother's larder. I never was more amused than by his carrying away your lunch under the full impression that it was meant for his own refreshment.

I have been to Chepstow with Ellis[3] – a beautiful journey. I do not know whether you ever travelled along the Wye: but I think the banks equal in beauty to anything that I have ever seen either at home or in Italy. The pleasure of our journey was however diminished towards the close by a circumstance which made us quite sad. The two other inside passengers were a lady and her daughter. The girl, a very nice looking girl of twenty, had been ill, and confined to her room two months. She was convalescent, and going to recruit in the fine Welsh air. The mother was anxious lest the journey should be too much for the poor child. At first they were very cheerful, but at last the girl became evidently exhausted. It was quite piteous to see the mother's anxiety. They sate holding each other's hand and pressing each other's fingers so tenderly. At last the mother began to cry: and then two or three drops ran down the girl's cheeks; but she was quite patient and sweet tempered. Ellis and I were ready to cry for company, and were much relieved when we came to the place where they were to leave us, and where a nice open carriage was in waiting for them to take them to a house two miles from the road. I hope poor Lizzy, as her mamma called her, had a good night's rest, and is now enjoying fresh air and glorious sunshine.

[1] Hendrik Jacob Van Der Heim (1824–90) edited *Het Archief van der Raadpensionaris Antonie Heinsius*, 2 vols., The Hague, 1867–74.

[2] A millenial, communistic sect, with special views on spiritual marriage, founded in 1846 by the Reverend Henry James Prince at Charlinch, Somerset, a few miles from the Trevelyans at Enmore.

[3] 6–8 September (Journal, IV, 240–3); they travelled by coach.

The next day was Sunday, and we meant to have gone to Church. But Ellis was taken very poorly.[1] So I sate with him all the morning, and made up my mind to missing all the sights of the neighbourhood. However in the afternoon he insisted on my going out. So I walked to Tintern Abbey through a scene of surpassing loveliness. I had travelled through it the day before, but had been so much distressed about poor Lizzy that I might as well have been on the railway between Ely and Cambridge. The only blemish on the beauties of the valley of the Wye is the Wye itself. It is at best not a river of sufficient dimensions for the place which it holds in the landscape: and, during half the day, when the tide is out, it is a miserable ditch, in no respect superior to Fleet Ditch, – a thin stream of dirty water trickling between two great masses of mud. Tintern, – I forget whether you ever saw it, – is the finest of Gothic ruins, as much superior to Netley as the Exhibition in Hyde Park is to the Soho Bazaar. I was here admiring and delighted when Ellis came pursuing me in a car. He was not well enough to walk, and yet would not abstain from the pleasure of seeing Tintern. We went back together. He was rather the better for his trip, and yesterday he rose pretty well. We came back with less interesting companions than had been with us when we went. There was an old Quaker lady who might have gone into fits in the coach without moving us as poor Lizzy had done. We got home to dinner; and I found on the table an invitation to a Soiree of Lady Gainsborough's[2] at eight. I sent an excuse. Indeed we were hardly at our second course by eight o'clock.

Ellis goes to morrow; and I shall be left with the hills and my books. I shall begin soon to wish to be in London, since you and Mamma are there. It makes me sad to think how few more walks we shall have through the Exhibition. Tell me what your plans are, and when George goes to school.[3]

Love to all.

Ever yours,
T B Macaulay

TO FRANCES MACAULAY, 10 SEPTEMBER 1851

MS: Trinity College.

Malvern September 10 / 1851

Dearest Fanny,

Thanks for the advertisement. I return it. I have enjoyed the country

---

[1] They were given bad sherry at their inn: 'Ellis made it into negus of which he drank largely, and boasted that he had corrected all the evil properties of the wine by his skilful cookery; but he was mistaken' (Journal, IV, 241: 6 September).

[2] See 19 August.

[3] George had entered Harrow in the Easter term this year.

air much, and have made several excursions, one of which occupied three
or four days. I have been with Ellis to Gloucester, Tewkesbury, and
Chepstow, – and, when he leaves me, I think of going to Hereford. This
place has many attractions. Yet on the whole I love the Isle of Wight
more.

Lord Lansdowne is here, more cheerful than when I saw him last in
town, yet perceptibly grown older and weaker. He very kindly took Ellis
and me to Madresfield,[1] a most curious old seat of Lord Beauchamp, to
which strangers are rarely admitted, and which we could not have seen
had we not been in Lord L's company. A strange old house washed on all
sides by a deep, dark coloured, stagnant, moat, and accessible only by a
bridge. There was something striking in the ancient halls and galleries,
but the whole aspect was gloomy and the place breathed of malaria.

Our uncle James continues to pester me. He cannot leave London, he
says, unless I send him thirty pounds to pay his debts; and at the same time
he sends me a pamphlet which he has printed against his nephews at
Bristol, and against a Judge who has, in the County Court, pronounced a
decision in their favour; – so that he begs money from one nephew to
spend it in libelling another. I have sent him no answer, and shall send
him none.

Love to Selina. There is no doubt of the Duke of Norfolk's conversion.[2]
I shall stay here a fortnight longer.

Ever yours
T B Macaulay

TO THOMAS FLOWER ELLIS, 12 SEPTEMBER 1851

MS: Trinity College. *Extracts published:* Trevelyan, II, 296–7.

Malvern September 12 / 1851

Dear Ellis,

I have sent William to look after your business. In the meantime I must
own that your ill luck rather titillates the malicious parts of my nature.
The taking of a place by a railway train, which the vulgar, myself included,
perform in thirty seconds, is with you an operation requiring as much
thought and time as the purchase of an estate. On two successive days
did I kick my heels in the street, first before the Railway Office, and then
before the Bellevue Hotel, while you were examining and crossexamining

---

[1] On 4 September (Journal, IV, 236–8). Madresfield Court is near Malvern.

[2] The Duke, concluding that he could not accept the new Catholic hierarchy without violating
his duty as a citizen, 'publicly became an Anglican by receiving holy communion in his
parish church' (Owen Chadwick, *The Victorian Church*, Part I, 2nd edn, 1970, p. 299). The
event is reported in *The Times*, 9 September.

the bookkeepers, and arranging and rearranging your plans. I must say that your letter is well calculated to make me uneasy as to my own return to London. For if all your forethought and anxiety, your acute inquiries and ingenious combinations have ended thus, how can such a careless fellow as I am hope to reach town without innumerable disappointments and losses?

I have had my troubles too. That rascal MacCann,[1] – we were quite right in putting *Shame* to his name,[2] – after trying to deceive me, tried to bully me. Yesterday he sent to say that, if I did not open my gate, he would break the padlock. I sent for the police, and told his foreman to tell him that, if he dared to touch the padlock, I would have him instantly before a Justice of the Peace. The fellow had not the pluck to persist. He afterwards came to William, growling and sneaking. He was not afraid of me, he said; but he did not like to get into a row which might be vexatious to Miss Hinds.[3] I enjoyed the victory over this insolent upstart, who is one of the petty tyrants of Malvern.

Lord Lansdowne goes to day. He sate here an hour yesterday. I said what was proper on your account. Senior also goes to day. Little did we think as we walked sighing by Trafalgar House that he was at Malvern. He was taken ill on his way to the Lewises, while we were at Chepstow, and returned to take another course of tubs and wet sheets. He now thinks himself well again.

As these go, others come. Do you remember a hideous Gothic gimcrack, called Oriel Villa, just opposite to the gate of my grounds? I charitably imputed the architecture to my friend MacCann. Dr. Holland has taken it. His wife and her girls came down yesterday; and he is expected to morrow.

Another arrival. I was sitting on the grass near the Wytche, and reading Wilhelm Meister when I heard my name uttered aloud. I saw nobody and thought of the voice of Pan in the mountains. But soon from behind a stone hedge emerged our valued friend William Wilberforce, looking like something between a varmint man[4] at a cockfight and an attorney just struck off the roll. Thank God, he is at Little Malvern, so that intercourse is out of the question.

I shall be delighted to see Adolphus.

Baba tells me that of all objects that ever she saw the queerest is George in stickups.[5] I hope that Walter[6] succeeds better.

---

[1] For the story of MacCann see 15 September.
[2] As Ellis did, with results described in 17 September.
[3] TBM's landlady at Malvern.
[4] 'A sporting amateur with the knowledge or skill of a professional' (*OED*).
[5] Stand up collars.
[6] Walter Ellis (1836?–75), Ellis's youngest living child, had entered Harrow earlier this year.

Your people have sent the Times of Monday and Tuesday to Chepstow; and the Chepstow Postmaster has forwarded them both hither. I suppose that they may be delivered over to the secular arm as waste paper.

Here is William at last with a letter, – a letter patent, – but no money. As to the three shillings, ουποτε ἥξουσι πρός σε ουποτε ηξουσιν.[1] I send the book keeper's explanations. You took your place in one coach: you rode to Worcester in another; you have paid the full fare to both; and you will not recover a halfpenny from either. Your case, if that is any comfort, is not a rare one. Indeed it seems to be the common practice at Malvern to travel in this way. And here we have an explanation of the extraordinary number of coaches at this place. There is room for a great many rival establishments when passengers pay both for the conveyance by which they go and for that by which they do not go.

Good bye – I miss you much, and I console myself as well as I can with Demosthenes, Goethe, Lord Campbell, and Miss Ferriar.[2] I hope that Marian will think you better for your trip. Lord Lansdowne tells me that he never remembers me looking so well. Kind regards to all at Bromley.

Ever yours

T B Macaulay

TO MARGARET TREVELYAN, 15 SEPTEMBER 1851

MS: Trinity College.

Malvern September 15 / 1851

Dearest Baba,

Thanks for your letter, and for all your letters. You are a dear good girl to think of me so often. I expect to be quite alone during the next fortnight. Dr. Holland came down on Saturday; and I drank tea with him yesterday. But to day he is off again on one of his rambles. Never was there such a traveller. He was in Hungary a fortnight ago; and a fortnight hence he will be in Andalusia. How you must envy him. He has been at all the places which you wish to visit, from New York to Babylon.

I have had a vexatious dispute here, and have got the better. My chief reason for giving so high a rent for this house was the beauty and seclusion of the grounds which are far the prettiest here. As to the mere house, I might have got one which would have suited me as well, nay better, for three guineas a week less. What then was my surprise when I came down to find the garden full of carts and workmen who were busy shooting

---

[1] Trevelyan translates: 'You will never get them back: never' (II, 297n).

[2] TBM was reading Demosthenes, *Pro Corona*; Goethe's *Wilhelm Meister*; Campbell's *Life of Lord Eldon*; and Susan Ferrier's *Marriage* (Journal, IV, 244–7: 10–12 September).

rubbish close under the windows, and at the very door. I remonstrated, and was told that the owner had determined to make a new approach, and that the work was going on by his orders. I now found that it had been thought a very ingenious trick to let the place to me while this insupportable annoyance lasted. I was determined not to be treated thus. I closed the gate of the grounds, and put a padlock on it. The person who had contracted for the works, a Mr. MacCan, found that his carts were stopped, and came to me to ask for admittance. I told him that I had not come a hundred and twenty miles from town, and agreed to pay eighty guineas, for the purpose of living in the midst of such noise and nastiness as never infested me in London; – that the place had been let to me; – that the agreement under which I was in occupation contained no stipulation that I should submit to such a nuisance, and that I was fully determined to stand on my legal rights. He owned that my case was a very hard one. He wished to avoid litigation, he said; and he ended by proposing a compromise. Would I allow the men to work one day more? They could, in that time, smooth the rubbish which they had already brought; and they should bring no more during my stay. I readily consented. The work went on during one day; and then I was left to the enjoyment of my quiet woods and turf for three weeks. At the end of three weeks the nuisance recommenced. Carts came full of earth, and were unloaded close to my drawing room. The workmen said that Mr. MacCan had ordered them to come, and, if I said anything to them, to take no notice. I instantly closed and padlocked the gate again. MacCan had the insolence to send a message that he would break the lock if I did not remove it. You should have seen how angry I was. Spetchley was nothing to it.[1] I told William to fetch the police; and I said to MacCan's foreman. "Go, and tell your master that the first person who dares to touch that lock shall sleep in Worcester gaol to night. –" This menace was completely successful. MacCan growled and threatened, but withdrew his people; and I have now the undisturbed possession of my little paradise.

What a long story. And I am afraid a dull one. But what can you expect from such a hermitage as mine?

Love to Mamma, Papa, George, and Alice. I long to see you all again, and to have two or three more rambles with you through the Exhibition before it closes. How much pleasure it has given. I shall always remember it with, I may say, affection, if it were only for your sake.

Ever yours
T B Macaulay

[1] Spetchley, TBM tells us, is where he was provoked to rage in 1846: see 10 August 1851.

TO THOMAS FLOWER ELLIS, 17 SEPTEMBER 1851

MS: Trinity College.

Malvern Septr. 17. 1851

Dear Ellis,

I have to give you joy on the extraordinary effect which your concise pencil note on Mr. MacCan's name has produced. The whole paper is now covered with similar remarks. One writer has summed up the character of the whole list in the words – "All bloody fools." Another has added — "More guts than brains." See how great a matter a little fire kindleth.[1] Pasquinades were utterly unknown in this innocent spot till you traced the single word "Shame;" and now it seems likely that the walls will be covered with inscriptions as numerous and as energetic as a Westminster election produces.

I went yesterday along the whole range of hills, quite at the top – the North Hill excepted. I passed an hour on the Herefordshire beacon, and regretted much that I had not visited it with you. The Roman works interested me greatly. I went on quite through Lord Somers's woods[2] to the other encampment which is hardly worth seeing. It was, I suppose, an outpost of the great cantonment. I have now quite got over all giddiness, and, with time, can climb as high as yourself. My powers of walking also increase perceptibly. Distances which knocked me up a month ago are nothing to me now. Yesterday my ramble was certainly of not less than twenty three miles. Yet I was scarcely sensible of fatigue. I hope that you are the better for your wanderings here.

If we meet at Peterborough it must be, I find, on Tuesday the 30th.[3] If you cannot manage to be there, let me know; and I will take some other route, and reserve Peterborough for some time when we may be able to go to Boston together.

I hear nothing of Adolphus.

Ever yours
T B Macaulay

TO MARGARET TREVELYAN, 18 SEPTEMBER 1851

MS: Trinity College. *Partly published:* Trevelyan, II, 205–6.

Malvern September 18. 1851

Dearest Baba,

I am extremely sorry to hear of your cold. However such things do

[1] James 3:5.
[2] At Eastnor Castle, near Ledbury.
[3] TBM left Malvern on the 29th via Birmingham for Peterborough; he met Ellis and Frank there on the 30th; on 1 October they went on to Boston and then returned to London (Journal, IV, 266–70).

not last. We have of late had as much fog here in the mornings as you can have had in London. The whole plain of the Severn, when I rise, is completely buried in mist on one side: the tops of the hills are capped with clouds on the other; and, instead of enjoying the most extensive prospect in England, I can but just distinguish the elms in my own grounds. The days continue to be dark and hazy till about one in the afternoon. Then the gloom disperses: the sky becomes blue: the sun shines out gloriously; and, from the top of the ridge all Herefordshire, Worcestershire and Gloucestershire lie spread out like a map before me. When I go to bed I see brilliant starlight: but when I wake again I again find everything covered with fog. This has been the regular course of every day since Sunday last. You, I am afraid from your account, have had our mornings, but not our afternoons.

I hope that you will be quite well on the 2nd of October, and that the weather will be fine. For I mean to take you on that day to the Exhibition.[1] I am impatient to see the Swedish contributions; and I am not a little curious to know whether the resort of foreigners be really such as to give anything like a new character to the streets of London. Your sketches of the strangers are very droll.

Tell me how you like Schiller's Mary Stuart. It is not one of my favourite pieces. I should put it fourth among his plays. I arrange them thus – Wallenstein, William Tell, Don Carlos, Mary Stuart, the Maid of Orleans. At a great interval comes the Bride of Messina; and then at another great interval Fieschi. Cabal and Love I never could get through. The Robbers is a mere schoolboy rant below serious criticism, but not without indications of mental vigour which required to be disciplined by much thought and study. But though I do not put Mary Stuart very high among Schiller's works, I think the Fotheringay scenes in the fifth Act equal to anything that he ever wrote, indeed equal to anything dramatic that has been produced in Europe since Shakspeare. I hope that you will feel the wonderful truth and beauty of that part of the play.[2]

Sintram[3] is trash – as unmeaning as the History of Jack and the Bean Stalk, and a great deal duller. Perhaps you may think otherwise. There is an age at which we are disposed to think that whatever is odd and extravagant is great. At that age we are liable to be taken in by such essayists as Carlyle, such orators as Irving, such painters as Fuseli,[4] such plays as the Robbers, such romances as Sintram. A better time comes,

---

[1] Margaret still had a cold and they did not go (Journal, IV, 271).
[2] TBM began re-reading Schiller's plays in March of this year and finished them in June (Journal, IV, 2; 137).
[3] By Friedrich, Baron de La Motte Fouqué, 1815.
[4] Henry Fuseli (1741–1825: *DNB*), Swiss-born romantic painter; Professor of Painting at the Royal Academy, 1799–1825.

when we would give all Fuseli's hobgoblins for one of Reynolds's little children, and all Sintram's dialogues with Death and the Devil for one speech of Mrs. Norris or Miss Bates.[1] Tell me however, – as of course you will, – quite truly what you think of Sintram. By the bye the author's name is not Touché but I believe Fouqué. And àpropos of orthography, who taught you to spell Cohinoor[2] in so queer a way? Is it one of your papa's odd forms of oriental words? I stick to the common practice, and continue to write *Mahomet,* though I see that the imposter figures as Mahommed, Mohammed, Mâhmet, Moûhmed, Mahômet, Mahmoud, and has in short as many aliases as one of the swell mob.

Love to Mamma and Papa and Alice.

Ever yours,

T B Macaulay

TO THOMAS FLOWER ELLIS, 21 SEPTEMBER 1851

MS: Trinity College.

Malvern September 21 / 1851

Dear Ellis,

I assent to the arrangements which you propose, and shall be delighted to have Frank's company. We shall therefore meet, nothing unforeseen preventing, at the Angel Inn in the City of Peterborough on Tuesday the 30th of this month of September, 1851. That, I think, is precise and business like.

Bravo Achilli![3] and bravo Newman! Two apostate priests are well matched. You never read Valentine MacClutchy.[4] There is just such a scene there, between an Orangeman who has turned Papist, and a Papist who has turned Orangeman. At last they, in their rage, forget their present positions, and talk their old language. "You ought to have staid among your damned heretics, and not come over to disgrace the true Church." "Why could not you stick to Popery and wooden shoes? It is a shame to see such a blackguard with an orange ribbon."

---

[1] In *Mansfield Park* and *Emma.*

[2] The diamond was presented to Queen Victoria in 1850 and was on display at the Great Exhibition.

[3] Giovanni Giacinto Achilli (1803–?: *Boase*), an Italian and a former Dominican priest, was employed by the anti-Catholic Evangelical Protestant Alliance in the agitation against 'papal aggression.' Newman printed a detailed list of charges against Achilli – mainly for sexual offences – in his *Lectures on the Present Position of Catholics,* 1851, pp. 197–9, whereupon Achilli brought suit against Newman for libel. In 1852 a jury found against Newman, and early in 1853 judgment was given against him, with a fine of £100 and costs of £12,000. Ellis was one of the counsel for the plaintiff.

[4] By William Carleton, 3 vols., Dublin, 1845. TBM read it in 1849 and again in August 1851 (Journal, II, 173; IV, 208). The scene he describes is in ch. 13.

Apropos of apostates. I suspect that the inestimable William Wilberforce will add to his other titles of honour that of Renegade,[1] if indeed he has not already. He, his wife, his children and his grandchildren, are all lodged at a house of Benedictines, near Little Malvern. You must remember the building and the pious inscription over the door. I met him two or three days ago sauntering before the porch of this monastery and looking like the very ἰδέα of a blackguard. What Plato said about virtue may be untrue:[2] but from the sensations and inclinations which the sight of William always raises in me, I feel assured that if Blackguardism could be exhibited to mankind in a visible form, they would all instantly begin to kick it *a posteriori*.

Ever yours
T B Macaulay

TO SELINA MACAULAY, 24 SEPTEMBER 1851

MS: Trinity College. *Envelope:* Miss Macaulay / Temple House / Brighton. *Subscription:* T B M.

Malvern September 24 / 1851

Dearest Selina,

I inclose a cheque for the quarter.

My stay here is drawing to a close. I expect to be in town again this day week. I have just returned from a ramble to Hereford, and am about to perform a pedestrian journey of a good many miles along the banks of the Severn. I seldom walk less than twenty miles a day; and I find that climbing which, when I came to this place seven weeks ago, tired me and affected my respiration, is now quite easy to me.

William Wilberforce is here, – that is to say at Little Malvern about four miles from me. He is lodged with his wife, son, and grandchildren, at a Benedictine Monastery. I found him sauntering the other day before the gate of this holy building, and looking, as he always does, like something between a pettifogging attorney and one of the swell mob. Whether our Church is to lose such an ornament I do not know. The only thing wanting to the perfection of his character was to be an apostate.

I have, with infinite difficulty, written an epitaph on our Uncle Babington,[3] and sent it to Hannah who will next week pay a visit to the Temple.

---

[1] He did join the Catholic Church, but not until 1863. When a report that Wilberforce was about to join the Roman Catholics was spread, TBM said that 'I advise him to go soon, for he will have a great deal to confess' (Alston, 'Recollections of Macaulay,' p. 64: this is told as though it referred to the elder Wilberforce, obviously by mistake).

[2] Perhaps TBM is recalling *Phaedrus*, 250–1, describing the sensations aroused by beauty.

[3] See 25 June 1851. TBM worked on it on 15 September and completed it on the 17th (Journal, IV, 249–50). The epitaph was not used.

I thought it better to let them see it in this way than to transmit it to them directly. They might have some delicacy in telling me that they did not like my composition. But when she shows it them as an attempt about which I have consulted her, they will probably speak frankly. I will write it on the other side. I should like to have your opinion and Fanny's. Give her my love.

Ever yours
T B Macaulay

Here lies
Thomas Babington
of Rothley Temple

Long the faithful representative of the Borough of Leicester in the
House of Commons.

He was born ————— A D 1758
He died ——————— A D 1838

From nature he received a just understanding and an amiable
disposition. Religion disciplined his passions, elevated
his moral and intellectual character, and fitted him to discharge with rare propriety all
the duties both of public and of private life.

In five eventful parliaments his judgment and moderation,
his indefatigable diligence and incorruptible probity, extorted
the esteem of contending factions.

But those only who lived in close intimacy with him under this
roof could know how nearly he attained on earth the goodness
and the happiness of heaven.

They still remember with tenderness and admiration that winning
courtesy which was in him merely the spontaneous expression of
Christian benignity, that childlike innocence on which the
temptations and cares of a long and busy life had left no stain,
and that angelic temper which adversity, age, and blindness
only made sweeter and more serene.

May the example of such an ancestor sustain the virtue
of those who inherit his blood, and who will one day be
laid here by his side.

TO CHARLES MACAULAY, 25 SEPTEMBER 1851

MS: University of London. *Published:* Rae, *Temple Bar,* LXXXVI, 202–3.

Malvern September 25 1851

Dear Charles,

Our Uncle James is an abandoned liar.[1] He called on me at the Albany a few days before I left town, and began haranguing about his plans touching the water supply.[2] I cut him short by telling him that his disreputable life, his frauds, his insolence and ingratitude to myself, and the manner in which he had abused my name by employing it to cheat innkeepers and to obtain admittance to public men had determined me to have no more to do with him. He stormed and ranted and blasphemed, after his ordinary fashion. I told him that my purpose was unalterable, but at parting, as he had said that he was in want of money, I put a cheque for twenty pounds into his hand. He took it and went on declaiming – "I do not want your money. The just God knows that I hate money. I despise money. Money is the root of all evil." He then thrust the root of all evil into his pocket and walked away. I gave immediate orders to the servants never again to let him pass the door.

Well, I came down to this place, and, in a few days, – about a fortnight, I think, certainly less than three weeks after this scene, I received a letter from him. He had spent the twenty pounds, and wanted thirty more immediately. In plain words he wants me to allow him ten pounds a week, five hundred and twenty pounds a year, near a third of my whole income, and twice as much as I allow to both my unmarried sisters. I sent him no answer. Then came letters upon letters. He could not quit London without my help. He did not know where to get a morsel of bread. Then he had the impudence to write to Elizabeth to ask her to inform him why his nephew did not send him any reply. I suppose that he thought poor Elizabeth was on the same footing with me on which his housekeeper formerly was with him. Then he sent me a libel which he has printed and circulated against our cousins, the sons of his brother John. It seems that, though he has not money to buy a roll, he can find money to publish lampoons against his nephews. I remained, and shall remain, obstinately silent. If he calls at the Albany, he shall not be admitted. If he makes a disturbance, which I think very likely, I shall send for the police. It is not very agreeable to figure in a Marlborough Street report. But I am confident that whoever knows anything about him will acquit me of harsh-

---

[1] TBM received a letter from Charles on this day: 'James Mills has been pestering him – lying worthless old scoundrel' (Journal, IV, 263).

[2] A metropolitan water bill had been before Parliament in this year and was the subject of considerable public debate.

ness: and at worst the story will be a nine day's wonder; and, if he once sees that I flinch, there will be no limit to his extortions.

I wish you a pleasant trip. I love the Isle of Wight dearly. The coast to Shanklin to the Black Gang Chine is one of the loveliest tracts in the kingdom. But I am much afraid that you have delayed your trip a little too long. We have had a glorious August and September. But to day the equinoctial weather seems to be beginning. The rain is falling in torrents; and my trees are tossing in the wind. Love to Mrs. Charles and the children.

Ever yours,

T B Macaulay

TO MARGARET TREVELYAN, 27 SEPTEMBER 1851

MS: Trinity College. *Partly published:* Trevelyan, II, 298.

Malvern September 27. 1851

Dearest Baba,

Thanks for your long pleasant letter. It is, I suppose, the last that I shall receive from you here, as this is the last that I shall write from hence. It is almost worth while to live away from my darling, in order to get so many kind amusing letters from her.

I am extremely diverted by poor Mamma's mishap about the Countess of Rudolstadt.[1] Papa would say that it was a judgment on her for reading such wicked books as those of George Sand. I once got through Consuelo and the sequel. But it was a heavy pull; and I shall never repeat the effort.

But the wedding[2] – I am quite delighted to have such a full, such a *graphic* account – (*graphic* is now the cant word.[3] Whenever you hear any man use it except in derision, set him down for an ass, on my authority) – but such a *graphic* account of the procession, dresses, and deportment of bridegroom, bride, bridemen and bridemaids. I see the whole – Aunt Margaret[4] in her fawn coloured silk, Miss Benson[5] in her ermine boa, my own Baba in white with blue ribbons, Mr. William Wakefield[6] with his hair just cut, and Mr. Willinch[7] with a boil on his nose. You should have

---

[1] By George Sand, 1843–5; it is the sequel to *Consuelo*, 1842–4.
[2] Of Mary Cropper to J. S. Howson (1816–85: *DNB*), later Dean of Chester.
[3] The *OED* gives an instance of the word in the sense of 'vividly descriptive' from 1669; but the first decade to produce two examples is the 1850s.
[4] Mrs Edward Cropper.
[5] Of the family in business partnership with the Croppers.
[6] Wakefield (1828–89) was a nephew of the Wakefield sisters who married into the Cropper family.
[7] Sarah, second daughter of John Cropper, married Arthur Willinck (1824–62), then Curate of Linslade, Buckinghamshire, and later Vicar of St Paul's, Tranmere, Cheshire.

mentioned your Mamma's dress. Was it the green? Or was it the dark velvet? And did she wear much lace? I do not ask whether she cried. For she always cries at weddings, as indeed most women do. Their tears on such occasions remind me of Goldsmith's saying – "We wept when we were born, and every moment tells us why."[1] There is a specimen of old bachelor's spleen for you.

I am beginning to prepare for my departure. It is time: for the delicious weather seems to be over. Never did I see seven such weeks together. But the equinox has come with its usual concomitants. The trees are yellower and yellower day by day: the wind roars: the rain falls; and I am forced to pass my evenings by the fire and to lay another blanket on my bed. However I have not given up my walks. Yesterday I rambled more than seventeen measured miles, – great part of the distance along the bank of the Severn. What odd things happen. Two gentlemen, at least men in good coats and hats, overtook me as I was strolling through one of the meadows close to the river. One of them stared at me, touched his hat, and said "Mr. Macaulay, I believe." I admitted the truth of the imputation. So the fellow went on. "I suppose, Sir, you are come here to study the localities of the battle of Worcester. We shall expect a very fine account of the battle of Worcester." I hinted with all delicacy that I had no more to do with the battle of Worcester than with the battle of Marathon. "Of course not, Sir, of course not. The battle of Worcester certainly does not enter into your plan." So we bowed and parted. I thought of the proverb which is often in our mouths: and I thought that on this occasion the name of Tom Fool might be properly applied to more than one of the parties concerned.[2]

Love to Mamma, and regards and kind wishes to all your friends.

Ever yours
T B Macaulay

TO JOHANN HEINRICH KÜNZEL,[3] 2 OCTOBER 1851

MS: Hessische Landes-und-Hochschulbibliothek, Darmstadt. *Published:* Walther Fischer, *Des Darmstädter Schriftstellers Johann Heinrich Künzel (1810–1873) Beziehungen zu England,* Giessen, 1939, p. 41.

Albany London / October 2. 1851

Sir,

I have just arrived in London after an absence of some weeks, and have

---

[1] *The Good Natur'd Man*, Act 1: 'We wept when we came into the world, and every day tells us why.' See the note on this in Goldsmith's *Works,* ed. Arthur Friedman, Oxford, 1966, v, 26.

[2] 'More people know Tom Fool than Tom Fool knows.'

[3] Künzel (1810–73) was a Darmstadt editor, translator, and historian, with a special interest in English history and literature.

found on my table your Life of Sir Robert Peel[1] and your obliging letter. I shall read with much interest the remarks of an enlightened foreigner on the character and conduct of my illustrious countryman. It is true that I was, during my whole public life, an opponent of Sir Robert Peel, and that there were two or three sharp contentions between us in the House of Commons. But I always did justice to his abilities and to the sincerity of his patriotism. We were on terms of personal friendship during the latter part of his life; and I entertain none but kind and respectful feelings towards his memory. With many thanks, / I have the honour to be, / Sir,

Your faithful Servant,

T B Macaulay

TO UNIDENTIFIED RECIPIENT, 7 OCTOBER 1851

MS: University of Washington.

Albany London / October 7. 1851

Sir,

The allusion about which you inquire is to Mrs. Sheridan.[2] She was celebrated both for her beauty and her voice. Sir Joshua painted her as St Cecilia. The portrait, one of his finest, is now in Lord Lansdowne's collection. Lady Seymour, the Queen of Beauty,[3] and Mrs. Norton are grand daughters of Mrs. Sheridan. / I have the honor to be, / Sir,

Your obedient servant,

T B Macaulay

TO MARGARET TREVELYAN, 11 OCTOBER 1851

MS: Trinity College. *Partly published:* Trevelyan, II, 206.

British Museum / October 11. 1851

Dearest Baba,

Thanks for your letter. It was very welcome. I should have gone to Westbourne Terrace to day in the hope of seeing your Mamma. But I am forced to sit here playing at doing business,[4] – Goulburn in the chair, – Inglis at my right hand, – the Bishop of London at my left, and further off Sir David Dundas. Here we shall stay dawdling till late in the afternoon,

---

[1] *Leben und Reden Sir Robert Peel's,* 2 vols., Braunschweig, 1851; it is item 205 in the sale catalogue of TBM's library.

[2] The reference is to TBM's elaborate allusion in the essay on Warren Hastings: 'There too was she, the beautiful mother of a beautiful race, the Saint Cecilia, whose delicate features, lighted up by love and music, art has rescued from the common decay' (*ER,* LXXIV, 242). Reynolds's portrait was painted in 1775.

[3] At the ill-starred Eglinton Tournament in 1839.

[4] 'After breakfast to the Museum. Long, stupid, useless sitting' (Journal, IV, 280).

and shall do as little for arts or letters or science as if we had been, like you, lounging on the beach, gathering shells, and counting the yachts and pleasure boats.[1]

You do not tell me how you are, a sad omission. Pray let me know. Ellis went to Harrow on Thursday and found George in bed, not at all seriously ill, but a little indisposed, and looking very comfortable with his book among the sheets and blankets.

Has Alice renewed her acquaintance with the coquettish Chairman, the property Chairman, the bearded Chairman, and the inquisitive Chairman? Pray make me sketches of them, especially of the bearded Chairman and the coquettish Chairman.

I have bespoken a Schiller for you. It is in the binder's hands, and will be ready, I hope, before your return.

Give my kindest love to your aunts and to dear little Alice. How changed you will find London when you come back. This is the last day of the great exhibition. It makes me quite sad to think of our many many happy walks there. The bustle and crowding of this week have been such as I never saw in my life. Next week all will be still – that is as still as in an ordinary London October.

I saw a description of myself yesterday in a New York paper.[2] The

[1] Margaret and Alice were at Brighton.
[2] The story, copied from the Inverness *Courier*, 31 July ('From Our Private Correspondent'), appears in the New York *Albion*, 6 September, p. 430, and is worth quoting: 'There is a common pedestrian of London streets, well known to all who are acquainted with their notabilities. He is a short, stout, sturdy, energetic man. He has a big round face, and large staring and very bright hazel eyes. His hair is cut short, and his hat flung back on the crown of his head. His gait is firm and decided, with a touch of pomposity. He is ever provided with an umbrella, which he swings and flourishes, and batters on the pavement with mighty thumps. He seems generally absorbed in exciting and impulsive thought, the traces of which he takes no pains to conceal. His face works, his lips move and mutter, his eyes gleam and flash. Squat as is the figure, and not particularly fine, in the features there is an unmistakable air of mental power and energy, approaching to grandeur, about the man. He is evidently under the influence of the strong excitement of fiery thought. People gaze curiously at him, and stop to stare when he has passed. But he heeds no one – seems indeed to have utterly forgotten that he is not alone in his privacy, and pushes energetically on, unwitting of the many who stare and smile, or of the few who step respectfully aside, and look with a curiosity and regard upon Thomas Babington Macaulay. Occasionally, however, the historian and the poet gives still freer vent to the mental impulses which appear to be continually working within him. A friend of mine lately recognized him dining in the coffee-room of the Trafalgar Hotel at Greenwich – a fashionable white-bait house, which it appears he frequently patronises. He was alone, as he generally is, and the attention of more than one of the company was attracted by his peculiar mutterings and fidgettiness, and by the mute gestures with which he ever and anon illustrated his mental dreamings. All at once – it must have been towards the climax of the prose or verse which he was working up in his mind – Mr. Macaulay seized a massive decanter, held it a moment suspended in the air, and then dashed it down upon the table with such hearty good will, that the solid crystal flew about in fragments while the numerous parties dining round instinctively started up and stared at the curious iconoclast. Not a whit put out, however, Mr. Macaulay, who was well known to the waiters, called loudly for his bill to be made at the bar, and then pulling

Yankee writer says that I am a stout man with hazle eyes, that I always walk with an umbrella, that I sometimes bang the umbrella against the ground, that I often dine in the coffee room of the Trafalgar on fish, that once he saw me break a decanter there, but that I did not appear to be at all ashamed of my awkwardness, but called for my bill as coolly as if nothing had happened. I have no recollection of such an occurence; but, if it did take place, I do not think that it would have deprived me of my self possession. This is fame. This is the advantage of making a figure in the world.

Ever yours, dearest,

T B Macaulay

TO MARGARET TREVELYAN, 14 OCTOBER 1851

MS: Trinity College. *Extract published:* Trevelyan, II, 206.

Albany London / October 14. 1851

Dearest Baba,

Thanks for your kind pleasant letter. I went on Saturday evening to Westbourne Terrace, and learned that your Mamma would not return till Monday week.[1]

When I got home I found on my table a ticket enabling me to go to the Exhibition on the 13th, 14th, and 15th. Yesterday I went, and passed two hours there; but I saw not a soul that I knew except General Fox and his wife. They directed me to a glorious piece of plate by Benevenuto Cellini in the Italian department. I had not seen it. It came while I was at Malvern. I scarcely ever saw anything so superb and so highly finished. Did you see it?

I observed another thing which I had not seen before, and round which there was an immense crowd. It was in the gallery, among the children's toys: but it was far too elaborate and costly to be a child's toy; nor would a child well understand it. Yet it was too childish to be much valued by a grown up person. I cannot conceive who would give for it a price at all proportioned to the labour and ingenuity of the performance; or where the purchaser of such a work could put it. It was Gulliver lying [on] his back, and Lilliputians all about him.[2] The figures seemed to be in some kind of

with a couple of jerks, his hat and his umbrella from the stand, clapped the one carelessly on his head, and strode out flourishing the other.' An article in the Chicago *Journal*, 18 March 1903, cites two other, much altered, versions of this story in illustration of the elasticity of legend, and prints a letter from G.O. Trevelyan calling the original anecdote an 'absurdity.' But one may wonder whether it was totally untrue.

---

1 Hannah had followed Alice and Margaret to Brighton.
2 The doll, displayed by a Bond Street dealer, was the work of a German named Fleishmann; item 126, class 29, United Kingdom, in the *Official Catalogue* of the Exhibition.

paste, – not wax. There must be hundreds of little dolls in various dresses and postures, climbing and dancing all over the great doll. Did you notice it? I never heard it mentioned; and yet yesterday it seemed to attract more gazers than anything in the whole Glass Palace.

To morrow I shall go to the final ceremony, and try to hear the Bishop of London's thanksgiving in which I shall very cordially join.[1] This will long be remembered as a singularly happy year, of peace, plenty, good feeling, innocent pleasure, national glory of the best and purest sort.

Meanwhile I am plagued with two bad things, a bad tooth and a bad uncle. Rogers Senior[2] is not in town: but to day I saw Rogers Junior. He pronounced the pain which I feel only occasionally and not very severely to be rheumatic. He would not take a fee; but he will have me next Friday when he is to perform some very innocent operations.

As to the uncle – talk of _____ as the proverb says. He came just as I was writing this page. I determined to have a full explanation and a final one. I told him that I would never again admit him, and that if he attempted to annoy me I would give him in custody. I did however put ten pounds into his hand at parting. I am not at all sure that I did right. He lied – never was there such a liar. He called heaven to witness that he is certain of having five hundred pounds as soon as parliament meets. I asked him whether he thought it reasonable that I should support him at the rate of 500£ a year. He said very coolly that it was not to be permanent; but only till the government gave him his due; – an agreeable prospect for me. However I have now done with him.

Kindest love to Mamma, Alice, Aunt Selina, Aunt Fanny. You do not say how you are.

Ever yours,
T B Macaulay

You know how many many happy returns I wished you on your birthday – a happy day for me. Pray give me a full account of the trial.[3]

TO BENJAMIN HAWES, 9 NOVEMBER 1851

MS: Trinity College.

Albany Nov 9 / 1851

Dear Hawes,

I am sorry that I cannot dine with you on Tuesday.[4] It would have

[1] It rained and TBM did not go (Journal, IV, 284).
[2] TBM's dentist: Arnold, Henry, and Thomas Rogers were all in practice at 16 Hanover Square (*Post Office London Directory*, 1851).
[3] I have not identified this.
[4] 11 November; TBM dined alone at home that day (Journal, IV, 306).

given me great pleasure to meet the young Under Secretary and to express to him my sincere good wishes for his father's sake and his own.[1]

> Ever yours truly,
> T B Macaulay

TO THOMAS FLOWER ELLIS, 13 NOVEMBER 1851

MS: Trinity College.

Albany Nov 13. 1851

Dear Ellis,

Thanks. No wonder that you are out of patience. Never was anything so provoking. If I were you I should gnash my teeth and roll my eyes à la Ramshay.[2] However good comes out of evil. I hope for a fine budget of Preston anecdotes when you return.

I shall drop no hint of your opinion. Mine, I own, is made up. Whether the commitment of Whitty were or were not legal, I do not presume to decide. But it will, I suppose, be conceded that the grossly indiscreet and intemperate use of a legal power may be reason enough for dismissing a Judge; and that a Judge who, in our age, sends a newspaper editor to prison for commenting, – no matter how acrimoniously, – on what passes in Court does act indiscreetly and intemperately seems to me perfectly clear. If a Judge of a superior Court were to do so, I think that parliament ought to request the Queen to dismiss him. Whatever would justify parliament in requesting the dismissal of a Judge of a superior Court would, in my opinion, justify Lord Carlisle in removing the Judge of a County Court.

> Ever yours
> T B Macaulay

---

[1] Hawes's eldest son was in the Indian army; I do not know who the 'young Under Secretary' can be. Hawes himself had been made deputy secretary to the War Department at the end of October.

[2] William Ramshay (1807–53: *Boase*), Judge of the Liverpool County Court. At the end of September Ramshay had sentenced Michael James Whitty (1795–1873: *DNB*), proprietor and editor of the Liverpool *Journal*, for contempt of court, Ramshay being offended by a placard advertising the newspaper containing a hostile report of one of his decisions. A few days later he sentenced Whitty's son on related charges. Ramshay's conduct clearly showed an unbalanced mind, and in response to petitions Lord Carlisle, Chancellor of the Duchy of Lancaster, held a court of inquiry at Preston that resulted in Ramshay's removal on 24 November. Ellis, as Attorney-General of the Duchy, was present at the inquiry as Carlisle's legal assistant.

TO SIR CHARLES WOOD, 23 NOVEMBER 1851

MS: The Earl of Halifax.

Albany November 23 / 1851

My dear Wood,

You will not, I hope, think that I take an improper liberty with you if, emboldened by the recollection of our old political connection, and of the constant kindness which has existed between us, I venture to offer a suggestion about the Solicitorship of the Treasury.

I did not know till to day that the Solicitorship was vacant.[1] I learned it from Trevelyan, on whom I called this afternoon; and we had some conversation about the importance of the office and the difficulty of finding a person perfectly qualified to fill it. The same thought struck us both at the same moment. I do not believe that there is at the bar any man fitter in any respect for such a post than Ellis, the Recorder of Leeds, and Attorney General of the Duchy of Lancaster. He has just been acting as Assessor to Lord Carlisle at Preston, and distinguished himself only last Thursday by an argument in the Queen's Bench which was praised by the judges, and which every body describes as excellent, on the criminal information against Newman.[2] He was in the Municipal Commission and in the Commission which went to the Channel Islands; and the reports which he drew up and which are among the blue books contain abundant proofs of research and ability. The report on the Channel Islands was commended by Guizot.

Ellis is one of my oldest and dearest friends, a friend of more than a quarter of a century. I lie under great obligations to him. A large part of the literary success which I have obtained I owe to the minute attention which he has bestowed on my writings, and to the kind severity of his criticism. But I should never think of recommending any man to such a place as the Solicitorship on personal grounds. Trevelyan, who is quite unbiassed, agrees with me. And I am confident that there is no Judge under whom Ellis has practised, no minister with whom he has done business, who will not confirm what I say. Lord Campbell, the Chancellor, Lord Carlisle, occur to me at once. If you are, as I collect from what Trevelyan said, looking out for a man of learning, of quick apprehension, of sure-footed judgment, I am certain that you cannot find a better.

Whether he would accept the place is a point about which I have some doubt. His professional income is larger than the salary: but a professional income is not a certainty; and his gains are as hardly earned as those of any man in the Inns of Court. Had he been in town, I would have seen him

---

[1] The Solicitor, George Maule (1777–1851), died on 14 November.
[2] Ellis's speech is reported in *The Times,* 21 November.

before writing to you. But he went into the country yesterday, and will not return till to morrow. In such cases every day is of importance. I have therefore determined to take the risk of being thought officious both by you and by him. / Ever, my dear Wood,

Yours very truly
T B Macaulay

TO THOMAS FLOWER ELLIS, [23 NOVEMBER 1851]

MS: Trinity College.

Albany Sunday

Dear Ellis,

I am afraid that you may think that I have been officious. But I have acted for the best. It was impossible to communicate with you; and I have taken care not to commit you.

This afternoon I called in Westbourne Terrace. There I learned that the Solicitorship of the Treasury was vacant, and that the Lords and Secretaries had been turning over the list of Queen's Counsel without finding any person both competent to fill the place and likely to accept it. The thought that you might not dislike it struck Trevelyan and me at the same moment. The salary is only 2000£ a year: but it is a certainty: there is a retiring pension: there is the opportunity of putting all sorts of good things in Frank's way; there is the prospect of being able to provide for Walter in the public service. The duties are less laborious, I imagine, by far than those which you now perform. They are also most important and honorable. We all thought that, on the whole, it would be a desirable thing for you. Trevelyan undertook to mention it to the Chancellor of the Exchequer, if you approved; and I was to see you to morrow as soon as you came to town, in order to know whether you approved or not. But, as I was going away, Trevelyan said that every hour was of importance, that, though nobody was fixed on yesterday, to morrow might be too late, and advised me to write to Wood this afternoon. With some hesitation I determined to do so. I have told Wood that I ventured to make the suggestion because I heard that he was looking out, and because the idea had struck both Trevelyan and me at the same moment. I have told him that I did not know whether you would accept the place if it were offered, that you were out of town, that I should not see you till to morrow, and that I had written because every minute was precious. I had exposed myself, I said, to be thought a meddler both by him and by you. I referred him to every judge under whom you had practised and to every minister with whom you had done business, particularly to Lords Campbell, Truro, and Carlisle.

If I hear anything from Wood or Trevelyan, I will immediately write again. Let me see you or hear from you; and if I have been indiscreet, excuse my rashness for the sake of my intention.

Ever yours
T B Macaulay

TO THOMAS FLOWER ELLIS, 24 NOVEMBER 1851

MS: Trinity College.

Albany November 24 / 1851

Dear Ellis,

I have written to Trevelyan to say that you will not take the Solicitor-ship. If he thinks it necessary, I shall write to the Chancellor of the Exchequer also.

Reynolds[1] will certainly not succeed Maule. I have not heard any other name mentioned.

I am engaged all this week, except on Tuesday and Wednesday. If on either of those days you can dine here I shall be glad to see you. Thank you for taking my intermeddling so kindly.[2]

Ever yours
T B Macaulay

TO SIR CHARLES WOOD, 25 NOVEMBER 1851

MS: The Earl of Halifax.

Albany November 25 / 1851

Dear Wood,

Thanks for the kind way in which you have taken my intermeddling.

I do not think that I can justly be accused of tardiness, at least by comparison with other historians. Robertson was ten years employed on the History of Charles the Fifth; and all Robertson's authorities were, I believe, in print. I do not remember that he consulted any M.S. I am confident that he made no journey to the scene of any event that he had to relate. I have to turn over thousands of pages of manuscript, French, Dutch and Spanish as well as English. I have been once to the Archives at Paris;[3] and I must go again. I have visited Londonderry, the Boyne, Cork, Limerick, Killicrankie, Glencoe; and I shall probably visit Steenkirk,

---

[1] Henry Revell Reynolds (1800–66), who had been at Trinity with TBM, succeeded Maule in the Solicitorship.

[2] 'On the whole,' TBM wrote, 'I have done no harm' (Journal, IV, 315).

[3] See 18 September 1849.

Landen and Namur.[1] If in five or six years I can produce a tolerable history of William's reign I shall think that I have done my duty.

Ever yours truly

T B Macaulay

TO LADY ASHBURTON,[2] 2 DECEMBER 1851

Text: Transcript from unlocated MS, furnished by Mr F. R. Cowell: dated Albany, 2 December 1851.

Dear Lady Ashburton,

Thanks for your kindness. I am really desirous to break the spell which has hitherto kept me from the Grange.[3] I will try to be with you on Wednesday the 17th. On Friday the 19th I must be in town again. / Believe me ever, Dear Lady Ashburton,

Yours very faithfully

T B Macaulay

TO WILLIAM WHEWELL, 2 DECEMBER 1851

MS: Trinity College.

Albany London / December 2. 1851

Dear Whewell,

Could you easily and readily let me know whether Newton stood for the University at the general election of $16\frac{89}{90}$; and, if he stood, by what majority he was beaten?[4] I find his name in a list of proscription which the Tories sent to all the constituent bodies on that occasion.

Remember me kindly to Mrs. Whewell.

Ever yours truly

T B Macaulay

I have looked at Brewster's book,[5] and learned nothing but Brewster's

---

[1] He did not.

[2] Lady Harriet Mary Montagu (1805–57) married the 2nd Baron Ashburton in 1823; she was one of the most famous of Victorian hostesses – 'the most conspicuous woman in the society of the present day' according to Greville (*Memoirs*, VII, 286). Thackeray and Carlyle among literary men were special ornaments of her circle. Lady Ashburton was regarded as the most brilliant talker among London hostesses, but TBM's Journal account of his visit records no distinct impression of her.

[3] Lord Ashburton's house near Alresford, Hampshire. TBM was there from the 17th to the 19th and found Carlyle among the guests: 'Carlyle and I tried to be mutually civil, but with mutual repulsion. His cant makes me sick' (Journal, IV, 330). For Carlyle's impressions of TBM on this occasion see Alexander Carlyle, ed., *New Letters of Thomas Carlyle*, 1904, II, 120.

[4] See 5 December.

[5] Sir David Brewster, *The Life of Sir Isaac Newton*, 1831.

ignorance of all the matters of which I am competent to judge in Sir Isaac's
life. I hope that the scientific part of the work is better than the historical.

TO LORD MAHON, 3 DECEMBER 1851

MS: Stanhope Papers, Chevening.

Albany Dec 3. 1851

My dear Mahon,

I shall have great pleasure in dining with you on Saturday.[1]

A mad world, to be sure.[2] I am much amused, and not at all frightened.
The Revolution of February 1848 was an earthquake. This Revolution
affects me merely like the transformations of a pantomime. I am, on the
whole, for the President and the army. I like neither priestly rule nor
military rule. But either is better than anarchy. In the 12th Century the
qualities which fit a class to govern were confined to the priests: and it was
therefore good that the priests should govern. At present, in France, it
seems to me that steadiness, subordination, trustworthiness, are pretty
nearly confined to the soldiers. It is therefore good that the soldiers should
govern. It is idle to complain that an army domineers over a society in
which whatever is not army is Chaos. I am sorry for Thiers;[3] and yet I
cannot help laughing at his situation. Of course he will be quit for a few
weeks of somewhat disagreeable seclusion.

Ever yours,

T B Macaulay

TO WILLIAM WHEWELL, 5 DECEMBER 1851

MS: Trinity College.

Albany Dec 5. 1851

My dear Whewell,

Many thanks for your kindness, and for Romilly's.[4] I was aware that
Newton was beaten at the election of 1705.

I am surprised that Newton should have voted for Sawyer. Perhaps, if

---

[1] The other guests were Sir Francis Baring, Sir John Walsh, and Dr Holland (*Journal*, IV, 325).

[2] The news of Napoleon's *coup d'état* reached London on the previous evening; TBM wrote then that 'I never cared so little about a revolution. Things were so bad that nothing could well make them worse as respects France' (*Journal*, IV, 320).

[3] Thiers was arrested and sent out of France but allowed to return in August of the next year.

[4] Joseph Romilly (1791–1864: *DNB*), Registrary of the University. Whewell no doubt referred TBM's request of 2 December to him. In the *History*, III, 536, TBM mentions that Newton did not stand in 1690 but voted for the Tory Sawyer, and adds this note from the University records: 'The votes were for Sawyer 165, for Finch 141, for Bennet, whom I suppose to have been a Whig, 87.'

we knew something about Bennett, the third candidate, we might be able to explain what now seems very strange.

My kind remembrances to Mrs. Whewell.

Ever yours truly,
T B Macaulay

TO UNIDENTIFIED RECIPIENT, 8 DECEMBER 1851

MS: Bonn University.

Albany London / Dec 8. 1851

Dear Sir,

If you were a candidate for any other situation than that of a Professor at Edinburgh, I should be truly happy in having an opportunity of saying what I think of your merits.[1] But I wish to be excused from taking any part whatever in any public matter affecting your city. I am the less inclined to interfere, because I know that you can easily command testimonies more valuable than mine, and because I strongly suspect that, by appearing to take an interest in your success, I should do you more harm than good. / Believe me, / Dear Sir,

Your faithful Servant,
T B Macaulay

TO SELINA MACAULAY, 13 DECEMBER 1851

MS: Trinity College.

Albany December 13 / 1851

Dearest Selina,

I am glad to be able to tell you that I am as well as a man of fifty one has any right to expect to be in an East wind and an orange coloured London fog at Christmas. I had a rheumatic attack; but Dr. Bright put me to rights in a day or two.[2] I wish that you were as well as I now am.

You know as much about the state and prospects of France as I, or, I believe, Lord Palmerston.[3] Of Louis Napoleon's conduct I am disposed to think less unfavourably than many [. . . .][4]

---

[1] The Professorship of Greek at Edinburgh was vacant. Of the nineteen candidates, seven were from Edinburgh (*Scotsman*, 31 December), and of these, the likeliest to be recipients of this letter seem to be Leonhard Schmitz (see 6 December 1845) or Dr William Veitch (1794–1885: *DNB*), neither of whom was successful.

[2] The attack, in the muscles of his neck, lasted from 28 November to 2 December (Journal, IV, 316–20).

[3] Palmerston had already expressed his approval of the *coup d'état* to the French ambassador, an act for which, at the end of the month, he was compelled to resign from the ministry. One of the consequences was that TBM was then offered cabinet office by Russell (Trevelyan, II, 299–301).

[4] The rest is missing.

TO WILLIAM WHEWELL, 13 DECEMBER 1851

MS: Trinity College.

Albany December 13 / 1851

Dear Whewell,

I am truly obliged to you and to Mrs. Whewell for thinking of me so kindly. I am sorry that I have such engagements as make it impossible for me to visit Cambridge next week.

The information which you sent me has been very useful. I am glad to say that it confirms me in the opinion which I had formed touching the state of parties in 1690.[1]

Ever yours,
T B Macaulay

TO SELINA MACAULAY, 23 DECEMBER 1851

MS: Trinity College.

Albany Dec 23. 1851

Dearest Selina,

I enclose a cheque. You of course understand that I mean to pay the calls to which you are still liable from the London and N W railway. I hope that you will contract no new liabilities.

I have been at Lord Ashburton's in Hampshire; and on Saturday I shall go to Bowood,[2] and thence to Lord Broughton's.[3] On New Year's day I hope to be settled for some months in town. Nothing indeed but a royal mandate will easily draw me forth till Easter.

Ever yours,
T B Macaulay

---

[1] See 5 December.

[2] 27–30 December: the guests were the Count and Mme de Flahault, Lord Elphinstone, Stirling of Keir, and Lord and Lady Seymour (Journal, IV, 341).

[3] Hobhouse had been created Baron Broughton earlier in this year. TBM spent 30 December– 1 January with Broughton at Tedworth House, Wiltshire, where the company were Samuel Whitbread and his wife (Broughton was partner in Whitbread's London brewery), John Benjamin Heath, Charles Cavendish Clifford, a Mr Fuller, and Thomas Love Peacock (Journal, IV, 345).

CRISIS IN HEALTH AND RETURN
TO PARLIAMENT
3 JANUARY 1852 – 24 DECEMBER 1853

1852 January 19
Offered cabinet post following Palmerston's dismissal

– March
Elected member of Academy of Turin

– April 8–12
Easter tour: Peterborough, Boston, Lincoln

– June [14]
Invited to stand for Edinburgh

– June 30
Crisis in his health begins

– July 13
Elected at Edinburgh

– July 22
Further heart attack

– August 3–September 27
Recuperating at Clifton

– August
Resumes work on *History* 'after a long intermission'

– November 2
Speech to Edinburgh electors

– November 6
Takes seat in Parliament

– November 16
Appointed to Committee on Indian Territories

– November 30
Elected to Royal Irish Academy

– November
Made Knight of Prussian Order of Merit

1853 January
Begins vol. 4 of *History*

— February
Elected to French Institute

— March 21
Finishes life of Atterbury for *Encyclopaedia Britannica*

— March 22–30
To Paris with the Trevelyan family

— June 1
Speech on Exclusion of Judges Bill

— June 7
Receives honorary D.C.L. at Oxford

— June 24
Speech on India

— July 12–August 19
At Tunbridge Wells

— July 19
Speech on Annuity Tax: last speech in Parliament

— August 26–September 19
European tour with Ellis: Cologne, Heidelberg, Geneva, Lyons, Paris

— December 2
Finishes life of Bunyan for *Encyclopaedia Britannica*

— December 7
Publishes *Speeches*

TO JOHN MURRAY,¹ 3 JANUARY 185[2]

MS: John Murray Ltd. *Mostly published:* Lord Mahon, *History of England from the Peace of Utrecht to the Peace of Versailles,* 3rd edn, 1853, V, Appendix.

Albany January 3. 1851

Sir,

I am much obliged to you for the new Number of the Quarterly Review. I cannot say that it has shaken my opinion.² I wonder a little indeed that so ingenious a person as the Reviewer should think that his objections have made any impression on the vast mass of circumstantial evidence which proves Francis to have been Junius. That evidence, I think, differs not only in degree but in kind from any evidence which can be adduced for any other claimant.

It seems to me too that one half of the arguments of the Reviewer is answered by the other half. First we are told that Francis did not write the letters because it would have been singularly infamous in him to write them. Then we are told that he did not write them because he did not own them. Surely this reasoning does not hang well together. Is it strange that a very proud man should not confess what would disgrace him? I have always believed that Francis kept silence because he was well known to have received great benefits from persons whom he had, as *Junius* or as *Veteran,* abused with great malignity.

It is odd that the Reviewer should infer from the mistake about Draper's half pay that Junius cannot have been in the War Office.³ I talked that matter over more than ten years ago, when I was Secretary at War, with two of the ablest and best informed gentlemen in the Department: and we all three came to a conclusion the very opposite of that at which the Reviewer has arrived. Francis was Chief Clerk in the English War Office. Every body who drew half pay through that Office made the Declaration which Junius mentions. But Draper's half pay was on the Irish establishment; and of him the Declaration was not required. Now to me and to those whom I consulted it seemed the most natural thing in the world that Francis, relying on his official knowledge, and not considering that there might be a difference between the practice at Dublin and the practice at Westminster, should put that unlucky question which gave Draper so great an advantage. I have repeatedly pointed out this circumstance to men who are excellent judges of evidence; and I never found one who did not agree with me.

---

¹ Murray (1808–92: *DNB*) became head of the publishing firm on his father's death in 1843.
² In his Journal for 2 January TBM writes that 'Murray sent me the Quarterly Review with a note asking my opinion of the paper on Junius' (IV, 351). The article, in the December *Quarterly*, was by David Trevena Coulton, and identified Junius with Thomas, second Baron Lyttelton (1744–79: *DNB*).
³ Page 99 of the article.

It is not necessary for me to say anything about the new theory which the Reviewer has constructed. Lord Lyttelton's claims are better than those of Burke or Barré, and quite as good as those of Lord George Sackville[1] or Single-Speech Hamilton.[2] But the case against Francis, or, if you please, in favour of Francis, rests on grounds of a very different kind, – on coincidences such as would be sufficient to convict a murderer.

There is however one strong objection to the theory of the Reviewer which strikes me at the first glance. Junius, whoever he was, wrote a long letter to George Grenville which was preserved at Stowe many years, and of which I have seen a copy in Lord Mahon's possession. The letter contains no decisive indications of the writer's situation. But on the whole it seems to be written by a man not very high in rank or fortune. The tone, though not by any means abject, is that of an inferior. The writer declares himself to be the author of a squib, then famous, called the Grand Council. He says that Grenville must soon be Prime Minister. "Till then I wish to remain concealed even from you. Then I will make myself known, and explain what I wish you to do for me." I quote from memory: but this is the substance. The original I have not seen: but I am told that it is in the handwriting of Junius's letters.

Now this circumstance seems to me decisive against Lord Lyttelton. He was George Grenville's cousin. The connection between the Stowe family and the Hagley family had, during two generations, been extremely close. Is it probable that George Grenville would not have known Lyttelton's hand? Is it possible that a letter written by Lyttelton should have lain at Stowe eighty years, and that none of the cousinhood should have been struck by the writing? Imagine, – for that is the parallel case, – that Sir George Grey's son[3] were to write a letter to Lord Grey, that Lord Grey were to treasure up this letter among his family archives at Howick as a great curiosity, that it were then to be inspected by all the branches of the family, and that none of them should ever suspect the true author.

But in truth the strongest arguments against the Reviewer's theory are the arguments which, in my opinion, prove that Francis was the real Junius.[4] / I have the honor to be, / Sir,

Your faithful servant,

T B Macaulay

[1] Lord George Sackville (1716–85: *DNB*), soldier and statesman, later changed his name to Germain and was afterwards created Viscount Sackville.
[2] William Gerard Hamilton (1729–96: *DNB*), M.P., famous for his maiden speech.
[3] Sir George Grey's only child was George Henry Grey (1835–74). Sir George Grey and the third Earl Grey were cousins.
[4] Coulton's notes in reply to TBM's argument are preserved with the MS of TBM's letter. Coulton concludes that TBM is simply 'unwilling to receive new ideas, and perhaps incapable of receiving them. Against that form of prejudice literary men of all others should most vigilantly guard.' But Coulton's case for Lyttelton is not now taken seriously.

TO RAIKES CURRIE,[1] 5 JANUARY 1852

MS: Royal Library, Copenhagen. *Published:* Enkvist, *Letters in Scandinavian Public Collections*, p. 98.

Albany January 5. 1852

Dear Mr. Raikes Currie,

I am truly sorry that I am forced to deny myself the pleasure of dining with you and of making the acquaintance of Lord Wodehouse.[2] I am still suffering from the Influenza,[3] and am advised to pass my evenings at home.

Very truly yours

T B Macaulay

TO CHARLES MACAULAY, 17 JANUARY 1852

MS: University of London. *Published:* Rae, *Temple Bar*, LXXXVI, 201.

Albany January 17 1852

Dear Charles,

Thank our cousin[4] in my name; and tell him that nothing will ever again tempt me to go through an election. Should I leave my oil? Should I leave my wine? – You remember the beautiful fable in the book of Judges.[5]

I return the letter.

Ever yours

T B Macaulay

TO FRANCES MACAULAY, 20 JANUARY 1852

MS: Trinity College.

Albany January 20. 1852

Dearest Fanny,

I am glad to hear that you are all frightened.[6] Your minds cannot be in a more salutary state. While we are afraid we are safe. Our danger is that we may be too secure. I am less uneasy than I have been for years. I have

[1] Currie (1801–81: *Boase*), a banker, was M.P. for Northampton, 1837–57.
[2] John Wodehouse (1826–1902), 3rd Baron Wodehouse; created Earl of Kimberley, 1866. A Gladstonian peer, he held various state offices and was ultimately the leader of the Liberals in the Lords. He was the nephew of Mrs Currie.
[3] There is no mention of illness in TBM's Journal at this time.
[4] Perhaps Kenneth Macaulay (1815–67: *Boase*), youngest child of Zachary Macaulay's brother Aulay. Kenneth was a successful barrister, and sat as Tory M.P. for the borough of Cambridge in 1852–4 and 1857–65.
[5] Judges 9:8–15.
[6] Following Napoleon's *coup d'état* there was a newspaper panic in England over the defenseless state of the country.

long known that there was danger, and that we had abundant means of guarding against that danger; and I was vexed that those means were not employed.[1] Now I believe that they will be employed; and then all will be right. As to Brighton it is as safe as Rothley Temple for the present.

I propose that we visit Peterborough, Boston, Lincoln, and perhaps Louth at Easter.[2] The Churches of Boston and Louth rank with Cathedrals of the second class. Of course, you will be of the party. We missed you much last year.

Love to Selina. You are quite right about George. He is a good boy.

Ever yours,

T B Macaulay

TO CHRISTIAN BERNHARD TAUCHNITZ, 20 JANUARY 1852

Text: Bernhard Tauchnitz, 1837–1887, p. 109.

Albany, London, Jan. 20, 1852.

I am glad that the first edition of the Essays has gone off. I have no change to suggest in the new impression. . . . I wish that I could tell you when my history of the reign of William the Third will be finished: but I am almost as ignorant about that matter as you can be. The road seems to lengthen before me as I proceed. . . .

TO DR KARL FRIEDRICH PHILIPP VON MARTIUS,[3] 20 JANUARY 1852

MS: Bavarian Academy of Science.

Albany London / January 20. 1852

Sir,

I have the honor to acknowledge the receipt of your most obliging letter, and of the Diploma which accompanied it.

I beg you to convey my warm and respectful thanks to the Academy of which I am now so happy as to be a member. I have read over the list of

---

1 In refusing Russell's offer of cabinet office, TBM took the opportunity to urge the need of a strong national defense: 'I spoke to him very earnestly – reminded him of the calamities of Holland in 1672, and of the fate of the DeWitts – a parallel case' (Journal, IV, 362: 19 January).

2 The Easter tour this year was to Peterborough, Boston, and Lincoln, 8–12 April (Journal, V, 27–9).

3 Von Martius (1794–1868), botanist and traveller, was secretary to the Royal Bavarian Academy of Science. TBM was elected to the Historical Section of the Academy on 2 August 1851 and received his diploma on 14 January (Journal, IV, 358).

my brethren with pleasure and pride. It shall be my earnest endeavour to vindicate the choice which they have made.

With sincere wishes for the prosperity of our Academy, I have the honor to remain, / Sir,

Your most faithful and obedient Servant,

T B Macaulay

The / Doctor Von Martius / etc. etc. etc.

TO LORD MAHON, 7 FEBRUARY 1852

MS: National Library of Scotland.

Albany February 7. 1852

Dear Mahon,

Will next Friday suit you and Lady Mahon? Ten is the hour.[1]

Ever yours truly
T B Macaulay

TO GEORGE CORNEWALL AND LADY THERESA LEWIS, 10 FEBRUARY 1852

MS: New York Public Library.

Mr. Macaulay is extremely sorry that he has an engagement which will make it impossible for him to have the honor of waiting on Mr. and Lady Theresa Lewis to dinner on Wednesday the 25th.[2]

Albany February 10. 1852.

TO LORD BROUGHTON, 29 FEBRUARY 1852

MS: British Museum. *Envelope:* The / Lord Broughton / etc. etc. etc. *Subscription:* T B Macaulay.

Albany February 29 / 1852

My dear Lord Broughton,

I am extremely sorry that I am engaged on Tuesday.[3]

Ever yours truly
T B Macaulay

[1] 'Breakfast party – Lord and Lady Mahon, Dr and Mrs Milman, Hannah, Lord Carlisle, Lord Broughton, Dundas and Hallam' (Journal, v, 8: 13 February).
[2] TBM dined on that night with the Trevelyans (Journal, v, 12).
[3] TBM stayed at home on that day (Journal, v, 14: 2 March).

TO LADY TREVELYAN, 1 MARCH 1852

MS: The Executors of the Late E. M. Forster. *Partly published:* E. M. Forster, *Marianne Thornton*, New York, 1956, pp. 200–1.

Albany March 1 / 1852

Dearest Hannah,

I will dine with you on Friday. On Wednesday, if it is fine, I shall walk with dear Baba.

I have sent the letter on to Fanny. I was at the Bank to day about business. The moment that I came, Labouchere[1] and Melville[2] began to talk of this miserable affair.[3] They seem to be most uneasy about it. I plainly told them that I thought it a serious matter as respected the Bank. They said that they wished me to speak to him, and talked about my influence. I told them that he knew my opinion, and that he carefully avoided the subject in my company. I could not with propriety introduce it; nor should I do any good by such officiousness.

They then asked whether I knew William Dealtry[4] enough to speak to him on the subject? I told them that I hardly knew him at all. They seem to think that he is the real prompter. They say that he declares this to be the only way of making his sister an honest woman. I can hardly believe that he is such a fool as to hold language which amounts to an admission that she has forfeited her honor. And how will such a marriage as this repair the evil? In truth it only makes the matter worse. For at present respectable ladies, you, for example, would not refuse to sit at table with her. But after this marriage, I apprehend, you would refuse.

We all agreed that he never will be able to bear a prolonged exile to the Continent. I told them that, if they could get him to go abroad alone for the purpose of taking a house and making preparations, he would come back so thoroughly sick of Bonn, or whatever other place he might try, that he would give up the whole scheme.

While we were talking he came. He looked unlike himself, gloomy,

---

1 John Labouchere (1799–1863), brother of Henry, and a partner in Williams, Deacon, Thornton, Labouchere and Co. He was a prominent Evangelical.

2 John Thornton Leslie-Melville (1786–1877), afterwards 11th Earl of Leven and Melville, was a partner in the bank. His first wife was one of Thornton's cousins and his second Thornton's sister Sophia.

3 Thornton had now determined to go ahead with his marriage to his deceased wife's sister, Emily Dealtry (see 27 October 1849). They left for the continent on 12 March, or, as TBM put it, 'he is off for the Continent with his trull' (Journal, v, 16: 7 March), and were married on the 22nd. His partners 'would not let him reside permanently abroad as he wished. . . .and for some years [he] hovered uneasily between England and the Continent, though eventually settling back in the family home in Battersea Rise' ('Henry Sykes Thornton,' *Three Banks Review*, No. 69 [March 1966], 36).

4 William, the only son of the elder William Dealtry, was in the Colonial Office, from which he retired as Chief Clerk in 1879.

anxious, and irritable. He tried to talk on ordinary subjects, but seemed constrained, and so, I have no doubt, did I. I went away in two or three minutes after his arrival.

Ever yours

T B M

TO [THOMAS LONGMAN?], 10 MARCH 1852

MS: Trinity College.

Albany March 10 / 1852

Dear Sir,

Many thanks for the Life of Jeffrey.[1] I received it last night; and I have already finished it. It is full of interest, and must, I think, be popular. I have been much affected, though not at all surprised by finding so many proofs of Jeffrey's great kindness for my self.

Ever yours truly

T B Macaulay

TO DAVID MACLAGAN, 10 MARCH 1852

MS: University of Kansas.

Albany London / March 10. 1852

Dear Dr. Maclagan,

I should be truly glad to serve you. But I have, as you may easily suppose, no interest at the Board of Control; nor is there any Director of the East India Company of whom I should chuse to ask a favour.

I wish that I were more competent than I am to appreciate the merit of your son's Thesis.[2] I have looked through it, however, with interest, – interest heightened perhaps by the fact that I have, within the last two years, been occasionally dosed with Colchicum.[3]

Ever yours truly,

T B Macaulay

TO THOMAS FLOWER ELLIS, 12 MARCH 1852

MS: Trinity College.

Albany London / March 12. 1852

Dear Ellis,

I write because I promised to write: for I have very little to tell you. As

[1] Not published until 31 March; Longman was the publisher.
[2] I have not identified this.
[3] The autumn crocus; the drug derived from it is used in cases of gout and rheumatism.

to politics, the chief news is that there was a meeting of M. P.s yesterday at Lord John's.[1] Near 170 came: – wonderful unanimity: – Cobden and Bright in the best temper; Hume and Duncombe a little mutinous, but borne down by general consent. I believe that there will be a dissolution in April, and that these people will all be kicked out before the end of June.[2] They are said to be squabbling furiously with each other; and I can easily believe it.

Lord St Leonards[3] begged hard that his wife might be received at Court, but was told that it was impossible. The reason assigned was that, in Ireland, she had never been presented to the Vice Queen. Lord St Leonards grumbled. Lord Derby consoled him. "Come, we'll compromise the matter. Your lady shall be received by Mrs. D'Israeli."[4]

What do you say to the case of Roebuck v Coppock?[5] Dundas, at our club on Tuesday, began, as soon as the cloth was removed, to display his magnanimity. "I am Roebuck's friend. This is the time for his friends to come forward. I should be ashamed of myself if I were to flinch now: and I do say, and it is the part of a friend who is a man of true spirit to say, that when Roebuck made that speech about his election dealings, he was dead drunk."

And what do you say to the newly discovered manufactory of literary forgeries.[6] Your minters and smashers are nothing to the artists who deal in bales of Byron, Shelley and Keats. These three poets are the persons whose names are generally used. The forger imitates the hand excellently, counterfeits an Italian postmark pretty well with a pen dipped in red ink, copies the matter of a letter from an old review or novel, and sells the fruit of two days of honest labour to Dicky Milnes[7] or some such wise-

---

[1] A notice of the meeting with a list of those attending appears in *The Times* of this day and is the subject of a leading article.

[2] Derby's administration, which succeeded Russell's at the end of February, lasted until the end of December. The dissolution and election were in July.

[3] Edward Sugden, the new Lord Chancellor, had been created Baron St Leonards on 1 March. His wife had originally been his kitchenmaid and had borne him several children before they were married.

[4] Famous for her good-humored ignorance and impulsive manners.

[5] On 16 February Roebuck had charged that elections to Parliament were generally corrupt; he was asked if he had ever tried to stop the activity of James Coppock (1798–1857: *DNB*), a leading election agent and a member with Roebuck of the Reform Club. Roebuck denied knowing anything of Coppock, moved that he be brought to the bar for examination, but at last withdrew the motion (*Hansard*, 3rd Series, CXIX, 620–2).

[6] These were the work of the man who called himself Major George Gordon Byron (d. 1882); the subject was exposed in the *Athenaeum*, 6 March, and in the *Literary Gazette* of the same date.

[7] Milnes not only bought several Keats forgeries, he published two of them as genuine items in the 1867 edn of his *Life, Letters and Literary Remains of John Keats*, long after he had recognized them as forgeries: see T. G. Ehrsam, *Major Byron: The Incredible Career of a Literary Forger*, 1951, pp. 100–1.

acre for a hundred guineas. I am afraid that some of these spurious compositions have been bought for the Museum. Moxon[1] has been done for four hundred pounds, it is said; Murray for nearly as much.[2] The joke is that Browning,[3] a ranting fool whom Moxon employed to write a preface to the works of the Pseudo Shelley, pronounces these letters invaluable, because they could proceed from no mind but that which produced the Revolt of Islam and the Cenci. There has been nothing so good of the kind since Ireland's Vortigern.[4]

As to me, I am much as you left me, except that I am a member of the Royal Academy of Turin, which I tell you, *rumpantur ut ilia Codria*.[5]

We hear that there is nothing to do at York, and that you will all be free by the end of the week. Do you mean to ramble about the country or to come up to town in the interval?

Ever yours,
T B Macaulay

TO JOHN RAMSAY McCULLOCH,[6] 21 MARCH 1852

MS: University of Reading.

Albany March 21. 1852

Dear Sir,

I am truly obliged to you for your kind present.[7] I shall, I have no doubt, find it most useful. Several of your works are always on my table; and I have perpetual occasion to refer to them.

Perhaps you could give me a piece of information which I have sought in vain from some great librarians and booksellers. Sir Dudley North, as his brother tells us, published in 1691 a pamphlet entitled "Discourses upon Trade, principally directed to the cases of Interest, coinage, clipping, and increase of Money." This pamphlet I have been unable to procure. There is no copy in the British Museum or in any other collection which

---

[1] Edward Moxon (1801–58: *DNB*), publisher of Southey, Wordsworth, Tennyson, Milnes and others.

[2] Moxon paid £115 for the Shelley letters; Murray, £123 for the Byron.

[3] Robert Browning (1812–89: *DNB*), the poet; *The Letters of Percy Bysshe Shelley, with an Introductory Essay by Robert Browning* was published by Moxon early in February. The letters were quickly recognized as forgeries, and the book was withdrawn, though not before it had been reviewed (*Athenaeum* and *Literary Gazette*, 21 February).

[4] William Henry Ireland (1777–1835: *DNB*), whose pseudo-Shakesperean *Vortigern and Rowena* was produced at Drury Lane in 1796.

[5] Virgil, *Eclogues*, VII, 26.

[6] The economist: see 15 April 1828.

[7] On the 20th TBM noted in his Journal that 'MacCulloch sent me his book on taxation with a civil letter' (v, 20). The book is *A Treatise on the Principles and Practical Influence o Taxation and the Funding System*, 1845.

I have examined. Have you ever fallen in with it? As far as I can judge from what Roger North says, Sir Dudley's opinion seems to have exactly agreed with Locke's.[1]

As to the combination of the booksellers,[2] I have a most decided opinion; and it gave me great pleasure to find that you agreed with me. In fact I have not spoken on the subject to a single person – booksellers excepted – who does not agree with me. The dispute will, I hope, be amicably terminated. Lord Campbell has undertaken to look into the matter and to say what he thinks ought to be done: and I believe that his award will be accepted.[3] / Believe me / Dear Sir,

Very truly yours,

T B Macaulay

TO FRANCES MACAULAY, 22 MARCH 1852

MS: Trinity College.

Albany London / March 22. 1852

Dearest Fanny,

I send you a letter for Guizot, though I believe that Dumont would do quite as well. I wish that Mr. Sortain[4] or anybody else could manage to infuse a little of the candour, benevolence and good sense of Grotius into our religious factions.

Every body has suffered from the March East winds; and I have passed a very disagreeable week.[5] But the equinox is come; the weathercock on Lord Anglesea's leads[6] has turned ninety degrees; and everything

---

[1] The reference to this pamphlet in the *History* makes it seem probable that TBM did not succeed in seeing it. TBM says of it only that North's plan for the restoration of the currency 'appears to have been substantially the same with that which was afterwards fully developed and ably defended by Locke' (IV, 631: ch. 21).

[2] The London Booksellers' Association, which controlled the retail price of books, had been challenged by the publisher and bookseller John Chapman in January of this year. Chapman managed to enlist many prominent authors on his side, the issue became public, and it was agreed, at TBM's suggestion, to submit the dispute to the arbitration of Lord Campbell, assisted by Grote and Dean Milman (*Publishers' Circular*, 15 April 1852, p. 141). Apart from suggesting the form of arbitrating the affair, TBM took no public part, though his support was claimed by both sides. It appears from this letter that he was in fact on the side of the free traders, though his publishers, Longmans, were prominent in the Association.

[3] On 19 May Campbell decided against the Association; it was thereupon dissolved, and so 'book publishing began a half-century of free trade' (James J. Barnes, *Free Trade in Books*, Oxford, 1964, p. 29).

[4] Joseph Sortain (1809–60: *Boase*), a popular preacher at Brighton, specializing in the denunciation of popery. TBM heard him in October of this year and found him 'not much to my taste' (Journal, v, 141). His church was the North Street Chapel, where the Macaulay family used to attend services when they resided for long periods at Brighton in the early years of the century.

[5] TBM stayed indoors, nursing a cold, from 17 through 19 March (Journal, v, 19–20).

[6] Which TBM saw from the windows of his study: see 24 October 1846.

indicates the speedy coming of bright sunshine, *soft showers, western breezes, green leaves and cream cheeses.* – A rhyme not intended. Charming: I shall give it to them at Westbourne Terrace as an extemporaneous effusion of the judicious poet. We shall, I hope, have fine weather at Easter. We missed you so much last year that we look forward with peculiar pleasure to having you with us.

Kindest love to Selina. I shall write to her in a day or two.

Yours ever
T B Macaulay

TO SELINA MACAULAY, 24 MARCH 1852

MS: Trinity College.

Albany London / March 24. 1852

Dearest Selina,

I inclose a cheque. I cannot tell whether I shall draw you another cheque on that unhappy bank. I am in great doubt whether to move my account or not. I became a customer of the house only because Thornton was a principal partner, and because I liked to do business with him. He will now be absent during great part of the year; and, when he comes, I shall have little pleasure in seeing him.[1]

Rely on it that there is more sense than you good ladies are disposed to allow in the old proverbs about wild oats, and reformed rakes, and young saints being old sinners. Thornton passed the most irreproachable youth that I ever heard of. Malden was very exemplary – but nothing to Thornton. No instance of excess or levity was ever observed in Thornton by those who saw him nearest. That he should ever have taken a drop too much, that he should ever have missed church, that he should ever have let an oath escape his lips, would have seemed to us utterly incredible. And now that he is in his fifty second year, – now that the most dissipated of our college contemporaries are patterns of both public and domestic virtue, – this poor fellow must give himself to a passion condemned by the laws of his country and by public opinion, and must commit follies which would be inexcusable in an ill educated lad of twenty. But there is no use in lamenting. The thing is done: and the punishment will not, I venture to predict, be long delayed.

Have you heard of a wonderful poet in livery who has been discovered in your neighbourhood.[2] There is a silly scribbler for the Magazines named

[1] See 1 March.

[2] In his Journal for 1 March TBM writes that he has been asked to sponsor the verses of a servant boy at Brighton by a Mr De la Pryme (v, 13). Charles De la Pryme (1815–99: *Boase*) was the son of TBM's Cambridge acquaintance, George Pryme: see [25 March], below.

De la Pryme who bores me with letters from the Marine Parade on your East Cliff. His last letter was about the poor Boy of Brighton,[1] a wonderful genius, a Burns, a Chatterton, whose compositions are about to be published by subscription. Mr. De La Pryme begged me to patronize this marvellous youth, to lend my name to the undertaking, and to give my advice as to the lad's future career. Specimens were sent me of the forthcoming volume. The best samples were of the most insipid mediocrity: the rest were detestable, nonsense, false rhythm, false English, trash which I should have been ashamed of at eight years old. If I had been asked only for a guinea I would have sent it: but I did not chuse to lend my name to so absurd a scheme; and therefore I told Mr. De la Pryme a little truth. I have not heard from him since, and shall never, I hope, hear from him again. Are you and Fanny subscribers to "The Poems of the poor boy of Brighton accompanied with a preface and notes by Mr. De La Pryme M. A."?

Love to Fanny. I hope to see her in a [. . . .][2]

TO THOMAS FLOWER ELLIS, [25 MARCH 1852]

MS: Trinity College.

Albany London. / The Feast of the Holy Annunciation. / Ave Maria
Dear Ellis,

This letter is not, as perhaps you will at first sight imagine, from the Reverend Ambrose Augustin Athanasius Alcock,[3] our Malvern friend. Alas, I well know how wide a difference there is between me and that great man, especially at present when I have been for a fortnight enjoying a very bad state of health, as the Morning Post has it.

I have had a vile cold, and am recovering slowly. The East wind is against me; and I shall not be quite right till the weather changes. I have stirred out seldom, and never except in the middle of the day. I have been neither at Lady Derby's nor at Lady Salisbury's. I have cut the Club at the Thatched House and the levee close by at the palace; and I have therefore scarcely any news political, fashionable, or literary. Milnes is in hopes of being a father.[4] So out with your tablets. Miss Sellon has pub-

---

[1] The Poor Boy of Brighton was Richard Realf (1834–78), whose *Guesses at the Beautiful,* Brighton, 1852, appeared with a preface by De la Pryme. Realf was taken up by Lady Byron, among others, later went to America, fought on the Union side in the Civil War, and died, a suicide, in California.

[2] The bottom of the last leaf has been cut away. Probably only part of a line, the closing, and the signature are missing.

[3] There are three Alcocks in the *Clergy List* for 1851 and 1852; none of them was from Malvern, though I suppose TBM means only that they met him there.

[4] Milnes married in July 1851; his first child, a daughter, was born on 3 August 1852.

lished a defence of her nunnery.[1] She says that crawling on all fours and licking a dirty carpet is a highly proper penance for people who presume to speak evil of Elect Ladies like herself. She has gone indeed deeper in Puseyism than the Bishop of Exeter chuses to follow. He has therefore to day put forth a pastoral epistle resigning the office of Visitor to her Beguinage.[2] I told you that a Mr. De La Pryme had pestered me to be one of the patrons of a new Pseudo Burns – the poor Boy of Brighton. I showed you, I think, Mr. De La Pryme's letter asking me to lend my "sacred name,"[3] and the samples which he sent of the Poor Boy's execrably middling verses. Who do you think this Mr. De La Pryme turns out to be? He is a son of Pryme, the old ass at Cambridge, and, thinking the hereditary name not euphonious enough, has turned it into De La Pryme.[4] This is the more droll because the father still keeps his old English surname. If I had the genius of the Poor Boy of Brighton I would write a poem on this subject. What do you think of this for a burden

"Stick to the name of your Papa.

Dele De La: Dele De La."

When shall you be in town again?

Ever yours

T B Macaulay

TO UNIDENTIFIED RECIPIENT, 25 MARCH 1852

MS: Mr F. R. Cowell.

Albany March 25. 1852

Sir,

I have this moment received the volume which you have had the goodness to send me; and I beg you to accept my thanks for it. I have opened it on the poem entitled Calamus; but I have only had time for a glance. The thought of making Calamus predict the fate of his country strikes me as very happy. I shall soon, I hope, have leisure to become better acquainted with your compositions. / I have the honor to be / Sir,

Your faithful Servant,

T B Macaulay

[1] 'Reply to a Tract by the Rev. J. Spurrell...Containing Certain Charges Concerning the Society of the Sisters of Mercy of Devonport and Plymouth,' 1852. TBM bought and read it on 20 March, concluding that 'she is evidently a puppet through which some man is squeaking' (Journal, v, 20). According to Thomas Jay Williams, *Priscilla Lydia Sellon*, 1965, p. 95, Miss Sellon was required by Phillpotts to write this reply to Spurrell's 'exposure.'

[2] 'Bought a letter of the Bishop of Exeter to Miss Sellon. His Lordship is forced to give her up, much against the grain' (Journal, v, 22: 25 March). Phillpotts' 'Letter to Miss Sellon, Superior of the Society of Sisters of Mercy, at Plymouth,' is dated 20 March.

[3] 'He...wishes to be allowed to quote my *sacred name* – booby!' (Journal, v, 14: 1 March).

[4] The blame is the father's not the son's, for De la Pryme's birth is registered in that name.

TO EDWARD MATTHEW WARD, 25 MARCH 1852

MS: Trinity College.

Albany March 25 / 1852

Dear Sir,

I am truly obliged to you for the engraving.[1] I am not a connoisseur: but to me it seems an excellent transcript of a very interesting original.

With very sincere thanks, I remain, Dear Sir,

Your faithful Servant

T B Macaulay

TO THOMAS FLOWER ELLIS, 29 MARCH 1852

MS: Trinity College.

Albany March 29 / 1852

Dear Ellis,

Will you dine here on Friday next?

I agree with you in thinking that the result of the classical examination at Cambridge is very odd and unsatisfactory.[2] Either the examination for the Tripos or the examination for the medal must be a very bad test of scholarship. That a seventh wrangler should be first Smith's prizeman would be thought a prodigy.

George comes back to morrow in good spirits. He wrote for a prize – Latin prose – and is one of seven who are named as having done themselves credit. The exercise is faulty enough, of course, but of very good promise indeed.

Ever yours

T B Macaulay

TO LORD MAHON, 23 APRIL 1852

MS: Stanhope Papers, Chevening.

Albany April 23. 1852

Dear Mahon,

Your nuzzur[3] has found favour in my eyes. So effectively indeed have you propitiated me that I will certainly breakfast with you on the 30th.[4]

Ever yours truly

T B Macaulay

---

1 According to Ward's endorsement of this letter, an engraving of Ward's 'The South Sea Bubble.' The painting was exhibited at the Royal Academy in 1847.

2 The senior Chancellor's Medal was won by the eighth Classic, E. W. Benson, the future Archbishop of Canterbury.

3 Cf. *nuzzer:* 'In India, a present made by an inferior to a superior' (*OED*).

4 The Comte de Rémusat, [Alexandre?] Thomas, Hallam, Gladstone, and Lady Craven were the company (Journal, v, 36).

TO [HENDRIK JACOB KOENEN?],[1] 30 APRIL 1852

MS: Royal Library, The Hague.

Albany April 30. 1852

Dear Sir,

I have just seen Hallam; and I find that he will be out of London on Wednesday: but I have engaged him to breakfast here on Friday, the 7th of May. On Friday therefore I shall hope for the pleasure of your company to breakfast, at ten o'clock. / Believe me, Dear Sir,

Your faithful Servant,

T B Macaulay

TO CHRISTIAN BERNHARD TAUCHNITZ, 8 MAY 1852

Text: Bernhard Tauchnitz, 1837–1887, p. 109.

Albany, London, May 8, 1852.

I apprehend that you are misinformed as to the terms of the convention between the French and English governments.[2] That convention has no retrospective effect. A day is to be fixed by the two governments for the commencement of the new system: and the stipulations are to apply only to books published after that day. Your editions of my works will therefore be admitted into France in exactly the same manner in which they have been admitted hitherto.[3]

TO PETER CUNNINGHAM, 10 MAY 1852

MS: Huntington Library. *Published: Catalogue* of the Alfred Morrison Collection, IV, 4.

Albany May 10. 1852

Dear Sir,

I have just got Nell Gwyn,[4] and have begun to make acquaintance with her.

[1] The only person who could not be called a familiar guest at TBM's breakfast party on 7 May was Major Thomas Larcom (Journal, v, 41). But the more likely recipient of this note is Koenen (1809–74), a Dutch historian and man of letters, the Secretary of the Royal Dutch Academy of Sciences. He called on TBM on this day (Journal, v, 36); as a historian he would have a particular interest in meeting Hallam.

[2] An act enabling a copyright convention with France passed its third reading in the Lords on 3 May and received the royal assent on 28 May.

[3] A note in the Tauchnitz *Festschrift* adds that, by a decree of Napoleon III, unauthorized editions of English works printed on the continent were forbidden in France, leaving the field to Tauchnitz.

[4] Cunningham's *The Story of Nell Gwynn,* published on 24 April.

From what I have seen I expect much pleasure and much information. I hope that our squeamish generation will not be shocked by some of your anecdotes. / I am, dear Sir,

Yours very truly

T B Macaulay

TO SIR JOHN POTTER,[1] 15 MAY 1852

MS: Manchester Central Library.

Albany London / May 15. 1852

Sir,

I am extremely sensible of the honor done me by the Committee of the Manchester Free Library; and I regret that it will be out of my power to be present at the opening of that Institution.[2] With sincere good wishes for the success of your judicious and benevolent design, I have the honor to be, / Sir,

Your faithful Servant,

T B Macaulay

TO HARRIET BEECHER STOWE,[3] 20 MAY 1852

Text: Introduction to *Uncle Tom's Cabin*, new edn, Boston, 1887 [1879], p. xix.

The Albany, London, May 20, 1852.

Madam,

I sincerely thank you for the volumes which you have done me the honor to send me. I have read them[4] – I cannot say with pleasure; for no work on such a subject can give pleasure, but with high respect for the talents and for the benevolence of the writer. / I have the honor to be, madam,

Your most faithful servant,

T. B. Macaulay.

---

[1] Potter (1815–58: *Boase*), a Manchester merchant, was Mayor, 1848–51.

[2] The opening ceremonies, with Potter in the chair, were held on 2 September. Dickens, Bulwer-Lytton, and Thackeray were present and all made speeches.

[3] Mrs Stowe (1811–96), the author, sent TBM a copy of her newly-published *Uncle Tom's Cabin* with a letter more or less inviting him to speak out on the subject of slavery: 'He who should direct the feelings of England on this subject wisely and effectively might do a work worthy of your father' (Introduction to *Uncle Tom's Cabin*, new edn, Boston, 1887, p. xviii).

[4] There is no mention of *Uncle Tom's Cabin* in TBM's Journal at this time; he read the book later in the year at Brighton: see 5 October.

TO ELIZA SUSAN QUINCY,[1] 26 MAY 1852

MS: Massachusetts Historical Society.

Mr. Macaulay presents his compliments to Miss Quincy, and begs her to accept his sincere thanks for the very interesting volume[2] which she has done him the honor to send him.

Albany. London
May 26. 1852

TO LADY TREVELYAN, 27 MAY 1852

MS: Scottish Record Office.

Albany May 27. 1852
Dearest H[annah],

I shall certainly not go abroad.[3] It would be the most paltry coquetry. The motive too would soon be detected or at least suspected: and I should make a most ridiculous figure when I returned, as I should probably return, just as I went.

The situation would be difficult if I had anything to conceal, – if I had any object or intention which I durst not avow. But I have not the smallest motive, on this occasion, to do anything but what is right or to say anything but what is true.

If I am asked to stand for Edinburgh, or any other place, – it matters not what – my answer is simple; – I will not stand. If I am asked whether I will authorise anybody to nominate me, my answer is equally simple; – I will give no such authority. If I am asked whether I will serve if I am elected, my answer is that I have no wish to be in parliament, that I have serious doubts whether my health will suffer me to give that attendance which constituents are entitled to expect from a representative, and that I would advise those who apply to me to make another choice; but that if, knowing all this, they should, at this conjuncture, elect me, I should think myself bound to make at least an effort to perform what I should

1 Miss Quincy (1798–1884) was the eldest daughter of Josiah Quincy, President of Harvard.
2 I do not know what this was. Josiah Quincy's *Memoir* of his father, Boston, 1825, was in TBM's library (sale catalogue, item 11).
3 People in Edinburgh had begun to talk about making amends to TBM by returning him to Parliament in the coming election, and he had great difficulty in determining how to act in response. This letter was in answer to one from Craig, who had been attempting to sound TBM through Hannah. She gave TBM's letter to her husband, who then sent it to Craig with a covering note imploring Craig not to tell TBM what he, Trevelyan, had done (28 May: MS, Scottish Record Office). Hannah also wrote to Craig, stating her belief that TBM would be pleased to be elected for Edinburgh (26 [28?] May: MS, Scottish Record Office). TBM's comment in his Journal of 27 May is that 'I should like the *amende*. I should dislike the trouble' (v, 53).

then consider as a plain duty. If I am asked questions about Maynooth, the ballot, triennial parliaments, or anything of that sort, my answer is that I am not a candidate, that I do not wish to be elected, and that I have no explanations to give. This seems to me to be the right course. However I will see you at lunch time to morrow; and perhaps Trevelyan had better not write till I have seen you.

Ever yours,
T B Macaulay

TO MRS SYDNEY SMITH, 29 MAY 1852

MS: The Viscount Knutsford.

Albany May 29. 1852

Dear Mrs. Sydney Smith,

I am not at all surprised that you should wish to join in paying honor to Mackintosh.[1] No person would have been more ready to do so than he who wrote that very interesting letter which you quote.

Sir Robert Inglis is our Secretary, and a most zealous Secretary. Subscriptions are received at Coutts's or at the house of Williams Deacon and Co in Birchin Lane. The precise nature of the memorial cannot be determined till we know what sum we shall have. A bust in Westminster Abbey, or perhaps in some corridor of the new House of Commons, is what I contemplate. We have, I suppose, about four hundred pounds in hand. / Ever, dear Mrs. Sydney Smith,

Yours most truly
T B Macaulay

TO FRANCES MACAULAY, 4 JUNE 1852

MS: Trinity College.

Albany London / June 4. 1852

Dearest Fanny,

Many thanks for your letter. I am much pleased by your account of John's parsonage and of the thriving state of the neighbourhood. That part of England has always seemed to me the pleasantest of residences. I remember telling poor Lord Kerry more than twenty years ago that only one thing was wanting to Bowood, and that if it were situated in North Lancashire it would be a paradise.[2] Nothing can reconcile me to the daily sight of squalidity and want. I would rather live on the plain

---

[1] A meeting about a monument to Mackintosh had just been held at Lansdowne House (Journal, v, 51: 22 May); TBM subscribed £10. The monument, a bust by the sculptor William Theed, was placed in Westminster Abbey in 1857.

[2] See 23 October 1849.

which lies between Boston and Lincoln than on the shore of the finest of the lakes of Killarney. John, however, has the happy peasantry and the fine scenery together. Love to him, his wife and his children.

Your stories about Miss Strickland[1] are most diverting. It would be a great happiness to me if I could feel but half as well satisfied with my performances as she is with hers.

Yesterday I took Hannah and Baba to a very fine sight. I wish that you had been with us: for, in one way at least, you would probably have enjoyed it more than any of us. It was the great annual meeting of the schools in St Paul's. There were seven thousand children in an immense amphitheatre under the dome, and about as many more visitors. The children are all taught to sing; and the peal which their voices made was quite astounding, and yet harmonious and pleasing. The spectacle was the finest that I ever saw within the walls of a building, except the coronation of William the Fourth, and the High Mass performed by Gregory the Sixteenth in St Peter's.[2] We lunched afterwards at the Deanery. I cannot tell you how much dear Baba was admired.

I begin to be tired of the bustle of the London season, and shall be glad when the dissolution comes to put an end to routs and dinner parties. I can tell you little about elections. Cardwell[3] seems to be confident. Gladstone, I am afraid, is in danger.[4] Bickham Escott[5] wanders about the country, seeking a seat and finding none. At Edinburgh they can get nobody to stand but candidates whom everybody is ashamed of. Leicester will, I believe and hope, be rid of Sir Joshua Walmesley[6] and his colleague Gardiner.[7] Lord John, I trust, is safe for the city.

Ever yours

T B Macaulay

---

[1] Agnes Strickland (1796–1874: *DNB*), author, with her sister Elizabeth, of the *Lives of the Queens of England*, 12 vols., 1840–8, and of the *Lives of the Queens of Scotland and English Princesses*, 8 vols., 1850–9. The *ER*, LXXXIX (April 1849), published a severe review of Miss Strickland by C. S. M. Phillipps to which TBM was invited to contribute. He refused, although he thought her 'a vulgar, mendacious, malignant scribbler as ever lived' (Journal, I, 420: 24 November 1848). She was Tory, and evidently disliked TBM as much as he did her, attacking him in her *Historic Scenes*, 1850, pp. 178–84.

[2] Christmas Day 1838.

[3] Cardwell was defeated at Liverpool; he was returned in 1853 for the city of Oxford.

[4] Two days later TBM attended a lecture by Alexandre Thomas on French history at Willis's Rooms, sat next to Gladstone, and was 'glad to learn that his election is safe' (Journal, v, 57).

[5] Escott (1800–53) had become something of a joke for his parliamentary ambitions. He unsuccessfully contested Westminster, Winchester, West Somerset, Cheltenham, and Plymouth between 1833 and 1852; he was elected for Winchester in 1841 but defeated there in 1847. Escott married a cousin of Trevelyan's.

[6] Walmsley (1794–1871: *DNB*), Radical M.P., held the seat for Leicester until 1857. In his Journal TBM defines a Walmsleyite as a 'mere flatterer of the rabble' (II, 224: 3 February 1850).

[7] Richard Gardner (1813–56: *Boase*) had been elected for Leicester in 1847 but unseated; he was returned with Walmsley in 1852.

TO NASSAU SENIOR, 7 JUNE 1852

MS: Trinity College.

Albany June 7. 1852

Dear Senior,

I shall have great pleasure in dining with you on Thursday the 17th.[1]
Will you breakfast here on Thursday the 11th at 10.[2]

Ever yours,

T B Macaulay

TO [WILLIAM BEHNES],[3] 11 JUNE 1852

MS: Morgan Library.

Albany June 11 / 1852

Dear Sir,

Nothing has been determined respecting Lord Lansdowne's bust.[4]
The only names that have been mentioned are yours and that of the Baron
Marochetti.

As far as I can judge the decision will probably rest with Lord Lansdowne himself. / I have the honor to be, / Dear Sir,

Your faithful Servant,

T B Macaulay

TO JOHN HILL BURTON, 16 JUNE 1852

MS: National Library of Scotland.

Albany London / June 16. 1852

Dear Sir,

Thanks for your kindness, which however is only what it always was.
I did not till within the last few hours think it possible that I should be
returned to parliament on the only terms on which I should chuse to sit
there.[5] But all that I learned yesterday and to day leads me to think it not

---

1 TBM's Journal names Lord Beaumont, Edward Ellice, and Lord and Lady Hatherton
among the guests (v, 63).
2 Thursday was the 10th: Senior did not come, but Lord Carlisle, Dundas, Sir John Boileau,
Hallam, and Bishop Wilberforce did (Journal, v, 59).
3 Identified from endorsement of the letter. Behnes (1795–1864: *DNB*) was a sculptor specializing in portrait busts.
4 A public subscription towards a bust of Lansdowne, to be presented to him in testimony of
his public services, was now in progress. Marochetti received the commission; his bronze
bust of Lansdowne is now at Bowood.
5 The *Scotsman*, 12 June, had announced the plan to nominate TBM. A public meeting
resolving on the nomination was held on the 14th.

improbable that I may be summoned back to public life in a manner which would make it my clear duty to obey. The sacrifice will be painful; and yet I must be a very insensible person if I were not gratified by a distinction which, all the circumstances considered, I believe to be unprecedented.

In any case I hope to have a good deal of leisure for pursuits which I greatly prefer to politics. I expect to have occasion soon to trouble you for information. Nobody is more competent to give it; and nobody is more liberal of it. During the last year I have been occupied with England, Ireland and the continent, and have had little to do with Scotland.

Ever yours truly,
T B Macaulay

TO LORD JOHN RUSSELL, 17 JUNE 1852

MS: Public Record Office.

Albany June 17. 1852

Dear Lord John,

I am sorry that I have no day at my command next week, except Saturday the 26th. Would that day suit you perfectly?[1] –

Nobody can have been more surprised than myself by this strange reaction of feeling at Edinburgh; and I still suspect that my friends there are too sanguine. I shall take no step whatever in the matter. Indeed I hardly know what I wish.

Ever yours truly
T B Macaulay

TO [JOHN WILLIAM SMITH COWARD],[2] 18 JUNE 1852

MS: Trinity College.

Albany June 18. 1852

Sir,

I am extremely sensible of your kindness, though I cannot avail myself of it. To be member for Finsbury would be a great honor;[3] but it

---

[1] TBM's Journal takes no notice of this interview. Perhaps Russell wanted to consult about the Edinburgh election.

[2] Identified from endorsement of the letter. Coward was a surgeon of Barnsbury Park, Islington.

[3] Thomas Wakley retired from the representation of Finsbury this month; as member for Finsbury TBM would have had the Radical Thomas Duncombe for a colleague.

would be an honor which, for many reasons, I could not accept, even if it were offered to me. With repeated thanks I have the honor to be, / Sir,

Your faithful Servant

T B Macaulay

TO FRANCES MACAULAY, 19 JUNE 1852

MS: Huntington Library.

Albany June 19. 1852

Dearest Fanny,

I have not made and do not mean to make the smallest move towards the people of Edinburgh. But they, to my great surprise, have suddenly found out that they used me ill five years ago, and that they are paying the penalty of their injustice and unreasonableness. They could find nobody of whom they were not ashamed to stand for a place which had got so bad a character; and it seemed that they were in danger of having members who would have made them regret not only me, but Cowan. Then, without any communication with me, it was suggested by some of the most respectable citizens that the town might recover its character and put to flight the cliques which domineered over it, by electing me without asking me to go down or to give any pledge or even any opinion on political matters. The hint was eagerly taken up; and I am assured that the enthusiasm in my favour is great, and that I shall probably be at the head of the poll. All that I have been asked to do is to say that, if I am chosen on those terms, I will sit. On full consideration, I did not think that I could, consistently with my duty, refuse. To me personally the sacrifice is great, though I shall not make a drudge of myself, and though I shall certainly never, in any event, accept office. The appearance of my next volumes may be postponed a year or two. But it seems to me to be of the highest importance that great constituent bodies should learn to respect the conscience and the honor of their representatives, should not expect slavish obedience from men of spirit and ability, and should, instead of catechizing such men and cavilling at them, repose in them a large confidence. The way in which such bodies have of late behaved has driven many excellent persons from public life, and will, unless a remedy is found, drive away many more. The conduct of Edinburgh towards me was not worse than that of several other places to their members, but it attracted more notice, and has been often mentioned, in parliament and out of parliament, as a flagrant instance of the caprice and perverseness of even the most intelligent bodies of electors. It is therefore surely not an unimportant nor an undesirable thing that Edinburgh should, quite spontaneously, make a very signal, I may say, an unprecedented, reparation. The event will be the more remarkable because the whole island, but more especially Scotland, is Maynooth-mad. Almost every member who is chosen by Scotland will be pledged to vote at least for inquiry into the Maynooth system. Several good men who have refused to give that pledge, have been forced to retire. Now, if I am elected, I shall be elected unpledged; and that though every body knows that I am for the Maynooth endowment, and that I lost my seat in 1847 chiefly for supporting the Maynooth endowment. I cannot think that, in these circumstances, I should be justified in saying that I will not serve. If the parliament should be a long one, I shall probably take the Chiltern Hundreds before it ends. I shall certainly never consent to be reelected. Having nothing to hope or to fear from my constituents I shall be as independent as if I were a peer. So the matter stands. If they elect me, you may be assured that it will be without the smallest advance or concession on my part. If they do not elect me, I shall be more than content.

Do not talk about this matter more than you find absolutely necessary; but treat it lightly, as I do in all companies where I hear it mentioned. I have a vexatious cold in the head about which I think a great deal more. Six weeks ago I was longing for rain; and now I am longing for dry weather. These are the signs of advancing age. Love to John, his wife, and children.

Ever yours,

T B Macaulay

TO UNIDENTIFIED RECIPIENT, [22? JUNE 1852][1]

Text: Scotsman, 30 June 1852.

[London]

I assure you that I feel as I ought to feel the very high honour done me by those electors of Finsbury in whose name you write. It is most gratifying to me to learn that I possess the esteem and confidence of so many of my countrymen, to whom I am personally a stranger. . . . I cannot accept the generous offer which you have conveyed to me,[2] but I shall always remember it with gratitude and pride.

---

[1] In his letter to Fanny on 23 June TBM says that he was invited 'yesterday' to stand for Finsbury 'free of charge'; this is presumably his response to the invitation. The recipient is perhaps the Doctor Coward of 18 June.

[2] The *Scotsman* adds: 'The latter paragraph is in allusion to a proposal to have held Mr Macaulay free of personal expense.'

TO FRANCES MACAULAY, 23 JUNE 1852

MS: Trinity College.

Albany London / June 23. 1852

Dearest Fanny,

I am glad that you do not blame the course which I have taken. What the result will be is of course doubtful. But as yet it is generally thought that I shall be returned at the head of the poll.

Selina has had a letter from the L and N W Railway company containing a call. Another letter for you came at the same time. As there could be no doubt about the contents I took the liberty of opening it. It is a call for £27 due on the first of next month. I have ordered my bankers to pay it on that day.

I shall be glad to know what you hear of the approaching election at Liverpool.[1]

Ever yours,

T B Macaulay

I forgot to tell you that I was yesterday invited to stand for Finsbury,[2] free of expense. I of course declined.

TO GEORGE LYON,[3] 23 JUNE 1852

Text: Scotsman, 30 June 1852. *Address:* To the Secretary of the Scottish Reformation Society, 6 York Place, Edinburgh.

Albany, London, June 23, 1852

Sir,

I must beg to be excused from answering the questions which you have put to me. I have a great respect for the gentlemen in whose name you write, but I have nothing to ask of them; I am not a candidate for their suffrages; I have no desire to sit again in Parliament; and I certainly shall never sit again there, except in an event which I did not till lately contemplate as possible, and which even now seems to me highly improbable. If, indeed, the electors of such a city as Edinburgh should, without requiring from me any explanation or any guarantee, think fit to confide their interests to my care, I should not feel myself justified in refusing to accept a public trust offered to me in a manner so honourable and so peculiar.

1 Charles Turner and W. F. Mackenzie defeated J. C. Ewart and Cardwell.
2 See 18 June and [22? June]. Two men called on TBM on 29 June to press him again to stand for Finsbury (Journal, v, 70–1).
3 Lyon was secretary of the Scottish Reformation Society and had written in the name of the Society to ask whether TBM would vote to repeal the grant to Maynooth and against any further grant (*Scotsman,* 30 June).

I have not, I am sensible, the smallest right to expect that I shall on such terms be chosen to represent a great constituent body. But I have a right to say that on no other terms can I be induced to leave that quiet and happy retirement in which I have passed the last four years.

I have the honour to be, etc.
T. B. Macaulay.

TO ADAM BLACK, 23 JUNE 1852

MS: National Library of Scotland.

Albany London / June 23. 1852

Dear Sir,

Many thanks. I have received the letter of the Secretary of the Reformation Society, and have answered him – civilly, I hope, but in such a manner as to put an end to questioning. I may as well transcribe my letter.

Sir,

I must beg to be excused from answering the questions which you have put to me. I have a great respect for the gentlemen in whose name you write: but I have nothing to ask of them: I am not a candidate for their suffrages: I have no desire to sit again in parliament; and I certainly shall never again sit there, except in an event which I did not, till very lately, contemplate as possible, and which, even now, seems to me highly improbable. If indeed the electors of such a city as Edinburgh should, without requiring from me any explanation or any guarantee, think fit to confide their interests to my care, I should not feel myself justified in refusing to accept a public trust offered to me in a manner so honorable and so peculiar. I have not, I am sensible, the smallest right to expect that I shall, on such terms, be chosen to represent a great constituent body. But I have a right to say that on no other terms can I be induced to leave that quiet and happy retirement in which I have passed the last four years. I have etc.

I shall attend to your hint about correspondents. The only person who has written to me lately is a crazy fellow named Pringle. I receive a letter from him almost every day. But I return no answers.

Ever yours truly,
T B Macaulay

TO ADAM BLACK, 30 JUNE 1852

Text: Composite from [Black], *Biographies by Lord Macaulay,* pp. xlii–xliii; *Scotsman,* 3 July 1852.

Albany, London, June 30, 1852.

Dear Sir,

I am truly sorry that you should have any cause for anxiety,[1] and I would gladly do my best to save you from any vexation. But what can I do? I despair of being able to use words which malice will not distort. How stands the case? I say that such a distinction is so rare, that I lately thought it unattainable, and that even now I hardly venture to expect that I shall attain it; – and I am told that I hold it cheap. I say, that to be elected member for Edinburgh without appearing as a candidate, would be a high and peculiar honour – an honour which would induce me to make a sacrifice such as I would make in no other case; and I am told that this is to treat the electors contemptuously. My language, naturally construed, was respectful, nay, humble. If any person finds an insult in it, the reason must be that he is determined to find an insult in everything that I write. My feeling towards the people of Edinburgh is the very opposite of unkind or contemptuous. I have been much gratified by what I have heard during the last week of their feeling towards me. I give the best proof of my regard for them by consenting to return to public life at their invitation, after repeatedly refusing to do so when invited on the most honourable and liberal terms by others; nor shall I cease to wish well to your fellow-citizens, or to think highly of their general character, even though they should be again estranged from me by misrepresentations, such as you describe. Remember me kindly to Craig when you see him. –

Ever yours truly,
T. B. Macaulay.

Adam Black, Esq., Edinburgh.

TO THOMAS FLOWER ELLIS, 4 JULY 1852

MS: Trinity College.

Albany July 4. 1852

Dear Ellis,

The bill could not have come at a better time:[2] for I have just received

---

[1] Black was anxious about the effect that TBM's letter to the Scottish Reformation Society might have. Both Duncan McLaren and Charles Cowan were actively campaigning in Edinburgh, while TBM wrote letters 'which his opponents perverted for the purpose of preventing his election' (Black, *Biographies,* p. xlii). When TBM saw that this letter to Black was published in Edinburgh he was vexed, for, as he wrote in his Journal, 'I cannot bear anything that looks like stooping' (Trevelyan, II, 313).

[2] A bill for £24 from Arthur Ellis (Journal, v, 73: 3 July).

from a Leipsic bookseller[1] 30£, the proceeds of the sale of an edition of my Lays of Ancient Rome which I authorised him to print. I inclose a cheque and Torrens's letter.[2]

I inclose also a German letter forwarded me by Bunsen of which I cannot make out a word. If you could at Bromley get it written in some intelligible character, I should be much obliged to you.[3] What a plague the German handwriting is. My bookseller at least has the grace to use the letters ordinary throughout Europe.

Ever yours,

T B Macaulay

TO THOMAS FLOWER ELLIS, 7 JULY 1852

MS: Trinity College.

Albany July 7. 1852

Dear Ellis,

Adam Black, though the most timid of politicians, now pronounces my election certain. The enthusiasm, he says, is strong and constantly increasing. He is very anxious that I should appear at the Declaration.[4] I therefore mean, if I learn by electric Telegraph on Tuesday afternoon that I am elected, shall run[5] to Edinburgh by the Express train that night, harangue in the High Street, and start for the south again on Thursday the 15th.

Nothing unforeseen preventing, I shall stop at York on the Thursday afternoon. I hope therefore that you will keep yourself disengaged to dine with me. I will then consult with you about the way of passing the next three or four days. For I do not wish to be in town again till the 20th, as my servant will be in Herefordshire discharging the duties of a freeholder. Do not mention my design of going down. If I should not be elected, it would make me ridiculous to have formed such a plan.

Lord John, I believe, is quite safe.

Ever yours,

T B Macaulay

[1] Tauchnitz.
[2] Probably (Sir) Robert Richard Torrens (1814–84: *DNB*), first Premier of South Australia, 1857. He had been in Australia since 1840 and was now Colonial Treasurer and Registrar-General of South Australia.
[3] Ellis's daughters more than once performed this service for TBM.
[4] Wednesday, 14 July.
[5] Thus in MS. TBM has changed his construction in mid-sentence.

TO SIR WILLIAM GIBSON CRAIG, 8 JULY 1852

MS: Scottish Record Office. *Envelope:* Sir W Gibson Craig Bart / etc. etc. etc. / Edinburgh. *Subscription:* T B M.

Albany London / July 8. 1852

Dear Craig,

I heard from our excellent friend Black yesterday, and, in reply, I told him that, though the exertion would be very trying to me at present, I would be at the Declaration if I could learn with absolute certainty before starting that I was chosen.[1] I will run no risk whatever of finding myself in a minority when I reach Edinburgh, or even of having to stop and turn back on the road. The ridicule would be intolerable. Even a considerable majority at two o'clock would not be to me sufficient warrant for incurring such a hazard.

The best course will be this. Say nothing about my coming, or speak of it as a thing barely possible, and not at all to be expected, which is the truth. Send me the best and speediest intelligence on Tuesday. I will be guided by circumstances. If I go down, it will be a compliment and a surprise to the citizens. If, as is much more probable, I do not go they will not take offence. Some time in October, before parliament meets, I can harangue them in the Music Hall.

For some reasons I should like to get the whole business over immediately. But I am not very well.[2] I am plagued by a slight asthma which forces me to put on mustard poultices every evening; and I fear that a night on the railway and a morning in the High Street would not mend matters.

Let me hear from you with speed; and let Black see this letter. Kindest regards to him and Rutherfurd. In spite of some mishaps, of which that at Liverpool[3] is the worst, the returns are good.

Ever yours,
T B Macaulay

Remember me kindly to Lady Craig.

---

[1] This letter is in answer to one from Craig 'dissuading me from going down and saying that Rutherfurd is of the same mind' (Journal, v, 78: 8 July).

[2] What TBM here calls a 'slight asthma' accompanied what was evidently a more general crisis in his health that began on 30 June. On that day he wrote: 'All day I have felt unstrung, – a weight at my heart, and an indescribable sense of anxiety' (Journal, v, 71–2). All of the evidence in TBM's Journal and letters, and in the testimony of others, agrees that his health never recovered after this attack.

[3] See *to* Frances Macaulay, 23 June.

TO ADAM BLACK, 10 JULY 1852

MS: Massachusetts Historical Society.

Albany July 10. 1852

Dear Sir,

I have to day received two letters from you and one from Sir William Craig. I have considered them fully, and have made up my mind not to appear at the Declaration. I am really unfit for a night journey by express train; and as to starting on Tuesday morning with the risk of being forced to turn back from Newcastle or Berwick, – you must excuse me if I say that I cannot bring my mind to it. The risk, you think, is small: but it is a risk of being placed in a situation singularly ludicrous and humiliating, and made more ludicrous and more humiliating by the reserve which I have hitherto maintained.

As soon as I know that I am chosen – if I am chosen – I will send you a letter to the Electors. In that letter I will explain my absence on the day of the Declaration, and I will promise to visit them before the meeting of parliament. The time of my visit I leave to be fixed by you and my other friends: only do not fix it without giving me a few days' notice; and do not fix it earlier than Thursday week. For I mean, as soon as this business is settled, to go down to Clifton in the hope that six or seven days of the air of St Vincent's rocks may enable me to speak. If I try to make a long harangue now, I am afraid that I shall only wheeze. I suppose that, after the election, Edinburgh will empty fast. In that case I should think it best that the meeting should be deferred till October. But, as I said, I leave this to you.

I shall write to Sir William Craig by this post to the same effect. / Ever, dear Sir,

Yours very truly
T B Macaulay

TO SIR WILLIAM GIBSON CRAIG, 10 JULY 1852

MS: Scottish Record Office. *Envelope:* Sir W Gibson Craig / etc. etc. etc. / Edinburgh. *Subscription:* T B M.

Albany London / July 10. 1852

Dear Craig,

This is a vexatious question. There cannot be two better advisers than you and Black. Yet you differ from each other; and you do not perfectly agree with yourselves. I must judge as well as I can; and I have determined not to appear at the Declaration. I am not well enough to run down by the night express train, and then to hold forth in the High Street. And I really cannot think of leaving town on Tuesday morning and going as far as Newcastle, or at least as far as York, without the slightest information as to the state of the poll. Only suppose a defeat, and that I am forced to turn back. Say that the chances are twenty to one against such a misfortune; – and that is a great deal to say in any matter which depends on popular feeling and on the combinations of several parties; – still I would not run the hazard. I have held my head high – too high, some people may think, – and the ridicule and humiliation would therefore be multiplied tenfold. On this point my mind is made up. On some other points I have written to our friend Black who will show you my letter.

In general the result of the elections is good. I think it certain that the days of Lord D[erby]'s administration are numbered. Then will come great difficulties, which we will discuss more fully when we meet.

Ever yours
T B Macaulay

TO THOMAS FLOWER ELLIS, 10 JULY 1852

MS: Trinity College.

Albany London / July 10. 1852

Dear Ellis,

I have been forced to give up all thought of going to Edinburgh for the Declaration. I cannot possibly learn the numbers at the close of the poll, or within some hours of the close, before starting: and I will not run the smallest risk of having to turn back. I have held my head pretty high; and therefore such a discomfiture would be far more ridiculous and degrading in my case than in the case of any other man. I shall therefore not see you at York. On Thursday[1] I go to Clifton where I hope to get rid of a vile asthmatic attack which has broken my rest during this week.

Ever yours,
T B Macaulay

I hear very good accounts of Walter. Your young ladies very kindly asked Baba to go with them up the Thames; and she would have been delighted to do so; but she was engaged on another party of pleasure, if any party ought to be so called with the thermometer at 89′ in the shade.

[1] TBM left on Wednesday the 14th and stayed at the Royal Hotel until the 20th, when he returned to London. He found and rented a house at 16 Caledonia Place during this time, and returned to it on 3 August.

TO LADY TREVELYAN, 13 JULY 1852

MS: Huntington Library.

Albany July 13. 1852

Dearest Hannah,
    At eleven the numbers stood thus
Macaulay   1014
Maclaren   894
Cowan   839
Bruce[1]   672
Campbell[2]   415.

Ever yours
T B Macaulay

TO LADY TREVELYAN, 13 JULY [1852]

MS: Huntington Library. *Envelope:* Lady Trevelyan. *Subscription:* T B M.

Albany July 13

Dearest H,
    At twelve –
Macaulay   1275
Maclaren   1110
Cowan   1090
Bruce   793
Campbell   497 –

I think that there can now be no doubt of the result now. I have gained on every one of the other candidates steadily. At 10 I was 74 before Maclaren, at 11 I was 120 before him. At twelve I was 165 before him. I have also increased my distance from Cowan, though not much. There is now very little probability that either will pass me, and no chance at all of my being passed by both.

I have been in Bright's hands yesterday and to day. He tells me that it is all bile: and Holland who looked in as a friend to ask about the election told me, without a fee, exactly the same – "I see by your look that you are

---

[1] Thomas Charles Bruce (1825–90: *Boase*), a son of the Earl of Elgin, contested Edinburgh, Portsmouth (twice), and Helston before being elected at Portsmouth in 1874.

[2] Alexander Campbell (1811–69: *Boase*), of Monzie, M.P. for Argyle, 1841–3, a Free Church of Scotland man. Cockburn says of this election that 'on the part of all the candidates, except Macaulay, it was chiefly a religious matter. Mr. Charles Cowan and Campbell of Monzie stood upon the Free Church alone; Mr. Duncan M'Laren upon the Dissenters; and Mr. Bruce, the Tory, on the Establishment; and with each of these the religious element was far more powerful than the political' (*Journal*, II, 284).

bilious." Bright has given me calomel enough to poison a gun elephant. To morrow I am off for Clifton. Unless I hear from you to the contrary I will call in Westbourne Terrace in the cool of the evening – say nine o'clock, and let you know the final result.

Ever yours,

T B Macaulay

TO SIR WILLIAM GIBSON CRAIG, 13 JULY 1852

MS: Scottish Record Office.

Albany July 13. 1852

Dear Craig,

I have your letter, and the telegraphic despatches down to twelve o'clock. All seems to be safe as far as I am concerned. But Cowan and Maclaren will have a desperate struggle for it.

The first intelligence which reached Brooks's produced a great ferment there. My name, by some strange mistake, was omitted altogether; and the oddest conjectures were formed during about ten minutes.

I am glad that you approve of my determination not to go down to the Declaration. I had, I find, no choice. For Dr. Bright, who has taken me in hand, and has given me calomel enought to set three bilious Mammoths to rights, says that it would have been positively dangerous to venture on such a journey, and on all that must have followed. If I am elected, which now appears to be highly probable, I will send off a letter to the Electors, short, warm, and kind, before I start for Clifton. I shall inclose it to our friend Black, of whose kindness I am extremely sensible.

I have received a letter from the Convenor of the Catholic Electors, inclosing a letter addressed to them by their Bishop, and urging them, not only to vote, but to plump for me. My answer shall be courteous, but properly guarded.

Ever yours,

T B Macaulay

TO THE ELECTORS OF EDINBURGH, 14 JULY 1852

MS: National Library of Scotland. *Published: Scotsman,* 17 July 1852.

To the Electors of Edinburgh

London July 14. 1852

Gentlemen,

At a late hour yesterday evening I learned that I was once more your representative.

I am truly sorry that it is impossible for me to appear before you to day in the High Street, and to give utterance to some part of the feelings with which I accept from you a trust, honorable in itself, and made doubly honorable by the peculiar manner in which it has been offered to me.

I hope that, before the meeting of parliament,[1] I shall have an opportunity of explaining to you the general view which I take of public affairs. But on this day, the day on which my old connection with you is, after an interruption of five years, to be solemnly renewed, I will avoid every subject which can excite dissension, and will only assure you that I am proud of your confidence, that I am grateful for your kindness, and that the peace, the prosperity, and the renown of your noble city will ever be to me objects of affectionate solicitude. / I have the honor to be, / Gentlemen,

> Your faithful Servant
>
> T B Macaulay

TO SIR WILLIAM GIBSON CRAIG, 15 JULY 1852

MS: Scottish Record Office. *Envelope:* Sir W Gibson Craig Bart. / etc. etc. etc. / Edinburgh. *Subscription:* T B M.

> Royal Hotel Clifton / July 15. 1852

Dear Craig,

Thanks for your congratulations, which I ought to return: for I do believe that you are more pleased than I am. Certainly we little expected this when we left the Merchants' Hall on the day of my defeat five years ago. I am not sure that I would not rather have had Maclaren for a colleague than Cowan. Maclaren is a cunning intriguer: but if he had been seated in company with a Whig, it would have been his interest to keep every thing quiet, and to avert any contest. His maxim of old was that the city ought to have one Whig and one Radical member. He might therefore have been inclined to serve me as to local business; and his intelligence and knowledge would have enabled him to do so. Now Cowan, however fair his intentions may be, has not sense enough to be depended upon. No man can expect to find twice such a colleague as I had in you. You must do what you can to help me, till you succeed me, which will be, I hope and trust, at the next dissolution. I feel that I am unequal physically to the work of the House of Commons, even though I should take that work easily, as I shall.

I suppose that the question of the Annuity Tax[2] will soon come on. I

---

[1] In the published text this is changed to read 'On as early a day as my health will permit': see *to* Craig, 17 July.

[2] A tax on house rents, providing the chief fund for the payment of the Edinburgh clergy; there had been agitation against it, particularly on the part of Dissenters, since the early

remember very little about it. Has any blue book been put forth on the subject.[1] I should like to lend the citizens a helping hand in that matter.

I shall stay here till next Tuesday, and then return for a short time to town. Then, I hope, I shall be able to go for two months to Malvern.[2] If you have occasion to write, it will for the present be best to direct to me at the Albany.

Ought I to write to Bailie Morrison.[3] He seems to have taken a very friendly part?

Kindest remembrances to Lady Craig.

Ever yours,

T B Macaulay

TO LORD RUTHERFURD,[4] 15 JULY 1852

MS: National Library of Scotland.

Royal Hotel Clifton / July 15. 1852

Dear Rutherfurd,

It was quite unnecessary for you to tell me either that you rejoiced in the event of the Edinburgh election, or that your house was at my service. The unvarying kindness which I have received from you during thirteen years made it impossible for me to doubt what your feelings would be.

It would be mere affectation in me to deny that I am pleased with an honor which, when all the circumstances are considered, may be called unprecedented. I am pleased too with the pleasure of my family and friends. I am pleased on account of the public. For, during some time past, the conduct of the great towns towards their representatives had made me seriously uneasy. There seemed to be among the electors a growing taste for mere sycophancy and assentation. I was afraid that this would go on till all the considerable cities and boroughs in the Kingdom were represented either by your effervescing demagogue or your still demagogue; – for demagogues are, like Champagne, of two kinds. George Thompson is the type of the one, poor Cowan of the other. No town had sinned more deeply than Edinburgh. I am therefore glad that Edinburgh has repented

---

1830s (see Cockburn, *Journal*, 1, 51–3). The bill brought in for its repeal in 1853 was unsuccessful. The question was not settled until 1860.

1 A report on the subject had been made by TBM's friend John Shaw Lefevre in 1849 (*Parliamentary Papers*, 1849, XLVI, 1–116).

2 On the 19th TBM learned that he could get nothing suitable at Malvern: 'I therefore began to look about me here; and I soon pitched on a most pleasant house in a pleasant situation' (Journal, v, 84).

3 Adam Morrison (d. 1876), Solicitor to the Supreme Court and a bailie in 1852, had made the motion for TBM's nomination at the meeting of the Liberal Committee on 14 June and had seconded Black's nomination of TBM on the hustings, 12 July.

4 Rutherfurd was made a Lord of Session in May 1851.

signally, and has, after the good old forms of Kirk discipline, had the courage to appear on the cutty stool. I am convinced by all that I hear that the effect on the public mind has been great: and I believe that this effect would have appeared in several places, had the Edinburgh election taken place a week earlier. Unfortunately it was the last town election, or nearly the last in the island.

For these reasons I am glad; and yet I am sorry. The sacrifice required of me is a severe one. I must now try to do what many others do better, and must leave half done, in all probability, what I did best. My health too is not what it was; and I look forward to the bad air and bad hours of the House of Commons with much apprehension. You will call me a querulous ungrateful fellow for murmuring at a lot which is generally thought enviable; and perhaps you will be right. / Ever, dear Rutherfurd,

Yours most truly
T B Macaulay

TO LADY TREVELYAN, 15 JULY 1852

MS: Trinity College. *Envelope:* Lady Trevelyan / 20 Westbourne Terrace / Hyde Park Gardens / London. *Subscription:* TBM.

Royal Hotel / Clifton July 15 / 1852

Dearest Hannah,

I am here in tolerably comfortable rooms, but not as yet much better for the change of air. That was indeed hardly to be expected. I received to day kind letters from Craig, Rutherfurd and others; and I have been all the morning employed in writing answers. I intend to be extremely courteous and gracious to the Edinburgh electors now. It was proper to be reserved and high while the event was at all doubtful. But what then was dignity would now be insolence.

William has left me for Herefordshire. He is to make inquiries at Malvern, but to conclude nothing.

How many old recollections this place calls up. Yet how things are changed: or rather how I am changed. In this very house Selina and I in the summer of 1811 breakfasted with my uncle Colin. The Royal Hotel was then the boast of Clifton. It was considered as the first house of the kind in the kingdom. The splendour of the plate, china, and furniture astonished me. On every dish and saucer was a picture of the hotel. Now this palace seems to me a great, rambling, shabby, caravansery, in which I can just make shift to get my meals and my sleep. Hard by is a villa built by Sir William Draper[1] with a cenotaph in the grounds. I well remember

---

[1] General Sir William Draper (1721–87: *DNB*), at Manilla Hall, Clifton Downs, 'erected a cenotaph to the thirty officers and one thousand men of the old 79th who fell in the East Indies in 1758–65' (*DNB*).

that the first time that I ever heard the word cenotaph was in 1811 from my uncle Colin when he showed me that monument. I did not know Greek enough to discover the meaning and supposed that it had something to do with Senate, and was spelt with an S. But I thought house, grounds, and cenotaph, magnificent. Now – On the other hand the rocks and woods which then interested me not at all give me now the greatest delight.

Ask Selina whether she remembers our breakfast at the Royal Hotel when we lodged at a certain Mrs. Anderson's about a hundred yards from where I am now writing, – and made acquaintance with a certain Mrs. and Miss Elliot, – and got an abominable religious novel, then just published, and entitled Self Controul,[1] – and saw my poor aunt Hannah[2] very pale and weak in a great arm chair, and how we were shown a most extraordinary dwarf – a woman of forty, less than Alice, and how Uncle Colin took up Elements of Morality,[3] and said that it was a Socinian book. These and hundreds of small events which happened here that summer I remember as if only a day, instead of forty one years, had passed since. Love to Trevelyan, Baba and Alice.

Ever yours,
T B M

TO THOMAS FLOWER ELLIS, 15 JULY 1852

MS: Trinity College. *Extract published:* Trevelyan, II, 315.

Royal Hotel Clifton / July 15. 1852

Dear Ellis,

You learned the result of the Edinburgh election yesterday, I suppose. I should have sent you the numbers on Tuesday evening by electric telegraph, had I received them myself in reasonable time. But, from whatever cause, I did not get my despatch till late at night.

In the midst of my triumphs I am but poorly. I have long been accustomed to oppression of the chest and difficulty of respiration in cold weather. But I have now for the first time been plagued by these maladies in the fiercest heat of summer. Bright says that the stomach is the seat of the disease, and has given me calomel enough to purge three bilious elephants. I hope that his pills and the fine air of these Downs will set me to rights. But I must not get into this style – τον γαρ καλον κἀγαθον ανδρα χρη, κἀν βαρεως νοσῃ, καρτερεῖν καὶ σιγᾶν, ου μεν ουν μαλακιζειν, ουδ'

---

[1] Mrs Mary Brunton, *Self-Control*, 1810.
[2] Hannah Mills, who died of tuberculosis that summer.
[3] See [12 September 1842].

εμψωνιζειν.[1] Translate this sentence. Explain the last word. What is known of the person alluded to? Whose daughter did he marry? What periodical work did he edite? In what college was he a teacher? – and of what? But it is a shame to laugh at so good a fellow and so true a friend.

I shall be in town again on Tuesday the 20th. When shall you be there? William started hence this morning for Herefordshire, and is to make inquiries at Malvern, carefully avoiding all dealing with Mr. MacCan.[2]

I hear everything good of Walter. Hannah was at Harrow on Tuesday. She says that he is working hard, and behaving well, and rising in every body's opinion.

Ever yours
T B Macaulay

TO FRANCES MACAULAY, 16 JULY 1852

MS: Trinity College.

Royal Hotel / Clifton July 16 1852

Dearest Fanny,

Thanks for your affectionate letter. I am glad that you are pleased. But there is little reason for congratulation. Even in this fine air and fine weather I am wheezing like a Grampus. What shall I do at two o'clock on a winter morning in the bad air of the House of Commons?

I brought down a prescription from Dr. Bright, and sent it to a druggist. The pills and mixtures however did not come. I went and complained. The druggist declared that he had sent them, but that my name was unknown at the Royal Hotel; and they had been brought back. "Impossible" said I. "Yes, Sir," said he. "Mr. Robert Hole, I believe, I have the honor of speaking to. It is in the prescription." "It is not so," I said, somewhat angrily: for I supposed that he had been so careless as to change my prescription for that of somebody else. He produced the paper, where I was described as

Rt Hoble
T B Macaulay

Looking only at the first line he made it out to be Robert Hole; and thus I very nearly missed my physic.

I must have done: for I have as many letters this morning as a Secretary of State. If I get a Scotch paper which would interest you, I

[1] 'A fine and good man should, even if he is very sick, endure and keep quiet and not grow soft or Empsonize.'
[2] See 15 September 1851.

will send it: but I do not learn that anything remarkable happened at the nomination. Love to George and Sarah Anne.

> Ever yours,
> T B Macaulay

TO JOHN THOMPSON GORDON,[1] 16 JULY 1852

Text: Mrs [Mary Wilson] Gordon, '*Christopher North*': *A Memoir of John Wilson*, New York, 1866, pp. 451–2.

> Royal Hotel, Clifton, / July 16, 1852.

My Dear Mr. Gordon: –

I am truly grateful for your kindness in letting me know how generous a part Professor Wilson acted towards me.[2] From my school-days, when I delighted in the *Isle of Palms* and the *City of the Plague*,[3] I have admired his genius. Politics at a later period made us, in some sense, enemies. But I have long entertained none but kind feelings towards him, and his conduct on Tuesday is not the first proof which he has given that he feels kindly towards me. I hope that you will let him know how much pleasure and how much pride I felt when I learned he had given me so conspicuous a mark of his esteem.

With many thanks for your congratulations, believe me, yours most truly,

> T. B. Macaulay.

TO SIR WILLIAM GIBSON CRAIG, 17 JULY 1852

MS: Scottish Record Office. *Envelope:* Sir W Gibson Craig Bart. / etc. etc. etc. / Edinburgh. *Subscription:* TBM.

> Royal Hotel Clifton / July 17. 1852

Dear Craig,

It is no very easy thing for a man in an asthma to tell you how soon he shall be able to harangue a great meeting for an hour. I am really afraid of disappointing the people of Edinburgh by fixing a time. However, I really feel myself better to day; and I think that the Clifton air is beginning to produce its effect. After ten miserable nights I have had a tolerable one. The earliest day, I am afraid, on which I could possibly make my appearance in the Music Hall is Saturday the 24th. I should leave town on the Thursday, divide my journey into two days, and have the Sunday to rest myself before returning. If this plan is objectionable, name any day in the

---

[1] Gordon (1813–65: *Boase*), Sheriff of Midlothian, was John Wilson's son-in-law.
[2] Though retired and invalid, Wilson had come into Edinburgh to vote for TBM.
[3] 1812 and 1816.

following week, and I will, if possible, do what you wish. Direct your answer to the Albany. I shall be there on Tuesday.

I do not doubt that you and Black judged wisely in altering my letter. Your kindness and his, through all this business, has been beyond praises or thanks; nor do I feel it the less because a seat in parliament has ceased to be an object of desire to me. If my own altered tastes and impaired health prevent me from enjoying this triumph as I should once have done, I have nevertheless great pleasure in the pleasure of my family and friends. My table here is covered with letters of congratulation. The most fervent, I think, is from Graham. Odd that, after so many vicissitudes, and such complete estrangement, he and I should again find ourselves seated together, as we were twenty two years ago, on the Speaker's left hand.[1]

Kindest regards to Lady Craig. In writing to you, I consider myself as writing to our friend Adam Black.

Ever yours,
T B Macaulay

to Lord Mahon, 17 July 1852

MS: Stanhope Papers, Chevening.

Royal Hotel Clifton / July 17. 1852

Dear Mahon,

I was just sitting down to write to you when I received your very kind letter. I did not mean to condole with you.[2] For, though I believe that you had much more taste for parliamentary life than I, I should have thought it absurd to condole with a man who has such sources of happiness as you are blessed with, on having more time to spare for literature, for friendship, and for the enjoyments of home. But I thought that it might be gratifying to you to know that at Brooks's, the head quarters of our party, though we regarded you as our enemy, and though we put down Chambers[3] among our gains, there was a general expression of regret at your defeat. Several Whigs with whom you never had any intercourse spoke of you in a way which gave me sincere pleasure. The conduct of Lord Salisbury[4] was the subject of universal blame and derision.

---

[1] Graham sat with the opposition to Derby and joined the coalition ministry formed at the end of this year.

[2] Mahon had been defeated at Hertford and did not again sit in the House of Commons.

[3] (Sir) Thomas Chambers (1814–91: *DNB*), a barrister, sat as Liberal M.P. for Hertford, 1852–7.

[4] The second Marquess (1791–1868), Mahon's political sponsor at Hertford, in this election 'participated in a political deal which involved bringing in a Radical for the constituency' (Aubrey Newman, *The Stanhopes of Chevening*, 1969, p. 265).

As to myself, my feelings about what has happened are of a very mixed nature. If I analyse them strictly, I find that I am very glad to be elected, but very sorry to have to sit. The election, all circumstances considered, was a great honor. The sitting will, I am afraid, bring me neither honor nor pleasure. I would very much rather sit with you under your beech tree. Indeed, as you quote *sub tegmine fagi*,[1] I think that a good parody might be made of the first Eclogue – you, Tityrus, lying at ease under the trees, – I poor Melibœus, driven from a quiet happy retreat, and regretting his lost ease and leisure. The dialogue ends by an invitation from Tityrus to a supper and a night's lodging: and this brings me to your kind invitation to Chevening. I wish that I could accept it: but the thing is impossible. I have come to this place in the hope of getting rid of an asthmatic complaint. As soon as I am tolerably well, I must go to Scotland and harangue my constituents; nor can I with any certainty say where I shall be next week or the week after.

Pray remember me most kindly to your family. I hope that Lady Mahon has not felt your defeat very painfully. In general I have observed that the sensibility of wives and sisters is the worst part of such defeats. All kind wishes to my Valentine.

Ever yours truly,
T B Macaulay

to Lord Broughton, 17 July 1852

MS: British Museum.

Royal Hotel Clifton / July 17. 1852

Dear Lord Broughton,

I am truly sensible of your kindness, and still more sensible of Miss Hobhouse's[2] kindness: for her proviso is a very judicious one. If I analyse my feelings strictly, the result is that I like very much the being elected, but that I do not at all like to sit. To be elected, as I was elected, is certainly a great honor. To sit is as certainly a great bore. I have been here two or three days trying to get rid of an oppression on the chest, before going down to Edinburgh. I have to make a speech to my constituents; and I much fear that, instead of speaking, I shall only cough and wheeze.

Ever yours truly
T B Macaulay

---

[1] Virgil, *Eclogues*, 1, 1.
[2] Charlotte (1831–1914), afterwards Lady Dorchester and the editor of her father's *Recollections*.

TO THOMAS FLOWER ELLIS, 17 JULY 1852

MS: Trinity College. *Partly published:* Trevelyan, II, 322.

Royal Hotel Clifton / July 17. 1852

Dear Ellis,

I am a little better, and must soon think of going to Edinburgh and haranguing. The probability is that I shall leave London for the north just as you are coming back from the north to London. The earliest day on which I can make a public appearance is Saturday the 24th. Early in the following week I hope to see you in town, and to be able to concert plans for the summer, or rather for the autumn.

Rely on it that I shall never be in office again. Every motive is against it, – avarice and ambition as well as the love of ease and the love of liberty. I have been twice a cabinet minister, and never made a farthing by being so. I have now been four years out of office; and I have added ten thousand pounds to my capital. So much for avarice. Then for ambition, – I should be a far greater man as M.P. for Edinburgh, supporting a liberal government cordially, but not servilely, than as Chancellor of the Duchy or Paymaster of the Forces.

Tell Campbell[1] that I am very sensible of his kindness. I receive congratulations from all quarters. The most fervent perhaps are from Graham. My own feelings are mixed. If I analyse them strictly I find that I am glad and sorry, glad to have been elected; sorry to have to sit. The election was a great honor. The sitting will be a great bore. I discriminate, you see, much more accurately than that pious old maid whose religious meditations are criticized in the Monthly Review. "For the sin of our first mother," says this lady, "our sex was justly punished with the cruel pains of conception."

I have a long story for you about my adventures with an apothecary here. They would furnish a good subject for a farce. But they must wait till we meet.

Ever yours
T B Macaulay

TO JOHN EVELYN DENISON, 20 JULY 1852

MS: University of Nottingham.

Albany London / July 20. 1852

Dear Denison,

Though you desire me not to answer you, I must send one line of

[1] Lord Campbell went the Northern Circuit in this summer's assizes.

thanks, and only one line; for I have a great deal on my hands. We shall have many opportunities now of talking politics together. My kindest regards and thanks to Lady Charlotte.

Most truly yours,
T B Macaulay

TO SIR WILLIAM GIBSON CRAIG, 21 JULY 1852

MS: Scottish Record Office.

Albany London / July 21. 1852

Dear Craig,

I returned to town yesterday, so much better for my sojourn at Clifton that I have determined to pass August and September there, in the hope of being able to collect health and breath for the Session. I was so much shaken by the journey up that it was a relief to me to find that I need not start again to morrow.[1]

I think it clearly desirable that the first public meeting which I attend at Edinburgh should be the meeting of electors. Since you leave it to me to name the day I will name Friday the 30th. I will try to be at Edinburgh on the evening of Tuesday the 27th. I should much wish to get away on the Saturday: but, if you think it right, I will stay till the Monday.

I hope that, during my visit, I shall enjoy one day at least with you at Riccarton.

I will write by to day's post to Bailie Morison.

I shall not be sorry to be at Edinburgh a day or two before the meeting: for I wish to consult you as to several topics and as to the best way of treating them.

Ever yours,
T B Macaulay

In writing to you I consider myself as writing to our friend Black.

TO SIR WILLIAM GIBSON CRAIG, 24 JULY 1852

MS: Scottish Record Office. *Envelope:* Sir W Gibson Craig Bart. / etc. etc. etc. / Riccarton / Edinburgh. *Subscription:* TBM.

Albany London / July 24. 1852

Dear Craig,

I am sorry to say that, since I wrote to you last, I have been very

---

[1] That is, for the meeting on the 24th that TBM proposed to Craig on 17 July. Craig wrote that TBM need not come down until the next week (Journal, v, 85).

unwell.[1] To day Bright after a very long and close examination with the help of a mysterious looking tube,[2] pronounced that the action of the heart was deranged, that quiet was absolutely necessary to me, and that it would be dangerous for me to make a long journey, and still more dangerous to make a long speech. He would hardly have prevented me from going to Edinburgh if my own sensations had not convinced me that the speech would be a matter of physical impossibility, and that I should be forced to sit down in five minutes. I shall remain a few days under his care, and then return by short journeys to Clifton. He encourages me to hope that some weeks of repose in that delicious air will set me up again. If I should want nurses my sister and niece will come down at an hour's notice.

I have no reason to doubt that this complaint will give way to proper treatment. But I feel that my health is giving way; and I look forward with much uneasiness to the late hours and bad air of the House of Commons. It is very probable that I shall, in no long time, be forced to apply to D'Israeli for the only place that I mean ever to take, the Steward-ship of the Chiltern Hundreds. Of course I shall do nothing of the sort without consulting you. But it would be desirable that you and our friend Black should even now begin to consider what course, in such an event, it would be proper for you to take.

Before I leave town I will send you my address at Clifton.

Ever yours truly

T B Macaulay

TO ABRAHAM HAYWARD, 24 JULY 1852

MS: National Library of Scotland.

Albany July 24. 1852

Dear Hayward,

Dr. Bright has positively forbidden me to go to Edinburgh, and has, after pulling me about and examining me with a strange looking tube, pronounced that I must keep myself quiet for some weeks. Instead of going northward to harangue I shall go westward, and nurse myself duing August and September at Clifton, in the hope that I may gather a stock of health sufficient for the parliamentary campaign.

Very truly yours,

T B Macaulay

[1] On the 22nd TBM wrote: 'Not well to day. The circulation deranged – something the matter with the heart. I felt a load on my breast. To Westbourne Terrace. I was much unstrung, and could hardly help shedding tears of mere weakness: but I did help it' (Journal, v, 86).

[2] 'He came with a stethoscope, I think they call it' (*ibid.*).

TO THOMAS FLOWER ELLIS, 24 JULY 1852

MS: Trinity College.

Albany July 24. 1852

Dear Ellis,

Bright has upset all my plans. He pronounces my heart deranged, – not dangerously – but so as to require rest and the absence of excitement. He positively interdicts me from going to Edinburgh at present. I am to be under his care during a few days, and then to go to Clifton. Now, if it would perfectly suit you that I should go to Bromley next Saturday – the 31st, and stay till Monday, I could easily manage it;[1] and your air would, I dare say, do me good. Come and dine here on Tuesday or Wednesday, and we will settle about it.

Ever yours,

T B Macaulay

TO LADY TREVELYAN, 26 JULY 1852

MS: Trinity College.

Albany July 26. 1852

Dearest Hannah,

I shall probably stay at home all day, as I feel very languid and as I expect Bright in the afternoon.

I had hoped that Craig would get my letter of Saturday last before the meeting in the Music Hall could be announced for Friday next. Unfortunately the announcement has been made:[2] and there will, no doubt, be much disappointment. I am a little uneasy lest the people there should think that I am making the most of a slight indisposition, and that, if I thought them worth a little exertion, I should have managed to go down. It has occurred to me that you might without impropriety write a line to Craig.[3] You have already corresponded with him about the election; and you could ask him to prevent his friends from urging me at present to make an effort which is really beyond my strength. I do not tell you what to say; for, if you have no objection to writing such a letter, you will of course acquit yourself with feminine skill and tact.

Ever yours

T B Macaulay

---

[1] TBM paid the visit, staying from the 31st to Monday the 2nd (Journal, v, 91–2).
[2] *Scotsman,* 24 July; a notice postponing the meeting appears on the 28th.
[3] Hannah's letter of the 26th to Craig explaining that TBM could not make the trip is now in the Scottish Record Office.

TO SIR WILLIAM GIBSON CRAIG, 27 JULY 1852

MS: Scottish Record Office. *Envelope:* Sir W. Gibson Craig Bart / etc. etc. etc. / Riccarton / Edinburgh. *Subscription:* TBM.

Albany London / July 27. 1852

Dear Craig,

Your kindness is what it has always been. Be assured that I will do my best to avoid all that can cause you the smallest embarrassment or annoyance.

I am certainly at present very languid and incapable of exertion. I find that a walk of a quarter of an hour, during which I am forced to lean on a stick, is as much as I can bear. But Bright tells me that a few weeks of quiet and country air will in all probability set me to rights for some time; and he said the same to my sister who, without my knowledge, called on him yesterday. She tells me that she has written to you: she saw that I was anxious lest my friends at Edinburgh should think that I was neglecting them.

I shall go a little way into the country on Saturday. On Tuesday I shall go down to Clifton. My sister will go with me; and my niece will afterwards come to me for some time. I want nothing that medical skill or feminine care and tenderness can do for me.

My address at Clifton will be 16 Caledonia Place. If, as I hope, I should be quite recovered by the beginning of October, it will be desirable that I should go down before the meeting of parliament. But on that subject we need not at present come to any decision. It is a great satisfaction to me to learn that, if I should be forced to retire, you think that you could bring in George Grey.[1]

I will own to you that I have been made a little uneasy by a letter which Lord Cockburn lately wrote to Empson, and which Empson sent to me, saying that it was the second to the same effect that Cockburn had written, and that it was evidently meant to be seen by me.[2] Cockburn expresses himself respecting me in the most friendly manner, but says that it is most important that I should understand my position. "Macaulay must pay the price which is exacted from other members for great constituent bodies. He must attend to all their jobs. He must flatter the self conceit of individuals. He must not imagine that any speech that he can make will do him so much good as the least neglect of these things will do him harm. He will now be more closely watched than ever. The electors are in a most touchy and punctilious temper about him, and are

---

[1] Grey lost his seat for North Northumberland in the election.
[2] TBM received this on the 21st and wrote that 'Cockburn says plainly... that the Edinburgh people think that they have got a slave.... They will find themselves grievously mistaken, I can tell them' (Journal, v, 85).

ready to construe anything into a slight." I sent the letter back to Empson, as he desired, and therefore I cannot give you the precise words: but this is the sense; and the words *job, touchy, punctilious,* I particularly remember. Now, if this really be the feeling of the citizens, or of a large part of them, it would surely be wise in me to make an early retreat on the plea, which I may most fairly urge, of delicate health, and not to produce an exacerbation of feeling among them which may be fatal to the Whig interest. Consider this well; – and, in any case, do nothing that can hurt Lord Cockburn's feelings: for it is evident that he can have had no motive for admonishing me thus except a wish to serve me.

 Kindest regards to Lady Craig.

Ever yours,
T B Macaulay

TO LORD MINTO, 30 JULY 1852

MS: National Library of Scotland.

Albany London July 30 / 1852

Dear Lord Minto,

 I am truly grateful for your kindness, and wish that I could avail myself of it. But I am under orders for Clifton where I am to pass the next two months, and to gather, if I can, breath and strength for the House of Commons. I hope to be able to go down to Edinburgh in October, certainly not earlier.

 I should indeed be glad to have an opportunity, before I say anything about politics to my constituents, of talking with Lord John.[1] The conjuncture is, as you say, one which calls for grave deliberation.

Ever yours truly
T B Macaulay

TO LORD JOHN RUSSELL, 30 JULY 1852

MS: Public Record Office.

Albany London / July 30. 1852

Dear Lord John,

 I am truly sensible of your kindness. My complaint is one for which quiet and fresh air will, I believe, do more than calomel or colchicum,

---

[1] Minto, Lord John Russell's father-in-law, wrote to TBM on this day 'inviting me to consult with Lord John who, Lord M says, is in need of counsel' (Journal, v, 90). The letter to Russell of this date was perhaps enclosed with TBM's reply to Minto.

though neither calomel nor colchicum has been spared. I hope that two months at Clifton will qualify me to visit my constituents and to harangue them. At present I am quite unequal to the exertion of a long journey or of a long speech.

I shall be truly glad if, before I make my public appearance at Edinburgh, which will not be till October, I could find an opportunity of talking with you. The conjuncture is an important and a perplexing one: and, though I am afraid that a speech from me could do little good, it might do much harm. It will be time however to think of this at Michaelmas. I have no more serious study at present than Grimm's correspondence and Goldoni's Comedies.

I heartily wish that George Grey were M.P. for Edinburgh in my stead. With kindest regards to Lady John, believe me

Ever yours most truly

T B Macaulay

TO JOHN EVELYN DENISON, 31 JULY 1852

MS: University of Nottingham.

Albany July 31. 1852

Dear Denison,

You are very kind to me, as you always are. I am not well: but Bright assures me that two months of perfect quiet and of Clifton air will set me up: and I shall leave town to day[1] in the hope that his predictions will be accomplished. My spirits are good: but I cannot walk a quarter of a mile without feeling faint; and I have been forced to take to the support of a stick, so that I am now in the third stage of the Sphinx's riddle. I hope however that I shall find strength for a passage of arms with D'Israeli before Christmas. I should like to give him back his phrase of *organized hypocrisy.*[2] "I thank thee, *Jew*, for teaching me that word."[3]

Remember me kindly to Lady Charlotte. I hope to see Ossington again, but not when I require nursing.

Ever yours truly,

T B Macaulay

---

[1] For Ellis's place at Bromley; TBM returned to town on the 2nd, spent the night at Westbourne Terrace, and went on to Clifton with Hannah on the next day (Journal, v, 92).

[2] Of Peel's government, in Disraeli's speech of 17 March 1845.

[3] *Merchant of Venice*, IV, i, 341.

TO THOMAS FLOWER ELLIS, [3 AUGUST 1852][1]

MS: Trinity College. *Mostly published:* Trevelyan, II, 322.

16 Caledonia Place / Clifton / Bristol

Dear Ellis,

Here I am not the worse, on the whole, for the journey. I already feel the influence of this balmy air; and I have proved that I am alive by eating a lunch – the first time for six months.

You are booked for the 10th of September. You will find a good bedroom, a great tub, a tolerably furnished book case, lovely walks, fine churches, a dozen of special sherry, half a dozen of special Hock, and a tureen of turtle soup.

I read this last paragraph to Hannah who is writing at the table beside me. She exclaimed against the turtle – "Such gluttons men are!" "For shame," I said. "When a friend comes to us, we ought to kill the fatted calf." "Yes," says she; "but from the fatted calf you will get only mock turtle."

Ever yours
T B Macaulay

TO SIR WILLIAM GIBSON CRAIG, [4 AUGUST 1852][2]

MS: Scottish Record Office. *Envelope:* Sir W Gibson Craig Bart. / etc. etc. etc. / Riccarton / Edinburgh. *Subscription:* TBM.

16 Caledonia Place / Clifton / Bristol

My dear Craig,

I am here, quiet, comfortable, and slowly recovering. I cannot yet bear much exercise; and the smallest flurry takes away my breath and sets my heart in quick motion: but my sleep, appetite, and spirits are good; and a few days of this air will make, I am assured, a great change.

I write chiefly to say what I ought to have said before. I will not offer to reimburse the expenses of my election, as I see that our friend Black made a strong declaration on that subject from the hustings.[3] But I am sure that my friends must have been put to some expense since that time on my account. There have been advertisements, placards etc. And possibly you may have been at some charge about the Music Hall. Now I rely on you to let me know exactly what I owe on these accounts. Indeed

---

[1] Dated from TBM's Journal for this day, which refers to his eating lunch: 'a wonder for me' (v, 93).
[2] Dated from Clifton postmark.
[3] Black congratulated the voters at the declaration of the poll for having 'taken on yourselves all the labour and expense which an election involves' (*Scotsman*, 17 July).

your kindness to me would not suffer you to conceal from me anything of the kind.

I have not been able to do any serious work during the last month. But I hope to resume my history this week.¹ Kindest regards to Lady Craig.

Ever yours
T B Macaulay

TO LORD RUTHERFURD, [4? AUGUST 1852]

MS: National Library of Scotland.

16 Caledonia Place / Clifton / Bristol

Dear Rutherfurd,

I have just received your most kind letter. Many thanks for it. I was a little shaken by my journey hither; but I am already reviving; and I fully expect to be a different man in six weeks or less. If not, I shall propose to myself the example of your fortitude and patience, when you were tried with suffering very much more severe than mine is likely to be.²

In October I shall, I hope, be able to appear before the electors and to harangue them for a good hour. The two pleasures which I promise to myself are a visit to Lauriston³ and a visit to Riccarton. It seldom happens to a man to make, after five and thirty, two such friends as you and Craig have been to me.

Ever yours most truly
T B Macaulay

TO LADY TREVELYAN, 7 AUGUST 1852

MS: Trinity College.

16 Caledonia Place / Clifton August 7. 1852

Dearest Hannah,

I am truly sorry that you should be detained so long at Enmore.⁴ If I

---

¹ TBM tried to write on the 6th but gave it up; on the 16th he managed 'a pretty fair quantity' (Journal, v, 97; 107).

² Rutherfurd was seriously ill at the beginning of 1851 and evidently never fully recovered. When TBM, after his own health had broken, once again called on Rutherfurd, he writes: 'It was a sad meeting. He cried; and when he ceased to cry, his sorrow was only the more affecting. But he seemed much pleased by my visit and my sympathy which God knows was sincere' (Journal, v, 161: 2 November 1852).

³ Rutherfurd's house near Edinburgh: 'a luxurious and splendid residence' according to Cockburn (*Journal*, II, 145).

⁴ Hannah left Clifton for Enmore on the 5th and returned from there to London on the 9th. TBM met her at the Bristol station on her return journey and 'had five minutes of talk.... Very precious to me – I do love her. I was unable to suppress my tears. But I tried to laugh' (Journal, v, 99–100).

had foreseen that you would not return to town till Monday, I should have tried to keep you here a day or two longer. It would have been a great – a very great – pleasure to me. Yet I can very well bear the utter solitude in which I now live. Indeed I prefer it to all but a very small and select society. I am, I think, better, indeed certainly better, though the weather is against me, and though Colchicum and blue pill are not of the nature of cordials. The showers came yesterday in such thick succession that I only ventured out once; and then I was caught in the rain and forced to change every thing. I tried to write, but found that the posture affected my chest disagreeably. So I lay on the sofa and read two lives of Julius Cæsar – Suetonius's and Plutarch's, and was much amused and interested by both.

Trevelyan is certainly a Μαντις Κακων.[1] Can you read that? But I am not, I own, quite easy about this dispute. The Americans are angry and unreasonable. Our foreign office is the weakest department of this weak government. And Lord Derby, who, I suppose, will, at such a conjuncture, take the helm out of Lord Malmesbury's[2] hands, is but a rash and ignorant steersman. I do not think it likely that there will be war, but very likely that our policy will be irresolute, undignified, and such as to lower the country in the eyes of other nations.

I should be very anxious about my dear Baba, if her complaint were at all serious. But it seems to be merely one of those common and trifling maladies which plague people for a few days and then disappear.

I will be at the station at $\frac{1}{2}$ after 2 on Monday.

Kind regards to Mrs. T[revelyan].

Ever yours
T B Macaulay

TO SELINA MACAULAY, 8 AUGUST 1852

MS: Trinity College. *Envelope:* Miss Macaulay / Temple House / Brighton. *Subscription:* TBM.

16 Caledonia Place / Clifton / August 8. 1852

Dearest Selina,

I am comfortably lodged here, and am getting better, in spite of the weather which prevents me from rambling all day as I did last year at Malvern and the year before at the Isle of Wight. Then I was never at home from ten in the morning till near six in the afternoon. Now I cannot venture out for half an hour without great risk of having to change

---

[1] Prophet of evils.

[2] James Howard Harris (1807–89: *DNB*), 3rd Earl, was Foreign Secretary in Derby's first and second administrations. A dispute over access to the Canadian fisheries was in progress between England and the United States but was soon peacefully settled.

everything when I come home. I have not had occasion to consult any physician here. Should I want one, I shall send for Dr. Symmonds.[1]

The great evil of coming to a place like this is that all sorts of bores think themselves entitled to intrude on you and to kill the time by lounging in your drawing room. Yesterday while I was quietly reading, a Mr. Wightwick[2] sent up his card. He told me that he had known John Macaulay at Plymouth I forget how many years ago; and on the strength of this connection he pestered me with his opinions about the weather, the waters, the scenery, and so forth. Scarcely was Mr. Wightwick gone when a Mr. Bruce[3] enters, – a horrible old twaddle. He told me that he had seen my name in the subscription book of a reading room here; and that he thought that he might venture to call, because twelve years ago he had seen me at an evening party at old Mr. Longman's. Then he told me his pedigree – how he was great grandson of Sir Something Bruce of Kinross. Then he informed me that Mrs. Bruce was in weak health – that he had lately made a tour in the Isle of Wight – that he was pleased with the Undercliff – that Prince Albert had a farm at Osborne. I could have kicked him down stairs with the greatest pleasure. As soon as he was gone I ordered William to let nobody in whom he did not know, or who did not come on particular business. Nothing is so intolerable as a watering place idler who, because he is weary of his own company, pesters others with it.

The Harfords have been very civil;[4] and I have a free admission to the grounds of Blaise Castle – a great favour. I intend to visit Barley Wood when the weather mends.

You are right about Miss Hay. I called her Miss Elliot in writing to Hannah.[5] I confounded her with a Miss Elliot who, about the same time lodged at Clapham – at Rippens's[6] or some such name.

Love to dear Fanny. It was very kind of her to offer to come and nurse me. But I hope that it will be long before I give so much trouble to anybody. Hannah is still at Enmore.

Ever yours
T B Macaulay

[1] John Addington Symonds (1807–71: *DNB*), in practice at Bristol since 1831 and the leading physician of the place. He was the father of the essayist and critic.

[2] George Wightwick (1802–72: *Boase*), an architect at Plymouth until 1851, when he retired to Clifton. He was a 'Shakespeare scholar, reader, lecturer and painter' (*Boase*). TBM says of his visit that 'he seemed to be an apothecary plying for practice' (Journal, v, 97).

[3] Thomas Bruce (d. 1 September 1852), a Commissioner of the Scottish Board of Customs.

[4] Harford called on 5 August (Journal, v, 95). Blaise Castle, his residence, is about four miles from Clifton.

[5] See *to* Lady Trevelyan, 15 July.

[6] A Joseph Rippen is in the 1827 Clapham directory.

TO LADY TREVELYAN, 10 AUGUST 1852

MS: Trinity College.

16 Caledonia Place / Clifton / August 10. 1852

Dearest Hannah,

I am decidedly better to day, probably in consequence of the change of weather. I have passed the whole morning in the open air, and have walked much further than you would think prudent, but without feeling myself at all the worse for it.

On Friday next I am to go over to Blaise Castle to lunch – that is to say, to see other people lunch. Harford has given orders that I and anybody whom I have in my company are to be admitted to the grounds. On Friday I shall go in a fly: but if I continue to mend I shall before long be able to walk thither and back.

Pray let me know how my dear Baba is, – how George liked his visit to Bromley, – and all the other news of Westbourne Terrace. On Friday week I expect Baba. As soon as she leaves me Malden comes for three days; and ten days after Malden's departure Ellis will pay me a visit. You know how glad I should be to see you here with Baba. But I will not ask you to do what might be inconvenient. Love to Trevelyan, Baba, George and Alice.

Ever yours
T B Macaulay

TO LADY TREVELYAN, 12 AUGUST 1852

MS: Trinity College.

Caledonia Place Clifton / August 12. 1852

Dearest Hannah,

Yesterday evening, after I had sent off a letter to Baba, I received one from Trevelyan accompanied by a few lines from you. Another letter from you arrived this morning. You are all very kind; and I am very sensible of your kindness.

On the whole, I am decidedly better than when I left town. I am not in force to day: but that is quite explicable. The rain is still pouring down in torrents. That foolish fellow Lord Maidstone[1] told the electors of Westminster that after Lord Derby would come the deluge. Unhappily we seem to have the deluge and Lord Derby too. I have not been out of doors these forty eight hours: and forty eight hours of strict confinement

---

[1] George James Finch-Hatton (1815–87: *Boase*), 11th Earl of Winchilsea, styled Lord Maidstone, 1826–58; Tory M.P., 1837–41. He stood for Westminster in the general election of this year but came in third of the four candidates.

to the house would at any time of my life have had a depressing effect on me. On Tuesday morning the weather was glorious; and I then felt myself almost perfectly well.

The society of my dear child is always delightful to me. If you can spare her next Monday,[1] it will be a great comfort to me to have her here. By that time, I hope, the sun will again favour us with his presence. As it is, the rain and mist equalise all landscapes. I might as well be living on that dead flat over which we travelled at Easter from Boston to Lincoln. Of course you will let me know all your arrangements, that I may be at the station in proper time.

I am glad that the visit to Walter turned out so well. I had a letter from Ellis this morning. He says — "I saw Georgy at Bromley, where he seemed to be very happy, and made himself much liked, particularly by his kindness to poor Tom,[2] who became much attached to him."
[. . . .]³
to Riccarton from a trip to the Highlands. The Scotch liberals are exulting in the victory which they have won in Orkney. The Lord Advocate,[4] they say, has spent four [. . . .]³

TO THOMAS FLOWER ELLIS, 12 AUGUST 1852

MS: Trinity College. *Extract published:* Trevelyan, II, 322–3.

16 Caledonia Place. / Clifton / August 12. 1852
Dear Ellis,

I am better than when I left town, but still far from well. The weather has been against me as yet. There has not, since I came down, been a single day without rain; and there have been only two or three days on which I could safely venture half a mile from shelter. During the last forty eight hours I have been close prisoner to the house. The deluge, which Lord Maidstone told us was to come after Lord Derby, has come already, so that we are cursed with Derby and deluge too.

I have very little to complain of. I suffer no pain. My mind is unclouded. My temper is not soured. I sleep sound. I eat and drink heartily. Nothing that care or tenderness can do for me is wanting. Indeed it would be

---

[1] Hannah had written to suggest that Margaret come to Clifton immediately (Journal, v, 101: 11 August); they both came on the 17th. Hannah returned the next day and Margaret stayed until the 23rd.

[2] Ellis's oldest son: see 15 December 1834.

[3] The lower half of the last leaf has been torn away, removing some seven or eight lines on the recto and perhaps as many on the verso, which would include the closing and the signature.

[4] John Inglis (1810–91: *DNB*), afterwards Lord Glencorse, Lord Advocate in Derby's administration.

unjust and selfish in me to accept all the sacrifices which those whom I love are eager to make. Hannah has gone back to town; and Baba comes down to me on Monday. I will transcribe a few lines from a letter which I received from Hannah two hours ago. "Georgy thoroughly enjoyed his visit to Bromley, and has returned quite in love with Marian. He says she is a perfect darling – she plays so beautifully at trap ball, is so kind, so clever, so agreeable. He liked Louise very much: but Marian is his favourite. Thomas was an object of the greatest interest, and of some very grave speculation." I did not know that trap ball was among Marian's accomplishments.

On the 26th, after Baba has left me, Malden comes for three or four days. The earlier you can run down in September, and the longer you can stay, the better. I reckon on you for the 10th at latest. The Trevelyans will then I hope be far on their way to the Tyrol. I shall absolutely insist on their going. For I can do very well without them; and Trevelyan cannot do without a short trip to the continent, and will not go to the continent without his wife. He cannot have a real holiday in England. Go where he will, red boxes and piles of papers tied up with tape follow him. Short as our Easter tours are, he has more than once had letters on the morning of Easter Sunday which have spoiled all our pleasure. He was forced to leave York[1] suddenly; and at Gloucester,[2] instead of going with us to the Cathedral, he had to sit at the inn all day, up to the knees in despatches. He is never sure of twenty four hours of entire relaxation till the sea is between him and the Treasury.

I am alone at present, but cheerful and agreeably employed. I do not venture to work on my history yet: but I read histories written by other people – Suetonius, Vulcatius,[3] Vopiscus, Lampridius, Plutarch, and Lord Campbell. Plutarch is the best of them. Which is the worst I hardly know. It lies, I think, between Vulcatius and Lord Campbell.

I have good news from Longman. He tells me that at Xtmas he shall have 1500£ for me, besides the 500£ which I am to have annually till Xtmas 1853.[4] I am beginning to give myself the airs of Mr. Peter Pounce.[5] At the same time, as Horace tells us, I find that anxiety grows with wealth.[6]

---

[1] In 1847.   [2] In 1846.

[3] This and the next two are among the traditional names assigned to the authors of the *Augustan History*, which TBM had been reading since the 10th. This was an old favorite of his. The family friend Selina Marriott, in her Journal account of TBM's conversation at Rothley Temple, [11] September 1832, reports TBM as saying: 'the Augustan History is very little read but it is very amusing, in fact the Journals of their H. of Commons' (MS., Lord Knutsford).

[4] On 4 November TBM reports the figure as £1568 plus the annual £500 (Journal, v, 162–3). An eighth edition of the *History*, 2,000 copies, had been printed in May.

[5] Lady Booby's steward in *Joseph Andrews:* see book III, ch. 13.

[6] 'Crescentem sequitur cura pecuniam,' *Odes*, III, xvi, 17.

I am troubled with very disagreeable palpitations of the heart when I think of some fifty thousand dollars which I have in Yankee securities. I comfort myself by the thought that, if Jonathan goes to war, he must borrow, and that, if he borrows, he must not begin by repudiating. But, in truth, I do not seriously anticipate war. The worst that I expect, – and that is bad enough, – is that the country will make a poor figure when the history of the dispute comes out. From what the Morning Herald says I infer that our ministers are as double tongued towards foreign powers as towards us. With the American government, as with the constituent bodies here, Lord Derby tries to carry a point, and, when he finds that he cannot carry it, turns round and declares that he has all along meant just the same thing with his antagonists.[1]

I shall be glad to hear from you whenever you have a spare half hour.

Ever yours
T B Macaulay

TO ADAM BLACK, 13 AUGUST 1852

Text: [Black], *Biographies by Lord Macaulay,* pp. xlv–xlvi.

16 Caledonian Place, Clifton, / August 13, 1852.

Dear Sir,

I am decidedly better than when I left London. Then, indeed, I could hardly crawl up and down stairs; and I can now walk miles, at a gentle pace, and on tolerably even ground. Still, however, any excitement, or any violent exertion, instantly brings on a derangement of the circulation and uneasy feeling of the heart. I should, I daresay, have made more rapid progress if the weather had been fine; but since I have been here the rain has been almost incessant. To-day the sun is bright, the western horizon clear, the St. Vincent rocks in full beauty, and the air delicious. I shall not despair of an entire recovery till I have tried what a succession of such days will do for me. I am not however sanguine. Perhaps my complaint depresses my spirits. But I will own to you, that I greatly doubt, judging by my own internal sensations, whether I shall ever be able to go through a session of Parliament in a manner which would satisfy even the most indulgent constituent body.

Ever, dear Sir, yours most truly,
T. B. Macaulay.

[1] The *Morning Herald,* having already defended Derby against charges of inconsistency on the policy of Protection, now had to perform the same service on this matter. On 6 August it approved the government's sending gunboats to protect the rights of the Canadians against the Americans, but by 11 August it had changed its tone from complaint to defense, arguing that the British action had left the matter just where it always had been and that no provocation had been given to the Americans.

TO LADY TREVELYAN, 15 AUGUST 1852

MS: Trinity College. *Extract published:* Trevelyan, 2nd edn, 1, 438n.

16 Caledonian Place / Clifton / August 15. 1852

Dearest Hannah,

I am more shocked than I can express by this report.[1] I would willingly hope that there is no ground for it: and yet it is but too probable. I shall wait anxiously for the newspaper to morrow.

It will be a great pleasure to me to see you and my dear Baba. You must have your way about the rooms: and Elizabeth will do her best to make you both comfortable.

I went to Blaise Castle on Friday and enjoyed my visit much. The weather was glorious, the scenery beyond all description lovely, the works of art in the house well worth looking at, and the people most kind and hospitable. On Thursday or Friday next they are to take Baba and me to lunch at Barley Wood. They have given me the most liberal admission to their grounds, so that I can go whenever I chuse and lose myself among the rocks and tufts of arbutus without calling at the house.

I was but poorly yesterday. Indeed the languor and sinking of the heart were so great that I thought it advisable to send for Dr. Symmonds. He came; and I found him a very clever man, a little of a coxcomb, but, I dare say, not the worse physician for that. He must have quoted Horace and Virgil six times at least àpropos of his medical inquiries. Horace says, in a poem in which he jeers the Stoics, that even a wise man is out of sorts when "pituita molesta est,"[2] which is being interpreted, "when his phlegm is troublesome." The Doctor thought it necessary to quote this passage in order to prove that phlegm is troublesome, a proposition of the truth of which, I will venture to say, no man on earth is better convinced than myself. However in essentials he seems to be a very skilful and attentive practitioner. He spent a good half hour in examining me, as if I had been a recruit, kept the stethoscope ten minutes at my breast in different positions, and interrogated me most strictly about my way of life. He made me give him the bill of fare of several successive dinners, would know the exact quantity of tea and wine that I took, and so forth. At last he pronounced that he was quite confident that I had no internal malady except a deficiency of tone. He approved of Bright's treatment,

---

[1] 'A note from H to say that there is a report of poor Parker's death' (Journal, v, 105: 15 August). Sir James Parker died, at Rothley Temple, on 13 August. On the 16th TBM wrote: 'The Times brought the news of Sir James Parker's death. He died of heart-complaint. Poor fellow! I feel for him. The attack came on just as he was made Vice Chancellor. Mine came on just as I was elected for Edinburgh. Mine may, very likely, end as his has ended; and it may be for the best that it should do so' (Trevelyan, II, 318).

[2] *Epistles,* 1, i, 108.

but said that the time was come when that treatment must be changed, as indeed Bright himself had predicted. He ordered me strengthening medicines, and a strengthening diet. Tea he prohibited, and, I really believe, with reason. Coffee and a little boiled bacon with eggs is the breakfast which he prescribes. He absolutely insists on a very little lunch; and, as everybody seems to be of a mind on this point, I intend to take a poached egg and a glass of sherry. For dinner he recommends firm and brown meats, and wishes me to give up for the present green vegetables and fruit tarts. As to wine he is very liberal: indeed he told me that I could not do without it. I have diminished the quantity of late; and he says that I have diminished it quite enough. I intend to give his precepts a fair trial. I have spoken to William and Elizabeth; and my first lunch is preparing. I have just come back from hearing rather a good sermon. The preacher's name I do not know.[1] He got a sovereign out of me for a charity.

There are two or three books which I should be much obliged to you to bring down – Shakspeare, no matter in what edition. I wish to read some of him with my dearest child. Bring Talents Improved.[2] I was in the middle of it when I gave it to you; and I want to finish it for Auld Lang Syne. The last commission will be the hardest. I want Herodian in the Greek. My copy is locked up in the Albany: and he is necessary to illustrate the history of the Emperors after Severus; for my studies, you see, go beyond those of the Miss Bertrams.[3] George will easily pick up a Herodian for a few shillings at any classical bookseller's. I generally deal with the King's College Bookseller opposite Somerset House. I will pay you when you come down.

I have something to tell you about your letter of Tuesday last which did not arrive till Wednesday evening; but that matter will keep. The wind has changed; and the sky is clearing fast. Love to Trevelyan, Baba, George and Alice.

Ever yours my darling
T B Macaulay

[1] James Marshall: see 22 August; and for an account of his sermon on this day, 31 August.
[2] By Harriet Corp, *c.* 1810. TBM bought it on the 9th and gave it to Hannah on her return to London: 'a trashy tale called Talents Improved which I remember to have read when I was nine or ten years old' (Journal, v, 99).
[3] Jane Austen, *Mansfield Park*, ch. 2.

TO FRANCES MACAULAY, 15 AUGUST 1852

MS: Trinity College.

16 Caledonia Terrace / Clifton / August 15. 1852

Dearest Fanny,

I am much obliged to you for the family news from Zetland.[1] I can tell you in return that I had the honor of a visit here from our respected Uncle James Mills, who came from Devonshire on the wings of love to inquire after my health. William kept him out; and I believe that he has gone back. I had also a card left here by Henry Mills.[2] Though he is my cousin I did not remember ever to have seen him. However I went yesterday to the Gazette office, and found him there among his Compositors, Correctors, and – saving your presence – Devils. I should have known him anywhere by his grotesque likeness to our uncle John. I was as civil and friendly as possible.

The bores here are dreadful. Here is a card from a Lieutenant General Wish or rather Whish[3] – a terrible old button holder, I will be bound for him, though I never saw him or heard of him in my life. As to that wretch Bruce, I met him in a bookseller's shop, and he instantly laid hold on me – all the shop, buyers and sellers and loungers, gaping and staring at us. "Oh Mr. Macaulay, I forgot to tell you the other day that I was a member of the Board of Customs in Scotland. Of course you know the gentlemen of the board of Customs. One of my colleagues was a very large man, Mr. Macaulay. I think he was the largest man I ever saw. Pray do you know him, Mr. Macaulay?" I gave him a cross look and a short answer and walked away; but soon I saw him coming after me down the street in full chase. Happily he was intercepted by another old twaddle like himself, and I got off while they were bestowing their tediousness on each other.

I have seen Dr. Symmonds who seems a very clever man. He assures me that I have no internal disease, that my complaint is merely want of

---

[1] The family of Zachary Macaulay's sister Penelope Hamilton lived in the Orkneys. Perhaps some of them had gone even further north.

[2] Henry James Mills succeeded his father John as printer and publisher of the Bristol *Gazette*; he was still living in 1872, when the *Gazette* expired. TBM says of his visit to Henry at his office that 'I was very friendly and cordial. There was a time when I was half ashamed of being related to vulgar people. That was when I was fighting my way against all sorts of difficulties. Now it is quite different' (Journal, v, 103–4: 14 August). A note in the *Gazette* for 19 August is no doubt a record of this visit. After quoting an item from the *Scotsman* on TBM's bad health the *Gazette* adds: 'It is with pleasure we can add that the right honourable gentleman has derived considerable benefit from his residence at Clifton, and in a few weeks we sincerely trust his health will be completely restored.'

[3] Sir William Sampson Whish (1787–1853: *DNB*), general in the Bengal artillery.

tone, and that I want only strengthening medicines and a nutritious diet.
I enclose the epitaph. Love to dear Selina.

Ever yours

T B M

TO LADY TREVELYAN, 22 AUGUST 1852

MS: Trinity College.

16 Caledonia Place / Clifton August 22. 1852

Dearest Hannah,

I was much better yesterday, indeed better than on any day since the
month of June. The weather was delicious. The Harfords called for us at
eleven, and brought a basket of superb grapes for Baba. We got into their
barouche, and had a most pleasant journey to Barley Wood.[1] The view of
Clifton and Ashton Court, the Rocks and the Avon rolling between
them, was delightful. I remembered well how it used to charm me in old
days. The valley in which Wrington lies was as rich and beautiful as ever.
I was pleased yet disappointed by Barley Wood. It is a very pretty place,
but it is not the place which I knew from my childhood. The fault is not
that of the owners who have shown great taste, and have preserved
whatever was capable of preservation. But the growth of the trees has of
itself changed the whole character of the grounds. The low shrubs which
were not as high as I was at eleven years old are turned into huge masses
of laurels and rhododendrons which rise so high as completely to shut
out the view of the surrounding country. The cottage is sunk down
amidst the wood, and cannot be seen till you actually drive up to the door.
It is certainly very well kept up; and the additions are in perfect harmony
with the original plan. Hannah More's bedroom is now Miss Harford's,
and of course I could not intrude myself into such a sanctuary. The
dining room was as it used to be, the old engravings excepted. I remembered the place of almost every one. The grounds have gained in beauty.
But the Temple of the Winds is in ruins. The *Tecta pauperis Evandri*[2] –
you remember – have utterly disappeared. That root house was my
favourite. It fell down in a storm not long ago. I should have regretted it
more, but for the growth of the plantations. Formerly that point commanded a charming view over the valley. Now you can see nothing but
the trees close to you. The other root house, near Bishop Porteus's urn,[3]
is still in good condition. We lunched and came back very pleasantly. The

---

[1] Barley Wood was now the residence of John Harford's brother William (1793–1877); a
widower, he lived there with his daughter Harriet (1831–55).
[2] A root house on the grounds of Barley Wood: see *Aeneid*, VIII, 359–60.
[3] Hannah More had set up urns dedicated to Bishop Porteus and to John Locke.

kindness and courtesy of everybody was very great. Mrs. Harford was charmed with my dear child, and told me that she had never seen a more intelligent and engaging girl. Indeed Baba looked very well, and behaved as she always does. She has quite got over the little pain which she felt the day before yesterday.

I still retain the ground which I got yesterday. We are just going to Mr. Marshall's[1] Church. Love to Trevelyan, Alice and George.

Ever yours
T B Macaulay

TO LORD MAHON, 23 AUGUST 1852

MS: Stanhope Papers, Chevening. *Partly published:* Stanhope, *Miscellanies*, p. 129.

16 Caledonia Place Clifton / August 23. 1852

My dear Mahon,

Thanks for your pamphlet.[2] It is excellent, – convincing, perspicuous, and eminently temperate and gentlemanlike. The mistakes which you acknowledge cannot by any man of common sense be made matter of charge against you. I am not sure that you do not concede too much. Some of the accusations which you still bring against Sparks are, in my opinion, quite as grave as the accusation which you withdraw.

I am certainly much better; and I begin to hope that six weeks more of the Downs will completely restore me. I have been reading a great quantity of exercrably bad Latin, Suetonius, Vulcatius, Spartianus, Trebellius Pollio, Julius Capitolinus, Lampridius, Vopiscus;[3] and I am going to try to take the taste of all the barbarisms which I have been devouring out of my mouth with the Andria and the Heautontimorumenos. I have read Herodian too. His Greek is not first rate, but is immeasurably superior to the Latin of his contemporaries. After all there is a great deal to be learned from these writers. Hume was quite in the right when he said that Gibbon ought to have made more of the materials for the history of the empire from the Antonines to Diocletian. Indeed Gibbon very candidly admitted the justice of Hume's criticism.[4]

---

[1] James Marshall (1796–1855: *DNB*), Vicar of Christ Church, Clifton. He did not preach on this day: see 31 August.

[2] 'Letter to Jared Sparks,' dated August 1852. Jared Sparks, biographer, historian, and President of Harvard, published an edition of the *Life and Writings of Washington*, 12 vols., 1834–7. In an appendix to vol. 6 of his *History of England*, 1851, Mahon had criticized Sparks's editorial practice, charging him with having made omissions, corrections, and additions without comment in his treatment of Washington's letters.

[3] TBM finished the *Augustan History* on the 20th and began Terence on the 24th (Journal, v, 111; 116).

[4] Hume said that Gibbon's narrative of the 'first reigns from Commodus to Alexander' was 'superficial.' Gibbon wrote that 'such an oracle might have been consulted and obeyed with rational devotion' (Gibbon, *Memoirs of My Life*, ed. Georges Bonnard, 1966, p. 156).

Pray remember me most kindly to Lady Mahon. I wish you and her a pleasant journey; and I can hardly doubt that my wish will be accomplished. My true love to my Valentine.

Ever yours,
T B Macaulay

TO JOHN SCANDRETT HARFORD, 25 AUGUST 1852

MS: Mr F. R. Cowell.

16 Caledonia Place Clifton / August 25. 1852
Dear Mr. Harford,

Your kindness is really indefatigable. I have to day availed myself of it by visiting the reading room.[1] On a future day I hope to make acquaintance with the Museum and with the Library in Old King Street.

I have written to remind my niece of what you told her about the König See.[2] Both she and I are extremely sensible of your kindness and Mrs. Harford's. Last Saturday[3] was indeed a day of pleasure, though of pleasure which to me was not unmixed with sadness.

With my kindest regards to Mrs. Harford, I beg you to believe me, / My dear Sir,

Yours most sincerely,
T B Macaulay

Thanks for good Mr. Whalley's tract.[4]

TO LADY TREVELYAN, 27 AUGUST 1852

MS: Trinity College.

16 Caledonia Place Clifton / August 27. 1852
Dearest Hannah,

This will be my last letter before your departure. I received your note and Baba's this morning, and was delighted to find that the dear girl is well. I am, I think, gaining ground daily. Yesterday I walked too quick, and was reminded of my error by a fit of my complaint, which lasted only

---

[1] 'To the Institution in Park St. where Harford has very kindly put down my name' (Journal, v, 116).
[2] The Trevelyans were just about to leave for the Continent; the Königssee is near Berchtesgaden.
[3] The visit to Barley Wood: see 22 August.
[4] Probably 'It is All True; or, the Grace and Truth of the Gospel Made Plain to Common Sense,' 1815, by Richard Chapple Whalley (1748–1816). Harford published a *Memoir* of Whalley, Vicar of Chelwood, Somerset, in 1846.

a quarter of an hour. I was soon quite right again. Malden is here.[1] He did ample justice to the turtle and Champagne, and seems to enjoy himself greatly. We are going to Blaise Castle to day. To morrow, if this lovely weather lasts, we shall visit Cheddar.

I met Serjeant Stephen[2] yesterday on his way to me. We shook hands very cordially, walked together, and had a pleasant chat. I like him and always did like him much.

I have begun to work on my history after a long intermission; and I find that I can write two hours at a time without any uneasy sensation.

Love to Trevelyan, Baba, George and Alice. A happy journey and a pleasant return to you. God bless you, my dearest sister.

TBM

TO [THOMAS FLOWER ELLIS, 28 AUGUST 1852][3]

MS: Trinity College.

[Clifton]

[. . .] I am glad that Marian and Frank had so pleasant a journey and are come back so well. The Trevelyans cross the sea to day, and I am glad of it. For the weather is fine and the water will be smooth.

By the bye,

"I have found out a dish for my friend

I have found where the turtle is fat."

After trying a Clifton pastry cook, who sent me some broth with dirt balls in it, and no green jelly at all, I explored the heart of old Bristol, and found that there the ancient traditions were not wholly lost. You shall judge for yourself on Wednesday[4] at seven. Malden will have drunk all my Champagne. But you shall have Hock, comme il y en a peu.

Ever yours,
T B Macaulay

TO THOMAS FLOWER ELLIS, 29 AUGUST 1852

MS: Trinity College.

16 Caledonia Place Clifton / August 29. 1852

Dear Ellis,

I shall be delighted to see you on Wednesday. Let me know by what

[1] He came on the 26th and left on the 31st (Journal, v, 117–21).
[2] Henry John Stephen, Commissioner of Bankrupts at Bristol: see 31 December 1823.
[3] The beginning of the letter is missing. Since TBM wrote to Hannah on the 27th and to Ellis again on the 29th, 28 August is the only date on which he could have written this.
[4] Ellis arrived on the 1st and left on the 4th, a brief visit preliminary to his longer one beginning on the 13th.

train you mean to come that I may meet you at the station. I would recommend the train which leaves Paddington at 12.30, and reaches Bristol at 4.55. If by any mischance we should not meet you will find your way easily.

I have been generally mending, though slowly. But I am not in force to day, having exerted myself a little too much yesterday. I took Malden to Cheddar and back over very rough cross roads, and was jolted from ten in the morning till six in the evening. It is therefore not strange that I should be somewhat languid this morning. I should not have undertaken the journey if I had known what it would be. But I must say that the sight was magnificent. We came into the pass at the tame end, and travelled about three miles through it till we came out between those noble precipices which you remember.

On the whole I am better, and can now write two or three hours at a time without uneasiness. I could hardly write at all three weeks ago.

Ever yours,

T B Macaulay

TO FRANCES MACAULAY, 31 AUGUST 1852

MS: Trinity College.

16 Caledonia Place Clifton / August 31. 1852

Dearest Fanny,

I am going on very well, and, if September does as much for me as August has done, may hope to get through the first part of the Session tolerably. Dr. Symonds assures me that I am making progress; and my sensations confirm his opinion. I have indeed nothing to complain of except an occasional faintness and sinking of the heart which either bodily exertion or mental excitement has a tendency to bring on. Malden left me to day; and Ellis comes to morrow. Malden's visit has not done me good: for, though I have a great value for him, it is matter of effort to keep up conversation with him. With Ellis I am perfectly at ease.

When I have done with Clifton I think of going to Brighton for a week, and seeing you and Selina and the dear children daily. But this will not be till about Michaelmas. Our cousin Mrs. Crinean has just called. I am glad to have so good an account of her situation. Her husband has got twenty pupils, – of respectable families, she assures me, and gives great satisfaction. She assists him by teaching French. This looks well.[1]

I called on Henry Mills, and found him begrimed with ink in his

---

[1] The Reverend J. Crinean, classical academy, Anglesea Place, Durdham Down, appears in the Bristol *Directory*, 1853 (but not in 1852); presumably the school was a new venture.

printing office – but the very image of his father. The resemblance was almost ridiculous.

I have heard Mr. Marshall, whom you or Selina recommended to me. He preached last Sunday fortnight an odd sermon on the word 'therefore' in the first verse of the 12th Chapter of the Epistle to the Romans.[1] There was some ingenuity and power of thought in what he said: but it was hardly consistent with good sense and good taste to tell us that this word contained the whole sum and substance of religion, the whole connection of Xtian faith with Xtian practice. He has not preached on any Sunday morning since; and I do not at all admire his substitute. Poor Bethune used to say that, if there were any sect whose principle was to attend the prayers and to go out before the sermon, he should be one of the fraternity; and I sometimes feel much inclined to agree with him.

Love to Selina and to both the children.

Ever yours,

T B Macaulay

TO LORD JOHN RUSSELL, 31 AUGUST 1852

MS: Bodleian Library.

16 Caledonia Place Clifton / August 31. 1852

Dear Lord John,

Many thanks for your kindness. I am really better; and, if September does for me as much as August has done, I shall hope to be at your side on the first night of the Session. I see no politicians here, and busy myself much more with the history of Caracalla and Heliogabalus than with that of Lord Malmesbury's negotiations.[2] I have been reading Spartianus, Vulcatius, Lampridius, Trebellius Pollio, and Flavius Vopiscus, till I am poisoned with their bad Latin, and am forced to take the taste out of my mouth with the Andria and the Heautontimorumenos. However, I can scarcely be wrong in wishing that the present administration may come to an end rather by a natural than by a violent death. Let them stay in till they have produced their budget, turned it inside out, and convinced the most credulous that there was never anything in it.

I am very curious to know whether they will let the Convocation sit for the despatch of business.[3] If they do, we shall have some singular scenes.

---

[1] 'I beseech you therefore, brethren, by the mercies of God, that ye present your bodies a living sacrifice, holy, acceptable unto God, which is your reasonable service.'

[2] See 7 August.

[3] See *to* Milnes, 20 November.

My kindest regards to Lady John Russell.[1] I am grateful to her for remembering me. / Ever, dear Lord John,

Yours most truly

T B Macaulay

TO FRANCES MACAULAY, 6 SEPTEMBER 1852

MS: Trinity College. *Extract published:* Trevelyan, ii, 316–17.

16 Caledonia Place / Clifton Septr. 6. 1852

Dearest Fanny,

I am going on well. Symonds paid me his weekly visit yesterday, and pronounced my pulse, my tongue, and my general appearance to be decidedly more satisfactory than on any former occasion. He is going to write to Bright about my case, and seems much inclined to recommend me to winter in Italy, – no very severe sentence to a man of my tastes. Do not talk about this: for, if I go to Italy, I must quit parliament; and the least rumour that I was going to quit parliament would produce a great agitation at Edinburgh, and set all the hostile factions canvassing, and quarrelling.

I have begun again to work at my history. It goes on slowly; but, if I live and have tolerable health, I shall finish the reign of William. I began it only in the autumn of 1849;[2] and it is now much more than half completed.[3] I should be sorry to leave it unfinished: for, though it is very far from satisfying me, it is better than any book that we have, or that we seem likely to have, on that subject. There is no great vanity in saying this. For Ralph,[4] Smollett, Kennett,[5] Somerville,[6] Boyer,[7] Belsham,[8] Lord Dungannon,[9] are all of them wretched writers of history: and Burnet, whose first volume, which ends with the Revolution, is most valuable and amusing, becomes as dull as any of them in [....][10]

[1] Frances Anna Maria Elliot (1815–98), Russell's second wife, the daughter of Lord Minto.

[2] TBM began the second part in February 1849, but much of the year he spent in collecting materials and he had done only parts of two chapters by the year's end.

[3] TBM was now working on the story of Sir John Fenwick – chapter 22, the last of volume 4 – but he worked on different parts out of sequence.

[4] James Ralph, *History of England during the Reigns of King William, Queen Anne, and King George I*, 1744–6.

[5] White Kennett, *Compleat History of England*, vol. 3, 1706.

[6] Thomas Somerville, *History of Political Transactions and of Parties from the Restoration of King Charles II to the Death of King William III*, 1792.

[7] Abel Boyer, *The History of King William the Third*, 1702–3.

[8] William Belsham, *History of Great Britain from the Revolution to the Accession of the House of Hanover*, 1798.

[9] Arthur Hill-Trevor, Lord Dungannon, *Life and Times of William the Third*, 1835–6.

[10] The rest is missing.

TO THOMAS FLOWER ELLIS, 6 SEPTEMBER 1852

MS: Trinity College. *Extract published:* Trevelyan, II, 212.

16 Caledonia Place / Clifton / September 6. 1852

Dear Ellis,

Let me know how you are. I thought that I heard you up in the night before your departure, and meant to have seen you in the morning, but overslept myself.

Let me also know, as soon as you have made up your mind, when you shall be here. Poor Bruce will never hold a button more. If you studied the deaths in the Times of last Saturday with the attention which you usually bestow on that corner of a newspaper, you must have seen that Thomas Bruce Esq, late a Commissioner of Customs in Scotland, died at Clifton of apoplexy on the 1st of September, – just while we were laughing at him, and you were begging me to point him out. So goes on the great Tragi Comedy of the world. I cannot think without tenderness and self reproach of the decent looking spruce old twaddle who is now lying no more. He has left bores enough behind him to keep up the breed. On Saturday I had a note from Lieut. Genl. and Mrs. Whish[1] of the Bengal Army, two people whom I never saw in my life, asking me to dinner. I civilly excused myself for disappointing such *Wishes* – Bravo! –

We treated the Zoo much too contemptuously. I lounged thither,[2] and found more than sixpenny worth of amusement. There is a pleasant garden with plenty of benches. The beasts are not so well worth seeing as those in Regent's Park. But there are a tolerable lion and lioness, and a superb leopard and leopardess. I observed the noise which the leopard made, and understood the force of Geta's admirable distinction. "Leones rugiunt – leopardi rictant."[3] There are two bears and two jackals, a pond covered with queer looking ducks, and a perfect wilderness of the most hideous monkeys, who have pulled off so many bonnets of ladies that a board is put up cautioning the fair sex not to approach these Lotharios in miniature too near. Time would fail me to speak of the Nyl Ghau,[4] the ostriches and the antelopes. We will certainly kill an hour at the Zoo.

I send you a line for Cawthorn's Library in Cockspur Street. Do not omit to bring the Prelude down. It is a glorious poem. The dear defunct Bruce might have written most of it. –

Ever yours
T B Macaulay

[1] See *to* Frances Macaulay, 15 August.
[2] TBM went there on the 4th and again on the 6th (Journal, v, 124).
[3] Aelius Spartianus, Life of Geta, v, 5, in the *Augustan History* (which TBM had just been reading: see *to* Ellis, 12 August, and *to* Russell, 31 August).
[4] A large Indian antelope: the common spelling is now *nilgai.*

TO THOMAS FLOWER ELLIS, 8 SEPTEMBER 1852

MS: Trinity College.

16 Caledonia Place Clifton / September 8. 1852

Dear Ellis,

How odd that our tributes to the great man who has been taken from us should have crossed each other! His fate has excited a great sensation. My sisters at Brighton saw the announcement in the Times with feelings not to be described. Galignani conveyed the mournful news to the Trevelyans at Frankfort; and I need not tell you that half the pleasure of their tour has been destroyed. In truth the last fortnight of this eminent person's life has done more for his renown than the preceding seventy seven years. His fame has gone out into all lands. For my own part I shall never while I live see a bore without a tender recollection of Thomas Bruce.

You have hit off the Morning Herald style capitally. You certainly write the best bred English going. In prose, I mean: for a copy of verses which I enclose and which has cost me half a crown to the poetess,[1] leaves all your metrical efforts far behind. Bring it me, when you come down. I must keep it for Hannah.

You shall find supper, or, if you please dinner, ready for you at half after eight on Monday.[2] I will put off my dinner till that hour, which, now that I lunch, I can do without the smallest inconvenience.

Your mention of the visit which your dark beauty[3] is going to make to London for the purpose of buying white dresses, suggests a disagreeable image. It is a great pity that the vestments which ladies wear on the most interesting of all occasions harmonize ill with the complexion of a brunette. If I were Lucy, I would break through so senseless a fashion. I would advise her to go to the altar in scarlet and gold, and to have plenty of red ribands in her night cap. –

Ever yours
T B M

TO FRANCES MACAULAY, 21 SEPTEMBER 1852

MS: Trinity College.

16 Caledonia Place Clifton / September 21. 1852

Dearest Fanny,

I hope to be at Brighton on Monday next, at what hour I do not know,

---

1 'A crazy woman has sent me an Acrostic and demands an interview. I told William to give her half a crown and send her away' (Journal, v, 125: 7 September).
2 Ellis arrived on the 13th and left on the 20th (Journal, v, 129; 132).
3 Lucy Haywood, only daughter of Ellis's friend Francis Haywood of Liverpool; she married Captain Charles Trigance Franklin, Royal Artillery, on 10 November.

and shall not know till I reach London. I must be at a hotel, as I cannot bring my servants with me. If you could secure me two comfortable rooms close together, a sitting room and a bedroom, not higher than the ground floor, I would take them for a week certain; and I should not be disposed to haggle about terms. The Bedford is, I suppose, the best house, and is certainly nearest to you. If you cannot succeed there, I should be inclined to go to the Bristol Hotel, though it is a good way off. I was once very comfortable there. But I will trust to your management.

I am pretty well: but my Doctors threaten me with the winter and the

[.   .   .   .   ]¹

advice on that subject. I have not made up my mind: and, if I had determined to vacate my seat, I should still think it right to keep that determination secret till a new writ can be issued; and a new writ cannot be issued till the parliament [. . . .]¹

TO MARGARET TREVELYAN, [22]² SEPTEMBER 1852

MS: Trinity College.

16 Caledonia Place Clifton / September 23. 1852

Dearest Baba,

Thank you for your letter from Vienna. I found it on my table when I came back from dining with the Bishop of Gloucester.³ He has a palace about four miles from Clifton. It is a large good house, not in the best style, but a very favourable specimen of that style. It is one of those somewhat stately buildings of red brick with stone facings which were fashionable in the days of William the Third, Anne, and the two first Georges. Kensington House and Marlborough House are good examples. Nothing could exceed the Bishop's civility and kindness. His daughter is an extremely fine girl, one of three whom you may remember to have seen conspicuous on the wall of the Royal Academy more than a year ago.⁴ The two sister Graces were from home.

I am alone at present, very well and very cheerful. Symonds however

---

¹ The top third of the last leaf has been torn away, probably for the signature on the verso; about four or five lines are missing from the recto and perhaps as many from the verso.
² This letter and the next are both clearly dated 23, but other evidence makes 22 almost certain. TBM says that he is going to Miles's at Leigh Court on Thursday – i.e., the 23rd. His Journal for the 22nd says that he walked with Stephen to his court on that day; and the furious equinoctial storm mentioned in the letter to Ellis was on the 21st according to the Journal.
³ TBM's old Trinity Tutor, James Henry Monk; he called on the 16th, and TBM dined with him on the 20th (Journal, v, 131; 133).
⁴ Richard Buckner's portrait of 'The Misses Monk' was exhibited at the Academy in May 1851.

tells me that he is uneasy about the winter and the Session; and Bright has written strongly to the same effect. They do not insist on my going abroad. But they are very urgent on the subject of parliament. I am disposed to agree with them. But this subject we will discuss when you return.

On Thursday I go to Miles's[1] to see the pictures, – a most celebrated collection. On Monday I run to London and thence to Brighton. I have written to your aunt Fanny to get me rooms at a good hotel. While I am there William and Elizabeth will lay down my new carpet, and get the chambers into order.

Serjeant Stephen is to call for me in a few minutes; and we are to walk together to his court at the Guildhall. Do you remember the Guildhall? It is a large Gothic building opposite the White Lion in Broad Street, near Brennus and Belinus.[2] Love to Mamma and Papa.

Ever yours, my dearest child
T B M

TO THOMAS FLOWER ELLIS, [22][3] SEPTEMBER 1852

MS: Trinity College. *One sentence published:* Trevelyan, II, 323.

16 Caledonia Place Clifton / Sep 23. 1852

Dear Ellis,

Answer me a legal question. The municipal bill,[4] I imagine, transferred to the Recorders of the new boroughs a large criminal jurisdiction which had previously belonged to the County Magistrates. Was the Transfer retrospective? I mean could the Recorders of Manchester try a pickpocket for a theft committed before the Statute passed? You see what I am driving at.

I dined with the Bishop. He was really more than civil – asked after you very kindly, and told me that you were one of the best scholars that he had known among young men. He was much pleased to hear that you still kept your scholarship up. The palace is a spacious and rather stately house, in a bad style, the style of Kensington House and Marlborough House, but a very good specimen of that bad style – red brick with stone facings, a long terrace with balustrades etc. etc. – The Chaplain looked very unlikely to emulate our friend Ambrose Augustin Athanasius.[5] But

---

[1] William Miles (1797–1878: *Boase*), afterwards first Baronet, a Bristol banker and M.P. for East Somerset, 1834–65. The notable collection of paintings at his residence, Leigh Court, near Taunton, had been formed by his father.
[2] Mythical founders of Bristol, whose figures are on the old city wall.
[3] See note on the date of the preceding letter.
[4] The Municipal Reform Act of 1835.
[5] See [25 March 1852].

the young lady, – for only one was there, – would have tempted Paul or St Hilarion. Nothing more attractive was ever made out of flesh, blood, hair, and muslin. I speak merely of the *physique*, without at all meaning to depreciate the *morale*, of which I know nothing.

To morrow I go to Leigh Court to see Miles's pictures. On Monday I pass through London on my way to Brighton. I shall be some hours in town; and, if I thought that you would be in Elm Court,[1] I would call there. But you will, I hope, be enjoying yourself at Bromley. After a furious equinoctial storm, we have one of the loveliest and most serene days that I ever saw. I hope that you are equally fortunate in your weather. I am really quite well, though Symonds adjures me not to take liberties, and Bright writes advising me to ask for the Chiltern Hundreds.

Ever yours

T B Macaulay

TO THOMAS FLOWER ELLIS, 25 SEPTEMBER 1852

MS: Trinity College. *Partly published:* Trevelyan, II, 323.

16 Caledonia Place Clifton / September 25. 1852

Dear Ellis,

I am much obliged to you for your learned and elaborate opinion. If I had guessed that you would have bestowed so much thought and trouble on my question, I would have indorsed my letter with Ten Guineas.

I shall be delighted to see you at Brighton on any day that may suit you. I do not yet know whether I shall be at the Bedford or the Norfolk. As soon as I am lodged I will write again.

The weather has been glorious during the last three days, and the rocks and woods in the highest beauty. On Thursday I walked to Leigh Court – Miles's place on the other side of the ferry, to see the famous collection of pictures, and found that report had not done them justice. Nothing struck me so much as Rubens's Woman taken in Adultery – one of his master-pieces which I saw so long ago as 1816, at Hope's[2] in Cavendish Square. It was then on sale, and went, I think, for 5000 Guineas.[3] I at once remembered the principal figures. In truth they have a look of life which I do not know that I ever saw elsewhere on canvass. There are other excellent pieces – a good Titian, a charming Murillo, and two Claudes which would be perfect if the figures did not in some degree spoil the landscape. On the road between Leigh Court and the ferry, however, I saw a more

---

1 Ellis had chambers at 3 Elm Court, Temple.
2 Thomas Hope (1769–1831: *DNB*), collector, patron, writer, and traveller.
3 Dr Waagen, *Treasures of Art in Great Britain*, 1854, III, 182, reports that it sold for £2,000.

delightful picture than any in the collection. In a deep shady lane was a donkey cart driven by a lad; and in it were four very pretty girls from eleven to six, evidently sisters. They were quite mad with spirits at having so rare a treat as a ride, and they were laughing, fondling each other, and singing in a way that almost made me cry with mere sense of the beautiful. They saw that I was pleased, and answered me very prettily when I made some inquiry about my route. I begged them to go on singing; and they all four began carolling, in perfect concert, and in tones as joyous as a lark's. I gave them the silver that I had about me to buy dolls: but I had some difficulty in getting them to take it. I should like to have a picture of the cart and the cargo. Gainsborough would have been the man. But I should not like to have an execrably bad poem on the subject, such as Wordsworth would have written.

I am glad that you found Miss Harford[1] so pleasant. You ought to send Frank off to the Lakes on speculation.

Ever yours,
T B Macaulay

TO THOMAS FLOWER ELLIS, 27 SEPTEMBER 1852

MS: Trinity College.

Norfolk Hotel Brighton / September 27. 1852

Dear Ellis,

I am here pretty well accommodated and shall be delighted to see you on Friday or Saturday, – whichever may suit you best.[2] The place is overflowing. The display of equipages and of fine women on fine horses equals that of Hyde Park on the loveliest afternoons of June. I am fortunate in having secured a small but comfortable sitting room which commands a view of the sea. This is a very good house, though one event which took place twenty three years ago nearly fastened on it the character of a bad house. It was here that Prince Schwartzenberg cuckolded Lord Ellenborough.[3] However, as there are now bibles in all the rooms, I hope that the pollution has been expiated.

Let me hear from you.

Ever yours
T B Macaulay

[1] TBM and Ellis met Miss Harford and her father at the station as Ellis was leaving Bristol (Journal, v, 133: 20 September).

[2] Ellis came on Friday and returned on Saturday, 1 and 2 October (Journal, v, 140–1).

[3] In February 1829. Prince Felix von Schwarzenberg (1800–52) was co-respondent in Ellenborough's suit for divorce in 1830. Ellenborough recovered £25,000, and Lady Ellenborough went on to end her days the wife of a sheik.

TO THOMAS FLOWER ELLIS, 5 OCTOBER 1852

MS: Trinity College.

Norfolk Hotel Brighton / October 5. 1852

Dear Ellis,

I am not quite certain on what day I shall return to town. My movements depend on Hannah's, and on her wishes about little Alice. But I fully intend to be in London on Saturday morning. I could, if that would perfectly suit you, go out to Bromley in the afternoon and return on the Monday. Let me know.[1]

On Sunday I heard a delightful sermon about the fate of the righteous man and the sinner, as exemplified in the cases of the Duke of Wellington and Buonaparte.[2] On Monday we had one of the most violent storms of wind and rain that I remember. I staid at home and read Uncle Tom's Cabin, cried a little, and was, on the whole, much pleased. The manner is too shocking, too Spagnoletto like for my taste, if I consider the book as a work of art. If I consider it as a political and moral work, I entertain some doubts whether it may not do more harm than good. But on the whole it is the finest work of the imagination that America has produced. There is some foolish ignorant trash about the way in which the English aristocracy oppress the working class here. I suppose that such a seasoning was necessary to make the mess palatable to the Yankees.

To morrow the fancy fair is held here, and I must buy some fairings for Baba and Alice.[3] Baba tells me that she expects to see Rica[4] at Stutgard. Poor Rica wrote a most touching letter expressing the greatest delight at the prospect of a meeting, and saying that her sisters accused her of loving the Miss Trevelyans more than them. Hannah has received your second letter and is most grateful for it.

Ever yours

T B Macaulay

---

[1] TBM left Brighton for London on the 8th, went to Bromley on the 9th, and returned to London on the 11th (Journal, v, 145–6).

[2] This was by Mr Sortain: see 22 March 1852. Wellington had died on 14 September.

[3] The fair was held at the Pavilion 'for the benefit of Trevelyan's emigration scheme.' TBM took Alice and 'bought forty shilling's worth of things which I did not want' (Journal, v, 142–3).

[4] Not identified.

TO JOHN PRESCOTT BIGELOW,[1] [11][2] OCTOBER 1852

MS: Harvard University.

Albany London / October 10. 1852

Sir,

I have just found here, on returning from the country to London, the volume which you were so good as to send me.[3] I have looked through it with real interest and pleasure. With the exception of Old England, there is no part of the world to which I am more attached than to New England. I rejoice in everything which tends to promote good will between two countries so closely connected by blood, language, laws, and religion: and it is truly gratifying to me to see that your sentiments are in perfect accordance with mine. / I have the honor to be, / Sir,

Your faithful Servant,
T B Macaulay

TO GEORGE OTTO TREVELYAN, 13 OCTOBER 1852

MS: Berg Collection, New York Public Library.

Albany October 13. 1852

Dear George,

I send you Hobbes's Thucydides,[4] which I hope you will study, and compare carefully with the original. Your Mamma tells me that you have some scruple about using a translation. There can be no possible objection to your doing so. Porson would not have thought it beneath him to consult a translation of such a writer as Thucydides. If there be a rule against translations at Harrow, it is a bad rule; and the more the boys break it the better. Deception there can be none. I defy any boy to use a translation in such a way as to prevent his masters from finding out whether he really understands the Greek or not. You will find Hobbes's English in some places as tough as the original or nearly so.

Your Mamma and sisters lunch with me to day. I wish that you could be of the party.

I am glad that you like Pope's Imitations.

Ever yours
T B Macaulay

---

[1] Bigelow (1797–1872) was Secretary to the Commonwealth of Massachusetts before serving as Mayor of Boston, 1849–52.

[2] TBM returned to London on the 11th (see note to the preceding letter).

[3] A copy of *Boston Railroad Jubilee: Opening of the Communication between Boston and Canada*, Boston, 1852, presented by J. P. Bigelow, late Mayor of Boston, is item 843 in the sale catalogue of TBM's library.

[4] Thomas Hobbes ,1629; reprinted 1822.

TO SELINA MACAULAY, 14 OCTOBER 1852

MS: Trinity College. *Envelope:* Miss Macaulay / Temple House / Brighton. *Subscription:* TBM.

Albany London / October 14. 1852

Dearest Selina,

I am as yet very well in spite of London fogs and of my staircase. I do not think that, on the whole, I have so much climbing here as at Clifton. For at Clifton I had to go from the ground floor to the drawing room or from the drawing room to the bedroom perhaps twenty times a day. Here all my rooms are on one floor; and my only climb, – a pretty tough one no doubt, – is when I come home after being abroad; and that is only once or twice in the twenty four hours.

The story about Penn is too long to tell you in a letter. Glynn has been misinformed. I still believe William Penn to have been the person to whom Sunderland wrote,[1] though a manuscript which has lately been discovered throws some doubt on the question. The spelling of the name is quite immaterial.

I am glad that your sale[2] succeeded so well. I think 350£ a very fair sum.

Everybody here is well and happy. Love to Fanny.

Ever yours,
T B Macaulay

TO NASSAU SENIOR, 16 OCTOBER 1852

MS: Yale University.

Albany October 16. 1852

Dear Senior,

I return the volume. It is highly interesting – important, if true, as the Yankee newspapers say.

I cannot but think that the account which Thiers gives of the transactions of 1840 is a complete vindication of Palmerston.[3]

Ever yours
T B Macaulay

---

[1] TBM's only evidence that Penn had a part in the ransom of the maids of Taunton was a letter from Sunderland (*History*, 1, 656n: ch. 5). Whether that letter was addressed to William or to some other Penn was the chief ground of dispute in the question. See *to* Frances Macaulay, 14 April 1851.

[2] The fancy fair at Brighton: see 5 October.

[3] It was Senior's practice to keep a journal record of his conversations with men of affairs and to circulate these notes among his friends; after his death, his daughter published parts of them. Thiers's remarks to Senior on the Eastern crisis of 1840, in which he complains

TO JOHN WATKINS,[1] 16 OCTOBER 1852

Text: New York *Times*, 5 November 1852.

Albany, Oct. 16, 1852.

Sir:

On returning to London a few days ago I found your letter. I did not immediately answer it, because I wished to have time for inquiry and consideration. I wished particularly to know in what state Mr. Hood had left his family – a matter about which I had no information, except what was derived from vague report. I have now learned that the children are provided for;[2] and I, therefore, have great pleasure in subscribing five pounds for the monument you propose to erect.

I have the honor to be, Sir, your faithful servant,

T. B. Macaulay.

John Watkins, Esq.

TO [ADAM BLACK], 21 OCTOBER 1852

Text: Scotsman, 23 October 1852: dated London, Thursday.

I am so much better that I think that I may, with some management, venture to make my appearance at Edinburgh before Parliament meets.[3] I think that Monday the 1st, or Tuesday the 2d of November would be the best day. I would start for the North on Friday the 29th, and divide the journey into two days, reaching Edinburgh on Saturday, stopping over the Monday and Tuesday, and leaving on Wednesday, so as to be in the House of Commons on Thursday afternoon. My kind friends must not expect from me more than one address, and that, I hope, I shall be able to get through pretty well. I am better certainly than in August I expected ever again to be.

that he was compelled to follow a policy not his own, appear in *Conversations with M. Thiers, M. Guizot, and Other Distinguished Persons, During the Second Empire,* ed. M. C. M. Simpson, 2 vols., 1878, I, 1–5.

1 Watkins was chairman of the committee for a public monument to the poet Thomas Hood (1799–1845: *DNB*), unveiled in Kensal Green cemetery in July 1854.

2 Hood's daughter married in 1849 and his son was to enter Oxford in 1853.

3 TBM heard on this date from Black: 'They wish me to go to Edinburgh – and I will go as soon as I come back from Bowood, if that will suit them' (Journal, v, 152). TBM adhered exactly to the schedule outlined in this letter, except that he did not manage to attend the House of Commons on Thursday, 4 November.

TO THE SECRETARY OF THE
ANTI-STATE CHURCH ASSOCIATION,[1] 25 OCTOBER 1852

Text: Glasgow *Constitutional,* 3 November 1852.

Albany, London, October 25, 1852.

Sir,

Your letter to me was sent, by some mistake, to Mr Cowan, and was consequently several days on the road to me. I am much obliged to you for the paper which you transmitted to me.[2] It is very ably drawn up, and contains much in which I cordially agree. As you have done me the honour to ask my opinion of what is called the movement for Religious Equality in Ireland, I must frankly say that, not as a friend of the Irish Church Establishment, but as a friend of civil and spiritual freedom, I look on that movement with extreme suspicion, and should be sorry to see the Protestant Dissenters of England and Scotland united in an unnatural coalition with men who defend those proceedings which have brought so much disgrace on the Tribunals and on the Government of Tuscany.[3] / I have the honour to be, Sir, your faithful servant,

T. B. Macaulay.

TO FRANCES MACAULAY, 27 OCTOBER 1852

MS: Trinity College.

Bowood[4] October 27 / 1852

Dearest Fanny,

A line to thank you for your kind letter. I am pretty well; and I am satisfied that it is better to go down now when everybody is in high good humour than to wait till Christmas when the weather will be colder, and

---

[1] A Dissenting organization, founded in 1844, and later known as the Society for the Liberation of Religion from State Control – the 'Liberation Society' for short.

[2] Probably the resolution passed by the Society to support the religious equality movement in Ireland if it should produce the 'complete removal of religious endowments' and put Church revenues to secular purposes (*Scotsman,* 16 October). A Religious Equality Association in Ireland had just been organized by several Irish M.P.s and was about to hold a conference in Dublin. The movement was, as the *Scotsman* said, 'deeply tainted with the suspicion of having for its real object the institution of a Roman Catholic hierarchy in place of the existing establishment' (3 November). At the end of his Edinburgh speech on 2 November TBM names the 'religious equality movement in Ireland' as one of the subjects he had meant to discuss had his strength allowed.

[3] The Madiai case: see 21 March 1853.

[4] TBM went down on the 25th and returned on the afternoon of this day (Journal, v, 154–5). The party included Lady Davy, Lord John Russell, Milman, Lord Clarendon, and George Cornewall Lewis and his wife.

when causes of dissatisfaction may have arisen. Besides, if I go then, I must stay at least a week: or I shall give offence. Now the necessity of being in my place at the opening of the Session is a valid plea for returning immediately. I am to harangue on Tuesday.

Love to Selina.

Ever yours
T B Macaulay

TO LADY TREVELYAN, 31 OCTOBER 1852

MS: Trinity College. *Extract published:* Trevelyan, II, 328.

Edinburgh October 31. / 1852

Dearest Hannah,

I arrived here at half after nine yesterday evening, rather tired, but pretty well. This is a fine day; and I feel quite equal to my work. I shall not dine out. I shall stay at home as much as I can during the day, and take a quiet walk in the evening when I shall not be seen. On Tuesday I am to harangue a great meeting. On Wednesday I go to York, and on Thursday to London. I may perhaps look in on you that evening.

I have just been to Guthrie's Church. It was Sacrament Sunday; and I saw the Presbyterian administration of the Eucharist which I had not seen for thirty five years.[1] Guthrie is a man of considerable ability and energy; but, to be sure, if the question between forms of prayer and extemporaneous effusions were to be decided by comparing the English Communion service with his performance, there could be little doubt as to the decision. "Lord, if thou hadst invited us to nothing but crumbs and cold water we ought to have been thankful. How much more for bread like this, and wine to make us of a cheerful countenance!" This is not quite in the vein of "Therefore with Angels and Archangels." Loves.

Ever yours
T B M

The town is as still as if it were midnight. It is a Sunday – a Presbyterian Sunday – a Presbyterian Sacrament Sunday. A person who opposes himself to the fanatical humour on this subject runs a great risk of being affronted. There was one person whom Christians generally mention with respect who, I am sure, could not have walked Prince's Street in safety, and who would have said to some of my grave constituents "Ye Hypocrites!"

[1] That is, on his first trip to Scotland, with his parents in 1817.

TO THOMAS FLOWER ELLIS, 31 OCTOBER 1852

MS: Trinity College.

Edinburgh October 31. 1852

Dear Ellis,

I arrived here in good health and in good heart yesterday evening. This is a day of profound rest; for it is not only a Sunday, and a Presbyterian Sunday, but a Presbyterian Sacrament Sunday. I have heard of several people who pass for religious in England, and who have been hooted and pelted here for Sabbath breakers. I am sure that one person who has generally been held in esteem by Xtians would have been mobbed all down Prince's Street. I daresay that I need not tell you whom I mean.

I am to harangue on Tuesday. On Thursday I shall be in town. Will you dine with me on Friday? I shall have a good deal to tell you. Your answer had better go to the Albany.

Ever yours,
T B Macaulay

Frank will have told you that he sent me a very civil letter of your friend Heywood.[1] Had I been asked to be bridesman to the gallant Captain, I might have accepted the invitation.

TO LADY TREVELYAN, 2 NOVEMBER 1852

MS: Trinity College.

Edinburgh Nov 2. 1852

Dearest Hannah,

I have just returned from the meeting.[2] I spoke an hour with immense applause. I found myself at last getting faint, partly with heat and partly with exertion, and ended rather abruptly. But the success was complete, and the enthusiasm of the audience such as I have hardly ever seen. I got better as soon as I was in the fresh air; and I now feel quite a load taken off my heart. I have entirely satisfied myself as to this – that my mental vigour, about which I care very much more than about my bodily health, has not been diminished by my illness. I wish that you and my dear Baba could have heard me. Love to all.

Ever yours
T B M

---

[1] Probably an invitation to Lucy Haywood's wedding: see 8 September.
[2] TBM spoke at 1 p.m. in the Music Hall. The speech is included in the authorized *Speeches*, 1853.

TO SELINA MACAULAY, 6 NOVEMBER 1852

MS: Trinity College. *Envelope:* Miss Macaulay / Temple House / Brighton. *Subscription:* TBM.

Albany London Nov 6. 1852

Dearest Selina,

Thanks for your kind letter. I am glad to have got so well through a very ticklish business which must have been got through sooner or later.

I have not compared the reports of my speech; nor indeed have I read any report through. I knew that the Times had sent one of the best short hand writers down from London;[1] and I therefore thought it unecessary to order the Scotsman for you.

What a fool poor Lord Maidstone is![2] I am really ashamed of having mentioned the name of so wretched a creature. But it is worth while to observe how very little anybody else can do to make us ridiculous, compared with what we can do ourselves. Three Dunciads would not have hurt this silly fellow so much as his own two letters.

I am pretty well recovered from the fatigue of my journey, and am in hopes that a moderate and cautious attendance in the House of Commons will not disagree with me.

Love to dear Fanny.

Ever yours,
T B Macaulay

TO GEORGE CORNEWALL LEWIS, 6 NOVEMBER 1852

MS: National Library of Wales.

Albany London / Nov. 6. 1852

My dear Lewis,

Thanks for your kind letter. I value your approbation much. To my great surprise Hume is pleased with my speech, and talked to me yesterday about the state of parties and the desirableness of a change of ministry with more moderation and good sense than he usually shows.

I should have been glad if I could have joined the very pleasant party at the Grove. But, though I am gaining strength daily, I find it necessary to be quiet after my late journey.

[1] His report in *The Times*, 4 November, begins by observing that TBM 'looked pale and thin, and was evidently affected by the warmth and cordiality of his reception.'

[2] In his Edinburgh speech TBM referred to Maidstone's inconsistency on the question of Protection and incidentally made fun of Maidstone's *Free Trade Hexameters* (a copy of which I have not been able to find). Maidstone replied in two rather silly letters to *The Times*, 5 and 6 November; the first of these inspired a leading article treating his Lordship with amused contempt.

Poor Lord Maidstone! I am really ashamed of having attacked him. How little anybody else can do to make us ridiculous, compared with what we can do ourselves. Ten Dunciads would not have hurt this silly man so much as his own two letters.

Ever yours truly

T B Macaulay

TO CHARLES BERTRAM BLACK,[1] 6 NOVEMBER 1852

MS: Dr Howard R. Seidenstein.

Albany London / November 6. 1852

Dear Sir,

It is very gratifying to me to learn that, in one of the most remote parts of the civilised world, I have countrymen who derive pleasure from my writings and take an interest in my fortunes. It is in a particular manner gratifying to me to know that among the readers whose approbation I prize so highly is the son of one of my most valued friends.

I was much interested by the very little that you say about the country where you reside. I should have been glad to have had more information as to the government and the state of manners and morals. Perhaps you will, on some future occasion, have the kindness to send me the results of your observations on those subjects. / Believe me, / My dear Sir,

Your faithful Servant,

T B Macaulay

TO UNIDENTIFIED RECIPIENT, 6 NOVEMBER 1852

MS: National Library of Scotland.

Albany Nov 6. 1852

Sir,

I beg you to accept my thanks for the work which you have had the goodness to send me. I hope soon to have leisure to become better acquainted with the contents. / I have the honor to be, / Sir,

Your most obedient servant,

T B Macaulay

1 The letter is endorsed 'to C. B. Black, Esq. / Serena / Coquimbo / Chile.' Black (1821–1906) was Adam Black's eldest son; his health 'was not strong and he went as a young man to Chile where he stayed many years, first in a shipping-office in Valparaiso, and later as Professor of English in Santiago; he returned to live in southern Europe, to write Black's guides to Spain, Holland, Belgium and much of France, and to accompany his aged father on visits to Italy and Spain' (*Adam & Charles Black 1807–1957*, p. 24).

TO FRANCES MACAULAY, 9 NOVEMBER 1852

MS: Trinity College.

Albany November 9 / 1852

Dearest Fanny,

You are mistaken about Lord Maidstone's allusion to Bruton Street.[1] He has, I imagine, a sporting acquaintance with Charles Greville, the Clerk of the Council, who is on the turf, and who is well known to furnish intelligence to the Times. Charles Greville has a suite of rooms in Lord Granville's house in Bruton Street.[2] Lord Maidstone therefore tells the Editor of the Times to drive to Bruton Street and ask the Clerk of the Council what sort of person his Lordship is. I do not imagine that Greville will be at all pleased to be thus mentioned.

You are right about Lord Winchelsea.[3] But I wonder that you should forget that the person with whom he fought was the Duke of Wellington. It was in 1829 about the Roman Catholic Emancipation Bill.

I am pretty well – all the better for having paid the visit which I owed to the electors of Edinburgh. Till that debt was discharged I never should have been easy; and I might possibly have been forced to go at Easter which would have destroyed my plan of an excursion. I mean to take you to Paris for a week. Trevelyan thinks that he can manage to get a sufficiently long holiday to be of the party. Hannah and Baba anticipate with great delight George's ecstasy when he hears that he is to see Paris. We shall be just the number for a railway journey – six – the complement of a carriage. Love to Selina.

Ever yours
T B M

TO JOHN HILL BURTON, 20 NOVEMBER 1852

MS: National Library of Scotland.

Albany November 20 / 1852

Dear Sir,

Many thanks. I expect the sheets impatiently.[4] I have looked into the question of the commercial relations between England and Scotland after the Restoration. You were quite right; and the subject is full of interest.[5]

---

[1] In his letter to *The Times* of 6 November: see *to* Selina Macaulay, 6 November.
[2] Greville moved there in 1849 and remained until his death in 1865.
[3] George William Finch-Hatton (1791–1858: *DNB*), 10th Earl of Winchilsea, Lord Maidstone's father.
[4] Of Burton's *History of Scotland, 1689–1748*. TBM had called on Burton – 'very kind and useful' – when in Edinburgh on 2 November (Journal, v, 160).
[5] TBM touches on this subject, with a reference to Burton's 'valuable history,' early in ch. 13 of the *History*, III.

I am pretty well: but I look forward with some anxiety to next week.[1] After that time, I anticipate no very severe trial of my strength before Christmas.

> Ever yours truly
> T B Macaulay

TO SIR HENRY ELLIS, 20 NOVEMBER 1852

MS: British Museum.

> Albany November 20 / 1852

Dear Sir Henry,

I shall be ready to attend a meeting of the Library Sub Committee at eleven on Saturday next. I do not know what authority you require to enable you to summon such a meeting. If I have any authority in the matter, I put my powers into your hands.

> Very truly yours,
> T B Macaulay

TO JOHN VAIZEY,[2] 20 NOVEMBER 1852

MS: Trinity College. *Envelope:* J Vaizey Esq / Gray's Inn. *Subscription:* TBM.

> Albany Nov 20. 1852

Sir,

I am much obliged to you for your kind offer. I have the volume which you mention. / I have the honor to be, / Sir,

> Your faithful Servant
> T B Macaulay

TO RICHARD MONCKTON MILNES, 20 NOVEMBER 1852

MS: Trinity College. *Published:* T. Wemyss Reid, *The Life, Letters, and Friendships of Richard Monckton Milnes, First Lord Houghton*, 2 vols., New York, 1891, I, 477.

> Albany November 20 / 1852

Dear Milnes,

I am sorry that I have made an appointment on business which will make it impossible for me to breakfast with you on Monday.[3]

[1] To the debate on a resolution in support of free trade intended to embarrass the Derby government. The debate lasted for three nights, 23, 25, and 26 November. TBM attended on the last night, voted, and did not get home until 2 in the morning: 'a few such nights will make it necessary for me to go to Clifton again' (Journal, v, 178: 26 November).

[2] Vaizey (1800?–55), of Gray's Inn and Denmark Hill, was a solicitor.

[3] TBM met his brother Charles at his solicitor's in the City to look into 'the question of the mortgage on which he wishes to lend some money' (Journal, v, 175).

You might almost as well have asked Sir Benjamin Hall[1] as me to meet my Lord of Oxford. For, if the Convocation[2] had gone on wrangling a day longer, I should have broken forth like Elihu.

"I will answer also my part: I also will show my opinion. For I am full of matter: the spirit within me constraineth me. I will speak that I may be refreshed: I will open my lips and answer. Let me not, I pray you, accept any man's person: neither let me give flattering titles unto man."[3] There certainly are some great Ecclesiastical personages to whom I should not have given flattering titles.

Ever yours truly
T B Macaulay

TO UNIDENTIFIED RECIPIENT, 26 NOVEMBER 1852

Text: Maggs Brothers Catalogue 445, Christmas 1923, item 2678, 2¾ pp. 8vo: dated Albany, London, 26 November 1852.

I know nothing about the North American Screw Steamer Ship Company; nor can I at all judge whether it would or would not be desirable that the responsibility of the shareholders should be limited.

TO FRANCES MACAULAY, 1 DECEMBER 1852

MS: Trinity College.

Albany London / December 1. 1852

Dearest Fanny,

I begin with a lie. For I am not at the Albany, but in the library of the House of Commons writing with a public pen and public ink on public paper, under a superb Gothic roof. I am very well on the whole. The divisions of last Friday night threw me back a little.[4] I was at the House till past two – almost squeezed to death during half an hour in the lobby; and then I had to walk home through the mire in a cold winter morning. But this will not happen again, or will happen very seldom.

---

[1] Hall (1802–67: *DNB*), first Baronet, and afterwards Baron Llanover, was liberal M.P. for Marylebone and an inveterate enemy of ecclesiastical sinecures and episcopal incomes.

[2] Bishop Wilberforce was the leading spirit in the effort to revive Convocation, which had not met except *pro forma* since 1717. A newly-elected Convocation had met four times between 5 and 17 November to debate Church business, a decisive event in the restoration of the body: see Chadwick, *The Victorian Church*, Part I, pp. 309–24. Laodiceans like TBM mistrusted the revival of Convocation as a step towards a new authoritarianism in the Church.

[3] Job 32: 17–21.

[4] See *to* Burton, 20 November.

You are right about that foolish address of the English ladies.[1] Hannah would not voluntarily have signed it; and I am rather sorry that she signed it at all. But the Duchess of Sutherland wrote to her; and it was awkward for a daughter of Z[achary] M[acaulay] to refuse. I believe too that the wish to see the most beautiful palace in England[2] had something to do with the matter. I never heard of the business till it was all over.

I do not think it at all unlikely that, in the Xtmas recess, I may go down to Brighton for a few days, if you can get me good accommodations. But this depends on many contigencies.

The King of Prussia has named me a Knight of the Order of Merit on the presentation of the Royal Academy of Sciences at Berlin;[3] and the nomination has been communicated to me in a most flattering letter from the famous Baron Von Humboldt,[4] Chancellor of the Order. I do not suppose that I shall be permitted by the government to accept this honor. I have written to Walpole,[5] not to ask permission, but to submit the case to the decision of the ministers; and I have told him that I do not wish him to relax any wholesome rule on my account. In truth it would be a mere plague to me to have a cross at my buttonhole, though I should never wear it except in Germany, or at Chevalier Bunsen's parties here.[6] Love to Selina.

                                                              Ever yours
                                                              T B Macaulay

TO LORD MAHON, 3 DECEMBER 1852

MS: Stanhope Papers, Chevening.

                                                       Albany Dec 3. 1852
Dear Mahon,
    Lord Seymour, Inglis and I propose to meet at the Museum on Monday

---

[1] Inspired by *Uncle Tom's Cabin*, Lord Shaftesbury composed an 'Address of the Women of England to the Women of the United States' asking for legal marriage and religious teaching for American slaves (*The Times*, 9 November). On the 26th the Duchess of Sutherland held a public meeting to form a committee to collect signatures to the address. Hannah, Margaret, and 'Mrs. Macaulay' – presumably Charles's wife – were among those present (*The Times*, 29 November). The address, with 562,448 names, was presented to Mrs Stowe at Stafford House on her visit to England in the next year; TBM was one of the guests on the occasion. Mrs Stowe he thought 'an ugly commonplace woman' but deserving 'great praise for not quite losing her head' (Journal, VI, 68: 6 May 1853).

[2] Stafford House, now Lancaster House.

[3] The first reference to this in TBM's Journal is on 27 November, when he wrote to the Home Secretary to inquire whether it were proper to accept the decoration (V, 178).

[4] Alexander von Humboldt (1769–1859), scientist and explorer.

[5] Spencer Walpole (1806–98: *DNB*), M.P., 1846–82, and Home Secretary in Derby's three cabinets.

[6] TBM went to a party at Bunsen's on this evening and found a 'great crowd of soldiers with Prussian orders' (Journal, V, 180).

– at two precisely. We shall have half an hour's talk and be able to consult Ellis and Panizzi before going to Downing Street.[1]

Ever yours,

T B Macaulay

TO WILLIAM WHEWELL, 4 DECEMBER 1852

MS: Trinity College.

Albany London / December 4. 1852

Dear Whewell,

I have been thinking over your very kind invitation; and I am sorry to say that it is very doubtful whether I shall be able to attend at our Festival,[2] and still more doubtful whether I shall be able to leave town till the morning of the 16th. In these circumstances it would be very wrong in me to prevent you from extending your hospitality to some other guest. If I am able to get to Cambridge on the evening of the 15th I will make my appearance at your breakfast table on the 16th. If not, I will try to be in time for Chapel.

I had a very pleasant breakfast party on Monday:[3] but we all missed you greatly.

Ever yours,

T B Macaulay

TO WILLIAM WHEWELL, 8 DECEMBER 1852

MS: Trinity College.

Albany London / December 8. 1852

Dear Whewell,

I am afraid that the change of day will make it impossible for me to attend our Commemoration. The debate on the budget will in all probability last till two or three o'clock on Wednesday morning;[4] and, if that is the case, I shall hardly venture to run down early in the day to Cambridge.

---

[1] A delegation of the Museum trustees met Lord Derby and the Chancellor of the Exchequer, Disraeli, on 6 December to call 'the special attention of the Government to the urgent necessity of providing space for the Printed Book Department and for the accommodation of Readers' (Minutes of the Trustees). The meeting was part of the negotiations leading to the building of the Museum's reading room. The Museum was so crowded already that in March 1853 it had to suspend all purchase of books (Edward Miller, *Prince of Librarians*, 1967, p. 211).

[2] The Trinity Commemoration. TBM did not go.

[3] The party were Lord Carlisle, Lord Mahon, Lord Glenelg, Dundas, and Milman (Journal, v, 179).

[4] The debate, ending in the defeat of the Government, lasted until the early morning of Thursday, the 17th; TBM stayed until nearly 4 a.m. (Journal, vi, 8).

I have just received a line from Lord Monteagle which tells me that Empson is very ill[1] – hopelessly so. I know no particulars: but I am greatly concerned.

> Ever yours truly
> T B Macaulay

TO THOMAS FLOWER ELLIS, 8 DECEMBER 1852

MS: Trinity College. *Partly published:* Trevelyan, II, 354.

> Albany December 8 / 1852

Dear Empson,

I meant dear Ellis. But my mind is full of poor Empson. He is dying. I expect every hour to hear that all is over. Poor fellow – he was a most kind generous friend to me, and as unselfish and unenvious as yourself.

The Cambridge scheme is over, as far as I am concerned. It is probable that the debate on the budget will last till two or three o'clock on Wednesday morning; and, if so, I shall be in no humour to rise before my usual time in order to go down to the Commemoration.

We are all pleased with George's place at the trials. I hope that you are not dissatisfied with Walter's.

> Ever yours
> T B Macaulay

To make this calamity worse, poor Mrs. Empson is expecting to be confined again after an interval of twelve years.[2]

Longman has just been here – sorry for Empson, and anxious about the Review. I recommended Cornwall Lewis; and I have little doubt that the offer will be made to him.[3] Now that he is out of place, out of parliament, and minus 8000£ for election charges,[4] 1000£ a year certain is likely to be acceptable. But say nothing about this.

TO JOHN HILL BURTON, 9 DECEMBER 1852

MS: National Library of Scotland.

> Albany London / December 9. 1852

Dear Sir,

I have received the first eight sheets of your book.[5] Very good it is and

---

1 He died on the 10th.
2 TBM's mistake: see 13 December.
3 Lewis accepted the editorship later this month.
4 After being defeated this summer in the election for Herefordshire Lewis stood for Peterborough and was again defeated. £8000 was the figure for his expenses according to the talk at Brooks's (Journal, VI, 1: 5 December).
5 See *to* Burton, 20 November.

very interesting. I hope that it will have the success which it deserves.

I am glad to find that our views generally agree. Where they differ I should be disposed to distrust my own judgment. Two or three of your sentences are so like sentences which I wrote more than a year ago that I must alter my words for fear of being thought as impudent a felon as the Chancellor of the Exchequer.[1]

Ever yours truly,
T B Macaulay

TO THOMAS FLOWER ELLIS, 13 DECEMBER 1852

MS: Trinity College. *Partly published:* Trevelyan, II, 354.

Albany December 13. 1852

Dear Ellis,

It is quite impossible that I can dine with you on Tuesday. If I venture out at all, it will be to the House of Commons. I have written to Hayter[2] desiring him to pair me for this evening. I am better, but still unfit to face such weather as this.

The government, to my great relief, has decided that I cannot be permitted to become a Knight of the Prussian Order of Merit.[3] To be sure I should not have had to carry my cross and ribband at my button hole more than once or twice a year: but that would have been once or twice too much. However I have written most politely to Humboldt, and have told him, with not less truth than civility, that his letter will be as much valued by me as the Insignia which I have been forced to decline.

Poor Empson died with admirable fortitude and cheerfulness. I find that his wife was lately brought to bed.[4] I thought that she had been still expecting her accouchement. He spoke to her, to his friends, to his other children, with kindness, but with perfect firmness. But when the baby was put on his bed, he burst into tears. Poor fellow! – For my part, I feel that I should die best in the situation of Charles the First or Lewis the Sixteenth or Montrose. I mean quite alone – surrounded by enemies, and nobody

---

[1] A part of Disraeli's eulogy in the House of Commons on the Duke of Wellington, 15 November, had been shown by the *Globe* to be plagiarized from a speech by Thiers (see Robert Blake, *Disraeli*, 1967, p. 335). Later in the month the *Morning Chronicle*, 25 November, showed that Disraeli had borrowed from TBM's essay on Byron in his *Venetia, or the Poet's Daughter*, 1837: 'the fellow has plundered me impudently' TBM wrote of this (Journal, VII, 65: 10 September 1853).

[2] William Goodenough Hayter (1792–1878: *DNB*), first Baronet, Whig M.P., 1837–65, and Whig Whip, 1850–8.

[3] Yet the decoration arrived on 8 February 1853 (Journal, VI, 32); and the *Gentleman's Magazine*, 1853, I, 285, notes that the honor has been conferred on TBM.

[4] Frances Charlotte Jeffrey Empson was born on 9 May.

that I cared for near me. The parting is the dreadful thing. I do not wonder at Russell's saying – "The bitterness of death is past."[1]

Will you dine here on Friday? The debate cannot last so long, nor my Influenza. And then we will do justice to the Champagne.[2]

[no signature]

TO JOHN HILL BURTON, 16 DECEMBER 1852

MS: National Library of Scotland.

Albany Dec 16. 1852

Dear Sir,

I have been a sincere mourner for poor Empson. He was one of the best of men, and to me especially one of the truest and most generous of friends. His poor widow bears up, I hear, better than could have been expected.

I feel assured that your book will succeed. If I should be disappointed, I shall be forced to think worse, not of my own taste, but of the taste of the public.

By the bye where did you find that Ferguson turned Episcopalian.[3] Jacobite of course: – but I do not remember that he ever recanted his antiprelatical opinions.

Ever yours truly
T B Macaulay

TO FRANCES MACAULAY, 17 DECEMBER 1852

MS: Huntington Library. *Extract published:* Trevelyan, II, 328n.

Albany London / December 17. 1852

Dearest Fanny,

I am glad that these poor creatures are out, though the difficulties of the conquerors are only beginning.

I was in the division at four this morning, in spite of an attack of Influenza, and am not the better for my patriotic exertions.

I have a great mind to go down to Brighton in the week after Xtmas. Could you get me good accommodation at the Norfolk? But make no

---

1 See Hume, *History of England*, ch. 69.
2 Ellis did not come until Sunday, the 19th, when they had 'oysters – turkey – snipes' (Journal, VI, 10).
3 Burton says that Robert Ferguson turned 'high episcopalian and Jacobite' (*History of Scotland*, 1853, I, 84n). TBM does not accept the statement in his *History*.

agreement till you hear from me again. I may be unable to go down from various causes.

One good thing the Derby ministry did before they went out. They refused me permission to wear the Prussian cross; and I bless them for it. I told Walpole that he had decided the matter exactly as I should have done. I wonder that you do not see how improper it is that an Englishman should go about with German and Russian decorations dangling from his button-hole. As to the Duke of Wellington and other military men, that is quite a distinct case. But I have not time to argue the matter.

Your old parson is a dunce. There is nothing in Homer or Hesiod either about the observation of every seventh day. Hesiod, to be sure, says that the seventh day of every month (a very different thing) is a holiday; and the reason which he gives is that on the seventh of the month Latona brought Apollo into the world[1] – a pretty reason for Christians. As to your Greek inscriptions, one of them I can make out. It means simply "a holiday"; and the words, I dare say, come over fifty times in Homer. The other inscription I am absolutely unable to decipher. Ask your friend just to give you the book and the line of Homer to which he refers; and that will make everything plain.

Poor Empson. I have been a most sincere mourner for him. He was a noble, amiable, generous, man as ever lived. The question about the Edinburgh Review is not absolutely settled. I hope that Cornwall Lewis will take it. Love to Selina.

Ever yours
T B Macaulay

TO FRANCES MACAULAY, 22 DECEMBER 1852

MS: Huntington Library.

Albany London / December 22. 1852

Dearest Fanny,

I was tolerably comfortable in the rooms which I had at the Norfolk in the autumn. But I should prefer the first floor, if apartments are to be had there. I think of going down on Monday the 27th, and staying till the Monday following. I shall carry down plenty of work with me.

I believe that we shall have a very good and a very strong ministry. I have seen something of what has been going on behind the scenes, – more indeed than I can venture to trust to paper.[2] Lord Lansdowne's behaviour has been incomparably good.

---

[1] *Works and Days,* 771.
[2] TBM had exhorted Lord John Russell to take part in a coalition government: his Journal account of the interview is printed in Trevelyan, II, 331–3.

Cornwall Lewis has accepted the Edinburgh Review. I am truly glad of it. But I am afraid that Price[1] will be disappointed. I was sorry to hear that he had set his heart on being editor. I do not think him at all fit for such a post. He is full of Arnoldian and Bunsenian crotchets about religion and politics; and he has no connection with the heads of the Whig party with which the Edinburgh Review has long been so closely allied. I should think Price hardly to be trusted as a contributor without very strict revision of his papers. And to trust him with the office of revising all the papers of other contributors would, in my opinion, be most hazardous. Love to Selina.

Ever yours

T B Macaulay

TO THOMAS FLOWER ELLIS, 24 DECEMBER 1852

MS: Trinity College.

Albany Dec 24 / 1852

Dear Ellis,

I send Pendennis.[2] I cannot lay my hand at this moment on the Paston Letters.

I have little news for you except that Molesworth comes into the cabinet.[3] I am glad of it.

Ever yours,

T B Macaulay

The reports are strong about Cranworth:[4] but he knew nothing about his fate himself yesterday evening.

TO FRANCES MACAULAY, 25 DECEMBER 1852

MS: Trinity College. *Extract published:* Trevelyan, II, 331.

Albany London / Dec 25. 1852

Dearest Fanny,

I shall be at Brighton on Tuesday, probably in time to see you on that day. William will be with me. They must find room for him in the house or near it.

I shall not be sorry to stay over Monday, and to hear Lord Aberdeen's

---

1 Bonamy Price: see 10 November 1849.
2 TBM had begun reading Thackeray's novel, evidently for the first time, on the 16th and finished it on the 23rd: 'very clever and powerful book' (Journal, VI, 14).
3 As First Commissioner of the Board of Works.
4 Lord Cranworth was Lord Chancellor in Aberdeen's administration.

explanation of his intentions.[1] The ministry is a very good one: but I am afraid that the feelings of many valuable men will be wounded by the way in which they have been passed over. There was a superabundance of good materials, and it was necessary to make a choice.

I should doubt whether so many members of the two houses have been in town on Christmas day since 1783, sixty nine years ago. Then, as now, there was a change of ministry in Christmas week. Indeed there was a great debate in a full house of commons on the 22nd of December; and Lord North made a very celebrated speech.

I will see about Shakspeare. You ought to have one always in your library. I gave Hannah a very pretty edition for her journey to the Tyrol. She liked it much. I will get one of the same edition for you.[2]

Give the inclosed with my love to Selina. A happy Xtmas to you both.

[no signature]

TO THOMAS FLOWER ELLIS, 30 DECEMBER 1852

MS: Trinity College. *Extract published:* Trevelyan, II, 355.

Norfolk Hotel / Brighton Dec 30. 1852

Dear Ellis,

I am here walking, writing, reading, eating, drinking and sleeping, easily and comfortably enough.[3] I suppose that you see all the papers; and I can add but little to what they will tell you. I have had a letter from Wood,[4] who was nettled, and not altogether without reason at what seemed to be a slight on the part of Lord Aberdeen. But every thing has since been satisfactorily explained; and Wood takes the Vice Chancellorship with great contentment. I have also seen Hayter who was here this morning lounging along the beach, and who seems to think that the Peelites have had more than their share of the plunder. The elections, I

---

[1] TBM attended the House on the 27th, and, after learning of the ministerial arrangements, wrote that 'Lord John, I am afraid, has not looked as he should have done after the interests of his friends or consulted their dignity....There is a disposition to murmur among our people. My business however is to allay their discontent, though I cannot help thinking it reasonable' (Journal, VI, 17).

[2] The edition, a copy of which TBM gave to Fanny on the 28th (Journal, VI, 17), was the Lansdowne Shakespeare, a one-volume edition published late in 1851.

[3] TBM went to Brighton on the 28th and returned to London on 3 January (Journal, VI, 17–18).

[4] William Page Wood (1801–81: *DNB*), afterwards first Baron Hatherley and Lord Chancellor, a contemporary of TBM's at Trinity and elected to a fellowship with him; Whig M.P., 1847–53; Solicitor-General under Russell; succeeded Lord Cranworth as Vice-Chancellor in Aberdeen's ministry. At the House of Commons on the 27th TBM had spoken to Wood: 'He was somewhat excited and seemed to think that he had been ill used' (Journal, VI, 16).

understand, are likely to go smoothly. Cardwell is in some danger, brought on by his own shuffling about the ballot.[1]

I do not much like the arrangement about the Duchy.[2] Strutt is a man who ought to have an active office. It would have been wiser to give Molesworth the Duchy and Strutt the Woods and works.

Was ever anything so lucky as Denison's letter,[3] coming just when the cry of Puseyism was setting up against the new Ministry?

I shall be in town again on Monday. I am disengaged all next week. Fix some day for dining with me in honor of 1853. I hope that it will be as happy a year as, in spite of some bodily suffering, 1852 has been to me. It is odd that, though time is stealing from me perceptibly my vigour and my pleasures, I am growing happier and happier. As Milnes says – It is shocking – it is scandalous – to enjoy life as I do.

Ever yours,
T B Macaulay

TO UNIDENTIFIED RECIPIENT, 10 JANUARY 1853

MS: Trinity College.

Albany London / January 10. 1853

Madam,

I have very great pleasure in complying with your request. I sincerely wish that you may always preserve, in spite of the distressing infirmities which you mention, the amiable and cheerful temper which your letter indicates. / I have the honor to be, / Madam,

Your faithful Servant,
T B Macaulay

TO THOMAS FLOWER ELLIS, 11 JANUARY 1853

MS: Trinity College.

Albany Jany. 11. 1853

Dear Ellis,

I found, on returning hither, that I had made a mistake. I am engaged to

---

[1] He was elected for the city of Oxford, in succession to William Page Wood, on 4 January 1853.

[2] The Chancellor of the Duchy of Lancaster, Edward Strutt, was not in the cabinet.

[3] A letter from George Denison, Archdeacon of Taunton, to Gladstone, announcing that, in consequence of Gladstone's taking office with Whigs like Russell and Lansdowne, Denison could 'place no confidence in you as a representative of the University of Oxford, or as a public man' (*The Times*, 30 December).

dinner on Thursday, but disengaged to morrow. I will therefore dine with you to morrow, if that perfectly suits you.[1]

Hannah and Baba extol Louise's acting to the skies. They were quite delighted by her cleverness.

Ever yours,

T B Macaulay

TO FRANCES MACAULAY, 13 JANUARY 1853

MS: Huntington Library.

Albany London / Jan 13. 1853

Dearest Fanny,

I am not much amiss, yet not quite well. My respiration now and then gives me trouble, and I suffer from want of exercise: for there has been scarcely one tolerable day this week. At present, to be sure, the weather is fine, and I have had a pleasant walk this morning. After all I have little reason to complain.

I hope and believe that Gladstone is safe.[2] The animosity of the ex ministers is without bounds. But their followers are much less rancorous. I fully expect a considerable addition to our numbers from the other side of the House. I am afraid that Lord John has vexed and disgusted some of his old friends, – not by leaving them out, – but by omitting to give them any explanation or to express any regret. I hear, indeed I know, that Lord Carlisle, Baring, and Labouchere are hurt by his conduct.[3] They will however support him as steadily as if they were in the cabinet: but it is a great mistake to throw away the personal attachment of such men. There are others whose discontent is as great and who are not equally honorable and public spirited. These may give the government serious annoyance. However things on the whole look well.

George went back to school yesterday. It was a sad parting. Love to Selina.

Ever yours

T B Macaulay

[1] TBM dined with Ellis on the 12th and with Sir Robert Inglis the next day (Journal, VI, 21–2).

[2] Gladstone, Chancellor of the Exchequer in the new ministry, had a difficult struggle at Oxford, where his opponents kept the polls open for fifteen days. The contest was 'reported daily in the national papers with all the excitement of a horse race' (J. B. Conacher, *The Aberdeen Coalition, 1852–1855,* 1968, p. 50).

[3] This is more or less confirmed by the evidence of Russell's papers: see Conacher, *The Aberdeen Coalition,* pp. 27–8.

TO LORD ABERDEEN, 22 JANUARY 1853

MS: British Museum.

Albany January 22. 1853

My dear Lord,

Mr. James Simpson,[1] an Advocate at Edinburgh and a very good friend of the government, has begged me to convey to you a work which he has just published.[2] Part of his book you probably read thirty seven years ago. It was the first account of the field of Waterloo that appeared; and I remember well that at Christmas 1815, everybody was talking about it. / Believe me, / My dear Lord,

Yours very faithfully

T B Macaulay

The / Earl of Aberdeen / etc. etc. etc.

TO UNIDENTIFIED RECIPIENT, [JANUARY?][3] 1853

Text: Maggs Brothers Catalogue 522, Summer 1929, item 1036: dated 1853.

I am glad you take so just a view of the question of national defence. It is, in my opinion, all important, and I am glad that the government, the parliament, and the country are agreed as to the essential points.

TO FRANCES MACAULAY, 3 FEBRUARY 1853

MS: Huntington Library.

Albany London / February 3. 1853

Dearest Fanny,

Your letter came while I was at Bowood.[4] I am sorry that I cannot help your friend. If I can get to Somerset House when the choice is made, I must vote for a gentleman who was strongly recommended to me by Dr. Bright.[5] My promise was given ten days ago.

---

[1] Simpson (1781–1853: *Boase*) was among TBM's active supporters at Edinburgh. He was interested in many reform enterprises and devoted much time to giving lectures in the cause of popular education.

[2] *Paris after Waterloo: Notes Taken at the Time and Hitherto Unpublished including a Revised Edition of 'A Visit to Flanders and the Field,'* 1853.

[3] This extract is one of three printed together in Maggs's Catalogue under the summary date of January–May 1853; two of the three are evidently later than January, and this one may plausibly be dated in January. The fear of France was then still intense, and, in the new session of Parliament about to meet, fresh military expenditure would be called for.

[4] TBM left London on 29 January and returned on 1 February (Journal, VI, 26–9). The party were Lord and Lady Granville, Lord and Lady Mahon, General Sir Edward and Mrs Kerrison (Lady Mahon's parents), their son Edward, and Sir James Lacaita.

[5] A new examiner in *Materia Medica* for the University of London was to be elected on 6 April; the election went to Dr G. O. Rees (1813–99: *DNB*). TBM had been a member of the Senate of the University since April 1850.

I came back through a fog which did not permit us to see the hedges on each side of the Great Western Railway. When we got to Paddington things were worse. The mist of the river and the cloud of sea coal combined made London darker than I ever saw it – one single evening excepted. I was an hour and a half in getting from the station to the Albany, by the help of link boys who led the horse. I am forced to keep at home, particularly in the evenings, for fear of bronchitis; but I am pretty well and very comfortable.

I do not know who wrote the article in the Edinburgh Review which you mention; nor do I remember to have read it.

I have had a letter from Guizot.[1] He has proposed me as a member of the Institute of France; and the proposition has been universally approved. The formal election, about which no doubt seems to be entertained, will be on Saturday.[2] This is really a great honor, as great as any honor of the sort can well be. The vacancy was caused by the death of Lingard who would not have been particularly pleased if he had known who was to be his successor. Love to Selina.

Ever yours
T B Macaulay

TO THOMAS FLOWER ELLIS, [3 FEBRUARY 1853]

MS: Trinity College.

[London]

Dear Ellis,

Saturday at seven.[3] On Tuesday I will dine with you if the weather and my chest agree.

Thanks for the papers.[4] They shall be returned to morrow. You little know the dignity of your correspondent. I now sign myself

T B Macaulay FRS, MRIA, M P late fellow of Trin Coll Cambridge late Lord Rector of the University of Glasgow, Knight of the Order of Merit of Prussia, Member of the Royal Academies of Munich and Turin, Member of the Historical Society of Utrecht, and, – die of envy –

Member of the French Institute in the
Department of Moral Science ! ! ![5]

[1] 2 February (Journal, VI, 30).
[2] TBM received nineteen of the twenty-two votes (*Literary Gazette*, 19 February, p. 181).
[3] 5 February: Ellis dined with TBM then, as TBM did with Ellis on the Tuesday following (Journal, VI, 31–2: 5 and 8 February).
[4] See 4 February.
[5] The dates of TBM's honors not previously mentioned are these: Fellow of the Royal Society, December 1849; of the Royal Irish Academy, November 1852. I have not been able to learn the date of his election to the Historical Society of Utrecht.

TO THOMAS FLOWER ELLIS, 4 FEBRUARY 1853

MS: Trinity College.

Albany Feb 4. 1853

Dear Ellis,

I like the speech[1] much – particularly the terseness and conciseness of the style. Finlason's book[2] is a prodigy of absurdity.

Ever yours
T B Macaulay

TO LORD ABERDEEN, 12 FEBRUARY 1853

MS: British Museum.

Albany February 12. 1853

My dear Lord,

I am sorry to be under the necessity of occupying even a small portion of your valuable time. But I must beg you to grant me an interview of a few minutes on the subject of the Edinburgh Annuity Tax.[3] There are two plans for the settling of that much disputed matter, one framed by Lord John Russell's government, and the other framed by the late Lord Advocate Mr. Inglis. Neither can be adopted without the consent of the Crown.

I will attend you at any hour or place. I propose to bring nobody but Tufnell, who was Chairman of a Committee of the Commons which thoroughly investigated the whole question. / Believe me, / My dear Lord,

Yours very faithfully
T B Macaulay

The / Earl of Aberdeen / etc. etc. etc.

TO SIR EDWARD BULWER-LYTTON, 14 FEBRUARY 1853

MS: Hertfordshire County Council.

Albany February 14 / 1853

Dear Sir Edward Lytton,

I looked round the House of Commons on Friday and again to day in

---

[1] Perhaps a speech by Ellis at some point in the Newman-Achilli trial, or perhaps the speech of Mr Justice Coleridge, 31 January, delivering sentence upon Newman (*The Times*, 1 February).

[2] William Francis Finlason, *Report of the Trial and Preliminary Proceedings in the Case of the Queen on the Prosecution of G. Achilli v. Dr. Newman*, 1852. Finlason, who writes as a partisan of Newman, provides not merely a report of the trial but an introduction, copious notes, and stage-directions.

[3] TBM, with Tufnell, called on Aberdeen on 17 February: 'We agreed very well' (Journal, VI, 35).

the hope of seeing you, and of being able to tell you how much I am obliged to you for My Novel.[1] But, as I was disappointed I will not defer my acknowledgments longer.

I did not read a line of your book while it was coming out in monthly parts,[2] though I often heard it praised by good judges. I like to sit down to a hearty meal, and not to be tantalized with nibbles and sips which irritate the appetite instead of satisfying it. As soon as the publication was announced I sent for a copy, and was deep in the second volume when your kind present arrived.[3] In some respects I prefer My Novel to anything that you have written. The multitude of characters powerfully and discriminatingly drawn is extraordinary. To be sure you took a larger canvass than usual. There are tragic scenes of exquisite pathos, and much genial and mirthful comedy. What pleased me least was Dr. Morgan's Homœopathy[4] and Burley's one eyed perch.[5] The perch I could excuse if Burley were not a masterpiece. However I am grateful to you for him, perch and all; and I should be glad to pass my life in reading works with twenty times the faults of My Novel and half the beauties.

Ever yours truly
T B Macaulay

TO THOMAS FLOWER ELLIS, 19 FEBRUARY 1853

MS: Trinity College.

Albany Feb 19. 1853

Dear Ellis,

I cannot venture to go to you to day. I tried yesterday evening to get to the House and found my chest so much irritated by the cold evening air that I came back without hearing Dizzy's eloquence.[6] I find that I must stay at home after sunset while the frost continues.

Will you breakfast here on Tuesday, and meet Lord Carlisle?[7]

Fix any day for dining here next week.

Ever yours
T B Macaulay

---

[1] *My Novel, or, Varieties in English Life,* 4 vols., published on 19 February. TBM began it on 6 February and finished it on the 13th, calling it 'one of B's best' (Journal, VI, 31–4).

[2] *Blackwood's,* September 1850–January 1853.

[3] Bulwer-Lytton sent TBM a copy of the book on the 9th (Journal, VI, 32).

[4] E.g., Book VI, ch. 13.   [5] Book VI, ch. 8.

[6] Disraeli's first attack on the new government, criticizing its French policy (*Hansard,* 3rd Series, CXXIV, 246–81).

[7] Ellis is not named among the guests, who were Hallam, Carlisle, G. C. Lewis, and Lord Glenelg (Journal, VI, 37).

After all Hallam's little grand child is still alive and likely to do well.[1] I hope that you will meet him on Tuesday.

TO UNIDENTIFIED RECIPIENT,[2] 21 FEBRUARY 1853

MS: Trinity College.

Albany London / February 21. 1853

My dear Sir,

Ellis mentioned your book to me in such terms that I fully purposed to read it. I am truly obliged to you for ordering a copy to be sent to me; and I shall expect it with impatience.

Mrs. Franklin does me great honor. My congratulations on her change of name are now rather out of season; but I assure you that they are perfectly sincere.

Yours very truly,
T B Macaulay

TO MRS WODEHOUSE CURRIE,[3] 21 FEBRUARY 1853

MS: Trinity College.

Albany February 21. / 1853

My dear Mrs. Wodehouse Currie,

I assure you that I am extremely sensible of your kindness. I have very little reason to complain. I do not suffer much; and I have much to enjoy. But I find that I cannot safely expose myself to the evening air in cold weather. I have refused all invitations to dinners and routs for some time past, and have been forced to give up my attendance in parliament while the frost and east wind last. I must therefore, very reluctantly, deny myself the pleasure of dining with you.

Very truly yours,
T B Macaulay

---

[1] One of the twins born to Hallam's daughter, Mrs Cator, was earlier thought to be dying (Journal, VI, 34: 16 February).

[2] His name is evidently Franklin (see the second paragraph of the letter), but I have no clue to his identity. Neither the shelf list nor the sale catalogue of TBM's library contains any book by a Franklin other than Ben. The reference to Mrs Franklin suggests Lucy Haywood (see 8 September 1852), but I can find no book associated in any way with her husband, Captain Charles Trigance Franklin.

[3] Laura Sophia, daughter of the second Lord Wodehouse and wife of Raikes Currie (see 5 January 1852).

TO THOMAS FLOWER ELLIS, 24 FEBRUARY 1853

MS: Trinity College.

Albany Feb 24. 1853

Dear Ellis,

It is very kind of you to think of coming to me. There is no chance of my being out; and I shall be delighted to see you.

I have not left my rooms since Sunday, and shall not leave them till the weather is better. I am mending daily under Dr. Bright's care. Hannah and Baba sate with me the day before yesterday. Hannah dined and drank tea here yesterday; and Trevelyan looks in about ten to make a second breakfast on some potted char which I do not venture to touch.

I have Ihne's book,[1] and have looked at it, but am not much attracted by it. I have read Reid[2] with interest, but I have learned nothing from him except that he held, under another name, precisely that theory of innate ideas which Locke attacked in his first Book. There are very good things in the chapters about Vision: but I had read or heard or thought most of what I found there. I ought to except his account of the way in which a man born blind might become a geometrician, and even a master of the science of optics.[3] That is new to me, and very ingenious.

Ever yours
T B Macaulay

TO JOHN HILL BURTON, 26 FEBRUARY 1853

MS: National Library of Scotland.

Albany February 26 / 1853

Dear Sir,

I am glad that Lord Breadalbane[4] has so far complied with your wishes. I did my best to persuade him to let you print all his papers.[5] You owe me

---

[1] Wilhelm Ihne, *Researches into the History of the Roman Constitution,* 1853, is item 526 in the sale catalogue of TBM's library. This was translated by Ellis's friend Francis Haywood of Liverpool. Ellis evidently knew Ihne, for a letter from Ellis introducing Ihne to Whewell, 6 December 1851, is at Trinity.

[2] Thomas Reid, *Inquiry into the Human Mind, on the Principles of Common Sense,* 1764; TBM read it on 21 February (Journal, VI, 37). Reid is regarded as the father of Scottish philosophy.

[3] Chapter 6, section 2 of the *Inquiry.*

[4] John Campbell (1796–1862: *DNB*), second Marquess of Breadalbane; Lord Chamberlain, 1848–52 and 1853–8. His ancestor was also John Campbell (1635–1716: *DNB*), first Earl of Breadalbane, one of those concerned in the massacre of Glencoe.

[5] In the Appendix to volume one of his *History of Scotland,* 1853, Burton prints two letters regarding the Glencoe massacre from 'a collection of papers in the Charter Chest of Breadalbane'; they were made available, he says, after most of the book was in type.

no thanks. I should have thought it shabby to act otherwise by any man of letters; and to act otherwise by you would have been not only shabby but ungrateful.

To me Lord B was extremely kind. I told him in the plainest words that I had formed an unfavourable opinion of his ancestor's character, that I must speak the truth, and that I should not at all complain if, after hearing this, he thought fit to deny me access to the family papers. Lord B said that he had no wish that anything should be concealed or softened, and promised that the papers should be sent to me as soon as they could be brought to London.[1]

I entertain a confident expectation that your book will succeed. Thanks for the two curious volumes which you sent me. Both are interesting. But one of them is beyond all price.

Ever yours truly
T B Macaulay

TO LORD MAHON, 3 MARCH 1853

MS: Stanhope Papers, Chevening.

Albany March 3. 1853

Dear Mahon,

Will you breakfast here on Monday?[2] And will you do me the very great honor and pleasure of bringing Lady Mahon? Such a visit would be an act of charity to a prisoner, as I have been since we last met.[3]

Very truly yours,
T B Macaulay

TO THOMAS FLOWER ELLIS, 4 MARCH 1853

MS: Trinity College. *Partly published:* Trevelyan, II, 354–5.

Albany London / March 4. 1853.

Dear Ellis,

I am not much amiss, and the weather is so fine to day that I hope to be soon quite well.

---

[1] TBM makes no acknowledgement of this source in his *History*.

[2] Neither Mahon nor his wife were of the party, which consisted of Hannah, Mr and Mrs Price, Lord Carlisle, James Moncrieff, Hallam, and his son-in-law, Captain Cator (Journal, VI, 41).

[3] I.e., 19 February. On the 21st TBM determined to stay at home until his health improved (Journal, VI, 37); he ventured out on the 28th, and again on 3 March.

Hannah gave me an account of your dinner party at Strutt's. Poor Lady Theresa imputed her fever to her husband's two defeats and to his having accepted the Editorship of the Edinburgh Review.[1] She cannot bear this last humiliation. She feels like one of the old noblesse of France at the thought of keeping a shop. A strange weakness in so clever and accomplished a woman.

Unless I should be very poorly, I mean to start for Paris on Wednesday the 23rd.[2] I have engaged our old courier. I shall be away just a week. I promise myself great pleasure from showing so noble a city and such fine works of art to my dear Baba, and to George whose curiosity is excited to the highest point.

So my cousin is out of parliament,[3] – the best thing for him, I believe; – for he is very likely to come in for the largest share of parliamentary practice; and, as his friends are out, and not likely to be soon in, he would have had little chance, even if he had distinguished himself in debate, of becoming Solicitor General or a Judge.

I am glad that you like Beaumarchais. The result was that the Goëzmans were utterly ruined; the husband forced to quit his office, the wife driven to a convent.[4] Beaumarchais was *blâmé* by the Court. The effect of that *blame* was very serious. It made a man legally infamous, I believe, and deprived him of many civil rights. But the public feeling was so strongly with Beaumarchais that he paraded this stigma as if it had been a mark of honor. He gave himself such airs that somebody said to him, "Monsieur, ce n'est pas assez que d'être blâmé: il faut être modeste."[5] Do you see the whole finesse of this untranslatable *mot?* What a quantity of French words I have used. I suppose that the subject Frenchifies my style.

I have not read the article on the Indian army in the Edinburgh Review.[6] I find that India occupies the thoughts of people more than I had expected.[7] The nation generally is indifferent; and I do not suppose that a single election will turn on any Indian question. But in the political circles there

---

[1] See *to* Ellis, 8 December 1852.

[2] See *to* Frances Macaulay, 17 March.

[3] Kenneth Macaulay was unseated by an election committee on 1 March for bribery (*Hansard*, 3rd Series, CXXIV, 800–1).

[4] In his suit against the Comte de la Blache, Beaumarchais sent bribes to the wife of the judge, Valentin Goëzman; Mme Goëzman accepted the bribes but Beaumarchais lost his suit. He thereupon exposed all the details of the story in a series of four *Mémoires*, 1773–4. In February 1774 both he and Mme Goëzman were '*blâmé*' by the court. TBM tells the story in the essay on Bacon.

[5] M. de Sartine to Beaumarchais: 'Ce n'est pas tout d'être *blâmé*... il faut encore être modeste' (Sainte-Beuve, *Causeries du Lundi*, 'Beaumarchais,' 14 June 1852).

[6] G. R. Gleig, 'The Indian Army,' *ER*, XCVII (January 1853), 183–220.

[7] The charter of the East India Company was due for renewal this year; TBM had been appointed in the preceding November to the Select Committee on the Indian Territories.

is a good deal of stir and a wish to do something without any clear notion either of what now exists or of what is wanted.

Ever yours,
T B Macaulay

TO SIR ROBERT ADAIR,[1] 7 MARCH 1853

MS: Trinity College.

Albany March 7 / 1853

My dear Sir,

I beg you to accept my thanks for your pamphlet.[2] The publication is well timed. I knew both Mr. Fox's letter and your comment upon it: but I am glad to have them in this form, especially at a time when, as you justly say, the authority of his name is employed in support of doctrines which he would have disowned.

I remember with melancholy pleasure the evenings which we passed together at Holland House. All my recollections of you are recollections of kindness; and I assure you that I prize few things more than the Memoirs of the Count de Dohna, which frequently remind me of you.[3] / Believe me ever, / My dear Sir,

Yours most truly
T B Macaulay

TO EDWARD STRUTT, 11 MARCH 1853

MS: Harvard University.

Albany March 11. 1853

Dear Strutt,

I must beg you to excuse me on Saturday week. I hope to be able to go

---

1 Adair (1763–1855: *DNB*), diplomat, the friend of Charles James Fox, was an intimate of Holland House. He was now the last survivor of a vanished generation; Greville writes of Adair that 'he lived in great intimacy with all the "great of old, who still rule our spirits from their own," and I believe possesses a great store of anecdotes of bygone days' (*Memoirs,* VI, 95: 31 July 1848).

2 Fox's 'Letter to the Electors of Westminster in 1793, with an Application of Its Principle to Subsequent Events,' 1853; first published on the signing of the Treaty of Amiens in 1802. Adair now reprinted the pamphlet in protest against Cobden's attempt to use Fox's authority in support of his pacifist policies.

3 Christophe, Comte de Dohna, *Mémoires Originaux sur le Règne et la Cour de Frédéric I.,* Berlin, 1833. TBM writes in a note to the *History,* ch. 11, that this book is 'almost unknown in England. The only copy that I have ever seen of it was kindly given to me by Sir Robert Adair' (III, 53).

to France at Easter; and I am carefully husbanding all my strength for the effort.

Ever~yours truly
T B Macaulay

TO GEORGE CORNEWALL LEWIS, 12 MARCH 1853

MS: National Library of Wales.

Albany March 12 / 1853

Dear Lewis,

I send you a line from my friend Ellis who is on the circuit.[1] I know Alford to be a very good scholar, and a clever man. I have no personal acquaintance with him: but I have heard him preach well in the University Church.

Ever yours truly,
T B Macaulay

TO THOMAS FLOWER ELLIS, 12 MARCH 1853

MS: Trinity College.

Albany March 12. 1853

Dear Ellis,

I have sent your letter to Lewis with a line from myself. I know Alford to be a good scholar; and I once heard him preach in St Mary's.

I am much better since the weather became fine; but I have paired till Easter. I shall be back from Paris by the 1st of April. I suppose that I shall find you in town.

I am writing about the national debt, and rather pique myself on the view which I have taken of it. I am also writing at odd minutes a life of Atterbury,[2] and, in order to do him justice, I have read over again his best work, Boyle v. Bentley. It is really a masterpiece. I think that you never

[1] Ellis's letter calls Lewis's attention to Henry Alford among the candidates for the position of examiner in classics to the University of London (MS, National Library of Wales). Lewis, like TBM, was a member of the University Senate. Alford (1810–71: *DNB*), Fellow of Trinity, biblical scholar, miscellaneous writer, editor, and preacher, was Vicar of Wymeswold, Leicestershire, until this year, when he became minister of Quebec Chapel, Marylebone; in 1857 he was appointed Dean of Canterbury. Alford was unsuccessful on this occasion, the examinership going to Dr William Smith on 6 April.

[2] The first of the biographies that TBM contributed to the eighth edition of the *Encyclopaedia Britannica,* the property of his friend and political guide in Edinburgh, Adam Black. Shortly after TBM's death, Black republished in a separate volume all of TBM's contributions to the *Encyclopaedia,* saying that it had been TBM's own intention to do so after he had 'increased the number of his contributions.' Black adds that, at TBM's request, 'remuneration should not be so much as mentioned' (Preface to *Biographies by Lord Macaulay Contributed to the Encyclopaedia Britannica,* 1860). TBM began the life of Atterbury early in March and finished it on the 21st (Journal, VI, 40–7).

read it. I never saw such an exhibition of cleverness. Bentley's learning is not more wonderful than the show which Atterbury makes with his ignorance. What do you think of this for example? Phalaris, says Bentley, would have reckoned by Sicilian talents. But the author of these letters reckons by Attic talents – Ergo – Q.E.D. Atterbury answers that Sicilians often reckoned by Attic talents. Diodorus Siculus always so reckons.[1] Now how neat and complete that answer looks to a superficial scholar, such as almost all the scholars of England were in those days; and yet how utterly contemptible it is in the sight of any man of real learning. There are a hundred such parries, which must have seemed completely su ccessful to ninety nine readers out of a hundred.

Have you finished Beaumarchais? What do you think of him and of French justice?

Ever yours,
T B Macaulay

TO FRANCES MACAULAY, 14 MARCH 1853

MS: Trinity College. *Extract published:* Trevelyan, II, 323.

Albany March 14. 1853

Dearest Fanny,

I meant to vote for Mr. Alford, – that is, if I am able to vote at all. I have also written to Cornwall Lewis to advise him to do the same.

I hope to see you well on Monday. I am much easier since the weather became mild. But last July was a crisis in my life. I became twenty years older in a week, and shall never be young again. A mile is more to me now than ten miles a year ago. But it matters little if I can keep my faculties and my affections, and if my temper does not sour. I am not sure that I do not enjoy life more than I ever did. Though I am confined to my rooms except for two hours in the middle of the day when it is fine, I never feel the time heavy. I have been writing much. I have done with the national debt; and am pretty well satisfied.

I am taking the greatest care of myself that I may be able to go to Paris with you. The exertion of the first day is the only thing that I doubt about. I shall probably sleep the preceding night in Westbourne Terrace. Love to our friends at Rothley.

Ever yours
T B Macaulay

[1] Charles Boyle, *Dr. Bentley's Dissertations on the Epistles of Phalaris and the Fables of Æsop Examin'd,* 1698, p. 85. This detail appears in TBM's summary of the effect that Atterbury created as one who 'wrote with so much pleasantry and good breeding about the Attic dialect and the anapaestic measure, Sicilian talents and Thericlean cups' (*Biographies by Lord Macaulay,* p. 9).

TO FRANCES MACAULAY, 17 MARCH 1853

MS: Trinity College.

Albany London / March 17. 1853

Dearest Fanny,

Thanks for your affectionate letter. Do not be uneasy about me. If I find it necessary, I will go down to Folkstone on Tuesday and wait there for you. But I had much rather that we should perform the whole journey together. There will be much change of exercise which is a very good thing for me. We shall leave town at six in the morning, – land in France at half after one, – walk about Boulogne and dine there, – start for Paris at five and arrive there at ten.[1] Rooms will be ready for us;[2] and I have engaged a good courier.

I dined out yesterday, the first time for several weeks. It was, as you may suppose, in Westbourne Terrace where there was a pleasant party, Lord Glenelg, the Chancellor of the Exchequer, Goulburn, the Lefevres.

By the bye did I not lend you two volumes of lives – Pococke, Bishop Pearce, Bishop Newton, and Skelton?[3] I lent them to somebody, and I cannot remember to whom. Love to our friends.

Ever yours,

T B Macaulay

I saw Miss Pert Rude[4] again yesterday after many years, – a very agreeable young lady now.

TO DUNCAN MCLAREN, 17 MARCH 1853

Text: Mackie, *Life of McLaren,* I, 191–2n.

Albany, London, March 17, 1853.

My Lord,

The Annuity-Tax Bill has been drawn as we agreed that it should be,[5]

[1] TBM did go down to Folkestone a day ahead of the others, but the rest of this plan was followed; they reached Paris on the 23rd and returned on the 30th (Journal, VI, 48–54).

[2] At the Hotel de Wagram.

[3] *The Lives of Dr. Edward Pocock, the Celebrated Orientalist, by Dr. Twells; of Dr. Zachary Pearce, Bishop of Rochester, and of Dr. Thomas Newton, Bishop of Bristol, by Themselves; and of the Rev. Philip Skelton, by Mr. Burdy,* 2 vols., 1816. This is among the titles in the shelf-list of TBM's library.

[4] In her 'Memoir' of TBM, his niece Margaret says that this was a daughter of Baptist Noel who 'was enchanted by finding him notice her and was constantly saying pert things to him. At last Uncle Tom christened her "Miss Pert-Rude," her name being Gertrude, which provoked her extremely, I remember' (MS, Lord Knutsford). Gertrude Noel (1835?–58) married Sir Henry Flower Every in 1855 and died in childbirth, 1858.

[5] The bill was not brought in until late in the session, when TBM spoke on it: see 16 July. On 5 March TBM had met with McLaren, Tufnell, Cowan, E. F. Maitland, and James Moncrieff, the Lord Advocate, to discuss the question: 'The Provost [McLaren] and I were perfectly civil' (Journal, VI, 41). This was presumably their first meeting since they had opposed each other in last July's election. McLaren was Lord Provost, 1851–4.

and yesterday the Lord Advocate mentioned the subject to Lord Aberdeen. Lord Aberdeen seems disposed to do everything that we could wish, always, however, under one reservation. He and the Chancellor of the Exchequer[1] will not consent to lay any charge in any event on the general revenues of the kingdom for the support of the ministers of Edinburgh. The matter has not yet been mentioned in Cabinet, and therefore we must not consider the Government as irrevocably bound, though I hope there is little danger in that quarter. I should have thought it desirable that the Lord Advocate should take charge of the bill. I find, however, that he, and, if I understand him rightly, Lord Aberdeen, would much rather that I should bring it in. I am perfectly willing to do so, if, on a full consideration, that shall be thought the best course. The difficulty about the standing orders remains as it was; and whether we shall be able to get over it seems to be very doubtful. I have had the honour of receiving a letter from your Lordship on the subject of probates and letters of administration. I need hardly say that I entirely agree with the Town Council as to that matter. / I have the honour to be, my Lord,

> Your Lordship's faithful servant,
> T.B. Macaulay.

The Lord Provost, etc.

TO THOMAS FLOWER ELLIS, 18 MARCH 1853

MS: Trinity College.

Albany London / March 18. 1853

Dear Ellis,

I inclose a letter which I have just received from Hawes.[2] It is not satisfactory; yet it might have been much worse.

I mean to start for Paris next Wednesday.

> Ever yours,
> T B Macaulay

TO THOMAS FLOWER ELLIS, 21 MARCH 1853

MS: Trinity College.

Albany London / March 21. 1853

Dear Ellis,

I think that you take quite the right view of the letter which I sent you.[2]

[1] Gladstone.
[2] 'Letter from Hawes about Arthur Ellis – sent it to his father' (Journal, VI, 46: 18 March).

It is plain that the poor fellow has done nothing bad or dishonorable; and, as I told Hawes, if the diggings have turned so young a head, this is not a thing to wonder at: for older and steadier people have been ranting and frolicking like the Athenian peasants in Aristophanes when they have found Plutus.[1] By the bye did it ever occur to you that the state of things in Australia is a striking comment on the lecture which Poverty reads to Charidemus and Blepsidemus?[2]

I am glad that Hawes's letter has cheered you. For yours of Friday was sad, and made me sad. I should have been glad to be able to be with you.

I am wonderfully well, by means of care and valetudinarian precautions. We start for Paris at daybreak on Wednesday and shall be, I hope, in the Rue Rivoli that night. I have taken a very pleasant suite of rooms in the Hotel de Wagram. The cuisine is said to be good; and our windows will command the garden of the Tuilleries. It was just at the entrance of the Hotel de Wagram that we heard that delightful dialogue – "Jalousie de femme" . . . "Ce soldat! . . ."

I am sorry for Arnold.[3] Another Trinity man is gone – your junior and my senior – Southern.[4] He was a coxcomb, but a clever fellow, unlucky at college, but successful both in literature and in business.

We are to have a more bustling season than even that of 1851. There is no Exhibition in Hyde Park, to be sure. But we are to have two great sights from beyond sea, Mrs. Becher Stowe from America, and the Madiai[5] from Tuscany. At Westbourne Terrace the other day three or four ladies, Mrs. Lefevre, Mrs. Drummond, Mrs. Merivale, Mrs. Price, were asking me what I meant to give to the Becher Stowe Testimonial. I told them to read through Goldsmith's Minor Poems; and they would find. Mrs. Price understood, and so did Hannah; but none of the others.

[1] *Plutus,* 750–63.
[2] *Plutus,* 415ff (Charidemus should be Chremylus). Poverty explains that if all were wealthy nobody would produce goods, there would be nothing to buy, and life would be grim. Gold was discovered in Australia in 1851.
[3] Thomas Kerchever Arnold (1800–53: *DNB*), Fellow of Trinity, 1823; Rector of Lyndon, Rutlandshire, and a prolific author of schoolbooks in the classics and modern languages. He died on 9 March.
[4] Henry Southern (1799–1853: *DNB*), B.A., Trinity, 1819, founded the *Retrospective Review* in 1820 and edited the *Westminster Review* and the *London Magazine* before going to Spain with George Villiers, the ambassador, as his private secretary in 1833. He was thereafter in the diplomatic service and died in Rio de Janeiro, 28 January. Southern was to have collaborated with TBM on a history of England for the SDUK in 1828: see Appendix to [August? 1828].
[5] Francesco and Rosa Madiai, residents of Tuscany and converts to Protestantism, were imprisoned by the Grand Duke in 1852 under an old law against Protestants. The case aroused great indignation in England, the British government officially intervened, the Madiai were released in March, came to England, and were provided with an annuity through popular subscription.

Mrs. Merivale and Mrs. Drummond are thumbing Goldsmith indefatigably, and have not yet made out the riddle. You, I suppose, remember
the lines in question.[1]

If you have any occasion to write till Sunday inclusive, direct to me at
the Hôtel de Wagram, Rue de Rivoli, Paris. On Wednesday the 30th, or,
at latest, on the following day, I shall be here again.

Ever yours,
T B Macaulay

TO SELINA MACAULAY, 21 MARCH 1853

MS: Trinity College.

Albany London / March 21. 1853

Dearest Selina,

I send you a cheque for the quarter.

The day after to morrow we start for Paris. It is not impossible that I
may go to Folkstone to morrow.[2]

By taking great precautions I have got pretty well through the cold
weather. I hope that our tour will do me good. We shall be pleasantly
lodged at the Hôtel de Wagram, Rue de Rivoli, where you had better
address any letter that you may have occasion to write. We are *au second*;
and our windows will look into the garden of the Tuilleries. Hannah and
Baba are bent on seeing the Empress,[3] about whom I am not at all curious.

Ever yours
T B Macaulay

TO LORD MAHON, 31 MARCH 1853

MS: Stanhope Papers, Chevening.

Albany London / March 31. 1853

Dear Mahon,

I returned to London late yesterday evening, and found your letter and
my young friend's prize on the table. I have done what you wished, and
have sent the book to Grosvenor Place.[4]

I am much the better for my trip to Paris. It was cold there; but the air
was clear, and suited my lungs better than the coal smoke which we
breathe here.

[1] 'The Gift,' last stanza: 'I'll give thee something yet unpaid, / Not less sincere, than civil:
/ I'll give thee – Ah! too charming maid; / I'll give thee – To the Devil.'
[2] He did.
[3] Napoleon had married Eugénie on 29 January.
[4] Mahon lived at 41 Grosvenor Place.

I had occasion to consult you a good deal while writing a paper on Atterbury for the Encyclopædia Britannica, and I always found both instruction and pleasure. We do not quite agree in our estimate of the Bishop's character. I am afraid that he was a very bad man.

By the bye I noted one slight mistake which you may as well correct, if you have not already done so. Clarendon's history was edited, not by Atterbury, Smalridge and Aldrich, but by the Earl of Rochester, Bishop Sprat and Aldrich.[1] Neither Atterbury nor Smalridge ever saw the M.S. You will find this in Atterbury's excellent refutation of Oldmixon.[2]

I hope that you will soon be in town again, and well. My kindest regards to Lady Mahon and the children, more especially to my Valentine.

Ever yours,

T B Macaulay

TO SELINA MACAULAY, 5 APRIL 1853

MS: Trinity College.

Albany London / April 5. 1853

Dearest Selina,

I am glad that the gloves suit you. It would have been a great addition to the pleasure of our very pleasant excursion, if we could have had your company.

The letter which took you in[3] produced a most comical effect on Lydia Price. She was quite cross at having been deceived, and excited about nothing at all.

I am beginning to attend the House of Commons again. Some questions are coming on which will make it necessary for me to say something, if I am in force: but I shall be very prudent.

Dumont is an excellent fellow; but I am sorry to say that he is becoming a bore. At least I thought so on Tuesday evening last. For we had to pack, and to start by daybreak the next morning; and he went on haranguing in bad English hour after hour till Fanny gave him a hint to take himself off. However I have a great regard for him. His politics are the politics of the party that is uppermost. I do not however materially

---

[1] Mahon's mistake appears at the end of ch. 15 of his *History of England from the Peace of Utrecht,* the third edition of which had just been published.

[2] 'The Late Bishop of Rochester's Vindication of Bishop Smallridge, Dr. Aldrich, and Himself, from the Scandalous Reflections of Oldmixon, Relating to the Publication of Lord Clarendon's History,' 1731.

[3] TBM wrote an April fool's letter to Hannah telling 'how Mrs. Becher Stowe had come to my Chambers and invited herself to lunch to morrow – how she had brought with her a parson – a man of colour – the Rev Cæsar Ugbark and his wife etc. etc.' The letter, TBM learned, 'took in several people – Trevelyan, Lydia Price and Selina among the rest' (Journal, VI, 55–6: 31 March; 3 April).

dissent from the view which he takes of the interest of France at present. I think the existing government as good as any that is likely to rise in its place.

I do not think that you apprehend correctly the nature of the objection to the Address which was presented to Napoleon the Third.[1] The sentiments expressed are very proper. But what business have Englishmen to lay addresses at the foot of a foreign throne? I believe that the proceeding was illegal. Lord Campbell, you see, thinks so;[2] and he is the first lawyer living. But, legal or illegal, I am sure that such acts are humiliating and that they tend rather to encourage than to prevent aggression on the part of our neighbours.

Kindest love to Fanny, and thanks for her letter.

Ever yours,
T B Macaulay

TO LADY TREVELYAN, 8 APRIL 1853

MS: Trinity College.

Albany April 8 / 1853

Dearest Hannah,

I send you the third and fourth Volumes of Moore's Life.[3] I got them yesterday evening.

I was surprised to see this morning that Trevelyan was the chief subject of debate in the House of Commons yesterday.[4] He got off very well. Lucky man to be praised by Gladstone, Wood and Napier,[5] and to be abused by French,[6] Moore,[7] and Scully.[8]

1 An address from the 'Merchants of London' to the 'French People,' appealing for peace, was presented to Napoleon on 28 March. It had no official sanction.
2 As he said in the House of Lords on 4 April.
3 Thomas Moore, *Memoirs, Journal and Correspondence*, 8 vols., 1852–6, edited by Lord John Russell, began publication in December; the first volumes were sent to TBM on 10 December, when he read them 'with great zest,' finding the 'Diary most interesting. . . . I suspect that he wrote a little for the public eye. Had he been as frank as poor Pepys who trusted to his shorthand we might have found some very odd disclosures' (Journal, VI, 4).
4 The debate was on a motion to remit part of the Irish public debt incurred in providing famine relief. Trevelyan, who had determined the fiscal policies resulting in those debts, and who had argued before a select committee of inquiry that they ought not to be remitted, was a primary object of attack, being called, among other things, 'a dogmatist whom no experience can instruct' (*Hansard*, 3rd Series, CXXV, 737). The motion was defeated.
5 Joseph Napier (1804–82: *DNB*), afterwards first Baronet, was Tory and Protestant M.P. for the University of Dublin.
6 Fitzstephen French (1801–73: *Boase*), M.P. for Roscommon, 1832–73. On the day of the debate TBM overheard 'French and another Irish blackguard and jobber abusing Trevelyan. I spoke pretty coolly and resolutely to them' (Journal, VI, 57).
7 George Henry Moore (1811–70: *DNB*), M.P. for County Mayo, the father of the novelist. Moore led the attack on Trevelyan in this debate.
8 Vincent Scully (1810–71: *DNB*), M.P. for County Cork.

I breakfasted this morning at Wood's, and held a long consultation with him and George Grey about India. I like their plan much on the whole.

Never was there a more wretched figure than that which Sir Erskine Perry[1] made yesterday. The universal impression is that he is an ass and a coxcomb.

If you are at home send a line to say how you all are.

Ever yours
T B Macaulay

TO [DUNCAN McLAREN], 11 APRIL 1853

Text: Scotsman, 27 April 1853.

[London] 11th April 1853.

I have received the petition from the Magistrates and Council on the subject of the University Tests Bill;[2] and I will take care to present it at the proper time. I do not at all like the provisions to which the petitioners object; but I must reserve to myself the liberty to consider whether, by voting against these provisions, I may endanger the bill.

Yours, etc.,
T. B. Macaulay.

TO LORD MAHON, 11 APRIL 1853

MS: Stanhope Papers, Chevening.

Albany April 11 / 1853

Dear Mahon,

I have no objection to your printing my letter.[3] But I should wish you to omit the passage which I have put between brackets.

---

[1] Before the India Committee of the House of Commons. Sir Thomas Erskine Perry (1806–82: *DNB*) served as a judge of the Supreme Court of Bombay, 1841–52; he was opposed to continuing the existence of the East India Company. TBM cross-examined him before the Committee on 7 April and concluded that 'never was there a more complete smash' (Journal, VI, 57): see *Parliamentary Papers,* 1852–3, XXVII, 214–26, for TBM's questions.

[2] On 5 April the Town Council voted to petition for the alteration of parts of the new Scottish Universities Bill (see 16 July 1853), especially the clause requiring all professors to make declaration that they would not act 'to the prejudice or subversion of the Church of Scotland' (*Scotsman,* 6 April). TBM presented the petition on 28 June.

[3] Of 3 January 185[2] to John Murray. Mahon published it in the new edition of his *History of England,* which appeared in August of this year.

Poor George Grey is not, I am afraid, very happy in his son; and the illustration might give him pain.[1]

Ever yours truly

T B Macaulay

TO FRANCES MACAULAY, 12 APRIL 1853

MS: Trinity College.

Albany London April 12 / 1853

Dearest Fanny,

You need not be ashamed of your ignorance. Few ladies have studied this subject; and I do not pretend to be deeply versed in it. But I can assure you that your friends are angry and frightened without a cause. The plan of the government is anything but prejudicial to them.[2] Since Gladstone moved his resolutions the price of stocks has risen. Your widows and single ladies can now sell their funded property for more than they could have got for it a fortnight ago. They are therefore richer; and it is strange that they should complain of the Chancellor of the Exchequer for making them so.

You do not seem to be aware that the government has no power to reduce the interest of the debt without the free consent of the creditors of the state. Every one of your friends who holds 3 per Cent stock will continue to receive 3 per Cent per annum till she is paid off, unless she chuses to give up some part of her interest in return for some advantage which she thinks a fair equivalent. Gladstone tries to tempt the fund-holders to give up some part of their interest by the offer of various advantages. But he puts no force on any body. Those who chuse to remain as they are will remain as they are. He says – "You are entitled to 3 per Cent till we can pay you off. Interest is low, and may be lower. If it becomes much lower we shall be able to borrow at 2 1/2 per Cent; and then we can pay you off. If that should happen you will be unable to get more than 2 1/2 per Cent on government security. Perhaps you would like to insure yourselves against the risk of so great a diminution of your

---

[1] The passage, in the next to the last paragraph of TBM's letter, was omitted in Mahon's reprinting. George Henry Grey (see 3 January 185[2]) entered Trinity College, Cambridge, in 1852 but left it for the army, becoming Lt Colonel in the Grenadier Guards and equerry to the Prince of Wales.

[2] The plan, described in a speech by Gladstone on 8 April (*Hansard*, 3rd Series, cxxv, 810–78), was for a conversion and consolidation of the national debt: 'the only stock available for such an operation was three percent Consols, which by their nature were protected against forced conversion. Nevertheless, he proceeded to offer several options to holders of Consols in an endeavour to obtain an arrangement in the long run more economical for the government' (Conacher, *The Aberdeen Coalition*, p. 62).

income. What do you say to abating nine pence in the pound on your interest, if we will engage not to pay you off for forty years. If you are willing, we are. But it is quite optional. Take your chance, if you please; and insist upon your clear right to receive 3 per Cent till we are able to pay you your principal."

Very likely I may not have succeeded in making this matter intelligible to you. On such subjects, a little talking goes further than a great deal of writing. You ask me what I shall do with my own money. I have no money in those stocks which will be affected by this scheme. What I have in the funds is in a stock which cannot be paid off for more than twenty years. If I had three per Cent stock I should probably consent to give nine pence in the pound in return for the forty years' guarantee. But I have not considered the matter much, as it is one in which I have no interest.

You are quite mistaken as to the relation in which the government stands to the fundholders. There can be no panic, no pressing to be paid off. Nobody has a right to be paid off as long as he receives his interest duly. The only way in which a man can remove his property from the funds to some other investment is by selling his stock for what it will fetch in the market.

The weather is not very genial here; and I have been plagued with pains in the teeth and face: but I have not much to complain of. Love to Selina.

Ever yours
T B Macaulay

TO JOHN EVELYN DENISON, 25 APRIL 1853

MS: University of Nottingham.

Albany April 25 / 1853

Dear Denison,

Tuesday week, the 3d of May, is, I am afraid, the earliest day that I can spare.[1] I am sitting to another artist[2] for a group which Prince Albert has ordered.

---

[1] Denison had commissioned Sir Francis Grant (1803–78: *DNB*), a leading portrait painter and President of the Royal Academy, 1866–78, to do TBM's portrait; TBM sat to Grant seven times between 3 May and 22 June (Journal, VI, 67–98). The portrait was exhibited at the Royal Academy Exhibition in 1854; TBM saw it there and found it 'excellent' (Journal, VIII, 51: 29 April 1854). I have no information about its present location; a study in oil for the portrait is now in the National Portrait Gallery. Charles Macaulay considered the Grant portrait 'not at all like Tom either in feature or expression' (to Mary Macaulay Booth, 9 July 1879: MS, University of London).

[2] John Partridge: TBM sat to him on the 26th (Journal, VI, 63), probably in connection with Partridge's work on 'The Fine Arts Commissioners' (see 21 February 1849). Partridge may have hoped that Albert would purchase the painting, but it was never sold.

Half after twelve is the hour which would suit me best.
Can you breakfast here on Wednesday at ten?[1]

> Ever yours,
> T B Macaulay

TO LADY TREVELYAN, 27 APRIL 1853

MS: Mrs Michael Millgate.

> Albany April 27 / 1853

Dearest Hannah,
I have the tickets for the private view of the Exhibition.[2] The doors
open at ten on Friday morning. At what hour will you call? I wish you
could bring Baba.

> Ever yours
> T B Macaulay

TO THOMAS FLOWER ELLIS, 29 APRIL 1853

MS: Trinity College.

> Albany April 29 / 1853

Dear Ellis,
Can you dine here to morrow – Saturday – or on Monday?

> Ever yours,
> T B Macaulay

The Speaker wishes me to oppose Lord Hotham's[3] Bill for excluding the
Master of the Rolls from the House of Commons; and I shall do so.[4]
Do not mention this, as I am very desirous that it should not be known
till I rise. But I should like to talk the matter over with you. The debate
will be at twelve on Wednesday next.[5]

[1] The party were Denison, Hallam, Bishop Wilberforce, Milnes, the Duke of Argyll, Lord
Mahon, and Inglis (Journal, VI, 63).
[2] Of the Royal Academy. TBM and Hannah went on Friday the 29th; among other things –
'Capital Landseers, one excellent Stanfield, a very good Roberts' – TBM also found 'much
PræRaphaelite trash' (Journal, VI, 65–6).
[3] Beaumont Hotham (1794–1870: *DNB*), third Baron Hotham, Tory M.P. for the East
Riding.
[4] TBM spoke against the bill on its third reading, 1 June (*Hansard*, 3rd Series, CXXVII, 996–
1008). Trevelyan provides a detailed account of the occasion (II, 333–7).
[5] TBM went down to the House on that day to find that the bill did not come on (Journal,
VI, 67).

TO DUNCAN MCLAREN, 29 APRIL 1853

Text: Scotsman, 11 May 1853.

Albany, 29th April 1853.
My Lord,

I presented the petition of the Town Council in favour of the Budget yesterday, before the debate.[1] I am happy to find that on that subject the opinion of my constituents agrees with mine.

I have the honour to be, etc.

T. B. Macaulay.

TO HENRY HART MILMAN, 3 MAY 1853

MS: McGill University.

Albany May 3. 1853
Dear Dean,

Lady Mahon does me the honor to breakfast here on Monday next. Will you come? And can you prevail on Mrs. Milman to accompany you?[2] If you can, I shall always remember the day with as much pride as Lady Margaret Bellenden felt in talking about the disjune which His Sacred Majesty condescended to take at Tillietudlem.[3]

Ever yours truly
T B Macaulay

TO UNIDENTIFIED RECIPIENT, [3 MAY][4] 1853

Text: Maggs Brothers Catalogue 522, Summer 1929, item 1036; dated 1853.

I spoke to Gladstone yesterday in the House about the opium duty; and to-day I have sent him your memorial. I have told him that I think your case a stray[5] one; and I cannot help thinking that he will be of the same opinion.

[1] The Town Council passed a resolution on 26 April approving the 'general principle of the new Budget' (*Scotsman,* 27 April). This was Gladstone's first budget, outlined to the House of Commons in a five-hour speech on 18 April.
[2] Neither Milman came: the guests were Lord and Lady Mahon, Lord and Lady Hatherton, Hannah, Dundas, Lord Glenelg, Hallam, and Bishop Wilberforce (Journal, VI, 69–70).
[3] Scott, *Old Mortality,* ch. 3.
[4] See next letter.
[5] Thus in text.

TO WILLIAM EWART GLADSTONE, 3 MAY 1853

MS: British Museum.

Albany May 3. 1853

Dear Gladstone,

I send you three memorials,[1] which, I am sure, you will consider with every desire to do justice.

The strongest case, I think, is that of the manufacturer of Morphia. There seems to [be] something contrary to principle in taxing the British manufacturer four times, nay eight times as heavily as we tax the foreign manufacturer.

The Cork cutters put their case well. But I admit the force of what you said yesterday on that subject.

The complaint respecting the licenses is one of the justice of which I am quite unable to judge.

Very truly yours,
T B Macaulay

TO JOHN LEYCESTER ADOLPHUS, 18 MAY 1853

MS: Trinity College.

Albany May 18. 1853

Dear Adolphus,

I hope to be able to have the pleasure of dining with you on Wednesday the 1st of June.[2]

Ever yours truly
T B Macaulay

TO FRANCES MACAULAY, 19 MAY 1853

MS: Trinity College.

Albany London / May 19. 1853

Dearest Fanny,

In the time of Edward the Third a mark contained as much silver as forty shillings of our time. I have not leisure to give you a lecture on the causes and nature of the change which followed.

Of course forty shillings then commanded a much greater quantity of food, labour, etc. than forty shillings now.

---

1 According to the clerk's endorsement on the letter these were protests against the proposed reductions of duty on morphia and cork and against the increase in fees for excise licenses. The proposals were part of Gladstone's budget, presented in his famous speech of 18 April.
2 TBM did not go: the 1st was the day of his speech on Lord Hotham's bill, and after the excitement of that he went home to dinner (Journal, VI, 80).

You are quite right not to take the new North Western shares. You have still some shares on which all the calls have not been made. Those calls, as I have told you, I mean to answer.[1]

TO SIR WILLIAM GIBSON CRAIG, 20 MAY 1853

MS: National Library of Scotland.

Albany London / May 20. 1853

Dear Craig,

Jamie Simpson has written to ask me to be one of a Committee for arranging a great Industrial Exhibition at Edinburgh.[2] I cannot help thinking that, if there were any design of this sort which excited much interest and promised well, I should have been apprised of it by somebody in whose judgment I could place confidence. I have told Jamie that I was taken by surprise and that I must beg him to let me have a few days for inquiry and consideration. If the plan be deserving of encouragement, I will most readily give my name. But I am unwilling to appear before the public as one of the authors of an absurd project.

Jamie informs me that the Exhibition is to be opened next year and that the place is to be a huge permanent building of brick and stucco on the Calton Hill. Is it possible that the funds can be raised and such a building completed within the year? The year after next is fixed for the great Parisian Exhibition;[3] and it would be absurd to attempt a competition with that magnificent show.

I am better since the summer began here – which was on Monday last. Kindest regards to Lady Craig.

Ever yours,
T B Macaulay

TO WILLIAM EWART GLADSTONE, 27 MAY 1853

MS: British Museum.

Albany May 27. 1853

Dear Gladstone,

I forward you another memorial about the Opium and Morphia.[4] In

---

[1] The bottom half of the leaf has been torn away; probably only the closing and signature are missing.

[2] The suggestion for a 'Great Industrial Exhibition for Scotland' had been brought before the Town Council in March and referred to a committee for study; the committee's report in September concluded that there was not sufficient support for the plan and it was dropped (*Scotsman*, 23 March; 23 April; 7 September 1853).

[3] It duly took place then and was the occasion of a state visit from Queen Victoria.

[4] See *to* Gladstone, 3 May.

my private opinion, my constituent[1] has made out his case; and I really think that opium might well be put into the list of articles which are to be imported duty-free.

Very truly yours,
T B Macaulay

TO UNIDENTIFIED RECIPIENT, [MAY?] 1853

Text: Maggs Brothers Catalogue 522, Summer 1929, item 1036: dated 1853.

I will deliver your memorial; but I am not very sanguine. On Thursday I spoke about this matter to Mr. Cardwell.[2] He referred me to Mr. Wilson,[3] to whom the details of the new Tariff seem to be left; for, of course, the Chancellor of the Exchequer cannot do everything himself. Mr. Wilson . . . spoke as if there was no importation of morphia into the island. You, he said, and another manufacturer really supplied the whole British market. I, of course, could not contradict him. I suggested the possibility that much morphia might be smuggled. He said that, as far as he could learn after the last inquiry, this was not the case. It was true that a small quantity of morphia went a great way and fetched a high price: but then circumstances in his opinion tended to prevent smuggling. People, he said, do not buy morphia as they buy cigars. They will not have an article about the quality of which there is any doubt; and, therefore, they go to dealers of established character.

TO JOHN KENT, 4 JUNE 1853

MS: Trinity College. *Envelope:* J Kent Esq / The Earl of Carnarvon's / Highclere Castle / Newbury. *Subscription:* T B M.

Albany June 4. 1853

Sir,

I am much obliged to you for your criticisms, though I cannot admit that they are just. It is really rather hard that I may not assert that Oxford condemned the writings of Milton and Buchanan without adding that she also condemned those of Bellarmine.[4] Surely I may say that the Council

1 J. F. Macfarlan, according to the clerk's endorsement on this letter. Macfarlan may also be the recipient of the letters of [3 May] and [May?] 1853 on this subject, but the evidence is not clear.

2 Cardwell was now President of the Board of Trade.

3 James Wilson (1805–60: *DNB*), a businessman and the founder of the *Economist*, was now M.P. for Westbury and financial secretary to the Treasury. He later became financial member of the Council of India, when his measures were opposed by Sir Charles Trevelyan in a way that led to Trevelyan's recall to England when he was Governor of Madras.

4 The reference here and in the next paragraph is to an Oxford decree of 21 July 1683 adopting the 'strange doctrines' of Sir Robert Filmer and ordering 'the political works of Buchanan, Milton, and Baxter to be publicly burned in the court of the Schools' (*History*, I, 270).

of Trent condemned the doctrines of Luther, without adding that the Council also condemned the doctrines of Arius, Socinus, Kniperdoling, and fifty other heretics. No person who has read my book can possibly imagine that I meant to represent Oxford as remiss in opposition to Popery.

Why too was I to take notice of those parts of the Oxford decree about which there is no controversy? When I say that Mahometanism is a false religion, no man of sense and candour understands me to mean that the Mahometans are wrong in asserting the Unity of God. Of course I mean only to condemn those Mahometan doctrines which are inconsistent with Christianity. And so when I speak of the Oxford decree of 1683 as servile and unconstitutional I speak of those parts of the decree about which there can be a difference of opinion, not of those parts to which Whigs and Jacobites would alike assent.

I have mentioned the servility of the Cambridge Address to James on his accession.[1] But I cannot think that an Address is so solemn an Act as the Decree of 1683. That Decree was constantly cited in the controversial pamphlets of the succeeding generation. It was read before both Houses in Westminster Hall. It was publicly committed to the flames, twenty seven years after it had been framed, by order of the highest Court of Judicature in the realm. It was in fact the most formal manifesto ever put forth by the High Church party, and therefore required special notice.

The authority for the fact about which your friend inquires is a despatch from the Dutch Envoy in London to the States General, dated June 25, 1688.[2] The dissenter in question was a Quaker. The despatch has never been printed; and so few people are able to read the original that I have had that rich mine almost entirely to myself. / I have the honor to be, / Sir,

Your most obedient Servant
T B Macaulay

TO MRS CHARLES JAMES BLOMFIELD,[3] 4 JUNE 1853

MS: Osborn Collection, Yale University.

Albany June 4. 1853

Dear Mrs. Blomfield,

I am sorry to say that the East wind and the hot and cold air of the

---

[1] *History,* I, 474.

[2] TBM twice cites the despatch of Van Citters of this date in his account of the trial of the seven bishops (*History,* I, 355 and 366). It is not clear what particular passage is in question here.

[3] Dorothy Cox, widow of Thomas Kent, married Blomfield as his second wife in 1819.

palace yesterday night[1] have given me a face ache which prevents me from exposing myself to the evening air. I am much disappointed by being forced to forego the pleasure of dining with you. / Believe me

Yours most truly

T B Macaulay

TO RICHARD MONCKTON MILNES, 11 JUNE 1853

MS: Trinity College.

Albany June 11. 1853

Dear Milnes,

I shall be most happy to breakfast with you on Wednesday.[2]

Ever yours truly

T B Macaulay

TO [HENRY REEVE],[3] 11 JUNE 1853

Text: Maggs Brothers Catalogue 275, December 1911, item 1076, 1p. 4to: dated Albany, 11 June 1853.

I give you joy on the success of your gallant enterprise.[4]

TO CHRISTIAN BERNHARD TAUCHNITZ, 14 JUNE 1853

Text: Bernhard Tauchnitz, 1837–1887, p. 109.

Albany, London, June 14, 1853.

I beg [you] to accept my thanks for your liberal and punctual mode of

---

1 TBM attended a concert at the palace but 'went home after the first Act with a pain in my face' (Journal, VI, 82).

2 The party were, besides Milnes, his wife, and his sister, Lord Stanley, the Duke of Argyll, and others unnamed (Journal, VI, 94: 15 June).

3 Reeve (1813–95: *DNB*), journalist and editor, was on the staff of *The Times,* 1840–55; in the latter year he succeeded Sir George Cornewall Lewis as editor of the *ER* and remained in that position until his death. Reeve was widely acquainted among writers and politicians in England and France and was much consulted by them. Charles Greville (he and Reeve were both officials of the Privy Council) entrusted the manuscript of his *Memoirs* to Reeve, who was its first editor. When TBM met Reeve in February 1849 at Lansdowne House, he noted then that Reeve was a man 'whom I had heard of a hundred times, but had never met before to my recollection' (Journal, I, 488).

4 According to the Maggs Brothers Catalogue, this note accompanied TBM's contribution to the public subscription that paid for Baron Marochetti's equestrian statue of Richard I that now stands before the entrance to the House of Lords. Henry Reeve and Lord Hatherton were agents for the subscription, promoted as a memorial to the Great Exhibition (J. K. Laughton, *Memoirs of the Life and Correspondence of Henry Reeve,* 2 vols., 1898, I, 302).

dealing[1] . . . I shall be most happy to see you in England. I hope to publish two more volumes of my history late in the year 1854 or early in 1855.

TO DERWENT COLERIDGE, 15 JUNE 1853

MS: Cornell University.

Albany June 15. 1853

My dear Coleridge,

I shall be most happy to subscribe for a proof impression of the portrait.

I am sorry that I was not at home when you called. It always gives me pleasure to see you.

Ever yours truly
T B Macaulay

TO [T. USHER],[2] 20 JUNE 1853

MS: Trinity College.

Albany London / June 20. 1853

Sir,

Your petition shall be presented; and I will take care that it is noticed in the papers. I wish that every town in Scotland had a Museum. I fear however that in the course of this year nothing can be done on the subject.[3] The business already before parliament is more than enough to occupy us till the end of August. / I have the honor to be, / Sir,

Your faithful Servant,
T B Macaulay

TO SELINA MACAULAY, 28 JUNE 1853

MS: Trinity College.

Albany June 28 / 1853

Dearest Selina,

I inclose a cheque for the quarter.

We are all pretty well, myself included, except that I am plagued by

---

[1] TBM received a letter on this day from Tauchnitz 'inclosing bills for £114. 16. 0. These Germans are good customers' (Journal, VI, 93).

[2] President of the Edinburgh Young Men's Association; he had written to the *Scotsman*, 20 November 1852, calling attention to Ewart's act of 1850 enabling town councils to establish public libraries and museums and suggesting the passage of a similar bill for Scotland. TBM presented the petition on 23 June.

[3] A public libraries and museums bill was brought in on 25 July, too late in the session to be proceeded with. Another bill passed in the session of 1855.

face aches and toothaches, to which the moisture contributes not a little.

I hope soon to get out of town. I shall probably go to Tunbridge Wells[1] where I shall be within reach, if there should be any division on which I am particularly wanted. I do not foresee any occasion for my [. . . .][2]

TO LADY THERESA LEWIS, 29 JUNE 1853

MS: New York Public Library.

Albany June 29. 1853

Dear Lady Theresa,

I have seldom been more vexed than by finding myself unable to accept your invitation for Monday. I have, I grieve to say, been invited to attend a wedding in St George's Church on that morning; and go I must.[3]

Ever yours truly
T B Macaulay

TO FRANCES MACAULAY, 30 JUNE 1853

MS: Trinity College.

Albany London June 30 / 1853

Dearest Fanny,

I was a good deal exhausted by speaking last Friday,[4] and was forced to sit down without saying much that was in my mind. But I am now quite well except that I am plagued by pains in the teeth and face which will last, I am afraid, till the weather changes for the better. I have nothing now to keep me in town except a local bill in which the Edinburgh people are deeply interested, but which, I am afraid, we shall be unable to carry.[5] When the fate of that bill is decided, I shall go to Tunbridge Wells for

---

[1] See 11 July.
[2] The rest is missing.
[3] The wedding was of Mrs Gore's daughter, Cecilia, to Lord Edward Thynne, 4 July: 'Great crowd. But nobody seemed to care much about the matter. It was the noosing of a young – or rather ci devant young flirt to an old rake. The whole service was read without mercy. I never heard some parts of it before' (Journal, VI, 104).
[4] TBM spoke on the India Bill on the 24th, defending the provision that based appointments to the Indian Civil Service upon competitive examination (*Hansard*, 3rd Series, CXXVIII, 739–59). E. M. Whitty describes TBM on this occasion as 'broken down in health, uncontrollably nervous, unable to sustain the pitch of his voice' and calls the speech a failure: 'the great effort was frigidly talked about and cruelly criticised' (*St Stephen's in the Fifties*, 1906, p. 242). TBM concluded merely that 'I succeeded better than I expected' (Trevelyan, II, 341): as the entries in his Journal show, he had been very anxious about the result.
[5] The Annuity Tax Bill: see 16 July.

some time, and probably run up to London occasionally when I am wanted at the Museum or in the House of Commons.

All well at Westbourne Terrace. Yesterday dear little Alice brought her Mama fairly written out the prayers which the dear child says night and morning. They are her own composition – very good on the whole, but sometimes ludicrous beyond measure. There is a prayer that she may be forgiven for her besetting and most habitual sin – blasphemy. As you may suppose, her blasphemies are of no very heinous sort.

Love to Selina, Mary, Lydia, if she is with you, and everybody else.

Yours ever

T B Macaulay

TO THOMAS FLOWER ELLIS, 30 JUNE 1853

MS: Trinity College.

Albany June 30. 1853

Dear Ellis,

I am pretty well, though I do not expect to be free from tooth ache and face ache while this vile moisture fills the air.

As soon as a local bill in which the Edinburgh people take much interest has been carried through our House or kicked out of it, I shall go to Tunbridge Wells, and shall probably stay there till September. Then I shall run to Paris and Geneva; and I shall be very much out of humour if I have not your company.

Ever yours

T B Macaulay

As you are my friend, I send you a blotted envelope which I can send to nobody else. A penny saved etc.

TO LORD MAHON, 30 JUNE 1853

MS: Stanhope Papers, Chevening.

Albany June 30 / 1853

Dear Mahon,

I shall have great pleasure in breakfasting with you next Thursday.[1]

Lord Grenville's speech on Indian affairs, the best that he ever made, was on a motion of Lord Wellesley's in April 1813.[2]

Ever yours,

T B Macaulay

[1] The party were the Duke and Duchess of Argyll, Lady Evelyn Stanhope, Lord Henry Vane, and Henry Reeve (Journal, VI, 106: 7 July).

[2] 9 April 1813 (*Hansard*, XXV, 709–52), on the proposals for the renewal of the East India Company's charter in that year.

TO AUGUSTUS DE MORGAN, 30 JUNE 1853

MS: University of London.

Albany June 30. 1853

Dear Sir,

Thanks for the Memoranda. I was acquainted with Newton's letter to Covel.[1]

Do you happen to recollect any complimentary allusion to Somers in any of Newton's scientific works. I found in a letter of that time a passage indicating that there was such an allusion; and I looked over all those parts of Newton's volumes in which I thought it possible that anything of the sort could be found; – but to no purpose.

There is a curious passage in the Transactions of the French Academy of Sciences which perhaps you may not have seen. James II went to the Observatory in 1692, I think, and there got into conversation with the French savans about the Newtonian system, and particularly about Newton's opinion concerning the equatorial and polar diameters of the globe. The Frenchmen were all against Sir Isaac.

Very truly yours,

T B Macaulay

TO SYDNEY WILLIAMS,[2] 7 JULY 1853

Text: Bernhard Tauchnitz, 1837–1887, p. 108.

Albany, July 7, 1853.

If Mr. Tauchnitz wishes to reprint my speeches,[3] I shall very gladly treat with him. All my dealings with him have been of the most satisfactory kind; and I will not make any contract with any other German publisher.

TO THOMAS FLOWER ELLIS, 11 JULY 1853

MS: Trinity College. *Partly published:* Trevelyan, II, 355–6; 360; 363–4.

Albany London July 11. 1853

Dear Ellis,

On Friday I went down to Tunbridge Wells, and took a house in a

---

1 Perhaps Newton's letter of 12 February 1688/9 to John Covel, Vice-Chancellor of Cambridge, advising that the University proclaim William and Mary 'with a seasonable decorum. . .after ye example of ye London Divines' (H. W. Turnbull, ed., *Correspondence of Isaac Newton*, Cambridge, III [1961], 10). But there is a whole sequence of letters to Covel at this time on the question of accommodating the University to the new sovereigns.

2 Williams, of the London bookselling and publishing firm of Williams and Norgate, was London agent for Tauchnitz.

3 TBM had this day agreed with Longman to publish his speeches (Journal, VI, 106) because an unauthorized edition had just appeared (see 11 July).

delightful situation.[1] The accommodation is pretty good, – the drawing room excellent, – the dining room so much overshadowed by trees and a verandah that it is dark even in the brightest noon. The country looks lovely. The heath is close to the door. I have taken measures for drenching your outside with water and your inside with wine. On Tuesday, to morrow, I go down. You had better direct to me at

1 Wellington Place
Tunbridge Wells

I shall be glad to know how soon you will visit me and for how long. The sooner and the longer the better. Hannah comes on Tuesday week, and stays till Friday.

I have some work to do at Tunbridge Wells which I had not reckoned upon. A disreputable bookseller, a sort of Curll,[2] named Vizitelly,[3] has advertised an edition of my speeches, *by Special License,* and had the brazen impudence to write to Lord Lansdowne and to ask his Lordship to accept the dedication. I found that people really wished to have the speeches. I therefore, much against my will, determined to give a revised and corrected edition. The preparing of this edition will occupy me two or three hours a day during my holiday. Many of the speeches must be rewritten from memory and from the hints given by the reports. I think of adding two or three state papers, my minute on the education of the natives of India, and my minute on the Black Act.[4] By the bye I learned yesterday that Mr. Vizetilly was hard run for money the other day, and hanged himself, but was cut down. Confound the fellow who cut him down! How truly did a great master of wisdom observe on a similar occasion τὸ πολλὰ πράσσειν οὐκ ἐν ἀσφαλεῖ βίῳ.[5]

I hope that you are looking forward to our tour, and that, when we meet next, you will be able to fix the time for starting. Till we know how many days we have, it will be impossible to settle our route. What I should like best would be Paris – Geneva – Lausanne – Basle. Strasburg by railroad – the Rhine to Cologne – and from Cologne to Ostend by railroad. We should see a great deal of what is fine in art and nature, and that in a very small compass. I think that we might do the whole in three weeks.

[1] TBM stayed there until 19 August.
[2] Edmund Curll (1675–1747: *DNB*), bookseller, the butt of Pope's satire.
[3] Henry Vizetelly (1820–94: *DNB*), wood engraver, journalist, and publisher, now best remembered for his being jailed as the publisher of Zola in 1889. His edition of TBM's speeches appeared early in July; they had earlier been published in New York by J. S. Redfield in two volumes, January 1853. TBM's own edition appeared early in December but dated 1854.
[4] TBM finally decided against these additions.
[5] 'One may not do many things in a safe life.'

Read Haydon's memoirs.[1] Haydon was exactly the vulgar idea of a man of Genius. He had all the morbid peculiarities which are supposed by fools to belong to intellectual superiority, – eccentricity, jealousy, caprice, infinite disdain for other men; – and yet he was as poor commonplace a creature as any in the world. He painted signs, and gave himself more airs than if he had painted the cartoons. He had an odious currish nature. Whether you struck him or stroked him, starved him or fed him, he snapped at your hand in just the same way. He would beg you in piteous accents to buy an acre and a half of canvass that he had spoiled. Some good natured Lord asks the price. Haydon demands a hundred guineas. His Lordship gives the money out of mere charity, and is rewarded by some such entry as this in Haydon's journal – "A hundred guineas, and for such a work. I expected that, for very shame, he would have made it a thousand. But he is a mean sordid wretch." In the meantime the purchaser is looking out for the most retired spot in his house to hide the huge daub which he has bought for ten times its value out of pure compassion.

But I must stop. I hope that your Troades is proceeding. You may have an interesting scene altered from the Agamemnon –

Κασανδρα – within attended by Ajax Oileus
ὤμοι, πέπληγμαι καιρίαν πληγὴν ἔσω.

'Ημιχοριον
σῖγα · τίς πληγὴν ἀϋτεῖ καιρίως οὐτασμένη;

Then Ajax Oileus repeats the offence

Κασανδρα
ὤμοι, μάλ' αὖθις δευτέραν πεπληγμένη.

'Ημιχοριον
τοὔργον εἰργάσθαι δοκεῖ μοι τῆς κορης οἰμώγματι[2]

Good bye. Ever yours. Write and let me know when you are likely to come.

T B Macaulay

---

[1] *The Life of Benjamin Robert Haydon...from His Autobiography and Journals,* Tom Taylor, ed., 3 vols., published 24 June; TBM read the book on 4–6 July (Journal, VI, 104–5).
[2] Cassandra: 'Alas, I have been given a mortal wound within.'
Semichorus: 'Silence; who, mortally wounded, is screaming about her wound.'
Cassandra: 'Alas, stricken again a second time.'
Semichorus: 'The deed seems to me to have been done, judging by the scream of the girl.'

TO THOMAS FLOWER ELLIS, 14 JULY 1853

MS: Trinity College. *Partly published:* Trevelyan, II, 361.

1 Wellington Place / Tunbridge Wells / July 14. 1853

Dear Ellis,

On Saturday week I shall expect you here; and most happy I shall be to see you. The country looked very pretty the day before yesterday; and the sunshine and starlight seemed to me to promise fine weather. But yesterday was dull, and to day is stormy. The rain is falling in floods, and the trees are tossing and roaring awefully. It will be better, I hope, when you are here.

I dare say that you are right as to the route to Switzerland. Hannah tells me that it is much better to go up the Rhine than down. I own that all my experience of rivers is the other way; and I have had some experience.

I have determined to read through Plato again. I began with the Phædrus yesterday, one of the most eloquent, ingenious, fantastic and delicately ironical of the dialogues. I doubt whether there be any of Plato's works which has left so many traces in the literature and philosophy of Europe. And this is the more remarkable, because no ancient work is so thoroughly tainted with what in modern times is regarded [as] the most odious of all kinds of immorality. I am afraid that Plato's character may be summed up in the words in which our valued friend Abraham Hayward[1] was once described.

Ever yours,

T B Macaulay

TO DR JOHN LEE, 16 JULY 1853

MS: National Library of Scotland.

Tunbridge Wells / July 16. 1853

My dear Sir,

I sincerely hope that long before your place in the University of Edinburgh is vacant, the government will have seen the propriety of doing something for the Academical Institutions of Scotland. One great difficulty will be removed by the Abolition of the Tests.[2]

---

[1] Hayward is several times described as 'coarse' or 'indecent' in TBM's Journal but never in such a way as to suggest homosexuality: e.g., 'Hayward was more offensive than I ever saw any man in company – indecent while the women were present – insolently and angrily disputatious after they were gone' (v, 63: 16 June 1852).

[2] See 20 May 1845. The oath required of professors was modified by the Scottish Universities Bill passed in this session so that Free Churchmen were enabled to take it: see Sir Alexander Grant, *The Story of the University of Edinburgh*, 2 vols., 1884, II, 86–9.

But it is quite impossible for me to oppose the Annuity Tax Bill.[1] The citizens of Edinburgh would with reason accuse me of ingratitude if I were to intercept a boon which the Crown is willing to bestow on them. I have no selfish motive for courting their favour. I have nothing to hope or to fear from them. But for that very reason, I am desirous not to appear to disregard their interests or their feelings.

I shall go up to town for the purpose of supporting the second reading of the Bill. I do not think that we can, this year, get beyond the second reading. / Believe me, / My dear Sir,

Your faithful Servant

T B Macaulay

TO THOMAS FLOWER ELLIS, 20 JULY 1853

MS: Trinity College.

1 Wellington Place / Tunbridge Wells / July 20. 1853

Dear Ellis,

Send a line to say whether I am to expect you on Saturday.[2]

The best train for you would be that which leaves London Bridge at half past four in the afternoon, and arrives a few minutes after six.

I have killed the fatted calf – that is to say I have hired a great tub for you.

I ran up to town yesterday, harangued with tolerable success in favour of my constituents, and came back, bringing Hannah with me. We are just starting in an open carriage to explore the beauties of the neighbourhood. The fine weather seems to be come at last.

Ever yours

T B Macaulay

I will write another letter directed to York.

TO THOMAS FLOWER ELLIS, 20 JULY 1853

MS: Trinity College. *Partly published:* Trevelyan, II, 360; 361.

1 Wellington Place / Tunbridge Wells / July 20. 1853

Dear Ellis,

Write to let me know whether you shall come down on Saturday.

I would recommend the train which leaves London Bridge at half past four and arrives here a little after six.

---

[1] TBM went up to London on the 19th to speak in favor of the bill (*Hansard,* 3rd Series, CXXIX, 451–7). These were his last words in Parliament.

[2] Ellis came then and stayed to Monday, the 25th (Journal, VI, 118–19).

I have a very pleasant room for you, a large tub, half a dozen of the best Sherry, and a dozen of good Champagne, Plato and Lucian. I have read a good deal of Plato, and the more I read, the more I admire his style, and the less I admire his reasonings.

I have written to the Temple, that I may be certain to catch you.

Yours ever
T B Macaulay

TO THOMAS FLOWER ELLIS, 28 JULY 1853

MS: Trinity College. *Partly published:* Trevelyan, II, 356.

Tunbridge Wells / July 28. 1853

Dear Ellis,

I have just received your letter. I am sorry that you cannot come down this week. Try to manage it next week; and remember that Saturday is the day for Penshurst. On any day however which is fine I can show you some very pretty country which you have not yet seen. I am afraid that my Champagne and my best Sherry will go back untasted to London.[1]

If you cannot come pray keep me informed about your plans. I shall finally leave Tunbridge Wells on Monday the 22nd of August, and shall go for one night to Hatfield that my servants may have time to make arrangements at my chambers.[2] On Tuesday the 23d I shall be at the Albany, and shall proceed to hire a courier, to get passports, and so forth. My present notion of a route is Dover – Ostend – sleep at Bruges – Cologne – get on the steamer – Rhine to Strasburg – railway to Basle – voiturin or diligence to Berne, and from Berne to Lausanne – steam boat on the lake to Geneva, – post to Lyons, – up the Soane [*sic*] by steam to Chalons, – railway to Paris, – three or four days at Paris, – and back to London in one day.[3] But I shall readily agree to any modification which you may propose. If we could start on or before the 27th of August we could easily, I think, do all this, and be in town on the 18th of September, with a great stock of pleasant recollections and images of fine objects natural and artificial. I dare say that you will despise me for saying that, on the whole, I expect more pleasure from the Cathedrals of Cologne and Strasburg than from the Bernese Alps or the Lake of Geneva.

Dear Alice sent me a delightful letter about Sardanapalus, and the terrible spectacle of the fire in which he and his capital perished. I sent her

[1] Ellis did not visit TBM again at Tunbridge Wells.
[2] In the event, TBM left Tunbridge Wells on the 19th for Hatfield, where the Trevelyans were spending the summer.
[3] For the outline of TBM's tour with Ellis, see 16 August.

in return a most edifying moral song, fit for Dr. Watts's collection,[1] and sufficient of itself to prove that the theatre might be made a school of virtue. The last verse is as follows

> From this sad warning let us learn
> To quit our sins and follies,
> To mind our music and our French,
> And put away our Dollies.
> For if our lives we do not mend
> But little 'twill avail us
> To have beheld the aweful end
> Of poor Sardanapalus.

Alice is passionately fond of her dolls, and was heard the other day parodying to herself, not very properly, one of Watts's hymns

> "At nine years old she talked with dolls."[2]

This, I suppose, is one of the blasphemies of which she accuses herself.

Ever yours,

T B Macaulay

TO GEORGE OTTO TREVELYAN, 1 AUGUST 1853

MS: University of Newcastle. *Mostly published:* Trevelyan, II, 422–4.

Tunbridge Wells / August 1. / 1853

Dear George,

I am glad to hear that you are so pleasantly lodged, and that Mamma enjoys her palace and her park so much.[3]

I am glad that you are working hard. Did you ever read Paradise Lost? If not, I would advise you to read it now. For it is the best commentary that I know on the Prometheus. There was a great resemblance between the genius of Æschylus and the genius of Milton; and this appears most strikingly in those two wonderful creations of the imagination, Prometheus and Satan. I do not believe that Milton borrowed Satan from the Greek drama. For, though he was an excellent scholar after the fashion of his time, Æschylus was, I suspect, a little beyond him. You cannot conceive how much the facilities for reading the Greek writers have increased within the last two hundred years, how much better the text is now

---

[1] Isaac Watts, *Divine Songs for Children*, 1715.
[2] *Ibid.*, Song 14, stanza 3: 'At twelve years old he talk'd with men': the reference is to Jesus.
[3] The Trevelyans were spending the summer at North Place, Hatfield.

printed, and how much light the successive labours of learned men have thrown on obscure passages. I was greatly struck with this when at Althorpe,[1] I looked through Lord Spencer's magnificent collection of Aldine editions. Numerous passages which are now perfectly simple were mere heaps of nonsense. And no writer suffered more than Æschylus, for there is a lyrical obscurity, not only in his Odes, but even in his dialogue, as I dare say you have discovered.

Note particularly in the Prometheus the magnificent history of the origin of arts and sciences.[2] That passage shows Æschylus to have been, not only a poet of the first order, but a great thinker. It is the fashion to call Euripides a philosophical poet: but I remember nothing in Euripides so philosophical as that rapid enumeration of all the discoveries and inventions which make the difference between savage and civilised man.

The latter part of the play is glorious. I know nothing finer than the whole from the lines

> Σέβου προσεύχου, θῶπτε τὸν κρατοῦντ' ἀεί.
> ἐμοὶ δ' ἔλασσον Ζηνὸς ἢ μηδὲν μέλει
> δράτω κρατείτω τόνδε τὸν μικρον χρόνον
> ὅπως θέλει· δαρὸν γὰρ οὐκ ἄρξει θεοῖς.[3]

Or is it βραχὺν χρόνον? I rather think βραχὺν is better.[4]

I am very busy here getting some of my speeches ready for the press; and during the day I get no reading except while I walk on the heath; and then I read Plato, one of the five first rate Athenians. The other four are your friends Æschylus and Thucydides, Sophocles, and Demosthenes. I know of no sixth Athenian who can be added to the list. Certainly not Euripides, nor Xenophon, nor Isocrates, nor Æschines. – But I forgot Aristophanes. More shame for me. He makes six. And I can certainly add nobody else to the six. How I go on gossiping about these old fellows when I should be thinking of other things. Love to Mamma and Papa and Baba and Alice.

Ever yours,
T B Macaulay

[1] In December 1849.
[2] Lines 447–506.
[3] Lines 937–40: 'Worship, adore, and fawn upon whoever is thy lord. But for Zeus I care less than naught. Let him do his will, let him hold his power for his little day – since not for long shall he bear sway over the gods' (Loeb translation).
[4] 'For a short time' and 'short.'

TO FRANCES MACAULAY, 4 AUGUST 1853

MS: Huntington Library. *Extract published:* Trevelyan, II, 242n.

Tunbridge Wells / August 4. 1853

Dearest Fanny,

I have told William to send the Times to Brighton.

I am glad to hear that your rooms make so handsome an appearance.

I have been very busy here, – writing on an average six hours a day. I rather like the work, though it interrupts my history. But I am not sure that at this distance from libraries etc. I should have made much progress in my history; and the speeches go on as fast as if I were in London.

The article on Moore is Croker's.[1] It is dirty and spiteful, which is only saying in other words that it is Croker's. Moore however and Lord John afforded but too good an opportunity to a malevolent assailant. Moore's Diary, it is evident to me, was written to be published; and this destroys the charm proper to Diaries. His conduct with respect to Lord Byron's Memoirs is so differently represented by different people that I hardly know what to believe. Lord Broughton, who knew everything that passed, and who had no conceivable motive for being unjust to Moore, goes further than Croker.[2]

The truth, I believe, may be summed up in one word. Moore was an Irishman. And in an Irishman great frankness, openhandedness, carelessness about money is compatible with great laxity of assertion and slipperiness in dealing. Miss Edgeworth's Sir Terence O'Fay is a specimen of the character in its coarse form, – Sir Ulick O'Shane in its refined form. I have seen and see daily both Sir Terence and Sir Ulick.[3]

I shall stay here a fortnight longer – then go for three or four days to Hatfield, and then to the Continent.

Love to Selina. My accounts with Longman are in a very good state.[4] Remember to let me know when the London and North Western calls upon you for money.

Ever yours,

T B Macaulay

---

[1] '*Memoirs of Thomas Moore,*' *Quarterly Review,* XCIII (June 1853), 239–310, a review of the first four volumes of Russell's edition of Moore's *Memoirs, Journal and Correspondence.*

[2] Broughton's account of the destruction of Byron's memoirs had not yet been published, so that TBM presumably had it either from Broughton or from gossip. Croker represented Moore as interested only in making money from Byron, and made fun of Russell for revealing the fact so indelicately (*Quarterly Review,* XCIII, 268–75).

[3] Sir Terence O'Fay is from *The Absentee;* Sir Ulick, from *Ormond.*

[4] See 1 October.

TO THOMAS FLOWER ELLIS, 4 AUGUST 1853

MS: Trinity College.

Tunbridge Wells / August 4. 1853

Dear Ellis,

I am sorry that I must give up the hope of seeing you here. But I hope that the days which you take away from your intended visit to Tunbridge Wells you will add to your tour. I think that we shall probably find it more convenient to cross from Dover to Calais, and to go thence by railway, through Lille to Brussels. The boats to Calais always start at a fixed hour, as they carry the mails; and the voyage is not a third part of the voyage to Ostend, a matter which is of more importance to you than to me.

I write six or seven hours a day, and rather take to my work, and become partial to my speeches in their cleansed form. I walk on the heath two or three hours in the morning with Plato in my hand. I like the Theætetus much better than formerly, the Apology and the Phædon rather less. I have now begun the Republic. I think that I understand Greek better now than I ever did. Many passages which I could not make out in India now seem quite plain to me; and I have no more help in the way of notes here than there, indeed rather less.

I think of treating Vizitelly as Pope treated Curll;[1] – the vagabond! – Craig wants me to attack him in an equity court. But I shall content myself with putting forth a ballad on his hanging himself. What do you say to this –

> Devil who erst didst play a tune
>   At midnight to Corelli,
> Scrape loud thy fiddle while I sing
>   The fate of Vizitelly.

> Beset by duns and bums enough
>   To puzzle Machiavelli,
> He climbed the stool, he tied the noose,
>   Poor Henry Vizitelly.

> A while he stood as pale as death,
>   And quaking like a jelly.
> "Ah me," he said, "I'm rightly named.
>   I soon shall *visit hell-I.*"

[1] In 'A Full and True Account of a Horrid and Barbarous Revenge by Poison, on the Body of Mr. Edmund Curll,' 1716. Trevelyan, II, 364n, says that TBM had a 'strong relish for Pope's celebrated pasquinade...which, in its own rather questionable class, he held to be inferior only to Voltaire's "Diatribe of Doctor Akakia."'

> After a minute's strife between
>   The *Nolle* and the *Velle*,
> He kicked the stool, and high in air
>   Swung Henry Vizitelly.
>
> But the rope broke; and down he fell;
>   And his guts burst out of his belly:
> So did this second Judas die
>   The pirate Vizitelly.

I leave Tunbridge Wells on the 19th for Hatfield where the Trevelyans are. On Tuesday the 23d I shall be at the Albany again. I shall probably hear from you before the 19th.

Ever yours,
T B Macaulay

Is not the pun in the third verse Σουιφτικώτατον[1]

TO LORD MAHON, 9 AUGUST 1853

MS: Stanhope Papers, Chevening.

Tunbridge Wells / August 9. 1853

Dear Mahon,

I had fully meant to cross the country, and to pass one day with you. But I have found my work a good deal heavier than I expected. I have to write six or seven hours daily; and even so I shall not have my volume of speeches ready to go to press till near the end of September. I hope to steal three weeks for Switzerland, and I shall be delighted to meet you and Lady Mahon there. I mean to see the Bernese Alps; that is to say, to see them from the plain: for my climbing days are over, and I think, with Professor Wilson, that mountains are things to look from and not to look at.[2]

I have read a good deal of Plato on the heath, with more pleasure than I ever took before in reading him; not that I am in any danger of becoming a Platonist: for all my leanings are the other way.

Remember me most kindly to Lady Mahon and my young friends, especially my Valentine.

Ever yours truly
T B Macaulay

---

[1] 'Most Swift-like.'

[2] Perhaps something from John Wilson's writings is meant. A passage in 'Noctes Ambrosianae', *Blackwood's*, v (August 1819), 601, is a little, but only a little, like TBM's recollection.

TO THOMAS FLOWER ELLIS, 16 AUGUST 1853

MS: Trinity College. *Partly published:* Trevelyan, II, 356–7.

Tunbridge Wells / August 16. 1853

Dear Ellis,

I am glad to find that we shall have a clear three weeks for our expedition.[1] I hope to secure Wolmar.[2] At all events I shall have a good courier. I can afford to indulge myself. For Longman informs me that he shall have more than 1300£ to pay me on the first of December besides 500£ in the first week of January, so that my whole income this year will be about 3600£ clear of property tax. Like Dogberry I shall have two gowns and everything handsome about me. But alas! like Dogberry I have had losses.[3] The East India Company is going to pay me off some thousands; and I must take four per Cent instead of five, and be thankful even to get four. How justly has an ancient poet observed that

Crescentem sequitur etc.[4]

However as my Lord Smart says "Hang saving. We'll have a penn'orth of cheese."[5] I say Hang saving! We'll have a jolly three weeks on the Continent. On Friday I shall go to Trevelyan's. The address is

North Place
 Hatfield
  Herts.

On Tuesday I shall return to the Albany to make arrangements. Will you dine with me that day, or Wednesday that we may finally settle our plan, and that I may know exactly what to do about passports? The plague about passports is great; and, as we shall pass through the territories of several powers, we may lose some days if we do not take care to be quite en regle.

I never was more amused than with the trial in Smyth v Smyth.[6] You remember the seat which was in dispute. It is on the road to Barley Wood – an immense front, four hundred feet long I should think, the work of

---

[1] On 26 August TBM and Ellis began a tour that took them from London to Dover, Calais, Ghent, Cologne, Bonn, Mayence, Frankfurt, Heidelberg, Strasburg, Basle, Malleray, Berne, Fribourg, Vevey, Lausanne, Geneva, Nantua, Lyons, Chalons, Paris, and Boulogne; they reached London again on 19 September (Journal, VII, 1–95): see also the summary in 19 September.
[2] As a courier. Wolmar was unavailable but they got a good man anyway: see 9 September.
[3] *Much Ado about Nothing*, IV, ii, 87–9.
[4] Horace, *Odes*, III, xvi, 17: 'Crescentem sequitur cura pecuniam.'
[5] Swift, *Polite Conversation*, Dialogue 2: 'bring us a half-p'orth of cheese.'
[6] At Gloucester assizes, 8–10 August. One Thomas Provis, claiming to be the son by a secret marriage of Sir Hugh Smyth, of Ashton Court, near Bristol, and thus heir to the baronetcy and an estate worth £30,000 yearly, was exposed as an imposter and sentenced to twenty years' transportation (*Annual Register*).

Inigo, but deformed by modern improvements, with a superb background of wood. You climbed, I remember, through the Ashton Woods to the top of the rock, while I remained below.

I am working hard at my speeches, and am rather pleased with their appearance. I meditate another work – a piece of vengeance on Vizitelly after Pope's fashion. Do you think that a broadside would sell with a wood cut and the following title?

> "The history of Henry Vizitelly Bookseller of Gough Court Fleet Street, showing how he was tempted of the Devil, and hanged himself, but was cut down alive, and recovered by John Spinks Apothecary after the manner prescribed by the Royal Humane Society, his repentance, and confession of his sins, the whole compiled from the best materials by the Right Honorable Thomas Babington Macaulay M.P. One of Her Majesty's most honorable Privy Council F.R.S. M.R.I.A. LLD.[1] Corresponding Member of the Institute of France. Member of the Academies of Turin, Munich and Utrecht, Knight of the Prussian Order of Merit, one of the Trustees of the British Museum and late Fellow of Trinity College Cambridge, Author of a History of England, Lays of Ancient Rome etc. etc. etc. 1853."

I think that I should make more by this than Viz will make by my speeches.

Yours ever
T B Macaulay

TO HENRY HART MILMAN, 18 AUGUST 1853

MS: McGill University.

Tunbridge Wells / August 18. 1853

My dear Dean,

I am sorry to say that a visit to Formosa[2] is quite out of the question at present. I start for the Continent next week, and every day, till I start, is appropriated.

My visit to Oxford and many other things which I had meant to do have been postponed in consequence of the prank of a rascally bookseller who, by publishing a heap of nonsense and bad English which he is pleased to call my speeches, has forced me to spend the summer in preparing a correct edition. I shall however, I hope, get my first sight of the Alps in little more than a fortnight.

Kindest regards to Mrs. Milman.

Ever yours truly
T. B. Macaulay

[1] TBM had been given not an LL.D. but a D.C.L. at Oxford, 7 June, on the occasion of the installation of Lord Derby as Chancellor.
[2] Formosa island and the house there, in the Thames at Cookham.

I ought to have told you long ago that we have at the Museum papal correspondence as far back as the 13th Century. I do not know how it slipped my memory.

Happily you can now make researches for yourself.[1]

TO MARGARET TREVELYAN, 1 SEPTEMBER 1853

MS: Trinity College.

Heidelberg. September 1. / 1853

Dearest Baba,

I have not time to send you a history of my travels. But you will be glad to hear that they have been in the highest degree pleasant. We had one bad day, Monday; and that mattered little: for we only went from Cologne to Bonn through a country as flat as Lincolnshire. We have since had three glorious days. The first we spent in running up the Rhine by steam from Bonn to Mayence. At first I was a little disappointed: but after we had passed Coblentz and Ehrenbreitstein the scenery delighted me beyond description. I have gone down the Rhone, and both down and up the Loire; and neither deserves to be compared to the Rhine. From Mayence we went yesterday by railway to Frankfort, lounged about there during four hours, saw the house where Goëthe was born, the Cathedral where the Emperors were crowned, the cemetery with Thorwaldsen's[2] sculptures, and, what interested me more than all, the Jewry – the Judengasse. In the afternoon we came hither by railway through a fine country. This morning we have passed near six hours in seeing the castle and roaming through the woods. We shall stay here to day, that our linen may be washed in the beautiful Neckar, and shall dine at seven on trout from the fishponds of the castle and on glorious hock marked with Prince Metternich's seal.[3] To morrow we go to Strasburg, where I hope to find letters saying that you are all well. I know nothing about English matters. The Times of Saturday contained the last information that I possess. Perhaps the Queen is dead. Perhaps Lord Aberdeen is turned out. Perhaps there has been a Chartist insurrection; and the British republic has been proclaimed. God bless all at Hatfield.

Ever yours, dearest.

T B M

---

[1] For his *History of Latin Christianity, including that of the Popes, to the Pontificate of Nicolas V*, 6 vols., 1854–5. Milman had been appointed a trustee of the British Museum on 1 July.

[2] Bertel Thorwaldsen (1770–1844), Danish sculptor.

[3] Schloss Johannisberg was bestowed on Metternich after the Congress of Vienna.

TO LADY TREVELYAN, 9 SEPTEMBER 1853

MS: Trinity College.

Geneva Friday September 9 / 1853

Dearest Hannah,

I saw in a stray Galignani[1] which was at Vevay that there had been an accident on the Great Northern Railway, and to that very train by which Trevelyan ordinarily goes to Hatfield; but, as he was not mentioned, I felt quite at ease about him, for I was sure that he would have been named if he had been among the sufferers. Your letter and dear Baba's which I found here made me shudder.[2] However we have all great reason to be joyful and thankful.

I do not expect much more English news till I reach Paris which will be on Wednesday evening. On Monday the 19th I expect to reach London.

We had a dreadfully bad journey on Tuesday last from Berne to Fribourg. The journey from Fribourg to Vevay was but little better. As we approached the lake of Geneva however the weather cleared a little; and the scenery had a grand though very gloomy effect. The next morning we went from Vevay to Lausanne; and still the weather was unfavourable, but during the night it changed. When I looked out of my window at four the first signs of dawn were visible over the Alps. I wrapped myself up, opened the window, and sate three hours with Mont Blanc full in view. The effect of the sunrise on the snowy mountain tops and on the lake was glorious. I could have cried with pleasure. The day has ever since been worthy of such a commencement. We have had a delightful voyage by a steamer to Geneva, where we have Mont Blanc and his gigantic brethren before us. Mont Blanc is as far from our window as Brighton from London, and looks as if we could walk to the base in an hour. We shall stay here to morrow and Sunday, and start on Monday for Dijon. We met none of our acquaintance till to day. But on board with us were Merivale and his wife, Judge Talfourd and his son, etc. etc. Mrs. Merivale asked very tenderly after you.

Franz[3] has really been beyond all price. I never saw so good a servant; and everybody that sees him thinks the same. Yesterday he telegraphed from Lausanne to Geneva and secured us excellent rooms. Other people whose couriers were less provident are forced to lie in pothouses. At the railways he slips a franc into the hand of a functionary who gives us a coupé and puts nobody else into it. He pays all the bills, and, I believe,

---

[1] Galignani's *Messenger*, published in Paris for Englishmen on the Continent.

[2] The accident, a collision involving the express from King's Cross, occurred on 31 August at Hornsey. Trevelyan was on the train but escaped injury (Journal, VII, 55: 9 September).

[3] Identified only as 'a certain George Franz of Cologne' (Journal, VI, 134: 23 August). TBM's Journal of the tour is filled with praise of the efficiency and honesty of Franz.

honestly. But certainly I never in my life travelled so cheap though we live as well as possible. Love to Trevelyan, and to the dear children. I will soon write to Baba. Your letters directed to Strasburg have miscarried.

Ever yours
T B M

TO LADY TREVELYAN, 16 SEPTEMBER 1853

MS: Trinity College.

Paris September 16. 1853

Dearest Hannah,

I have found your letter of Tuesday here, and most happy I was to find it. I cannot imagine how it is that the letters to Strasburg have miscarried. I am afraid that the French post office has been playing tricks.

I hope to be in town on Monday, after a very pleasant journey. I am better than I have been for many months; and my tooth has quite left off plaguing me. I am glad that I did not part with it.

Lyons was delightful. I have seldom seen a more interesting city. I had been there before,[1] but for a very short time and in very bad weather. We had a last view of the snow on Mont Blanc from the heights above the town.

At Paris we found the Hotel de Bristol full and were consigned to a second rate house called the Hotel de Chatham, where I am now writing in an entresol so dark that I can hardly see my paper. We are promised better apartments in a few hours; and, as we shall dine out and pass most of the day out, it matters little.

Dear little Alice's letter has not reached me yet. It may arrive from Geneva to morrow. Whether it does or not, I will write to her. Love to her and Baba and George and their Papa.

Ever yours
T B M

TO FRANCES MACAULAY, 19 SEPTEMBER 1853

MS: Trinity College.

Albany September 19 / 1853

Dearest Fanny,

Here I am, just arrived. Nothing would be more pleasant than to write

---

[1] TBM was there both going and returning from his Italian tour in 1838–9. Recalling that time in his Journal for 14 September he writes that 'I was then very unhappy. Now I am as happy as any man can easily be – at least a man of near 53' (VII, 78).

you a long letter about my journey. But unhappily I have found my table covered with papers, the accumulation of three weeks; and I must spend a day or two in answering them. There are poets who send me their odes, constituents who want places, literary ladies who want autographs, etc. etc. etc. I must therefore be very concise. In a tour of three weeks and three days I went from London to Dover, from Dover to Calais, from Calais by railway to Cologne, from Cologne by railway to Bonn, from Bonn up the Rhine to Mayence, from Mayence by rail to Frankfort and thence to Heidelberg, Strasburg, and Basle, from Basle by voiturin to Vevay and Lausanne, from Lausanne across the lake to Geneva, from Geneva post to Lyons, from Lyons up the Saone to Chalons, from Chalons by rail to Paris, and from Paris home by Boulogne and Folkstone. We had delicious weather generally. The only ill luck of which we have to complain is that we never saw the Bernese Alps. From the passes of Jura to Vevay we were in constant mist and rain. But on the Rhine, at Heidelberg, through the Jura, and on the Lake of Geneva, we had the finest sunshine imaginable. I am very well at present, – much better than I, a year ago, expected ever to be. It is not unlikely that when you are again settled at Brighton I may pay you a short visit there. But my plans are not yet fixed. The first thing to be done is to answer about thirty letters which are on my [. . . .][1]

TO GEORGE CORNEWALL LEWIS, 20 SEPTEMBER 1853

MS: National Library of Wales.

                              Albany London / September 20. 1853
Dear Lewis,

I have just found your letter of the 29th of August on my table. While you were writing to me, I was admiring the banks of the Rhine. I hope that my silence has not caused any inconvenience, and that the Lord Advocate has undertaken to review the Life of Jeffrey.[2] No man is so fit. For myself, it is quite impossible for me to do anything at present in that way. I have been forced by a scoundrelly pirate to publish, in self defence, an edition of my speeches; and this work, to which I have not the least inclination, will occupy me during some weeks and will interrupt pursuits much more important and interesting.

I had the greatest affection for Jeffrey, and sincerely admired his eloquence, his wit and his ingenuity. But I do not think myself well qualified to draw his character. For I never saw him, except during two or

---

[1] The second leaf of the second sheet has been torn away; probably only the closing and signature are missing.

[2] The Lord Advocate was James Moncrieff. No review of Cockburn's *Life of Lord Jeffrey* appeared in the *ER*.

three days, in what our modern jargonists would call his normal state.[1] Edinburgh was his home; and it so happened that I was never but once under his roof at Edinburgh, and then only for half an hour. I have seen him in rural retirement; and I have seen him as a lion in London. But in his own peculiar sphere I scarcely caught a glimpse of him. You are therefore likely to obtain from the Lord Advocate much more valuable assistance than I could have given you, even if I had been at liberty.

Ev[. . . .][2]

TO SELINA MACAULAY, 26 SEPTEMBER 1853

MS: Trinity College. *Envelope:* Miss Macaulay / Temple House / Brighton. *Subscription:* TBM.

Albany London / September 26 1853

Dearest Selina,

Are you at Brighton? – One line, that I may know where to send a cheque.

Ever yours,

T B M

TO AUGUSTUS DE MORGAN,[28 SEPTEMBER 1853][3]

Text: Augustus De Morgan, *Newton: His Friend: and His Niece,* 1885, pp. 68–70.

[Albany]

I return your paper.[4] It is very interesting; but there are some important facts which seem to have escaped your notice. Mrs. Barton was a most intimate friend of Swift. "I love her better than anybody," is the expression he uses about her in one of his letters to Stella.[5] She is mentioned perhaps twenty times in his journal. He never hints the least suspicion of her virtue;

[1] See 15 April 1828 for TBM's description of his visit to Jeffrey in Edinburgh.

[2] The rest of the closing and the signature have been cut away.

[3] TBM records the letter in his Journal for this date (VI, 139–40).

[4] On the question whether Catherine Barton (1680–1739), Sir Isaac Newton's niece, was the mistress of Newton's patron, Charles Montagu (1661–1715: *DNB*), first Earl of Halifax. The paper, published in *Notes and Queries,* 5 November 1853, argues that contemporary scandal about Mrs Barton was wrong and that she was secretly married to Halifax. De Morgan persisted in his conviction on this question; it is repeated in his posthumously-published essay on *Newton: His Friend: and His Niece,* 1885. Newton's latest editor says merely that 'there is no doubt that [Catherine Barton] lived in [Halifax's] house, though in what capacity it is impossible to establish with certainty' (J. F. Scott, ed., *The Correspondence of Isaac Newton,* IV [1967], Cambridge, 350n).

[5] *Journal to Stella,* 3 April 1711. The fact that Swift mentions Mrs Barton was not known to De Morgan until TBM called his attention to it; it was, De Morgan says, 'unnoticed by all the scientific biographers' (*Newton,* p. 67).

and his regard for her must be supposed to have been very strong since it overcame his party feeling. He was then completely estranged from Halifax, and was the great literary champion of the Tories. Yet he suffered Mrs. Barton to talk Whiggism to him, and seems not to have liked her the less. She evidently lived at that time, not with Halifax, but in a lady-like manner by herself, seeing the best company, and giving handsome dinners. I cannot believe that Swift, who, though he had no religion, had a great deal of professional spirit,[1] would have haunted the house, and sate at the table of any man's kept-mistress, above all the kept-mistress of his enemy. But you can look at the letters to Stella, and judge for yourself. Swift mentions the brother, an officer, a sad dog, who was killed in Hill's unlucky expedition to Quebec.[2]

You must not, I think, say much about the purity of Halifax's morals. He is accused of libertinism by Davenant;[3] and though Davenant was a malignant fellow, and little to be trusted, I do not know that we have the means of refuting the accusation. I am very unwilling to believe that Mrs. Barton was Halifax's mistress; but I cannot think that she was his wife. There was no conceivable reason for his not avowing the marriage, if it had really taken place. There would have been no *mésalliance*. He was a younger son of a younger brother, and had been educated for the Church. Dorset's patronage, and his own abilities, raised him in the world. But in all the lampoons of the time Montague is spoken of as a *parvenu*. The sister of a colonel in the army, the niece of a member for the University of Cambridge, was surely a match for any man. My own belief is that Mrs. Barton was neither Halifax's mistress nor his wife, and that the *liaison* between them was of the same sort with that between Congreve and Mrs. Bracegirdle, with that between Swift and Stella, with that between Pope and Martha Blount, with that between Cowper and Mrs. Unwin. But, whether it were so or not, I have no doubt it was so considered by Newton, who, sagacious as he was in his own sphere, was the last man in the world to have discovered an amour, if the parties took the most ordinary precautions. With all his genius, he was as simple as a child; and the coldness of his own temperament would have made him slow to believe that others had been led astray by their passions. If anything more occurs to me, I will write again.[4]

---

[1] De Morgan interpolates at this point the remark: 'I have worded this very differently'; but whether he means that he has altered TBM's text or has described Swift's 'professional spirit' in different terms in his own narrative is not clear.

[2] *Journal to Stella*, 9 October 1711: 'He was a lieutenant-colonel and a coxcomb.'

[3] Charles Davenant (1656–1714: *DNB*), political economist and Tory M.P. TBM calls him 'an acute and well informed though most unprincipled and rancorous politician' (*History*, I, 314: ch. 3).

[4] In printing this letter De Morgan takes the opportunity to 'record the fairness of Macaulay's mind in a matter in which unfairness is neither sin nor shame. . . . Macaulay held equal

TO SELINA MACAULAY, 29 SEPTEMBER 1853

MS: Trinity College. *Envelope:* Miss Macaulay / Temple House / Brighton. *Subscription:* TBM.

Albany London / September 29. 1853

Dearest Selina,

I inclose a cheque. I am truly sorry that your head gives you trouble. I hope that you did not aggravate your complaint by writing to me. Never distress yourself on my account. A line will always be enough; and I shall understand why you are so short.

There are undoubtedly, both in the physical and in the political world, many things which may well cause anxiety. But I have lived through much darker times. The material prosperity of the country, in spite of a momentary interruption, exceeds anything ever known before. What is of still more consequence, the heart of the country is sound. High prices we shall have; indeed we have them: but of famine there is no danger. War, I hope and believe, will be averted.[1] As to the Cholera,[2] I can prophesy nothing.

Ever yours
T B Macaulay

TO MARGARET TREVELYAN, 1 OCTOBER 1853

MS: Trinity College.

Albany London / October 1. 1853

My dearest Baba,

I am working hard, in spite of interruptions. I have had to day a whole budget of letters asking for places. The Moneys want me to get a chaplainship for some canting man whom they call a Fellow of Oxford. The Evanses want me to get a place of 500£ a year for John Gisborne.[3] A Mrs. Acworth who informs me that she was formerly Miss Close wants an autograph. I know neither Mrs. Acworth nor Miss Close. But I remember two abominable parsons, an Acworth[4] at Rothley and a Close[5] at Cheltenham. If she is the sister of one and the wife of the other, I pity her.

rights to mean *quid pro quo*. He began by asking information from me, which I took pains to give; he took equal pains to return an equivalent when I asked of him. I then began to send him scraps, as I found them, unasked; and this he retorted in kind' (*Newton*, p. 71).

[1] The Eastern question was nearing a crisis; on 5 October Turkey declared war against Russia.
[2] Newcastle and other northern towns suffered from cholera in this month.
[3] Gisborne (d. 1869) was the second son of Thomas Gisborne, the Evangelical and poet, and the nephew of Mrs Evans of Allestree.
[4] William Acworth (1803–99) was Vicar of Rothley, 1836–53; of Plumstead, Kent, 1853–64; and of South Stoke, Somerset, until his death. None of his three wives was a Miss Close.
[5] See 14 October 1846.

Other interruptions are more agreeable. Here is my account from Longman – better than I expected.

£1547. 5. 2 due Dec 4
£500. 0. 0 due Jan 4

£2047. 5. 2. is the total for this year. This consoles me for the low price of North Western Stock and London Dock Stock, and for the probability of my being paid off by the East India Company.

I hope that Thackeray's literary enterprises may prove as profitable as mine. He has just published the first number of a new Novel.[1] I have bought it but not read it. He has I hear made a pretty good bargain with Bradbury and Evans, the booksellers. He is to have 3000£.[2]

But I must turn to my work again. Love to Mamma and Alice, and Papa, if he has come back to Enmore. Give all sorts of kind messages to Grandmamma and Uncle William.

Ever yours,
T B Macaulay

TO FRANCES MACAULAY, 4 OCTOBER 1853

MS: Huntington Library.

Albany London / October 4. 1853

Dearest Fanny,

I saw Palmerston's speech.[3] It was very civil. I wish that it had been as true.

I do not very well know what to say about Miss Cunninghame.[4] I should never think of trying to convert a Roman Catholic to Protestantism either in Tuscany or in England: for I think that, ten to one, I should make him an infidel, or, at least, unfix all his opinions. What I have seen of converted Roman Catholics has not made a favourable impression on me. But, I suppose, Miss Cunninghame thinks that the Pope is Antichrist, the Beast, the Man of Sin, and so forth; and, so thinking, she might, as it seems to me, defend her conduct by arguments which you would not find it easy

---

[1] The first number of *The Newcomes* appeared on this day.

[2] In fact £3,600 (Gordon Ray, ed., *Letters of Thackeray*, III, 280).

[3] On receiving the freedom of the City of Glasgow on 27 September Palmerston had said that he was gratified to share the honor with that 'eminent man Mr. Macaulay, a man with the rare faculty of combining in his person the sagacity, wisdom, and political experience of the statesman with that intellectual distinction which qualifies him to be one of the greatest historians this country has ever produced' (*The Times*, 29 September).

[4] A Miss Margaret Cunninghame, of Thornton, Ayrshire, had been arrested and imprisoned in Lucca for distributing Bibles and an Italian translation of *Pilgrim's Progress*; in response to popular feeling in Britain, the government had protested to the Grand Duke, but he pardoned Miss Cunninghame before the official protest was received (*The Times*, 26 September; 13 October).

to answer. The Laws of Tuscany forbid her to make converts, it is true: and the laws of Rome forbade the primitive Xtns to make converts; and the laws of England forbade our reformers to make converts. Why is she more bound to obey the Grand Duke than Peter was bound to obey Herod, or Lambert[1] to obey Henry the Eighth? As I am unable to prove to her that she is in the wrong, so I must own myself quite unable to prove to the Grand Duke that he is in the wrong. He might say – "You in England punish people for circulating impious tracts. You punished the bookseller who sold Paine's Age of Reason.[2] You sent Carlisle and Taylor,[3] the Devil's chaplain, and a good many of their underlings to prison for distributing Atheistical and Deistical works. You cannot possibly think worse of the Age of Reason than I think of the Pilgrim's Progress. Paine's doctrines can do no more than send a man to Hell; and, in my opinion, Bunyan's doctrines will assuredly send a man there. I have as good a right to my opinion as you have to yours. Abolish therefore your own laws against blasphemy, before you blame me for inforcing my laws against blasphemy." I am clear as to this, that we have no right to interfere in the matter, except by expostulation. Nevertheless, my English blood is so much stirred that I should rejoice, though I should not approve, if the government were to act as Old Noll would certainly have acted, and to send a squadron to Leghorn. It is highly probable that, in a few years, Italy will be on fire and the Grand Duke an exile.[4] I would not advise him to come to England. If he ventured into Exeter Hall, he would, I firmly believe, be torn in pieces.

The weather here is very variable. Yesterday and the day before were beautiful. It is now blowing and raining. I shall pass the day by my fire in correcting my speeches. I do not suppose that they will have any great success. But I do not think that they will lower my character. I am vexed to find how little I have improved in the course of twenty years. I spoke as well in 1831 as I could do now.

Ever yours,

T B Macaulay

Pray remember me kindly to your hostess.

A certain W. Money[5] writes to me from France to ask me to get something for somebody. What is he? Is he a clergyman? Mrs. Evans has also written to ask me to get something for John Gisborne. I am afraid that the case is hopeless.

---

[1] John Lambert (d. 1538: *DNB*), martyr.
[2] Thomas Williams, in 1797.
[3] See 14 June 1831.
[4] Leopold II, the Grand Duke, was expelled in 1859.
[5] Probably William Money (1802–90), one of the clerical sons of Mrs Eugenia Money (see *to Fanny*, 14 October 1846); he was chaplain at St Servan, France, 1858–87.

TO AUGUSTUS DE MORGAN, 14 OCTOBER 1853

MS: University of London.

Albany October 14. / 1853

Dear Sir,

Many thanks for the papers. Vous me comblez, as the French say. I am afraid that I shall not live to write the history of the American war. Indeed heaven knows when I shall have done with King William. A piratical bookseller has published a heap of trash which he calls my speeches, and has forced me to publish a genuine edition in self defence. The business of correcting and revising has occupied me during some weeks, and has made it impossible for me to proceed with my history.

Ever yours truly

T B Macaulay

TO UNIDENTIFIED RECIPIENT,[1] 14 OCTOBER 1853

Text: Unidentified newspaper clipping in volume of miscellaneous clippings about TBM at Harvard.

Albany, London, Oct. 14, 1853.

Sir,

I am obliged and at the same time diverted by your kind solicitude. I assure you that you need not be uneasy. The story which is going the rounds of your papers is an impudent lie,[2] without the slightest shadow of a foundation. All the opium that I have swallowed in a life of fifty-three years does not amount to ten grains. I affirm, on my honor, that I never took even a drop of laudanum, except in obedience to medical authority; and the last time that I took any, to the best of my remembrance, was when the cholera was here in 1849.

My health, it is true, is delicate. I am very well at present. But, with the cold weather my maladies will probably come back. My chest suffers most from the winter air. But everybody who knows me, knows that my faculties and spirits have never flagged, and that, in spite of indisposition, I lead a most happy life. I cannot help feeling some indignation at the

---

[1] No doubt the American from whom TBM received a letter of advice on this date regarding the charge that he was an opium addict: 'I was rather glad of the opportunity of contradicting the impudent slander' (Journal, VI, 146).

[2] On 11 October TBM learned that the New York *Tribune* had published a story 'about my having destroyed my faculties with opium' (Journal, VI, 144). The story, over the initials A.P.C., reports that the third volume of the *History* is about to appear, though TBM's friends 'never believed that he would be able to finish it, as the excessive use of opium, to which he is addicted, has destroyed his health, and prevents him from any continued mental exertion' (*Tribune*, 12 August).

villany of the low-minded and bad-hearted man who could send such a calumny across the Atlantic.[1] However, my indignation has already cooled into contempt, or nearly so. I will venture to say that the writer of the letter in which this falsehood appeared never approached even the outskirts of the society in which I live, or he would have made his fiction a little more probable.

I have the honor to be, sir, your obedient servant,

T. B. Macaulay.

TO THOMAS FLOWER ELLIS, 17 OCTOBER 1853

MS: Trinity College.

Albany October 17. 1853

Dear Ellis,

I think that I am to dine with you on Wednesday, and you with me on Thursday. Have you a party on Wednesday.[2]

These Yankees plague me to death. I shall succeed to De Quincy's name of the Opium Eater. I send you a letter which I have received from an honest New Yorker. Do not lose it, as I shall want to show it to Hannah.

I have sent a short and civil answer which, ten to one, will be in all the newspapers of the United States within six weeks.

George is certainly getting on better this quarter. Harris[3] says that there is a decided improvement.

Ever yours,
T B Macaulay

TO FRANCES MACAULAY, 20 OCTOBER 1853

MS: Trinity College.

Albany London / October 20. 1853

Dearest Fanny,

I was sorry to find that you had called here in my absence. Perhaps, when my work is done, I may be able to steal a week for a trip to Brighton. But I am afraid that it will be some time before I can escape from the printer and his imps.

The Trevelyans are all here, and well and happy. We talk of going to Paris and Rouen at Easter, and reckon on your company.

[1] TBM supposed that Horace Greeley was the author of the story (Journal, XI, 321: 24 May 1858), but Greeley was not then in England.
[2] Adolphus and Sir William Atherton were of the party (Journal, VI, 149: 19 October).
[3] George Frederick Harris (1812–69: *Boase*), Second Master at Harrow ,1836–68.

The article on Church parties[1] is very good indeed, – much above what I thought that Conybeare[2] could have written. But what possessed him to tell us that he heard the parson say, "Saddle me the ass, and they saddled *him*."[3] And if Conybeare was guilty of such folly, how could Lewis let it pass? It is an old Joe Miller. I could show it you printed in a book which appeared in 1784, thirty years, I suppose, before Conybeare was born.

Love to Selina.

Ever yours
T B Macaulay

TO FRANCES MACAULAY, 27 OCTOBER 1853

MS: Trinity College.

Albany October 27. 1853

Dearest Fanny,

You did quite rightly in sending me the paper.[4] I have kept the first leaf. The second leaf you must fill up and send to the Secretary. Selina should send me the first leaf of her paper, and send the second, properly filled up, to the Secretary. I will take care that the money shall be paid in proper time. It matters little indeed whether I pay it or not at present. And I should probably gain a few pounds by waiting till the call is imperative. But I very much wish you to be free from all the liabilities contracted in that unhappy season of Railway speculation. I am truly glad that it has been in my power to extricate you without inconvenience to myself.

Love to Selina.

Ever yours
T B Macaulay

TO SELINA MACAULAY, 31 OCTOBER 1853

MS: Trinity College.

Albany October 31 / 1853

Dearest Selina,

Thank you for the paper. I will take care that the needful shall be done, as the bankers phrase it. The sale of my books keeps up so well that I can pay this sum without the smallest inconvenience.

---

[1] 'Church Parties,' *ER*, xcviii (October 1853), 273–342. TBM called it 'a very clever paper' and at first thought that it was by Stephen (Journal, vi, 145: 11 October).

[2] William John Conybeare (1815–57: *DNB*), Vicar of Axminster and Edinburgh Reviewer his wife was Eliza, daughter of TBM's cousin Lydia Babington Rose.

[3] Conybeare says that he had heard this from 'a clergyman of the "Low and Slow" school' (*ER*, xcviii, 327n).

[4] 'Letter from Fanny. 128 pounds to pay for her and Selina' (Journal, vi, 154: 26 October).

I like Conybeare's paper much, and am very far from thinking it too severe. Miss Cunninghame's letter is exquisite.[1]

As to libels on the dead, I remember several cases in which they have been prosecuted. When the Queen's business was pending, the John Bull brought an infamous charge against Lady Caroline Wrottesley, wife of my old friend Sir John Wrottesley who was afterwards made Lord Wrottesley.[2] Lady Caroline had long been dead. But her husband obtained a criminal information; and the publishers were convicted and sentenced to fine and imprisonment. I could mention other instances. I do not know that I ever heard of a civil action in such a case; and I should doubt whether it could be maintained, unless there were some special damage to some living person. But I have no doubt that, if there were special damage to a living person, the action would lie. Suppose, for example, that a young lady were engaged to be married. Some malignant person publishes a libel blackening the character of her deceased mother. The lover, who, like Lord Colambre,[3] is very squeamish on that point, breaks off the engagement. I have no doubt that, in such a case, the lady might recover damages from the libeller.

Hannah and Baba, I hear, go down to you on Wednesday. I should be obliged to Fanny to send me by them Warren's Ten Thousand a Year,[4] if she has done with it.

My love to her.

Ever yours
T B Macaulay

TO FRANCES MACAULAY, 5 NOVEMBER 1853

MS: Trinity College.

Albany London / November 5. 1853

Dearest Fanny,

There is not the smallest difficulty about getting anything copied on very moderate terms at the Museum. Some poor but respectable people

---

[1] Miss Cunninghame (see 4 October) wrote that she wished to refuse the Grand Duke's pardon in order to bring her case to trial and that she left her prison only under duress (*Scotsman*, 26 October).

[2] Sir John Wrottesley (1771–1841: *DNB*), first Baron Wrottesley; TBM would have known him in the House of Commons, where he sat as Whig M.P. at various times between 1799 and 1837. His first wife died in 1818; in 1821 the *John Bull* alleged that she had once been 'detected in a criminal intrigue with a menial servant,' whereupon Sir John brought his action (*The Times*, 5 and 12 February 1821).

[3] 'Lord Colambre had the greatest dread of marrying any woman whose mother had conducted herself ill' (Maria Edgeworth, *The Absentee*, ch. 7, the end).

[4] Samuel Warren, *Ten Thousand a Year*, 1841. See *to* Fanny, 21 November 1853.

who have admissions to the reading room, and write excellent hands, earn their bread by copying. I paid half a guinea the other day for a copy of what would, I think, make eight or ten octavo pages. I can easily manage the matter for your friend's friend. But in truth any eminent bookseller in London could do the thing as well as I.

Do not imagine that the Scotch trouble themselves about Lord Eglington's fooleries.[1] Not a single man of the smallest consideration at Edinburgh exhibited himself at the meeting. The thing is as much laughed at as his Lordship's tournament.[2]

Hannah and Baba have come back delighted with their visit. I should be glad to get to Brighton. But at present many things detain me here. Love to Selina.

Ever yours
T B Macaulay

TO HENRY HART MILMAN, 12 NOVEMBER 1853

MS: Bodleian Library.

Albany Nov 12. / 1853

My dear Dean,

Thanks to you and Mrs. Milman. On Saturday at ten I shall be delighted to see you here. Be assured that I shall not forget Tuesday.[3]

Yours ever
T B Macaulay

TO LORD MAHON, 15 NOVEMBER 1853

MS: Stanhope Papers, Chevening.

Albany London / November 15. 1853

Dear Mahon,

I am much obliged to you for remembering me when you were enjoying Italy. I shall paste the sketch which you have kindly sent me into Flaxman's fine Volume.

---

[1] Lord Eglinton presided at a meeting in Edinburgh on 2 November of the Association for the Vindication of Scottish Rights, organized to protest against English indifference towards Scotland; his speech appears in *The Times,* 4 November, and is the subject of a leading article on 5 November. For the Association's program, see William Ferguson, *Scotland: 1689 to the Present,* New York, 1968, pp. 320–2.

[2] The famous re-creation of a medieval tournament held at Eglinton Castle in 1839.

[3] TBM was forced to excuse himself from dinner with the Milmans on Tuesday the 15th (see the next letter). At breakfast on Saturday the 18th he entertained Hannah, the Milmans, Dundas, Sir Charles Wood, Hallam, and Sir John Macleod (Journal, VI, 163; 165).

I have been very well till within the last few hours. The coming of the wintry frosts and fogs begins to affect me disagreeably. I am just correcting the last proof sheets of a volume which has given me a great deal of trouble and from which I expect very little credit, but which I have been forced to publish in mere self defence. I shall desire Longman to send it you; but I do not desire you to read it. I have now returned to pursuits which are much more to my taste.

All our friends, I believe, are well. Hallam called yesterday, and was in great force. I shall dine with the Dean of St Paul's if the fog which is at once blinding and choking me will let me venture out.[1]

My kindest regards to Lady Mahon and to my Valentine.

Ever yours truly
T B Macaulay

TO FRANCES MACAULAY, 21 NOVEMBER 1853

MS: Trinity College.

Albany November 21 / 1853

Dearest Fanny,

I have a great longing for Brighton. But I have work to do which can be done only in the neighbourhood of great libraries. I feel too some doubt whether the benefits of your air, which are great, are not more than compensated by some inconveniences inseparable from life at an inn. Here I step at once from my warm sitting room into my snug, well carpeted bedroom. At the Norfolk my sitting room did very well. But I had to go up stairs to my bedroom with the wind blowing on me in all directions; and the bedroom was cold, ill lighted, ill ventilated. You will think that I am becoming a querulous old valetudinarian. But in truth I find that, if I pass my winters in this climate, I must be careful of myself. When I have published the next two volumes of my History, and when the railway communication is completed from Boulogne to the Mediterranean, I shall, I think, become a bird of passage, and get over the cold months at Naples or Palermo. It is now a week since I have drawn an easy breath. Nevertheless my spirits are excellent; and I have very much to enjoy. Love to Selina.

Ever yours,
T B Macaulay

Ten Thousand a year came safe. The author[2] is the very strangest of

---

[1] TBM excused himself on account of the fog (Journal, VI, 163).

[2] Samuel Warren (1807–77: *DNB*) was a barrister on the Northern Circuit and a writer of fiction, legal manuals, lectures, and tracts. He joined the Circuit long after TBM had left it,

human beings, – a man of some cleverness, a liar, a buffoon, as mutable and as little in the habit of suppressing emotions or keeping secrets as a child of three years old.

TO THOMAS FLOWER ELLIS, 21 NOVEMBER 1853

MS: Trinity College.

Albany Nov 21 / 1853

Dear Ellis,

I find that I must keep close prisoner in the evenings for some time. I have not drawn a perfectly easy breath since Monday last;[1] and I attribute my sufferings to my having dined on that day in Westbourne Terrace.

I am anxious to hear what passed between you and Wood.[2] Name any day this week that will perfectly suit you for dining here; and fix your own hour. Friday alone is excepted.

Ever yours
T B Macaulay

Longman is dancing with delight at the scourging which I have administered to Vizetelly.[3] The old story – καὶ κεραμεὺς κεραμεῖ[4]

TO FRANCES MACAULAY, 24 NOVEMBER 1853

MS: Trinity College.

Albany London / Novr. 24. 1853

Dearest Fanny,

I have been dreadfully plagued with cough and difficulty of breathing during the last week. Dr. Bright has now made me better; and I think of going down to Brighton on Saturday for a week. On the following Saturday I must be in town, and on Monday week I must go to Bowood.

Could you get me a comfortable lodging for a week, with accommodation for William? I would bring down wine. Every thing else, I suppose, I ought to find in the house. I should like a sitting room and bed room,

but perhaps TBM knew him through Ellis. Warren had been awarded an honorary degree at Oxford at the same time as TBM; they sat together then at a banquet, when TBM found him 'intolerable' (Journal, vi, 87: 7 June 1853). Warren was especially noted for what Sir Francis Doyle, another Northern Circuit barrister, called his 'foolish and restless vanity' (*Reminiscences and Opinions*, 1886, p. 235).

1 The 14th.
2 Respecting Ellis's appointment to the Commission on the Reform of Judicial Establishments, Judicial Procedure, and Laws of India: see 30 November. Wood was President of the Board of Control.
3 In the preface to his *Speeches*, which TBM finished on the 17th (Journal, vi, 164).
4 'potter [is angry with] potter': Hesiod, *Works and Days*, line 25.

warm and on the first floor. If the sitting room overlooks the sea, so much the better. Money is no object.

If you cannot find such lodgings, try to get me good rooms at the Norfolk or the Bedford. Love to Selina.

> Ever yours
> T B Macaulay

TO THOMAS FLOWER ELLIS, 26 NOVEMBER 1853

MS: Trinity College.

Albany Nov 26. 1853

Dear Ellis,

I have got very good lodgings at 32 Regency Square Brighton.[1] I am much better. I could not go to my sister's yesterday. She and Baba have breakfasted here to day.

I am glad to see that Vizetelly's rule has been discharged.[2] Quick work – a trial on the Wednesday. Motion for new trial and rule *nisi* on the Thursday. Cause shown and rule discharged on the Friday. Bentham could have wished for nothing more.

> Ever yours
> T B Macaulay

I shall be back in town to dinner on Friday. Will you dine here?

TO THOMAS FLOWER ELLIS, 30 NOVEMBER 1853

MS: Trinity College.

32 Regency Square / Brighton / Nov 30. 1853

Dear Ellis,

Pray let me know whether you will dine with me on Friday. Name your own hour.

I am curious to hear the history of your banquet. I see that you are all gazetted.[3]

---

[1] TBM went down to Brighton on this day and returned on 2 December; in the interval he wrote most of his life of Bunyan for the *Encyclopaedia Britannica*.

[2] This refers to a suit brought by William Hazlitt (son of the essayist) against Vizetelly for payment for a translation of a *Life of Louis XVII*. Judgment was given against Vizetelly, whereupon he moved for a new trial. The motion was argued on Thursday, the 24th; Vizetelly abandoned the matter on the next day (*The Times*, 25 and 26 November).

[3] To the Commission on the Laws of India. Ellis's fellow-commissioners were Sir John Romilly, Sir John Jervis, Sir Edward Ryan, C. H. Cameron, J. M. McLeod, J. A. F. Hawkins, and Robert Lowe. The Commission's business was with the many unsettled questions of Indian law reform dating back to the days of TBM's work on the India Law Commission in 1835–7. Sir Charles Wood originally thought of including TBM on it: see R. J. Moore, *Sir Charles Wood's Indian Policy, 1853–66*, Manchester, 1966, pp. 65–71.

A strange blind story this about Sir John Mactaggart.[1] Surely the Counsel never would have mentioned his name at random. All members of parliament whose names begin with Mac have reason to tremble.

Ever yours

T B Macaulay

I have had vile weather, and have scarcely stirred out. But, whether from change of air or from some other cause, I am better than I was in town.

TO UNIDENTIFIED RECIPIENT, 3 DECEMBER 1853

Text: Wilbur C. Abbott, review of *History of England*, III (ed. Firth), in *American Historical Review*, XX (1914–15), 431: dated 3 December 1853.

[London]

I hope that early in 1855, I shall be able to publish two more volumes. I have little hope of being able to tell the story of the Irish wars in such a manner as to satisfy the bigots of any party. But I do not think that I shall be accused by any candid man of injustice towards the defenders of Londonderry.

TO LADY TREVELYAN, 6 DECEMBER 1853

MS: Trinity College.

Bowood[2] / Dec 6. 1853

Dearest Hannah,

When I had got into my seat in the railway train yesterday, and was preparing to read the third number of the Newcomes, I was surprised by the appearance of Mrs. Milman at the carriage door. I supposed of course that she was going down to Bowood. But I soon learned that she had been summoned to the bedside of her eldest son – a clergyman who had been thrown out of a gig and had broken his arm. She was very low; and I felt for her much. However the accident seemed by her account to be as little dangerous as such an accident could be – a simple fracture – and the medical man not alarmed. One of her younger sons was with her. At Faringdon Road they left the train and set off on a journey of nine miles

---

[1] A story in *The Times*, 25 November, reports a quarrel before the police magistrate at Guildhall between two men over a woman who had been the mistress of both. On questioning by the magistrate she admitted that she had formerly lived with Sir John McTaggart, who gave her an allowance of £50 per annum. A letter from the woman in *The Times* for 30 November contradicts the report, saying that the name was misunderstood and was not McTaggart's, only that of an M.P. whose name was like McTaggart's. Sir John McTaggart (1789–1867: *Boase*), first Baronet, was M.P., 1835–57.

[2] TBM left London on the 5th and returned on the 7th.

across the Downs. Here I found a small but pleasant party – the Lewises, Senior, and two very clever artists.[1] My cough plagued me a good deal, and forced me to leave the dinner table for five minutes. It tormented me also a good deal at night. I shall return to town to morrow, though they are most kind and attentive here. The day is dull; and I cannot walk: but I find plenty of amusement within doors.

I had a disagreeable accident. I broke my spectacles, and should have been, as far as books are concerned, a blind man during forty eight hours, had not Senior, who always carries two pair for fear of accidents, been able to supply me with a pair which make me look like an owl, but serve my purpose perfectly.

Lewis has seen the minute on the public offices which was got up by Trevelyan and Northcote,[2] and praises it highly.

Love to all. Lady Theresa talks most kindly about you and my dear Baba.

Ever yours
T B Macaulay

TO LADY THERESA LEWIS, 9 DECEMBER 1853

MS: New York Public Library.

Albany December 9 / 1853

Dear Lady Theresa,

You are very kind to interest yourself about me. I have reason to think that I judged wisely in returning when I did.[3] Yesterday I suffered a good deal: but medical discipline has subdued my cough and restored my rest for the present. If I go any more out of London during the winter, it will be to the southern coast.

Ever yours truly
T B Macaulay

---

[1] Identified in the Journal as 'Philipps and Watts' (VI, 173) – i.e., Henry Wyndham Phillips (1820–68: *DNB*), portrait painter, and George Frederick Watts (1817–1904: *DNB*), the protégé of Lord and Lady Holland and already one of the most successful of Victorian artists.

[2] Sir Stafford Northcote (1818–87: *DNB*), afterwards first Earl of Iddesleigh, Tory statesman, collaborated with Trevelyan on a series of investigations of government departments and on the general report, dated 23 November 1853, that became the basis of the nineteenth-century reforms of the civil service: see 4 March 1854.

[3] Two days earlier, on account of his cough: see the preceding letter.

TO SELINA MACAULAY, 14 DECEMBER 1853

MS: Trinity College. *Envelope:* Miss Macaulay / Temple House / Brighton. *Subscription:* TBM.

Albany London / December 14. 1853

Dearest Selina,

I had a very pleasant day at Bowood; and then I thought it necessary to return to town to nurse myself. I have not stirred out of my rooms during three or four days; and in this way I get on pretty well. I am a very cheerful happy invalid. I work at my history several hours a day. I read much; and I have pleasant visitors. Yesterday Baba and George dined with me. Hannah will dine here to morrow or the day after; and so I shall get through the season of fog and east wind.

Vizetelly is furious, and threatens to bring an action.[1] I heartily wish that he would. William Longman,[2] the wit of the house, says that Vizetelly is not the greatest rogue unhanged; for that he has hanged himself.

As to Respirators, there is something to be said for them and against them. They warm the air which we breathe, no doubt. But they increase the difficulty of inhaling it. On the whole I think it best to stay by my fire till the weather mends.[3]

Kindest love to Fanny.

Ever yours

T B Macaulay

Alice has a little dog, and is out of her wits with delight.

TO LORD LANSDOWNE, 14 DECEMBER 1853

MS: The Marquess of Lansdowne.

Albany London / December 14 / 1853

Dear Lord Lansdowne,

I have just seen Hallam who told me that you were kindly anxious about me. I am not sorry that I left Bowood, though it is worth while to be ill there, merely to experience Lady Shelburne's[4] goodness. An invalid

---

[1] A letter from Vizetelly in the *Athenaeum*, 17 December, concludes by saying of TBM's personal remarks in the preface to the *Speeches* that 'these I shall leave to be dealt with, as advised, by a court of law.'

[2] Longman (1813–77: *DNB*), younger brother of Thomas, had been a partner in the publishing firm since 1839.

[3] TBM later did get a respirator and found it useful. A respirator is a 'device of gauze or wire covering the mouth, or mouth and nose, and serving to warm the inhaled air' (*OED*); it was invented in 1835.

[4] Emily (1819–95), the daughter of Auguste, Comte de Flahault, and the second wife of Lord Shelburne (see *to* Lord Shelburne, 19 December).

is best situated in his own home. I am close prisoner to the fire side, and shall be so till the fog and east wind abate. But I sleep pretty well; I cough little; I work all day; I have my niece or my sister to dinner; and I am a very cheerful valetudinarian.

It will not be long, I hope, before I publish two more volumes of my history. Then I shall think that I have earned my liberty. I shall probably become a bird of passage, and pass my winters on the shore of the Mediterranean. Naples and Palermo will soon be nearer to us than Harrowgate and Scarborough were to our grandfathers. Indeed a medical man told me yesterday that, unless he was mistaken, Malaga would soon be as much an English colony as Boulogne. / Ever, dear Lord Lansdowne,

Yours most truly

T B Macaulay

TO THOMAS FLOWER ELLIS, 15 DECEMBER 1853

MS: Trinity College.

Albany December 15 / 1853

Dear Ellis,

Huzza – Vizetelly threatens an action. I retain you. With you Sir Frederic Thesiger.[1] I never was either plaintiff or defendant yet: and I much enjoy the prospect of having a lawsuit of my own, particularly with so good a case.

I am still, as you may suppose, a prisoner, much better however, and working with great energy and enjoyment. I really begin to think that my next two volumes will succeed. Hannah dines with me to morrow. You, I suppose, will be at Bromley on Saturday and Sunday. Would it suit you to come on Monday? In short name your own day.

Ever yours

T B Macaulay

There is one thing that I enjoy in poor Vizetelly's situation. In his rage, he wishes to run down my speeches. But he dares not, for fear of spoiling the sale of his own edition of them. So he puts forth curses on me and puffs on me mingled in the most ludicrous way possible. Here again he much resembles Curll, who could not vent his spleen against Pope without diminishing the profits of his own piracies.

[1] Thesiger and Ellis had acted together in Achilli v. Newman.

TO LORD MAHON, 19 DECEMBER 1853

MS: Stanhope Papers, Chevening.

Albany December 19. 1853

Dear Mahon,

Thanks for your corrections. The blunder about Lord Hotham[1] was very stupid.

I give you and Lady Mahon joy most sincerely.[2] I hardly know whether I may venture to send congratulations and good wishes to the future Lady Bateman. I hope that there is no danger of such an interruption as prevented the marriage of an ancient Lord Bateman, celebrated in our ballad poetry.[3]

I have suffered a good deal from cough and cold, but am now pretty well. I am working hard and with great enjoyment.

Kindest regards to my Lady and to my Valentine.

Ever yours truly
T B Macaulay

TO LORD SHELBURNE,[4] 19 DECEMBER 1853

MS: The Marquess of Lansdowne.

Albany London / December 19. 1853

My dear Lord Shelburne,

Your kind letter has gratified and affected me much. The obligations under which I lie to your father must necessarily attach me to all his family. But it is not only on his account that I am sincerely interested in your welfare. When I could hardly say that I knew you, I was your friend for his sake. Since I have known you, I have been your friend for your own sake; and it is a great pleasure to me to find that the regard which I have long felt for you is not unreturned. A happy Christmas to you and yours.

Ever yours most truly
T B Macaulay

---

[1] In the headnote to his speech of 1 June 1853 TBM identifies Hotham as M.P. for Kent; Hotham in fact sat for the East Riding. The *Speeches* were published on 7 December.

[2] On the engagement of Lady Mahon's sister Agnes to William Bateman-Hanbury (1826–1901), 2nd Baron Bateman. They were married in May 1854.

[3] 'The Loving Ballad of Lord Bateman': his wedding was interrupted by the Turk's daughter who had freed him from captivity in return for a promise of marriage.

[4] Henry Thomas Petty-Fitzmaurice (1816–66: *DNB*), second and surviving son of Lord Lansdowne, whom he succeeded as fourth Marquess. Shelburne was M.P. for Calne, 1837–56, and Foreign Under-Secretary, 1856–8.

TO ADAM BLACK, 19 DECEMBER 1853

MS: Trinity College.

Albany London / December 19. 1853

My dear Sir,

I send you Bunyan[1] by this day's post. I am afraid that the M.S. may now and then puzzle the printers. But I will set all right when I get the proofs. I rather like the paper, though I say it who should not say it.

Ever yours truly

T B Macaulay

TO CHRISTIAN BERNHARD TAUCHNITZ, 23 DECEMBER 1853

Text: Bernhard Tauchnitz, 1837–1887, p. 109.

Albany, London, Decbr. 23, 1853.

I do not doubt that it[2] will be useful to me; and I shall value it on your account.

TO SELINA MACAULAY, 24 DECEMBER 1853

MS: Trinity College.

Albany Dec 24 / 1853

Dearest Selina,

I inclose a cheque.

I have been during the last fortnight almost a close prisoner to my room, but working very cheerfully, and, I think, not unsuccessfully. To day I go, with all precautions, to our Christmas dinner at Westbourne Terrace. All the heads there have been turned by a little Mexican spaniel which seems to be quite as much an object of attention as a baby could be. Alice is droll beyond description. Love to Fanny.

Yours ever

T B Macaulay

[1] The life of Bunyan for the *Encyclopaedia Britannica*, begun at Brighton (see 26 November); according to TBM's Journal, he finished it 'or nearly so' on 2 December (VI, 170). It was published in volume 5 of the eighth edition of the *Encyclopaedia* on 29 April 1854.
[2] According to the note in the Tauchnitz *Festschrift*, this was a copy of Camill von Behr's *Genealogie der Europäischen Fürstenhäuser*, Leipzig, 1854.

THE HISTORY OF ENGLAND, PART II
JANUARY 1854–29 DECEMBER 1855

1854 March
Appointed chairman of Committee on Indian Civil Service
– April 13–17
Easter tour: York, Castle Howard, Durham
– May 17
Elected president of the Edinburgh Philosophical Institution
– June
Further crisis in health
– July 5–September 30
At Thames Ditton
– September 7–18
French tour with Ellis: Bourges, Orléans, Tours, Paris: examines French War Office records
– September 30–October 6
Reading MSS at All Souls, Oxford
– December 27
Report on Indian Civil Service published
1855 January–November
Concentrated work on finishing *History*, volumes 3 and 4: ceases to keep Journal, reduces correspondence, rarely ventures out during winter
– June 28–September 29
At Richmond
– August 27
Finishes life of Goldsmith for *Encyclopaedia Britannica*
– November 21
Finishes proofs of *History*, volumes 3 and 4
– December 17
History, volumes 3 and 4, published: first edition of 25,000 copies

TO ADAM BLACK, [EARLY JANUARY? 1854]

Text: Scotsman, 28 January 1854.

Albany

My Dear Sir,

In the main I cordially agree with your resolutions; and I can have no scruple about avowing my opinion.[1]

To whom shall I address my letter on the subject?

Ever yours truly,
T. B. Macaulay.

Adam Black, Esq.

TO FRANCES MACAULAY, 10 JANUARY 1854

MS: Trinity College.

Albany London / January 10. 1854

Dearest Fanny,

I inclose a letter from a man of whom, I think, I have heard a very bad report from you or Selina. How is that? If he was a decent person, I should willingly send him a trifle.

I am well, but it is on condition of my keeping my room, and having great fires blazing. On Sunday, which was a delicious day, I hoped that my imprisonment was over. But yesterday the cold weather came back; and the wind is now N N E. There are splendid festivities in Westbourne Terrace to night: but I cannot go to them.

Love to Selina.

Ever yours,
T B Macaulay

TO FRANCES MACAULAY, 17 JANUARY 1854

MS: Trinity College. *Extract published:* Trevelyan, II, 368.

Albany London / January 17. 1854

Dearest Fanny,

I am amused by Lord Shaftesbury's discomfiture.[2] I hate Puseyites and Puritans impartially; and I think that they are never so well employed as in worrying one another.

---

[1] A meeting in favor of national education was about to be held at Edinburgh (originally scheduled for the 12th, it was postponed to the 25th). The resolutions, published in the *Scotsman,* 25 January, are all directed to the support of non-sectarian education and urge the passage of a comprehensive bill.

[2] I cannot explain this reference.

The yelping against Prince Albert[1] is a mere way of filling up the time till Parliament meets. If he has sense and fortitude to despise it, the whole will blow over and be forgotten. I do not believe that he has done anything unconstitutional; and I am sure that those who are loudest in bawling know neither what he has done nor what is unconstitutional. I hear that the ministers have with difficulty dissuaded him and the Queen from insisting that the Attorney General should file an information against the Morning Advertiser.[2] It would have been a most unwise step. What is any man the worse for all that is written against him? I am sure I have reason to say this.

I am pretty well, with care; and I write several hours every day. I am now upon the establishment of the Presbyterian Church in Scotland;[3] and I have found much that is new and interesting to me, and that will probably be so to other people.

So Inglis retires.[4] I have sent him a handsome letter.

Ever yours,
T B Macaulay

Love to Selina.

TO THOMAS FLOWER ELLIS, 17 JANUARY 1854

MS: Trinity College.

Albany January 17. 1854

Dear Ellis,

Dine here on Thursday, Friday, or Saturday, at your choice.

I hear that the Chancellor[5] was forced to leave his Court the other day and to hasten to Windsor, and that he spent some hours there in dissuading the Queen and Prince Albert from insisting that the Attorney General should file a criminal information against the Morning Advertiser. What a foolish step it would have been.

I inclose a letter from a girl in her teens, a charming one, I am sure.[6]

---

[1] In the excitement before the declaration of war against Russia the Prince was the subject of wild rumors, based on the suspicion of him as a foreigner. He was accused of unconstitutional interference in domestic and foreign affairs, and it was both said and believed that he had been sent to the Tower for high treason. TBM's prophecy was exactly fulfilled.

[2] The *Advertiser*, under the slogan of 'England for the English,' was particularly virulent against Albert; on 9 January, e.g., it asserted (without naming him) that he had made English policy subservient to Russian aims, had contrived Palmerston's dismissal, and had nearly provoked war with France.

[3] *History*, III, ch. 16.

[4] Inglis's resignation is reported in *The Times* of 16 January.

[5] Lord Cranworth.

[6] 'A queer letter from a Yankee Girl – in her teens, she says – enough to turn a young man's head' (Journal, VIII, 3–4: 17 January).

Pray bring it me when you come next. For I must answer it: and I have not yet shown it to my ladies.

Ever yours

T B Macaulay

TO ADAM BLACK, 20 JANUARY 1854

MS: National Library of Scotland. *Mostly published:* [Black], *Biographies by Lord Macaulay,* pp. xlviii–xlix.

Albany London / January 20. 1854

My dear Sir,

To whom ought I to write on the subject of education?[1]

What I should be inclined to say would be that I thought to this effect. I have always thought it the duty of the State to provide education for the people of every religious persuasion. My wish would be to see a national system of secular education established, and to leave the religious education of the young to their own parents and pastors. The state of public feeling in England has hitherto made such an arrangement impossible. Many persons whom we should have thought our natural allies are violently opposed to all state education. Of those who are friendly to state education a majority will not hear of a purely secular education. In England therefore the system of Privy Council grants, imperfect as it is, is the best that unfortunate circumstances permit us to adopt. But if the public feeling of Scotland be in favour of a system free from all sectarianism, I should be delighted to see such a system established, and should hope that the success of such a system on one side of the Tweed would remove the prejudices which now exist on the other.[2] These are my views. I am sorry that the Scotsman, – an excellent paper as any in the Kingdom, – blames Lord John for having taken the only course which the unreasonableness both of Churchmen and of Dissenters left open to him.[3]

I had heard about the Glasgow dispute: but I am afraid that I can do nothing in the matter.

Thanks for the letter and papers from Chile. They have interested me much. I will soon write to your son.[4]

[1] See [Early January? 1854]. Black presumably told TBM to write to Lord Panmure, who presided at the meeting of the 25th; it was stated then that Panmure expected a full communication from TBM on the matter of national education (*Scotsman,* 28 January).

[2] A Scottish Education Bill, proposing to raise the stipends of teachers, to remove religious tests, and to make religious instruction voluntary, was introduced on 12 February; it was defeated on its second reading, 12 May, 'to the disgrace of the House, but to the relief, I suspect, of the ministers' (Journal, VIII, 56).

[3] The *Scotsman* supported 'national' education – i.e., education free of all ties to religious denominations – and opposed the government scheme as a 'Presbyterian plan.'

[4] See *to* Charles Black, 6 November 1852.

379

My correspondent at Florence is Mr. Stuart Montgomery.[1] His address is

Casa Orfei: Borg'Agni Santo

The next favour that I ask of Lord Canning[2] shall be for Mr. Law's protégé.

Very truly yours,
T B Macaulay

TO FRANCES MACAULAY, 6 FEBRUARY 1854

MS: Trinity College.

Albany London / February 6. 1854

Dearest Fanny,

I have had an anxious fortnight.[3] But now thank God – things look well. Hannah is getting better and better daily. Baba is still safe. We were alarmed about her yesterday. But to day she appears to be well again.

I have had other causes of distress which would have been serious at another time. Hallam has had a touch of paralysis. And, though it has not affected his speech or his faculties, and will probably yield to medical treatment, such a shock at his age is a grave matter. I am afraid that his friends can hardly hope to enjoy his society as they have hitherto done. I have seen him, poor fellow, and was greatly affected. I shall try to see him again to day.

Public affairs seem to me to be going on well. There is no opposition to speak of; and I am not without hopes that the peace of Europe will be preserved. The cry against Prince Albert has gone down as fast as it rose, and will be forgotten in a week. Love to Selina.

Ever yours,
T B Macaulay

---

[1] Not Stuart Montgomery but James Montgomery Stuart (1816–89), resident in Italy since 1841, an attaché of the British legation in Florence, and later, for many years, the Italian correspondent of the *Morning Post*. His 'Mornings with Macaulay' in *Reminiscences and Essays,* 1884, gives an authentic record of TBM's conversation.

[2] Charles John Canning (1812–62: *DNB*), second Viscount Canning and afterwards first Earl Canning and Governor-General of India, was Postmaster-General in Aberdeen's ministry.

[3] TBM learned on 29 January that Hannah had scarlet fever: 'Baba too exposed. I was quite overset – could eat nothing – could do nothing but weep for half an hour' (Journal, VIII, 7). Margaret's death in 1834 was from scarlet fever.

TO THOMAS FLOWER ELLIS, 13 FEBRUARY 1854

MS: Trinity College.

Albany February 13 / 1854

Dear Ellis,

I shall be delighted to see you on Saturday at *seven,* unless I hear that you wish the hour to be later. I will dine with you on the 21st if I can. This East wind keeps me a prisoner. I was forced to excuse myself to Lord Lansdowne yesterday; and I am forced to stay away from the House of Commons to night. I see that it is meant to put the Reform Bill off *sine die,*[1] and that the only question is how the retreat may be most gracefully made. A very different day this from the 1st of March 1831 when the old Reform Bill was brought in by the same man.

I am glad that your knee is going on well.[2] All is right at Westbourne Terrace. Baba has not had the rash, and will therefore be out of Quarantine before her Mamma. Hannah writes that she looks at present like the new Court of Baliol College.[3] Do you remember the appearance of that stone. If you do not, the young ladies will.

Ever yours,
T B Macaulay

TO FRANCES MACAULAY, 15 FEBRUARY 1854

MS: Trinity College.

Albany London / February 15. 1854

Dearest Fanny,

I send off to day a parcel containing dear little Alice's books. Let me hear whether you get it safe.

Hannah and Baba have got wonderfully well through their malady, Baba especially. I am impatient to see them. They are in trouble about Mrs. Trevelyan.[4] The good old lady is ill; and Trevelyan has been summoned down to Enmore. Of course at her age every attack is alarming.[5]

---

1 The Reform Bill introduced by Lord John Russell on this day fell a victim to the approaching war and never reached its second reading.
2 Ellis was troubled with rheumatism.
3 Designed by Anthony Salvin and erected in 1852–3.
4 TBM received news of her death later on this day (Journal, VIII, 17).
5 The top third of the second leaf has been cut away; probably only the closing and signature are missing.

TO FRANCES MACAULAY, 17 FEBRUARY 1854

MS: Trinity College.

Albany February 17 / 1854

Dearest Fanny,

I find my weekly bills very high of late; and my servants have asked for an addition to their board wages while the present prices last.[1] It has occurred to me that you and Selina may be a little pinched in your house-keeping. I therefore send you a cheque[2] which will, I hope, cover the difference in the cost of living. Next harvest will set everything to rights if the weather should be as propitious as it has been hitherto.

I have seen Baba this morning. She has been a good deal pulled down; and her grandmother's death has affected her much. But I have so much to be thankful for that I will not complain. A week of sea air will, I trust, set both her and her Mamma to rights. Poor Trevelyan looks very ill with sorrow, watching and [. . . .][3]

TO THOMAS FLOWER ELLIS, 20 [FEBRUARY][4] 1854

MS: Trinity College.

Albany Saturday 20 / 1854

Dear Ellis,

I feel that I cannot prudently venture out in the evening at present. So I must deny myself the pleasure of dining with you to morrow.

Come and dine here on your first open day – Wednesday, Thursday Friday or Saturday.[5]

Lady Trevelyan and Margaret are gone to Brighton.

Have you read Victor Hugo's eloquence.[6] I wonder whether English

---

[1] 'I have added half a guinea a week among the three. More than they asked' (Journal, VIII, 13: 4 February).

[2] For £20 (Journal, VIII, 17).

[3] The bottom half of the second leaf has been cut away for the signature.

[4] The letter is clearly dated 'Albany Saturday 20 / 1854', but the only Saturday 20 in 1854 is in May, when TBM was freely moving about London, when he had no engagement with Ellis on the 21st, and when Hannah and Margaret were not in Brighton. The likeliest explanation is that 'Saturday' is TBM's error for Monday, 20 February. Hannah and Margaret had gone to Brighton on that day, and on the next day TBM was, according to his Journal, unable to keep a dinner appointment with Ellis (VIII, 18; 19). The reference to Victor Hugo also fits the 20th.

[5] Ellis dined with TBM on Thursday, 23 February (Journal, VIII, 21).

[6] A very long and very rhetorical letter addressed to Lord Palmerston appears in *The Times* of this day; it protests about an execution just carried out on the isle of Guernsey, describes it in grisly detail, and hints that Palmerston allowed it to take place in deference to the wishes of Napoleon III.

fine writing reads to a Frenchman as Victor's does to me. To me he seems a greater ass than Carlyle.

Ever yours
T B Macaulay

TO SELINA MACAULAY, 21 FEBRUARY 1854

MS: Trinity College. *Envelope:* Miss Macaulay / Temple House / Brighton. *Subscription:* T B M.

Albany London / February 21. 1854

Dearest Selina,

I was much interested by your letter. No doubt, the dear little child[1] requires care and skilful management. Her organization is wonderfully delicate and her sensibility and imagination dangerously quick. I will say nothing to Hannah till she is quite well; and that, I hope, will be soon. I am curious to hear how your quarantine regulations are framed. Do you nod to each other from opposite sides of the street? Do you stand on the cliff and talk to her and Baba on the beach? I shall go down in a week or so, and shall hope to find all restrictions removed. I must write to Alice, so that I will only send my love to Fanny.

Ever yours
T B Macaulay

TO FRANCES MACAULAY, 25 FEBRUARY 1854

MS: Trinity College.

Albany London / February 25. 1854

Dearest Fanny,

Do not be uneasy about me. I hold the danger of infection very cheap; and have already run more risk than there can now be. For I repeatedly saw Baba in almost every stage of her complaint.

I do not wish to make you anxious about Alice. I shall therefore go to Temple House before I go to Bedford Square,[2] and not visit you after I have been in the region of contagion.

Could you get me rooms at the Norfolk or the Bedford for one night. I shall dine there late. I expect to be down by the train which leaves town at 12 on Tuesday. You know what sort of rooms I want. There must be a

---

[1] Alice Trevelyan.
[2] Where Hannah and Margaret were staying. TBM went down to Brighton on the 28th, stayed at the Norfolk Hotel, and returned on 1 March (Journal, VIII, 23–4).

fireplace in the bedchamber. Prospect on this occasion will be of little consequence, as I shall hardly be at my inn except when it is dark. If the rooms opened into one another *tant mieux.*
William will go with me.
Love to Selina and Alice.

Ever yours,
T B Macaulay

TO ÉMILE DE BONNECHOSE,[1] 26 FEBRUARY 1854

MS: The Carl H. Pforzheimer Library.

Albany February 26 / Sunday – 1854
Sir,
Any gentleman whom M. Guizot esteems must be most welcome to me. I am extremely sorry that the shortness of your stay and my own engagements make it impossible for me to have the pleasure of presenting to you some persons whom, I am sure, you would be glad to meet. I am forced to leave London on Tuesday morning for the purpose of visiting a sick relation. But to morrow I shall be at home till two o'clock in the afternoon, and shall be most happy to see you. / I have the honor to be, / Sir
Your faithful Servant,
T B Macaulay
I am truly grateful to you for your valuable present. I have no doubt, from what M. Guizot tells me, that I shall be both instructed and interested by your volumes.

TO WILLIAM WHEWELL, 27 FEBRUARY 1854

MS: Trinity College. *Extract published:* D. A. Winstanley, *Early Victorian Cambridge,* 1940, p. 397.

Albany London / February 27. 1854
Dear Whewell,
Goulburn showed me your Letter to the Vice Chancellor[2] some days

---

[1] Bonnechose (1801–75) was a French Protestant historian. TBM received him on the 27th: 'He had sent me his book – Les Quatre conquêtes. I liked it much. We talked together for an hour or so in French' (Journal, VIII, 23). The book referred to is *Les Quatre Conquêtes d'Angleterre,* 2 vols., Paris, 1851. Later TBM received the first two volumes of Bonnechose's *Histoire d'Angleterre,* Paris, 1858–9, from which he discovered that 'He has merit – and particularly the merit of being very civil to me' (Journal, XI, 225–6: 9 December 1857). Bonnechose calls him 'observateur érudit, penseur spirituel et grand artiste' (*Histoire d'Angleterre,* I, xvi).

[2] Thomas Charles Geldart (1797?–1877: *Boase*), Master of Trinity Hall, 1852–77, and Vice-Chancellor, 1853–4.

ago. I think it quite satisfactory on all the points to which it refers. There are other points, not raised by Lord Palmerston's communication,[1] about which I have a very strong feeling, so strong a feeling that, if my health were better, I should probably take the sense of the House of Commons upon them. I have the greatest possible objection to the rule which requires the fellows of our college to take orders.[2] It is a rule of which the tendency is to drive good scholars out of the University and to give bad priests to the Church. Porson is ejected and forced to live on the charity of the merchants of London; and great parishes are committed to the care of – I will not mention names. You will remember two reverend gentlemen who were high in college office when I was an undergraduate. One of them never opened his mouth without an oath; and the other had killed his man.[3] This is not, I know, one of the questions at issue: but I am strongly tempted to raise an issue upon it when we go into Committee.

Ever yours truly
T B Macaulay

TO THOMAS FLOWER ELLIS, 27 FEBRUARY 1854

MS: Trinity College.

Albany Feb 27. 1854

Dear Ellis,

I shall be only twenty four hours at Brighton.

I return Walter's lines. They are of very great promise indeed. I th nk nothing of the inaccuracies of so young a scholar. What he does not know he has ample time to learn. But what cannot be learned he seems to me to have got. The Vālentine is certainly unlucky.

Ever yours,
T B Macaulay

---

1 Palmerston had sent a letter to Prince Albert, Chancellor of the University, on 12 December 1853 setting forth the ministry's 'essential points' of University reform and asking for the University's response to the program proposed. The Vice-Chancellor had then asked the various colleges to reply to the points in Palmerston's letter to assist the University in preparing its answer (Winstanley, *Early Victorian Cambridge*, pp. 274–7). Trinity's – that is, Whewell's – letter of reply is dated 10 January (Mrs Stair Douglas, *Life of Whewell*, 1881, pp. 386–7).

2 Whewell was opposed to lay fellowships; they were not established at Trinity until 1861.

3 By the second of these two reverend gentlemen TBM may mean William Clark (1788–1869: *DNB*), made a Fellow of Trinity in 1809, ordained in 1818, and Professor of Anatomy in the University from 1817. Clark killed George Payne in a duel on Wimbledon Common, 6 September 1810. Clark was not in fact 'high in college office,' but he otherwise fits the case (information from Dr R. Robson, of Trinity).

TO SIR EDWARD BULWER-LYTTON, 1 MARCH 1854

MS: Hertfordshire County Council. *Partly published:* Lytton, *The Life of Edward Bulwer, First Lord Lytton,* II, 198.

Albany March 1 / 1854

Dear Sir Edward,

When your note was left here yesterday, I was at Brighton. I have but just returned.

Your invitation is very tempting: but I dare not venture as yet into the evening air. I have excused myself to the Speaker whose requests are commands, and above whom, in such matters, there is nobody but the Queen. For pleasure I would much rather go to you than either to the Queen or the Speaker.

Thanks for the Addresses.[1] I have already read them with much interest and admiration. I really do not think that my judgment is corrupted by your praises,[2] when I say that I have seen no compositions of the sort that have pleased me so much. My constituents were delighted, as I hear from all quarters, and no wonder.

Ever yours truly
T B Macaulay

TO THOMAS FLOWER ELLIS, 4 MARCH 1854

MS: Trinity College. *Partly published:* Trevelyan, II, 357–8.

Albany London / March 4. 1854

Dear Ellis,

I went to Brighton on Tuesday and came back on Wednesday. I had a most happy day. Hannah and Baba are still weak, but getting well fast; and we cried a little and laughed a great deal, walked a little, and drove about a great deal. On my return I found on my table, among other things, the inclosed precious little volume.[3] Whether the theological or

[1] Bulwer-Lytton spoke on classical education to the Associated Societies of the University of Edinburgh on 18 January, and described his career as a writer at a public dinner in Edinburgh on the 20th. Both speeches were published.

[2] In the address of 18 January Bulwer-Lytton speaks of 'the great orator and author, whose luminous genius, whose scholastic attainments, whose independence of spirit, whose integrity of life, so worthily represent not only the capital, but the character of the people who claim their countryman by descent in Macaulay' (p. 5).

[3] Two pamphlets in French by 'a mad German named Lipke' who had 'discovered that money is only a commodity like other commodities' (Journal, VIII, 36: 28 March). The pamphlets in question are Wilhelm Lipke, 'Notion de la Monnaie,' Paris, 1853, and 'Lettre sur la Notion de la Monnaie,' Berlin, 1854. On the 27th TBM received a letter from Lipke, 'the most important part of which was that he threatened to murder all the Bunsens, except *une bonne brin de fille*' (Journal, 28 March).

the philosophical part be superior I am in doubt. The manner in which the Book of Joshua and Strabo are reconciled is great, – the rule for squaring the circle still greater. Why do you not win his thousand pounds?

I am afraid that Trevelyan's plans about the civil service[1] will be frustrated by the opposition which strong interests and strong prejudices are raising up in all quarters. The pear, as I always told him, is not yet ripe.

In the meantime there is one good appointment made. Gladstone has named my brother Charles Secretary to the Board of Audit. The place is worth 1000£ a year, and Charles gets away from the Board of Health, from Chadwick,[2] who is a knave, and from Lord Shaftesbury who is one of the tools that knaves do work with. All my brothers and brothers in law are now comfortably quartered on the public, and I alone remain without a halfpenny of the Queen's money.

We have given up our plan of going to France at Easter. We may probably go to York and Durham. Apropos, I wish that you would learn what is the best inn at Durham

ὅθι

κορεις ὀλιγιστοι[3]

as Aristophanes has it. When I was there last, now twenty one years ago,[4] the accommodation was detestable; but there has probably been a great change there as elsewhere.

Glorious news! Robert Montgomery writes to Longman that there is a point at which human patience must give way.[5] Since the resignation and Xtian fortitude of a quarter of a century have made no impression on the hard heart and darkened conscience of Mr. Macaulay, our injured poet

---

[1] Embodied in the so-called Northcote-Trevelyan report (see 6 December 1853) 'On the Organisation of the Permanent Civil Service,' submitted to Parliament on 24 February (*Parliamentary Papers*, 1854, XXVII). The Report, whose main recommendation was for competitive examination, is a key document in the history of civil service reform, though the government did not bring in a bill on the plan this year, and though its proposals were enacted only slowly and piecemeal. Trevelyan himself was energetically and indiscreetly active in propagandizing for reform.

[2] Chadwick, 'with his incessant attacks upon the vested interests in the way of sanitary reform, made himself and the board as unpopular as the poor-law commissioners' (Sir Llewellyn Woodward, *The Age of Reform, 1815–70*, 2nd edn, 1962, p. 464).

[3] 'Where there are the fewest bedbugs' (*The Frogs*, 114–15).

[4] When TBM and Hannah were on their way to Edinburgh in September 1833: see *to* Zachary Macaulay, 26 August 1833.

[5] Probably the point was reached on the publication of the 'People's Edition' of TBM's *Essays*, issued in seven parts beginning in February 1854. A new edition of the three-volume *Essays*, the seventh, had also appeared in January. On 24 February Longman had called on TBM with 'a letter from the wretched Robert Montgomery, begging hard to be taken out of the pillory. Never, with my consent. He is the meanest as well as the silliest scribbler of my time, and that his books sell among a certain class is a reason for keeping my protest on record' (Journal, VIII, 21).

must appeal to the laws of his country, which will doubtless give him a redress the more signal because he has been so slow to ask for it. I retain you. Consider yourself as feed. You shall chuse your own junior, I shall put nobody over your head in this cause. Will he apply for a criminal information? Imagine Jack[1] – "I have *thee graitest* respect for the very eminent poet who makes this application and for the very eminent critic against whom it is made. It must be very satisfactory to Mr. Montgomery to have had an opportunity of denying on oath the charge that he writes nonsense. But it is not the practice of this Court to grant criminal informations against libels which have been a quarter of a century before the world."

I do not see why we might not meet at Oxford about the 27th of March.[2] Let me know your arrangements.

> Ever yours,
> T B Macaulay

TO RICHARD MONCKTON MILNES, 6 MARCH 1854

MS: Trinity College.

Albany March 6 / 1854

Dear Milnes,

I shall be most happy to breakfast with you on Thursday.[3]

> Ever yours,
> T B Macaulay

TO UNIDENTIFIED RECIPIENT, 11 MARCH 1854

MS: Mr W. Hugh Peal.

Albany London / March 11. 1854

Sir,

I am sorry that I can be of no use to you. I have no connexion with any newspaper. I know the editor of the Edinburgh Review; but, as it is not in my power to give him any assistance, I feel a delicacy about asking anything of him.

There is at present no international treaty about copyright between England and the United States; nor do I much expect that there will be

---

1 Trevelyan's note reads: 'It is to be feared that this unceremonious reference is to no less a personage than Lord Campbell' (*Life*, II, 357).
2 This trip was not made.
3 'To breakfast with Milnes. Stupid – I knew nobody but Lowe and the Lord Advocate' (Journal, VIII, 27: 9 March).

such a treaty.[1] Some of my friends however are more sanguine than myself. / I have the honor to be, / Sir,

Your faithful Servant
T B Macaulay

TO SIR CHARLES WOOD, 17 MARCH 1854

MS: The Earl of Halifax.

Albany March 17 / 1854
Dear Wood,
I readily acquiesce in what you propose about Melville.[2]

As to instructions, – it seems to me that you had better not limit us.[3] Refer the Act to us; and request us to suggest what we think the best mode of carrying it into execution.

I called at the Treasury to day to consult Trevelyan. He told me that he had been turning the subject over in his mind during some days, and had come exactly to the same conclusion with me.

Of course if there be any limitation which you wish to impose on us, you will impose it. But I do not think that any is necessary.

Ever yours truly
T B Macaulay
Right Honorable Sir C Wood
etc. etc. etc.

TO THOMAS FLOWER ELLIS, 18 MARCH 1854

MS: Trinity College. *Partly published:* Trevelyan, II, 369–70.

Albany London / March 18. 1854
Dear Ellis,
Thanks for the information which you sent me. It agrees with what I

---

[1] An international copyright treaty was submitted to the United States Senate in February, but no such treaty was approved until 1891.

[2] The Reverend Henry Melvill (1798–1871: *DNB*), Principal of Haileybury College from 1843 until its closing in 1857; he was a member of the Committee on the Indian Civil Service (see next note).

[3] Wood had just appointed a Committee, consisting of TBM as chairman, Lord Ashburton, Benjamin Jowett, John Shaw Lefevre, and Henry Melvill, to consider means for effecting the provision in the new India Charter Act for appointing civil servants through competitive examination. Its instructions were just what TBM suggests here. The Committee's report, dated November and published in *The Times*, 27 December, and in *Parliamentary Papers*, 1854–5, XL, 112–20, was written by TBM in July of this year and adopted in January 1855. This was TBM's last piece of official writing.

have obtained from Ingham.[1] I rather think that we shall take up our quarters at York, and run to Durham and back in the course of the same day.[2] This will be the best way of escaping the Dean's[3] hospitality. For I should not chuse to plague him with our whole party – George and Baba included; and I do not wish to leave them during our short trip.

George by the bye has been confined some time to his room with a sprain, and has at last been sent home. His sister is nursing him: for his Mamma has been forced to go down into Somersetshire to divide the inheritance which good old Mrs. Trevelyan has left.

What do you think of the Oxford scheme?[4] I should like to talk it fully over with you before I pronounce positively; and, as far as I can, I will keep my thoughts to myself for the present. But I own that I think it mischievous in the highest degree. There are good parts. But the general effect, I am convinced, will be bad. I may vote for the second reading, but, unless great changes are made, certainly not for the third.

Poor Talfourd![5] I wish to God that you were to succeed him. The seat has been offered to Thesiger and refused.

I am pretty well – have dined out once,[6] and shall dine out again next week.[7] I went to the House on Monday, but, for any pleasure I got, might as well have staid away. I heard Bright say everything that I thought, and I heard Palmerston and Graham expose themselves lamentably.[8] Palmerston's want of temper, judgment and good breeding was almost incredible. He did himself more harm in three minutes than all his enemies and

---

[1] Perhaps (Sir) James Taylor Ingham (1805–90: *DNB*), London magistrate, who was a veteran of the Northern Circuit and might have advised TBM about lodgings in Durham (see 4 March).

[2] This is the plan they followed: they left for York on the 13th, made side trips to Castle Howard on the 14th and to Durham on the 15th, spent Easter Sunday, the 16th, in York, and returned to London the next day (Journal, VIII, 44–7).

[3] George Waddington (1793–1869: *DNB*), a Fellow of Trinity, Dean of Durham, 1840–69.

[4] The Oxford University Bill, introduced on 17 March, proposed a number of reforms, including a reorganization of the Hebdomadal Board, extension of the University, the institution of competitive examination for fellowships, and the establishment of a Statutory Commission. The Bill, much modified, passed both Houses and received the royal assent on 7 August. It began the major reforms of nineteenth-century Oxford.

[5] He died suddenly on 13 March.

[6] At Vernon Smith's, 15 March (Journal, VIII, 30).

[7] At Sir Charles Wood's, 23 March (Journal, VIII, 33).

[8] Three ministers – Palmerston, Graham, and Molesworth – had gotten into trouble by talking lightly of the impending war in speeches at a farewell dinner given at the Reform Club on 7 March to Admiral Sir Charles Napier, about to sail in command of the Baltic fleet. On 13 March Bright attacked them in the House of Commons for their indiscretion. TBM attended the debate and found 'Bright disagreeable but in the right and powerful. Palmerston lost his temper and good manners and disgusted me, and, I dare say, others. Graham was rather shabby[?] on the other hand. Molesworth, who indeed had less to excuse, was spirited and said nothing improper' (Journal, VIII, 29).

detractors throughout the world have been able to do him in twenty years. I came home quite dispirited.

> Ever yours
> T B Macaulay

TO THOMAS FLOWER ELLIS, 22 MARCH 1854

MS: Trinity College.

Albany London / March 22. 1854

Dear Ellis,

I quite agree with you about the fellowships.[1] I have spoken both to Lord Lansdowne and to Gladstone[2] on the subject; and I am to see Gladstone again. If I could get the bill set to rights quietly, I should be very glad. If not, as Sancho says, the deaf shall hear me.[3] Do not commit me. For I keep my opinion to myself, except when I see any of the Ministers.

I was at the levee to day, not having paid my Court these two years, and having been forced to let my court dress out two inches. The Queen and Prince most graciously hoped that I was better.

Poor George's accident is very disagreeable.[4] He must pass at least a month on the sofa. I have furnished him with Lucian and Quintus Curtius, that he may not lose his time. His Mamma is still in Somerset-shire dividing old Mrs. Trevelyan's hoards of shawls, plate and jewels. But it is quite charming to see how his sisters nurse him. They are never tired of reading to him, talking to him, playing chess with him, running on errands for him; and he is as grateful as can be. They are a wonderfully happy family. I never once, during the last three years, heard a word that was not affectionate uttered by any one of the three to any other. It is worth a boy's while to be laid up a few weeks, if the effect is to strengthen such a tie.

I hear Crowder's[5] name mentioned. But I doubt whether Grey's influence be now great enough to make a Judge. I wish to God that mine were.

Macleod tells me that the Indian Law Commission has come to a hitch,

---

[1] TBM objected to the provision in the Oxford University Bill that would normally require fellows to reside at Oxford. On 27 March TBM dined at Buckingham Palace, where, in company with Archbishop Musgrave, he argued to Lord John Russell against 'the abominable clause about the residence of Fellows' (Journal, VIII, 35).

[2] Gladstone, then M.P. for Oxford University, was responsible for framing the University Bill.

[3] *Don Quixote,* Part 2, ch. 3.

[4] He had sprained an ankle.

[5] (Sir) Richard Burden Crowder (1795–1859: *DNB*) succeeded Talfourd as a judge in the Court of Common Pleas.

and will be forced to apply to the Board of Control for directions. Your colleagues miss you much, I imagine.

Your ladies, I suppose, are at Bromley. If you return, as you propose on Tuesday, dine here on Wednesday.

Ever yours
T B Macaulay

TO SELINA MACAULAY, 24 MARCH 1854

MS: Trinity College.

Albany London / March 24. 1854

Dearest Selina,

I inclose a cheque. I hope that the weather suits you better than it does me. I have, in spite of the N E wind, ventured to dine out twice, and I am *not* the worse for it.

There is no end to our troubles. As soon as Hannah and Baba get well, George must hurt his foot, and lay himself up for a month or more. Nothing can be kinder than the way in which his sisters nurse him, or more grateful and affectionate than he is. I hope and believe that he will be able to go with us at Easter, when we count on Fanny's company.

Of course you have congratulated our brother Charles on his good fortune. Nothing could be kinder than the way in which Gladstone spoke to me about the appointment at the levee on Wednesday. I told him that I would not thank him, for that I was certain that he had acted from a sense of public duty. He said "Thank you for not thanking me. I really did act as you say. But it was most gratifying to me that the fittest man was a brother of yours."

Love to Fanny.

Ever yours,
T B Macaulay

TO [J. F. MACFARLAN], 13 APRIL 1854

MS: Berg Collection, New York Public Library.

Albany April 13 / 1854

My dear Sir,

I hope and believe that we shall get rid of the objectionable parts of Mr. Crawford's Bill.[1]

---

[1] A bill introduced by E. H. J. Craufurd, M.P. for Ayr, to enable the execution of the judgments of any court in the United Kingdom in any part of the United Kingdom; it passed its second reading unopposed on 28 March but was referred to a select committee and was not heard of again in this session. At its meeting of 4 April the Edinburgh Chamber of Commerce, of which Macfarlan was secretary, resolved to protest about that part of the bill extending the jurisdiction of English courts to Scotland (*Scotsman*, 5 April).

As to the other matter mentioned in your letter I entertain very great doubts.[1] Is not every bill that is brought into the House of Commons now sent to the Lord Advocate and to every Scotch member? What more can be necessary to prevent a surprise? And was there ever such a surprise? You say that, in this case, a surprise was attempted. Be it so. But the attempt did not succeed. You charge the contrivers of the scheme with very discreditable disingenuousness. But, surely, the more disingenuous their conduct was, the more clear it is that we have at present abundant securities against disingenuousness. For with all their cunning they have gained nothing at all. We have had ample time to prepare to meet them in Committee. I am therefore at a loss to conceive on what grounds you ask for new safeguards, when the old safeguards have just been found perfectly sufficient to prevent even an artful and unscrupulous enemy from stealing a march upon us.

I am however quite willing to attend to anything that you may wish to represent on this or any subject.

Ever yours truly
T B Macaulay

TO [J.F. MACFARLAN], 17 APRIL 1854

MS: Berg Collection, New York Public Library.

Albany London / April 17. 1854

My dear Sir,

I asked you to give me some instance in which an enactment injurious to Scotland had been carried by a surprise. You give me instances in which enactments injurious to Scotland, after going through some stages by surprise, were detected, opposed, and thrown out. That is just what I say. The present machinery of legislation has, by your own showing, been found sufficient to prevent the evil which you apprehend. Are we then to alter our whole system of legislation from top to bottom in order to provide against a chimerical danger? You demand nothing less than a total revolution in the whole procedure of both Houses. You say that a bill relating to Scotland ought to be referred to certain Scottish functionaries for a report before it is entertained; and you say also that a bill which, on the face of it, has no relation to Scotland, may contain some clause which may directly or indirectly affect Scotland. Every bill therefore, without distinction, must be referred to certain Scotch functionaries for a report. The Irish of course will not be content with less. And thus we

---

[1] The same meeting agreed 'to petition Parliament to hand over all English bills containing provisions relating to Scotland to the law officers of this country for their inspection' (*ibid.*).

shall have, on an average, a month added to the time now necessary for the passing of a bill. Legislation is difficult enough now. You would make it impossible; and all this from fear of an evil which has never happened, and which is every day less and less likely to happen.

I tell you my first thoughts just as they rise in my mind. If I am wrong I am quite willing to be set right.

Very truly yours

T B Macaulay

TO THOMAS FLOWER ELLIS, 18 APRIL 1854

MS: Trinity College.

Albany April 18. / 1854

Dear Ellis,

I have come back from a trip[1] which would have been very pleasant, if the East Wind had not affected my respiration cruelly.

I have no engagement this week. Dine here to morrow, or on Thursday, or on Friday.[2] Gladstone has written to tell me that they have determined to modify the Oxford Bill so as to meet our views.

Ever yours,

T B Macaulay

TO THOMAS FLOWER ELLIS, 21 APRIL 1854

MS: Trinity College.

Albany April 21. 1854

Dear Ellis,

I send you Bristed's book.[3] I am plagued with tooth ache which is not very severe unless I eat or speak, but which is roused into most cruel activity by any attempt to masticate or to articulate. I breakfasted on nothing but coffee, and an egg which I with great difficulty managed to

---

[1] The Easter trip to York and Durham; TBM had returned to London on the day before.
[2] Ellis came on Thursday, when they had 'the first asparagus' (Journal, VIII, 48: 20 April).
[3] Charles Astor Bristed, *Five Years in an English University*, 1852; Ellis's copy of the book, which was inherited by G. M. Trevelyan from his father, is now at Trinity. Bristed (1820–74), a grandson of John Jacob Astor, after graduating from Yale went on to Trinity College, Cambridge, and took a degree there in 1845, the year before Frank Ellis. Bristed intruded himself into a breakfast party that TBM gave on 19 June 1850, when TBM described him as a 'raffish Yankee,' 'ill bred and impertinent.... It was all that I could do to be civil. Though educated here at Cambridge he had the vilest nasal twang and all the manners of a thorough Jonathan' (Journal, II, 345–6).

swallow. But I mean to dine on turtle soup, which will, I hope, suffice for the support of nature. I feel the firmest confidence in this sign that abundance of rain is coming.

The lines which you had forgotten in Denham's masterpiece are
"Rolled up in wanton swine's feet
The Devil might have crep into thee."[1]
I follow the poet's own orthography.

Ever yours
T B Macaulay

TO JOHN HILL BURTON, 21 APRIL 1854

MS: National Library of Scotland.

Albany April 21 / 1854

My dear Sir,

To whatever immunities I may pretend as M.P. for Edinburgh, I do not at all wish to be left out when you have any occasion for the services of your friends.[2] Just let me know who is the person to whom application should be made.

Ever yours
T B Macaulay

TO THOMAS FLOWER ELLIS, 24 APRIL 1854

MS: Trinity College.

Albany April 24. 1854

Dear Ellis,

I am sorry that I was not at home when you called. I was running about to find somebody to present Mrs. Adolphus[3] to the Queen on Thursday next. A pretty errand! Lady Trevelyan undertakes the office more graciously than I expected: for she does not much admire her god daughter. "I will do anything for a friend of yours. But I wish it had been Marian instead." This answer I have had to translate into the florid complimentary style. By the bye, I know of no more fertile cause of quarrels among old friends, than this matter of presentations. Men who are intimate have

---

[1] Misquoted from Sir John Denham's 'News from Colchester, or, a Proper New Ballad of Certain Carnal Passages Betwixt a Quaker and a Colt,' stanza 6.

[2] Burton was applying for the post as Secretary of the Prison Board that he succeeded in obtaining later this year: see 7 July.

[3] Adolphus married Clara, daughter of Rowland Richardson, of Streatham, Surrey, in 1822. I suppose that calling her Hannah's 'god daughter' is TBM's joke for Hannah's standing sponsor for Mrs Adolphus at court.

wives who are in perfectly different sets. A lady who affects the highest breeding does not care to see her name coupled in all the newspapers with that of a vulgar woman who never pronounced an H in the right place. Then the husbands are drawn into the feud. I remember several instances.

I have been living three days on things which can be swallowed with little or no use of the teeth, soups, sweetbreads, asparagus, jelly, etc. I am now again equal to solids. I am engaged to dinner to day and to morrow. Any other day in the week I shall be delighted if you will dine here. What do you do on the fast day?[1] Do you go to Bromley? If not let us mingle our tears for our poor country.

Ever yours

T B Macaulay

Let me know in time, For whatever is to be eaten on Wednesday must be laid in on Tuesday.

TO JOHN LEYCESTER ADOLPHUS, 24 APRIL 1854

MS: Swarthmore College.

Albany April 24. 1854

Dear Adolphus,

Lady Trevelyan is delighted to have an opportunity of being of any use to Mrs. Adolphus, and is sorry only that she has made such arrangements as prevent her from offering to take Mrs. Adolphus to the Palace. This however matters little. It is not necessary that the lady who presents and the lady who is presented should make their appearance together.

Ever yours truly

T B Macaulay

TO THOMAS FLOWER ELLIS, 25 APRIL 1854

MS: Trinity College.

April 25. 1854

Dear Ellis,

I will fast with you to morrow.

Lady T. is perfectly aware of the probability of her being outshone by Mrs. A.

Ever yours

T B Macaulay

---

[1] A day of 'Solemn Fast, Humiliation, and Prayer' proclaimed by the Queen for 26 April, on the declaration of war against Russia. TBM attended St Anne's church that day, heard the special prayer written for the observance, and then dined at Ellis's house (Journal, VIII, 50).

TO LORD PALMERSTON, 26 APRIL 1854

MS: Osborn Collection, Yale University.

Albany April 26. 1854

Dear Lord Palmerston,

Dr. Robert Renton,[1] one of the most valued of my friends at Edinburgh, is now here, deputed by the College of Physicians of that City to press on you the expediency of bringing in a bill for the regulation of the Medical Profession.[2] He much wishes to see you. I know how much your time is occupied at the present moment. But if you could allow him a quarter of an hour, you would gratify him and the respectable body which he represents. His views as to the general principles on which this question ought to be settled seem to me perfectly correct. As to details there is of course room for improvement. But his plan, if adop[ted][3] just as it stands, would, in my opinion, be highly beneficial. / Ever, my dear Lord Palmerston

Yours very truly
T B Macaulay

The / Viscount Palmerston / M.P. / etc. etc. etc.

TO SIR RODERICK MURCHISON, 28 APRIL 1854

MS: British Museum.

Albany April 28. 1854

Dear Sir Roderic,

Is the lady to whom you did me the honor to introduce me the other day Lady Malcolm, or Mrs. Malcolm?[4]

Ever yours truly
T B Macaulay

---

1 Renton (1794?–1884: *Boase*), educated at Edinburgh, had been in practice there since 1814.
2 A medical bill to regulate the licensing of doctors had already been introduced in this session but died on 10 May, when Palmerston opposed it, as did the Scottish medical profession. A medical act did not pass until 1858.
3 Letter torn.
4 TBM dined with Murchison on the 25th, when the company included a 'Mrs. Malcolm. I remembered her as Miss Georgiana Vernon in 1828 – a handsome girl then – a handsome woman still' (Journal, VIII, 50). Georgiana (1807–86: *Boase*), sixteenth and youngest child of Edward Vernon, Archbishop of York, married Major (afterwards General) George Alexander Malcolm in 1845.

TO BISHOP SAMUEL WILBERFORCE, 29 APRIL 1854

MS: Bodleian Library.

Albany April 29 / 1854

Dear Bishop of Oxford,

I shall be most happy to breakfast with you on Tuesday.[1]

Ever yours truly,

T B Macaulay

The / Bishop of Oxford / etc. etc. etc.

TO FRANCES MACAULAY, I MAY 1854

MS: Trinity College.

Albany May 1. 1854

Dearest Fanny,

I return the Spiritual Play Bill. It is an old acquaintance of mine. I know well the shop in Queen Street at which it was published. It was there that I got the Spiritual Railway Guide and the Spiritual Banker's Directory.[2]

The speech of Mr. Pitt about which you inquire must have been that in which he explained the reasons of his retirement in March 1801.[3] But I rather think that Mr. Thornton's[4] account of the debate is not quite accurate. That Pitt spoke with admirable art and propriety I do not doubt at all. I have heard our Uncle Babington mention that speech as a wonderful instance of skill in handling very ticklish matters.

Love to Selina. The drawing room[5] went off excellently.

Ever yours,

T B Macaulay

---

[1] On the morning of that day, 2 May, TBM felt ill, excused himself from the breakfast, and sent for the doctor, who told him that 'the liver is in fault and gave me strong doses of calomel' (Journal, VIII, 52).

[2] I cannot find any record of these publications. Lord Carlisle reports hearing TBM quote 'several strange couplets from some professed religious poetry; one instance was

"The ticket Faith a first-class seat to gain;
Thy works will follow in a luggage-train"'

(*Journal,* p. 247: 8 May 1857). Perhaps the lines were from 'The Spiritual Railway Guide'?

[3] 25 March 1801.

[4] Probably the elder Henry Thornton, the close friend of Pitt and M.P. for Southwark in Pitt's time.

[5] At which not only Mrs Adolphus but also Margaret Trevelyan were presented.

TO SIR GEORGE GREY, 15 MAY 1854

MS: Osborn Collection, Yale University.

Albany May 15. 1854

My dear Grey,

Many thanks. I shall soon pay a visit to the State Paper Office; and then the list which you have been so kind as to send will be of great use to me. Some of the papers are in print: I have seen manuscript copies of others. The initials J.M., which have puzzled the people at the State Paper Office, are, beyond all doubt, those of Sir James Mackintosh.

Ever yours truly

T B Macaulay

TO HENRY BOWIE,[1] 18 MAY 1854

Text: Scotsman, 20 May 1854.

Albany, May 18, 1854.

Dear Sir,

I beg you to inform the members of the Philosophical Institution that I accept, with pride and gratitude, the honourable office to which I have been elected.[2]

With sincere thanks for the manner in which you have communicated to me the result of the election, I request you to believe me, dear Sir, ever yours faithfully,

T. B. Macaulay.

TO EDWARD MATTHEW WARD, 27 MAY 1854

MS: Trinity College. *Published:* James Dafforne, *Life and Works of Edward Matthew Ward R.A.,* p. 39.

Albany May 27 / 1854

My dear Sir,

Lord Mahon must have misunderstood me. I am at present too busy to spare a single hour for a sitting;[3] and I am likely to be very fully occupied during some weeks.

---

[1] Bowie was secretary of the Edinburgh Philosophical Institution.
[2] TBM was elected on 17 May to succeed Professor Wilson as president of the Philosophical Institution; this, he wrote, was done 'in spite of my excuses' (Journal, VIII, 59: 18 May).
[3] Perhaps Ward wanted a further sitting for the portrait he had done a year earlier: see *to* Ward, 12 August 1851, note.

I congratulate you on the success of your picture of Argyle.[1] I hear no dissentient voices.

Very truly yours

T B Macaulay

TO EDWARD EVERETT, 30 MAY 1854

MS: Massachusetts Historical Society. *Extract published: New York Ledger,* 25 February 1860.

Albany London / May 30. 1854

My dear Everett,

Your letter has given me much pleasure, and yet has made me very sad. I never imagined that you had forgotten or neglected me. I well know that the intermission of correspondence does not at all imply any intermission of friendly feeling.[2]

I have nothing to complain of. My health is indeed not good. But I suffer no pain; and, though my pleasures are fewer than they were, I retain the great sources of happiness. My mind is as clear and my affections as warm as ever. Nothing can exceed the tenderness of those who are nearest and dearest to me. On the whole I find life quite as pleasant, now that I am confined, during many months every year, to my room, as when I was in the vigour of youth.

My book goes on. I hope in a few months to bring out two more volumes. I have not promised myself a great success. I know that the world punishes no offence so severely as that of having been overpraised; and, as my first two volumes were extravagantly overrated, I fully expect that my next two volumes will be underrated.

I say nothing of my parliamentary duties. In truth I never go down to the House except in a case of life and death. The late hours and the bad air would kill me in a week, if I attended as I used to do seven years ago. Why then, you will ask, continue to be a member? Solely because the people of Edinburgh wish me to do so. They think that they used me unjustly in 1847. They elected me, in my absence, without a farthing of expense, in 1852; and they now treat me with a delicacy and an indulgence hardly to

---

[1] 'The Last Sleep of Argyll,' painted for the House of Commons and based on TBM's description of the scene in the *History*: see *to* Ward, 12 August 1851, note. The picture was at the Royal Academy, where TBM saw it and thought it 'very good' (Journal, VIII, 51: 29 April).

[2] Everett's letter was in reply to TBM's letter of 9 December 1850, three and a half years earlier. TBM wrote that Everett's belated response 'brought tears into my eyes' (Journal, VIII, 62: 30 May). Everett, as senator from Massachusetts, had acted weakly in the struggle over the Kansas-Nebraska Bill earlier in the year, had suffered much personal abuse, and had lost whatever chance he had had of the presidency.

be expected from gentlemen, and perfectly astonishing in a constituent body composed of six thousand ten pound householders.

In spite of the melancholy close of your letter, I will continue to cherish the hope that we shall meet here again. Till then let us occasionally, as you propose, exchange a few lines. God bless you.

Ever your affectionate

T B Macaulay

TO COLONEL WILLIAM MURE, 1 JUNE 1854

MS: National Library of Scotland.

Albany June 1. 1854

My dear Sir,

I have just received your valuable present.[1] Pray accept my best thanks. The volumes, I see at a glance, will afford me abundance both of information and of amusement.

Ever yours truly,

T B Macaulay

TO THOMAS FLOWER ELLIS, 13 JUNE 1854

MS: Trinity College.

Albany June 13. 1854

Dear Ellis,

This execrable weather – not June – but alternately March and April – does not suit me. I am at present suffering under calomel, and must cut the Club. When will you dine here? I shall not dine out this week.

I am anxious to know how you acted about the matter which perplexed us on Saturday. The more I think about it, the more awkward it seems to me. For it must – constituted as your office is, – be known to some very bitter enemies of the Government; and I expect every day to see a Screamer, as the Yankees call it, in the Herald.[2]

Ever yours,

T B Macaulay

---

[1] Probably the two volumes of *Selections from the Family Papers Preserved at Caldwell, 1496–1853*, published by Mure through the Maitland Club in 1854; they are item 639 in the sale catalogue of TBM's library.

[2] I do not know what business TBM is talking about; possibly it is something to do with Ellis's work on the Commission on the Laws of India.

TO FRANCES MACAULAY, 14 JUNE 1854

MS: Trinity College.

Albany June 14 / 1854

Dearest Fanny,

I never saw Mr. Philip's book.[1] But I do not see why, on the grounds which you mention, we should give up the belief that the Pilgrim's Progress was begun, – and that is all that I have said[2] – in Bedford Gaol. If the Pilgrim's Progress was published in 1676, it does not follow that it was begun in that year or even two years before. Bunyan says that he spent only "vacant seasons" on it, and that, when at last it was finished, he did not print it without much hesitation, and long consultation with numerous friends. We may therefore I think reconcile the date given by Mr. Philip with the tradition which is certainly very ancient.

It is almost incredible to me that the Pilgrim's Progress should have sprung out of the Strait Gate.[3] There is much more affinity between the Pilgrim's Progress and the Holy City[4] which was certainly written in prison.

However, after all, the question is of no real importance.

Ever yours

T B Macaulay

Love to Selina and your host and hostess. I am truly glad to have so good an account of George.[5]

TO RICHARD MONCKTON MILNES, 19 JUNE 1854

MS: Trinity College.

Albany June 19 / 1854

Dear Milnes,

I am truly vexed to find that I must stay at home to day under medical discipline.

Ever yours truly

T B Macaulay

Will you breakfast here next Monday?[6]

---

[1] Robert Philip, *The Life, Times, and Characteristics of John Bunyan,* 1839. The chapter on 'Bunyan's Bibliography' (the work of an unnamed 'literary friend,' Philip says, p. 565) conjectures that *Pilgrim's Progress* followed *The Strait Gate* and was published in 1677. The date accepted now is 1678.

[2] In his life of Bunyan for the *Encyclopaedia Britannica* TBM says that the publication date of *Pilgrim's Progress* is unknown but that the book was begun before Bunyan left prison.

[3] 1676.   [4] 1665.   [5] Babington.

[6] The party that day were Milnes, Goulburn, Mahon, Milman, Bishop Wilberforce, and a Mr Payot or Fayot (?) (Journal, VIII, 74: 26 June).

TO THOMAS FLOWER ELLIS, 20 JUNE 1854

MS: Trinity College.

Albany June 20 / 1854

Dear Ellis,

You must allow me to retract as to Friday. I have been forced to send for Bright to day;[1] and he is of opinion that I ought for some days to eat only of very simple dishes. It would therefore be impossible for me to do justice to your great artist at the University Club.

I shall, I think, soon retire to Kingston,[2] where I can be near both London and the Trevelyans.

Ever yours,
T B Macaulay

TO SELINA MACAULAY, 24 JUNE 1854

MS: Trinity College.

Albany London / June 24. 1854

Dearest Selina,

I inclose a cheque. I am delighted to hear that you are going to pay a visit at Esher. I have taken a small hermitage about two miles from them, and hope to remove thither in ten days.[3]

Ever yours,
T B Macaulay

---

[1] TBM describes himself in his Journal for this day as 'Miserable. . . . Weak as a child, could hardly walk without holding the table' (VIII, 72). Later in the week he wrote that 'I feel that the fund of life is nearly spent' (VIII, 74: 26 June), a feeling that had grown upon him in the last two months. Several passages in the Journal for this period express the sense that death is very near, and, sometimes, the hope that it will not delay.

[2] See the next letter.

[3] To be near the Trevelyans, who were spending the summer at Esher, TBM took a house called Greenwood Lodge at Thames Ditton. He went there on 5 July and remained until 30 September, though making frequent trips to London and, in early September, a tour of France (Journal, VIII, 74–128).

TO PAOLO EMILIANI-GIUDICI,[1] 24 JUNE 1854

Text: Facsimile in *L'Autographe,* Number 45 (1865), 374. *Envelope:* À Monsieur / M. Paolo Emilio Giudici / Florence. *Subscription:* T B Macaulay.

Albany London / June 24. 1854

Sir,

I beg you to accept my thanks for your valuable present,[2] and for the very kind letter which accompanied it. I have read great part of your appendix with much interest and pleasure. I can easily conceive how much such documents as you have collected must delight a Florentine. I have always had a great love for your city, a city second only to Athens in the history of arts and letters.

I am most sensible of the obligations under which I lie to you; and I rejoice to learn that your translation has been successful. I fear that my two next volumes will hardly interest foreigners as much as the two which have already appeared; and I am quite sure that you will be more usefully employed in original composition than in acting as my interpreter.

I shall accept most gratefully the dedication with which you propose to honor me. Before many months have elapsed, I hope to have the pleasure of making acquaintance with you at Florence.[3] / I have the honor to be, / Sir,

Your faithful Servant
T B Macaulay

TO THOMAS FLOWER ELLIS, 26 JUNE 1854

MS: Trinity College.

Albany June 26 / 1854

Dear Ellis,

I shall be delighted to see you on Friday.

I am impatient to be in the country. I hope to migrate on Wednesday

---

[1] Emiliani-Giudici (1812–72), literary critic and historian, published a translation of the first two volumes of TBM's *History,* Florence, 1852–3. His own major work was a *Storia della Letteratura Italiana,* 2 vols., Florence, 1855, dedicated to TBM in these terms: 'all'uomo onorando, all'inclito storico, in argomento di riverenza pel suo carattere, e di ammirazione pel suo ingegno, intitolo la Storia della Letteratura Italiana' (see W. T. Bandy, 'Macaulay and His Italian Translator: Paolo Emiliani-Giudici,' *Italica,* xxv (1948), 129–30).

[2] According to TBM's Journal, 'Savanarola's process and a Life of Beccaria – not much in it – by Villari' (VIII, 74); the title is *Le Opere di Cesare Beccaria, Precedute da un Discorso sulla Vita e le Opere dell' Autore di Pasquale Villari,* Florence, 1854.

[3] TBM did not revisit Florence.

week. As a pièce de résistance, I mean to carry Photius[1] down. How I shall manage with him I do not know. For I have neither a Latin version nor a single note.

> Ever yours
> T B Macaulay

TO LORD MAHON, 27 JUNE 1854

MS: Stanhope Papers, Chevening.

Albany June 27 / 1854

Dear Mahon,

I send back the book in which I have written a few words which, I hope, your amiable child will read in the twentieth century.

Many thanks for your Volume.[2] I give you joy on having come so successfully to the close of so arduous and valuable a work.

I will with the greatest pleasure breakfast in Grosvenor Place next Tuesday.[3] On Wednesday morning I hope to leave town.

> Ever yours truly
> T B Macaulay

TO CHRISTIAN BERNHARD TAUCHNITZ, 1 JULY 1854

Text: Bernhard Tauchnitz, 1837–1887, p. 109.

Albany, London, July 1, 1854.

I have had every reason to be satisfied[4] . . . and shall be very willing to treat with you for the next two volumes of my history. As far as I can judge, I shall publish before next Easter.

---

[1] At TBM's breakfast party on this day 'Milman recommended me to read Photius' (Journal, VIII, 74). TBM's copy, ed. Bekker, 2 vols. in 1, Berlin, 1824–5, is item 940 in the sale catalogue of his library. According to Trevelyan, 'the rumour that he read Photius for pleasure was current in the Athenæum Club, and was never mentioned without awe' (II, 385n).

[2] The seventh – and last – volume of Mahon's *History of England from the Peace of Utrecht to the Peace of Versailles* was published in this week.

[3] The company that day were Lady Evelyn Stanhope, Lady Crewe, and Van de Weyer (Journal, VIII, 78: 4 July).

[4] TBM received £50 from Tauchnitz on 29 June (Journal, VIII, 76).

TO THOMAS FLOWER ELLIS, 6 JULY 1854

MS: Trinity College. *Extracts published:* Trevelyan, II, 378.

Greenwood Lodge / Thames Ditton / July 6. 1854

Dear Ellis,

Here I am in a pleasant small dwelling, surrounded by geraniums and roses – the house so clean that you might eat off the floor. The only complaint which I have to make is that the view from my front windows is blocked by a railway embankment at the distance of a hundred yards.[1] By way of compensation I have numerous stations near me. The Trevelyans have a very pleasant place only a mile and a half off. I passed yesterday afternoon there most pleasantly and happily. To day I have been working four or five hours on our report about the civil service,[2] and am rather fagged. I shall take my first walk, and, when I return, shall sit down to my history.

I have taken my walk down to the Thames, and have seen Hampton Court and the woods of Bushy on the other bank. There are pleasant boats in abundance, and I shall often cross when I am less busy and the weather is less Aprilish than to day. The Trevelyans have a key of Claremont,[3] which however they do not use at present, because the Ex Queen of the French is there. When she is gone that beautiful pleasure ground will be open to us. I have not seen it since 1818; but I then thought it the loveliest of all gardens; and I still retain a most vivid recollection of the avenue of cedars and of the walk along the little lake.[4]

Let me know when you expect to be in town. I purpose to go thither twice a week, to examine books and M.S.S. I can bring you out with me some day.

I am cruelly embarrassed about Hallam. He writes me letters – poor fellow! – which I cannot decipher and do not know how to answer. I could just make out that his last was an invitation to his house in Kent, or rather to Cator's house.[5] I think that I will write to Cator or his wife on

---

[1] Trevelyan, in his Macaulayesque vein, says that TBM's house, where he 'settled himself, with infinite content,' was 'exactly in the middle of the only ugly square mile of country which can be found in that delightful neighbourhood' (II, 378). TBM took the house without seeing it (Journal, VIII, 73).

[2] The task of writing the report of the Committee on the Indian Civil Service had been assigned to TBM on 1 July; he began it the next day (Journal, VIII, 76–7).

[3] Built by Lord Clive, it had been granted to Louis Philippe and his family in 1848; his widow continued to live there.

[4] TBM went to Claremont on 11 August and again recalled his visit in the summer of 1818: 'I remember as if it were yesterday the place and my thoughts, and the castles in the air that I was building' (Journal, VIII, 96).

[5] (Sir) John Farnaby Cator (1816–99: *Boase*), first Baronet, who later took the name of Lennard, married Hallam's daughter and only surviving child, Julia, in 1852; they lived

the subject. Will you give me their address; and tell me whether Cator is now a Colonel or only a captain?

Ever yours
T B Macaulay

TO JOHN HILL BURTON, 7 JULY 1854

MS: National Library of Scotland.

Greenwood Lodge / Thames Ditton / July 7. 1854

My dear Sir,

I am truly glad that you have succeeded;[1] and I do not doubt that, in pressing your claims on the government, I did a service to the public. There was, however, very little for me to do. The Lord Advocate,[2] at the very first word, admitted your claims, and would, I dare say, have used his influence in your favour, even if I had never mentioned your name.

I have been forced to leave town for the country where I breathe rather more freely than in smoke and river fog.

Ever yours truly
T B Macaulay

TO BISHOP SAMUEL WILBERFORCE, 7 JULY 1854

MS: Trinity College.

Greenwood Lodge / Thames Ditton / July 7. 1854

My dear Bishop of Oxford,

My address will sufficiently explain why I cannot have the pleasure of breakfasting with you on Tuesday. I am smelling hay, listening to birds, and eating my own green peas and currants.

Ever yours truly
T B Macaulay

at Wickham Court, Beckenham, Kent. Cator had been Lieutenant-Colonel of the Kent Militia since 1853.

[1] See *to* Burton, 21 April. Burton was appointed Secretary to the General Board of Directors of Prisons in Scotland, a post that, according to the *DNB*, gave him 'pecuniary independence'; the appointment was gazetted on 24 July.

[2] James Moncrieff.

TO DAVID STEVENSON,¹ 10 JULY 1854

Text: Scotsman, 15 July 1854.

Greenwood Lodge, July 10, 1854.

Sir,

I was absent from the division² which you mention, because my health did not suffer me to venture out late.

I am most sensible of the indulgence which has been shown to me by my constituents; and I assure you that I would instantly vacate my seat if I thought that they generally wished me to do so.

But it would be disingenuous in me not to add that if I had been able to attend the House, I should certainly have voted, and probably have spoken, in favour of the grant to the Roman Catholic chaplains of jails, and against Mr Spooner's motion concerning Maynooth.³

It is impossible for me to believe, on your authority, that all the Protestant electors of Edinburgh are surprised and indignant because I did not vote against the Government on these points. The Protestant electors of Edinburgh, when they did me the high honour to elect me to represent them, knew well what my conduct had been in times of great religious excitement, and yet they did not think it necessary to require from me any assurance that I should act in a manner different from that in which I had always acted.

The young men in whose name you write are, I presume, too young to remember the passing of the Maynooth Bill for 1845. If they will take the trouble to inform themselves as to my votes and speeches on that occasion, they will not, I believe, think it necessary to ask me for any further explanation. – I have the honour to be, Sir, your most obedient servant,

T. B. Macaulay.

¹ Stevenson is identified by the *Scotsman* as Secretary of the Edinburgh Young Men's Protestant Society. He had written to ask TBM why he was absent from the House 'when the vote was taken on the important question of paying Popish chaplains in Great Britain. The Committee desire me to add, that this request is made from a conviction that some explanation is necessary to remove that strong feeling of dissatisfaction which is entertained on the subject by all the true Protestant electors of Edinburgh.' TBM calls this 'a most absurd and impudent letter from some foolish boys' (Journal, VIII, 80: 9 July).

² 12 June, when a motion by Richard Spooner, M.P. for North Warwickshire and perennial opponent of Maynooth, against the provision in the Estimates for £550 to pay Catholic chaplains in the prisons, was passed (*Hansard,* 3rd Series, CXXXIII, 1395–1422).

³ 3 July; Spooner unsuccessfully moved to withdraw the Maynooth grant from the Consolidated Fund in order to subject it again to annual revision in Parliament (*Hansard,* 3rd Series, CXXXIV, 1041–53).

TO THOMAS FLOWER ELLIS, 11 JULY 1854

MS: Trinity College. *Partly published:* Trevelyan, II, 380.

Greenwood Lodge / Thames Ditton / July 11. 1854

Dear Ellis,

I have been working four or five days at my report on the Indian Civil Service, and have at last finished it. It is much longer than I anticipated that it would be, and has given me great trouble. I am just going to send it to John Lefevre, who will convey it to a private press of which the government has the command.

On the 22nd I am to be in town for the purpose of considering the report in company with my colleagues. Let me know whether, if I can get to the Temple on that day, I shall be likely to find you there.

To morrow I go vigorously to work on my history. I have been so busy here with my report that I have read nothing but comedies of Goldoni and novels of Eugene Sue.[1]

The weather is very strange; sometimes gloriously fine; then nothing but clouds, rain and storm. On two successive days I have been ready to drop with the heat of the sun at three in the afternoon, and have been forced, at eight in the evening, to have a roaring fire. I walked yesterday to Hampton Court along the Middlesex bank of the Thames, and lounged among the avenues and flower beds about an hour. I wonder that no poet has thought of writing a descriptive poem on the Thames. Particular spots have been celebrated. But surely there is no finer subject of the sort than the whole course of the river from Oxford downward, – the noble University, – Clifden, – Windsor, – Chertsey, the retreat of Cowley, – St Anne's Hill, the retreat of Fox, – Hampton Court with all the recollections of Wolsey, Cromwell, William and Mary, Belinda's hair, the Cartoons, the Beauties; – then Strawberry Hill – then Twickenham and Pope's grotto – then Richmond, – and so on to the great City, – the forest of masts, – the Tower, – Greenwich Hospital, – Tilbury fort and the Armada. Is there any river in the world which, in so short a space, affords such subjects for poetry? Not the Tiber, I am sure, nor the Seine.

Do you know the river between Hampton Court and Richmond? If not we will make a voyage down, look at the ruins of poor Strawberry Hill, and at Pope's house and grotto, and dine at the Star and Garter. As to dining at the University Club, that would make it necessary for me to

---

[1] TBM began *Le Veau d'Or* on 5 July; between the 7th and the 11th he read Goldoni's *Le Smanie per la Villeggiatura* – 'long a favourite play of mine' – *Le Avventure della Villeggiatura*, and *Il Giocatore* (Journal, VIII, 79–81).

sleep in town, which I would gladly avoid. However we will discuss that matter when we meet.

Ever yours,

T B Macaulay

TO LORD MAHON, 13 JULY 1854

MS: Stanhope Papers, Chevening.

Greenwood Lodge / Thames Ditton / July 13. 1854

My dear Mahon,

Thanks for your letter. Miss Seward was a very great fool; and perhaps you construe her meaning rightly. If so, I admit that she leaves the case exactly where it stood.[1]

I do not think her volumes tiresome. They are amusing from their very badness. The most absurd of the Femmes Savantes of Moliere was a miracle of good sense and good taste compared to her. I do not think that you have, as I have, a very keen relish for very absurd books. They please me just as it pleases me to see Justice Shallow or Sir Andrew Ague Cheek on the stage. I could better spare many very well written volumes than Miss Seward's Life of Darwin[2] or Charles Phillips's Memoirs of Curran.[3] One half of the charm of Boswell's works is their absurdity. So is one half of the charm of Bishop Newton's Life of himself.[4] There is a delightful book of the same sort – the Autobiography of Percival Stockdale.[5] But I shall never have done if I try to make a catalogue of the books which I value for their faults. I am afraid that I have this taste pretty much to myself.

Ever yours,

T B Macaulay

---

[1] The question was of Washington's part in the execution of Major André; TBM told Mahon that Miss Seward had printed a letter from Washington on this subject that vindicated his conduct. Mahon had run the letter down through what he found the 'tiresome' volumes of her *Letters* but concluded that she left the matter where she found it (Mahon to TBM, 11 July: copy, Chevening). In the recently-published final volume of his *History of England* Mahon had blamed Washington for condemning André: 'certainly by far the greatest, and perhaps the only blot in his most noble career' (*History of England*, VII, end of ch. 62).

[2] *Memoirs of the Life of Dr. Darwin*, 1804.

[3] *Recollections of Curran and Some of His Contemporaries*, 1818.

[4] See *to* Frances Macaulay, 17 March 1853.

[5] *Memoirs*, 2 vols., 1809; TBM's annotated copy is in the library at Wallington.

TO THOMAS FLOWER ELLIS, 14 JULY 1854

MS: Trinity College.

Greenwood Lodge / Thames Ditton / July 14. 1854

Dear Ellis,

I send you the draft of my report on the Civil Service, and shall be glad to have your opinion and suggestions. It is, as you will see, not in a finished state; and my colleagues may alter it, though Lefevre, who is the only person that has as yet seen it, approves of the whole. I wish you, therefore, to let no human being see it in its present form.

I am very happy here, in tolerable health, within a mile and a half of Hannah and her children, writing, reading, walking, or chatting, from eight in the morning till half after ten at night. The weather is not exactly what I could wish. Yet I have had beautiful half days.

Ever yours,

T B Macaulay

TO GEORGE MILNER STEPHEN,[1] 17 JULY 1854

MS: Mitchell Library, Sydney. *Envelope:* G M Stephen Esq / 29 Western Villas / Blomfield Road / London. *Subscription:* TBM.

Mr. Macaulay presents his compliments to Mr. Stephen, and will be at home next Friday from twelve to three, if it should suit Mr. Stephen to call at that time.

Greenwood Lodge / July 17. 1854

TO LORD MURRAY,[2] 21 JULY 18[54][3]

Text: Sotheby's Catalogue, 31 May 1912, item 87, 3½ pp. 8vo: dated Thames Ditton, 21 July 1835.

For vagrant children, as far as I have seen anything of them, have no more religion than cats or dogs. Their parents too have generally abdicated all parental functions; and when this is the case, I do not see why the State, being *in loco parentis*, may not teach its own religion.[4]

---

[1] Stephen (1812–94), Australian barrister and politician, and a cousin of Sir James Stephen, was in England promoting the British Australian Gold Mining Co. He later became a spiritualist and faith healer of great notoriety.

[2] Sir John Archibald Murray (1779–1859: *DNB*), sat in the House of Commons for Leith, 1832–9, and was a Judge of the Scottish Court of Session as Lord Murray from 1839; he was one of the original contributors to the *ER*.

[3] The date of 1835 in the catalogue which is the source of the text is obviously wrong; 1854 alone is possible.

[4] This letter is listed again in C. A. Kyrle Fletcher, Catalogue 233, 1971, item 186, where it is dated 1837. The summary given there says that the letter is written regarding Mr Dunlop's

TO THOMAS FLOWER ELLIS, 26 JULY 1854

MS: Trinity College.

Greenwood Lodge / Thames Ditton / July 26. 1854

Dear Ellis,

On Saturday morning I go into town. At one I must be at Lefevre's. As soon as I have despatched my business there I will go to the Temple. We might start either by the four o'clock train, or by the train which sets out at ten minutes after five. The run will in either case be only of twenty five minutes. I have ordered a tub, rough ice, and other necessaries of life to be provided for you.[1]

Have you seen Mrs. Stowe's absurd book.[2] Every body abuses it except Alice who is so much delighted at being called in print a charming young lady[3] that she runs about the house to show the book to the housekeeper and the ladies' maids.

We shall, I hope, be able to pass Sunday under the shade of the gardens of Hampton Court and of the old elms in Bushy Park. We may also make the round of the palace and have a look at the Beauties and the Cartoons. I love the place extremely.

Ever yours
T B Macaulay

bill on education. The summary adds that TBM expresses his doubts whether the state's religion should be taught to vagrant children whose parents have another religious preference and then quotes his words: '. . .such cases are, I imagine, very rare.' Dunlop's bill, to provide reformatory schools in Scotland, passed in this session. In the debate in committee on 19 July some Irish M.P.s had expressed suspicion that the bill was a plot to put Catholic children in Protestant schools (*Hansard*, 3rd Series, CXXXV, 432–7).

[1] Ellis stayed with TBM over the weekend of 29–31 July, when TBM provided him with 'Excellent turtle, good ham, good wine and plenty of it, good fruit' (Journal, VIII, 90).

[2] *Sunny Memories of Foreign Lands*, 2 vols., published 15 July; TBM bought the book on the 22nd and found it 'a mighty foolish impertinent book' (Journal, VIII, 86). Letter XIX contains a lengthy description of TBM as Mrs Stowe observed him at a breakfast party at the Trevelyans' on 11 May 1853: 'Macaulay's whole physique gives you the impression of great strength and stamina of constitution. He has the kind of frame which we usually imagine as peculiarly English; short, stout, and firmly knit. There is something hearty in all his demonstrations. He speaks in that full, round, rolling voice, deep from the chest, which we also conceive of as being more common in England than America. As to his conversation, it is just like his writing; that is to say, it shows very strongly the same qualities of mind' (Boston edn, II, 4). TBM wrote of this meeting in his Journal at the time that 'I was next the lioness and found her simple and sensible' (VI, 71).

[3] 'Some very charming young lady relatives seemed to think quite as much of their gifted uncle as you might have done had he been yours' (II, 5).

TO UNIDENTIFIED RECIPIENT, 28 JULY 1854

MS: University of California, Berkeley.

Greenwood Lodge / Thames Ditton / July 28. 1854

Sir,

I have very little interest at the India House. I will however speak to one or two of the Directors in your son's favour. But I should deceive you if I did not add that I am by no means sanguine as to the result. / I have the honor to be, / Sir,

Your most obedient Servant

T B Macaulay

TO THOMAS LONGMAN, 3 AUGUST 1854

MS: Longman Group Ltd.

Greenwood Lodge / Thames Ditton / August 3. 1854

My dear Sir,

I am more than satisfied by the account of my annual gains. I had not expected 1000£.[1]

I am willing, if you have no objection, that our new engagement should be, like the former, for a term of six years;[2] and I only hope that it may be, in every way, as satisfactory as our former arrangement was. I am very sensible of your kindness; and I assure you that I cordially return the feelings which your letter expresses.

Ever yours truly,

T B Macaulay

TO SIR ALEXANDER DUFF GORDON, [5 AUGUST 1854]

MS: University of Texas.

Greenwood Lodge

Dear Sir Alexander,

I shall be most happy to be of any use to Lady Gordon.[3] A fly will be at my door at six to morrow, as I must be at Richmond in time to dress for dinner. If Lady Gordon will do me the honor to come at that hour, I

---

[1] He was to receive £1500 at the end of the year (Journal, VIII, 92: 3 August).

[2] The term of the original agreement for the *History* having expired, Longman now wished to negotiate a new one. The agreement, for six more years on the original terms, was signed on 16 August (Longman Archive).

[3] TBM and Lady Duff Gordon, who lived at Esher, had both been invited to Lord Lansdowne's house at Richmond; on 5 August TBM wrote that he was 'vexed by a note from Sir Alexander Gordon which disturbs all my Richmond arrangements' (Journal, VIII, 93). This letter is evidently his answer to that note. For TBM's impressions of Lady Gordon during the visit to Lansdowne, see 2 April 1850, note.

will, with pride and pleasure, take charge of her. I stay at Richmond that night: but on Monday morning I go to Hampton Court with Lord Lansdowne;[1] and I shall probably walk from Hampton Court home. If I had seen Lady Gordon, as I had hoped to do, at my sister's to day, or if we had a longer time to make our arrangements, I should have been most willing to alter my plans to suit her convenience. But, as I am afraid that I shall hardly receive an answer to these lines early enough to make any change in the orders which I have given, I may as well say that, unless I hear from you to the contrary, I shall wait for Lady Gordon till a quarter past six.

Yours very truly,

T B Macaulay

TO THOMAS LONGMAN, 11 AUGUST 1854

MS: Longman Group, Ltd.

Greenwood Lodge / Thames Ditton / August 11. 1854

My dear Sir,

Nothing can be clearer than the agreement as you have drawn it.[2] I am perfectly willing to sign it, whenever it suits you to do so.

I agree with you as to the expediency of printing three thousand more copies. The next edition will, I hope, be in a smaller form.[3]

I am working regularly, and see my way distinctly to the close of my work. But when? I sometimes have misgivings that I shall scarcely bring out two volumes till October year. The number of books and M.S.S. to be consulted can hardly be imagined by anybody who has not tried his hand on this part of history.

In any case I shall want an amanuensis[4] when I return to town six weeks hence.

Ever yours truly,

T B Macaulay

---

[1] Lady Gordon went with them, embarrassed TBM by talking of a passage in Pepys about the Duchess of Cleveland's smocks, and made him wonder about Lord Lansdowne's relation to her: 'I cannot understand his liking for Lady Gordon – whether I look at it as friendly or as amorous' (Journal, VIII, 95).

[2] Renewing the agreement for the first part of the *History*: see 3 August.

[3] The three thousand copies were of the tenth edition of volumes 1 and 2, August 1854. The *History*, volumes 1 and 2, reached a thirteenth edition in the original format, a total of 36,570 copies, before the publication of the small octavo edition of 1857–8.

[4] To copy the first two volumes of the *History* Longman had provided an amanuensis in the person of W. Parker Snow (see 21 April 1849); the same service was performed for parts of the second two volumes by Patrick Cumin (1823–90: *Boase*), a graduate of Balliol, a newly-made barrister, and later an official in the Department of Education. He had left the work on TBM's manuscript at the beginning of July: I do not know who succeeded him.

TO THOMAS FLOWER ELLIS, 14 AUGUST 1854

MS: Trinity College. *Extract published:* Trevelyan, II, 385n.

Greenwood Lodge / Thames Ditton / August 14. 1854

Dear Ellis,

How are you? – Have you premonitory symptoms? Are you provided with aromatics and opiates? Poor Lord Jocelyn's case[1] has frightened many people out of their wits. It is a consolation to know that he had, in spite of the advice of physicians, persisted during some time in a regimen which seemed expressly intended to prepare him for the Churchyard. He was afraid of being fat: so, like a fool, he lived on nothing but acids. With his stomach full of cucumbers and lemonade, he took up his abode in rooms close to the Tower Ditch. The stench without and the sourness within soon did his business. Your heroine Lady J.[2] has now a place in her gift for which I advise you to become a candidate.

Seriously, however, I want to know how you are. It is no joke, at this time, to pass burning days in bad air; and that, I apprehend, is what you are doing. You had better come away as fast as you can, and inhale the breezes here. I have some delicious walks and drives for you. George has written to ask Walter to Sandown Lodge.[3] I hope that there will be nothing to prevent the visit. For I should like to have some talk with Walter in a quiet way, and without the forms of a lecture.[4] George is reading the Plutus with me; and very well he gets on. His construing is remarkably precise. It is quite evident that Greek is thoroughly well taught at Harrow. George too seems to enjoy the jokes, the parodies, and the allusions to living people much more than I had hoped. The edition is an expurgated one, just printed at our University press.[5] I am rather glad of it: for it is not agreeable to read with a virtuous boy those unutterably beastly lines in which Scholefield used to examine and cross examine.[6]

[1] The summer was again a season of cholera in London. Lord Jocelyn died of the disease at Lord Palmerston's house on 12 August. Robert Jocelyn (1816–54), styled Viscount Jocelyn, eldest son of the third Earl of Roden, was Tory M.P. for King's Lynn, 1842–54, and Colonel of the East Essex Militia. He was stationed at the Tower with his regiment when he fell ill.

[2] Lady Jocelyn (1820–80), née Frances Elizabeth, daughter of the fifth Earl Cowper, married Jocelyn in 1841. She was one of the Ladies of the Bedchamber and the favorite of the Queen. GEC, *Complete Peerage,* quotes Sir Arthur Rumbold's description of her as the 'most charming and lovable of women'; Dickens, in 1840, writes facetiously to Maclise of being in love with her (*Letters of Charles Dickens,* II, 28).

[3] The name of the Trevelyans' house in Esher.

[4] In the recent examinations at Harrow, Walter Ellis stood very low; George Trevelyan, by contrast, was third in his form (Journal, VIII, 91: 1 August).

[5] TBM must mean the edition of Aristophanes' *Comedies* edited by H. A. Holden, Fellow of Trinity, 'usibus scholarum accommodabat,' and published by Parker in 1848; the work was printed at Cambridge and the parts were available separately.

[6] No doubt lines 149–54. They are omitted from Holden's edition.

I have been reading Aulus Gellius and Pliny the younger. I think more highly of Pliny than I did. There are to be found in his letters wonderfully happy illustrations and turns of expression. I do not get on with Photius. I read chiefly while walking; and my copy of Photius is not one which I can conveniently carry in my hand.

The harvest is going on gloriously. The sheaves look beautiful here among the rich verdure of the woods and meadows. I suppose that most of the wheat crop south of the Thames is already gathered in.

Ever yours,

T B Macaulay

TO THOMAS FLOWER ELLIS, 22 AUGUST 1854

MS: Trinity College.

Greenwood Lodge / Thames Ditton / August 22. 1854

Dear Ellis,

I learned yesterday that you had returned from the circuit, and rather expected to have heard from you to day.

I have sent your letter about Pashley[1] to Wood, and have added a few words from myself. Wood is in the Highlands wandering from place to place. Some time may therefore elapse before he can return an answer. I am glad to say that he cordially concurs in all the suggestions of the Civil Service Committee.

I hope that you will be able to fix a day for coming here again.[2] Come on Saturday and stay till Tuesday. I wish you to be here on a week day. Lady Trevelyan has set her heart on showing you some delightful heath and wood, – the very finest common scenery in England. Your commons in Kent are good, but nothing to those round St George's Hill here.[3] Or could you come on Friday and stay till Monday? But the longer you stay the better I shall be pleased, as you well know.

I hope that you will be able to go with me to France, under our old conventions. I remember that pleasant day at Lyons[4] most vividly. And I

[1] Robert Pashley (1805–59: *DNB*), a Fellow of Trinity, author of two volumes of *Travels in Crete,* 1837, and a barrister on the Northern Circuit.

[2] Ellis spent the weekend of September 1–4 with TBM at Thames Ditton (Journal, VIII, 108–10: see 30 August).

[3] They went to St George's Hill on 2 September, 'exploring like Mrs. Elton in her barouche landau' (Journal, VIII, 109: TBM had just finished re-reading all of Jane Austen at Thames Ditton).

[4] 13 September 1853, when TBM and Ellis rambled over the city from top to bottom (Journal, VII, 71–7).

think that we may well have equally pleasant days at Blois and Tours.
I am glad that Marian had such fine weather in Ireland.

Ever yours,
T B Macaulay

TO CHARLES MACAULAY, 23 AUGUST 1854

MS: University of London. *Mostly published:* Rae, *Temple Bar*, LXXXVI, 201.

Greenwood Lodge / Thames Ditton / August 23. 1854
Dear Charles,
The Report on the Indian Civil Service is printed. That is to say there
are four or five copies in print. Some corrections are still to be made: and
my only copy is marked in many places and cannot well be spared. Charles
Wood has seen it as it now stands, and decidedly approves of it. If I can
get another copy I will send it to you.
I am sorry that you should visit Cambridge without me. Nor is this a
good time of the year. You ought to go when the place is full, and to dine
in our hall and attend evening service in our chapel. At present the Colleges
are as desolate as the streets of Pompeii. I still remember our visit to
Oxford with much pleasure. That was, I think, in the winter of 1840.[1]
I think it much better that you should be where you are than that you
should return to the Board of Health. Though Chadwick is gone there will
be plenty of vexation and obloquy for his successor to endure. Nor is my
opinion of Hall[2] by any means high.
You do not mention your wife and children. My love to them, if they
are with you.

Ever yours,
T B Macaulay

TO THOMAS FLOWER ELLIS, 24 AUGUST 1854

MS: Trinity College.

Greenwood Lodge / Thames Ditton / August 24. 1854
Dear Ellis,
I shall be delighted to see you to morrow week. I shall probably be in
town on Saturday morning. If so I will call in the Temple, and bring away

---

[1] Charles wrote to his daughter Mary, after her visit to Oxford in 1881, that 'I never
attended service at Magdalen, but I lounged through the gardens with my brother Tom one
charming afternoon, and had altogether a pleasanter time with him there than any other
that I can now look back upon' (3 November 1881: MS, University of London).
[2] Sir Benjamin Hall was now President of the remodelled Board of Health.

Warren's present.[1] How shall I return thanks for it? The book is a clever book, but a very blackguardly book; and it goes desperately against the grain with me to commend such a performance. Besides the fellow is very likely to show or to print my letter.

I am sorry that your time in France must be so short. As to our arrangements something will depend on the tides and the hours at which the packets start. I confess that I should much prefer getting to Boulogne on Saturday evening, if possible. I shall try to engage either Franz or Wolmar. Short as the time is, I do not think that either of them would object to going with us.

The Emperor is in the south of France, I imagine. I hope that he will not be at Paris when we are there.

I am going to day with the Trevelyans to John Lefevre's house – a most curious old place, I am told, built by the brewer of Henry the Eighth, and still retaining its original appearance.[2]

I am charmed with this country. It is not at all unlikely that I shall settle not many months hence in one of the new houses which are building near Weybridge. Delicious commons, – fine woods, – air which it is a luxury to breathe, – a railway station close at hand, – the distance from your chambers, for all practical purposes, about as great as if I lived in Belgravia or Tyburnia. But all this must be well considered.

Ever yours

T B Macaulay

I have killed three wasps while writing this letter. I generally kill eighteen a day. There must be a nest near me.[3]

TO LORD CLARENDON, 26 AUGUST 1854

MS: Corpus Christi College, Cambridge.

Greenwood Lodge / Thames Ditton / August 26. 1854

Dear Lord Clarendon,

I am quite ashamed to trespass on your time, occupied as you are with the care of us all.[4] But I am sure that you will excuse me. I mean to go to Paris in a fortnight for the purpose of examining the Archives of the War Department. My particular object is to see the despatches which the

---

[1] A copy of *Ten Thousand a Year*; 'though the book is clever, there are things in it which are open to objections more serious than those of mere criticism. However I thanked him civilly' (Journal, VIII, 112: 6 September).

[2] Sutton Place, north of Guildford.

[3] On 19 August, being plagued by wasps, TBM writes that 'I was at last forced to exert a skill for which I was famous in my school days' – i.e., wasp-killing (Journal, VIII, 101).

[4] Clarendon was now Foreign Secretary.

Generals of Lewis the Fourteenth, Lauzun and St Ruth, wrote from Ireland in the years 1690 and 1691.[1] I have always been most courteously treated by official people at Paris; and I dare say that I might, without any assistance, obtain, with some little delay, the permission which I want. But every day is of importance to me. If you would be so kind as to desire Lord Cowley[2] to make an application, so that I may, as soon as I arrive, be able to go to work, I should be greatly obliged to you.

To the French foreign office I already have had access.

Ever yours truly
T B Macaulay

TO THOMAS FLOWER ELLIS, 27 AUGUST 1854

MS: Trinity College.

Greenwood Lodge / Thames Ditton / August 27. 1854

Dear Ellis,

Your notion of starting on Thursday the 8th is a great improvement.[3] As to stopping for the night at Boulogne, that must depend on the tides. I do not think that the time table for September is yet published. At all events I have it not.

Surely the Hotel des Bains is that at which we have always taken up our quarters. I hope that, before we meet on Friday next, I shall have engaged a courier and made all needful arrangements. I have already written to Lord Clarendon about the special object of my journey.

Boulogne may be full: but Paris, I hear, is empty. However, I will try to secure good accommodation there. I should much like to show you Beauvais. But that can hardly be in going. I shall certainly show you Bourges, Orleans, Blois and Tours, all places of great interest – Orleans the least so though the largest town.

The Trevelyans expect Walter on Tuesday, and are laying schemes for entertaining him. There is to be a pic nic one day. And Trevelyan means to stay at home one day in order to give the boys a shooting excursion. George is a terrible destroyer of thrushes and rabbits: but, in spite of the

---

[1] TBM spent two days, 15–16 September, making extracts from the records of the War Office. He had some difficulty in obtaining official permission, but once admitted he was well treated (Journal, VIII, 118–21). In the *History*, III, 160n (ch. 12), he acknowledges the 'liberality and courtesy with which the immense and admirably arranged storehouses of curious information at Paris were thrown open to me.'

[2] Henry Richard Charles Wellesley (1804–84: *DNB*), second Baron and first Earl Cowley, was ambassador at Paris, 1852–67.

[3] They left on 7 September, going by Folkestone and Boulogne to Paris; on the 10th they went to Beauvais; between the 11th and 14th they went to Orléans, Blois, and Tours. TBM then spent two days in research, after which they retraced their steps from Paris to Folkestone on the 17th and to London the next day (Journal, VIII, 112–21).

authority of Aristophanes and Horace, he does not chuse to eat the thrushes which he kills.[1]

Walter should go by a train which stops at Esher. Almost all the trains stop there. He will then be within five minutes' walk of Sandown Lodge; and there are always flies. But if he will let the Trevelyans know by what train he may be expected, I dare say that George will meet him.

Ever yours,
T B Macaulay

TO THOMAS FLOWER ELLIS, 30 AUGUST 1854

MS: Trinity College.

Greenwood Lodge / Thames Ditton / Aug 30. 1854
Dear Ellis,

I shall be in town on Friday; and, if you have no objection I will be at the Temple at three. I shall appoint the Courier[2] to be there at that hour, in order that we may both have an opportunity of seeing him and giving him his instructions.

On Saturday, if Saturday should be, as I hope, a fine day, I shall take you a delightful walk to Claremont and through the grounds. Then we shall lunch at Sandown Lodge, and Lady Trevelyan will take us a long drive in an open carriage through much charming scenery. She insists on our dining with them, and will not hear of dressing. If you are tired we will have a fly to bring us home at night.[3] For Trevelyan's horses will have had a good day's work. But probably you may prefer a cool walk by moonlight for twenty or five and twenty minutes. It is not more.

I suppose that Walter is at Sandown Lodge by this time.

Ever yours,
T B Macaulay

TO THOMAS FLOWER ELLIS, 18 SEPTEMBER 1854

MS: Trinity College.

Greenwood Lodge / Thames Ditton / September 18. 1854
Dear Ellis,

I mean to remain here a week longer than I at first intended. I shall not

[1] Perhaps Horace, *Epistles*, I, xv, 40–1: 'nothing better than a fat thrush'; and Aristophanes, *Clouds*, 339, and *Peace*, 1149, where the thrush is listed among good things to eat.
[2] His name was Kloss. TBM calls him 'a queer looking fellow, and not alert' (Journal, VIII, 112: 7 September).
[3] The program was carried out as outlined here, and Ellis and TBM returned to Greenwood Lodge in a fly (Journal, VIII, 109–10).

leave my cottage till I start with Hannah for Ulverstone[1] this day fortnight. When I return thence I shall go to Oxford; and I hope that we shall have at least one pleasant Sunday there.[2]

I inclose you two letters, – prodigies of impudence in their different styles. Enjoy Warren's; but do not talk about it. The manner in which you and he are joined in his concluding sentence is delightful.

The impudence of the Reverend Joseph Brown[3] is, in its way, as good a thing as Warren's.

Ever yours,

T B Macaulay

TO THOMAS FLOWER ELLIS, 20 SEPTEMBER 1854

MS: Trinity College.

Greenwood Lodge / September 20. 1854

Dear Ellis,

My plans have again been altered in consequence of intelligence from Ulverstone.[4]

I mean to go to Oxford on Saturday the 30th; and I hope that you will be able to accompany me, and to stay till the Monday. On the Monday I go to work, in All Souls' Library, for how many days I cannot of course positively say.[5] But on the following Monday, the 9th, I must be off for Ulverstone.

If this suits you, let me know when you can start on Saturday week. The days are shortening; and we ought, if possible, to have time for a walk before dinner.

I am glad that Walter has got on so well. I hope that he will not relax. He has read ten books, it seems, in about a fortnight. At that rate he would finish both Odyssey and Iliad by the middle of November; and he ought to get on with constantly accelerating velocity.

I am much pleased by George's diligence, and still more by finding that he has a great enjoyment of the manner of Aristophanes, and likes even the nonsense. He has promised me to begin Herodotus as soon as gets back to

---

[1] To see John Macaulay, whose living of Aldingham is a few miles south of Ulverston.

[2] See next letter.

[3] Perhaps the Joseph Brown (1800?–67: *Boase*) who was Rector of Christ Church, Southwark, 1849–67.

[4] Instead of leaving on the 2nd of October, Hannah, Margaret, and TBM left London on the 9th and returned on the 12th on this visit (Journal, VIII, 132–5).

[5] Ellis and TBM went to Oxford on Saturday, 30 September. Ellis returned to London on the Monday, while TBM remained until Friday, 6 October, reading both at All Souls and at the Bodleian (Journal, VIII, 128–30).

Harrow, and to read the nine books straight through. I told him not to trouble himself about passages which did not readily yield their meaning, but to go resolutely forward.

I should think that any master would be glad to assist a boy who showed a real taste for study. If however George should be shy about applying for help, I shall myself write to Vaughan.

I give you joy on having got your favourite stick again.[1]

Ever yours,

T B Macaulay

TO JOHN HULBERT GLOVER,[2] 22 SEPTEMBER 1854

MS: Huntington Library.

Greenwood Lodge / Thames Ditton / September 22. 1854

My dear Sir,

I remember with gratitude the kind assistance which I received from you when I had occasion, in 1848, to examine the Stuart papers.[3] It is now necessary that I should again look into them; and I should be glad to do so as early as possible. Is there any day next week, Saturday excepted, on which it would be convenient to you that I should call on you at Windsor for that purpose?[4] If not, could you fix any time after the 14th of October? / Believe me, / My dear Sir,

Your faithful Servant

T B Macaulay

TO THOMAS FLOWER ELLIS, 4 OCTOBER 1854

MS: Trinity College. *Partly published:* Trevelyan, II, 219n; 370.

Oxford October 4 / 1854

Dear Ellis,

I have ordered dinner for you at seven on Friday – herrings, goose, and game. Remember the 'Ελενης ὁρμηματα τε στοναχας τε[5] to morrow

---

[1] The courier had lost TBM's umbrella and Ellis's orangewood stick on the first day of their French tour (Journal, VIII, 113).

[2] Glover (*d.* 1860: *Boase*) was Royal Librarian from *c.* 1837. In his Journal, VIII, 125, TBM says that he wrote to Glover on the 23rd, but since he often wrote up his Journal after an interval its dates are sometimes mistaken.

[3] For the Stuart Papers, see 15 September 1846. TBM acknowledges Glover's assistance in a note to the *History*, II, 136: ch. 6.

[4] TBM went to Windsor on the 26th and was pleased to find that there was 'scarcely anything of earlier date than George I. A good hearing: I have now got to a point at which there is no more gratifying discovery than that nothing is to be discovered' (Journal, VIII, 126).

[5] *Iliad*, II, 356: 'Helen's longing to escape and her lamentations' (Lattimore translation). I do not know what TBM is talking about in this sentence.

evening; and utter such short ejaculations as a Christian owes to a sister in extremis, even when he has not the honor of being personally known to her.

Glorious news[1] – too glorious, I am afraid, to be all true. However there is room for a large abatement. One effect, and a most important one, of these successes, is that the war, which has not yet been national in France, will become so, and that, consequently, neither the death of the Emperor nor any revolution which may follow, will easily dissolve the present alliance with us.

As soon as you were gone I left a card and a note at the house of the Warden of All Souls.[2] He was the only Soul – good that – in residence. He was most kind, took me to the library, got out the M.S.S. which I wanted, provided me a comfortable room with all accommodations, and left me to myself. I worked till sunset, returned again yesterday after breakfast, and did not stir till near six. I have now done with Narcissus Luttrell,[3] and am going to the Bodleian. To give you a specimen of the things which I found – The Jacobites, about 1694, invented a new way of drinking treasonable healths. They got up and limped about the room with the glasses at their lips. The secret sense of this proceeding you will hardly guess. It meant

> L   Lewis XIV
> I   James II
> *M*   Mary of Modena
> P   Prince of Wales.

I hear nothing of Adolphus yet.

> Ever yours,
> T B Macaulay

to Lady Trevelyan, 4 October 1854

MS: Trinity College. *Extract published:* Trevelyan, 2nd edn, 1, 469n.

> Angel Inn Oxford / October 4. 1854

Dearest Hannah,

I have had a most successful and pleasant visit here. I passed a most

---

[1] The news of the battle of the Alma reached London on the evening of Saturday, 30 September; it was first believed that Sebastapol itself had fallen, and this was not definitely known to be false until 6 October. On the day that TBM is writing *The Times* announced that the fall of Sebastapol had been confirmed.

[2] Lewis Sneyd (1788–1858: *Boase*), Warden of All Souls from 1827.

[3] Luttrell's diary, a 'compilation based on the newsletters and newspapers of the period' (Firth, *Commentary on Macaulay's History of England*, p. 84), is one of TBM's favorite authorities in the *History*. Part of it he had available to him through a copy in the Mackintosh papers; the rest he saw 'through the kindness of the Warden of All Soul's College, where the original MS. is deposited' (note added to *History* (1857), 1, 622: ch. 5).

agreeable Saturday and Sunday in the cloisters and gardens with Ellis. He
went early on the Monday; and I set to work. The place is empty. I found
not a soul at All Souls except the Warden. But he was most kind, took me
to the library, got me out the M.S.S. which I wanted, seven thick volumes
of cramped writing, and put me into a comfortable room where I worked
all day. I returned at ten yesterday morning, and, at near six, completed
my extracts. To day I attack the Bodleian. I shall call at Worcester to see
whether Chambers[1] is there. Jowett[2] is absent; and indeed I hardly expect
to fall in with my acquaintance; nor do I much wish it. For I came to work
and not to chat and feast.

I had a very kind and welcome letter from Trevelyan yesterday. I cannot
but be pleased to find that, at last, the Code on which I bestowed the
labour of two of the best years of my life has had justice done to it.[3] Had
this justice been done sixteen years ago, I should probably have given
much more attention to legislation and much less to literature than I have
done. I do not know that I should have been either happier or more useful
than I have been.

Glorious news – so glorious that I am afraid it cannot all be true. But
half is more than we had a right to expect.

I return to town on Friday. Send a line with your final and precise
directions. Love to all.

Ever yours

T B Macaulay

Felicitations to our friends the Mangleses.[4]

[1] William Chambers (1826?–1910), Fellow and later Tutor of Worcester, 1851–65; Rector of
Blandford St Mary, Devon, 1881–1907. He had been very attentive to TBM and his family
on the occasion of TBM's receiving an honorary degree from Oxford the year before.
TBM found him 'a very intelligent and well read man, with a little of Academic stiffness
about his manner particularly with ladies, to whom he is Academically attentive. I liked him
much' (Journal, VI, 84–5: 7 June 1853).

[2] Benjamin Jowett (1817–93: *DNB*), then Tutor of Balliol; in the next year he was appointed
Regius Professor of Greek, and, in 1870, Master of Balliol. In this last position Jowett
became the dominant personality in the Oxford of his time. Jowett had been working with
Trevelyan on civil service reform and was a member of TBM's Committee on the Indian
Civil Service, where TBM seems to have met him for the first time. In August TBM had
called on Jowett at his summer residence near Twickenham and had 'much talk about the
Epistles of St Paul, the early history of Xtnity, Bunsen's Hippolytus etc. Jowett is certainly
a superior man' (Journal, VIII, 101).

[3] This refers to the decision of a committee of the Indian Legislative Council to recommend
the adoption of TBM's draft Penal Code. The decision had been compelled by the work of
the Commission on the Laws of India, on which Ellis sat, since it had been charged with the
preparation of a Code of Criminal Procedure and needed to know what Penal Code was to
be its basis: see the reference to the decision (undated) in the *First Report* of the Commissioners, *Parliamentary Papers*, 1856, XXV, 94. Thus, after long delay and severe
criticism, TBM's Code was vindicated, though it was not enacted until 1860 (see Eric
Stokes, *The English Utilitarians and India*, pp. 260–2).

[4] Their eldest daughter, Ellen, married John Lowis on 5 October.

TO MRS EDWARD CROPPER, 6 OCTOBER 1854

Text: Sir Joseph Arnould, *Memoir of Thomas, First Lord Denman,* 2 vols., 1873, II, 355.

Albany, London: October 6, 1854.

Dear Mrs. Edward Cropper,

I have only this morning returned to town, after some days of wandering, and I have found on my table your letter of Monday. You will believe that I was much affected by Lord Denman's death.[1] His many noble qualities, his fine talents, and his great kindness to myself when I was young and unknown, were forcibly brought back to my recollection.

Yet I could scarcely think it matter for condolence that, full of years and full of honour, he should have been released, by the most placid of all deaths, from sufferings which must have severely tried even his fortitude and suavity.

I can wish nothing better to myself or to those whom I love, than such a dissolution. Love to Edward and the children.[2]

Very truly yours,
T. B. Macaulay.

TO SELINA MACAULAY, 7 OCTOBER 1854

MS: Trinity College.

Albany October 7. 1854

Dearest Selina,

I inclose a cheque which ought to have been sent before. It was put out of my head by the troubles attending my removal from Greenwood Lodge – William's niece[3] was very ill – I thought, dying; and, in such circumstances we had to pack, and go through all the plagues incident to a change of residence. I went off to Oxford leaving my cheque book locked up, and could not get at it till to day. There has been, I am afraid, some irregularity in the transmission of the newspapers, in consequence of the unsettled state in which we have been. But I hope that all will go right now.

On Monday I take Hannah and Baba to Ulverstone. On Thursday I hope to be again in town. On the Tuesday following, the 17th, I shall go for two days to Woburn to meet Lord Lansdowne and Lord John.

---

1 On 22 September; Mrs Cropper was Denman's daughter.
2 Her two children by Henry Macaulay and the first of her three by Edward Cropper, born in May of this year.
3 She fell ill of 'bilious fever' on 25 September (Journal, VIII, 126). Her name was Louisa, and her age is given as 14 in the census return of 1851.

I had a most successful hunt in the Bodleian Library and at All Souls, and worked there several days with great delight. Love to Fanny.

Ever yours,

T B Macaulay

TO FRANCES MACAULAY, 14 OCTOBER 1854

MS: Trinity College.

Albany October 14 / 1854

Dearest Fanny,

We had a very pleasant visit to Aldingham. The house and grounds are most enviable and enviably situated. We saw Furness Abbey, and had a very handsome dinner at the inn there. I had not expected such a table in the wilderness. I liked what I saw of the children – especially of Arthur.[1] Selina's[2] suitor is a cross between a Lancashire clown and a Yankee pedlar. He has been much in the United States, and has brought home the genuine Connecticut twang of the nose to grace his utterance. However I dare say that he will make a good husband.

I do not understand what ground the Baptists have for complaining that Bunyan has no monument in the Abbey. I should never dream of complaining because Bishop Butler[3] or Archbishop Leighton has not a monument in a Baptist meeting. The Abbey is a religious edifice. No man, however eminent, who has publicly separated himself from the Church, who denies the validity of the initiatory sacraments of the Church, who writes and preaches against the Church, has any claim to funeral honors in the Church. You might as well blame the Russians for not erecting monuments to our brave fellows who were killed at the Alma as blame the Dean and Chapter of Westminster for not erecting a monument to a man who was the enemy of the religious society to which they belonged. His place in heaven has nothing to do with the matter. You may as well say that his arms ought to be put up among the arms of the Knights of the Garter at Windsor because he is in heaven, or that a picture of him ought to be put among the pictures of the Scotch Kings at Holyrood because he is in heaven. A man in heaven has no right to have his arms at Windsor unless he was a Knight of the Garter. A man in heaven has no right to have his

---

[1] Arthur Babington Macaulay, John's second son. He seems to have died in foreign parts while yet young, though I have found nothing about him. When John Macaulay lay dying he was 'troubled by doubts about Arthur – fancying that he may, after all, be still alive and turn up again somewhere or other' (Charles Macaulay to Mary Booth, early 1874? : MS, University of London).

[2] Selina (b. 1834), John's eldest child, married the Reverend William Henry Fell, curate of St John's, Lancaster, in April 1855.

[3] Joseph Butler (1692–1752: *DNB*), author of the *Analogy of Religion.*

portrait at Holyrood unless he was a King of Scotland. And a man in heaven has no right to a monument in the transept of a Church, unless he was a Churchman.

William's niece is well again, except that she is very weak. I go to Woburn next Tuesday,[1] and then I shall settle in town for some months. I shall meet the Chancellor at Woburn; and I am glad of it. For, though little in the habit of asking favours, I mean to ask him to do something [. . . .][2]

TO SIR EDWARD RYAN, 30 OCTOBER 1854

MS: Trinity College.

Albany / October 30. 1854

Dear Ryan,

Will you breakfast with me at ten on Thursday?[3]

Ever yours
T B Macaulay

TO SELINA MACAULAY, 15 NOVEMBER 1854

MS: Trinity College.

Albany London / November 15. 1854

Dearest Selina,

I am settled here for a long time. I hope to have my history ready for the press before I stir. I work hard every day, and am tolerably satisfied with the part which is finished.

As to the Greek Church, I am no great authority on such points. But I can answer most of your questions. The Greek Church holds the real presence. It does not acknowledge the Pope. There is not a single Patriarch, but several; nor does any Patriarch pretend to anything like Papal authority. The Greeks worship Saints, and pay homage to pictures, but not to statues, which they think forbidden by the second commandment – a most

---

[1] Among the large party at Woburn were Lord and Lady Cranworth, Charles Howard, Charles Cavendish, Sir Robert Adair, Dundas, Lord and Lady Parke, Lord and Lady Howe, Sir George Hamilton Seymour, and Lord John Russell (Journal, VIII, 136–40: 17–19 October).

[2] The bottom third of the last leaf has been torn away for the signature. The favor that TBM asked of the Chancellor was the gift of a living to Edward Rose, son of his cousin Lydia Babington Rose (see 19 December 1849). The Chancellor responded with the offer of a living in Warwickshire, but Rose refused it (Journal, VIII, 140; 145: 19 and 27 October).

[3] The party, besides Ryan, were Hannah, Margaret, Ellis, Dundas, Lord Glenelg, and Macleod (Journal, VIII, 146).

judicious distinction. They allow a married man to be ordained: but he must be married to a woman who had not had a former husband; and he must marry only once. After he is ordained he cannot marry. Besides the secular clergy there are monks who do not marry at all. The service is in Greek. Indeed even Greek Roman Catholics perform the service in Greek. It is quite a mistake to imagine that the Roman Catholic Church ascribes any particular virtue to the Latin. The rule, as it was explained to me in the English College at Rome, is this. Every nation must perform the services in the language in which it originally performed them. There must be no change. Consequently the Greek Roman Catholics say mass in Greek, the Syrian Roman Catholics in Syriac, the Roman Catholics of Western Europe in Latin.

The paper on my speeches[1] was written by an excellent person, Henry Rogers of Birmingham, the author of a book entitled the Eclipse of Faith.[2] There are few people whom I value more.

Love to Fanny.

Ever yours,

T B Macaulay

By the bye – the great distinction between the Greek and Latin Churches relates to the procession of the Holy Spirit. The Greeks hold that the Spirit proceeds from the father only; and this was, beyond all doubt, the way in which the Nicene Creed was originally framed.

TO LADY HOLLAND,[3] 17 NOVEMBER 1854

MS: New College, Oxford.

Albany November 17 / 1854

My dear Lady Holland,

Thanks for your most kind and welcome present.[4] I have already read most of the volume with great interest and with pleasure, sometimes, I am afraid, the effect of selfish vanity. Your father's opinion of me was far higher than I deserve.[5] In one thing, however, he was unjust to me. He

---

[1] *ER*, c (October 1854), 490–534. TBM described the review as 'very kind and judiciously so' (Journal, VIII, 136: 13 October).

[2] Published anonymously in 1852.

[3] Saba, wife of Sir Henry Holland and daughter of Sydney Smith.

[4] Her *Memoir* of her father; it was not published until 30 May 1855. This presentation copy of the book is now in the library at Wallington.

[5] The praise was usually mingled with some acid but was always high praise, e.g.: 'I always prophesied his greatness from the first moment I saw him, then a very young and unknown man, on the Northern Circuit. There are no limits to his knowledge, on small subjects as well as great; he is like a book in breeches' (*Memoir*, 2nd edn, p. 366).

fancied that I did not listen to him;[1] and I was not so tasteless and senseless as to be inattentive when he talked.

I will observe your injunctions. But I hope that you will suffer me to consider my sister's house as my own. It is indeed my house; and she will be most impatient to see the book: for she greatly admired your father. I shall not however let her have it till to morrow, in order that you may have time to object.[2]

TO FRANCES MACAULAY, 18 NOVEMBER 1854

MS: Trinity College. *Partly published:* Trevelyan, II, 371.

Albany London / November 18. 1854

Dearest Fanny,

I had the Eclipse of Faith;[3] but I must have lent it to somebody. For I do not see it anywhere. To be sure, my books are in sad disorder, and must for the present continue so. If the Eclipse turns up to day or to morrow, I will send it by Hannah.

The interest excited by the war is as great as that which in my boyish days used to be excited by the Duke of Wellington's operations. I am well pleased on the whole. It is impossible not to regret so many brave men and to feel for the distress of so many families. But it is a great thing that, after the longest peace ever known, our army should be in a higher state of efficiency than at the end of the last war. The spirit of the soldiers and of the whole country is a complete guarantee against those plagues with which we were threatened two or three years ago. Nobody will be in a hurry to invade England for a long time to come.

I do not know how many men go to a regiment now. The number varies; for the army is increased or diminished by increasing or diminishing the companies. I remember when a battalion of the line had only about 600 rank and file. Then it was raised to more than 800 rank and file. Sometimes a regiment consists of two battalions. At present, I think, no regiment of the line has more than one. You must remember too that the whole regiment is never abroad. A part of it, called the depôt, remains at home for the purpose of recruiting. "Rank and file" means the men as distinct from the officers.

Regiments are never commanded by their Colonels, but by their Lieutenant Colonels. If you will look into an army list or a Court Kalendar,

---

[1] "'Oh yes! we both talk a great deal, but I don't believe Macaulay ever did hear my voice,' he exclaimed, laughing. "Sometimes, when I have told a good story, I have thought to myself, Poor Macaulay! he will be very sorry some day to have missed hearing that"'" (*ibid.*, p. 371).

[2] The closing and signature have been cut off.

[3] By Henry Rogers: see 15 November.

you will see that the Colonels of Regiments are all, without a single exception, Generals or Field Marshals.

[.　　.　　.　　.　　.　　.　　.　　.　　.　　.　　.　　.　　.]¹

officers look forward after many years of service. A colonelcy may be worth 1300£ or 1400£ a year. A few are worth more. The real command is always with the Lieutenant Colonel.

[.　　.　　.　　.　　.　　.　　.　　.　　.　　.　　.　　.　　.]¹

eighty rank and file under his command.

Love to Selina.

Ever yours,
T B Macaulay

TO LORD JOHN RUSSELL, 21 NOVEMBER 1854

MS: British Museum.

Albany November 21 / 1854

Dear Lord John,

Mr. Alexander Russell,² editor of the Scotsman, wishes much to have an opportunity of explaining to you his views respecting the much disputed question of the newspaper stamps.³ I need not tell you how high among newspapers the Scotsman stands, or how much service it has rendered to you and your friends. Russell's arguments have completely convinced me; and I think that they would produce the same effect on you. He wrote an excellent article on the subject not long ago in the Edinburgh Review.⁴

If you could spare him a quarter of an hour without inconvenience, you would oblige a very deserving and powerful friend.

Ever yours truly,
T B Macaulay

¹ The top third of the last leaf is cut away, removing four or five lines from each side of the leaf.
² Russel (1814–76: *DNB*) had been editor of the *Scotsman* since 1848; he succeeded not only in maintaining but in strengthening the paper's position as the most powerful in Scotland. TBM calls him 'both a good and a clever fellow' (Journal, v, 161: 2 November 1852).
³ The penny stamp on newspapers, the special object of attack by the Association for the Repeal of Taxes on Knowledge (see *to* John Smithson, 11 August 1832). The stamp tax was abolished in 1855. According to E. E. Kellett, the *Scotsman* suffered particularly from this tax; before it was repealed the paper came out twice a week and had a circulation of 2,500; afterwards it became a penny daily and by 1865 reached a circulation of 25,000 ('The Press,' in G. M. Young, ed., *Early Victorian England*, 1934, II, 38).
⁴ 'The Newspaper Stamp,' *ER*, xcviii (October 1853), 488–518.

TO UNIDENTIFIED RECIPIENT, 21 NOVEMBER 1854

MS: Mr T. S. Blakeney.

Albany Nov 21. 1854

Dear Sir,

I am much obliged by the interest which you take in my health. I have no great reason to complain.

There is no reason to wonder either that a statue should have been erected to James II,[1] or that it was not pulled down. It was erected, not by popular subscription, but at the royal charge while James was King, and was put up in his garden, and within the gates of his palace. At the time of the Revolution there were two days of rioting in London: but, during those days, the mob never got into Whitehall, which was always strongly guarded. And after that short fit of turbulence was over, the capital was as quiet as it had ever been. / Believe me, / Dear Sir,

Your faithful Servant,

T B Macaulay

TO SIR CHARLES WOOD, 27 NOVEMBER 1854

MS: The Earl of Halifax.

Albany Nov 27. 1854

Dear Wood,

I am truly glad that you are satisfied with our report. By all means transmit it to the Directors. Sooner or later, it must come out. It will be violently abused, of course. But for abuse I am perfectly prepared.[2]

Jowett, in a letter which I received from him two or three days ago, mentions his friend Temple[3] as a man eminently qualified to set the machinery of the examinations going. I believe Temple to be a very

---

[1] The life-size bronze of James as a Roman emperor by Grinling Gibbons, 1686, now standing in front of the National Gallery.

[2] The Report on the Indian Civil Service proposed to raise the minimum age of entry to Haileybury from 17 to 18 and the maximum age to 23, with the intention of opening the Civil Service to university graduates. It recommended that examinations for entrance should be in 'those branches of knowledge to which it is desirable that English gentlemen who mean to remain at home should pay some attention' and that the successful candidates should then study the history of India, jurisprudence, economics, and the Indian vernaculars. The scoring of the examinations was designed to insure that no one specialization should be given undue advantage. The Report was published in *The Times* of 27 December; a leader on that day, and another on 3 January 1855, are certainly friendly on the whole.

[3] Frederick Temple (1821–1902: *DNB*), Archbishop of Canterbury, 1896–1902, at this time was Principal of the teacher training college at Kneller Hall, Twickenham, where TBM had met him during the summer just past. Temple was successively Headmaster of Rugby, Bishop of Exeter, Bishop of London, and Archbishop. The post of civil service commissioner was offered to Temple but declined.

superior man; and my only doubt is whether his present duties would leave him leisure to pay much attention to any other business.

Ever yours truly,

T B Macaulay

TO GUSTAV ADOLF SCHOELL,[1] 28 NOVEMBER 1854

MS: University of California, Berkeley.

Mr. Macaulay presents his compliments to Dr. Schoell, and will be most happy to see Dr. Schoell on Thursday at eleven, if that hour should be perfectly convenient.

Albany Nov. 28. 1854

TO THOMAS FLOWER ELLIS, 3 DECEMBER 1854

MS: Trinity College.

Albany December 3. 1854

Dear Ellis,

Remember that you dine here on Tuesday. I particularly wish to have some talk with you about your Indian Supreme Court.[2] Macleod was here yesterday, and gave me an account of your doings which, I must say, seriously alarmed me. I saw Trevelyan to day, and repeated to him what Macleod had told me. Trevelyan is as much surprised and displeased as either Macleod or I. I would willingly hope that there is some misapprehension; and this seems to me the more probable, because you told me on Friday that Macleod stood alone against the other Commissioners. Now I will tell you in confidence, what Macleod told me in confidence, that Hawkins[3] talks of resigning if the plan is not altered, and says that he cannot, without forfeiting his character, suffer such a monstrous arrangement to be announced in India as sanctioned by him. If Macleod's account of the scheme be accurate, I have no hesitation in saying that you are going to introduce frightful jobbing and corruption into the Indian administration, and into that very department of the Indian administration which it is most important to keep pure. Do not mention to anybody that I have

[1] Schoell (1805–82), a critic and literary historian, was librarian to the Grand Duke of Weimar.
[2] The Commissioners on the Laws of India proposed to remodel the Indian Supreme Court but disagreed about how the judges should be selected and from what eligible groups they should be drawn. Macleod's dissenting minute to the proposed arrangement is Appendix D to the *First Report* of the Commissioners, *Parliamentary Papers*, 1856, xxv.
[3] John Abraham Francis Hawkins (d. 1879), in the East India Company's service, 1822–48; he was Register of the Courts of Sudder Dewanny and Nizamut Adawlut at the time of his retirement.

written to you on this subject; and above all keep secret what I have told you about Hawkins; and pray commit yourself as little as you can till we have talked the matter over.

Ever yours

T B Macaulay

TO LORD JOHN RUSSELL, 15 DECEMBER 1854

MS: Public Record Office.

Albany Dec 15. 1854

Dear Lord John,

    I have no information about the number of English and foreign troops in Marlborough's battles, except what is to be found in books which you have no doubt consulted.[1]

    If you wish for an instance of the cooperation of English and French troops look at the "True and Just Relation of Major General Sir Thomas Morgan's progress in France and Flanders with the six thousand English, in the years 1657 and 1658, at the taking of Dunkirk and other important places, as it was delivered by the General himself."[2] You will find it in the Harleian Miscellany. The account of Turenne's delight in the intrepidity of the English soldiers is very interesting.[3] Since that time the two nations have never, that I recollect, acted together by land, except in the ignominious war of 1672 against Holland, of which the less we say the better.[4]

Ever yours truly

T B Macaulay

---

[1] Russell's query was evidently part of his preparation for a speech on the Enlistment of Foreigners Bill on 19 December (see *to* Frances Macaulay, 23 December). In the speech, Russell argued that England had not relied on its own forces alone in past European wars and cited the examples of Cromwell, William III, and Marlborough (*Hansard*, 3rd Series, CXXXVI, 507–19).

[2] First published in 1699; the *DNB* account of Morgan says that this pamphlet's historical value is 'very doubtful.'

[3] Among other anecdotes, Morgan tells that Turenne and his officers, after allowing the English to charge the Spanish unsupported, said that 'They never saw a more glorious action in their lives, and that they were so transported with the sight of it, that they had no power to move, or do any thing' ('True and Just Relation,' *Harleian Miscellany*, III [1809], 346).

[4] In finding illustrations Russell said that he passed over 'the disgraceful reign of Charles II' (*Hansard*, 3rd Series, CXXXVI, 508).

TO ADAM BLACK, 23 DECEMBER 1854

MS: National Library of Scotland. *Envelope:* Adam Black Esq / etc. etc. etc. / Edinburgh.
Subscription: T B M.

Albany Dec 23. 1854

My dear Sir,

I have written to Lord Canning in behalf of Robert Gray.[1]

Mr. Gilchrist I have not seen. I am afraid that it will be quite out of my power to serve him.

We dragged the government out of the scrape into which it had got.[2] I could not venture to sit in the House till two. But I got excellent pairs for both the divisions.[3]

I have been a sincere mourner for Rutherfurd.[4] I have heard many people speak of him as harsh and overbearing. To me he always was the kindest, most gentle, most assiduous of friends. Another tie between me and Edinburgh is gone. But some still remain, and among them, my very sincere regard for you.

Ever yours truly
T B Macaulay

TO SELINA MACAULAY, 23 DECEMBER 1854

MS: Trinity College.

Albany London / Dec 23. 1854

Dearest Selina,

I inclose a cheque. I hope that you are pretty well this fine day. Christmas is seldom so mild as this year.

Have you the last volume of Wilberforce's Life?[5] I do not want it at present. I only want to know where it is.

George has done excellently at Harrow. I have no doubt that he will make a figure at Cambridge. He has a real taste for classical literature, and is beginning to imitate the ancient writers not unsuccessfully in their own languages. He is also a very good boy, and causes as little anxiety as any lad of sixteen. But at best it is a critical age.

[1] Not identified, but perhaps the 'Mr. Law's protégé' mentioned in *to* Black, 20 January 1854. He and the Gilchrist mentioned in the next sentence of the letter were no doubt candidates for post office appointments.
[2] In the debate on the Enlistment of Foreigners Bill.
[3] On 19 and 22 December.
[4] He died on 13 December.
[5] TBM was re-reading this between 5 and 10 December (Journal, VIII, 153–4).

I work some hours every day on my history. I am in tolerable spirits about it. But I do not think that it will be as much liked as the first part. I write to Fanny by this post.

Ever yours

T B Macaulay

TO FRANCES MACAULAY, 23 DECEMBER 1854

MS: Trinity College.

Albany Dec 23 / 1854

Dearest Fanny,

Thanks for your letter of last week. I have got very easily through our short parliamentary campaign.[1] Everybody on both sides was very kind about giving me facilities for pairing, so that I have not once had to sit up till midnight.

The government is, I think, very unfairly abused, and yet is not free from blame. The Foreign Enlistment Bill[2] is in itself unobjectionable. Yet I do not wonder that a storm was raised against it. People asked why it was not mentioned in the Queen's speech, and why it was brought in without the slightest notice. They suspected a trick, and began to look for all sorts of bad designs. Then it was a great error to bring such a Bill first into the House of Lords where the ministers are not strong in debate. Lord Derby and Lord Ellenborough had a great superiority in the discussion, and when the Bill came down to us it was already grievously damaged. If it had originated in the Commons, it would have been thoroughly explained and ably defended, and would have gone up to the Lords with every advantage. To say the truth, the ministry is but a bad one. The component parts are excellent; but they do not work well together. Sidney Herbert[3] has rather risen in my opinion as a speaker. But he is very unequal.

I inclose a cheque for twenty pounds to assist you and Selina in your housekeeping, as prices keep up, and do not seem likely to go down soon.

Ever yours

T B Macaulay

[1] A special session, 12–23 December, called to pass measures for reinforcing the army.

[2] Authorizing the government to recruit troops abroad and to train up to 15,000 in England for service in the Crimea; after the first debates the number was reduced to 10,000. *The Times* was opposed to it, and it met much opposition in both Houses of Parliament.

[3] Herbert (1810–61: *DNB*), afterwards first Baron Herbert of Lea, was Secretary-at-War, and the official sponsor of Florence Nightingale. He took a leading part in the debates of this session and made a notable speech defending the conduct of the war (*Hansard*, 3rd Series, CXXXVI, 129–60).

TO CHARLES BERNARD GIBSON,[1] 4 JANUARY 1855

MS: University of Washington.

Albany London / January 4. 1855

Sir,

I have just received the volumes[2] which you have been so good as to send me; and I hope that I shall soon have leisure to become acquainted with them.

I am not aware that I ever used the expression which you attribute to me. It is liable to be misconstrued: but it is, no doubt, true in a certain sense.

With sincere thanks and good wishes believe me, Sir,

Your faithful Servant,
T B Macaulay

C B Gibson / etc. etc. etc.

TO THOMAS FLOWER ELLIS, 9 JANUARY 1855

MS: Trinity College.

Albany January 9 / 1855

Dear Ellis,

Will you dine here to morrow, – Wednesday – or indeed any day this week, except Thursday. I have been all but a close prisoner to my room since I saw you last.[3]

Did you notice among the advertisements in the Times of this morning the notice about the examinations for the Indian Civil Service. My plan is adopted almost to the letter.[4] I shall be very anxious till the number and quality of the candidates is known.

Ever yours,
T B Macaulay

---

[1] Gibson (1808?–85: *Boase*) was a minister of the Irish Evangelical Society at Mallow, County Cork, 1834–56; he was ordained priest of the Church of England in 1867, after which he held various livings in London.

[2] *The Last Earl of Desmond, a Historical Romance of 1599–1603,* 2 vols., Dublin, published anonymously in October 1854; it is item 189 in the sale catalogue of TBM's library.

[3] TBM was suffering rheumatic pains late in December; there is no entry in his Journal between 1 and 10 January 1855.

[4] There was, however, one material alteration: see 19 January.

TO HENRY HALLAM, 12 JANUARY 1855

MS: Mr E. E. Smith.

Albany January 12. / 1855

Dear Hallam,

How are you? – I heard only yesterday that you were in town. I should try to see you to day, but that I am, and have been ever since Sunday, close prisoner to my room.

Ever yours,
T B Macaulay

TO SELINA MACAULAY, 14 JANUARY 1855

MS: Trinity College.

Albany London / January 14. 1855

Dearest Selina,

The 5th volume of Wilberforce's Life came quite safe.[1] Thanks. I am more amused than surprised or shocked by Miss Preston's Escapade.[2] If her father managed her as he managed me, her freaks were the natural effects of his discipline. Do you remember that, some eight or nine years ago, he was shocked at George's easy ways, and said, with one of his gloomy looks, that, if the young gentleman were not more restrained, he would bring down Charles's and Hannah's grey hairs etc. etc. – after the usual singing. I want Hannah to write him a letter of delicate condolence returning him his advice. George is doing excellently, and will, I really hope, make a figure at Cambridge. But all depends on his perseverance. I have scarcely stirred out of doors during the last fortnight. But I am not amiss. I work hard. Love to dear Fanny.

Ever yours,
T B Macaulay

TO THOMAS FLOWER ELLIS, 16 JANUARY 1855

MS: Trinity College.

Albany Jany. 16 / 1855

Dear Ellis,

Thanks for the devotional volume. I will take care of it. I fear that I cannot get to you this week. Next week I shall hope to see you.

[1] See *to* Selina Macaulay, 23 December 1854.
[2] In her Memoir of TBM Hannah says of Preston that 'he made his home so trying to his children that one girl certainly ran away, and I think became a governess, though the mother had a large fortune' (p. 27).

I have had some chat with Walter.[1] I hope that he will do well. I take a great interest in him.

Ever yours,
T B Macaulay

TO SIR CHARLES WOOD, 19 JANUARY 1855

MS: The Earl of Halifax. *Extract published:* R. J. Moore, *Sir Charles Wood's Indian Policy, 1853–66,* Manchester, 1966, p. 94.

Albany January 19 / 1855

Dear Wood,

I have been, during some days, hoping that I should soon be able to call on you. But I am, and, while this frost[2] lasts, shall be a close prisoner. I have therefore at last determined to write.

I am a good deal vexed by the change which you have made in our plan.[3] It is a change of great moment. By reducing the age of the candidates from twenty three to twenty two, you will, I am satisfied, exclude a very large number of the very best men. The alteration which you have made will tell greatly against Oxford and Cambridge, which, much as they need reform, are still the first schools in the empire, and in favour of the London University, the Scotch Universities, and the Queen's Colleges in Ireland.

Perhaps it may be true that a servant of the Company ought to go out to India at an age not later than twenty four. But, if this be so, you should, in my opinion, have amended our plan by shortening the period of probation, and not by making an alteration which will shut the most valuable talents and acquirements out of the original competition.

I have not communicated with Lefevre: but I am quite certain that he will agree with me. In this hermitage I see, as you may suppose, very few people. But I have seen some who are well entitled to speak on such a subject; and they all think that the change which you have made will, as respects the English Universities, have a very pernicious effect.

I cannot help saying that I think that you should have mentioned this matter to me, and heard what I had to say about it before you decided. You did consult me about some other alterations of much less importance

---

[1] Walter was evidently not doing well at Harrow; on 13 December TBM, after noting George's successes, added: 'But I am sorry for Walter Ellis' (Journal, VIII, 155).

[2] A record cold spell persisted through most of January and February this year – the 'Crimean winter.'

[3] In the notice of the examinations published in *The Times,* 9 and 18 January, the maximum age for candidates is given as under 22 whereas TBM's Report had proposed to allow candidates up to age 23.

than this; and I was generally able to satisfy you. I make this complaint, –
if it is to be called a complaint, – solely on public grounds. You will not,
I am sure, suspect me of being so punctilious, or so forgetful of the past,
as to take personal offence on such an account. I need not tell you how
much I value your friendship, or with what pleasure I reflect that it has
never, during as many years, been interrupted by the smallest misunderstanding.

Ever yours,
T B Macaulay

P.S. I do not like the change the better, because I strongly suspect that it
has been made at the instance of the Directors. You should never forget
that their object is that the whole plan may fail discreditably, and that the
Indian Judgeships and Collectorships may again be apanages for the
younger sons and nephews of the Chairman and Deputy Chairman.

TO SIR CHARLES WOOD, 19 JANUARY 1855

MS: The Earl of Halifax.

Albany January 19 / 1855

Dear Wood,

If you will read my letter again you will see that, though I was writing
under what I find to be an erroneous impression, I was not under the
influence of any unkind feeling. It never occurred to me that you could
have meant to offer me a personal slight; and I do assure you that my
regard for you was never stronger than while I was, on public grounds,
complaining.

It is clear that I was under a mistake. I had overlooked the substitution
of 23 for 22.[1] How I came to overlook it I do not know. It was careless,
no doubt. But I am confident that not a word was said on the subject
when we met at the Board of Control. And I never was more surprised
than when I saw the advertisement in the Times.

So much as to the personal question, as to which you are plainly in the
right. As to the public question I own that I entertain a very strong opinion, which even Lefevre's authority, much as I respect it, does not shake.

I return the paper. Ever with great truth and sincere kindness

Yours,
T B Macaulay

[1] I do not know what this refers to. The notices in *The Times* (see preceding letter) give 22,
not 23. On 25 January a notice appeared in *The Times* stating that the Board of Control, in
response to many protests, would alter the maximum age for candidates from 22 to 23.

TO THOMAS FLOWER ELLIS, 23 JANUARY 1855

MS: Trinity College.

Albany Jany. 23. 1855

Dear Ellis,

I hardly need tell you that you must not expect to see me to morrow, unless there should be such a change of weather as would make the meteorologists stare. I have not stirred from my fireside since I saw you. I have however seen some people who know what is going on, – Charles Wood, among them. I have carried my point – 23 years v. 22 – and the alteration will be announced as soon as Wood has seen Lefevre. Printed copies of the amended notice are to be sent forthwith to all colleges etc. throughout the United Kingdom and the Colonies. In the meantime I continue to receive the most delicious letters. The best is that of a clerk in a cornfactor's house at Limerick who begs that I "will send him a prospectus informing him in what he is capable of undergoing an examination, for admission into above Service."

You know how welcome you will be here when ever you happen to be disengaged.

Ever yours
T B Macaulay

TO THOMAS FLOWER ELLIS, 25 JANUARY 1855

MS: Trinity College.

Albany Jany. 25 / 1855

Dear Ellis,

As you seemed a little anxious about me yesterday, I write to tell you that I am pretty well this morning. These attacks come from time to time during the cold weather and, while they last, are distressing to me, and more distressing to those who witness them. But abstinence, mustard and Ipecacuanha soon set me to rights.

Any evening, except next Saturday, when you feel inclined, I shall be delighted to see you, and shall be, I hope, better company than I was last night. On Saturday the Trevelyans will be here.

Ever yours
T B Macaulay

TO ADAM BLACK, 25 JANUARY 1855

Text: [Black], *Biographies by Lord Macaulay,* p. L.

Albany, London, / January 25, 1855.

My dear Sir,

I must very earnestly beg you to think about finding some person to succeed me as member for Edinburgh.

I really can remain titular member no longer; I feel that I am every winter becoming more and more unfit for parliamentary life. It is now the ninth day since I have stirred out of my chambers. Twice this week I have been forced to use blisters, to relieve my chest; and this is likely to be my life till the warm weather returns. Public affairs, meanwhile, are every day looking blacker and blacker.[1] The members for the great cities of the empire ought all to be at their posts; and it is my plain duty to attend the House or to vacate my seat. I must be resolute; the question really troubles my conscience and my reputation. What good reason can I assign to the world, for keeping the title of M.P., while I perform none of the duties of a representative. The unexampled indulgence of my constituents is an additional reason for my doing what I feel to be my duty by them.

Every yours truly,
T. B. Macaulay.

TO SELINA MACAULAY, 29 JANUARY 1855

MS: Trinity College.

Albany London / January 29. 1855

Dearest Selina,

John will carry down with him to Brighton Southey's Life of Wesley,[2] which will, I hope, entertain you and your reader.

We are all in confusion here. That is, the political world is in confusion. For Cowper was not more a hermit at Olney nor Cowley at Chertsey than I within a hundred yards of Piccadilly and a hundred yards of Regent Street. I have scarcely stirred out during the last month, not at all during the last fortnight. I am rather glad that the state of my chest makes it impossible for me to venture to the House of Commons this evening.

---

[1] The disastrous failures to maintain proper supply and care of the army in the Crimea were about to cause the overthrow of the ministry; Aberdeen resigned on 30 January.

[2] 2 vols., 1820. In his essay on Southey TBM says of the book that 'The Life of Wesley will probably live. Defective as it is, it contains the only popular account of a most remarkable moral revolution' (*ER*, L, 531).

For I could not in conscience vote for the ministers, and it would be very painful to me to vote against them.[1] Love to Fanny.

Ever yours,

T B Macaulay

TO UNIDENTIFIED RECIPIENT, 31 JANUARY 1855

MS: William L. Clements Library, University of Michigan.

Albany. London / January 31. 1855

Sir,

I have much pleasure in complying with any wish of a citizen of Edinburgh. / I have the honor to be / Sir

Your faithful servant

T B Macaulay

TO THOMAS FLOWER ELLIS, 3 FEBRUARY 1855

MS: Trinity College.

Albany February 3 / 1855

Dear Ellis,

I shall be delighted to see you on Monday.

Could you lend me for a few hours Coke's Institutes.[2] I want to look at what he says about subsidies. The passage, I think, is in the Fourth Book.

Ever yours,

T B Macaulay

TO SIR CHARLES WOOD, 6 FEBRUARY 1855

MS: The Earl of Halifax.

Albany February 6. 1855

Dear Wood,

Look at Clause II of the India Act of 1833.[3] You will see that all enactments, provisions, matters and things, which might, under the India Act of 1813, have been construed to continue only till 1833, are to last till the end of the new lease, unless repugnant to the terms of the new lease. And if you will then turn to Clause CIII and the clauses which follow,

---

[1] They were defeated by a majority of 157 on this evening.

[2] TBM cites Coke's *Institutes*, Part IV, ch. 1, on the matter of subsidies, in *History*, IV, 314n (ch. 19).

[3] Wood had perhaps raised a question about a statement in the Indian Civil Service Commissioners' Report to the effect that one part of the India Act of 1853 clearly implied 'that the College at Haileybury is to be kept up' but that another part of the Act gave power to the Board of Control to admit to the civil service persons who had not studied at Haileybury (*Parliamentary Papers*, 1854–5, XL, 120).

you will, I think, be of opinion that the Act of 1833 contains nothing repugnant to the provisions of the Act of 1813, as respects Haileybury.

Nevertheless I submit my opinion to that of professional lawyers, among whom, though I am a bencher of Lincoln's Inn, I do not presume to rank myself.

I have now been close prisoner for nearly a month; and I do not regret it. I have been spared much that would have given me acute pain.

Ever yours truly,
T B Macaulay

Our plan, thank God, has been wonderfully well received, on the whole.

TO THOMAS FLOWER ELLIS, 21 FEBRUARY 1855

MS: Trinity College. *Partly published:* Trevelyan, II, 324.

Albany February 21 / 1855

Dear Ellis,

I am still, as you may suppose, a prisoner. I have now had nearly three months of it, with rather less range than Sir Francis Burdett had in the Tower,[1] or Leigh Hunt in Newgate.[2] I am however pretty well – better than I was a fortnight ago.[3]

Any day that you may wish to have an excuse for avoiding some disagreeable party, I shall, as you know, be glad to see you.

Ever yours,
T B Macaulay

TO SIR GEORGE CORNEWALL LEWIS,[4] 23 FEBRUARY 1855

MS: National Library of Wales.

Albany February 23 / 1855

Dear Lewis,

If you will send me the M.S. I will read it, and tell you, in general, what

---

[1] Burdett was in the Tower on political charges in 1810.

[2] Hunt spent two years, 1813–15, in Surrey jail for libelling the Prince Regent.

[3] Between 1 January and 2 March 1855 there are only six entries in TBM's Journal, and after 2 March he ceased altogether to keep it until he resumed it on 6 November of that year. The enforced solitude of the winter months, his weak health, and his determined effort to complete the next two volumes of the *History* all combined to put him out of the mood for journalizing.

[4] Lewis succeeded as second baronet in January.

I think of it.[1] I am afraid that I shall not have leisure for the discussion of details.

I hope that this weather suits you and Lady Theresa better than it suits me. I am entering on my ninth week of imprisonment.

Will you breakfast here at ten on Tuesday?

Ever yours,
T B Macaulay

TO LORD MAHON, 28 FEBRUARY 1855

MS: Stanhope Papers, Chevening.

Albany February 28 / 1855
Dear Mahon,

Many thanks. I cannot be satisfied by Mr. Nichols's explanation.[2] Observe that he alters ten of the twelve characters, and alters every one of those ten in such a way as to destroy all resemblance. What likeness is there between Y and X, or between Θ and 3, or between ୪ and Λ, or between Y and I, or between I and T? What likeness indeed is there between Σ and S? It is true that Σ is the Greek for S. But nobody who was not acquainted with the Greek character would ever guess that Σ is the Greek for S. And, if the copyist was acquainted with the Greek character, how came he to make ten blunders in twelve letters? I do not pretend to guess the meaning of the inscription. But I am strongly of opinion that Sir Michael was a student of astrology and cabala, and that the characters are talismanic, and have some reference to some horoscope, probably his own. The character which stands alone, ୪, is very like the symbol used for the sign of Taurus in the Zodiac; and the watch would have been a most useful part of the apparatus of an astrologer. The closed book may be supposed to have been a volume on the occult sciences. There is my guess, such as it is.

Ever yours truly,
T B Macaulay

[1] Probably Lewis's *Inquiry into the Credibility of the Early Roman History*, 2 vols., 1855. A skeptical treatment of Niebuhr's position on the subject, Lewis's book makes frequent reference to the *Lays of Ancient Rome* and to TBM's Preface to the *Lays*.

[2] This letter has to do with a portrait of Stanhope's ancestor Sir Michael Stanhope (d. 1552: *DNB*) which bore an inscription of twelve cabalistic letters. Stanhope had submitted the puzzling inscription to the antiquarian John Gough Nichols (1806–73: *DNB*), who conjectured that it was a blundering copy of the Greek for 'Jesus Christ the Son of God.' The portrait also showed a watch in one of Sir Michael's hands, while his other hand rested on a closed book. See Stanhope, *Notices of the Stanhopes as Esquires and Knights*, privately printed, 1855, pp. 25–7.

TO SIR JAMES GRAHAM, 2 MARCH 1855

Text: Charles Stuart Parker, *Life and Letters of Sir James Graham*, 2 vols., 1907, II, 275.

Albany, March 2, 1855.

I can hardly condole with you on your retirement;[1] but I heartily condole with the public, and, much as I love Charles Wood, I can wish him nothing better than that he may equal you as an administrator.

TO JOHN HILL BURTON, 12 MARCH 1855

MS: National Library of Scotland.

Albany London / March 12. 1855

My dear Sir,

I send you by this post the two books which you were so kind as to lend me. Both are curious and have been very useful to me. Many thanks for them.

Very truly yours
T B Macaulay

TO UNIDENTIFIED RECIPIENT, 12 MARCH 1855

MS: Mr F. R. Cowell.

Albany London / March 12. 1855

Sir,

I am not sure that *however*, standing as it does, is incorrect: but it is certainly very inelegant. "But, notwithstanding every effort," would be far better.[2] / I have the honor to be, / Sir,

Your obedient Servant
T B Macaulay

TO UNIDENTIFIED RECIPIENT, 13 MARCH 1855

Text: Facsimile in *Autographic Mirror*, 1 (1864), 122.

Albany London / March 13. 1855

Sir,

I will frankly own to you that I am not satisfied with the paper which you have drawn up. You have made us too humble. We are addressing

---

[1] Graham was First Lord of the Admiralty in Aberdeen's ministry and continued in that office under Palmerston until late February, when he resigned with Gladstone and Sidney Herbert over the appointment of a committee of inquiry into the conduct of the war. Sir Charles Wood succeeded him.
[2] Perhaps this refers to the memorial discussed in the next letter.

Lord Palmerston not as beggars, but as advisers. We ask nothing of him for ourselves. We offer to him a suggestion in the belief, (or we ought not to offer it,) that it is a suggestion which it will be for the public good and for his own honor to adopt. We therefore ought to take the tone of gentlemen addressing a gentleman.

Then I do not think that it is desirable to mention Mr. [   ]¹ lectures; and I am quite sure that it is not desirable to mention the eulogies which, as a lecturer, he has obtained from the editors of provincial newspapers. In men who know the world and whose taste in literature is refined, a long string of puffs from newspapers always excites a strong prejudice against a book.

I have hastily scribbled a few lines which seem to me to be in the proper style and I inclose them to you. Make what use of them you will. I return the Memorial. / I have the honor to be, / Sir,

Your most obedient Servant
T B Macaulay

TO ADAM BLACK, 15 MARCH 1855

MS: National Library of Scotland. *Envelope:* Adam Black Esq / etc. etc. etc. / Edinburgh. *Subscription:* T B M.

Albany London / March 15. 1855

My dear Sir,

I have not yet seen Mr. Gilchrist. I wrote to Lord Canning about Grey; and he promised to bear the recommendation in mind.² He has had other things to think of since; and I can hardly write to him again at present on such a subject.

I have of late been able to go out occasionally in the middle of the day. But I am forced to take the greatest care. The smallest imprudence makes it necessary for me to blister my chest; and I suffer if I read aloud for an hour. I work hard however, and have no doubt that I shall soon be a free man. Then I will try to pay off arrears to the Encyclopædia.

It would be a great relief to me to be out of parliament. Nevertheless, if Craig thinks it possible that he may be able to come in next year, I will go on this Session. That is the very utmost that I can do. Next spring I shall probably pass in a warmer climate.

Ever yours truly
T B Macaulay

¹ The name has been deleted in the facsimile. This sounds as though a memorial for the grant of a pension is in question, but no likely person appears among the pensioners of 1855; the only one granted for literature after March in 1855 was to Thomas Dick (1774–1857: *DNB*), the scientific writer.
² See *to* Black, 23 December 1854.

TO CYRUS R. EDMONDS,[1] 15 MARCH 1855

MS: Trinity College.

Albany March 15 / 1855

Sir,

I am obliged to you for the very handsome manner in which you allude to the disagreeable correspondence which formerly took place between us.[2]

I will make some inquiries about the M.S.S. which you mention. But I have little hope that I shall be able to discover anything of value. / I have the honor to be, / Sir,

Your most obedient Servant,

T B Macaulay

C R Edmonds Esq / etc. etc. etc.

TO ADAM BLACK, 16 MARCH 1855

MS: National Library of Scotland. *Envelope:* Adam Black Esq / etc. etc. etc. / Edinburgh. *Subscription:* T B M.

Albany London / March 16. 1855

My dear Sir,

Though I wrote to you yesterday, I must write again to day. A Mr. Snody[3] has been asking me to contribute to a Saturday Half Holiday Association. I would gladly have sent him ten pounds if I had not felt some misgivings. I see no name which I much respect among the members; and I rather infer from the papers that the object of the Institution is to promote the Pharisaical observance of the Sunday. Indeed Mr. Snody all but says that one of his objects is that the poor may have no excuse for breathing fresh air and walking into the country on a Sunday afternoon. Now, if this be so, I cannot honestly lend my name to such a plan. Will you have the kindness to give me your advice. I shall not answer Mr. Snody till I hear from you.

Ever yours truly

T B Macaulay

---

[1] Edmonds wrote biographies of Washington and Milton and made translations of Cicero and Livy for the series published by Henry Bohn.

[2] I have no information about this. Edmonds' *Milton*, 1851, contains a number of references to TBM, but all of them are complimentary.

[3] Andrew Snody (d. 1881), Solicitor to the Supreme Court.

TO UNIDENTIFIED RECIPIENT,[1] 19 MARCH 1855

MS: Mr W. Hugh Peal.

Albany March 19 / 1855

My dear Sir,

I have sent 5 £ to the Saturday Association.[2] I inclose a cheque for ten, which I shall be obliged to you to convey to the Treasurer of the Infirmary.

Very truly yours,
T B Macaulay

TO THOMAS FLOWER ELLIS, 22 MARCH 1855

MS: Trinity College. *Extract published:* Trevelyan, II, 358.

Albany London / March 22. 1855

Dear Ellis,

How are you? What have you been doing? Where are you lodged? When do you come back? I am pretty well, – that is, for an invalid. I pine for the summer and the country. I shall get out of town early this year, and pass the warm weather at Roehampton or some such place, within a short distance of the Museum and of my printer's office. I see land: but there is a very hard pull still before me.

As far as I can learn, the ministry may very well remain in office, unless there should be some great reverse in the Crimea. If that should happen, Lord Derby will have everything his own way.

By the bye his son[3] made a gallant speech against the Pharisees the other night. He is really a young man of great spirit and sense.

I send you some exquisite lines which I saw placarded on a wall the other day. The versification and diction seem to me perfect. Byrom's "My time, oh ye Muses,"[4] is not so complete in its kind.

"Although it is wrong, I must frankly confess,
To judge of the merit of folks by their dress,
I cannot but think that an ill looking hat
Is a very bad sign of a man, for all that;
Especially now, when James Johnson is willing

---

[1] Perhaps the letter is to Black, but the style is not quite that which TBM uses with him.
[2] See the preceding letter.
[3] Edward Henry Stanley (1826–93: *DNB*), afterwards fifteenth Earl of Derby, was M.P. for King's Lynn, 1848–69; he held high office under various Tory administrations and under Gladstone in 1882–5, ending his political life as a Liberal Unionist. On 20 March he had spoken in support of a motion to open the British Museum and the National Gallery on Sundays, a motion defeated by a majority of 187 (*Hansard*, 3rd Series, CXXXVII. 927–32). Stanley had been TBM's neighbor in the Albany since 1851.
[4] *Spectator*, No. 603, 6 October 1714.

To touch up our old ones in style for a shilling.
And gives them a gloss of so silky a hue
As makes them look newer than when they were new."
Àpropos of poetry. Joe Hume's son[1] has written a poem on his father, and
has sent me a copy. I inclose it. But pray bring it back safe. It makes me
wish to have a son –

ὡς ἀγαθὸν καὶ παῖδα καταφθιμένοιο λίπεσθαι
ανδρος.[2]

Who but a son would have pronounced Joe the model of beauty?[3] This
son, I hear, was a prodigious[4] son, and had but lately returned from his
harlots and his hog trough to the fatted calf when the old gentleman died.[5]

Ever yours,
T B Macaulay

TO MRS CHARLES BUXTON,[6] 22 MARCH 1855

MS: Osborn Collection, Yale University.

Albany March 22 / 1855

Dear Mrs. Buxton,

I am truly glad to learn that you were amused and interested by what
you saw on Tuesday.

You have however looked at only a small part of our treasures. On
some future occasion I shall be delighted to escort you again to the
Museum.

Ever yours truly,
T B Macaulay

[1] Joseph Burnley Hume (b. 1818?), B.A., Trinity College, Cambridge, 1840; he published
Poems of Early Years, 1851, and 'Joseph Hume: A Memorial,' 1855 ('Price One Penny'),
the poem TBM refers to here. A letter of Charles Tindal, son of the Chief Justice, to his
father in the late 1830s speaks of Hume as one 'whose presence, I regret to say, disgraces the
College' (quoted in R. Robson, 'Trinity College in the Age of Peel,' in *Ideas and Institutions of Victorian Britain*, New York, 1967, p. 332n).
[2] *Odyssey*, III, 196–7: 'so good a thing is it that a son be left behind a man at his death' (Loeb
translation).
[3] 'His body was a master-piece; for force, endurance, speed, / And every kind of action
perfect; beautiful indeed' ('Joseph Hume: A Memorial').
[4] Thus in MS.
[5] Hume died on 20 February.
[6] Emily Mary (d. 1908), eldest daughter of Sir Henry Holland, married Charles, son of Sir
Thomas Fowell Buxton, in 1850. After the Trevelyans moved to Grosvenor Crescent in
1856 they had the Buxtons as their next-door neighbors.

TO ADAM BLACK, 6 APRIL 1855

MS: National Library of Scotland. *Envelope:* Adam Black Esq / etc. etc. etc. / Edinburgh.
Subscription: T B M. *Partly published:* [Black], *Biographies by Lord Macaulay*, pp. l–lii.

Albany London / April 6. 1855

My dear Sir,

I hope that you will not think me importunate if I again and very earnestly beg you to consider seriously the state of the representation of the City. I feel every day more and more that my public life is over. I am, not, thank God, in intellect or in affections, but in physical power, an older man by some years than I was last Easter. I see no chance of my being able again to take part in debate. By the bye, I hoped till lately that I might be able to go down to Edinburgh in the course of the summer and give a lecture at the Philosophical Institute. But the thing is impossible. My voice would not hold out a quarter of an hour. I have been forced to give up reading aloud to my sister; and I seldom pass an evening in animated conversation without suffering severely afterwards. The little that I can do for mankind must be done at my desk. I try to flatter myself with the hope that a sojourn at Palermo or Malaga may set me up again; and I shall probably try that experiment as soon as I have brought out the next part of my history. But in the meantime the feeling that I ought to be in the House of Commons preys upon my mind. I think that I am acting ungenerously and ungratefully to a constituent body which has been most indulgent to me. However, I will, as I have said, remain an M.P. till the end of this Session. But I must positively declare that I will, on the first day of next Session, at the very latest, take the Chiltern Hundreds. It would be a great relief to me if our excellent friend Craig would consent to stand at present. Pray let him know what I say.

I hope that I have managed Baillie Kay's[1] affair to his satisfaction.

Ever yours truly,
T B Macaulay

TO SELINA MACAULAY, 7 APRIL 1855

MS: Trinity College.

Albany London / April 7. 1855

Dearest Selina,

Anything that is likely to be of use to your health I shall, as you well know, have true pleasure in supplying. I dare say that you have judged rightly about Mr. Leggatt.[2] You will soon feel, I hope, the effect of the

---

[1] John Kay, wine and spirit merchant, and Bailie of Edinburgh in 1855.
[2] Perhaps a physician, though none of that name was then in Brighton.

change of weather. I have no right to complain. It is true that every year steals away some source of enjoyment. I am now forced to give up reading aloud; and I find that even animated conversation, if prolonged, affects my respiration painfully. I retain however, thank God, my intellect and my affections; and if I am suffered to keep them entire to the last, I shall account myself a happy man.

I am pleased at George's success. His lines too are highly creditable to him. They show more thought and more power of expression than I expected. He is a most amiable and excellent boy.

You are right about Sense and Sensibility. It is a remarkable circumstance that Jane Austen went on improving to the very last. Her first work was Northanger Abbey;[1] her second Sense and Sensibility. She was an excellent writer from the very first. But her manner became better and better, till, just before her death, she produced Persuasion, beyond which it seems impossible to go.

Love to Fanny.

Ever yours,
T B Macaulay

TO HENRY BOWIE, 9 APRIL 1855

MS: Trinity College.

Albany London / April 9. 1855

My dear Sir,

I am most deeply sensible of the continued kindness of the members of the Philosophical Institution; and I wish that I could offer them in return something more than thanks and good wishes.

I did hope that it would have been in my power to appear among them in the summer; and I turned over in my mind several subjects about which I might perhaps have been able to give them some information which would have interested them. But the trying season through which we have gone has left my chest in such a state that I am quite unable to speak for a quarter of an hour together even in tones much lower than those which would be necessary to fill a large room. I have been forced to give up reading aloud, which was one of my pleasures. For I found that the continuous exertion of the voice, even with a single hearer, soon threw me into a convulsion of coughing and wheezing. Even in conversation I am under the necessity of indulging very cautiously. In truth I feel that I have done with speaking, and that, if I can be of any use to the world, it must be with my pen.

[1] Most scholars would now put it third in order of composition.

Again and again I return my thanks for the kindness with which I have been treated by the members of the Philosophical Institution, and by you personally; and I beg you, my dear Sir, to believe me ever

Your faithful Servant

T B Macaulay

H Bowie Esq / etc. etc. etc.

TO RICHARD MONCKTON MILNES, 26 APRIL 1855

MS: Trinity College.

Albany April 26. 1855

Dear Milnes,

I shall have great pleasure in dining with you on Wednesday the 9th.

Ever yours truly,

T B Macaulay

TO UNIDENTIFIED RECIPIENT, 27 APRIL 1855

MS: Trinity College.

Albany London / April 27. 1855

Sir,

You do not mention the day for which you wish to have an order. I send one for Monday next. / I have the honor to be, / Sir,

Your faithful Servant,

T B Macaulay

TO THOMAS FLOWER ELLIS, 5 MAY 1855

MS: Trinity College.

Albany May 5. 1855

Dear Ellis,

I shall be delighted to see you on Tuesday.

Your lines are very good lines, but, I must say, out of place. I hate the mixture of prose and verse in an inscription. I hate still more the mixture of English and Latin; and how you are to describe the young gentleman in Latin, if his military rank and his regiment are indispensable, I do not know. I wish that you could avoid the last word *rogo*. It reminds me of Hammond.

"Wilt thou with sighs thy lover's corpse attend?

With eyes averted light the funeral pyre?"[1]

[1] James Hammond, Elegy IX, stanza 7, of his 'Love Elegies,' 1743, slightly misquoted.

I doubt about "debueras tribuisse." You may say "debebas tribuisse," or "debueras tribuere." But "quod debueras tribuisse" is, in English, "which it had been your duty to have paid to us." Is that quite correct?

Donec, as you use it, has the authority of Horace – "Donec gratus eram tibi."[1] But I remember no other authority; and it always jars on my ear. To be sure there is "Donec virenti canities abest."[2] But I have a strong impression that some M.S.S. read *adest,* which is certainly more agreeable to the general sense, and to what I take to be the etymology of *donec.*

Do not put

marmor mosti munus.

It is too alliterative. "Hunc lapidem" will do as well.

Ever yours
T B Macaulay

I have looked into Forcellini,[3] and I see that your use of *donec,* though he allows it to be a perversion, has the authority of Livy and Ovid. I therefore withdraw my objection. Forcellini says

"Ponitur et pro quamdiu, qua notio facile cum priori confunditur."

TO FRANCES MACAULAY, 18 MAY 1855

MS: Trinity College.

Albany May 18. 1855

Dearest Fanny,

I heard yesterday of poor Sir Robert's bequest to you.[4] It was most kind, and delicate, and like himself. There is a remarkably good portrait of him by Richmond in the exhibition of the Royal Academy.[5] It is in oil. I should not at all wonder if Richmond should now take entirely to oil, and aspire to the throne of portrait-painting, a throne vacant since Lawrence's death.

I have been struggling on through this bleak Marchlike May. To day the wind is in the south, – a good thing for me, since I must be at the palace this evening. My friends and acquaintance have been dropping fast

---

[1] *Odes,* III, ix, 1.

[2] *Odes,* I, ix, 17.

[3] Egidio Forcellini, *Lexicon Totius Latinitatis,* first published Padua, 1771; TBM's copy was of the edition by J. Furlanetti, Leipzig, 1839 (sale catalogue, item 340).

[4] Inglis died on 5 May.

[5] Inglis had been Richmond's steadiest patron. The portrait is reproduced in E. M. Forster, *Marianne Thornton,* opposite p. 74. Forster says that two engravings of this portrait 'so oppressed my youth that when they came into my possession I took one of them out of its frame, tore it into small pieces, and burnt them in the kitchen range. Duplicate Sir Roberts were too much' (*ibid.,* p. 73). But he adds that he later came to appreciate the integrity of Inglis.

during the ungenial weather – Sir Robert, Lady Davy,[1] Lord De Mauley,[2] and others whom you never heard of.

You are quite right about Southey's Life of Wesley.[3] When it first came out, I used to be disgusted by the nonsense which was talked about it. Southey said that Wesley loved to govern. Then all the Methodists and friends of the Methodists – Watson[4] – Alexander Knox,[5] Hannah More, – I am sorry to say our father, accused him of imputing Wesley's whole conduct to ambition. They could not deny that, in many passages Wesley was represented as sincerely pious. But this, they said, only showed how little Southey understood what piety meant. For no person could be at once pious and ambitious. What ignorance of human nature! What forgetfulness of the very doctrines which Wesley himself taught! It is curious too that though Whitfield,[6] Toplady[7] and Romaine[8] said stronger things against Wesley than ever Southey said, [the evangelical party would have resented any aspersion on Whitfield, Toplady or Romaine. The explanation was merely this. They were][9] of the clique; and Southey was not. They might therefore steal a horse; and he might not look over the hedge [. . . .][9]

TO FRANCES MACAULAY, 21 MAY 1855

MS: Trinity College.

Albany London / May 21. 1855

Dearest Fanny,

The fire[10] was quite as destructive as was reported. Nothing was saved.

1 She died on 8 May.
2 William Francis Spencer Ponsonby (1787–1855), first Baron De Mauley, died on 16 May.
3 See 29 January.
4 Richard Watson (1781–1833: *DNB*), Wesleyan minister and director of Wesleyan missions. He was commissioned to write a reply to Southey's *Life*, 'Observations on Mr. Southey's "Life of Wesley"', 1820, and published his own *Life of Wesley*, 1831.
5 Knox (1757–1831: *DNB*), theological writer, was a friend of Wesley and, later, of Hannah More and Wilberforce. TBM calls him 'that very remarkable man...whose eloquent conversation and elaborate letters had a great influence on the minds of his contemporaries' (*History*, II, 348n: ch. 8). His 'Remarks on the Life and Character of John Wesley' were added to the second edition of Southey's *Wesley*.
6 George Whitefield (1714–70: *DNB*), leader of the Calvinistic Methodists.
7 Augustus Toplady (1740–78: *DNB*), Calvinistic Methodist, violent in controversy against Wesley.
8 William Romaine (1714–95: *DNB*), the leading London clergyman of Whitefield's party.
9 The bottom half of the last leaf has been cut away for the signature; the text in brackets is from a copy of the lines in Fanny Macaulay's hand accompanying the letter.
10 The manor house of Widmore, near Bromley, on the property where Ellis had his house, was completely destroyed by fire. It was the residence of some cousins of Ellis's wife – Sarah, Susanne, and Mary Anne Telford, sisters of the Telford who was partner in the sherry business with John Ruskin's father. Ruskin speaks of 'the refinement of their highly educated, unpretending, benevolent, and felicitous lives' (*Praeterita*, I, ch. 1).

A Spanish book of mine which Louise Ellis was reading perished in the flames. Marian was not there. She was dining with Hannah and Baba at Sir Edward Ryan's when the misfortune happened, and went down the next day.

The calamity is serious, no doubt. It is melancholy to think that three good old ladies should be burned out of a favourite residence, where they had lived long, and where they fully expected to die. But the thing might have been worse.[1] They are

[.   .   .   .   ]2

money cannot replace.

You are right about Wesley's sermon against Predestination.[3] It is one of the finest things in English pulpit [. . . .]2

to Thomas Flower Ellis, 24 May 1855

MS: Trinity College.

Albany May 24. 1855

Dear Ellis,

I wish that you would dine here on Monday or Tuesday.

I have not been well this week; and to night I must sit up late in the House of Commons,[4] and am not likely to be much benefited by the air and the bustle.

I think of going in a fortnight or so to Wimbledon. By that time I hope it will be summer.

Ever yours,

T B Macaulay

Did you see that our poor friend Miss Harford[5] – Mrs. Sitwell – died only two days after the birth of her baby – only twenty seven. I could hardly help crying. The family and the husband are in great distress.

---

[1] The sisters were wealthy enough to build a new house nearby, called Widmore Court.
[2] The bottom half of the last leaf has been cut away, taking about six lines on the recto and probably a line or two and the closing on the verso.
[3] Number LVIII in Wesley's *Sermons on Several Occasions*, Second Series.
[4] For the vote on Disraeli's motion of censure on the government for its conduct of the war and condemning the negotiations then in progress at Vienna. It was defeated by a majority of one hundred on the 25th, but TBM's name is not in the division list.
[5] See 25 September 1852. Harriet Harford married William Sitwell in 1853 and died on 18 May 1855 (the *Gentleman's Magazine* gives her age as 27; Burke, *Landed Gentry*, says she was born in 1831).

TO UNIDENTIFIED RECIPIENT, 24 MAY 1855

MS: Trinity College.

Albany London / May 24. 1855

Sir,

I ought to have acknowledged earlier your letter of the 18th. I assure you that, though I think defensive war perfectly justifiable, and though I think that the present war was on our side really defensive, I am earnestly desirous to see peace restored. But I am fully convinced that, by voting for Mr. Milner Gibson's motion,[1] I should have rendered no service to the cause of humanity. If that motion had been carried, the consequence would have been, in my opinion, a dissolution of the close friendship by which we are happily bound to France. There would have been a strong, and, I must say, a just impression on the mind of the French people that we had used them ill, that we had acted towards them with bad faith, that no confidence could safely be placed in us. Now, though I think the war with Russia a great evil, I think that a hostile feeling between England and France would be a greater evil still, and would, in all probability, produce, in no long time, a contest more disastrous than that which is now taking place in the Crimea. I could say much more. But I am afraid that, as we reason on principles fundamentally different, we shall not succeed in coming to the same conclusion. Believe me, with sincere respect,

Your faithful Servant,

T B Macaulay

TO WILLIAM WHEWELL, 30 MAY 1855

MS: Trinity College.

Albany London May 30. 1855

My dear Master,

I am sure that you will be delighted to become acquainted with M. de Montalembert.[2] He is a most able and liberal man; – a strong Roman Catholic, but not the less estimable on that account. You will do him the honors of our Protestant University in the best style. Guizot introduced him to me for which I am grateful to Guizot; and I trust that you will be grateful to me for sending him down to Cambridge.

Ever yours,

T B Macaulay

[1] Gibson, an opponent of the war, had given notice of a motion to address the Crown on the subject of the Vienna negotiations; he withdrew it on 21 May.

[2] Charles Forbes, Comte de Montalembert (1810–70), French liberal Catholic politician and religious historian.

TO RICHARD MONCKTON MILNES, 31 MAY 1855

MS: Trinity College.

Albany May 31. 1855

Dear Milnes,

If I can, I will join your party soon after nine on Sunday evening. I will, as you desire, keep the secret[1] till the meeting is over. But I must then be allowed to speak.

Ever yours truly
T B Macaulay

TO SIR CHARLES EASTLAKE,[2] 1 JUNE 1855

MS: Mr F. R. Cowell.

Albany June 1. 1855

My dear Sir,

I was occupied all this morning at the British Museum, and did not see your letter till it was too late for me to obey your summons. I shall be very sorry if I find that my absence has caused any inconvenience.

Very truly yours,
T B Macaulay

Sir C L Eastlake / etc. etc. etc.

TO RICHARD MONCKTON MILNES, 5 JUNE 1855

MS: Trinity College.

Albany June 5. 1855

Dear Milnes,

I shall be delighted to breakfast with you on Monday.

Yours ever
T B Macaulay

TO BISHOP SAMUEL WILBERFORCE, 15 JUNE 1855

MS: Trinity College.

Albany June 15. 1855

My dear Bishop of Oxford,

I alone was to blame. I shall be delighted to breakfast with you on Thursday next.

[1] I have no clue to this.
[2] Eastlake (1793–1865: *DNB*) was President of the Royal Academy from 1850 and Director of the National Gallery from 1855; TBM had known him earlier as Secretary to the Fine Arts Commission. Presumably the summons was on Royal Academy business.

Hayward did not invent the circumstance which he mentioned; but I suppose that he related it to you more maliciously than I had related it to him. I certainly understood one of the two persons whom I found on your stairs to say that you were not up yet. But I really think that, in London, even a Bishop may be in bed at ten without incurring any censure.

Ever yours,

T B Macaulay

TO HENRY ALWORTH MEREWETHER,[1] 23 JUNE [1855][2]

MS: Corporation of London Records Office. *Published: Archives,* II (1954), 124.

Albany June 23. 1689

Sir,

Sir Francis Palgrave informs me that among the papers which are under your charge are some highly curious materials for history. I trust that I may without impropriety ask you to let me have an opportunity of examining them at any time which may be perfectly convenient to you. / I have the honor to be, / Sir,

Your faithful Servant

Mr. Serjeant Merewether / etc. etc. etc.

TO SELINA MACAULAY, 24 JUNE 1855

MS: Trinity College.

Albany London / June 24. 1855

Dearest Selina,

I inclose a cheque as usual. I add another cheque for 20£ which I wish you and Fanny to employ in your joint housekeeping.

You will both of you be glad to hear that the Chancellor has given Edward Rose a very pleasant living, that of Weybridge,[3] – the very thing Lydia tells me. I suppose that he will soon marry.[4]

I have taken a small but comfortable house at Richmond near the brow of the hill. Lord Lansdowne promises me the key of his beautiful grounds, so that I shall be as well off as if I were myself the proprietor of them. I hope that the air will set me up after the sufferings of the last eight months.

[1] Merewether (1780–1864: *DNB*), serjeant-at-law, was town clerk of London, 1842–59.
[2] This letter shows TBM in an unusually pre-occupied state, being dated 1689 and unsigned. Merewether has written at the top that he 'Sent to Sir Francis Palgrave to know from whom / Mr. Thomas Babington Macaulay.'
[3] He held this living for the rest of his life.
[4] In September he married his cousin Ellen Mary, elder daughter of Sir James and Mary Babington Parker.

I shall come daily or almost daily into town in order to work here and at the Museum. My two volumes, nothing unforeseen preventing, will be out before Xtmas. The orders, I hear, are very numerous. My book-sellers – but this is a secret – talk of printing fifteen thousand at once.[1]

Kindest love to Fanny.

Ever yours

T B Macaulay

TO THOMAS FLOWER ELLIS, 29 JUNE 1855

MS: Trinity College.

6 Upper Park Place / Richmond Hill / Surry / June 29. 1855

Dear Ellis,

Here I am luxuriating in the loveliest weather and in the loveliest scenery, and reading Cicero's epistles under magnificent old oaks with the most charming valley and river in the world beneath me.[2] I have hardly once remembered during the last twenty four hours that I had lungs, – a fact which I have during seven or eight months been very seldom able to forget even in my dreams.

When will you come down. You will find a tolerable room, your own sherry, your own claret, a tub, and plenty of ice. Any day but next Wednesday. For then I entertain a large family party. Fix your day; and come to the Albany at a quarter to six and you will find a carriage which will take us down most pleasantly. This is a luxury with which I mean frequently to treat myself during the summer. I shall generally come into town in the morning, work with my outer door sported during four or five hours, and then return. Here I shall do nothing that is of the nature of work, except writing a sketch of Goldsmith's Life[3] for the Encyclopædia Britannica.

Ever yours

T B Macaulay

---

[1] Later raised to 25,000: see 19 October.

[2] TBM stayed at Richmond until 29 September.

[3] Finished next month (see 27 August) and published in vol. 10 of the eighth edition at the end of February 1856.

TO THOMAS FLOWER ELLIS, 30 JUNE 1855

MS: Trinity College.

6 Upper Park Place / Richmond Hill / June 30. 1855

Dear Ellis,

I must add another limitation to the one which I mentioned in my letter of yesterday. On Thursday the 5th I must dine and sleep in town. Any day but Wednesday and Thursday I shall be delighted to see you.

I hear that Walter's verses were thought very good by everybody who understood such things at Harrow yesterday. My information comes from Hannah and Baba who could only repeat what they heard said.

When you write mention how he is going on.

Ever yours,
T B Macaulay

TO THOMAS FLOWER ELLIS, 3 JULY 1855

MS: Trinity College.

Richmond Hill / July 3. 1855

Dear Ellis,

Your letter made me uneasy. However I was comforted by learning this morning when I called in Bedford Place that you were well enough to prosecute minters and smashers.[1] I really think that quiet and country air would do you good. Suppose that you come down on Saturday. I will call for you in Bedford Place at half after five; and I will bring you back on Monday, if you can stay here no longer. The longer the better, as you well know.

I am curious to hear how Jerome solves the question which he raises about the pious King's warming pan.[2]

I am charmed with Cicero's letters. Unhappily they are quite fatal to his character as a public man, and do not give any very high notion of his probity in private life. The style is perfection. Do you remember Middleton's execrable translations?[3] They are as incorrect as inelegant. I note mistakes in every page.

Ever yours,
T B Macaulay

Though I mentioned Saturday, I should be delighted to bring you down on Friday, if that suited you.

---

[1] Ellis had for many years been employed as an attorney for the Royal Mint.
[2] I have not identified Jerome.
[3] Conyers Middleton, trans., *The Epistles of M. T. Cicero to M. Brutus and of Brutus to Cicero,* 1743.

TO THOMAS FLOWER ELLIS, 7 JULY 1855

MS: Trinity College.

Albany July 7. 1855

Dear Ellis,

I am truly sorry to have so bad an account of you. I shall hope to find a line here on Monday morning, to tell me how you are going on.

Thanks for the Epistles.

Ever yours

T B Macaulay

Have you tried Sarsaparilla? That is the great specific for boils,[1] which are now quite epidemic.

I wish Lord John had been laid up with a boil yesterday evening.[2] This cannot go on.

TO LADY TREVELYAN, 9 JULY 1855

MS: Trinity College.

Richmond Hill / July 9. 1855

Dearest Hannah,

I am not quite sure what you finally determined as to the time of your arrival here and the time of dinner on Thursday. Pray let me have a line. Ellis could not come on Saturday. He passed his Sunday in bed. He is not seriously ill. But he is in pain to which he is not much used; and he is consequently low spirited.

I hope that there will be a fine day for you and another for my dear Baba's sketching. Yesterday the park was glorious. Lord John called on me.[3] What an exhibition he made on Friday in the House of Commons. I had not had a tête a tête with him since his strange freak in the winter.[4] We talked about Lord Robert's Bill,[5] Wilson Patten's Bill,[6] and the history of Sabbatical superstition. Not a word about the great political questions of the time.

[1] Sarsaparilla is 'pharmacologically inert and therapeutically useless' (*Encyclopaedia Britannica,* 13th edn).

[2] Evidence that Russell had approved the terms of peace proposed by Austria was published shortly after he had made a speech urging the prosecution of the war. The apparent contradiction exposed him to a storm of criticism, he defended himself weakly on 6 July, and, in the face of a motion of censure, resigned on the 13th.

[3] When not in London, Russell lived at Pembroke Lodge in Richmond Park.

[4] His resignation from Aberdeen's ministry in January.

[5] Lord Robert Grosvenor's bill for regulating Sunday trading in London, intended not to enforce Sabbatarianism but to secure a holiday for workers; it was withdrawn on 2 July.

[6] A bill introduced by John Wilson-Patten, M.P. for North Lancashire, to restrict the sale of beer on Sunday, had been passed in the previous session, but Parliament had reconsidered and was on the point of repealing the act.

I had a begging letter to day from a man who says that his maternal uncle was acquainted with our uncle Aulay sixty five years ago, and sends a letter of our uncle's to prove the fact. A sufficiently remote tie, I think. The beggar adds that in 1818 he was at the University of Edinburgh, and that there his morals were looked after by my respected Aunt Miss Mary Macaulay, – that in his younger days he constantly met our father, then Governor of Sierra Leone at Inverary, – etc. etc. etc.[1] He concludes by asking me to get him a place.

Ever yours,
T B Macaulay

TO EDWARD PLEYDELL-BOUVERIE,[2] 10 JULY 1855

MS: Osborn Collection, Yale University.

Richmond Hill / July 10. 1855

My dear Bouverie,

I shall certainly give no notice till after the debate on the second reading.[3] You will, I hope, in that debate announce changes which will make any such notice on my part unnecessary. I own that I have great doubts whether it would not be better to withdraw the bill altogether, and to introduce a new one in the House of Commons next Session. When poor Pope used the exclamation "God mend me!" a waterman said "Much easier to make another, master."[4] And so, I think of this creation of Lord Monteagle.

Yours very truly,
T B Macaulay

[1] The point of this is that Zachary Macaulay had no sister Mary and that the Macaulay family left Inverary when Zachary was six years old.

[2] Bouverie (1818–89: *DNB*), Whig M.P. for Kilmarnock, 1843–74, was Vice-President of the Board of Trade at this time and shortly later became President of the Poor-Law Board.

[3] This probably refers to the Cambridge University Bill passed by the Lords on 14 June and given its first reading in the Commons on 15 June; it did not proceed beyond that point. Early in the next session another bill substantially like it was brought in by Pleydell-Bouverie and passed in July. Monteagle does not seem to have been primarily responsible for the first bill, but he was one of the Statutory Commissioners provided for in it. TBM had originally been intended as one of the commissioners but had refused (Winstanley, *Early Victorian Cambridge*, p. 46n). The opinion that TBM expresses in this letter had some effect, according to his own testimony. On 9 February 1856 he talked to Pleydell-Bouverie about the bill shortly to be brought in and concluded that the ministers, 'remembering how much I had to do with throwing out the bill of last year, do not wish me to be a Commissioner' – a wish with which he eagerly agreed (Journal, ix, 77).

[4] The anecdote, with a hackney coachman rather than a waterman, is told in an article attributed to Richard Owen Cambridge in *The World*, 13 December 1753: see Alexander Chalmers, *The British Essayists*, 1808, xxvi, 272.

TO THOMAS FLOWER ELLIS, 19 JULY 1855

MS: Trinity College.

Richmond Hill / July 19. 1855

Dear Ellis,

I am truly sorry that I have engaged myself to dine with Lord Lansdowne on Sunday. Nevertheless come. We shall have Saturday evening,
and Sunday till seven. You shall have a comfortable dinner alone; and to
make you amends for my desertion, I will leave you the proof sheets of
my first Chapter,[1] which I much wish you to see. Nobody has yet read it
except Longman and his wife; and they are in ecstasies, and certain that it
will succeed. I accept the omen: for there are many Longmans and Mrs.
Longmans in the world.

If you do not object to this plan, I will call for you at five on Saturday
in Bedford Place. Write immediately.

Ever yours,
T B Macaulay

TO [HENRY BOWIE],[2] 27 JULY 1855

MS: Dr Howard R. Seidenstein.

Albany July 27. 1855

My dear Sir,

I have been able to procure, to my great joy, a copy of Howell's State
Trials for little more than twenty guineas. It is in thirty four volumes, and
will be, unless I deceive myself, a most useful and agreeable addition to
your library.

I have also procured Scott's Dryden, Roscoe's Pope, Burnet's History
of the Reformation and History of His own Times in the Oxford
Edition, Clarendon's Life of himself, Gifford's Ben Jonson, and Whitelock's Embassy. The whole will cost less than sixty pounds. I shall go to
Longman's to see the books in the course of next week; and then I will
order them to be sent to you.

Very truly yours,
T B Macaulay

[1] The third volume of the *History* begins with ch. 11.
[2] TBM had recently consulted with Bowie, Secretary of the Edinburgh Philosophical
Institution, over the Institution's library catalogue (see 15 August) and was assembling a
gift of books to the library. The list of those that he sent is printed in the 'Report of the
Philosophical Institution,' Edinburgh, 1856, p. 7, and agrees exactly with the enumeration
in this letter. The books have now been dispersed by the sale of the Institution's library.

TO UNIDENTIFIED RECIPIENT, 14 AUGUST 1855

MS: University of Chicago.

London August 14. 1855

Sir,

I beg you to accept my thanks for the volumes which you have had the kindness to send me. The history of your province is peculiarly interesting to an Englishman. For you and we are, as the resemblance of our languages proves, very near akin. I promise myself great pleasure and profit from the perusal of your work. But I am sorry to say that it will be a matter of time. For, though I read Dutch, I read it with difficulty; and I find the style of your modern writers very different from that of your diplomatists of the seventeenth century, with whose despatches I am better acquainted than with any other part of your literature.

With repeated thanks for the honor which you have done me, I beg you to believe me, / Sir,

Your most faithful Servant
T B Macaulay

TO HENRY BOWIE,[1] 15 AUGUST 1855

Text: 'Report of the Philosophical Institution,' Edinburgh, 1856, p. 6.

Richmond Hill, August 15, 1855.

Dear Sir,

When we looked together, a few weeks ago, over the Catalogue of our Philosophical Institution, I was, as I told you, much pleased to find that so good a collection had been formed. Yet, though great credit is due to the gentlemen who have managed that part of the business of our Society, I could not but notice some deficiencies. What seemed to me the most important of those deficiencies I have tried to supply. You will, I trust, about the time at which this letter reaches you, receive a box of books, none of which, in my opinion, ought to be wanting to a Library such as ours. These books will, I hope, be read by many with pleasure and profit. At all events, I am sure that the Institution, from which I have received so many marks of kindness, will receive graciously this small token of the good-will of a sincere friend.

Believe me ever, my Dear Sir, your faithful servant,

T. B. Macaulay.

Henry Bowie, Esq.

[1] This is the formal letter of transmittal accompanying TBM's gift of books to the Edinburgh Philosophical Institution: see 27 July.

TO THOMAS FLOWER ELLIS, 16 AUGUST 1855

MS: Trinity College.

Albany / August 16. 1855

Dear Ellis,

By this day's post I send you Chapter XIV. It still requires much correction.

Be so kind as to return it so that I may have it on Tuesday morning; and, if you please, send a few lines separate, as I do, by the same post. Tell me when you expect to be in the South again. We have glorious weather; and so, I suppose, have you; for sunshine like this cannot be confined to one part of the island. I am working very hard, but enjoying my work.

Ever yours,
T B Macaulay

TO FRANCES MACAULAY, 22 AUGUST 1855

MS: Trinity College.

Richmond Hill / August 22. 1855

Dearest Fanny,

I inclose a letter from Hannah which she wishes you to see. I am not quite easy about her husband.

I am very hard worked, but not the worse for it. In a few days the whole of my third Volume will be in print. I think it as good as either of the former two, whatever that praise may be worth. But we authors are said to be bad judges of our own compositions. About the fourth volume, which will not go to the printers for some time, I have great misgivings. I really do not know how it will look when the scattered scrawls are put together and printed fair. At present some of them are hardly legible. Connecting passages are wanting, – and the style requires much correction.

Love to Selina and Alice. I hope that you let the dear child have plenty of Miss Austen. All her lessons will not do her half so much good.

What do you think of a verse which I saw here over the shed of a man who lets out donkeys to the young ladies here.

> "One angel came to Balaam's ass,
>   And met him by the way.
> My asses do through Richmond pass
>   With angels every day."

I assure you that this is not the judicious poet's, though, I think, well worthy of him.

Ever yours
T B Macaulay

TO LOUISA ELLIS, 25 AUGUST 1855

MS: Mr F. R. Cowell.

Albany August 25 / 1855

Dear Louise, –

For so I hope so old a friend may call you. I pronounce chivalry as an English word, and not as a French word. That is, I say Tschivalry, and not Shivalry. The Yankees, I believe, say Shivalry, – an additional reason for adhering to the good old English fashion.

Ever yours most truly,

T B Macaulay

TO ADAM BLACK, 27 AUGUST 1855

MS: Colby College.

Richmond Hill / August 27. 1855

My dear Sir,

I send you the article on Goldsmith by this post. Pray let me have a proof. You must indeed let me have one for the sake of the Encyclopædia: for the M.S. is by no means so legible as I could wish.

Ever yours truly

T B Macaulay

TO UNIDENTIFIED RECIPIENT, 21 SEPTEMBER 1855

MS: Massachusetts Historical Society.

Albany September 21 / 1855

Sir,

My time is very fully occupied; and I have not leisure to write more than a very few lines in answer to your letter.

You will find a concise and popular account of the Troubadours, and some specimens of their poetry in Sismondi's Literature of the South of Europe.[1] If I remember rightly, he refers his readers to other works where fuller information may be found. / I have the honor to be, / Sir,

Your obedient Servant

T B Macaulay

[1] Chs. 3–6.

TO SELINA MACAULAY, 27 SEPTEMBER 1855

MS: Trinity College.

Albany September 27 / 1855

Dearest Selina,

I inclose a cheque. I am now on the point of going into winter quarters. On Saturday I leave Richmond. I pass the Sunday with Ellis at Bromley. On the Monday I go to St Leonard's, that my servants may have a day or two to put my chambers to rights. On Thursday next I take up my abode here for the winter, or at least till my book is out. I have had no holiday. Every day I am at my desk here before eleven; and I seldom get to Richmond again till past six. On the whole I am better satisfied with my work than I was some months ago. How very far short it is of excellence nobody knows better than I, perhaps nobody so well. Two thirds of it are now printed; and one third has received the last corrections. Love to dear Fanny.

Ever yours
T B Macaulay

TO LADY TREVELYAN, 5 OCTOBER 1855

MS: Trinity College.

Albany London / October 5. 1855

Dearest Hannah,

I came home safe, through torrents of rain and reached town just as a furious thunderstorm was coming to a close.

I have since had a Yankee negotiator with me, and have agreed to let my proof sheets go to New York for 300£.[1] It is too little; but I am not skilful in driving bargains.

I should be much obliged to you to send me by Baba the proof sheets of the first three Chapters. I forgot to bring them with me.

The subscription, as it is called, for the book is opened to day. The price is to be 36 shillings.* The Longmans expect to get rid of 15000 the
[.   .   .   .   ][2]
all surprised if it should prove little more than half what they talk of.

Love to the dear children. I hope that Trevelyan is with you
[.   .   .   .   ][2]

---

[1] The third and fourth volumes of the authorized American edition of the *History* were published by Harpers, as were the first two volumes. The Harpers' London agent was Sampson Low – not a Yankee but perhaps a 'Yankee negotiator.'

[2] The bottom of the second leaf has been cut away, taking about four lines on the recto (including TBM's footnote) and a line or two plus the closing and signature on the verso.

TO CHRISTIAN BERNHARD TAUCHNITZ, 10 OCTOBER 1855

Text: Bernhard Tauchnitz, 1837–1887, p. 109.

> Albany, London, Octbr. 10, 1855.

... There will never be any misunderstanding between you and me.[1]

TO ADAM BLACK, 18 OCTOBER 1855

MS: National Library of Scotland.

> Albany London / October 18. 1855

My dear Sir,

I fear that I can hardly expect the Secretary of the Treasury[2] to pay much attention to any request of mine at present. I will see however what can be done.

You understand, I hope, that it is my fixed determination to take the Chiltern Hundreds before Parliament meets. I feel that I have delayed too long to do what my constituents had a right to expect; and I am now convinced that I shall never again be able to take a part in debate. Yesterday evening, for the first time after a long interval, I was persuaded to read aloud; and in less than half an hour I was forced to stop by cough and difficulty of breathing. Whatever I can do for the public must henceforth be done at my desk. I earnestly hope that Craig will be prepared to take my place.

In six weeks or little more my third and fourth volumes will come out. I have not promised myself a great success, and therefore shall not be disappointed if they are coldly received.

> Ever yours truly,
> T B Macaulay

TO FRANCES MACAULAY, 19 OCTOBER 1855

MS: Trinity College.

> Albany London / October 19. 1855

Dearest Fanny,

I believe that the apprehensions of your bankers and brewers are absurd; and I am quite sure that to keep gold in the country if anything is to be got by sending it abroad is impossible.[3] A few years ago every-

---

[1] No doubt this refers to the arrangement between TBM and Tauchnitz for the *History:* see 19 July 1856.

[2] Presumably TBM means W. G. Hayter, Patronage Secretary of the Treasury, 1850–8.

[3] The Bank of France was buying gold and the price had risen sharply in Paris. *The Times* suggested that there was a conspiracy to 'create a panic' (5 October).

body was crying out that gold would be as common as slate, and so cheap that all fortunes would be turned topsey turvy. Now we have a different set of evil predictions just as unfounded. I believe that things will go right if they are let alone. At all events I am sure that I never can be better prepared for a crash among the banks than at present. For I have just borrowed sixteen hundred pounds from my bankers to make a purchase on favourable terms. And if they break before next January, I shall have no balance at all in their hands.

I am thinking a great deal more of the state of the currency and of the banks in 1696 than of what is doing in the City at present. I work hard every day and all day long. I fully expect that the two volumes will appear in the first week of December. I am almost ashamed to tell you what a sale is expected. The orders from London booksellers alone are already near thirteen thousand; and the orders of the Piccadilly district, including Hatchard's[1] and many other large establishments, have not come in. The first edition is to be of twenty five thousand copies; and the Longmans expect to get rid of them all by New Year's day. Do not talk about this.

Ever yours
T B Macaulay

TO THOMAS FLOWER ELLIS, 27 OCTOBER 1855

MS: Mr F. R. Cowell.

Albany October 27. 1855

Dear Ellis,

I send you Chapters XVII and XVIII. I should be glad to have Chapter XVII back on Monday; for this is the last revise; and the printers want to work off the sheets. Chapter XVIII you may keep as long as you will.

My work, according to the best calculation that I can make, will be over this day fortnight. Then the printers, binders, index makers, etc. must have a month; and on the 10th of December or thereabouts, I come out.

Come and dine with me on Monday, or any other day next week which may suit you better; and let me know as soon as you can.

Ever yours,
T B Macaulay

---

[1] Hatchard's, 187 Piccadilly, was founded by a resident Claphamite who was publisher to the Sect for many years.

TO THOMAS FLOWER ELLIS, 5 NOVEMBER 1855

MS: Trinity College.

Albany Nov 5 / 1855

Dear Ellis,

I am truly sorry that I cannot dine with you on Saturday. The Trevelyans wanted to make up a party this week for Lord Canning who is going to India,[1] and asked me to fix the day. I named Saturday,[2] supposing it to be the only day on which you could not possibly have your party, as I had no doubt that you would go to Bromley. I return your letter to Campbell. Any other day will suit me; and I will not engage myself anywhere till I hear from you.

Come and dine with me on any day this week that you like best – Saturday excluded.

Ever yours
T B Macaulay

TO LORD JOHN RUSSELL, 1[9][3] NOVEMBER 1855

MS: Mr T. S. Blakeney.

Albany London, November 18. 1855

Dear Lord John,

The story which you have heard is utterly destitute of foundation.[4] The subjects for the corridors are not chosen by Ward. They were settled, some years ago, by the Commissioners, at a meeting at which I was present. If any changes have been made, they have been made without my assent or knowledge.

Ward has twice or thrice consulted me about the mode of treating his subjects. But he never consulted me about the subjects themselves. They were chosen for him by higher authority; and, even if I had thought them ill chosen, I should not have been so absurd as to object to them.

---

[1] He had in July been appointed Governor General in succession to Lord Dalhousie.

[2] The dinner on that day was 'a large and pleasant party – Sir C. Wood and Lady Mary – George Grey and Lady Grey – Lord and Lady Canning – Merivale – Mangles and his wife – C. Buxton and his wife. I was in very good spirits and, I thought, amused the party' (Journal, VIII, 165–6).

[3] The letter is probably misdated. The Journal entry in which the letter from Lord John is described (see next note) is mistakenly dated Monday November 18 and then corrected to 19.

[4] TBM received on this day 'a very odd absurd letter from Lord John, to which I hardly knew how to frame an answer. He has taken it into his head – God knows why – that I wish to prevent Ward from painting a picture of Lord Russell's parting with Lady Russell' (Journal, VIII, 171). For Ward and his paintings for the House of Commons, see *to* E. M. Ward, 12 August 1851.

I think that the last Communion of Lord Russell, or his parting from his wife, would be an excellent subject. But I do not remember that I ever had any conversation with Ward about the matter.

Ever yours very truly,

T B Macaulay

TO LORD STANHOPE,[1] 19 NOVEMBER 1855

MS: Stanhope Papers, Chevening.

Albany London / November 19. 1855

Dear Lord Stanhope,

I am truly glad to have so good an account of Lady Stanhope[2] from the best authority. I had already heard from two or three quarters that all was going on well. I assure you that I felt for you much.

Thanks for the Proceedings of the Society of Antiquaries.[3] I am glad that a copy of the Wicked Bible is extant; but I have, I own, some misgivings. It would be well worth the while of a clever knave to insert in a Bible of Charles the First's time a leaf with the Seventh Commandment misprinted, and then to sell his handiwork for fifty guineas. I have seen, and you no doubt have seen, lost pages of old books restored in such a way as to be quite similar in appearance to the genuine pages.

I rather suppose that the famous *erratum,* which very justly excited Laud's indignation, was the work of some waggish printer who escaped detection.

I do not know whether you ever read Madan's Thelypthora,[4] a work once very famous, or, if you please, infamous. Madan laments the horrible profligacy of fashionable manners. This, you must remember, was seventy or eighty years ago. The ladies, he says, either do not read their bibles at all, or read only, to judge by their practice, the edition of 1631.[5]

I have been working hard and steadily. My last revise of the last Chapter will go, I hope, to the printer to morrow. Then there must be

---

[1] Mahon succeeded to the earldom on 2 March 1855.

[2] She had suffered some accident to her arm. Perhaps this was one of the two times that she broke her arm in disembarking at Calais (Aubrey Newman, *The Stanhopes of Chevening,* p. 314).

[3] The MS of TBM's letter is accompanied by two printed pages from the *Proceedings* of the Society of Antiquaries, III (1855), 213–14: they describe the exhibit of a copy of the so-called 'wicked Bible,' 1631, in which the Seventh Commandment reads 'Thou shalt commit adultery.' On Bishop Laud's complaint the printers were fined and the edition ordered to be destroyed. The copy, bought for 50 guineas, is identified as unique.

[4] Martin Madan, *Thelyphthora or a Treatise on Female Ruin,* 2 vols., 1780, an argument for polygamy.

[5] *Ibid.,* I, 68.

three weeks at least for binding, etc. etc. On the 15th of December we hope to be out. Kindest regards to Lady Stanhope, and to my Valentine.

Ever yours,

T B Macaulay

I have just received a very kind, but very sad letter from Everett.[1]

TO HENRY BOHN,[2] 20 NOVEMBER 1855

Text: Maggs Brothers Catalogue 439, Summer 1923, item 839, 2pp. 8vo: dated Albany, 20 November 1855.

I beg you to accept my thanks for the portion of your edition of Addison[3] which you have been so kind as to send me. I have only been able to glance at a few pages; but all that I have seen leads me to believe that you have rendered a real service to literature.

TO CHRISTIAN BERNHARD TAUCHNITZ, 21[4] NOVEMBER 1855

Text: Bernhard Tauchnitz, 1837–1887, p. 109.

Albany, London, Novbr. 21, 1855.

I wonder that you have not found more typographical errors... *Catharine* is the right spelling, as the word comes from the Greek καθαρος. You are right about *couleur,* no doubt, though the word is written *douleur* in the copy from which I took the quotation.[5]

TO FRANCES MACAULAY, [22?][6] NOVEMBER 1855

MS: Trinity College.

Albany London November 21. 1855

Dearest Fanny,

Thanks for the advertisement. It is a jewel. I have sent it to Hannah, and charged her to take care of it and to send it safe to you.

---

[1] See 29 November.

[2] Bohn (1796–1884: *DNB*), London bookseller, publisher, and collector, was best known for his reprints in series, including the 'Standard Library' and the 'Classical Library.' He edited a number of handbooks and compilations, and an amplified edition of Lowndes' *Bibliographer's Manual,* 6 vols., 1857–64.

[3] A new edition by Bohn of Richard Hurd's edition of Addison's *Works,* 6 vols., 1854–6; the book is now in the library at Wallington.

[4] See note on date of next letter.

[5] Tauchnitz was evidently reading proofs of the *History,* vol. 3: Catherine (p. 391) and *douleur* (p. 533n) are altered to Catharine and *couleur* after the first edition.

[6] TBM has misdated the entries in his Journal for 19–22 November as 18–21 November and very likely has misdated this letter in the same way; at any rate it is clear that he finished his work on the *History* on 22, not 21, November (Journal, VIII, 172).

I have been kept close prisoner some days by the fog and east wind, to say nothing of the rain. On the whole, my chest is less irritable than last year; and I think my general health rather improved. My work will finish to day. The last page will receive the last correction; and then what remains must be left to the printers, binders, etc. etc. Longman thinks that we shall be out on the 15th of December.[1] I am enjoying a holiday after a year of almost uninterrupted work, and am reading [. . . .][2]

TO RICHARD MONCKTON MILNES, 22 NOVEMBER 1855

MS: Trinity College.

Albany Nov 22 / 1855

Dear Milnes,

I am truly sorry to give up your party to morrow. But I really dare not stir out after dusk.

Ever yours
T B Macaulay

TO UNIDENTIFIED RECIPIENT, 23 NOVEMBER 1855

MS: Colby College. *Published: Colby Library Quarterly,* Series IV, No. 5 (February 1956), 97–8.

Albany London / November 23. 1855

Sir,

I am in possession of no particular information about Royston. It is very probable that there may have been a press there in the days of the Commonwealth. At that time no Episcopalian divine would have been able to get his writings printed at the University of Cambridge. It was therefore very natural that some friends of the oppressed Church should establish in the neighbourhood of the University a press to which such a man as Jeremy Taylor[3] might have recourse. But I should be much surprised to find that, after the Restoration, a press at Royston had been licensed; and I observe that all the works which, as you inform me, bear

---

[1] Next day Longman called to announce a new arrangement: 'Monday Dec 17 is to be the day. But on the evening of the preceding Saturday those booksellers who take more than a thousand are to have their books' (Journal, VIII, 174).

[2] A part of the second leaf has been cut away for the signature.

[3] The reference to Taylor suggests that TBM's correspondent has raised a question based on a mistake; none of Jeremy Taylor's works was published at Royston, but his regular publisher was the prominent London bookseller, Richard Royston (1599–1686: *DNB*).

the date of Royston, were printed before the passing of the Licensing Act.[1] / I have the honor to be, / Sir,

Your obedient Servant,

T B Macaulay

TO HENRY HART MILMAN, 23 NOVEMBER 1855

MS: McGill University.

Albany November 23. 1855

My dear Dean,

I am sorry to say that this dull raw weather affects my chest so much that I am forced to remain by my fireside. It is very much against my will that I give up the hope of being able to breakfast with you to morrow.

Ever yours truly,

T B Macaulay

TO WILLIAM HICKLING PRESCOTT,[2] 26 NOVEMBER 1855

MS: Massachusetts Historical Society.

Albany London / November 26. 1855

My dear Sir,

Your most kind and most welcome present[3] reached me just as I had finished my own long labours, and was beginning to take a holiday which I had fairly earned. I have to thank you for a day or two of great enjoyment. At this season I am almost close prisoner to my room; and I sometimes can hardly help repining at my confinement. But I deduct from this dreary period of restraint and suffering the happy hours which I have passed over your volumes. / Believe me, my dear Sir,

Yours very faithfully,

T B Macaulay

---

[1] 1662.

[2] Prescott (1796–1859), American historian of the Spanish empire, was one of the Boston circle that included Everett and Ticknor. TBM had met Prescott in June 1850 (Journal, II, 336).

[3] The first two volumes of *The History of the Reign of Philip the Second*, just published in Boston. TBM began them on the 22nd, finding them 'well enough: but I read through half the first volume without finding anything that much altered my notion of the events or men of that time; and I have never studied that part of history deeply' (Journal, VIII, 173).

TO EDWARD EVERETT, 29 NOVEMBER 1855

MS: Massachusetts Historical Society. *Partly published: New York Ledger*, 25 February 1860.

Albany London November 29. 1855

Dear Everett,

Your letter of the 6th gave me pleasure and pain, pleasure because it is full of kindness, and pain because the writer does not seem to be happy.[1] I hope that your sadness was merely the effect of temporary depression of spirits. I still look forward to the pleasure of seeing you again in the old country. You well know how gladly you will be welcomed by all that remains of the circle in which we passed so many agreeable hours together.

We shall hardly meet in the Albany. My lease expires in a few months; and, as I am a much more wealthy and a much less healthy man than when I took up my abode here, I mean to change my quarters. I should like to settle very near London within an easy distance of the Clubs, of the British Museum, and, above all, of my sister and her children, and yet beyond the reach of the coalfog and riverfog which, during six months of the year, make it difficult for me to breathe. I must have room for near ten thousand volumes. I must have, if possible, an acre of green turf where I can walk up and down among lilacs and laburnums with a book in my hand. I must also have a spare bed for a friend; and I need not tell you that no friend will be more welcome to it than you.

Possibly, before I settle, I may visit Italy again. I shall vacate my seat in parliament on the first day of the approaching Session, and shall thus be freed from a tie which, though in my case singularly easy, nevertheless imposed some little restraint on my movements. I have corrected the last proof sheet of the second part of my History, and am fairly entitled to a holiday. You shall have a copy which will sometimes remind you of a very sincere friend. I have not promised myself that the book will be popular. The public has extravagantly overpraised me: it expects miracles: and it will probably punish me for its own folly. In the meantime I am enjoying my newly recovered liberty. I have been reading two very much better historians than myself, Herodotus and Thucydides. I ought not to forget our friend Prescott, over whose volumes I passed a very pleasant day by the fireside, while London was covered with one of our orange coloured fogs.

Thanks for your sketch of American politics. Our politics are not what you remember them. The ballot, free trade, Maynooth, the Irish Church, are scarcely mentioned. The only talk of the Clubs is about ports in the

---

[1] Everett had resigned from the Senate in 1854 and was now living in retirement, a 'disappointed and defeated man' according to his biographer (Frothingham, *Everett*, p. 373).

Euxine and fortresses on Mount Caucasus, the depth of the water in the sea of Azov, and the state of the roads between Sympherapol and Percop. A friend of ours said not long ago that my chambers were the only place where a man could pass a quarter of an hour in company without hearing the Crimea mentioned.

As to the great question of peace or war, there are few politicians here so peaceably disposed as myself; and yet I do not think the present moment a moment for making peace. But I will not inflict on you a dissertation in defence of my opinion. In truth I, like you, take little pleasure in contemporary politics. I am sometimes half afraid that I trouble myself about them less than a good citizen should. But my excuse is that the state of my health makes it impossible for me to take an active part. I am doomed to my desk and my fireside. I live much in the past; and I am therefore less violently excited than my neighbours about the present. But I must have done with this egotism. God bless you, my dear Everett: write to me a little oftener; and believe me always yours affectionately,

T B Macaulay

TO LORD STANHOPE, 4 DECEMBER 1855

MS: Stanhope Papers, Chevening.

Albany December 4. 1855

Dear Lord Stanhope,

I am prisoner to my room, and can only tell you what my own recollections and my own books supply me with. You know of course that the nobleman about whom M. Cousin[1] inquires was the first Earl of Holland,[2] Bassompierre's Earl,[3] the Earl who ratted from the Parliament to Charles, from Charles to the Parliament, and from the Parliament back to Charles, and to whose tricks the High Court of Justice at last put an end. He was a younger son of Rich Earl of Warwick.[4] In the next generation the earldoms were united, and the elder title only was used, except in formal instruments. I believe that both earldoms became extinct towards the close of the reign of George the Second.[5] To whom the property and the

---

[1] Cousin was at work on his *Madame de Chevreuse*, Paris, 1856, which briefly summarizes the affair between Lord Holland and Mme de Chevreuse in 1624–5 (pp. 15–17).

[2] Henry Rich (1590–1649: *DNB*), favorite of James, negotiated the marriage of Charles and Henrietta Maria; he wavered between sides in the Civil War and was beheaded on the sentence of a Parliamentary court.

[3] François de Bassompierre (1579–1646), courtier and Marshal of France; his *Mémoires* (1665) describe frequent visits to Lord Holland at Kensington during Bassompierre's embassy to London in 1626.

[4] Robert Rich (1559–1619), first Earl.

[5] The titles were united in 1673 and became extinct in 1759.

papers of the Rich family descended I have no means of learning in my cell here.

I am surprised to learn that Lord Holland was suspected of having been the lover of Anne of Austria.[1] There was much scandal about him and Henrietta Maria, whose marriage he negotiated while he was only Lord Kensington. He was, to be sure, a man of distinguished gallantry, a man of much taste and magnificence, and a very great rascal.

I cannot think that the family papers of the Riches are at all likely to be found at Holland House. They do not seem to have considered that House as their principal seat. It was often let; and it was the jointure house of the Countess Dowager. It does not appear to have been the residence of any Earl of Warwick and Holland, during the seventy or eighty years which preceded the extinction of those titles.

You do not mention Lady Stanhope. I hope that I may infer that she has quite recovered from the effects of her accident. My kindest regards to her and to my Lady Valentine.

Ever yours truly

T B Macaulay

TO SIR GEORGE CORNEWALL LEWIS, 11 DECEMBER 1855

MS: National Library of Wales.

Albany December 11. 1855

Dear Lewis,

Trevelyan has just told me that you wish to have my opinion on two points relating to the Museum. I will tell you quite frankly what I think as to both.

First, as to Sir Henry Ellis; – he is a faithful and laborious public servant. He has been very useful during many years. But he is now too old and infirm for his post. It is enough to say that, at the meetings of the Trustees, it is painful to see and hear him. We generally relieve him by reading the letters for him. He has most fairly earned a pension sufficient to make his last years comfortable.[2]

As to Hawkins's medals,[3] I am decidedly of opinion that we ought not to buy them. It is the duty of the chief officers of the Museum to be constantly on the look out, each in his own line, for rare and valuable

---

[1] Louis XIII's queen. Cousin says only that she and Buckingham carried on a flirtation in which Holland was interested.

[2] Ellis resigned with a pension in February 1856; he 'lived thirteen years more almost in the shadow of the museum, full of geniality, urbanity, and anecdote to the last' (*DNB*).

[3] Edward Hawkins (1780–1867: *DNB*), Keeper of Antiquities at the British Museum since 1826. His collection of British medals was purchased by the Museum in 1860.

articles, Madden[1] for curious Manuscripts, Carpenter[2] for curious prints, Panizzi for Alduses and Caxtons, Hawkins for medals. It is to these gentlemen that we look for such information and advice as may enable us to expend judiciously the money entrusted to us by Parliament. But if our agents are to be our competitors at sales, if our agents are to forestall us, if they are to use that skill, which of right belongs to us who pay them, for the purpose of forming collections which they may afterwards sell to us at an advanced price, it is quite impossible that the public can be well served.

I tell you my own opinion. If you have any doubts, you cannot do better than consult the Duke of Somerset[3] who thoroughly understands the business of the Museum.

Ever yours truly
T B Macaulay

TO RICHARD MONCKTON MILNES, 12 DECEMBER 1855

MS: Trinity College.

Albany Dec 12. / 1855

Dear Milnes,

I am sorry that I cannot breakfast with you on Saturday.

Ever yours,
T B Macaulay

TO [THOMAS LONGMAN], 18 DECEMBER 1855

MS: Osborn Collection, Yale University.

Albany December 18 / 1855

My dear Sir,

I send the second Volume with corrections.[4] Pray let the printers be told to be careful.

---

[1] Sir Frederic Madden (1801–73: *DNB*), in the employ of the British Museum from 1826, was Keeper of the Department of Manuscripts, 1837–66, a noted paleographer, and editor of early English texts. A dissatisfied and ill-tempered man, he bitterly hated Panizzi and, as the references in his copious MS diary show, had no very high opinion of TBM.

[2] William Hookham Carpenter (1792–1866: *DNB*), Keeper of Prints and Drawings since 1845.

[3] Lord Edward Seymour succeeded as twelfth Duke of Somerset in August of this year.

[4] Longman had called the day before to say that they must begin reprinting: 'He was for 5000. I insisted that there should only be 2000' (Journal, VIII, 187). Longmans' records show that 2000 copies were printed in January and a further 1000 in October 1856.

Be so kind as to send a copy from the author to

Walter Ellis Esq
Trinity College[1]
Cambridge.

Let it, if convenient, be sent to day.

Very truly yours,
T B Macaulay

TO UNIDENTIFIED RECIPIENT, 18 DECEMBER 1855

MS: Boston Public Library.

Albany London / Dec 18. 1855

Sir,

I have had much pleasure in signing the certificate. I return it with the letters.

I am glad that you have found any thing to approve in my book. I feel very painfully how much better it might have been. Believe me

Yours very faithfully
T B Macaulay

I shall be much interested, I do not doubt, by what you have written about India.

TO FRANCES MACAULAY, 19 DECEMBER 1855

MS: Trinity College.

Albany London / December 19. 1855

Dearest Fanny,

I have directed my bankers to put for the future fifty pounds, instead of twenty five pounds, to your credit every quarter day, beginning from this Christmas. I mean also to give Selina two hundred a year. Hannah will add fifty pounds for your joint housekeeping. I hope that your income will now be such as to make you quite comfortable.

All that I hear about my book as yet is laudatory. I have seen several newspaper critiques, some from quarters in which my opinions are not likely to find favour; and I have not observed a word indicating that the new volumes are thought inferior to the old ones. We are already reprinting. Indeed it is necessary to reprint the first two volumes too.[2]

[1] Walter Ellis went up to Trinity in the Michaelmas term this year.

[2] An eleventh edition of 3000 copies was printed in January 1856. Trevelyan reports that the sale of the first two volumes in the year before the publication of the second installment was 1172 copies; in the year after, 4901 (II, 386n).

For the demand for them has within the last three days become exceedingly brisk, near a hundred a day. You see therefore that I can very well afford to allow my sisters four hundred a year.

Ever yours,
T B Macaulay

TO SELINA MACAULAY, 19 DECEMBER 1855
MS: Trinity College.

Albany London December 19 / 1855
Dearest Selina,

I inclose a cheque for fifty pounds; and I mean to send you henceforth fifty pounds every quarter day. I am now what I should once have considered as a rich man; and I cannot use my money more to my own satisfaction than in adding to your comforts. I mean to make the same allowance to Fanny. Hannah, whom I have consulted, proposes to add fifty pounds a year for your joint housekeeping. You will therefore have between you four hundred and fifty pounds a year, free of income tax, in addition to your own property. I hope that this sum will enable you to live quite comfortably.

I am truly sorry to hear that you are poorly. I have got through the winter tolerably, by remaining shut up in my room. I bear my imprisonment well; and never have a moment of ennui. All that I hear about my book is as yet favourable.

Ever yours
T B Macaulay

Would it suit you to have your allowance paid quarterly into some bank at Brighton, or to have it put on the same footing with Fanny's? That arrangement would secure punctuality; and I may be forgetful; or may be out of England on a quarter day.

TO FRANCES MACAULAY, 24 DECEMBER 1855
MS: Trinity College.

Albany December 24 / 1855
Dearest Fanny,

Thanks for the *errata.* They come too late. For two thousand additional copies are, I believe, already printed. In any case, I should not, on account of errors merely verbal, have made any change in the first Volume, which is stereotyped. The second volume, being in moveable type, may be corrected without difficulty.

I am truly glad that you are pleased with the book, though of course I make a very large allowance for your kind partiality. As far as I can learn, empty as London is, and imprisoned as I am, the general opinion is that there is no falling off. It is much not to have disappointed expectations wound up to an unreasonably high point.

Longman sends me all the newspaper articles on the book which come to his knowledge; and I cut them out and keep them for you. They are generally very laudatory; but there is a mixture of abuse. The praise and the abuse are of nearly equal value. For I have long known that the place of a book is settled by what is written in it, and not by what is written about it. Love to dear Selina.

Ever yours

T B Macaulay

TO LORD LANSDOWNE, 24 DECEMBER 1855

MS: The Marquess of Lansdowne.

Albany London December 24 / 1855

Dear Lord Lansdowne,

You are so kind, and I am so desirous to see Bowood again, that I will not positively decline your invitation. Yet my hopes of being able to accept it are very small. I suffered severely from the cold weather last week; and the West wind and sunshine have not yet begun to restore me. If I should be much better, and if the air should continue to be mild, I will venture down next Monday, the 31st. But I feel that, in writing thus, I am merely flattering myself.[1]

You will find Milman's new volumes[2] excellent, – superior, I think, to anything that he has written. / Ever, dear Lord Lansdowne,

Yours most truly

T B Macaulay

TO HENRY BOHN, 24 DECEMBER 1855

MS: Mr D. R. Bentham. *Published:* Henry G. Bohn, ed., W. T. Lowndes, *The Bibliographer's Manual of English Literature*, 1861, p. 1433***.

Albany December 24 / 1855

Dear Sir,

I beg you to accept my warm thanks for your present.[3] It is a valuable

---

[1] See *to* Lansdowne, 29 December.

[2] Volumes 4–6 of Milman's *History of Latin Christianity* were published in late December. TBM read them on the 20th: 'Very good indeed' (Journal, IX, 1).

[3] Another volume of Addison's *Works:* see *to* Bohn, 19 November.

addition to any library. Yet I am sorry to see that you have omitted some papers which were undoubtedly Addison's, though he did not own them. I mean particularly The Spectator Number 623[1] – the richest and broadest specimen of his humour. It is a little indelicate; and that no doubt was his reason for not claiming it. He also abstained from claiming Number 608,[2] though most undoubtedly his, and one of his best, because he could not have avowed it without avowing also Number 623. If any person can doubt that both those papers are Addison's, either that person or I must be an exceedingly bad critic.

With repeated thanks for your kindness, I beg you to believe me, / Dear Sir,

Your faithful Servant
T B Macaulay

TO LADY HOLLAND,[3] 26 DECEMBER 1855

MS: New College, Oxford.

Albany December 26. 1855

Dear Lady Holland,

I am most deeply sensible of the kind feeling which impelled you to write what you knew would give me pleasure. Your approbation is very gratifying to me, though I know, or rather because I know, that your judgment is in some degree perverted by your good will. The judgment of the public is not to be so perverted; and what the public will say remains to be seen. / Ever, dear Lady Holland,

Very truly yours
T B Macaulay

TO SIR CHARLES WOOD, 26 DECEMBER 1855

MS: The Earl of Halifax.

Albany London December 26 / 1855

Dear Wood,

I am truly gratified by your approbation. What you say of the public men of William's reign is too true. Many times I have wished that I had

---

[1] 22 November 1714, by Thomas Tickell, about incontinent widows and the burlesque legal ceremony of the 'benefit of the ram.'

[2] 18 October 1714, by Tickell, on the claims of married couples to the prize of the flitch of bacon. Addison's latest editor says that this may possibly be worked up from materials left by Addison (Donald F. Bond, ed., *The Spectator*, Oxford, 1965, v, 78n). The essay is one of those that TBM said he knew by heart 'before I was nine' (Journal, XI, 230: 21 December 1857).

[3] Sir Henry Holland's wife.

taken some subject more pleasing, some subject which I could treat without violating truth, and yet without disgusting and, I am afraid, sometimes wearying my readers by such a dreary, monotonous, spectacle of depravity. However, I have now got through the worst part of my task. If I should live seven or eight years longer, and should retain my faculties, I may hope to bring my narrative down to the accession of the House of Hanover. There I shall stop. In this way only I can now hope to be of use to my country. Every year I feel my bodily infirmities increasing. But while my intellect and my affections are spared to me, I shall not think myself unhappy.

All kind Christmas wishes to Lady Mary and to all in whom you and she are interested.

Ever yours truly
T B Macaulay

TO LORD LANSDOWNE, 29 DECEMBER 1855

MS: The Marquess of Lansdowne.

Albany London / December 29. 1855

Dear Lord Lansdowne,

Within the last forty eight hours I have breathed more freely than during the preceding month. Dr. Bright however positively forbids me to go to Bowood; and I feel that he is right, though I murmur a little.

On the first day of the Session of Parliament a new writ will be moved for Edinburgh. I shall then be at perfect liberty. The years which remain to me are not likely to be many: but I hope to be able to give them to my friends, to my family, to letters and to whatever is most beautiful in art and nature.

A happy new year, and many happy years to you and all yours. / Ever, dear Lord Lansdowne,

Yours most truly
T B Macaulay

TO HENRY HART MILMAN, 29 DECEMBER 1855

MS: McGill University.

Albany December 29 / 1855

My dear Dean,

I did not till this day altogether give up the hope of meeting you next week at Bowood. But as Bright has just laid his final orders on me not to

483

stir, I cannot any longer defer my thanks for your last three volumes.[1] I think this quite your best work; and that is saying a great deal. That the History of Latin Christianity will have a high and permanent place in literature I have not the slightest doubt. I mean to read all the six volumes again with more attention than formerly; and I promise myself many happy evenings over them.

I have had a most pleasant month of mere literary idling and luxury. I have finished Photius, after digressing from him repeatedly to the authors whom he mentions, particularly Isocrates and Lysias. I have also read again Cicero's philosophical works, and think, as I thought at twenty two, when I read him under the chestnuts at Trinity, that the De Finibus is the best, that then comes the De Natura Deorum, and that the Tusculan Disputations are the least valuable, – mere anointing for broken bones. A pleasant new year to you and Mrs. Milman.

Ever yours,
T B Macaulay

---

[1] See *to* Lansdowne, 24 December. TBM's Journal for 29 December reports that 'Milman called and sate half an hour' (ix, 12), so it seems probable that this letter or the Journal has been misdated, or that TBM has put the visit on the wrong day.